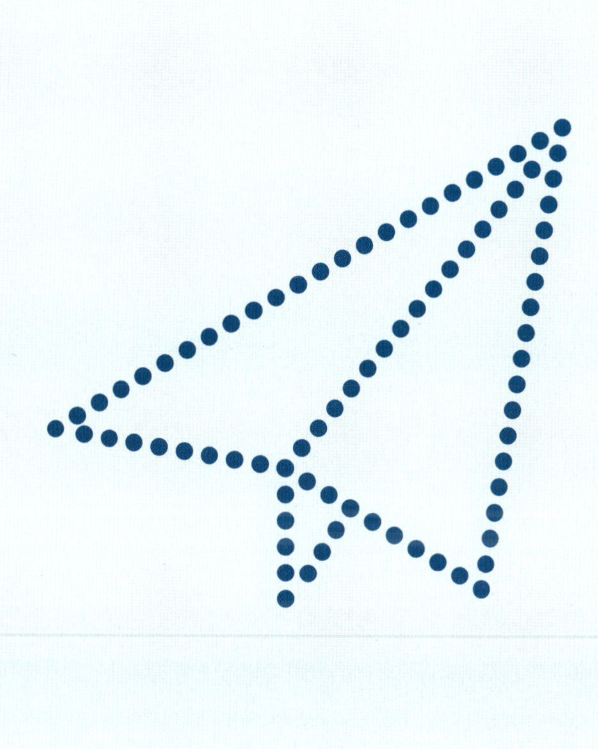

SEND ME AN IMAGE
From Postcards to Social Media

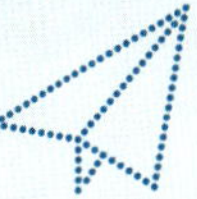

Herausgegeben von / **Edited by**
Felix Hoffmann & Kathrin Schönegg
für / **for** C/O Berlin Foundation

C/O Berlin   **Steidl**

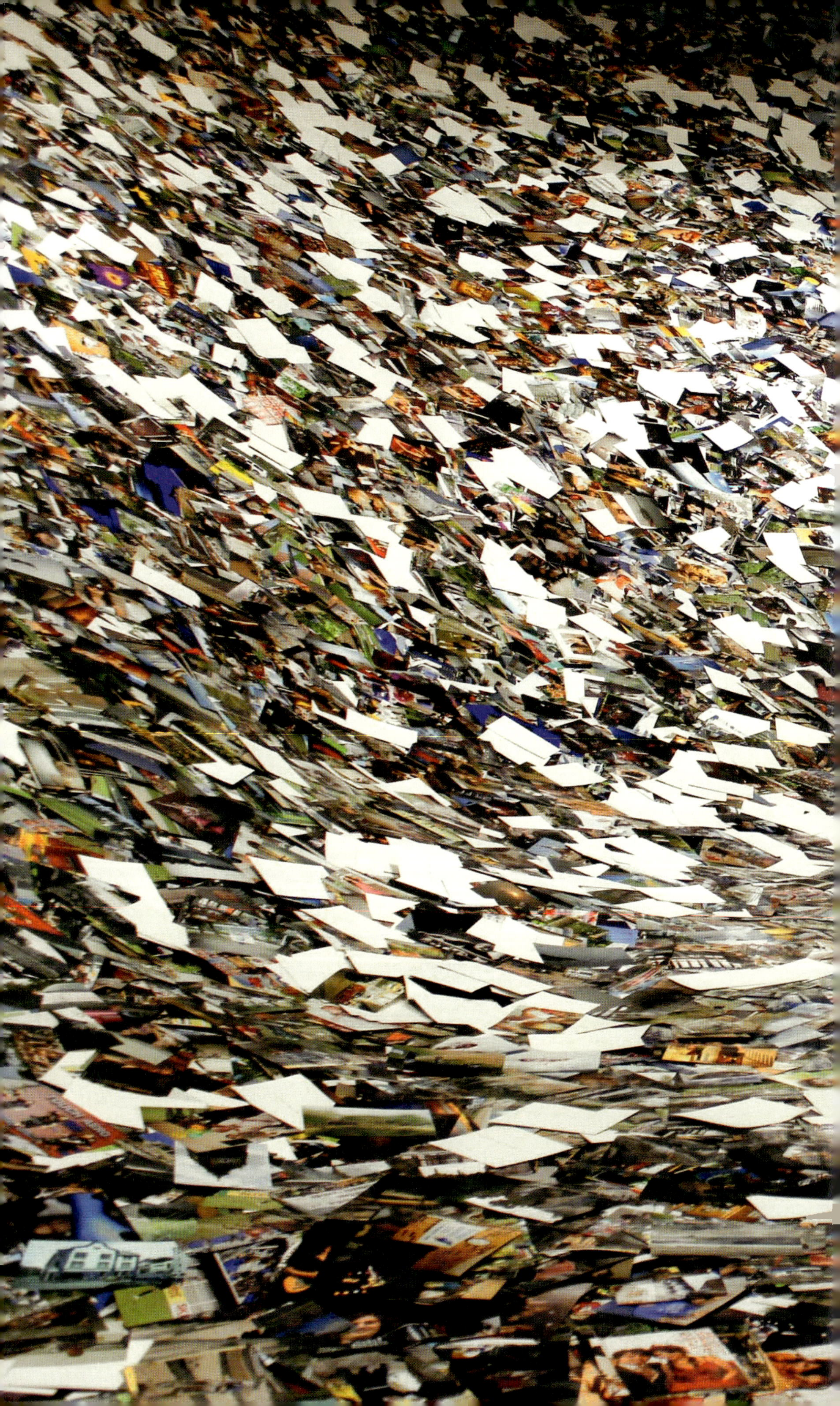

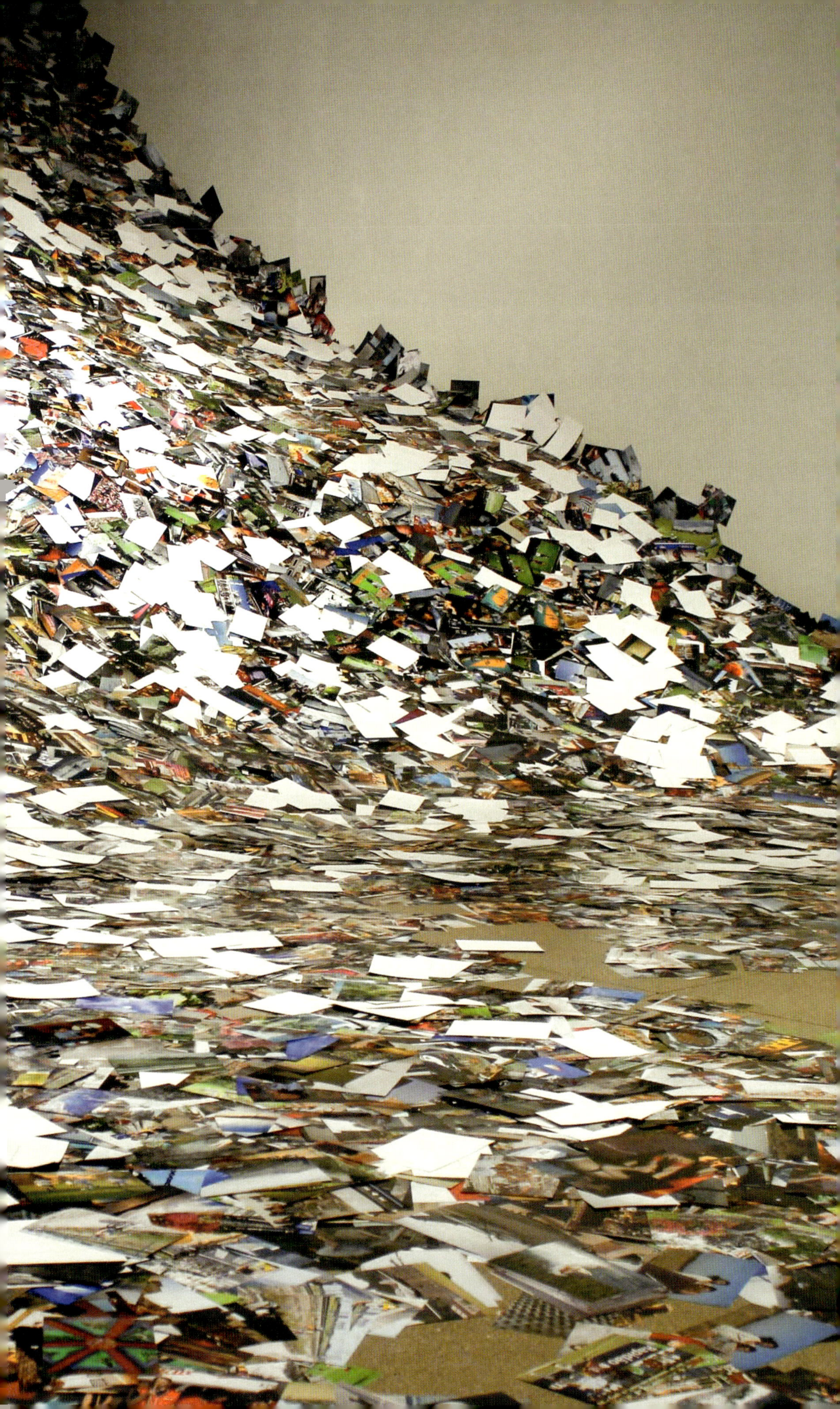

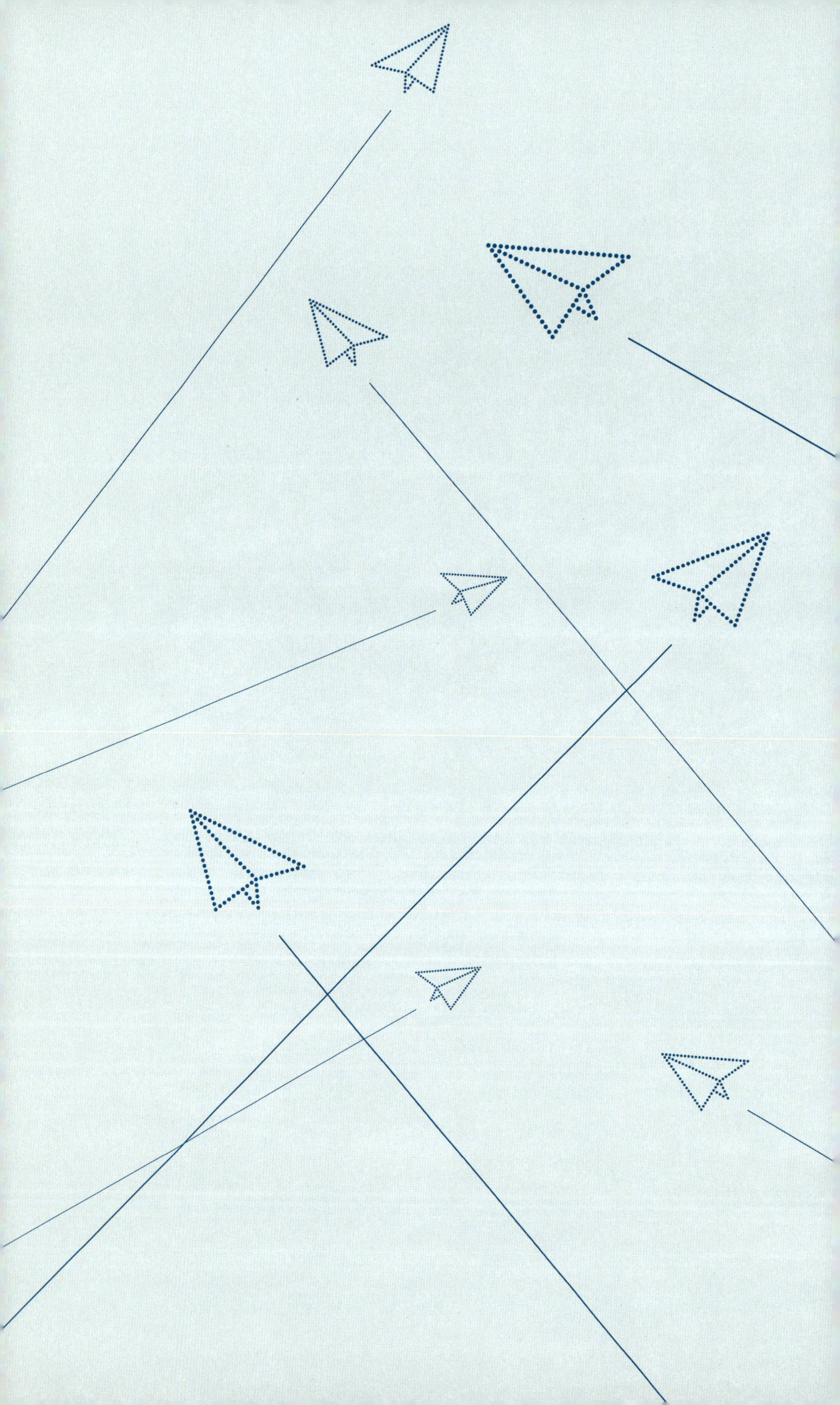

VORWORT

Seit 20 Jahren setzt sich C/O Berlin mit der erzählerischen, der Reportage-, der Mode-, der Werbe- und der Kunstfotografie auseinander. Gegründet, um in der Hauptstadt eine Institution für Fotografie zu etablieren, tragen wir die geläufige Zustellanweisung zur Präzisierung des Adressaten im Briefverkehr in unserem Namen: c/o (care of) Berlin. Als wir im Jahr 2000 mit *Magnum°. Betrachtungen über die Welt* im ehemaligen Kaiserlichen Postfuhramt in Berlin-Mitte unsere erste Ausstellungseröffnung feierten, versinnbildlichte das c/o in unserem Namen eben diesen Vorgang: das Verschicken von Bildern aus der Welt nach Berlin, um sie hier präsentieren zu können. Mehr denn je ziehen heute, da C/O Berlin im Amerika Haus sesshaft geworden ist, die Bildwelten international renommierter Künstler*innen in unsere Räumlichkeiten ein und in Form eigens produzierter Ausstellungen wieder aus diesen aus. So tragen sie zu einer Verbreitung der Sichtweisen bei, wie die Welt wahrgenommen werden kann.

Da das Thema der Post also eng mit unserer Institution verbunden ist, hat uns dies zu einer Ausstellung inspiriert, die sich Geschichte und Gegenwart des Bildversandes widmet. Anlässlich des 20-jährigen Jubiläums von C/O Berlin thematisiert *Send Me an Image. From Postcards to Social Media* eines der spannendsten Phänomene unserer heutigen Bildkultur: Kommunikation mit und Verteilung von Fotografien in der Gegenwart. Ausgehend von der aktuellen Foto- und Medienkunst wirft die Ausstellung einen Blick zurück und erzählt sowohl von Praktiken des Bilderversandes im 19. und 20. Jahrhundert als auch von den zirkulierenden Bildern unserer Tage.

Dieses Ausstellungsthema hat in den vergangenen Monaten weiter an Aktualität und Relevanz gewonnen. Denn seit die globale Covid-19-Pandemie Europa erreicht hat, ist unser Leben von Abstand und Distanz geprägt. Den mobilen Bildern kommt in diesem Kontext eine zusätzliche Bedeutung zu. In Ablösung von klassischen Medien wie der Postkarte spiegeln die im Netz zirkulierenden Bilder den Zeitgeist wider: Ist momentan das an Familie und Freund*innen per Nachrichtendienst versandte oder auf einer Plattform der sozialen Medien gepostete Selfie oder sonstige Bild doch eine der wenigen Möglichkeiten, ein Lebenszeichen zu geben, um zu zeigen, dass wir in Gedanken bei den Menschen sind, die wir während der Pandemie nicht treffen können.

FOREWORD

For twenty years, C/O Berlin has engaged with photography used for storytelling, reportage, and fashion as well as commercial and fine-art photography. Founded in order to establish an institution for photography in Germany's capital, our name bears the typical delivery instructions used to make clear the recipient when posting letters via a third party: we are "care of"—c/o—Berlin. When we celebrated the opening of our first exhibition in 2000 with *Magnum°. Observations on the World* in the former royal post office in Berlin-Mitte, the "c/o" that forms our name epitomized precisely this process of sending images from around the world to Berlin so that they could be shown here. Now more than ever, since C/O Berlin has become a permanent fixture in Amerika Haus, internationally renowned artists send their visual interpretations of the world to our exhibition rooms, only to have them sent back out into the world in the form of the exhibitions we put on, thus contributing to a broadening of visual ways of perceiving that world.

The close connection between the postal service and our institution inspired us to put on an exhibition devoted to the sending of images both in the past and present. Held to mark C/O Berlin's twenty-year anniversary, *Send Me an Image . From Postcards to Social Media* addresses one of the most exciting phenomena in visual culture today: the communication with and distribution of photographs in the present day. The exhibition begins with current media art and fine-art photography, then takes a retrospective approach, investigating both established ways of sending images in the nineteenth and twentieth centuries and of circulating images in our current time.

The topic of this exhibition has become increasingly relevant and topical in recent months. Since the global COVID-19 pandemic reached Europe, our lives have become defined by distance and separation. The circulation of images takes on a new meaning in this context. Moving away from classical media such as postcards, it is images circulating online that reflect the zeitgeist: at the moment, selfies and other images shared with family and friends online using messaging apps or on social media represent one of the few ways of sending a sign of life, in order to show that we are thinking of those individuals we are unable to meet in person during the pandemic.

Da auch das Ausstellungsprogramm von C/O Berlin aufgrund der Pandemie verschoben werden musste, findet unsere Jubiläumsausstellung *Send Me an Image . From Postcards to Social Media* erst im Jahr 2021 statt. Noch im Jubiläumsjahr 2020 aber begann unsere Kooperation mit der Forschungsstelle *Das Technische Bild* an der Humboldt-Universität zu Berlin, um das 20-jährige Bestehen beider Institutionen mit dem Symposium *Return to Sender. Grenzen und Utopien zirkulierender Bilder* zu feiern, das als Live-Stream übertragen wurde und dessen Beiträge für diesen Katalog publizistisch aufbereitet wurden. Bei dem Symposium analysierten die Teilnehmer*innen nicht nur erhellende Beispiele zirkulierender Bilder in Geschichte und Gegenwart, sondern zeigten auch auf, wie sich visuelle Grußbotschaften im Laufe der Jahrzehnte weiterentwickelt haben, wie sie abhängig von den politischen Rahmenbedingungen untersucht wurden, um heutzutage nun neuartige digitale Erscheinungsformen und Übertragungswege zu besetzen. Durch den Live-Stream wurden diese Diskurse direkt digital an Bildproduzent*innen, Follower*innen und Distributor*innen der heutigen Bildkultur weitergegeben. So hat C/O Berlin ein Beispiel gegeben, wie sich auch in Zeiten sozialer Distanz die öffentliche Teilhabe am visuellen Diskurs über Medien wie Fotografie und Video fortsetzen lässt.

Mein besonderer Dank gilt der Leiterin der Forschungsstelle *Das Technische Bild*, Katja Müller-Helle, und allen Autor*innen des vorliegenden Kataloges. Ebenfalls bedanken möchte ich mich bei allen ausgestellten und hier publizierten Künstler*innen, die, wie so oft, als Barometer aktueller Entwicklungen fungieren und uns mit ihren Arbeiten helfen, unsere alltägliche Verwendung der Fotografie zu hinterfragen und zu debattieren. Maßgebliche Impulse verdankt die Ausstellung Clément Chéroux, der 2019 als Kurator des SFMOMA in San Francisco die Schau *Snap + Share. Transmitting Photographs from Mail Art to Social Networks* gezeigt hat. Mein Dank gilt ebenso der Schweizer „Art Mentor Foundation Lucerne" für die großzügige finanzielle Unterstützung des Symposiums *Return to Sender . Grenzen und Utopien zirkulierender Bilder* sowie für die Förderung dieser Publikation. Nicht weniger herzlich möchte ich der LOTTO-Stiftung Berlin für ihre umfangreiche Förderung danken, die diese Ausstellung bei C/O Berlin ermöglicht hat.

Stephan Erfurt,
Vorstandsvorsitzender C/O Berlin Foundation

C/O Berlin's exhibition plans have also been affected by the pandemic and our anniversary exhibition *Send Me an Image . From Postcards to Social Media* is now taking place in 2021. But what did begin in our anniversary year of 2020 was our cooperation with the research center "The Technical Image" at the Humboldt University in Berlin. The symposium *Return to Sender: Utopias and the Limits of Circulating Images* celebrated the twenty-year anniversary of the founding of both our institutions and took place via livestream. The talks given there form the basis for the essays presented in this catalog. In the symposium, participants not only analyzed illuminating examples of circulating images in the past and present, but also showed how visual forms of greetings have developed over the decades, how they have been studied within the context of the current political situation, and consequently, how they have come to inhabit new digital forms and means of transmission today. The livestream meant this discussion was instantly shared digitally with producers of images, followers, and distributors in current visual culture. C/O Berlin thus demonstrated how public participation in a visual discourse on such media as photography and video can still be maintained in the days of social distancing.

Special thanks go to Katja Müller-Helle, head of the research center "The Technical Image," and to all the authors who contributed to the present volume. Moreover, I would like to thank all the artists involved in the exhibition and this publication, who, as ever, keep their fingers on the pulse of current developments and whose work helps us to query and debate our everyday use of photography. The exhibition was occasioned in part by SFMOMA curator Clément Chéroux, whose exhibition *Snap + Share: Transmitting Photographs from Mail Art to Social Networks* took place in San Francisco in 2019. Equally, my thanks go to the Art Mentor Foundation Lucerne in Switzerland for their generous financial support of the symposium *Return to Sender . Utopias and the Limits of Circulating Images* and of this publication. I am equally grateful to LOTTO Stiftung Berlin for the extensive funding that made possible the exhibition at C/O Berlin.

Stephan Erfurt,
CEO of the C/O Berlin Foundation

VOM SENDEN UND TEILEN

Seit die Fotografie im 19. Jahrhundert reproduzierbar wurde, hat sie sich mit verschiedenen Medien verbunden, um auf die Reise zu gehen. Sie wurde als papierner Abzug per Post [✍ Friedrich Tietjen], auf Briefmarken gedruckt, als Lithografie und Offsetdruck, als telegrafisch zerlegtes Bild über Leitungen und Funkwege [✍ Christian Kassung] und schließlich als digitale Datei per Netzverbindung im Echtzeitstreaming versendet [✍ Simon Rothöhler]. All diese Spielarten des Fotografischen haben den mobilen Bilderberg kontinuierlich anwachsen lassen: Schon 1870, während des Deutsch-Französischen Krieges, wurden über 10 Millionen Feldpostkarten innerhalb von knapp fünf Monaten versandt.[1] Ab den 1910er-Jahren wuchs der Markt für Illustrierte und Magazine. Um 1930 wurden allein in Deutschland Zeitungen in einer Gesamtauflage von 5 bis 6 Millionen Exemplaren wöchentlich aufgelegt und in ihnen eine enorme Anzahl von Bildern verbreitet.[2] 2004 wurden innerhalb von 24 Stunden 350.000 Bilder auf die neu gegründete Plattform Flickr geladen.[3] Nach Angaben des Unternehmens wuchs das Volumen bis 2012 auf gesamt rund 8 Milliarden Bilder an.[4] 2013 wurden auf dem Onlinedienst Facebook täglich 343 Mio. Fotos hinzugefügt.[5] Im Jahr 2020 feierte nicht nur die Bildpostkarte ihr 150-jähriges Jubiläum, sondern auch Instagram sein 10-jähriges Bestehen. Angesichts solcher Auflistungen mag der Eindruck entstehen, die viralen Fotografien unserer Tage würden sich in eine zielgerichtete Fortschrittserzählung zunehmender Bildmobilität fügen. Doch unsere Bildkommunikation über soziale Netzwerke wie Facebook (2004), Twitter (2006), Instagram (2010), Snapchat (2011) oder TikTok (2016) ist keine dynamisierte Fortführung von geschichtlichen Parametern, sondern eine Zäsur.

Unsere Ausstellung *Send Me an Image . From Postcards to Social Media* unternimmt den Versuch, das neue Terrain zirkulierender Bilder zu vermessen, und zwar aus der Perspektive gegenwärtiger künstlerischer Praktiken mittels des Mediums Fotografie. Dabei fragt sie sowohl nach Brüchen als auch nach Kontinuitäten zu traditionellen „reisenden" Bildwelten.

In der Fotografie hat sich jüngst ein tiefgreifender Wandel vollzogen. Als die Digitalisierung in den 1990er-Jahren einsetzte, standen die Produktionsbedingungen des verän-

Text: Felix Hoffmann & Kathrin Schönegg

ON SENDING AND SHARING

Photography has joined forces with different media since it became reproducible in the nineteenth century. Photographs have been shared as paper copies by post [✎ Friedrich Tietjen], printed on postage stamps, made into lithographs and off-set prints, transmitted via telegraph wires and radio waves [✎ Christian Kassung], and most recently streamed online as digital files transmitted in real time [✎ Simon Rothöhler]. This plethora of ways to make and share photographs has caused the mountain of mobile images to grow continuously: in less than five months in 1870 during the Franco-Prussian War, over ten million postcards were sent from the front.[1] The market for newspapers and magazines began to grow from the 1910s. In 1930 in Germany alone, over five to six million newspapers were printed each week, distributing a staggering number of images.[2] In 2004, 350 thousand images were uploaded onto the newly founded photo-sharing service Flickr in just twenty-four hours.[3] According to Flickr, the site was hosting roughly eight billion images by 2012.[4] In 2013 people were uploading an average of 343 million photos onto Facebook each day.[5] The year 2020 was the sesquicentennial of the picture postcard, and also marked the tenth anniversary of Instagram's launch. In light of such lists, one might have the impression that viral photography today fits into a teleological history of progress toward increasingly mobile images. Yet our visual communication via social media including Facebook (2004), Twitter (2006), Instagram (2010), Snapchat (2011), and TikTok (2016) marks not a dynamic continuation of historical parameters, but a break with them.

Our exhibition *Send Me an Image . From Postcards to Social Media* attempts to chart the new terrain of circulating images from the perspective of contemporary art practices using photography as a medium. This raises questions about disrupting and perpetuating the traditional world of "traveling" images.

More recently, a profound change has taken place in photography. As digitalization took hold in the 1990s, the production conditions of the changing medium were in flux. So were the possibilities for manipulating photographs and thus tampering with the much-ballyhooed belief, one underpinning the medium since its invention,

derten Mediums, seine Manipulationsmöglichkeiten und damit der vielbesungene Wirklichkeitsglaube zur Diskussion, der die Fotografie seit ihrem Aufkommen gestützt hatte. Obwohl schon damals das „Ende der Fotografie"[6] heraufbeschworen wurde, fiel erst die zweite Phase der Digitalisierung mit einem realen Niedergang zusammen – dem der analogen Fotoindustrie, die sich um 2005 im Produktionsstopp von Papieren, Filmen und weiterem Equipment durch traditionsreiche Firmen wie Kodak zeigte. Im künstlerischen Bereich führte das Ende der analogen Fotografie zu einer Wiederkehr und verstärkten Reflexion ihrer Anfänge. Die Arbeit in der Dunkelkammer, altehrwürdige Apparate wie die Plattenkamera und Verfahren aus der fotografischen Frühzeit erleben eine neue Aktualität.[7] Unter dem Begriff „Fotografie" werden heute allerlei Spielarten des Mediums subsumiert: Verschiedenste digitale Varianten, die als codierter Datensatz bestehen oder über Bildschirme und Projektoren visualisiert werden, existieren neben Bildern, die an einen physischen Träger wie Papier, Zelluloid oder Metall gebunden sind. Die Digitalisierung hat der materiellen Vielfalt der historischen Fotografie neue mediale Formen hinzugefügt. In der dritten und jüngsten Phase der Digitalisierung in den 2010er-Jahren steht nicht mehr die veränderte Materialität des Mediums, sondern seine Einbindung in digitale Infrastrukturen zur Debatte:

Der Vernetzung und Verteilung von Bildern kommt in der Gegenwart die zentrale Rolle zu.

Der Diskurs hat sich von der Bildproduktion hin zur Bildzirkulation verschoben: Nicht mehr der technologische Wandel und die veränderten Herstellungsbedingungen der Fotografie werden diskutiert, sondern die Praktiken, die sich mit der Einbindung der Bilder in digitale Infrastrukturen etabliert haben.[8]

Fraglos ist eine zentrale Bedingung der „Fluidität"[9] der neuen Fotografie ihre Ablösung vom physischen Träger. Doch erst der Zusammenschluss von Kamera und Internet hat das gegenwärtige Zeitalter der Bildkommunikation eingeläutet und Fotografie „sozial" werden lassen. Es sind tragbare Devices wie das Smartphone, in denen Aufnahme (Kamera), Speicherung (Datei) und Vernetzung (Distribution im Netz) in einem Gerät verschmelzen. Damit lassen sich unsere Bilder in „social photographs"[10] und „networked images"[11] verwandeln, die uns im Alltag als mobile und zirkulierende Bilder begegnen. Stille und bewegte Fotografien sind in neuen Formen wie GIFs und Live-Fotos zusammengewachsen. Die Motive, die sie zeigen, sind oftmals banal. Bildproduzent*innen stellen Schnappschüsse und persönliche Fotos, domestizierte und vernakuläre Ansichten her, um sie im digitalen Äther mit anderen zu teilen. Neue Bildgenres wie Foodfotografie und das Selfie sind entstanden [↗ Wolfgang Ullrich]: Wir fotografieren Essen, Katzen, Sonnenuntergänge und uns selbst. Wir verarbeiten die Bilder anderer, die wir online finden, fertigen Screenshots an und verwenden Re-Posting-Apps, um uns fremde Bilder zu eigen zu machen. Vielerorts hat die Appropriation den Akt der Aufnahme ersetzt und – etwa in Form des Internetphänomens Meme, bei dem Bild und Text immer wieder neu zusammengesetzt, interpretiert und verteilt werden, – die Tradition der satirischen, gesellschaftskritischen und politischen Bild-Text-Kombinationen im ort- und zeitlosen, digitalen Raum re-aktualisiert [↗ Kerstin Schankweiler]. Gefundene Bilder aus dem Netz können beschnitten, mit Filtern belegt, gelikt und verlinkt, getaggt und kommentiert, mit neuer Schrift versehen und immer wieder aufs Neue in diverse Plattformen eingespeist werden, um sie auf den Displays unserer Digital Devices zu betrachten, erneut bearbeiten und wieder verteilen zu können.

that photographs represent reality. Although the "end of photography" was discussed even then,[6] its true downfall came with the second phase of digitalization, ushered in around 2005, when the production of photographic papers, films, and other equipment long produced by such established firms as Kodak was halted. In the world of fine-art photography, the end of analog photography meant a return to and reflection on photography's roots. Darkroom work, old-fashioned equipment such as plate cameras, and processes used in the early days of photography regained relevance.[7] Today, the term *photography* covers a huge variety of approaches to the medium: a wide array of digital uses such as encoded data sets and on-screen visualizations exist alongside images that inhabit the physical realm, such as paper, celluloid, and metal. Digitalization has added new medial forms to the material diversity of historic photography. The third and latest phase of digitalization in the 2010s does not call into question the changed materiality of the medium, but rather its entrenchment in digital infrastructures:

the networking and sharing of images has now taken on a central role.

The discourse has moved on from the production of images to their circulation: it is no longer photography's technological transformation and changed production methods that are the focus of debate, but rather the increasingly established practices of embedding images in digital infrastructures.[8]

The decoupling of new photography from a physical medium is doubtless a central aspect in its "fluidity."[9] The coupling of camera and internet has ushered in the present era of visual communication and "social" photography, with portable devices such as smartphones unifying the functions of taking a picture (with their built-in cameras), saving it (as a data file), and circulating it (through online distribution). Thus our images metamorphose into the "social photographs"[10] and "networked images"[11] we encounter in our everyday lives as mobile and circulating images. Static and moving images have merged into such new formats as GIFs and Live Photos. The subjects shown are often banal. Image producers create snapshots and personal photographs, domesticating and vernacularizing their images in order to share them with others by digital means. New genres of photography such as food photography and the selfie have become established [⊲ Wolfgang Ullrich]. We photograph food, cats, sunsets, and ourselves. We edit photographs we find online, take screenshots, and use reposting apps to appropriate the images of others. In many places, appropriation has replaced the act of taking a photograph. Internet phenomena such as the meme, which continually recombines, reinterprets, and shares images and texts, reinvigorates the tradition of satirical, societally critical, and political pairings of images and texts, in a digital space untethered from space and time [⊲ Kerstin Schankweiler]. Images found online are cropped and filters applied; they are liked and linked; tagged and commented on; written on with new typefaces and constantly uploaded across various sites in order to be viewed on the screens of our digital devices, only to be once again edited and shared.

The feedback loop in which images in online circulation also appear in physical space has been well established for some time. Images that have gone viral appear in cities as tags, stickers, and graffiti, only to be photographed out

Längst ist die Rückkopplung der digital zirkulierenden Fotografie in den physischen Raum gängige Praxis, wenn viral gegangene Motive in Form von Tags, Stickern oder Graffitis in die Städte und von dort, wiederabfotografiert, zurück in die sozialen Netzwerke migrieren oder wenn sich, wie zuletzt bei den globalen Black-Lives-Matter-Protesten, Bilder des Widerstands und von politischen Aktionen über das Internet verbreiten und dann am anderen Ende in der physischen Welt Nachahmer*innen und Verbündete finden.

Die aktuelle Bildpraxis lässt sich kaum mehr in tradierten fotografischen Paradigmen beschreiben, die das Medium längste Zeit als Repräsentation der Welt verstanden haben. Denn Motiv und Einzelbild sind heute in den Hintergrund getreten – auf Plattformen wie Snapchat werden sie nach 24 Stunden gelöscht; andere Netzwerke ordnen nach Aktualität, so dass die Aufmerksamkeit für jedes erscheinende Bild direkt vom nächstfolgenden überschrieben wird. Heute sind Fotografien fragmentierte Da-Seins-Behauptungen, deren Funktion in der eigenen Präsenz, aber nicht mehr der Repräsentation der Welt liegt. Wenn aktuell also von der Allgegenwart des Fotografischen, der „Ubiquität"[13] der Fotografie die Rede ist, ist an die Stelle ihres Abgesangs und Endes ein Motiv getreten, das auf eine lange Tradition in der Fotogeschichte zurückblickt und die Entwicklung des Mediums kontinuierlich begleitete. Schon in ihren Erfinderjahren 1839/40 sprach man von einer „Daguerreotypomanie"[13], auf die im weiteren Verlauf des 19. Jahrhunderts eine durch günstige, standardisierte Carte-de-Visite-Papieraufnahmen ausgelöste „Kartomanie"[14] folgte; in den 1980er-Jahren versuchte man, der „Bilderberge"[15] Herr zu werden; in den 1990er-Jahren wurde ein „Bilderstrom", ja eine „Bilderflut" konstatiert[16]. Und obschon die Anzahl der heute durch die sozialen Kanäle flimmernden Bilder alle vorherigen Massen in den Schatten stellt – online kursiert die Schätzung, aktuell würden in zwei Minuten mehr Fotos geteilt, als im gesamten 19. Jahrhundert aufgenommen – haben wir es doch mit einem neuen Phänomen zu tun.

Nicht die Erfüllung des in den 1990er-Jahren ausgerufenen „Pictorial"[17] bzw. „Iconic Turn"[18] wird darin erlebbar, sondern eine neue Form der Fotografie.

Plädierte man in den 1990er Jahren für eine Bildhermeneutik, um Bilder wie Texte zu lesen, unterlagen diesem Impuls gängige Ordnungsschemata und Kategorien der Kunst- und Bildgeschichte, die angesichts der Praktiken der sozialen Netzwerke nicht mehr greifen. Sowohl bei kunsthistorischen Werkbetrachtungen als auch bei tradierten linearen Sendungen wie der Postkarte, waren Autor und Rezipient bzw. Absender und Adressat noch klar zu bestimmen. Im digitalen Bilderzirkel sind diese Differenzen obsolet geworden: Öffentlicher und privater Raum, professionelles und amateurhaftes Handeln, das Gewollte und das Kontingente sind miteinander verschmolzen. Das ikonische Einzelbild ist obsolet geworden. Wichtiger als das, was das geteilte Bild zeigt, ist dessen Zirkulation in der Welt und dessen Verteilung im digitalen Äther.

Neue Bedeutung kommt Metadaten zu [✐ Estelle Blaschke] und damit all jenen in den Apparaten präfigurierten und zusätzlich hinzugefügten Informationen wie Kameramarke, -modell und -einstellungen, aber auch Zeitpunkt und GPS-Location der Aufnahme, die in unseren Bildern hinterlegt sind. Diese werden von Algorithmen und Maschinen

in the world and uploaded back onto social media. Photographs of resistance and political action during Black Lives
Matter protests were circulated online, finding imitators
and sympathizers at the other end of the real world.

Using traditional photography paradigms that frame the medium as a representation of the world is barely an option anymore when describing current
image-making practices. The subject and the individual image are of secondary
importance today. Social media apps such as Snapchat delete photographs after
twenty-four hours whereas others rank images by topicality, so that the attention one
pays to every image posted is displaced by the one immediately following. Photographs today are fragmentary "I-was-there" claims whose function rests in asserting
one's presence rather than representing the world. So if, at the moment, the "ubiquity"[12] of photography is under much discussion, a new subject is coming into view even
as traditional photography fades out and ceases to exist, a subject that may also look
back over an equally long tradition in the history of photography, one that has been
present in the years the medium has evolved. In the very years of the daguerreotype's
invention, there was talk of a "daguerreotypomania,"[13] which was succeeded by a "car-
tomania"[14] as cheaper, standardized paper *cartes de visite* supplanted daguerreotypes
over the course of the nineteenth century. In the 1980s, people sought to master the
"mountain of images";[15] in the 1990s, people spoke of a flood, even a torrent of photographs.[16] Yet even as the sheer mass of photographs flickering across social media
sites puts all the past masses of images to shame—an online estimate suggests that at
the moment, more photos are shared every two minutes than were taken in the whole
of the nineteenth century—we are experiencing a new phenomenon.

This is not the realization of the "pictorial"[17] or "iconic turn"[18] mooted in the 1990s, but rather a new form of photography.

The plea in the 1990s for a hermeneutics of the image that allowed images to be
read as texts was predicated on the impulse to draw on established schemata of ordering and categorization in the fields of art history and visual studies, schemata that
no longer apply within the practices of social media. Author and recipient, or sender
and recipient, may be clearly defined when viewing artworks in art history or in traditional and linear means of transmission such as postcards. But the circuitous routes
taken by images online have rendered such differences obsolete. Public and private
spheres, professional and amateur actions, and the intended and the contingent have
melded. The iconic single image has become obsolete. The fact that an image is circulating in the world and shared in the digital ether has become more important than
its visual content.

Metadata [⊿ Estelle Blaschke] have taken on new meaning. So too does all the
associate information preset and added by the devices we use, such as camera brands,
models, and settings, as well as the time and GPS coordinates of images. This data is
processed by algorithms and machines, calculated and classified, thus keeping circu-
lar transmission and networking technologies busy. These technologies remain—for
now—supported by humans who are working as content moderators and censors.
These individuals take on the task of sorting out the masses of images and, in doing
so, train machines to perform these jobs autonomously [⊿ Katja Müller-Helle]. Our

prozessiert, errechnet und klassifiziert und halten so die zirkuläre Übertragungs- und Vernetzungstechnologie am Laufen, die – zumindest heute noch – von menschlichen Akteuren unterstützt wird, die als Content-Moderator*innen und Zensor*innen das Aussortieren der Bildermassen übernehmen und im gleichen Zuge die Maschinen trainieren, dies künftig selbstständig zu tun [◁ Katja Müller-Helle]. Unsere Bilder sind ein Kapital, von dem in erster Linie die großen Internetkonzerne profitieren. Wie denken Künstler*innen über diese gegenwärtigen Bildkulturen nach? Wie finden die neuen Phänomene zirkulierender Bilder und Post Pictures [◁ Matthias Bruhn] Eingang in die Foto- und Medienkunst? Und inwieweit lassen sich von dort Verbindungen in die Fotogeschichte ziehen? Dies sind die Fragen, vor denen wir heute stehen, und die dieses Buch und die Ausstellung diskursiv zu erhellen versuchen.

....

1   Vgl. Robert Lebeck, Gerhard Kaufmann, *Viele Grüße. Eine Kulturgeschichte der Postkarte,* Dortmund 1985, S. 404ff.

2   Konrad Dussel, *Bilder als Botschaft. Bildstrukturen deutscher Illustrierter 1905–1945 im Spannungsfeld von Politik, Wirtschaft und Publikum,* Köln 2019, S. 47ff.

3   Vgl. dazu Erik Kessels *24HRS in Photos* (2004)

4   Vgl. https://blog.flickr.net/de/2012/12/12/flickr-noch-besser-nutzen-besser-navigieren-und-fotos-entdecken/ [Zugriff am 11. Oktober 2020]

5   Vgl. https://de.statista.com/statistik/daten/studie/312268/umfrage/taeglich-auf-facebook-hochgeladene-und-geteilte-fotos/ [Zugriff am 15. Oktober 2020]

6   William J. Mitchell, *The Reconfigured Eye. Visual Truth in the Post-Photographic Era,* Cambridge/Mass. 1992, S. 20; Geoffrey Batchen, "Phantasm: Digital Imaging and the Death of Photography", in: *Aperture,* 136, 1994, S. 47–51; Hubertus von Amelunxen (Hg.), *Fotografie nach der Fotografie,* Dresden/Basel 1996

7   Ruth Horak, "The Analog Turn", in: *Eikon. International Magazine for Photography and Media Art,* 88, 2014, S. 49–58. C/O Berlin hat diesem Thema die Gruppenausstellung *Back to the Future. From the 19th Century in the 21st Century* gewidmet (29. September–1. Dezember 2018)

8   Siehe dazu u.a. Winfried Gerling, Susanne Holschbach, Petra Löffler, *Bilder verteilen. Fotografische Praktiken in der digitalen Kultur, Bielefeld 2018, S. 8ff.;* Daniel Rubinstein, Katrina Sluis, "The Digital Image in Photographic Culture. Algorithmic Photography and the Crisis of Representation", in: Martin Lister (Hg): *The Photographic Image in Digital Culture,* London/New York 2018, S. 22–40 sowie Hito Steyerl, "In Defense of the Poor Image", in: *e-flux journal,* 10, 2009, S. 1–9 (https://www.e-flux.com/journal/10/61362/in-defense-of-the-poor-image/)

9   André Gunthert, "Einführung. Das fluide Bild", in: Ders., *Das geteilte Bild. Essays zur digitalen Fotografie,* Göttingen 2019, S. 13–21, hier S. 16

10 Nathan Jurgonson, *The Social Photo: On Photography and Social Media,* London/New York 2019.

11 Daniel Rubinstein, Katrina Sluis, "A Life More Photographic: Mapping the Networked Image", in: *Photographies,* März 2008, S. 9–28

12 Arlid Fetveit, "The Ubiquity of Photography", in: Ulrik Ekman (Hg.), *Throughout. Art and Culture Emerging with Ubiquitous Computing,* Cambridge Mass./London 2013, S. 89–102

13 Vgl. Th. Maurisset, "Daguerreotypomanie, 1839/1840, Lithografie", publiziert in: Rolf H. Krauss, *Die Fotografie in der Karikatur,* Seebruch am Chiemsee 1978, S. 8f.

14 Jochen Voigt, *Faszination Sammeln. Cartes de Visite. Eine Kulturgeschichte der photographischen Visitenkarte,* Chemnitz 2006, S. 28

15 Joachim Schmid, "Keine neuen Fotos bis die alten aufgebraucht sind!" [1987], in: *Hohe und niedere Fotografie,* Hafensalon Köln 1988, S. 21–26

16 Vilem Flusser, "Bilderstatus", in: ders., *Medienkultur,* Frankfurt am Main 1997, S. 69–82, hier S. 73

17 William J. Thomas Mitchell: "The Pictorial Turn", in: *Artforum,* März 1992, S. 89ff.

18 Gottfried Böhm: "Die Wiederkehr der Bilder", in: Ders. (Hg.): *Was ist ein Bild?* München 1994, S. 11–38

images are a form of capital from which major internet firms are most likely to profit. How do artists reflect on contemporary image culture? Where do the new phenomena of circulating and post pictures [✒ Matthias Bruhn] make themselves felt in the fields of fine-art photography and media art? And to what degree is it possible to tie these to the history of photography? These are the questions facing us today, the questions that the discourse presented in this book and exhibition seeks to illuminate.

1   See Robert Lebeck and Gerhard Kaufmann, *Viele Grüße: Eine Kulturgeschichte der Postkarte* (Dortmund: Harenberg, 1985), 404ff.

2   Konrad Dussel, *Bilder als Botschaft: Bildstrukturen deutscher Illustrierter 1905–1945 im Spannungsfeld von Politik, Wirtschaft und Publikum* (Cologne: Herbert von Halem Verlag, 2019), 47ff.

3   See also Erik Kessels's *24HRS in Photos* (2004).

4   See Markus Spiering, "Flickr noch besser nutzen: Besser Navigieren und Fotos entdecken," Flickr Blog, accessed October 11, 2020, https://blog.flickr.net/de/2012/12/12 /flickr-noch-besser-nutzen-besser-navigieren-und-fotos-entdecken/.

5   See "Anzahl der täglich bei Facebook hochgeladenen Fotos in den Jahres 2008 bis 2014," Statista, accessed October 15, 2020, https://de.statista.com/statistik/daten/studie/312268 /umfrage/taeglich-auf-facebook-hochgeladene-und-geteilte-fotos/.

6   William J. Mitchell, *The Reconfigured Eye: Visual Truth in the Post-Photographic Era* (Cambridge, MA: MIT Press, 1992), 20; Geoffrey Batchen, "Phantasm: Digital Imaging and the Death of Photography," *Aperture* 136 (1994): 47–51; Hubertus von Amelunxen, ed., *Photography After Photography: Memory and Representation in the Digital Age* (Amsterdam: G&B Arts, 1996).

7   Ruth Horak, "The Analog Turn," *Eikon: International Magazine for Photography and Media Art* 88 (2014): 49–58. The C/O Berlin group exhibition *Back to the Future: The 19th Century in the 21st Century* (September 29–December 1, 2018) was devoted to this theme.

8   On this subject, see, for example: Winfried Gerling, Susanne Holschbach, and Petra Löffler, *Bilder verteilen: Fotografische Praktiken in der digitalen Kultur* (Bielefeld: transcript Verlag, 2018), 8ff.; Daniel Rubinstein and Katrina Sluis, "The Digital Image in Photographic Culture: Algorithmic Photography and the Crisis of Representation," in Martin Lister, ed., *The Photographic Image in Digital Culture* (London and New York: Routledge, 2018), 22–40; Hito Steyerl, "In Defense of the Poor Image," *e-flux journal* 10 (2009): 1–9, https://www.e-flux .com/journal/10/61362/in-defense-of-the-poor-image/.

9   André Gunthert, "Einführung: Das fluide Bild," in Gunthert, ed., *Das geteilte Bild: Essays zur digitalen Fotografie* (Göttingen: Konstanz University Press, 2019), 13–21, here 16.

10 Nathan Jurgonson, *The Social Photo: On Photography and Social Media* (London/New York: Verso Books, 2019).

11 Daniel Rubinstein and Katrina Sluis, "A Life More Photographic: Mapping the Networked Image," *Photographies* (March 2008): 9–28.

12 Arlid Fetveit, "The Ubiquity of Photography," in Ulrik Ekman, ed., *Throughout: Art and Culture Emerging with Ubiquitous Computing* (Cambridge, MA, and London: MIT Press, 2013), 89–102.

13 See Théodore Maurisset, "Daguerreotypomanie, 1839/1840, Lithografie," in Rolf H. Krauss, *Die Fotografie in der Karikatur* (Seebruch am Chiemsee: Heering Verlag, 1978), 8–9.

14 Jochen Voigt, *Faszination Sammeln: Cartes de Visite; Eine Kulturgeschichte der photographischen Visitenkarte* (Chemnitz: Edition Mobilis, 2006), 28.

15 Joachim Schmid, "Keine neuen Fotos bis die alten aufgebraucht sind!" (1987), in *Hohe und niedere Fotografie* (Cologne: Hafensalon Köln, 1988), 21–26.

16 Vilem Flusser, "Bilderstatus," in *Medienkultur* (Frankfurt am Main: Fischer Taschenbuch Verlag, 1997), 69–82, here 73.

17 William J. Thomas Mitchell, "The Pictorial Turn," *Artforum* (March 1992): 89ff.

18 Gottfried Böhm, "Die Wiederkehr der Bilder," in Böhm, ed., *Was ist ein Bild?* (Munich: Wilhelm Fink Verlag, 1994), 11–38.

Text: Wolfgang Ullrich

VON DER IKONE ZUM SELFIE
Über die Mobilmachung des Gesichts

Die Geschichte der Bilder war immer auch die Geschichte einer Konkurrenz, gar eines Konflikts zwischen ortsfesten und mobilen Bildwerken. Wieder und wieder wurde versucht, den einen Typus gegen den anderen auszuspielen, so als komme entweder nur in immobilen Artefakten oder aber nur in transportablen Objekten zur Geltung, was Bilder ‚eigentlich' ausmache. Und natürlich ist die Geschichte der Bilder reich an Gattungen, die die Ortsfestigkeit oder die Mobilität voraussetzen: Grabmäler, Freskomalerei oder ‚site specific art' auf der einen Seite, Münzen, Reisealtäre oder Postkarten auf der anderen Seite. Dass diese Konkurrenz nie zugunsten eines Typs entschieden wurde, liegt an ihrerseits gegenläufigen Eigenschaften von Bildwerken. So kann ein Bild stabiler sein als das, was es darstellt, ist aber vielleicht beweglicher als sein Sujet.

Bezogen auf Porträts bedeutet das einerseits, dass das Aussehen eines Menschen dauerhaft fixiert wird. Dieser altert, verändert sich, stirbt, aber das Bild zeigt ihn immer gleich (bis es sich selbst auflöst). Indem es etwas Vergängliches unvergänglich werden lässt, eignet das Porträt sich zum Andenken – als Memorialbild –, weckt aber auch die Erwartung, mehr als nur eine Momentaufnahme zu liefern, ja das zu zeigen, was am Menschen selbst dauerhaft ist und sein Wesen

FROM ICONS TO SELFIES
On Setting Faces in Motion

The history of images has always been the history of the competition—or even the conflict—between static and mobile images. Over and again, attempts are made to set one in opposition to the other, as if only immobile artifacts or portable objects are capable of revealing what images "really" are. And naturally, the history of images is rich in variants that require either stability or mobility: tombs, frescoes, and site-specific art on the one hand, and coins, portable altars, and postcards on the other. The fact that this competition was never decided in favor of one or the other is due to the opposing qualities of images. An image can be more stable than its subject, but it can also be much more flexible than what it represents.

Looking at portraits, a person's appearance is, on the one hand, permanently fixed. A person ages, changes, and dies, but the way a portrait depicts him remains constant (until it disintegrates). By making something fleeting into something fixed, the portrait is an ideal memento—a memorial picture—but it is also expected to provide more than just a snapshot. It is expected to reveal that part of the person that remains stable; the essential part of his being. In this way, a portrait can be elevated to the ideal of the person being

ausmacht. Ein Porträt kann daher zum Idealbild des Porträtierten überhöht werden, das von allem bloß Beiläufigen gereinigt ist. Ein derart wahres Bild soll dann aber auch nur an ausgewählten Orten stehen und am besten dort einen festen Platz haben, wo es die porträtierte Person am besten repräsentieren kann. In der Ortsfestigkeit wird die Dauerhaftigkeit des Porträts eigens manifestiert, aus einer Eigenschaft, die das Bild qua Bild hat, wird ein Geltungsanspruch. Das gilt für ein ägyptisches Mumienbildnis in einem Grab genauso wie für die Gemälde einer Ahnengalerie oder für die Porträts der Kanzlergalerie im Berliner Bundeskanzleramt. (Und deshalb gehören zu jeder revolutionsartigen Bewegung Bilderstürze. Dass allein die Deportation eines ortsfesten Bildwerks dann schon als Zerstörung klassifiziert wird, zeugt von der Bedeutung des festen Ortes. Man denke etwa an zahlreiche Marx- oder Lenindenkmäler, die in der ehemaligen DDR nach 1990 entfernt wurden. Obwohl sie heute unbeschadet in Museumsdepots stehen, ist allein ihr Verschwinden für diejenigen, die dem untergegangenen Regime ideologisch nahestehen, ein ikonoklastischer Akt.)

Andererseits aber schätzt man es, dass sich das Porträt einer Person verschicken oder in beliebige Konstellationen bringen lässt, während die Porträtierten ihren Ort oft nicht oder nur schwer verlassen können und auch sonst vielfach unflexibel sind, was ihre Umgebungen und Kontakte anbelangt.

Als Bilder können sie vor allem an mehreren Orten präsent sein, zumal wenn diese in vervielfältigter Form vorliegen. So sorgte allein die Werkstatt Lucas Cranachs für hunderte von Luther-Porträts, die überall dort zum Einsatz kamen, wo man sich zur Reformation bekannte.

Im Lauf der Geschichte entwickelten sich aber auch Bildpraktiken, bei denen die beiden Eigenschaften von Porträts – ihre idealisierend-unveränderliche Erscheinungsweise und ihre Mobilität – gleichermaßen genutzt wurden. So entstand im römischen Kaiserreich ein Bilderkult, bei dem ein Porträt des Kaisers nahezu denselben Status hatte wie dieser selbst. Bildnisse von ihm vertraten ihn in den Provinzen, beim Militär und vor Gericht, „damit die Amtshandlungen bekräftigt werden", denn „da er ein Mensch ist, [kann er] nicht überall gegenwärtig sein", wie es in einem Text aus dem frühen 5. Jahrhundert heißt.[1] Die Bildnisse, „aus Gründen rascher Herstellbarkeit und bequemer Transportfähigkeit" üblicherweise „in Wachsfarben ausgeführt und auf Holztafeln gemalt", wurden zum Amtsantritt versandt; an den jeweiligen Zielorten fand der Bildempfang in Form eines aufwendigen Zeremoniells statt, gelegentlich kam es jedoch auch zu einer „Verweigerung der Annahme" (einer frühen Form von ‚Return to Sender'!), womit die kaiserliche Autorität unmittelbar infrage gestellt war.[2]

Ohne die Mobilität der Bilder wäre das Reich in seiner Größe also nicht oder nur viel schwerer zu regieren gewesen. Zugleich konnten die Porträts aber nur deshalb als Autoritäten anerkannt werden, weil man in ihnen die Essenz – die den beliebigen Moment transzendierende Gestalt – des jeweiligen Kaisers verkörpert sah. Daher bekamen sie an vielen Orten einen festen Sitz und wurden in eine institutionelle Infrastruktur eingebettet, innerhalb derer sie wirksam werden konnten. Die Praxis, ein Foto des Staatsoberhaupts in jeder Amtsstube aufzuhängen, ist ein spätes Echo dieses kaiserlichen Bilderkults; dahinter steht die Erwartung, allein mit einem Bild lasse sich die herrschende Ordnung stabilisieren.

portrayed, cleansed of anything merely incidental. But accordingly, such a true likeness should only be displayed in select places and should ideally have a fixed position from which to best represent the person portrayed. The static position represents that permanency of the portrait itself; a claim to validity arises from the quality of the image as an image. This is just as true of an Egyptian portrait of a mummy on a tomb as it is for portraits in a gallery of ancestral portraits or in the portraits of the chancellors' gallery in the Federal Chancellery in Berlin. (This is why iconoclasm forms part of every revolutionary movement. The fact alone that the "deportation" of a fixed image is deemed destruction illustrates the importance of fixed location. One need only think of the numerous statues of Marx and Lenin that were removed in the former GDR after 1990. Though they are now in museum depots unscathed, their disappearance alone is an iconoclastic act for those ideologically aligned with the fallen regime.)

On the other hand, the fact that a portrait of a person can be sent and arranged in any constellation is to be appreciated, whereas it is often difficult or impossible to so freely move the individuals depicted, inflexible as they are with regard to their surroundings and contacts.

Most importantly, they can be present in many places at once as images, especially if available as reproductions. Lucas Cranach's workshop alone produced hundreds of Luther portraits, which were displayed wherever people professed support for the Reformation.

But over the course of history, pictorial practices have also developed where the two properties of the portrait—its idealized, unchanging appearance and its portability—were exploited simultaneously. In the Roman Empire, a cult of image arose in which a portrait of the emperor had almost the same status as the emperor himself. Images stood in for him in the provinces, in the military, and at court, "to sign off on official acts," because "since he is a human, [he] cannot be present everywhere," as stated in a text from the early fifth century.[1] The portraits, "for reasons of quick producibility and convenient transportation," were usually "made in wax colors and painted on wooden panels," and were sent out when he assumed office; each image was received at its respective destination with an elaborate ceremony, but occasionally there would be a "refusal of acceptance" (an early "return to sender"!), which immediately called the imperial authority into question.[2]

Owing to the size of the empire, it would not have been possible to rule without portable images, or it would have been much more difficult. But the portraits could only be recognized as authorities because they were seen as the essence—a form transcending a particular moment—embodying the present emperor. As such, they took up a permanent seat in many places and were embedded in an institutional infrastructure within which they wielded power. The practice of hanging a photo of the head of state in every government office is a late echo of this imperial cult of image; behind this is the expectation that the prevailing order can be maintained with just one image.

Hans Belting has shown that the image cult of the Roman Empire also provided the basis for Christian icons. Through icons, the opposing qualities of images were further inflated. Out of an essentialist longing for a static image

Hans Belting hat gezeigt, dass der Bilderkult der römischen Kaiserzeit auch die Grundlagen für christliche Ikonen lieferte. Bei ihnen erfuhren die gegenläufigen Eigenschaften von Bildern eine weitere Überhöhung. Aus der essentialistischen Sehnsucht, ein statisches Bild möge das bleibende Wesen des Porträtierten offenbaren, erwuchs die Vorstellung, wirklich echt könne es nur sein, wenn es nicht von einem bloß menschlichen und damit fehlbaren Künstler stamme, sondern sich entweder göttlicher Sendung verdanke oder durch „den direkten Kontakt mit dem Körper, den es wiedergab, entstanden" sei.[3] Damit besaß die Ikone den Charakter einer Berührungsreliquie, was vor allem für Christus-Bilder eine große Rolle spielte, beglaubigten sie doch die Leibhaftigkeit von Gottes Sohn. Entsprechend mobilisierte ein solches Bild die Gläubigen, die zu ihm pilgerten, in der Überzeugung, es könne genauso Wunder vollbringen wie Christus selbst.

Die der Ikone immanente Heilkraft galt aber als so bedeutsam, dass man sich nicht damit begnügte, sie an einem festen Ort zu belassen; vielmehr schickte man sie selbst auf Reisen, veranstaltete Prozessionen und Feste, damit möglichst viele Menschen in Kontakt damit kommen konnten. Daher reichte aber auch nicht ein einzelnes Bild, und man bemühte sich um seine Vervielfältigung. Um die Echtheit nicht zu gefährden, musste es jedoch exakt kopiert werden, und noch besser war es, wenn es sich seinerseits durch Berührung mit einem weiteren Bildträger, also ohne Intervention durch einen Künstler reproduzierte. Da es ohnehin schon über spezielle Kräfte verfügte, lag es auch nahe, ihm die wundersame Fähigkeit einer selbständigen Übertragung zuzutrauen.

Ikonen waren also Bilder, die die dargestellte Person bestmöglich verkörperten und die deshalb selbst mobil sein mussten. An ihrem jeweiligen Einsatzort aber waren sie fest integriert: in Rituale eingebunden oder – etwa als Teil einer Bilderwand in einem Kirchenraum – eigens installiert. Den Gläubigen blieb jedoch bewusst, dass die Bilder – und damit die auf ihnen Verewigten – zu ihnen gekommen waren. Eine Ikone war Mission: geschickt, um von der Existenz des Heiligen zu zeugen und um seine Wirksamkeit zu erhöhen.

Die religiöse Funktion von Ikonen mag Parallelen zu heutigen Bildtypen und Bildpraktiken, die ihren Ort fast durchwegs in profanen Räumen haben, unwahrscheinlich wirken lassen. Doch über alle Unterschiede hinweg gibt es Gemeinsamkeiten zwischen Ikonen und digitalen Bildformaten wie Selfies, die zu analysieren wechselseitig erhellend sein kann.

> Eine erste Gemeinsamkeit besteht etwa darin, dass Selfies genauso wie Ikonen Bilder sind, die sich dem Dargestellten selbst verdanken. Dabei sind sie jeweils von Selbstporträts zu unterscheiden. Für ein Selbstporträt begibt man sich nämlich auf Distanz zu sich selbst, macht sich selbst zum Objekt, bringt sich in die Position von jemand, der von außen porträtiert wird. Diese Außenperspektive fehlt bei Ikonen und Selfies.

Christus hat gerade kein Bild von sich gemacht, ja er war kein Künstler, sondern er hat sich selbst zum Bild gemacht, als sein Gesicht in Kontakt mit einem Tuch – etwa dem Schweißtuch der Veronika – oder einem anderen Bildträger kam (Abb. 1). Ähnliches passiert bei einer Person, die ihr Smartphone auf sich

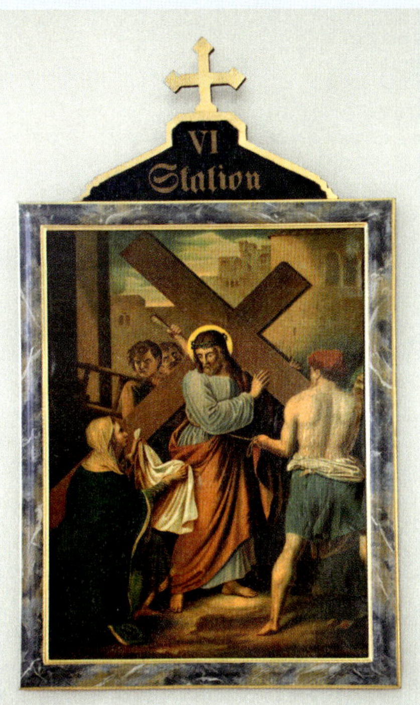

Abb. / **Fig. 1**
Anonym / **Anonymous**
Veronika reicht Jesus das Schweißtuch, Sechste Station des
Kreuzwegs der Kirche St. Nikolaus in Achern-Gamshurst /
**Saint Veronica Offers the Sudarium to Jesus, Sixth Station
of the Cross at St. Nicholas Church in Achern-Gamshurst,**
n.d., Öl auf Holz / **oil on panel**

to reveal the permanent essence of the person portrayed, the idea arose that the portrait could only be real if it did not come from a merely human and thus fallible artist, but was either the result of a divine missive or created by "direct contact with the body it reproduced."[3] Icons thus had the status of contact relics. This played a major role for images of Christ in particular, as they authenticated the corporeality of God's son. Accordingly, such an image mobilized believers who made pilgrimages to it, convinced that, like Christ himself, it could perform miracles.

The healing power innate to icons was considered so significant that they could not just be left in one place; instead, they were sent on trips, and processions and festivals were organized so that as many people as possible could come into contact with them. As such, a single picture was not enough, and efforts were made to reproduce it. In order not to endanger its authenticity, it had to be copied exactly, and was preferably reproduced by contact with an image carrier, i.e. without the intervention of an artist. Since it already had special powers, it was only logical to trust it to have the miraculous ability to make an autonomous transfer.

Icons were thus images that embodied the person depicted as closely as possible and also had to be mobile. At their respective places of use, however, they were firmly integrated: incorporated into rituals or installed as part of a picture wall in a church. Yet believers remained aware that the images, and those eternalized in them, had come to them. An icon was a mission: sent to testify of the existence of the sacred and to increase its efficacy.

Comparison of the religious function of icons to today's image types and image practices, which are almost entirely located in profane spaces, might seem dubious. But regardless of all the differences, the similarities between icons and digital images such as selfies make it instructive to analyze the two.

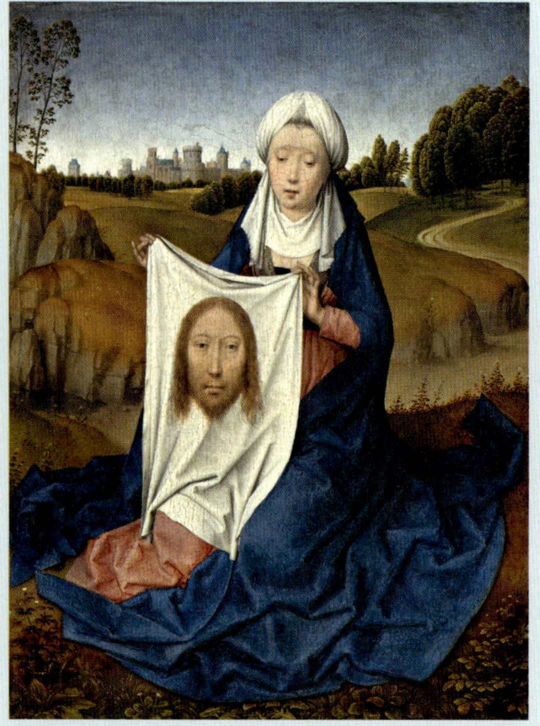

richtet und klickt, so dass ein Programm ausgelöst wird, welches das Licht, das auf den Sensor der Kamera trifft, in Daten überträgt, die in einer Datei gespeichert werden und die sich auf einem Screen als Bild darstellen lassen. Tatsächlich wurden Ikonen immer wieder mit Fotografien verglichen, da beides Bilder sind, die aus der Einwirkung von Körpern auf bildfähige Oberflächen hervorgehen.[4]

In beiden Fällen geht es auch nicht um einen Hintergrund oder um die Komposition des Bildes, innerhalb dessen das Gesicht auftaucht. Vielmehr macht das Gesicht selbst das Bild aus. Bei einer Ikone hat sich allein das Gesicht in den Bildträger eingedrückt (Abb. 2), und wenn man sein Gesicht vor das Smartphone hält, um ein Selfie zu machen, identifizieren die Programme es sogleich als solches, markieren es und widmen ihm mehr Rechenaufwand und damit eine höhere Darstellungsqualität als allem anderen innerhalb des Aufnahmebereichs der Kamera (Abb. 3). Entsprechend konzentriert man sich für ein Selfie auf die eigenen Gesichtszüge – auf die bildhafte Qualität der Mimik.

Wie Ikonen sind Selfies ferner dafür gemacht, verschickt zu werden. Üblicherweise fertigt man sie an, um mit anderen in Kontakt zu treten.

Sie fungieren als Lebenszeichen, die das aktuelle Befinden signalisieren, dienen oft aber auch dazu, die Adressaten zu einem bestimmten Verhalten oder Handeln zu bewegen. Vielleicht wünscht man sich nur, dass andere das eigene Bild liken oder ebenfalls mit Selfies antworten, doch genauso kann mit der Präsenz von Selfies politischer Druck ausgeübt werden. So sind etwa Selfie-Proteste zu einem gängigen Format der Demonstrationskultur geworden. Auf diese Weise kann es gelingen, „in Zeiten der Migration [...] insbesondere auch Menschen in der Diaspora [zu] integrieren, die Entwicklungen in ihren Heimatländern mit-

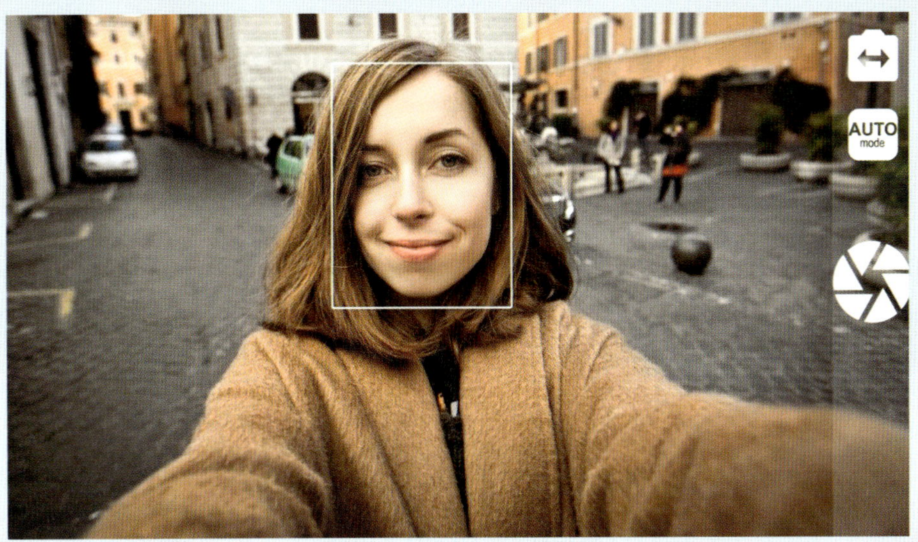

Abb. / **Fig. 3**
Anonym / **Anonymous**
Die / **The** App Selfie Camera Auto
von / **by** Konstantin Kachur, 2017,
Werbebild / **advertisement image**

The first thing they have in common is that selfies, like icons, are images that come directly from the depicted. As such, they are distinct from self-portraits. For a self-portrait, one creates distance from oneself, makes oneself into an object, and puts oneself in the position of someone being portrayed from the outside. This exterior perspective is not present in icons and selfies.

Christ did not draw a picture of himself, as he was not an artist, but when his face came into contact with a cloth—as in the sudarium of Saint Veronica—or with another support (fig. 1), he made himself into an image. Something similar happens when people point their smartphone at themselves and click, triggering a program that converts the light hitting the camera's sensor into data, which is then saved and displayed on screen as a picture. In fact, icons have been compared time and again with photographs; both are images emerging from the action of bodies imprinting on supports.[4]

In both cases, it is not about the background or the composition of the image within which the face appears. Instead, the face itself constitutes the picture. In the case of an icon, the face alone has impressed itself on the support (fig. 2). When a person positions their face in front of the smartphone to take a selfie, it is immediately recognized as such, selected, and given more processing power to capture it at a higher image quality than anything else within the frame (fig. 3). When taking a selfie, a person concentrates on their own facial features—on the visual quality of their facial expressions.

Like icons, selfies are also made to be sent. They are usually taken in order to make contact with others.

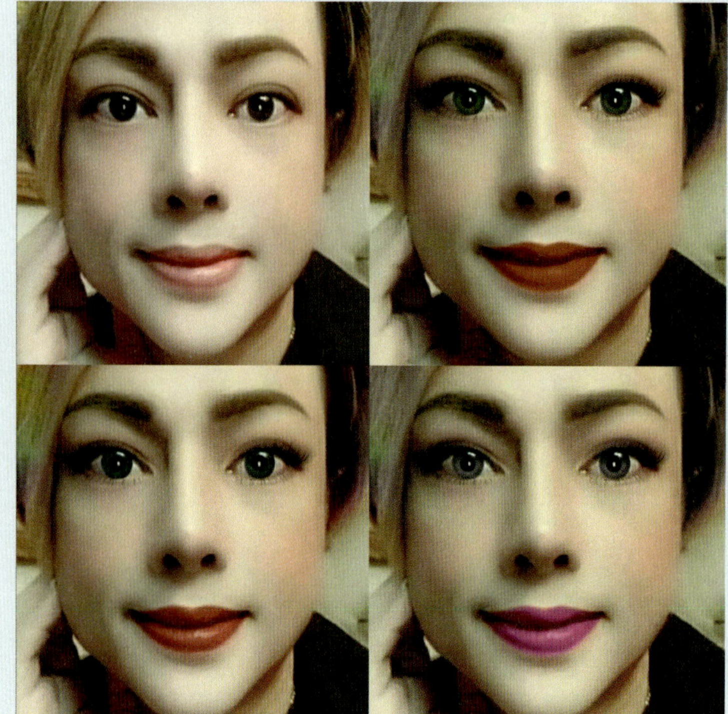

verfolgen [...] möchten", wie Kerstin Schankweiler gezeigt hat.[5] Vergleichbar mit Bildern innerhalb des kaiserlichen oder christlichen Bilderkults kann ein gesendetes Selfie also diejenigen, die es absenden, vertreten und so für mehr Verbindlichkeit sorgen – an etwas erinnern, schlechtes Gewissen wecken, motivieren oder trösten. Wer das Selfie sieht, wird in eigenen Überzeugungen gestärkt, zu einer anderen Meinung bekehrt oder dazu gebracht, sich selbst für etwas zu engagieren – und das vielleicht seinerseits mit einem Selfie zu bekräftigen.

Anders als in der analogen Welt ist es möglich, Bilder sekundenschnell und an beliebig viele Adressaten zu versenden. War schon mit einer Ikone die Idee – der Wunderglaube – verbunden, dass sie sich selbst immer wieder exakt reproduzieren kann, so ist das in der digitalen Welt die übliche Praxis. Auf unzähligen Bildschirmen können genau dieselben Daten in ein Bild übersetzt werden. In Form einer Datei können dieselben Daten aber auch auf beliebig vielen Rechnern gespeichert werden. Sendet man ein Selfie etwa über WhatsApp, wird die betreffende Datei automatisch in die Foto-Ordner der Adressaten kopiert. So erhalten die mobilen Bilder zugleich feste Orte, und je mehr sie zirkulieren, desto öfter reproduzieren sie sich, an desto mehr Orten sind sie präsent.

Doch gibt es hier auch einen großen Unterschied zwischen einem analogen und einem digitalen Bild. So schnell und so oft sich eine Bilddatei vervielfältigen lässt, so schnell lässt sie sich auch verändern. Dank Bildbearbeitungsprogrammen sowie Filtern und Masken ist eine Datei eine immer neu variierbare Datenmenge (Abb. 4). Neben der perfekten Reproduzierbarkeit ist also gleichermaßen die beliebige Veränderbarkeit ein Hauptkennzeichen digitaler Bilder. Stabilität und Mobilität kehren somit als gegenläufige Eigenschaften wieder, beziehen sich aber auf etwas anderes als in der analogen Bildkultur. Stabilität meint nun nicht mehr die Fixierung eines Bildes auf einem Bildträger, sondern bedeutet, dass jede weitere Reproduktion einer Datei als Sicherheitskopie fungiert. In der Redewendung

They act as signs of life that signal one's current status but often also elicit a certain behavior or action in those who see them. Perhaps one just want others to like one's picture or respond with selfies. But the presence of selfies can also exert political pressure. Selfie protests, for example, have become a common form of demonstration culture. In this way it is possible "in times of migration . . . to integrate those people, particularly members of a diaspora, who wish to follow developments in their home countries,"[5] as Kerstin Schankweiler has shown. Comparable to images within the imperial or Christian image cult, sending a selfie can represent the individual who sends it and thus ensure more accountability—reminding recipients of something, awakening a guilty conscience, motivating or comforting them. Those who see the selfie are strengthened in their own convictions, convinced of a different opinion or made to commit themselves to something—and perhaps confirm this by sending a selfie of their own.

Unlike in the analog world, it is possible to send images to any number of recipients in seconds. The idea of replicating oneself exactly countless times—a belief in miracles—was already present with icons, but in the digital world it is truly the case, and standard practice. The exact same data can be transmitted as an image on countless screens. In the form of a file, that data can also be saved on any number of computers. If one sends a selfie via WhatsApp, the file in question is automatically added to the recipient's gallery. In this way, mobile images are also given fixed locations, and the more they circulate, the more often they are reproduced and the more places they appear.

But this too is a major difference between an an analog image and a digital one. An image file can be changed just as swiftly and frequently as it can be copied. Image editing programs, filters, and masks mean that a file is a constantly variable set of data (fig. 4). Thus along with their perfect reproducibility, a defining feature of digital images is their endless variation. Stability and mobility are once again features in opposition, but they refer to something different here than in analog image culture. Stability no longer means the fixing of an image onto an image support, but rather that every further reproduction of an image file is a backup copy. The saying "The internet doesn't forget" speaks to the possibility of a comprehensive archive. And mobility no longer refers solely to transporting an image, but also to the fact that the data it consists of may constantly be set in motion.

A digital image is not a fixed entity, but rather an event, a process, a metamorphizing occurrence.

This also has consequences for the subject. The fact that the image resulting from an analog portrait of an individual is unalterable and therefore intended to show the typical nature of the individual, abstracted from individual moments, almost always led to an eschewal of eccentric or extreme facial expressions. What Belting has described as the conventional portrait's "stilling of the expressive life" lets "a face bring itself to its own emphatic definition."[6] Whether a photograph of the deceased, an icon, or a sovereign portrait, early forms of portraits are characterized by their attempts at

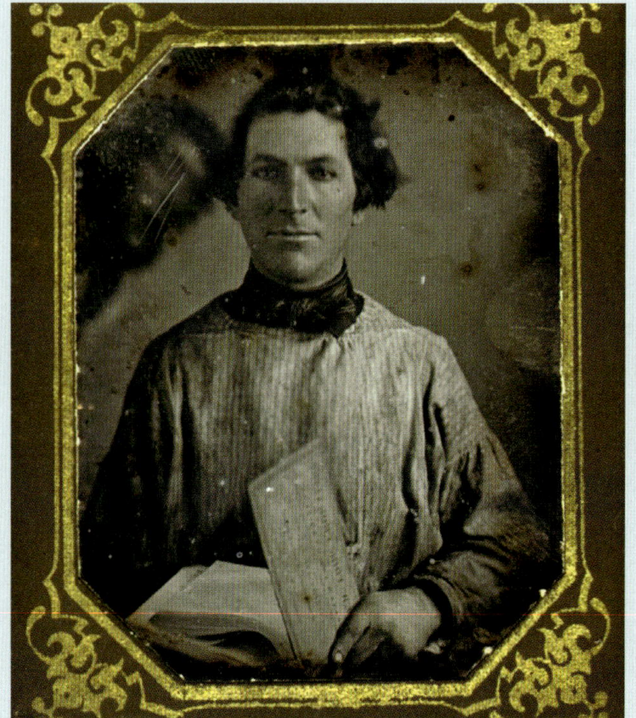

‚Das Internet vergisst nichts' ist die Möglichkeit einer Totalarchivierung angesprochen. Und Mobilität bezieht sich nun nicht mehr allein auf die Transportfähigkeit eines Bildes, sondern meint, dass die Daten, aus denen es besteht, jederzeit selbst in Bewegung versetzt werden können.

Ein digitales Bild ist keine feste Einheit, sondern ein Ereignis, ein Prozess, ein metamorphotisches Geschehen.

Das aber hat auch Folgen für die Sujets. Dass das analoge Porträt einer Person als Bild unveränderlich ist und daher gerade das zeigen soll, was für diese Person jenseits des bloß Momentanen typisch ist, führte etwa fast immer dazu, auf Exzentrisches, ja auf extreme Ausschläge in der Mimik zu verzichten. Das herkömmliche Porträt „legt [...] das mimische Leben still", und erst damit lasse sich, so Hans Belting, „ein Gesicht in emphatischer Weise auf den Begriff seiner selbst bringen"[6]. Ob Totenbild, Ikone oder Herrscherbildnis: Die frühen Formen des Porträts zeichnen sich dadurch aus, nach Zeitlosigkeit zu streben und die Gesichtszüge neutral zu halten. Das Gesicht sollte als Summe seiner mimischen Möglichkeiten erscheinen, weshalb es nicht eine einzelne von ihnen wiedergeben durfte. Die mimische Neutralität lässt ein Gesicht ernsthaft, ein wenig streng aussehen, und diese Darstellungskonvention blieb von den frühen Formen der Porträtkultur bis hin zum bürgerlichen Bildnis des 18. und 19. Jahrhunderts, aber ebenso noch lange Zeit in der Porträtfotografie prägend (Abb. 5).

Bei Selfies hingegen ist es anders. Bei ihnen trifft man fast nie auf einen neutralen Gesichtsausdruck, vielmehr häufig auf besonders überspitzte Mimiken, auf karikaturenhafte Übertreibungen und Praktiken wie das ‚duckface', die bis vor kurzem selbst jenseits von Bildern nicht üblich waren. So präsentiert man sich aber nur, wenn man weiß, dass das Selfie im Nu durch weitere Selfies überla-

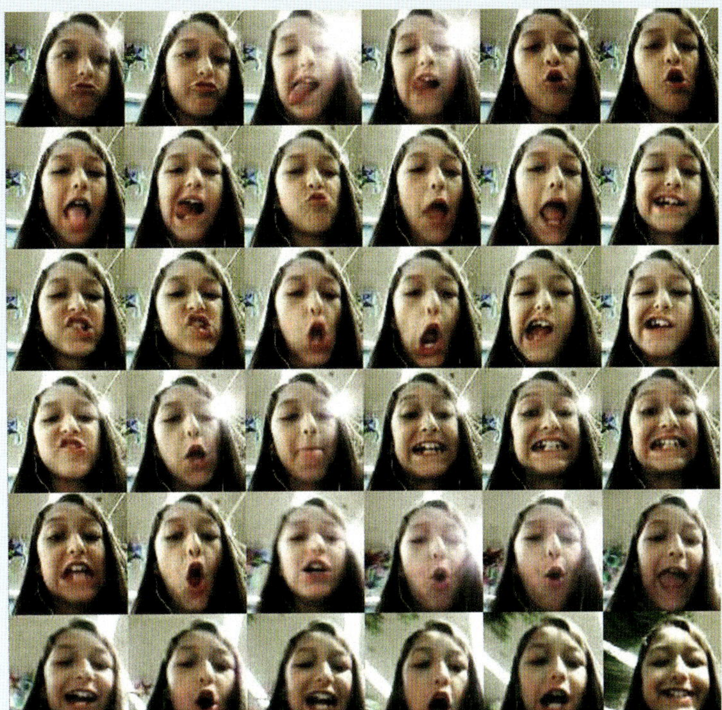

timelessness and a neutral arrangement of facial features. The face is meant to appear as the sum of all its expressive parts and as such should not express one single instance of those possibilities. This expressive neutrality makes a face appear serious, a little stern; a convention of portrayal that remained in place from early forms of portrait culture to the bourgeois portraits of the eighteenth and nineteenth centuries, and well into the era of portrait photography (fig. 5).

Selfies are different. They rarely show a neutral facial expression. Rather, they are far more likely to capture an exaggerated pose, with caricature-like expressions and popular trends such as the "duck face," which until recently was uncommon even outside of photography. But one only presents oneself in this manner when one knows that a selfie will shortly be relativized, superseded by further selfies, and that it need not remain in the form in which it was taken. Even when a file is kept in a stable way, one does not associate it with permanence, much less timelessness. Rather, selfies are taken and sent with an awareness that everything can be changed at any point in time and that the image need therefore do nothing more than represent a single instant. In contrast to an icon, one does not seek to make an image for all eternity; rather, a selfie is an icon in time, an icon for a moment.

With regard to selfies, one can also speak of a mobilization of the face. Everything one can offer by way of facial expressions is deployed and technical supports are also drawn on. As much as people over the millennia have sought the ideal—the single valid—portrait that set aside all fleeting expressions, people now want nothing more than to capture every possible random expression and to make a photograph that is uniquely calibrated to fit a specific situation (fig. 6). The fact that people can send photographs immediately after taking them and that one might receive photographs in response just

gert und relativiert wird und dass es in der Form, in der es aufgenommen wurde, nicht bleiben muss. Selbst wenn es in einer Datei stabil aufgehoben ist, assoziiert man damit nicht Dauerhaftigkeit oder gar Zeitlosigkeit. Vielmehr werden Selfies mit dem Bewusstsein produziert und gesendet, dass sich alles jederzeit ändern lässt und daher auch nicht mehr als einen Moment zu repräsentieren hat. Anders als bei einer Ikone macht man sich bei einem Selfie nicht zum Bild für die Ewigkeit, vielmehr ist ein Selfie eine Ikone in der Zeit, eine Ikone des Augenblicks.

Bezogen auf Selfies lässt sich daher auch von einer Mobilmachung des Gesichts sprechen. Alles, was man mimisch zu bieten hat, gelangt zum Einsatz, technische Hilfsmittel werden ebenfalls angewendet. So sehr man über Jahrtausende nach dem idealen – dem einen gültigen – Bildnis strebte, das allen momenthaften mimischen Ausschlägen gleichsam zugrunde liegt, so sehr geht es heute darum, so viel Akzidentelles wie möglich einzufangen und sich differenziert, passgenau, auf die jeweilige Situation abgestimmt zum Bild zu machen (Abb. 6). Dass man die Bilder unmittelbar nachdem sie entstanden sind auch schon versenden kann und dass man vielleicht schon nach Sekunden Antwortbilder empfängt, begünstigt das spontane und pointierte Agieren. Man geht dann so im Selfie-Dialog auf, dass man leicht vergisst, es nach wie vor mit Dateien, mit speicherbaren Bildern zu tun zu haben. Die Beschleunigung der Zirkulation von Bildern lässt die Mimik somit so wichtig werden, wie sie es in der physischen Begegnung zwischen Menschen schon immer war. Selfies sind also nicht nur Ikonen des Augenblicks, sondern bei ihnen ist die Differenz zu dem, was sie abbilden, geringer als jemals zuvor in der Geschichte der Porträts.

Die Konkurrenz zwischen ortfesten und mobilen Bildern ist damit aber sicher nicht beendet. So sehr die technischen Entwicklungen Praktiken begünstigen mögen, bei denen Bilder im doppelten Sinne mobil – nämlich transportabel und veränderbar – sind, so sehr wird es auch künftig das Bedürfnis geben, unveränderliche und fest an einem Ort installierte Bilder zu haben. So wurde das Einfrieren und Immobil-Machen nie nur als Verlust an Lebendigkeit und Flexibilität empfunden, sondern stellte oft auch eine Form von Ermächtigung dar. Je mobiler Bilder zirkulieren, desto attraktiver wird es also werden, sie auch wieder einzufangen.

1 Severian von Gabala, *De mundi creatione*, VI, 5, zit. nach Helmut Kruse, *Studien zur offiziellen Geltung des Kaiserbildnisses im römischen Reiche*, Paderborn 1934, S. 79f.
2 Ebd., S. 26, 49
3 Hans Belting, *Bild und Kult. Eine Geschichte des Bildes vor dem Zeitalter der Kunst*, München 2011 [Erstausgabe 1990], S. 66
4 Vgl. z.B. Horst Bredekamp, *Theorie des Bildakts*, Berlin 2010, S. 173–191
5 Kerstin Schankweiler, *Bildproteste. Widerstand im Netz*, Berlin 2019, S. 41
6 Hans Belting, *Faces. Eine Geschichte des Gesichts*, München 2013, S. 175

seconds later bolsters this spontaneous and targeted approach. One can enter into a selfie dialogue in which one forgets that one is still exchanging files, saved images. The speeding-up of the circulation of images allows facial expressions to attain the same prominence they have always enjoyed in real-life interactions. Selfies are not merely icons of a moment; rather, the discrepancy between the selfie and that which it depicts is more minor than ever before in the history of the portrait.

This certainly does not, however, put an end to the competition between static and mobile images. Even as technical developments increasingly enable practices in which images are mobile in two senses—both portable and changeable—the desire for unchangeable and static images will nevertheless remain. The act of freezing an individual in place and immobilizing them was never solely about losing a lifelike quality and a flexibility, but also represented a form of empowerment. The more mobile images circulate, the more appealing it will become to once again hold them still.

1   Severian Gabala, *De mundi creatione*, VI, 5, quoted in Helmut Kruse, *Studien zur offiziellen Geltung des Kaiserbildnisses im römischen Reiche* (Paderborn: Schöningh, 1934), 79–80. Translated here from German by Sylee Gore.
2   *De mundi creatione*, 26, 49.
3   Hans Belting, *Likeness and Presence: A History of the Image before the Era of Art*, trans. Edmund Jephcott (Chicago, IL, and London: The University of Chicago Press, 1994), 53.
4   See for instance Horst Bredekamp, *Image Acts: A Systematic Approach to Visual Agency*, trans. Elizabeth Clegg (Berlin and New York: De Gruyter, 2018).
5   Kerstin Schankweiler, *Bildproteste: Widerstand im Netz* (Berlin: Verlag Klaus Wagenbach, 2019), 41.
6   Translated here from Hans Belting, *Faces: Eine Geschichte des Gesichts* (Munich: C.H. Beck Verlag, 2013), 175. Also available in English as *Face and Mask: A Double History*, trans. Thomas S. Hansen and Abby J. Hansen (Princeton, NJ, and Oxford: Princeton University Press, 2017).

Text: Friedrich Tietjen

MASSEN VON VERSCHIEDENEN BILDERN
Zu Produktion und Versand privater Fotografien bis etwa 1920

Gegen Ende der 1850er-Jahre existierte eine kaum überschaubare Vielfalt fotografischer Verfahren, doch in der Anwendung dominierte eines – die Daguerreotypie. Nachdem im Sommer 1839 die technischen Einzelheiten dieses Verfahrens veröffentlicht worden waren, hatten verschiedene Verbesserungen schnell dafür gesorgt, dass die Platten nicht mehr Minuten, sondern nur noch wenige Sekunden belichtet werden mussten. Damit war es möglich, Porträts aufzunehmen. In der Folge öffneten ab Anfang der 1840er-Jahre vor allem in europäischen und US-amerikanischen Städten zahlreiche daguerreotypische Studios. Weil sie die Porträts für relativ billiges Geld produzieren konnten, wurden diese bald auch in relativ großer Zahl hergestellt (Abb. 1).[1] Diese Daguerreotypien sind meist zwar nicht besonders groß (das gängigste Format war die 1/6-Platte und maß 7 x 8 cm),[2] aber es sind visuell außerordentlich attraktive Objekte: Sie sind bis in kleine Details hinein scharf gezeichnet, und weil sie auf versilberten Kupferblechen aufgenommen werden, sieht der Blick in diese Porträts die andere Person und wie in einem Spiegel auch sich selbst. Allerdings sind diese Bilder Unikate – weil es kein Negativ gab, ließen sie sich nicht reproduzieren. So erreichten sie nur ein begrenztes Publikum – die eigene Familie, die Ehepartner, gute Freund*innen.

MASSES OF DIFFERENT IMAGES
On the Production and Sending of Personal Photographs until circa 1920

Around the late 1850s, there was a dizzying array of photographic processes but one dominated in practice: the daguerreotype. After the technical details of this process were published in the summer of 1839, various improvements quickly meant that plates needed to be exposed for only a few seconds rather than minutes. This made it possible to take portraits. As a consequence, countless daguerreotype studios opened chiefly in European and American cities in the 1840s. Because portraits could be produced fairly cheaply, they were quickly being made in relatively large numbers (fig. 1).[1] Granted, these daguerreotypes were seldom particularly large (the most common size was one-sixth of a plate, measuring seven by eight centimeters),[2] but visually, they were extraordinarily attractive objects. The images were crisp down to the smallest details and because they were taken on silver-coated copper sheets, looking at these portraits one sees both the subject and oneself. But these pictures were one-of-a-kind and could not be reproduced because there were no negatives. Thus they reached only a limited audience: the subject's own family, spouse, and close friends.

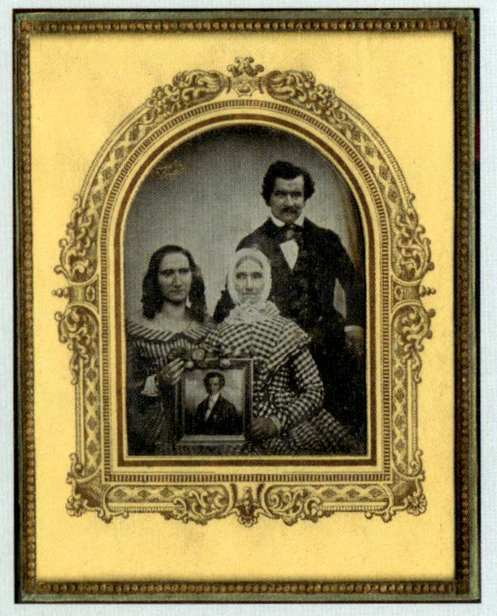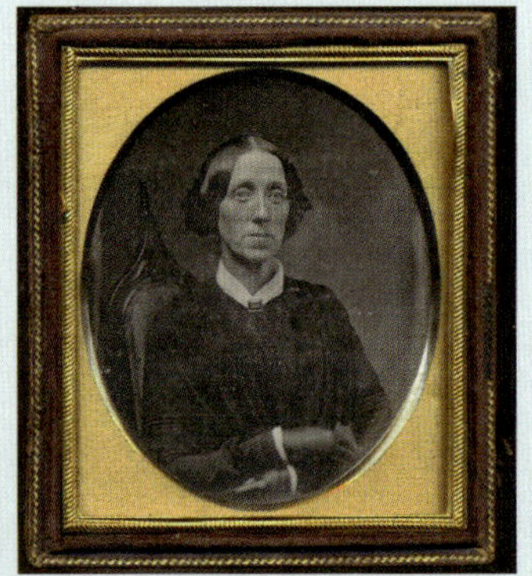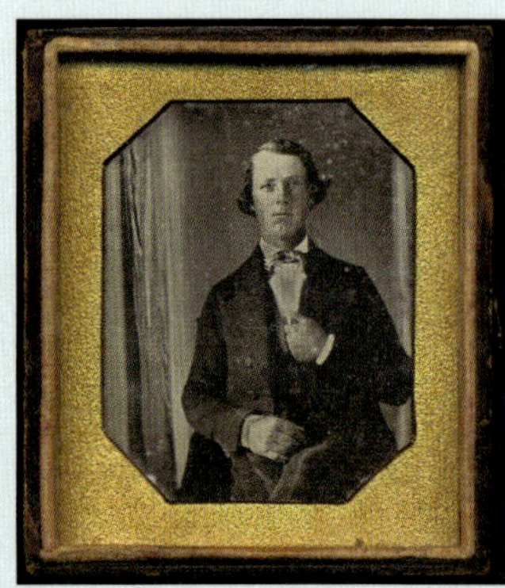

Abb. / **Fig. 1A–C**
Anonym / **Anonymous**
Familie mit gemaltem Porträt, Österreich / **Family with a painted portrait, Austria**
Frau im Sessel, USA / **Woman in an armchair, USA,** ca. 1850
Mann im Atelier / **Man in the studio,** USA, ca. 1850
3 Daguerreotypien / **3 daguerreotypes**

Ab Anfang der 1850er-Jahre waren nun Verfahren verfügbar, mit denen sich von Glasnegativen, wenigstens theoretisch, beliebig viele Abzüge auf Papier anfertigen ließen. Damit war es möglich, nicht nur – wie mit der Daguerreotypie – große Mengen verschiedener fotografischer Bilder zu produzieren, sondern von diesen konnten auch beliebig viele mehr oder weniger identische Kopien hergestellt werden. Diese Verfahren veränderten vor allem jenen Zweig des fotografischen Gewerbes dramatisch, der bei weitem die meisten Bilder produzierte – die Porträtstudios. Die Produktion wurde nochmals beschleunigt, als sich ab Ende der 1850er-Jahre mit den Cartes de Visite ein einheitliches Format für Porträtfotografien durchsetzte (Abb. 2). Diese Cartes de Visite unterschieden sich in mehrfacher Hinsicht substanziell von den Daguerreotypien. Ihnen fehlte das visuelle Spektakel – sie spiegelten nicht, kamen in der Regel nicht gerahmt in die Hände der Kund*innen, boten weniger Bildfläche, und auch die Auflösung konnte nicht unbedingt mit jener des älteren Bildmediums mithalten. Überdies wurden sie meist in zwölf oder mehr Abzügen hergestellt und waren damit pro Bild im Vergleich zu den Daguerreotypien noch preiswerter.[3] Obwohl sie also eher weniger ansehnlich waren, verdrängten die Cartes de Visite die daguerreotypischen Porträts binnen weniger Jahre fast vollständig. Verantwortlich dafür waren offenbar gerade nicht die ästhetischen Qualitäten der Bilder, sondern die auch durch den billigen Preis eröffneten Möglichkeiten ihrer Nutzung – mit ihrer Hilfe ließen sich Präsenz und Sichtbarkeit der eigenen Person in einer Weise herstellen, die mit den Daguerreotypien nicht zu haben war.

Aber dazu mussten die Bilder ihr Publikum auch erreichen. In einer Stadt ließen sich die Cartes de Visite einfach übergeben, doch in weiter gespannte soziale und auch geschäftliche Netzwerke mussten die Bilder verschickt werden. Die Voraussetzungen für einen solchen massenhaften Versand der Bilder wurden allerdings erst mit Reorganisationen des Postwesens um die Mitte des 19.

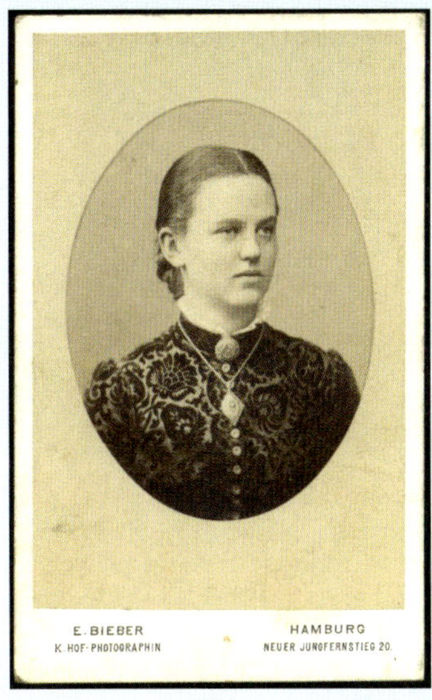

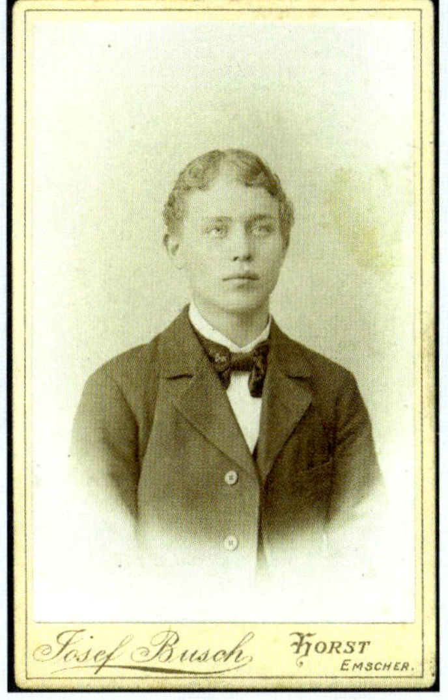

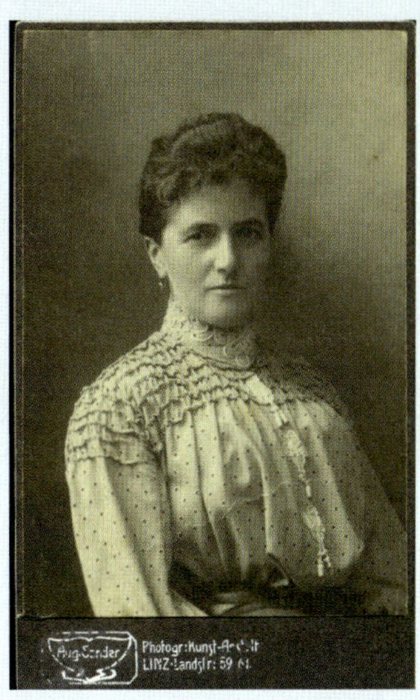

Abb. / **Fig. 2A–C**
Diverse Fotograf*innen / **Various photographers**
Porträts / **Portraits,** ca. 1870–1920, Abzüge in diversen fotografischen Verfahren /
prints in various photographic processes, Cartes de Visite

From the early 1850s, a process using glass negatives became available that made it possible to produce, at least in theory, a limitless number of prints on paper. With it came the possibility not only to produce large numbers of different photographic images—which the daguerreotype had already made possible—but also to make as many or few identical copies as one liked. This process dramatically changed the branch of commercial photography that produced the most images by far, that of the portrait studio. Production was once again accelerated, when the *carte de visite* established itself as the standard format for portrait photographs from the end of the 1850s (fig. 2). Such *cartes de visite* are substantially different from daguerreotypes in many respects. They are not visually spectacular: they do not have a reflective surface, they were seldom framed for customers, the pictorial surface was smaller, and the resolution was poorer than in the case of daguerreotypes. Moreover, they were usually produced in twelve or more prints and thus were cheaper than daguerreotypes per image.[3] So although they were rather less attractive, *cartes de visite* quickly supplanted daguerreotype portraits in the space of a few years. It was the cheap price that opened up possibilities for how such images were used, rather than the aesthetic qualities of such images. With this help, it was possible to make an individual person present and visible in a manner daguerreotypes could not achieve.

Yet for that, the images must actually reach their audience. In a city, *cartes de visite* could simply be handed out, yet in more decentralized social and business networks, the images had to be sent. Yet the conditions needed for such a large-scale sending of images was only made possible in the mid-nineteenth century with the reorganization of postal services. Until then, it was usual for the recipient, not the sender, to pay for postage; moreover, the fees were exorbitant, especially across greater distances.

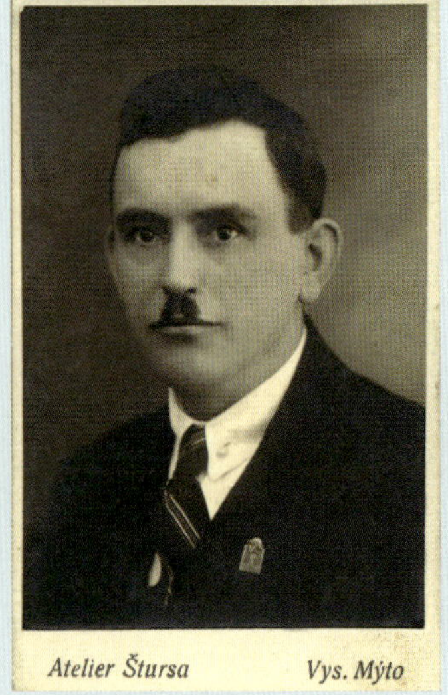

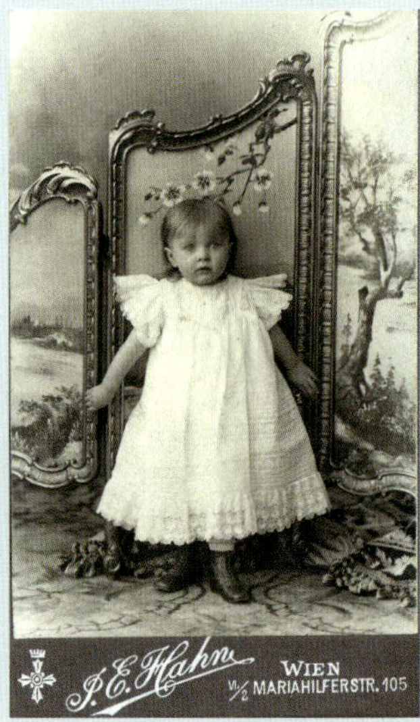

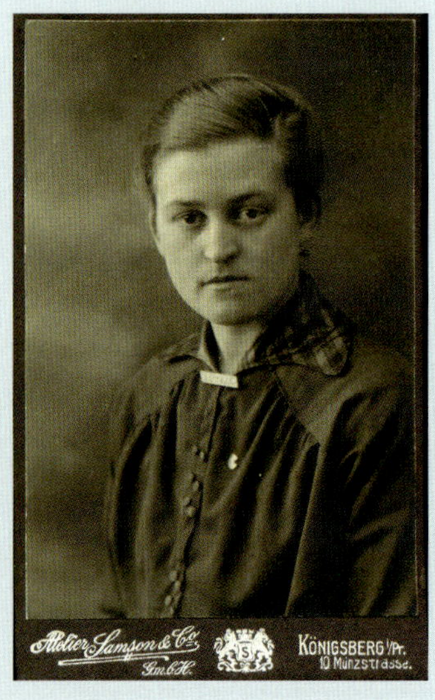

Abb. / **Fig. 2D–F**
Diverse Fotograf*innen / **Various photographers**
Porträts, ca. 1870–1920, Abzüge in diversen fotografischen Verfahren /
prints in various photographic processes, Cartes de Visite

Jahrhunderts geschaffen. Bis dahin war es allgemein üblich gewesen, dass für den Empfang eines Briefes gezahlt wurde, nicht für den Versand; zudem waren die Gebühren vor allem bei größeren Entfernungen exorbitant teuer. Die Nachteile eines solchen Systems lagen auf der Hand: Die hohen Gebühren standen wirtschaftlichen und auch wissenschaftlichen Entwicklungen im Weg, und wenn die Annahme eines Briefes verweigert wurde, blieb die Post auf den Kosten des Transportes sitzen. Im Mai 1840 wurden deshalb zuerst in Großbritannien nicht nur die Tarife drastisch gesenkt, sondern das Porto musste nun vom Absender bezahlt werden; als Beleg dafür wurden die Umschläge mit einer Marke beklebt und abgestempelt. In den USA wurden ab 1845 ähnliche Veränderungen in die Wege geleitet, so dass sich ab Mitte der 1850er-Jahre das Geschäftsmodell der Post grundlegend verändert hatte – damit sie kostendeckend arbeiten konnte, mussten nun möglichst viele Sendungen befördert werden und das hieß auch: möglichst viele private Briefe.[4] Dass mit diesen Briefen auch Fotografien in großer Zahl verschickt wurden, lässt sich beispielsweise den Jahresberichten des US-amerikanischen Postmaster General entnehmen: So waren im Jahr 1863 mehr als vier Millionen Briefe unzustellbar gewesen; immerhin knapp 70.000 davon enthielten Fotografien, Schmuck oder ähnliche Objekte. Erst mit einem solcherart organisierten Postwesen konnten die Bilder in Ländern wie den USA tatsächlich massenhaft ausgetauscht werden – wer ein Bild gab, konnte im Gegenzug auch eines erwarten, wer ein Dutzend an verschiedene Bekannte und Verwandte verteilte und verschickte, konnte hoffen, auch ein Dutzend zu bekommen.

Damit veränderten sich der Bildbesitz und auch der Modus der Bildbetrachtung. Weil daguerreotypische Porträts nur als Unikate existierten, waren sie offenbar nicht so sehr Objekte eines Austauschs als vielmehr Geschenke. Und weil sie im Vergleich zu den Cartes de Visite in deutlich geringerer Zahl hergestellt

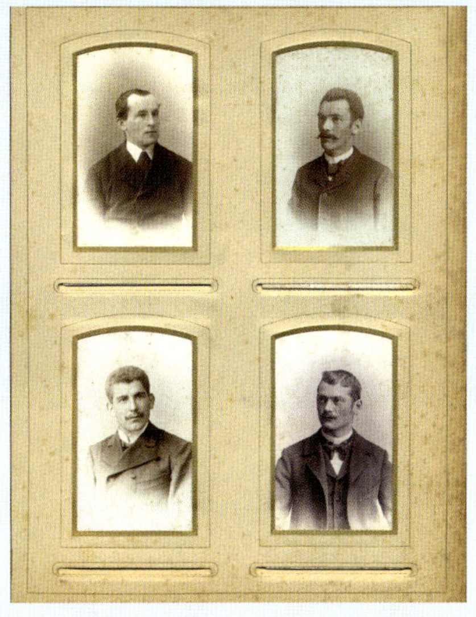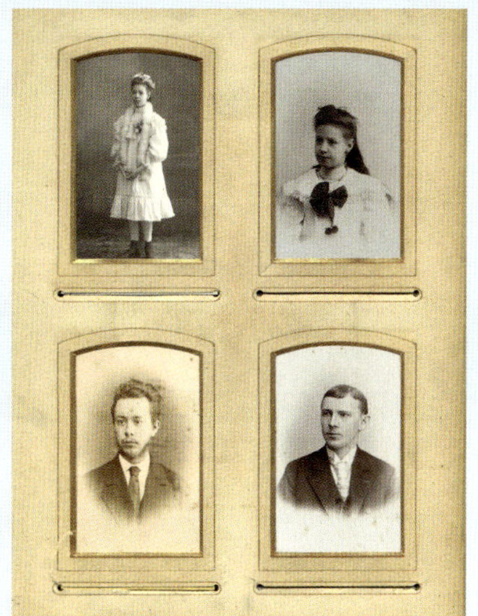

The disadvantages of such a system are easy to list: the high fees hampered economic and scientific developments, and when a recipient refused to accept a letter, the postal services had to bear the cost of transport. As a result in May 1840, initially in Great Britain, the cost of postage was dramatically lowered and the cost of postage was borne by the sender. Payment was documented with a postage stamp stuck onto the envelope and postmarked. Starting in 1845, similar changes were set into motion in the US, and the business model of the post office fundamentally changed from the mid-1850s. In order to be economically viable, as much mail as possible needed to be sent, which meant as many personal letters as possible.[4] That a greater number of photographs were being sent along with letters can be seen for instance in the yearly reports of the US postmaster general: in 1863, more than four million letters could not be delivered to their recipients; of these, 70,000 contained photographs, jewelry, or similar objects. Only with such an organized postal system could images in countries such as the US be exchanged on a large scale. A person who sent an image could in turn expect to receive one, and someone who distributed and sent a dozen images to various acquaintances and relatives could also hope to receive a dozen too.

This in turn changed which images were owned and how they were regarded. Because daguerreotype portraits only existed as one-of-a-kind images, they were naturally far less objects to be traded than given as gifts. And because they were produced in far smaller numbers than were cartes de visite, one may assume that an individual or family would at best own a few such images.

Cartes de visite in contrast were produced and distributed in such numbers and frequency that recipients could amass quite a collection. Individual such images may have also

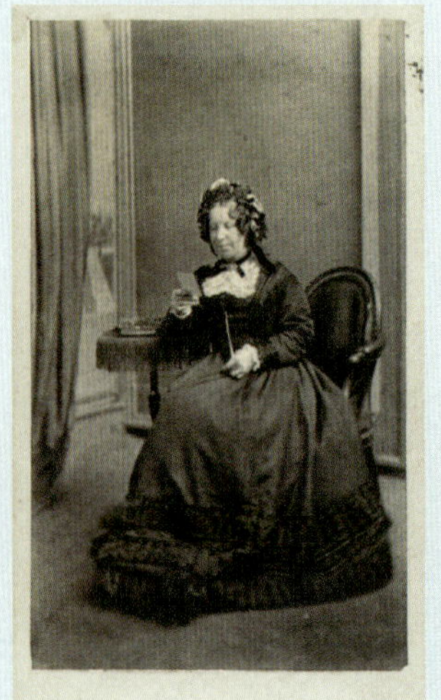 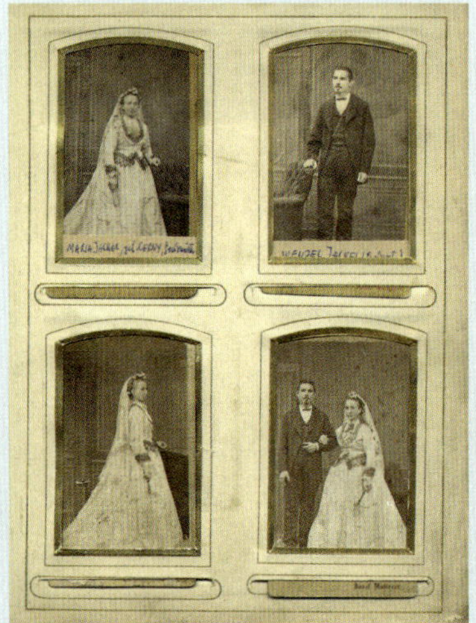 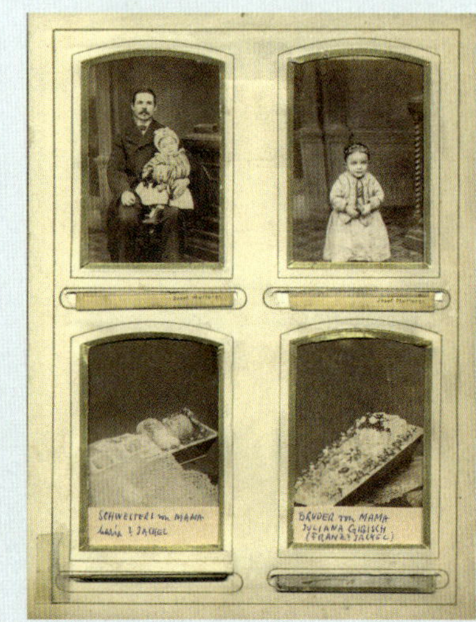

Abb. / **Fig. 4**
Anonym / Anonymous
Porträt einer Frau, eine Carte de Visite betrachtend /
Portrait of a woman looking at a carte de visite,
ca. 1880, Albuminabzug / **albumen print,** Carte de Visite

Abb. / **Fig. 5A–B**
Josef Mutterer und diverse Fotograf*innen / **and various photographers**
Bilder eines Hochzeitspaares und Porträts von lebenden und
verstorbenen Kindern, Österreich / **Pictures of a wedding couple
and portraits of living and deceased children, Austria,** ca. 1880,
Album, Cartes de Visite / **carte-de-visite album**

wurden, lässt sich davon ausgehen, dass eine Person oder eine Familie allenfalls
einige wenige solcher Bilder besaß.

Cartes de Visite dagegen wurden in solcher Zahl und
Frequenz hergestellt und verteilt, dass sie sich bei den Empfänger*innen ansammeln konnten. Zwar wurden einzelne
dieser Bilder auch gerahmt oder lose gesammelt; doch mit
den Cartes de Visite entwickelte sich auch das Fotoalbum
als Ordnungsmedium.

Alben mit Bildern hatte es auch vor der Fotografie gegeben. Etwa ab Anfang des 19. Jahrhunderts gehörte es zum gehobenen bürgerlichen Zeitvertreib,
scrapbooks anzulegen, in denen aus Zeitschriften und Büchern geschnittene Dru-
cke und Textpassagen, gepresste Pflanzen, Etiketten, Visitenkarten und andere
Ephemera eingeklebt wurden, oft in Form von Collagen und Montagen. Auffällig
ist allerdings, dass die Konstruktion der Visitkarten-Alben gerade nicht an dem
Modell dieser *scrapbooks* orientiert war (Abb. 3). Vielmehr gaben die Alben eine
feste Anordnung der Bilder vor, die nebeneinander und in festen Abständen in
dicke Kartonseiten eingeschoben wurden. Ermöglicht wurde dies durch das vor
allem in den ersten Jahrzehnten eigentümlich konstante Format der Cartes de
Visite, dessen Dominanz im Umkehrschluss von den massenproduzierten Alben
gestützt wurde: Damit Bildertausch und Bilderordnung gelingen konnten, mussten alle Porträts das gleiche Format haben. Nur so war es möglich, dass die Alben
die sozialen Beziehungen einer Person oder einer Familie in Form von Porträts
nicht nur aufnehmen, sondern auch abbilden konnten. Darüber hinaus ermög-
lichte diese Konstruktion auch, dass die Bilder beweglich blieben und bei Bedarf
den Alben entnommen und einzeln betrachtet werden konnten (Abb. 4). Und
noch eines kam hinzu: Als die Preise für ein Set Cartes de Visite durch technische
Innovationen und nicht zuletzt durch eine mörderische Konkurrenz sich gegen-

been framed or collected unframed, but the *cartes de visite* gave rise to the photo album as a means of organizing.

Albums with images existed before the advent of photography too. In the early nineteenth century, for instance, creating scrapbooks was a popular upper-middle-class pastime. Prints and snippets of text cut out of magazines and books were glued into these along with pressed plants, stickers, calling cards, and other ephemera, often as collages and montages. Yet it is notable that the construction of calling card albums was not figured on the model of such scrapbooks (fig. 3). Rather, the albums prescribed a fixed layout of images, which were to be slid in beside one another and at defined spaces into thick cardboard pages. This was all made possible due to the curiously consistent format of *cartes de visite* in the early decades, which in turn was made dominant due to the mass production of such albums. In order for images to be exchanged and filed, they had to be of the same size. Only thus was it possible for albums to not only record but also display the social connections of a person or family through portraits. Moreover, this construction made it possible for images to remain mobile and they could be removed from the albums and viewed individually as needed (fig. 4). Moreover, when prices for a set of *cartes de visite* sunk further as a result of technical innovations and not least due to a sense of cut-throat competition between photo studios undercutting each other, it became affordable to have portraits made of oneself not only once but repeatedly. People would be photographed as children, for their first communion, after completing military service, at their wedding, and with their first child, and if that child died—in the mid-nineteenth century child mortality remained very high—then that child would be brought into the photo studio for one final photograph (fig. 5).[5]

Above all, daguerreotypes bore witness to a person's existence, taken as they were far less often, sometimes perhaps just once in a person's life. In contrast, portrait photography became a biographical medium with *cartes de visite*, taken as they were at more regular intervals.

The first pages of an album, commonly filled gradually, would at first show one's own family and spouse before marriage, then pictures of the bridal couple, then children, grandparents, and in the series of subsequent photographs, how all these individuals aged; separated by some blank pages, further images of relatives and acquaintances might follow. These images often lack a temporal anchoring unique to weddings and similar such occasions. These portraits are generic and relatively lacking in temporal qualities, neither showing key moments in a person's life nor relating a story, unless a note on the front or back of the image mentions the time, place, or the people portrayed or with whom the image was shared (fig. 6). But placed in albums, these images make visible the size and the geographical reach of a family's social network—most of the photographs in the album shown here are from Saxony, but the top left image was taken in Odessa.

Cartes de visite were extraordinarily successful. Estimates suggest that 300 million *cartes de visite* were sold in the 1860s in Great Britain alone.[6]

MASSEN VON VERSCHIEDENEN BILDERN / *MASSES OF DIFFERENT IMAGES*

seitig unterbietender Fotostudios weiter sanken, wurde es bezahlbar, nicht nur einmal, sondern immer wieder porträtiert zu werden. Man wurde als Kind, zur Erstkommunion, nach dem Dienst beim Militär fotografiert, zur Hochzeit und mit dem ersten eigenen Kind,und wenn das der Mitte des 19. Jahrhunderts immer noch hohen Kindersterblichkeit zum Opfer fiel, brachte man es zuweilen für ein letztes Bild ins Studio (Abb. 5).[5]

Die deutlich seltener, oft genug vielleicht nur einmal in einem Leben aufgenommenen Daguerreotypien bezeugten vor allem die Existenz einer Person. Doch mit den in kürzeren Abständen aufgenommenen Cartes de Visite wurde die Porträtfotografie zu einem biografischen Medium.

Häufig sukzessive befüllt können die ersten Seiten eines Albums beispielsweise die Familie und die Ehepartner vor der Heirat zeigen, dann Bilder des Brautpaares, dann die Kinder, die Großeltern und in der Folge Bilder davon, wie alle diese Personen älter werden; zuweilen mit einigen Leerseiten Abstand kommen dann weitere Bilder von Verwandten und Bekannten. Diesen Bildern fehlt oft die zeitliche Verankerung, die den Bildern von Hochzeiten und ähnlichen Ereignissen eigen ist. Es sind generische und relativ zeitarme Porträts, die keinen biografischen Moment zeigen und keine Geschichte erzählen, es sei denn, dass eine Beschriftung auf der Vorder- oder Rückseite Ort und Zeit, Porträtierte oder Adressat*in benennt (Abb. 6). Aber diese Bilder ließen im Album den Umfang und auch die geografische Weite des sozialen Netzwerks einer Familie sichtbar werden – die meisten Fotografien des hier gezeigten Albums etwa stammen aus Sachsen, doch das eine Bild links oben wurde in Odessa aufgenommen.

Die Cartes de Visite waren ungeheuer erfolgreich. Schätzungen gehen davon aus, dass während der 1860er-Jahre allein in Großbritannien jährlich etwa 300 Millionen Cartes de Visite verkauft wurden.[6] Zwar zählen dazu auch die oft in Auflagen von mehreren tausend Exemplaren abgezogenen Porträts von Prominenz, Landschaftsaufnahmen, Kunstreproduktionen und anderen Sujets; dennoch muss der Anteil privater Porträts enorm hoch gewesen sein. Oliver Wendell Holmes hatte die Cartes de Visite Anfang der 1860er-Jahre als „social currency" beschrieben und damit auf die allgemeine Verfügbarkeit und Verbreitung angespielt.[7]

Anders als Münzen und Banknoten zirkulierten sie zwar nicht, sondern wurden verschenkt, gefordert, miteinander ausgetauscht. Doch gesammelt, geordnet und nicht selten im Wohnzimmer auch für Besucher*innen zugänglich, akkumulierten sie sich in den Alben als sichtbarer Ausdruck des sozialen Kapitals einer Familie.

Der Erfolg der Cartes de Visite war einer der Gründe, der auch zu ihrem Niedergang führte. Die Produktion solch gewaltiger Mengen von Bildern führte zur Industrialisierung der Herstellung der notwendigen Emulsionen, Papiere und Kameras; die Zwänge der Konkurrenz sorgten dafür, dass diese Produkte stetig weiterentwickelt wurden. Portable Kameras, magazinierbare Gelatinetrockenplatten und später Filme vereinfachten die Fotografie außerhalb der Studios, so dass neben den professionellen Fotograf*innen der Studios auch Amateur*innen und Knipser*innen Bilder aufnehmen konnten. Fotografie wurde damit zwar nicht zu einem Alltags-, doch zu einem Gelegenheitsmedium für das, was im Leben gut

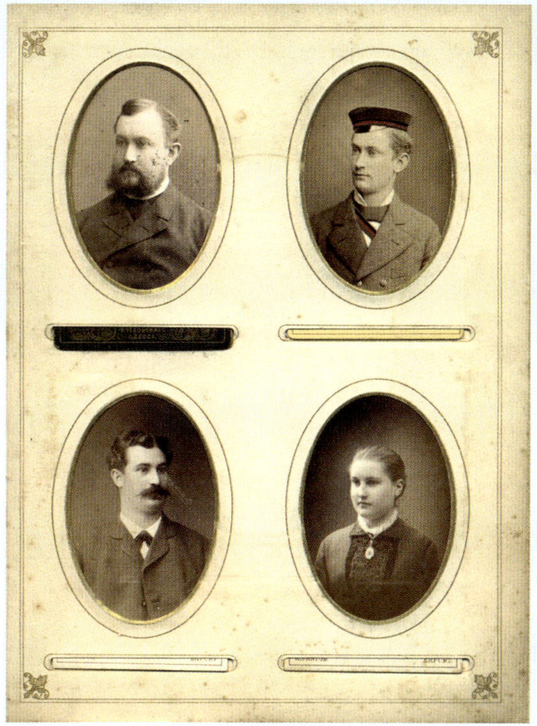

Admittedly, this number includes portraits of celebrities, landscapes, art reproductions, and other subjects, which were often produced in editions of several thousand copies; nevertheless, the percentage of personal portraits must have been significant. Oliver Wendell Holmes described *cartes de visite* as the "social currency" in the 1860s, referencing their widespread availability and distribution.[7]

Admittedly, they were gifted, requested, and swapped, and did not circulate, unlike coins and bank notes. Yet they were collected, organized, often displayed to visitors in living rooms, and accumulated in albums as the visible expression of a family's social capital.

The success of *cartes de visite* also contained the seeds of its downfall. The production of such huge numbers of images led to the industrialization of the manufacturing of necessary emulsions, papers, and cameras; the pressures of competition led to these products being constantly developed further. Portable cameras, shelf-stable dry plates, and later films simplified photography outside of the studio, making it possible for amateurs and hobbyists to take photographs as well as professional studio photographers. Accordingly, photography became a medium perhaps not to be used everyday, but now and again to capture what was good and beautiful in life. Admittedly, events such as weddings continued to be elaborately captured in photography studios; but smaller cameras made it possible for people themselves to take photographs of such occasions as well as of far more fleeting moments such as a Sunday stroll or a day spent in the garden (fig. 7). These images could take on more of a narrative character when such occasions were photographed repeatedly—and not just moments, but a series of events then became recognizable. Images alone would not tell the story:

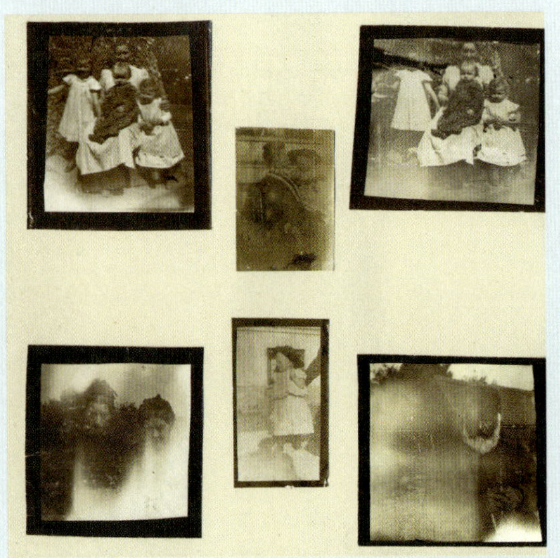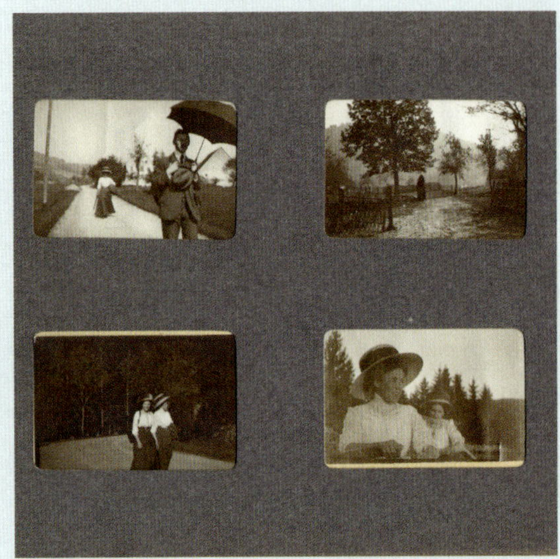

und schön war. Zwar wurden Ereignisse wie Hochzeiten weiterhin repräsentativ in Fotostudios inszeniert; doch mit den kleineren Kameras konnten nun Bilder solcher und auch viel flüchtigerer Momente wie ein Sonntagsspaziergang oder der Tag im Garten selbst aufgenommen werden (Abb. 7). Und die Bilder konnten erzählerischer werden, wenn bei einer solchen Gelegenheit immer wieder fotografiert und nicht nur Momente, sondern ein Geschehen erkennbar wurde. Nicht immer reichten dafür die Bilder allein; sie wurden beschriftet, auf der Rückseite oder im Album, sie konnten datiert werden, Ort, Anlass und Personen wurden benannt, und zuweilen deuten ein, zwei Zeilen an, was vor, nach oder während der Aufnahme geschah.

Mit diesem nochmals neuen Modus der Bildproduktion wurde die private Fotografie flüchtiger, beiläufiger und damit als biografisches Medium neu gefasst. Ein Carte-de-Visite-Porträt von sich anfertigen zu lassen war ein Ritual – mit dem Studio wurde ein Termin vereinbart, man zog sich den Sonntagsstaat an, und das Bild war das Resultat aus eigenen Vorstellungen und den Anweisungen der Fotograf*in. Fotografierte man selbst, konnten Situationen aufgenommen werden, die sich im Studio bestenfalls simulieren ließen: die Sommerferien am Strand, ein fröhliches Fest, das spielende Kind. Auch Zahl und Dichte der Bilder konnten andere sein – vom Fest gab es dann nicht nur das eine zeremonielle Gruppenfoto, sondern auch allerhand Schnappschüsse, nicht nur ein, sondern jeder Tag am Strand war wenigstens eine Aufnahme wert, und beim Kind ließen sich das erste Lächeln, die ersten Schritte und der erste Schultag dokumentieren.

Die Verbreitung der privaten Kameras, die Zahl der Bilder und vielleicht auch die Intimität der aufgenommenen Sujets mag dazu geführt haben, dass solche Bilder offenbar deutlich weniger versandt wurden. Cartes de Visite und später auch andere Studiofotografien waren produziert worden, um verteilt zu

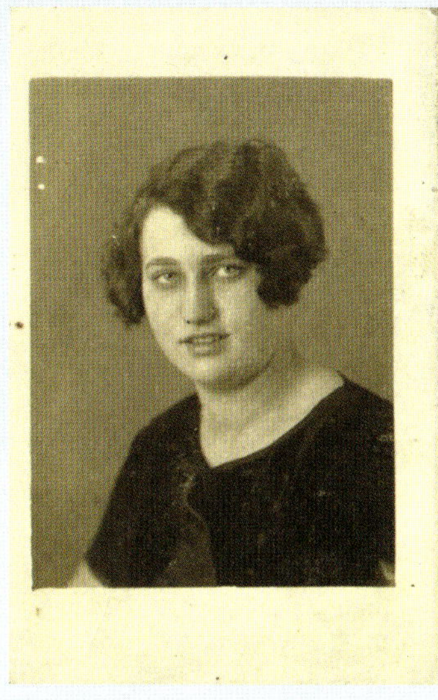

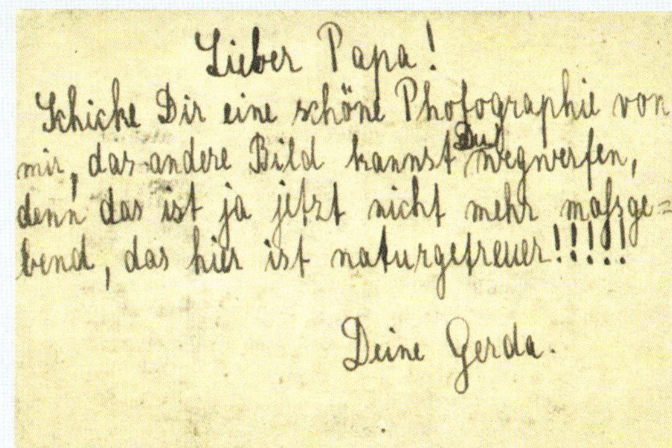

Abb. / **Fig. 8A–B**
Anonym / **Anonymous**
Porträt von Gerda, vermutlich Deutschland / **Portrait of Gerda, presumably Germany,** ca. 1930,
Silbergelatineausbelichtung / **gelatin silver print (recto / verso)**

handwritten notes would be added on the back of photographs and in albums, and the date, place, occasion, and people would be named; sometimes one or two lines would suggest what happened before, after, or during the moment when the photograph was taken.

This new mode of image production reframed personal photography as more fleeting and more casual, thus reinventing it as a biographic medium. To have a *cartes de visite* portrait taken of oneself was a ritual: one would arrange an appointment with a studio and don one's Sunday best; the image was a result of one's own ideas and the photographer's instructions. Taking photographs for oneself meant one could capture situations that could at best only be simulated in the studio: the summer holidays on the beach, a merry party, a child at play. A greater number and density of images was possible too: it was possible to have not just one single ceremonial group photograph at a party, but any number of snapshots; not just one single day, but every day at the beach merited at least one photograph; and people could document a child's first smile, first steps, and first day of school.

The spread of personal cameras, the number of images, and perhaps also the intimacy of the subjects photographed may have led to such images evidently being sent far less often. *Cartes de visite* and later studio photographs were produced in order to be distributed, and thus albums mostly contain images of other people rather than the album owner. But the albums of hobbyist and amateur photographers mostly contain photographs the owner has taken themselves. It seems that photography lost its significance as manifestations of a person's or family's social capital, and its worth began to lie above all in the ability to permanently preserve one's own life and good times. But the practice of sending photographs did not disappear altogether (fig. 8). "Dear Papa!," one young woman for instance wrote in the early 1920s, "I'm

werden, und so finden sich in den Alben vor allem Bilder anderer Personen als der jeweiligen Besitzer*innen. Die Alben der Knipser*innen und Amateur*innen sind dagegen in erster Linie mit selbst aufgenommenen Fotografien bestückt. Es scheint, dass die Fotografien ihre Bedeutung als Manifestationen des sozialen Kapitals einer Person oder einer Familie verloren und ihr Wert nun vor allem darin bestand, sich des eigenen Lebens und seiner guten Zeiten dauerhaft zu versichern. Die Praxis, sich Bilder zu schicken, verschwand darüber allerdings nicht vollständig (Abb. 8): „Lieber Papa!", schrieb eine junge Frau etwa Anfang der 1920er-Jahre, „Schicke Dir eine schöne Photographie von mir, das andere Bild kannst Du wegwerfen, denn das ist ja nicht mehr maßgebend, das hier ist naturgetreuer!!!!! Deine Gerda." Das Bild selbst ist nichts besonderes – unter einer Wellenfrisur blickt eine junge Frau leicht lächelnd in die Kamera, und es ist so unklar wie unwichtig, ob dahinter eine Freundin stand oder ein/e Fotograf*in.[8] Die sechs Rufzeichen unterstreichen dagegen die Dringlichkeit des Anliegens – dieses Bild soll auch physisch ein anderes ersetzen, das Gerda nicht mehr zeigt wie sie gesehen werden möchte, mit anderen Worten: Es soll ihre Präsenz im Leben des Vaters aktualisieren. Für die Absenderin ist so nicht allein der Moment der Aufnahme von Bedeutung, sondern auch jener des Empfangs und des Blicks auf die Fotografie, der das Bild Gerdas prägnant verändern soll.

Und ganz von ferne deutet sich in solchen und anderen Bildern an, was erst Jahrzehnte später in den digitalen sozialen Medien zur Entfaltung kommen sollte – dass Fotografien nicht allein vom Gewesenen, vom ça-a-été erzählen, sondern Gegenwärtigkeit herstellen können.

1 Zwischen 1840 und 1860 wurden allein in den USA etwa 20 Millionen Daguerreotypien aufgenommen, die Mehrzahl davon Porträts. Vgl. Amy K. DeFalco Lippert, *Consuming Identities. Visual Culture in Nineteenth Century San Francisco*, Oxford 2018, S. 143

2 „About 70 percent of the millions of daguerreotypes made were sixth-plate [...]", ebd., S. 383

3 Gegen Ende der 1850er-Jahre kostete eine Daguerreotypie in den USA 2,50 Dollar; ein Dutzend Cartes de Visite kostete zwischen 1 und 3 Dollar. Vgl. Robert Taft, *Photography and the American Scene*, New York/Dover 1938, S. 80

4 Zur Geschichte der Reorganisation des Postwesens in den USA vgl. ausführlich David M. Henkin, *The Postal Age. The Emergence of Modern Communication in Nineteenth-Century America*, Chicago/London 2006

5 Zu Fotografie und Tod vgl. ausführlicher Felix Hoffmann, Friedrich Tietjen (Hg.): *Das letzte Bild: Fotografie und Tod / The Last Image: Photography and Death*, Ausst.-Kat. C/O Berlin, Berlin/Leipzig 2018

6 Vgl. William C. Darrah, *Cartes de Visite in 19th Century Photography*, Gettysburg 1981, S. 4. Zur gleichen Zeit hatte Großbritannien etwa 20 Millionen Einwohner.

7 Vgl. Wendell Holmes, "Doings of the Sunbeam", in: *Soundings of the Atlantic*, Boston 1864, S. 228–281, hier S. 255

8 Pose und Ausleuchtung sprechen für eine Studiofotografie, Format und Bildqualität für eine private Aufnahme.

sending a nice photograph of myself, you can throw away the other picture, it's not representative anymore, this one is truer to nature!!!!!! Your Gerda." The photograph itself is nothing special: a young woman with waved hair gently smiles into the camera, and it is as unclear as it is unimportant whether it was taken by a female friend or a photographer.[8]

Yet the six exclamation points underscore the urgency of the matter: this photograph was meant to physically replace another one that no longer showed Gerda as she wished to be seen. In other words: it was meant to bring up to date her presence in her father's life. For the sender, the significant moment was not only when the photograph was taken, but also the moment when it was received and in which the photograph was regarded, which was intended to substantially change Gerda's image.

And at a great remove, these and other such images hint at what fully came to fruition with digital images on social media decades later—that photographs did not merely convey the past, *ça a été,* but could also create the present moment.

1 Between 1840 and 1860, approximately twenty million daguerreotypes were taken, the majority of them portraits. See Amy K. DeFalco *Lippert, Consuming Identities: Visual Culture in Nineteenth Century San Francisco* (Oxford: Oxford University Press, 2018), 143.

2 "About 70 percent of the millions of daguerreotypes made were sixth-plate," Lippert, *Consuming Identities,* 383.

3 Around the end of the 1850s, a daguerreotype cost 2.50 dollars in the US; a dozen *cartes de visite* cost between one and three dollars. See Robert Taft, *Photography and the American Scene: A Social History, 1839–1889* (New York and Dover, DE: Dover Publications, 1938), 80.

4 For detailed information on the history of the US postal service's reorganization, see David M. Henkin, *The Postal Age: The Emergence of Modern Communication in Nineteenth-Century America* (Chicago, IL, and London: University of Chicago Press, 2006).

5 To read about photography and death in greater detail, see Felix Hoffmann and Friedrich Tietjen, eds., *Das letzte Bild: Fotografie und Tod / The Last Image: Photography and Death* exh. cat. C/O Berlin (Berlin and Leipzig: Spector Books, 2018).

6 See William C. Darrah, *Cartes de Visite in Nineteenth Century Photography* (Gettysburg, PA: Darrah-Smith Books, 1981), 4. At the same time, Britain had around twenty million inhabitants.

7 See Wendell Holmes, "Doings of the Sunbeam," in *Soundings from the Atlantic* (Boston, MA: Gale, Sabin Americana, 1864), 228–81, here 255.

8 The pose and lighting suggest a studio photograph, the format and image quality a private snapshot.

MASSEN VON VERSCHIEDENEN BILDERN / **MASSES OF DIFFERENT IMAGES**

Text: Christian Kassung

GLEICH(ZEITIG)E BILDER
Über Anfänge und Störungen der Bildübertragung

Etwa um 1700 änderte sich das europäische Strafsystem radikal. An die Stelle der Marter, die körperliche Vergeltung eines verbrecherischen Angriffs auf die Macht des Souveräns, trat ein streng reguliertes System der Verteidigung der Gesellschaft. Die Qual wurde durch die „Vorstellung der Qual" ersetzt – zumindest war dies der Grundgedanke.[1] Aus diesem weiten Rahmen des Verhältnisses von Macht und Wissen, das Michel Foucault 1975 in seinem Werk *Überwachen und Strafen* entfaltet hat, möchte ich hier ein einzelnes Element herausgreifen: Die Gewissheit, dass die im Gesetz kodifizierte Strafe auch tatsächlich vollzogen wird. Aber was hat dies mit zirkulierenden Bildern zu tun?

Erst ein entsprechendes Überwachungsorgan konnte garantieren, dass jedes noch so kleine Vergehen ans Tageslicht kommt „und mit vollkommener Gewißheit" bestraft wird.[2] Dass dieses Moment des modernen europäischen Strafsystems in aktuellen Debatten wieder an die Oberfläche tritt, sei an dieser Stelle nur angemerkt. Im Folgenden jedoch möchte ich zwei Punkte diskutieren: Zum einen, dass technische Bilder im Kontext von „Überwachen und Strafen" von Anfang an, nämlich seit Mitte des 19. Jahrhunderts, eine zentrale Funktion besitzen. Und zum zweiten, dass diese Funktion unlösbar mit der Idee der Gleichzeitigkeit bzw. Synchronizität von Bildern verbunden ist.

SIMILAR (AND SIMULTANEOUS) IMAGES
On the Inceptions and Interruptions of Image Transmission

Around 1700, the European penal system changed radically. In place of torture and corporal punishment as a response to a criminal attack on sovereign power, a stringently regulated system was implemented to defend society. Pain was replaced by the "idea of pain"—this, at least, was the fundamental idea.[1] I would like to single out just one element within the broad framework that Michel Foucault developed on the relationship between power and knowledge in his 1975 work *Discipline and Punish*: the certainty that the punishment codified in the law will actually be carried out. But what does this have to do with circulating images?

Only an appropriate monitoring body may guarantee that even the smallest offense will come to light and be punished "in all certainty."[2] It is worth mentioning at this point that this aspect of the modern European penal system is surfacing again in current debates. In the following, however, I would like to discuss two points: The first is the fact that images transmitted by means of technology have always had a central function in the context of "surveillance and punishment" since the mid-nineteenth century. And the second is that this function is inextricably linked to the idea of simultaneity or synchronicity of images.

Die Idee zirkulierender Bilder ist stets auch eine Idee der Gleichzeitigkeit. Damit Bilder zirkulieren, also zur selben Zeit an verschiedenen Orten sind, müssen sie medial übertragen werden. Solange wir uns im Paradigma des Analogen befinden, setzt die Übertragung von Bildern eine technische Synchronisation von Sender und Empfänger voraus. Das heißt also, dass der eine Pol zirkulierender Bilder durch die Gleichzeitigkeit bestimmt ist: durch das große Imaginäre ubiquitärer Bilder. Am anderen Pol jedoch, der Synchronisation, scharrt und kratzt beharrlich das Reale. Was ist damit gemeint? Und was bedeutet es, heute in einer Welt vermeintlich gleichzeitiger Bilder ohne Synchronisationsprobleme zu leben?

Das erste Medium, das mit dem Versprechen einer Gleichzeitigkeit der Bilder auftrat, ist die Bildtelegraphie. Was jedoch zu der Frage zurückführt, was in diesem Kontext überhaupt unter Gleichzeitigkeit zu verstehen ist. Die einfachste Antwort auf diese Frage lautet, wie bereits gesagt, dass zwei gleiche Bilder zur gleichen Zeit an verschiedenen Orten sind. Kompliziert wird diese einfache Antwort, sobald man „zwei gleiche Bilder" nicht als ein Faktum, sondern als einen Prozess versteht: Ob etwas gleich ist oder nicht, diese Entscheidung kann nur das Ergebnis eines Vergleiches sein, sei dies ein Vergleich von Bildern, Mustern oder Daten. Jeder Vergleichsprozess aber ist ein Vorgang in der Zeit; das heißt, dass das Urteil der Gleichheit dem Eindruck der Differenz notwendigerweise hinterherhinkt. Mit anderen Worten: Gleichzeitigkeit ist seinerseits kein zeitloses Kriterium, kein augenblickshafter Befund, sondern ein komplexer Effekt von Übertragungsmedien und Vergleichsoperationen. Gleichzeitigkeit in der Antike, unter den Bedingungen marathonlaufender Boten, ist keine Gleichzeitigkeit optischer Telegraphensysteme, und diese wiederum ist keine Gleichzeitigkeit vernetzter Glasfaserkabel. Dass Albert Einstein diesen medienhistorischen Überlegungen 1905 einen ahistorischen Strich namens Spezielle Relativitätstheorie durch die Rechnung gemacht hat, lasse ich an dieser Stelle außen vor.[3]

Springen wir vor diesem Hintergrund in die Mitte des 19. Jahrhunderts, so ist klar, dass sich gleiche Bilder dann zu gleicher Zeit an verschiedenen Orten befinden, wenn alle anderen Übertragungen langsamer vonstatten gehen; wenn wir also Bilder nicht mit Boten, Pferdekutschen, Schiffen oder Eisenbahnen übertragen, sondern mit Elektrizität. Das Denken von Gleichzeitigkeit ist auf das Engste mit der Elektrizität verbunden, weil alle Dinge buchstäblich hinterherhinken.[4]

Anders formuliert: Wenn es gelingt, Bilder durch Elektrizität zu übertragen, dann ergibt sich daraus geradezu zwangsläufig das Phantasma, dass diese Bilder immer schon ihren Empfänger erreicht haben werden, bevor dort auch die Schicksalswellen des Realen anbranden.

Der Tsunami folgt den Bildern seiner Zerstörung nähergelegener Orte, einfach weil die Dinge und mit ihnen auch wir Menschen den elektrischen Bildern nicht mehr hinterherkommen. Und wenn die Bilder auch noch per Funk übertragen werden, dann zirkulieren sie im Wortsinne: als kugelförmige Bildwelle, die sich

THE PHANTASM OF SIMULTANEITY

The idea of circulating images is also always about simultaneity. In order for images to circulate, that is to be in different places at the same time, they have to be transmitted medially. As long as we are in the paradigm of the analog, the transmission of images requires a technological synchronization of sender and receiver. This means that one pole of circulating images is determined by simultaneity: by the great imaginary of ubiquitous images. At the other pole, however, synchronization steadfastly chips away at the real. What do I mean by that? And what does it mean today to live in a world of supposedly simultaneous images without synchronization problems?

The first medium that appeared to promise a simultaneity of images is phototelegraphy. This, however, leads back to the question of what is meant by simultaneity in this context. As stated, the simplest answer to this question is that two identical images are in different places at the same time. This simple answer becomes complicated as soon as one understands "two identical images" not as a fact but as a process: of whether something is the same or not, a decision that comes only from comparison, be it of pictures, samples, or data. But every process of comparison is an event in time; that is, a verdict on similarity must inevitably lag behind the impression of difference. In other words, simultaneity is not a timeless criterion, not an instantaneous finding, but a complex result of transmission media and comparison operations. Simultaneity in ancient times, under the conditions of marathon-running heralds, is not the same as the simultaneity of optical telegraph systems, and this in turn is not akin to the simultaneity of fiber optic cable networks. I will leave out the fact that Albert Einstein dashed these media-historical considerations with his special theory of relativity in 1905.[3] Against this backdrop, if we jump to the middle of the nineteenth century, it is clear that the same images are located in different places at the same time if all other transmissions take place more slowly: that is, if we transmit images not with messengers, horse-drawn carriages, ships, or trains, but with electricity. The idea of simultaneity is intimately related to electricity because all things are literally lagging behind.[4]

In other words, if it is possible to transmit images through electricity, then the phantasm inevitably arises that these images will have reached their recipient before the waves of fate crash down upon them.

Following the images is a tsunami that destroys everything surrounding them because things and with them we humans can no longer keep up with electronic images. And if the images are transmitted by radio, then they literally circulate: as a spherical image wave that engulfs the respective event at the speed of light —faster than any event itself.

This notion of a spherical wave, in which images surround their place of origin almost instantaneously, now fits perfectly into Foucault's initial scenario: "Consider those first movements in which the news of some horrible act

mit Lichtgeschwindigkeit um das jeweilige Ereignis herumlegt – schneller als jedes Ereignis selbst.

Diese Vorstellung einer Kugelwelle, mit der sich Bilder um ihren Ursprungsort quasi instantan herumlegen, fügt sich nun passgenau in das Foucault'sche Eingangsszenario ein:

„Betrachtet die ersten Augenblicke, in denen sich die Kunde von einer gräßlichen Tat in unseren Städten oder auf dem Lande verbreitet: die Bürger gleichen Menschen, die den Blitz hinter sich einschlagen sehen; jeder ist durchdrungen von Entrüstung und Schauer… Das ist der Moment zur Bestrafung des Verbrechens: laßt ihn nicht vorübergehen! Laßt den Untäter nicht entwischen!"[5]

Würden sich also Informationen über den Täter schneller als dieser selbst um ihn herum ausbreiten, wäre sein Entwischen ausgeschlossen und die Bestrafung sicher. Ich werde darauf zurückkommen. Zuvor jedoch einige Worte zur Technikgeschichte der Bildtelegraphie.

DIE GESCHICHTE DER BILDTELEGRAPHIE

In der Geschichte der Bildtelegraphie verweben sich zwei Hauptnarrative: Zeit und Bild. Diese Erzählstränge vollständig zu entflechten, wurde bereits andernorts geleistet.[6] Für hier reicht es aus, das überaus komplexe Geflecht auf einen einzigen Satz zu verkürzen: Seit ihrem Gründungspatent vom 27. Mai 1843 besteht die Bildtelegraphie in der Transformation von Bild in Zeit (Abb. 1). Im Sender wird Raum in Zeit verwandelt, im Empfänger dann Zeit wieder in Raum. Bilder zu übertragen, heißt Zeit zu übertragen, heißt zwei räumlich voneinander getrennte Bewegungen vollständig zu synchronisieren: Ein Bild wird in derselben Weise im Sender abgetastet wie es im Sender angeschrieben wird. Wo also gleichzeitige Zeitsignale vorhanden sind, da sind auch die Bilder gleich. Und wo es Synchronisationsprobleme gibt, da wird die Störung zum Bild im Bild. Das erklärt, warum die Übertragung von Zeit und die Übertragung von Bildern historisch besehen so lange das gleiche technische Problem darstellen, bis schließlich die Digitalisierung den Status von Bildern grundsätzlich neu definiert.

Entsprechend schreibt Carl August von Steinheil, einer der Pioniere der elektrischen Uhren, dass seine Zeit-Telegraphen „alle nur Eine und Dieselbe Zeit zeigen", man sie also als „Spiegelbilder der *Einen Uhr*" ansehen kann.[7] Es ist gerade keine rhetorische Figur, wenn Steinheil das Synchronisationsproblem mit der Abbildung von Uhren identifiziert, durch die der Raum zwischen Sender und Empfänger „verschwindet".[8]

Die menschlichen Hauptakteure der Bildtelegraphie lassen sich schnell an einer Hand aufzählen: der erfolglos gebliebene und 1877 vollkommen verarmt gestorbene Schotte Alexander Bain; sein erbitterter Konkurrent, der englische Physiker Frederick Bakewell; dann Giovanni Caselli, ein italienischer Physiker, Erfinder und Geistlicher, den man durchaus als lachenden Dritten dieser Geschichte bezeichnen kann; und schließlich Arthur Korn, der als Professor an der Technischen Universität Berlin die Bildtelegraphie so weit technisch stabilisieren konnte, dass ihr kommerzieller Einsatz möglich wurde, dann jedoch 1939 vor den Nationalsozialisten in die USA fliehen musste. Entlang dieser Akteure skandiert die Technikgeschichte im Normalfall die Entwicklungslogik immer schnel-

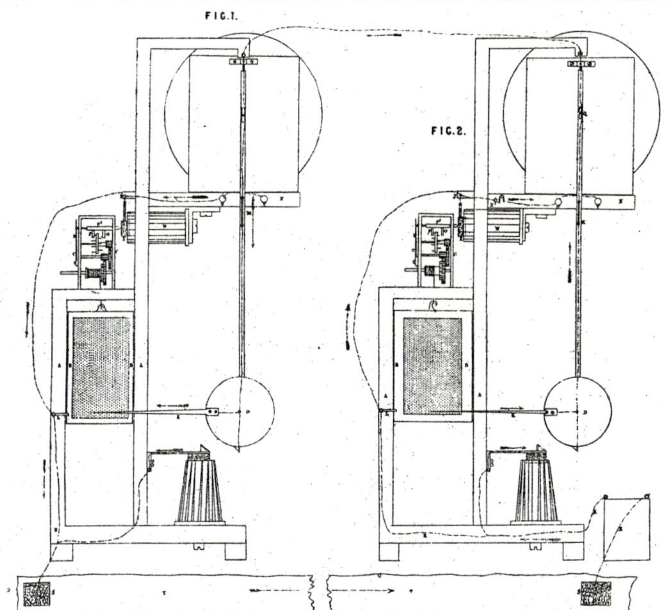

Abb. / **Fig. 1**
Alexander Bain
Copying Telegraph,
Konstruktionszeichnung /
construction drawing, 1843

spreads through our towns and countryside; the citizens are like men who see lightning falling about them; everyone is moved by indignation and horror … That is the moment to punish the crime: do not let it slip by; hasten to prove it and judge it."[5]

If information about the perpetrator were to move faster than the perpetrator himself, his escape would be impossible and the punishment inevitable. I will come back to that. But now a few words on the technical history of phototelegraphy.

THE HISTORY OF PHOTOTELEGRAPHY

Two main narratives interweave in the history of phototelegraphy: time and image. Completely disentangling these narrative strands has already been done elsewhere.[6] It suffices here to summarize the extremely complex web in a single sentence: since its founding patent on May 27, 1843, phototelegraphy has consisted of the transformation of image into time (fig. 1). The transmitter transforms space into time, the receiver transforms time into space again. To transmit images is to transmit time, entailing the complete synchronization of two spatially distinct movements: an image is scanned in the transmitter in the same way it is written in the transmitter. So where there are simultaneous time signals, the images are the same. And where there are synchronization problems, the disturbance to the picture is evident in the picture. This explains why, until digitization finally redefined the status of images, the transfer of time and the transfer of images historically represent the same technical problem. On this Carl August von Steinheil, one of the pioneers of digital clocks, writes that his time telegraphs "all only show one and the same time" such that they can be viewed as "mirror images of *one clock*."[7] When Steinheil identifies the synchronization problem with an image of clocks,

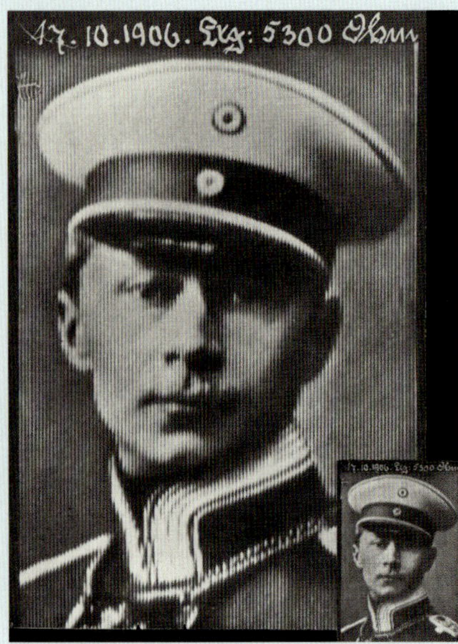

Abb. / **Fig. 2**
Arthur Korn
Wilhelm von Preußen / **of Prussia,** 1906,
Telegrafisch übertragene Fotografie /
photograph transmitted by telegraph

lerer und störungsfreierer Apparate. So berichtet bereits am 22. Februar 1862 die britische *Times* aus Frankreich:

„A new system of telegraph has been submitted to the Emperor, to which its inventor, M. Caselli, has given the name of 'pantelegraph'. This telegraph has been already worked at Florence and Leghorn [Livorno]. It transmits autograph messages and drawings with all the perfections and defects of the originals. An inhabitant of Leghorn wrote four lines from *Dante*, and they appeared in the same handwriting at Florence. A portrait of the same poet was painted at Leghorn, and it was reproduced at Florence line for line and shade for shade."[9]

Und auch Arthur Korn, der 1923 den ersten Rückblick auf die Entwicklungsgeschichte der Bildtelegraphie schrieb,[10] verzeichnete in seinen zahllosen, auch internationalen Publikationen unermüdlich die Fortschritte dieses neuen Mediums (Abb. 2). So gelang die juristisch wichtige Übertragung einer Handschrift laut Korn in wenigen Minuten.[11] Meteorologische Karten halfen der Wettervorhersage, aber auch, neben anderen Karten, dem Militär.[12] Zu den ersten zirkulierenden Bildern zählten selbstverständlich auch wichtige Ereignisse, die tagesaktuell verbreitet werden konnten (Abb. 3, 4). Beispielsweise berichtete *Le Matin* bereits am folgenden Morgen in Paris mit einer Bildübertragung von den Flugversuchen mit dem Voisin Standard-Doppeldecker, die Armand Zipfel zwischen dem 28. Januar und dem 4. Februar 1909 auf dem Tempelhofer Flugfeld ausführte.[13] Bereits zwei Jahre zuvor war die Einrichtung eines regelmäßigen Bildverkehrs zwischen Berlin, Paris und London beschlossen worden.[14]

Was lag angesichts dieser Erfolge näher, als auch über den Einsatz der „Bildtelegraphie im Dienste der Polizei" nachzudenken? Unter diesem Titel hielt Arthur Korn im September 1926 auf dem zweiten internationalen Polizeikongress zu Berlin einen Vortrag über den Einsatz der Bildtelegraphie im Polizeidienst.[15] Darin verwies er auf einen Fall, der sich bereits knapp 20 Jahre zuvor in London

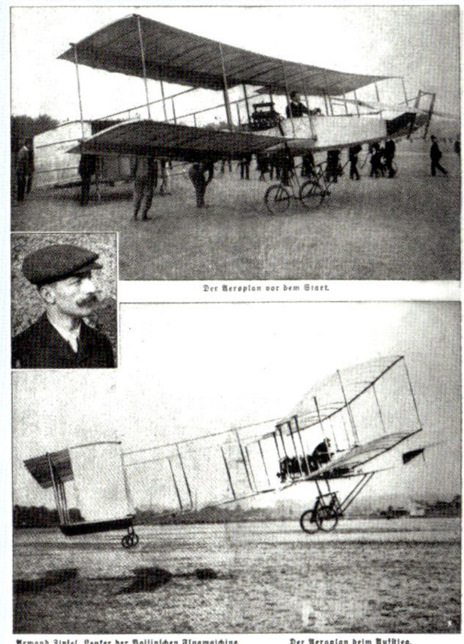

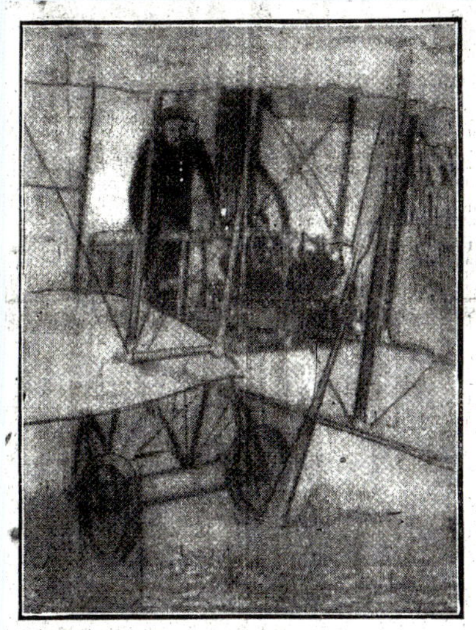

Abb. / **Fig. 3**
Die Woche
„Armand Zipfel, Lenker der Voisinschen
Flugmaschine", Tempelhofer Flugfeld, 1909,
Magazinseite / **magazine page**

Abb. / **Fig. 4**
Le Matin
„L'Aviateur Zipfel sur son Aéroplane", 1909,
Bildtelegrafische Übertragung /
phototelegraphic transmission

through which the space between transmitter and receiver "disappears," it is not a mere rhetorical flourish.[8]

One can quickly name the people involved in telephotography: Alexander Bain from Scotland, who remained unsuccessful and died in poverty in 1877; English physicist Frederick Bakewell; Italian physicist, inventor, and intellectual Giovanni Caselli, who can accurately be described as the laughing third party in this story; and finally Arthur Korn, professor at Technische Universität Berlin, who succeeded in stabilizing the technology behind telephotography such that it could find commercial application, but who had to flee from the Nazi party to the United States in 1939. Following these key players, technological history, usually the logic of development, heralds ever-faster apparatus with ever-fewer interference problems. Already in February 22, 1862, the London *Times* reported from France: "A new system of telegraph has been submitted to the Emperor, to which its inventor, M. Caselli, has given the name of 'pantelegraph.' This telegraph has been already worked at Florence and Leghorn [Livorno]. It transmits autograph messages and drawings with all the perfections and defects of the originals. An inhabitant of Leghorn wrote four lines from Dante, and they appeared in the same handwriting at Florence. A portrait of the same poet was painted at Leghorn, and it was reproduced at Florence line for line and shade for shade."[9]

Arthur Korn tirelessly made reports in countless publications, some international, on the progress of this new medium (fig. 2). In 1923, he wrote the first résumé of the history of phototelegraphy.[10] According to Korn, the first transmission of handwriting, significant in juristic terms, was successful after a few minutes.[11] Meteorological maps helped to predict the weather, as did military and other maps.[12] Inevitably among the first circulating images (figs. 3, 4) were reports on important events, which could be distributed daily.

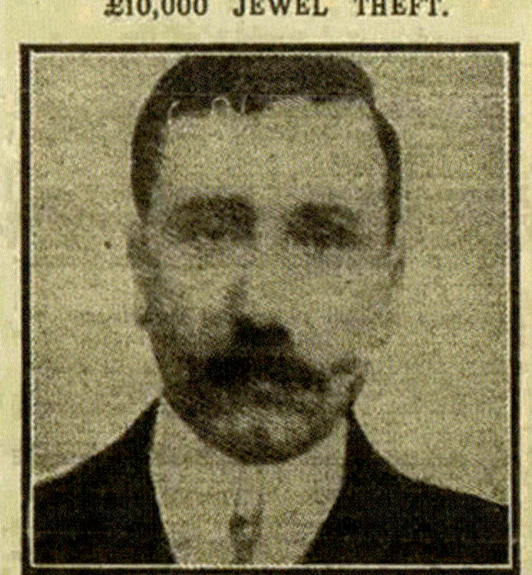

Abb. / **Fig. 5, 6**
The Daily Mirror
„Juwelendiebstahl im Wert von 10.000 Pfund" / "£ 10,000 Jewel Theft,"
„Identifiziert durch eine Korn-Fotografie" / "**Identified by Korn Photograph**"
1908, Zeitungsausschnitte / **newspaper clippings**

ereignet hatte (Abb. 5, 6): Am 17. März 1908 wurde ein Porträtfoto des bis dahin noch namenlosen Täters Maurice G. Guttman mittels Korn'scher Apparatur von Paris nach London telegraphiert und im „Daily Mirror" unter der Überschrift abgedruckt: „£ 10,000 JEWEL THEFT."[16] Bereits am folgenden Tag war die Sensation perfekt, da Guttmann anhand des Fotos identifiziert werden konnte:

„Calling at the *Daily Mirror* office yesterday, Mr. O. F. Weisse said that he immediately and unmistakably recognised the photograph of Guttman as a former lodger."[17]

Erfolgreicher im Sinne Foucaults können zirkulierende Fahndungsbilder nicht sein. Entscheidend sind die Signalwörter „immediately" und „unmistakably": Das System zirkulierender Bilder kann gar nicht versagen, die Technik überholt und kreist den Verbrecher mit Sicherheit ein. Seine gerechte Bestrafung ist gesichert. Insofern verwundert es kaum, dass der *Daily Mirror* bei dieser Gelegenheit auch noch einige „Crime Experts' Eulogies" abdruckte, freilich ohne dass dabei die Wichtigkeit der Zeitung selbst als Verbreitungsmedium unter den Tisch fiel.

DIE STÖRUNG DER SYNCHRONISATION

Erstaunlich ist allerdings, dass die Idee der zirkulierenden Fahndungsfotos Alexander Bain schon Mitte des 19. Jahrhunderts gekommen war. Sie war von Anfang an mit der Bildtelegraphie verwoben, also bereits zu einem Zeitpunkt, als von hinreichend stabilen, schnellen und störungsfreien Übertragungen noch keine Rede sein konnte: „My 'Copying Telegraph' is capable of transmitting the fac-simile of any communication in writing or printing, or of any other figure, including the profile of the 'human face divine,' so that the physiognomy of a runaway could be sent to all the outports of the kingdom in two or three minutes. The 'Copying Telegraph' has not yet been put in practical operation […]: but these difficulties are not insurmountable."[18]

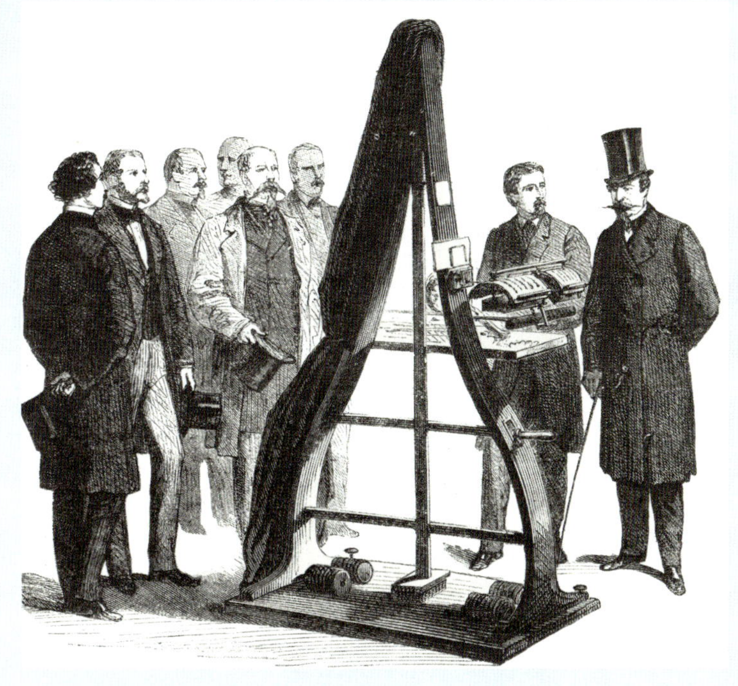

Le Matin, for example, reported on Armand Zipfel's attempts to fly the Voisin biplane between January 28 and February 4, 1909, on Tempelhofer Feld in Berlin the following morning in Paris, images included.[13] The establishment of regular image transmission between Berlin, Paris, and London had already been agreed upon two years prior.[14]

In view of this success, what would be more logical than to explore utilizing phototelegraphy for police work? Korn gave a talk at the second international Berlin police conference on employing phototelegraphy for police matters.[15] In it, he made reference to a case some almost twenty years previous in London (figs. 5, 6). On March 17, 1908, Korn's apparatus was used to telegraph a portrait photo of the then nameless criminal Maurice G. Guttman, which was printed in the *Daily Mirror* under the headline "£10,000 JEWEL THEFT."[16] The sensational case was concluded the following day when Guttmann was identified on the basis of the photograph: "Calling at the *Daily Mirror* office yesterday, Mr. O. F. Weisse said that he immediately and unmistakably recognized the photograph of Guttman as a former lodger."[17]

The circulating "wanted" images could not have been closer to the way that Foucault described them. The key words "immediately" and "unmistakably" are decisive: the system of circulating images is foolproof, and technology can be relied on to locate and capture criminals, whose deserved punishment is guaranteed. Thus it is hardly surprising that the *Daily Mirror* used this case to print other "crime experts' eulogies," without, of course, negating the newspaper's own importance as a means of mass communication.

A DISTURBANCE IN THE SYNCHRONIZATION

It is astonishing then to consider that Alexander Bain first had the idea of circulating "wanted" photography in the mid-nineteenth century. It was woven into

Doch die Euphorie für das neue Medium wurde von beständigen Rückschlägen gedämpft. Bains Apparate funktionierten nie, Bakewell musste mit der Hand nachhelfen. Und nach den anfänglichen Erfolgen der Telegraphenlinie Casellis (Abb. 7), die am 14. Februar 1865 mit den Strecken Paris–Amiens, Paris–Marseille und Paris–Lyon debütierte und bereits im Sommer in den solcher Übertragungstechnologien besonders bedürftigen Flächenstaat Russland exportiert wurde, nahmen dessen finanzielle Schwierigkeiten zu, und Caselli stirbt schließlich verarmt.[19] Die mit dem „Fernsehen" von Anfang an verbundene Hoffnung, „die Schranken von Raum und Zeit zu brechen", zerrieb sich immer wieder aufs Neue an der nackten Materialität von Bild und Zeit:[20] Je länger der Übertragungsweg sein sollte, umso stärker machten sich die Synchronisationsprobleme als Störungen bemerkbar. Und je detailreicher die Bilder waren, umso länger dauerte die Übertragung. Arthur Korn brachte den Stand der Dinge 1923 wie folgt auf den Punkt: „Man mußte sich daher, wenn man die Transmissionszeit nicht erhöhen wollte, was mit Rücksicht auf die zu lange Inanspruchnahme der Fernsprechleitungen nicht ratsam war, im allgemeinen mit der Übertragung von verhältnismäßig einfachen Bildern, wie Portraits, begnügen; nur in seltenen Fällen konnte man bei etwas komplizierteren Vorlagen, wie Gruppen und Landschaften, auf genügende Übertragung der Einzelheiten rechnen."[21]

Anders formuliert:

Der Teufel lauerte im Detail. Die Vermeidung oder Korrektur von Störungen benötigte Zeit. Genau das aber machte eine gleichzeitige Zirkulation der Bilder unmöglich.

Denn selbst wenn sich die Störungen und damit das Synchronisationsproblem mit endlichem Aufwand minimieren ließen – durch unterschiedlichste Technologien wie Korrekturlinien, mannshohe Pendel, Zwischenklischees, Kompensationsschaltungen bis hin zu direktem menschlichen Eingreifen in den Apparat –, die Gleichzeitigkeit und Idee der zirkulierenden Bilder war damit nicht vereinbar.

Es mutet wie ein Treppenwitz der Geschichte an: Zuerst gab es zu wenig Bilder und zu viel Störung, dann gab es, im Digitalen, keine Störung mehr, aber zu viele Bilder.

Lorenz Engell formulierte diesen Querstand bereits 2004: „Wenn alles schon immer da ist, macht Übertragung keinen Sinn mehr."[22] Warum eigentlich, könnte man pointiert fragen, widersetzen sich Bilder ihrer Übertragung bis heute? Denn seien wir ehrlich, wer heute Instagram, Pinterest oder Flickr aufruft, der hat vor allem eines: ein Filter- und damit Zeitproblem. Nochmals Engell: „Das schon früher beobachtete Phänomen der Sättigung an Sichtbarkeit zieht den Zwang zur Wahl, zur Selektion nach sich."[23] Die digitale Gleichzeitigkeit der Bilder bedeutet zwar eine technische Lösung des Übertragungsproblems, aber eben nur dies: eine technische Lösung. Das Technische ist jedoch nur ein Aspekt von Bildern, zumal von technischen Bildern. Dass uns gerade dies die Technikgeschichte der Bildübertragung lehrt, sollte zu weiterem Nachdenken Anlass geben.

the fabric of phototelegraphy from the very beginning; at a time before adequately stable, fast, and reliable transmission technologies were available: "My 'Copying Telegraph' is capable of transmitting the facsimile of any communication in writing or printing, or of any other figure, including the profile of the 'human face divine,' so that the physiognomy of a runaway could be sent to all the outports of the kingdom in two or three minutes. The 'Copying Telegraph' has not yet been put in practical operation … : but these difficulties are not insurmountable."[18]

Yet excitement over the new media was dampened by continual setbacks. Bain's device never worked, and Bakewell had to make improvements later. And despite the early successes of Caselli's telegraph lines (fig. 7), which debuted from Paris to the cities of Amiens, Marseille, and Lyon on February 14, 1865, and were already being exported to the Russia—a vast country in need of such communications technologies—by the summer, he encountered financial difficulties and ultimately died poor.[19] The hope initially pinned on "television" to "break the boundaries of space and time" repeatedly came up against the stark materiality of image and time:[20] the greater the distance between two transmission points, the worse the synchronization and the more disturbances there were. And the more detailed the image, the longer transmission took. In 1923, Korn succinctly summarized the state of affairs: "In order to avoid increasing transmission time, which is advisable in view of the fact it blocks the phone lines for too long, one needs to limit oneself generally to the transmission of relatively simple images, such as portraits. It is unusual that one can rely on more complicated images, such as those of groups and landscapes, being transmitted in sufficient detail."[21] To put it another way:

The devil is in the detail. Avoiding or compensating for disturbances requires time. Yet this is precisely what makes it impossible to achieve a simultaneous circulation of images.

Even if disturbances and with them synchronization problems could be minimized with finite effort—using widely disparate technologies such as guidelines, human-sized pendulums, intermediary clichés, compensatory switches, and direct human intervention in the devices—it would still not be possible to unite simultaneity and the idea of circulating images.

It seems a strange irony of history that at first there were too few images and too many disturbances, whereas now in the digital era there are no longer disturbances but too many images.

Already in 2004, Lorenz Engell summarized this state of affairs: "When everything is always there, transmission no longer makes sense."[22] One could press the point and ask why images still resist transmission today? If we take an honest view, anyone who uses Instagram, Pinterest, or Flickr has a problem of time that results from a filter problem. In the words of Engell: "The phenomenon of visual oversaturation, which was observed early on, makes it necessary to select."[23] The digital simultaneity of images may mean a technical solution to the problem of transmission, but it is just a technical solution. The

1   Michel Foucault, *Überwachen und Strafen. Die Geburt des Gefängnisses,* Frankfurt am Main 2010 [frz. Erstausgabe 1975], S. 120

2   Ebd., S. 123

3   Vgl. Peter Galison, *Einsteins Uhren, Poincarés Karten. Die Arbeit an der Ordnung der Zeit*, Frankfurt am Main 2003

4   Vgl. hierzu immer noch lesenswert Christoph Asendorf, *Ströme und Strahlen. Das langsame Verschwinden der Materie um 1900*, Gießen 1989, S. 119–63

5   Zit. nach Foucault 2010 (wie Anm. 1), S. 141

6   Vgl. Christian Kassung, *Das Pendel. Eine Wissensgeschichte*, München 2007, S. 309–387

7   Carl August von Steinheil, „Beschreibung und Abbildung der von dem K. Akademiker und Conservator, Professor Dr. Steinheil Erfundenen Galvanischen Uhren", in: *Kunst- und Gewerbeblatt des Polytechnischen Vereins für das Königreich Bayern*, 2, 1843, S. 127–142, hier S. 139

8   Carl August von Steinheil, „Noch ein Wort über den Galvanischen Telegraphen zu München", in: *Schumachers Astronomisches Jahrbuch*, 1, 1839, S. 162–179, hier S. 165

9   *The Times,* 22. Februar 1862, S. 10

10   Vgl. Arthur Korn, *Bildtelegraphie*, Berlin/Leipzig 1923

11   Vgl. ebd., S. 37f.

12   Vgl. ebd., S. 39f.

13   Vgl. auch *Die Woche*, 4, 23. Januar 1909, S. 135–137

14   Vgl. Korn 1923 (wie Anm. 10), S. 84f.

15   Vgl. Arthur Korn, *Die Bildtelegraphie im Dienste der Polizei. Vortrag gehalten auf dem Zweiten Internationalen Polizeikongreß zu Berlin im September 1926*, Wien 1927

16   *Daily Mirror,* 17. März 1908, S. 4

17   *Daily Mirror,* 18. März 1908, S. 3

18   Alexander Bain et. al., „Bain's Patent Electro-Chemical Copying Telegraph", in: *Mechanics' Magazine, Museum, Register, Journal, and Gazette,* 52, 1378–1403, 1850, S. 101–105, 143f., 163–165, 187f., 217f., 223–125, 273f., 359, hier S. 102

19   Vgl. die skeptische Diskussion des Pantelegraphen z. B. bei: Anonymus, „Der Autographische oder Copir-Telegraph von Caselli", in: *Polytechnisches Journal*, 177, 1865, S. 1–13, hier S. 12f.; Anonymus, „Der Pantelegraph von Caselli in Florenz", in: *Polytechnisches Centralblatt*, 14, 1859, S. 1006–1008, hier S. 1008 sowie Philippe Bata, Patrice A. Carré, „Presse, Photographie et Télécommunications de 1850 à 1940", in: *Revue Francaise Des Télécommunications,* 56, 1985, S. 54–61 und Julia Zons, „Giovanni Casellis Bildtelegraphische Patente als Geschichtenerzähler (1855–1867)", in: *Figurationen*, 2, 2016, S. 89–102

20   Peter Lertes, *Fernbildtechnik und elektrisches Fernsehen*, Frankfurt am Main 1926, S. I

21   Korn 1923 (wie Anm. 10), S. 87f.

22   Lorenz Engell, „Vom Bild zur Zahl, oder: Wie Die Stellen Ihre Objekte verließen", in: *Das Gesicht der Welt. Medien in der digitalen Kultur*, hrsg. von Lorenz Engell und Britta Neitzel, München 2004, S. 185–201, hier S. 193

23   Ebd., S. 194

technical consideration is only one aspect of the image, especially images transmitted by means of technology. The fact that it is precisely the technical history of image transmission that teaches us this lesson is reason for further reflection.

1   Michel Foucault, *Discipline and Punish: The Birth of the Prison*, trans. Alan Sheridan (New York: Random House, 1995), 94.
2   Foucault, *Discipline and Punish*, 96.
3   See Peter Galison, *Einstein's Clocks, Poincaré's Maps: Empires of Time* (New York: W. W. Norton, 2003).
4   In relation to this, it is also worth reading Christoph Asendorf, *Ströme und Strahlen: Das langsame Verschwinden der Materie um 1900* (Giessen: Anabas-Verlag, 1989), 119–63.
5   Quoted in Foucault 1995 (see note 1), 110.
6   See Christian Kassung, *Das Pendel: Eine Wissensgeschichte* (Munich: Wilhelm Fink Verlag, 2007), 309–87.
7   Carl August von Steinheil, "Beschreibung und Abbildung der von dem K. Akademiker und Conservator, Professor Dr. Steinheil Erfundenen Galvanischen Uhren," in *Kunst- und Gewerbeblatt des Polytechnischen Vereins für das Königreich Bayern* 2 (1843): 127–42, here 139.
8   Carl August von Steinheil, "Noch ein Wort über den Galvanischen Telegraphen zu München," in *Schumachers Astronomisches Jahrbuch* 1 (1839): 162–79, here 165.
9   *The Times,* February 22, 1862, 10.
10 Arthur Korn, *Bildtelegraphie* (Berlin and Leipzig: De Gruyter, 1923).
11 Korn, *Bildtelegraphie,* 37–38.
12 Korn, *Bildtelegraphie,* 39–40.
13 See also *Die Woche* 4, January 23, 1909, 135ff.
14 Korn, *Bildtelegraphie* (see note 10), 84–85.
15 See Arthur Korn, *Die Bildtelegraphie im Dienste der Polizei: Vortrag gehalten auf dem Zweiten Internationalen Polizeikongreß zu Berlin im September 1926* (Vienna: Moser, 1927).
16 *Daily Mirror,* March 17, 1908, 4.
17 *Daily Mirror,* March 18, 1908, 3.
18 Alexander Bain et. al., "Bain's Patent Electro-Chemical Copying Telegraph," in *Mechanics' Magazine, Museum, Register, Journal, and Gazette* 52, 1378–1403 (1850): 101–05, 143–44, 163ff., 187–88, 217–18, 223–25, 273–74, 359, here 102.
19 See skeptical discussions of the pantelegraph, for example, in anonymous, "Der Autographische oder Copir-Telegraph von Caselli," *Polytechnisches Journal* 177 (1865): 1–13, here 12–13; anonymus, "Der Pantelegraph von Caselli in Florenz," *Polytechnisches Centralblatt* 14 (1859): 1006ff., here 1008; see also Philippe Bata and Patrice A. Carré, "Presse, Photographie et Télécommunications de 1850 à 1940," *Revue Francaise Des Télécommunications* 56 (1985): 54–61; and Julia Zons, "Giovanni Casellis Bildtelegraphische Patente als Geschichtenerzähler (1855–1867)," *Figurationen* 2 (2016): 89–102.
20 Peter Lertes, *Fernbildtechnik und elektrisches Fernsehen* (Frankfurt am Main: H. Bechold, 1926), 1.
21 Korn, *Bildtelegraphie* (see note 10), 87–88.
22 Lorenz Engell, "Vom Bild zur Zahl, oder: Wie Die Stellen Ihre Objekte verließen," in *Das Gesicht der Welt: Medien in der digitalen Kultur*, ed. Lorenz Engell and Britta Neitzel (Munich: Wilhelm Fink Verlag, 2004), 185–201, here 193.
23 Engell, "Vom Bild zur Zahl," 194.

Text: Simon Rothöhler

REAL TIME
Anmerkungen zur ‚Echtzeitlichkeit' der Streambildzirkulation

Ende Juli 2020 informierte der Streamdienstleister Netflix seinen Kundenstamm über ein neues Feature namens „playback control". Hinter der Ermächtigungsformel „tweak the speed" verbarg sich ein in ähnlicher Form bereits auf der Videosharingplattform Youtube verfügbarer Algorithmus. Dieser erlaubt es dem „possessive spectator",[1] wie Laura Mulvey die mit immer invasiveren Instrumenten spielerisch-manipulativen Bildzugriffs ausgestattete Rezipientin digitaler Medieninhalte genannt hat, die Geschwindigkeit der Content-Wiedergabe auf die halbe Playbackzeit zu verlangsamen oder mit dem Faktor 1,5 zu beschleunigen. Nicht nur weil dabei auch die Tonspur eine entsprechende Retardierung bzw. Akzelerierung erfährt, die etwa Dialoge einigermaßen alkoholisiert oder comichaft klingen lässt, ist nicht sofort ersichtlich, warum diese Form der „Kontrolle" tatsächlich ein nutzerseitiges Desiderat sein sollte. Netflix selbst hat aber, wie es sich für ein hegemoniales Big-Data-Unternehmen gehört, ganz andere Einsichten in die – als granulare Datenspurgeschichten von rund 180 Millionen Abonnent*innen vorliegenden – empirischen Rezeptionspraktiken und verwies, als das empörte Feedback ausgewiesen digitalskeptischer Kreativarbeiter wie Christopher Nolan deutlich vernehmbar wurde, auf ein ausgeprägtes Flexibilisierungsbegehren der eigenen Kund*innen: "our tests show that consumers value the flexibility it provi-

REAL TIME
Remarks on Real Time in Streamed Videos

In late July 2020 the streaming service Netflix informed its customers of a new feature called "playback control." The self-empowering catchphrase "tweak the speed" indicated an algorithm already available in a similar form on the video sharing site YouTube. This feature allows what Laura Mulvey has termed the "possessive spectator,"[1] equipped with ever-more-invasive instruments for casually manipulating digital media image content, to slow the playback speed of a video to half as fast or to speed it up by 50 percent. It is unclear whether and why users would truly desire such a form of control, not least because the feature causes the audio to slow down or speed up, causing dialogues, for instance, to sound either tipsy or cartoonish. But Netflix, as befits a hegemonial big-data company, is able to draw on very different insights using the empiric data on how its users consume its services, examining the granular data history of its 180 million subscribers, and referring to their customers' strong desire for flexibility when countering the outraged feedback of self-avowed digital skeptics and creatives such as Christopher Nolan: "Our tests show that consumers value the flexibility it provides whether

des whether it's rewatching their favorite scene or slowing things down because they're watching with subtitles or have hearing difficulties."[2]

Steigerung von Flexibilität klingt irgendwie immer kundenfreundlich – und passt natürlich zur Vermarktung des Etiketts „on demand", das im Kern eine Entlassung aus zeitgebundenen Rezeptionsschemata in Aussicht stellt. Aber wie ist die Temporalität von Streaming – dem gegenwärtig dominanten Modus, Bewegtbilder in Bewegung zu versetzen – eigentlich medientechnisch verfasst? Welche Zeitlichkeit geht mit der inzwischen ubiquitär verfügbaren Übertragung digitaler Bildströme einher und wie kommen diese bei den Rezipient*innen an?

Das Versprechen digitaler Streambilder bezieht sich zunächst auf ihre aufwandlose und unverzügliche Mobilisierbarkeit.

Entsprechende Endgeräte und Konnektivität vorausgesetzt, sollen digitale Bilder generell – ob usergenerierte oder von global agierenden Medienkonzernen produzierte – instantan konsumier- und teilbar sein. Dass Netflix wirklich ein Interesse daran hat, die zeitlichen Abläufe der hier gerade nicht reziproken, nicht auf Multiplikation via Sharing-Praktiken ausgerichteten, sondern einbahnstraßenartig als Downstream formatierten Streambildübertragung an User*innen zu delegieren, überzeugt allerdings schon mit Blick auf das Interface des Anbieters nur bedingt. So zielten die zuvor eingeführten Features gerade nicht auf invasivere Eingriffe in den streamästhetischen Content, nicht auf das erweiterte Verfügbar- und Fungibelmachen filmisch-serieller Inhalte, sondern vor allem auf Automatismen, die Konsumptionspraktiken ohne Unterbrechungen und Interventionen („binge-watching") stabilisieren und popularisieren sollten – man denke an voreinstellbare Optionen wie „skip intro" und „play next episode", die auch seriell zäsurierte Erzählformate mit einem Buttonklick in den unendlichen Spaß kontinuierlich fließender Bildströme verwandeln.

Die Übertragung digitaler Streambilder – ob als On Demand bzw. Live Streaming Content (Netflix, Youtube, Twitch), Social Media Feature (TikTok, Facebook Watch) oder als videotelefonische bzw. -graphische Kommunikate (FaceTime, Zoom) –, macht insgesamt rund 75 % der Gesamtdatenlast des weltweiten Internet-Traffics aus.

Dies wirft jenseits rezeptionsästhetisch unmittelbar wahrnehmbarer Zeitmodalitäten Fragen des bildversandgebundenen *time shiftings* auf. Zunächst ist festzuhalten, dass Streambilder gerade in ihrer Eigenschaft als Versandbilder nicht als sessile Objekte, sondern immer nur als fluide, hochgradig distribuierte Prozesse zu verstehen sind. Grundsätzlich lässt sich hier beobachten, dass die mittlerweile weitgehend kommerziell überformte Utopie einer irgendwie neuen demokratischen Qualität massenweise teilbarer Null-Grenzkosten-Bilder schnell an die Grenzen der realen Distributionsverhältnisse stößt. Dort stehen radikal vertikal integrierte Downstream-Giganten wie Netflix – 2019 war der Konzern für 12,9 % des weltweiten Internet-Traffics verantwortlich und verursacht zur abendlichen Prime Time Peaks bis zu 40 % des Datenvolumens – neben einigen wenigen Social Media-Anbietern, bei denen Features der Bildzirkulation im Wesentlichen als werbewirtschaftliche Köder für die mitlaufende Selbstverdatung Bilder ver-

it's rewatching their favorite scene or slowing things down because they're watching with subtitles or have hearing difficulties."[2]

Somehow, increasing flexibility always sounds customer-friendly—and naturally accords with marketing a service labelled "on demand," one that at heart posits a liberation from the time-based schemata of reception. But how does media technology author the temporality of streaming—the mode of setting moving images into motion that is so dominant today? What temporality goes hand in hand with the broadcasting of digital image streams that has become ubiquitously accessible, and what do the recipients make of it?

At first, the promise of streamed images has at its heart an ease and an ability to be immediately mobilized.

Assuming the necessary devices and connectivity are available, digital images should as a rule be instantaneously capable of being consumed and shared, whether they are user-generated or produced by media companies working on a global scale. But a look at the Netflix interface only partially convinces one that Netflix is truly interested in shunting the temporal pace of the images being streamed to the user in a one-way street as a downstream rather than in a multiplication system using sharing practices. The recently introduced features aim not to invasively intervene into the aesthetics of streamed content or the expansion of making films and TV series available and fungible, but rather most of all for an automatization that stabilizes and popularizes practices of consumption without interruption or intervention (i.e., binge-watching). One need only think of the preset options such as "skip intro" and "play next episode," which transform the serially divided narrative structures into the constant fun that is the continuously flowing stream of images at the press of a button.

The broadcast of digital streamed images, whether as on-demand or live-streamed content (Netflix, YouTube, Twitch), social media features (TikTok, Facebook Watch), or as a means of communicating by voice and/or video (FaceTime, Zoom) comprises roughly 75 percent of data use across all global internet traffic.

This raises questions about time shifting related to the circulation of images quite apart from temporal modalities that are immediately perceptible in the aesthetics of reception. First of all, one must note that streamed images, as accords with sent images, have the trait of being not sessile objects, but rather constantly fluid, highly distributed processes. Fundamentally one may observe here that the now largely commercially determined utopia of a somehow democratic new quality of images, which are mass-produced with no marginal costs, quickly come up against the limits of real distribution practices. Radically vertically integrated downstream behemoths like Netflix—which is responsible for 12.9 percent of global internet traffic worldwide and up to 40 percent of data volume at peak prime time—sit alongside those few social media providers whose features of image circulation are chiefly programmed to be commercial bait for the simultaneous self-datatization of users sending and

    REAL TIME / **REAL TIME**

sendender und empfangener User*innen programmiert werden. Während die dazugehörigen Ermächtigungsutopien noch in den Nullerjahren weitgehend unwidersprochen von „Prosumern" und „Sharing Culture" sprachen und an eine tatsächliche Umverteilung klassisch massenmedialer Sender-Empfänger-Hierarchien zu glauben schienen, haben sich in den letzten Jahren zunehmend kritischere Perspektiven durchgesetzt – mit Blick auf Datafizierungsagenden, intransparente Empfehlungsalgorithmen und das gegenüber dem Zensurbegehren autoritärer Regime oftmals recht entgegenkommende ökonomische Kalkül einer letztlich oligarchisch operierenden Gruppe digitaler Medienkonzerne. Spätestens „post Snowden" gilt auch im öffentlichen Bewusstsein die Vermutung: Black Boxing und Data Mining, wohin man schaut und klickt – egal, ob Streambilder aus Sicht der User*innen lediglich on demand bezogen oder tatsächlich auch nutzerseitig herstellbar, uploadbar und teilbar sind.

Die davon relativ unabhängige medientechnische Utopie, für die Streambilder oftmals einstehen, gerät hingegen deutlich seltener in den Blick. Gemeint ist eine Vorstellung, die sich auf die Zeitlichkeit dieses digitalen Bildtypus' bezieht: Die Utopie einer nicht nur qua ubiquitärer Konnektivität überall verfügbaren, sondern auch instantanen Übertragung. Aufschlussreicher als die temporale Verfasstheit konkreter Nutzungspraktiken – als wie auch immer am Frontend interaktiv gestaltbare Wiedergabe-, Rezeptions- und im weitesten Sinn: Zugriffszeit – ist aus dieser Perspektive die Temporalität eines in nahezu allen Bereichen digitaler Medienkulturen an Dominanz gewinnenden Übertragungsvorgangs, der Digitalbilder als streamförmig prozessierte Datenpakete versendet und empfängt.

Denn Streaming bedeutet zunächst einmal vor allem das: ein die Speicherkapazitäten von Endgeräten schonendes Datenverteilungsverfahren, bei dem Übertragungs- und Wiedergabeprozesse zwar nicht ohne Rückstände zusammenfallen, aber spezifisch enggeführt werden.

Die informationstechnische Aufbereitung und Präsentation des ikonisch manifestierbaren Datenmaterials werden instanziiert, während laufend weitere Bestandteile des – nur in der Rückschau als solches fasslichen – Gesamtpakets empfangen werden. Streaming kommt aus Sicht des Empfängers jenseits bestimmter Prozesse der Zwischenablage ohne unmittelbar evidente speichermediale Funktionalität aus. Unter Computernetzwerkbedingungen verläuft die entsprechende Operation über eine ‚Echtzeitlichkeit', die sich vom klassischen wie vom sogenannten progressiven Download eines Files – die mediengeschichtlich ältere Form des Digitalbildversands bzw. -bezugs – vor allem dadurch unterscheidet, dass auf der serveranfragenden Seite zu keinem Zeitpunkt eine vollständige Kopie des bezogenen Datensatzes existiert. Das spart nicht nur Speicherressourcen, sondern auch Zeit – die man etwa nicht warten muss, bis ein File vollständig auf einem lokalen Festplattenspeicher hochgeladen ist.

Die Bestandteile eines Streamdatenpakets strömen als Datagrammserie aus und fließen zeitnah wieder ab: eine – heutzutage meist bitrateadaptiv rückgekoppelte – Doppelbewegung, die über den Transportkanal moderiert wird und erst seit Mitte der 1990er-Jahre von den Rechen- und Zwischenspeicherleistungen allgemein verfügbarer Endgeräte prozessiert werden kann. Kurz

receiving images. If the attendant utopias of empowerment largely continued to speak without the contradiction of "prosumers" and "sharing culture," and truly appeared to believe in an actual redistribution of classical mass-media sender/receiver hierarchies in the first decade of the millennium, then perhaps more critical perspectives would not have made themselves heard in recent years,with an eye to datatization agendas, untransparent suggestion algorithms, and the fact that the group of digital media companies—which ultimately act as oligarchs—have shown themselves to be all too obliging with regard to authoritarian regimes' desire for censorship, driven by economic calculation. Since the Snowden case, there is the sense in the public consciousness that black boxing and data mining exist everywhere one looks and clicks, whether regarding streamed images only accessed (from the users' point of view) on demand or images which are actually creatable, downloadable, and shareable by users.

The relatively independent technological media utopia that streamed content often demands is much less likely to be subjected to scrutiny—that is to say the idea that relates to the temporality of this digital image type: the utopia not only of a ubiquitous connectivity accessible from everywhere, but also of an instant transmission. Viewed from this perspective, the temporality of a transmission process that is gaining in dominance across almost all realms of digital media culture, one that sends and receives digital images and streams and processes data packets, is more revealing than the temporal state of concrete usage practices, such as the playback time, retention time, and in the broadest sense, access time of interactively designed front-end interfaces.

For, first and foremost, streaming denotes a means of distributing data without overextending the memory space on the end-user devices, in which transmission and playback are conflated, albeit not without deficits, but reduced.

The processing and presentation of data manifested as icons using information technology is instantiated, while further components of the overall unit—only apprehensible as such in ex post facto—are constantly being received. From the recipient's point of view, streaming does not appear to require any immediately evident storage media functionality beyond certain clipboard functions. Computer network conditions allow the corresponding operation to take place in real time, a manner distinct from both the traditional and the progressive downloading of a file—the more ancient form of digital image transmission or retrieval with regard to media history—above all in that at no point does a complete copy of the data set retrieved on the device making the request to the server exist. This not only saves memory space, but also time— time that does not have to wait until a file has been completely uploaded to a local hard drive. The components of a streamed data packet are transmitted as a series of datagrams, only to be streamed back shortly thereafter: this double motion, which at present is one of mostly bitrate adaptive feedback, is moderated via the transport channel and has only been able to be processed by commonly available end devices' computing and buffering capacities of intermediary memory space since the mid-1990s. Succinctly put, streaming

gesagt: Streaming unterläuft umfangreichere Speichernotwendigkeiten auf Seiten der Endgeräte und Clientanwendungen durch einen Übertragungsvorgang, der Medienserverdaten nicht nur kontinuierlich anfragt, verteilt und entgegennimmt, sondern ebenso kontinuierlich verwirft. Je breiter und unverzüglicher dieser Strom flüchtiger Daten fließen soll – bei audiovisuellem Streamingcontent bedeutet das in der Regel: hochaufgelöster, stabiler und bufferfreier –, desto effizienter müssen nicht die Langfristspeicher, sondern die Prozesszeiten im Übertragungskanal organisiert sein. Zusammengefasst wird dies unter dem Begriff *adaptive bitrate streaming*.[3] Dieser bezeichnet einen Vorgang der Datenübertragung, dessen „real time" sich auf die infrastrukturelle Leistungsfähigkeit des Transportkanals bezieht. Entscheidend ist hier, dass die Übertragungskapazitäten dieses Kanals nicht feststehen, sondern sich aus den versandbegleitend erhobenen und evaluierten Messdaten ergeben. Im Ergebnis handelt es sich um ein adaptives Feedbacksystem: Algorithmisch und quasi-echtzeitlich kalkuliert wird das Maximum an störungsfrei übertragbarer Datenlast, die als Bewegtbild mobilisiert und wahrnehmbar werden kann.

Die hier nur angedeutete Geschichte des „verteilten Bildes"[4] kann als postalische Geschichte der Versanddatenlaststeigerung und Datenversandbeschleunigung erzählt werden. Dies scheint einerseits offenkundig, wirft andererseits aber unweigerlich die üblichen Rückfragen an teleologische Fortschrittserzählungen auf – zumal im vorliegenden Fall der in digitalen Medienkulturen vorgeblich erreichte Zustand instantaner Übertragung als immer schon avisierte Zielgröße erscheint. Gleichwohl – es stimmt ja auch: So war Akzelerierung etwa in der Entwicklung bildtelegrafischer Technologien von Anfang an ein erklärtes Desiderat, wie man etwa bei Arthur Korn nachlesen kann.[5] Dauerte die bildtelegrafische Übertragung einer Porträtfotografie über die Telefonschleife München-Nürnberg 1904 beispielsweise noch 42 Minuten, beanspruchte der gleiche Vorgang zwölf Jahre später nur noch rund 6 Minuten – und kostete, wie Marius Hug rekonstruiert hat, umgerechnet 66 Euro.[6] Das muss nicht nur Instagram-, TikTok- und FaceTime-Nutzer*innen wie eine unendlich weit entfernte Urzeit (und ziemlich teuer) vorkommen.

Grundsätzlich können schon die für den Versand spezifisch aufbereiteten Fotografien der Bildtelegraphie insofern als ‚prädigitale' Streambilder verstanden werden, als sie nach einem übertragungstechnischen Kalkül diskretisiert wurden – und zwar in räumlicher wie in zeitlicher Hinsicht: als Datenpaket, das aus einzelnen Bildelementen bestand, die nacheinander übertragen und am Empfangsort als „Zeilen- und Spaltenbilder"[7] wieder zusammengesetzt werden mussten. Und auch die Bildübertragungsmodalitäten des frühen Fernsehens gehören, wie Albert Kümmel gezeigt hat, zur Geschichte des Digitalbildes als technisch übertragbar werdendes: „Digitale Bilder sind, was immer sie sonst sein mögen, aus diskreten Elementen zusammengesetzte Bilder, in Zeilen und Spalten zwecks buchstäblich punktgenauer Übertragbarkeit zerschnittene Bilder."[8]

Zerlegen, Übertragen und Zusammensetzen sind Prozesse, die Zeit benötigen. Allein schon deshalb hängen Segmentierung und Sequenzierung zusammen.

circumvents the need for end devices with extensive memory space and client applications by using a transmission process that not only continuously requests, distributes, and receives media server data, but also continuously discards it. The more broadly and instantaneously this stream of ephemeral data is intended to flow—in the case of streamed audiovisual content, this usually means at a high resolution, stable, and unbuffered level—the more efficiently organized the processing times in the transmission channel (not the long-term memory) need to be. This is subsumed within the term "adaptive bit-rate streaming,"[3] which describes a process of data transmission in which the idea of real time refers to the infrastructure performance of the transport channel. The decisive factor here is that the transmission capacities of this channel are not fixed, but result from the measurement values collected and evaluated during transmission. The result is an adaptive feedback system: the maximum data load transferable without interference that can be transmitted and perceived as a moving image is calculated using algorithms essentially in real time.

The history of the "distributed image"[4] only roughly adumbrated here can be narrated as a "postal" history of an increase in the transmission load of and the acceleration of data transmission. On the one hand, this might appear self-evident, yet it ineluctably raises predictable questions about a teleological narrative of progress, particularly as in the present example, digital media companies' desired goal of instantaneous transmission appears to have been achieved. Nevertheless, it is also the case that acceleration was a declared desideratum from the very beginning of the development of telephotographic technologies, as detailed by Arthur Korn.[5] For example, while the telephotographic transmission of a portrait photograph between Munich and Nuremberg took forty-two minutes in 1904, the same process took only about six minutes twelve years later—and, as Marius Hug has ascertained, cost the equivalent of sixty-six euros.[6] This must seem like a hopelessly old-fashioned and unfathomably long amount of time (not to mention quite a high price), and not just to users of Instagram, TikTok, and FaceTime.

In principle, telephotographs specially prepared for transmission can be understood as predigital streamed images in that they were divided according to a technical transmission calculation both in terms of space and time into discrete units as data packets comprised of individual image elements transmitted one after the other and reassembled at the reception location as "row and column images."[7] And as Albert Kümmel has shown, the image transmission modalities of the early days of television also form part of the history of the technically transferable digital image: "Whatever else digital images might be, they are always formed out of discrete elements arranged into rows and columns in order to achieve a transferability literally down to the exact point."[8]

This dissolution, transmission, and reassembly is a process that takes time. This alone links segmentation and sequencing.

An der zeitlichen Verfasstheit von Techniken der Bildübertragung interessiert aus medientheoretischer Sicht dabei sowohl die räumliche Entfernungen überwindende Versandzeit als auch die Mikrozeitlichkeit des räumlichen Bildaufbaus auf Screens und Displays am Empfangsort. ‚Zeitfrei‘ oder ‚zeitgleich‘ ist an diesen diskreten Operationen nichts. Umgesetzt werden diese in Gestalt einer datagrammatischen Sequenzierung, die jene kontinuierliche Übertragung audiovisuell materialisierbarer Daten informationstechnisch ist, die üblicherweise Streaming genannt wird und in ihrer Entstehungszeit, Mitte der 1990er-Jahre, insbesondere von einer Protokollfamilie abhing, die auf den Namen „real time" getauft wurde. Dass diese von einer zeitlosen oder zeitenthobenen Transmission träumende ‚Echtzeit‘ realiter keine, zumindest keine Gleichzeitigkeit ist, weil Versand wie Bildaufbau von Multimediastreams zwar keine 42 Minuten pro Einzelbild, aber doch prinzipiell messbare Mikrozeiten in Anspruch nehmen, hat Stefan Heidenreich folgendermaßen verallgemeinert: „Was in Datenströmen strömt, und das heißt hier: was in der Zeit abläuft und Zeit benötigt, ist das Einspeisen des Signals. Es besteht aus einer Folge von Veränderungen der elektrischen Feldstärke oder, in Glasfaserkabeln, der Lichtstärke.

> Eine Nachricht zu übermitteln dauert nicht deshalb eine gewisse Zeit, weil eine Entfernung zu überwinden ist, sondern weil das Nachrichtensignal als eine Folge von Impulsen abläuft."[9]

Noch fundamentaler theoretisiert Hartmut Winkler diesen Zusammenhang: Weil auch die Rechenvorgänge innerhalb des Computers (unabhängig von seiner Vernetzung) als Signalversandintervalle ablaufen, seien diese rechnenden Verkehrszeiten, so Winkler, als „interne Telegrafie" beschreibbar. Die computerinternen Prozesse erscheinen dann als Mikrozeiten beanspruchende Transportvorgänge, weil Komputation in zeitlichen Intervallen zwischen Festplatte, Arbeitsspeicher, Prozessor – und (zumindest manchmal) Bildschirm zirkuliert.[10]

Was bedeutet das für die ‚real time‘ heutiger Streambildphänomene? Zum einen, dass deren ‚Echtzeit‘ trotz aller Anmutung von Instantanität und ‚Liveness‘ aus Mikrozeiten seriell fortgesetzter Komputation besteht, obwohl sie aus Sicht menschlicher Akteur*innen auf den Interface-Oberflächen „pragmatisch synchron"[11] erscheinen kann. Weil dies auch bei besonders zeitkritischen Streambildübertragungen – man denke an die geringe Latenztoleranz von Videotelefonie – völlig ausreichend ist, geht es bei Streaming zum anderen nicht um eine tatsächlich ‚echt-‘ oder gar ‚gleichzeitige‘ *real time,* sondern um eine situative ‚Rechtzeitigkeit‘, die im Kontext konkreter Anwendungen einen geteilten und anschlussfähigen Rezeptions- oder Kommunikationsraum entstehen lassen kann. So gesehen handelt es sich dann lediglich um eine bildkommunikative ‚Echtzeitlichkeit‘, die sich als Reaktionszeit der Mensch-Maschine-Interaktion manifestiert.[12] Unterschiedliche Plattformen und Anwendungen haben deshalb je eigene ‚Echtzeitlichkeiten‘ und ergeben „distinctive real time cultures".[13]

Wie könnte es auch anders sein: Wäre die Übertragung von Streambildern realiter ‚zeitfrei‘, bliebe den Bildnachrichtentransporte bewirtschaftenden Unternehmen auch keine Zeit, die Transmission ökonomisch zu rationalisieren (und medientheoretisch gesehen wäre die Übertragung keine). Streambilder sind Rechen- und Prozessbilder, deren Versand, Empfang und rastergrafische Umset-

From the perspective of media theory, the temporal state of image transmission processes is of interest both in terms of the time required to traverse spatial distances as well as the micro-temporality of the way the images are spatially assembled on screens and displays at the point of reception. There is nothing "time-free" or simultaneous about these discrete operations. They are implemented in the form of a sequencing of datagrams, which calls for an uninterrupted IT transmission of audiovisual materializable data, commonly known as streaming, which was governed by a family of protocols dubbed "real time" when first used in the mid-1990s. Stefan Heidenreich has extrapolated that this timeless or time-delayed transmission that dreamed of simulating "real time" was nothing of the kind in reality, or was at least not a simultaneous process, because even if the transmission and image formation from multimedia streams no longer took forty-two minutes per image, the duration was still measurable in principle in microtime, and states as follows: "What is being streamed in these data streams—that is, what is taking place in time and requiring time—is the loading of the signal. It consists of a sequence of changes in the strength of the electric field or in fiber-optic cables, the light intensity.

To transmit a message takes a certain amount of time not because there is a distance to travel, but because the message signal travels as a series of pulses."[9]

Hartmut Winkler's theories on this relationship are even more fundamental, noting that the computing processes within a computer (independent of its networked state) also take place as signal transmission intervals, these computing traffic times can be described, according to Winkler, as an "internal telegraphy." The internal computing processes thus register as transport processes that take up intervals of microtime because the process of computation circulates at intervals between hard disk, RAM, processor, and (at least sometimes) monitor.[10]

What does this mean for the "real time" of contemporary streamed content? On the one hand, it means that their "real time," all claims of instantaneity and "liveness" notwithstanding, consists of microtimes of serially completed computations, even though they might appear to be "pragmatically synchronous"[11] to humans using the surface interface. On the other hand, because this is entirely sufficient even for especially time-critical streaming—consider, for instance, the low latency tolerance in video telephony—streaming is not about a truly "real" or even "simultaneous" real time, but rather about a situational "timeliness," which can create a shared and connectable, receptive or communicative space in the context of concrete applications. Thus seen in this light, the crux of the matter is a communicative "real time" that manifests itself as the reaction time of the human-machine interaction.[12] As a result, different platforms and apps each have their own "real time temporalities" and yield "distinctive real time cultures."[13]

And how could it be otherwise? If streaming were in fact "time-free," companies managing the transmission of streamed content would have no time to rationalize the transmission in economic terms (and viewed from a media theory point of view, there would be no transmission). Streamed images

zung auf konkreten Screens nicht nur Zeit, sondern eine Vielzahl distribuierter Akteure und Infrastrukturen in Anspruch nimmt. Insofern sind sie alles mögliche, aber sicher nicht 'immaterieller' als analoge Übertragungsmodi. So lässt sich über die „real time" digitaler Streambilder sagen, dass uns deren pragmatische Rechtzeitigkeit oftmals davon abhält, die beteiligten algorithmischen Kalküle, die bis hin zu proprietären Distributionsnetzwerken (was bei Netflix halb-ironisch „open connect" genannt wird) privatisierten Infrastrukturen (und deren *carbon footprint*) genauer in den Blick zu nehmen.[14] Wo Bildübertragung unverzüglich scheint, fehlt auch die Zeit, die postalischen Verlaufsbedingungen dieser 'echtzeitlichen' Bildtransmission epistemisch wahrnehmbar zu machen. „Playback control" ist so gesehen vielleicht gar kein schlechter Begriff für eine nachzügliche Heuristik des *reverse engineering*, die sich Zeit nimmt, wo (scheinbar) keine ist.

1   Laura Mulvey, *Death 24x a Second. Stillness and the Moving Image*, London 2006, S. 161–180

2   https://media.netflix.com/en/company-blog/player-control-tests [Zugriff am 2. Oktober 2020]

3   Vgl. Christian Sandvig, "The Internet as Anti-Television. Distribution Infrastructure as Culture and Power", in: Lisa Parks, Nicole Starosielski (Hg.), *Signal Traffic. Critical Studies of Media Infrastructures*, Champaign 2015, S. 225–245

4   Vgl. Simon Rothöhler, *Das verteilte Bild. Stream, Archiv, Ambiente*, Paderborn 2018

5   Arthur Korn, *Die Bildtelegraphie*, Berlin: De Gruyter, 1923. Vgl. dazu Albert Kümmel-Schnur, Christian Kassung, „Vorwort", in: dies. (Hg.), *Bildtelegraphie. Eine Mediengeschichte in Patenten (1840–1930)*, Bielefeld 2012, S. 7–12

6   Marius Hug, „Die Übertragung wagen. Der Patentanmelder Arthur Korn", in: ibid., S. 211–231, hier S. 212

7   Peter Berz, „Bitmapped Graphics", in: Axel Volmar (Hg.), *Zeitkritische Medien*, Berlin 2009, S. 127–154

8   Albert Kümmel, „Ferne Bilder, so nah (Deutschland 1926)", in: Jens Schröter, Alexander Böhnke (Hg.), *Analog/Digital – Opposition oder Kontinuum. Zur Theorie und Geschichte einer Unterscheidung*, Bielefeld 2004, S. 269–294. Siehe zur Vor- und Frühgeschichte televisueller Bildtransmission auch die medienarchäologische Studie: Doron Galili, *Seeing by Electricity. The Emergence of Television, 1878-1939*, Durham 2020

9   Stefan Heidenreich, *FlipFlop. Digitale Datenströme und die Kultur des 21. Jahrhunderts*, München 2004, S. 27

10 Hartmut Winkler, *Prozessieren. Die dritte, vernachlässigte Medienfunktion*, Paderborn 2015, S. 298

11 Ebd., S. 198

12 Wendy Chun hat dazu treffend angemerkt: "In computer systems, 'real time' reacts to the live: their 'liveness' is their quick acknowledgment of and response to users' actions. Computers are 'feedback machines', based on control mechanisms that automate decision making. As the definition of 'real time' makes clear, 'real time' refers to the time of computer processing, not the user's time. 'Real time' is never real time it is deferred and mediated." Wendy Hui Kyong Chun, *Updating to Remain the Same. Habitual New Media*, Cambridge/MA 2016, S. 79

13 Esther Weltevrede, Anne Helmond, Carolin Gerlitz, "The Politics of Real-time: A Device Perspective on Social Media Platforms and Search Engines", in: *Theory, Culture & Society*, 6, 2014, S. 125–150, hier S. 137

14 Vgl. Simon Rothöhler, „Stay Streaming. Netflix als Infrastruktur: Über das proprietäre Distributionsnetzwerk Open Connect", in: *cargo Film / Medien / Kultur*, 46, Juni 2020, S. 4–12

are images that have been computed and processed, whose transmission, reception, and transfer onto actual screens using raster graphics not only takes time, but also a multitude of distributing bodies and infrastructures. In this respect, they may be many things, but they are certainly not more "immaterial" than analog transmission methods. Thus one can say that the pragmatic timeliness of the "real time" of streamed digital images often prevents us from taking a closer look at the algorithmic calculations involved and that the infrastructures (and their carbon footprint) have been privatized up to proprietary distribution networks (which Netflix semi-ironically calls "open connect").[14] When image transmission appears instantaneous, no time remains to make the "postal" conditions of this "real-time" image transfer epistemically perceptible. Viewed in this light, "playback control" is perhaps not such an inapposite term after all for a retrospective heuristic of reverse engineering that takes time where (apparently) there is none to take.

1   Laura Mulvey, *Death 24× a Second: Stillness and the Moving Image* (London: Reaktion Books, 2006), 161–80.

2   "Player Control Tests," Netflix, accessed October 2, 2020, https://media.netflix.com/en /company-blog/player-control-tests.

3   See Christian Sandvig, "The Internet as Anti-Television: Distribution Infrastructure as Culture and Power," in Lisa Parks and Nicole Starosielski, eds., *Signal Traffic: Critical Studies of Media Infrastructures* (Champaign: University of Illinois Press, 2015), 225–45.

4   See Simon Rothöhler, *Das verteilte Bild. Stream, Archiv, Ambiente* (Paderborn: Wilhelm Fink Verlag, 2018).

5   Arthur Korn, *Die Bildtelegraphie* (Berlin: De Gruyter, 1923). See also the editors' foreword in Albert Kümmel-Schnur and Christian Kassung, eds., *Bildtelegraphie: Eine Mediengeschichte in Patenten (1840–1930)* (Bielefeld: transcript Verlag, 2012), 7–12.

6   Marius Hug, "Die Übertragung wagen: Der Patentanmelder Arthur Korn," in *Bildtelegraphie* 211–31, here 212.

7   Peter Berz, "Bitmapped Graphics," in Axel Volmar, ed., *Zeitkritische Medien* (Berlin: Kulturverlag Kadmos, 2009), 127–54.

8   Albert Kümmel, "Ferne Bilder, so nah (Deutschland 1926)," in Jens Schröter and Alexander Böhnke, eds., *Analog/Digital—Opposition oder Kontinuum: Zur Theorie und Geschichte einer Unterscheidung* (Bielefeld: transcript Verlag, 2004), 269–94. Translated here from German by Sylee Gore. For information on the background and early history of televisual image transmissions, see also Doron Galili's media-archaeological study *Seeing by Electricity: The Emergence of Television, 1878–1939* (Durham, NC: Duke University Press), 2020.

9   Stefan Heidenreich, *FlipFlop: Digitale Datenströme und die Kultur des 21. Jahrhunderts* (Munich: Carl Hanser Verlag, 2004), 27.

10 Hartmut Winkler, *Prozessieren: Die dritte, vernachlässigte Medienfunktion* (Paderborn: Wilhelm Fink Verlag, 2015), 298.

11 Winkler 2015, 198.

12 On this subject, Wendy Chun has made the apt remark: "In computer systems, 'real time' reacts to the live: their 'liveness' is their quick acknowledgment of and response to users' actions. Computers are 'feedback machines', based on control mechanisms that automate decision making. As the definition of 'real time' makes clear, 'real time' refers to the time of computer processing, not the user's time. 'Real time' is never real time it is deferred and mediated." Wendy Hui Kyong Chun, *Updating to Remain the Same: Habitual New Media* (Cambridge, MA: MIT Press, 2016), 79.

13 Esther Weltevrede, Anne Helmond, and Carolin Gerlitz, "The Politics of Real-Time: A Device Perspective on Social Media Platforms and Search Engines," *Theory, Culture & Society* 6 (2014): 125–50, here 137.

14 See Simon Rothöhler, "Stay Streaming: Netflix als Infrastruktur; Über das proprietäre Distributionsnetzwerk Open Connect," *cargo Film / Medien / Kultur* 46 (June 2020): 4–12.

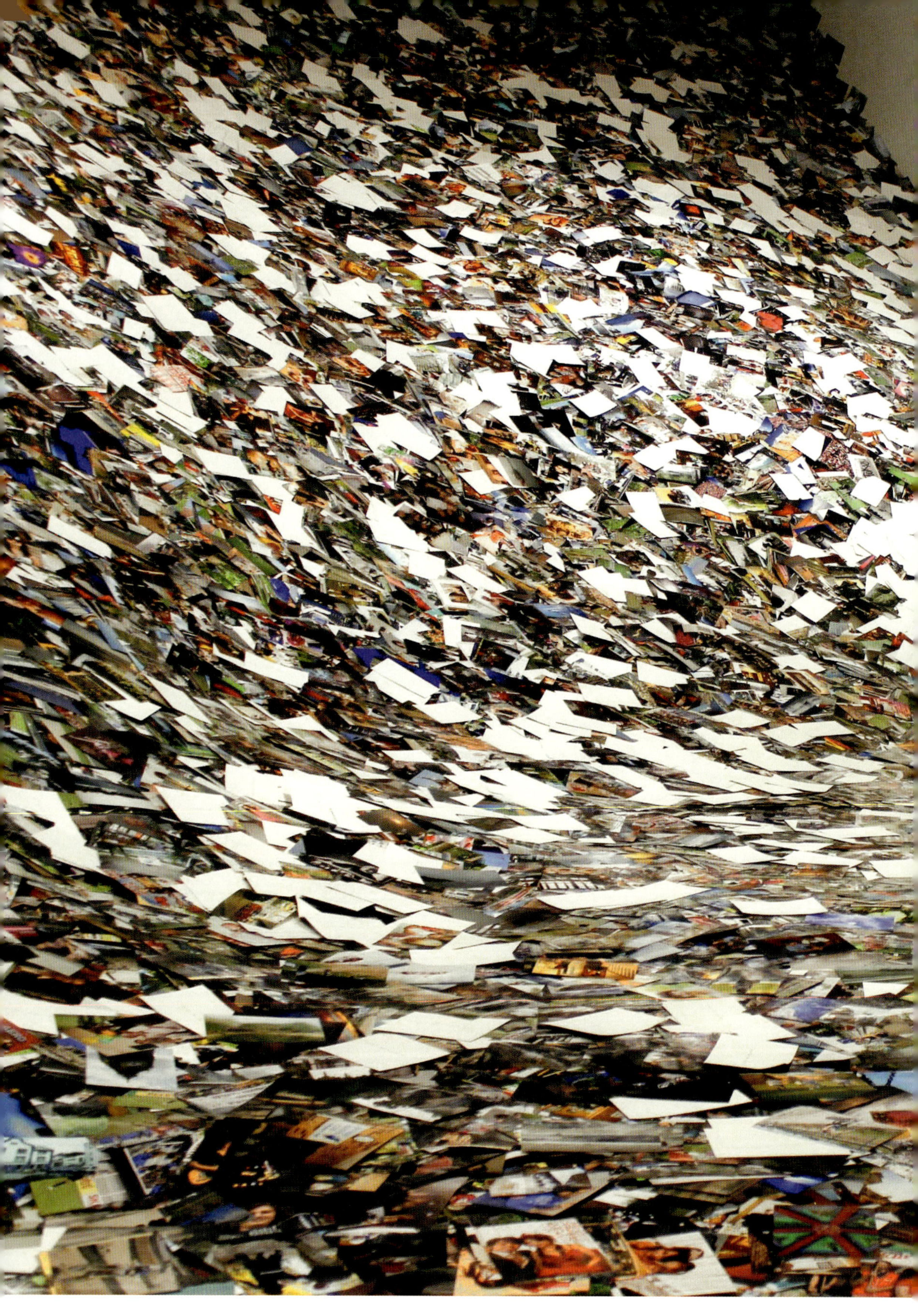

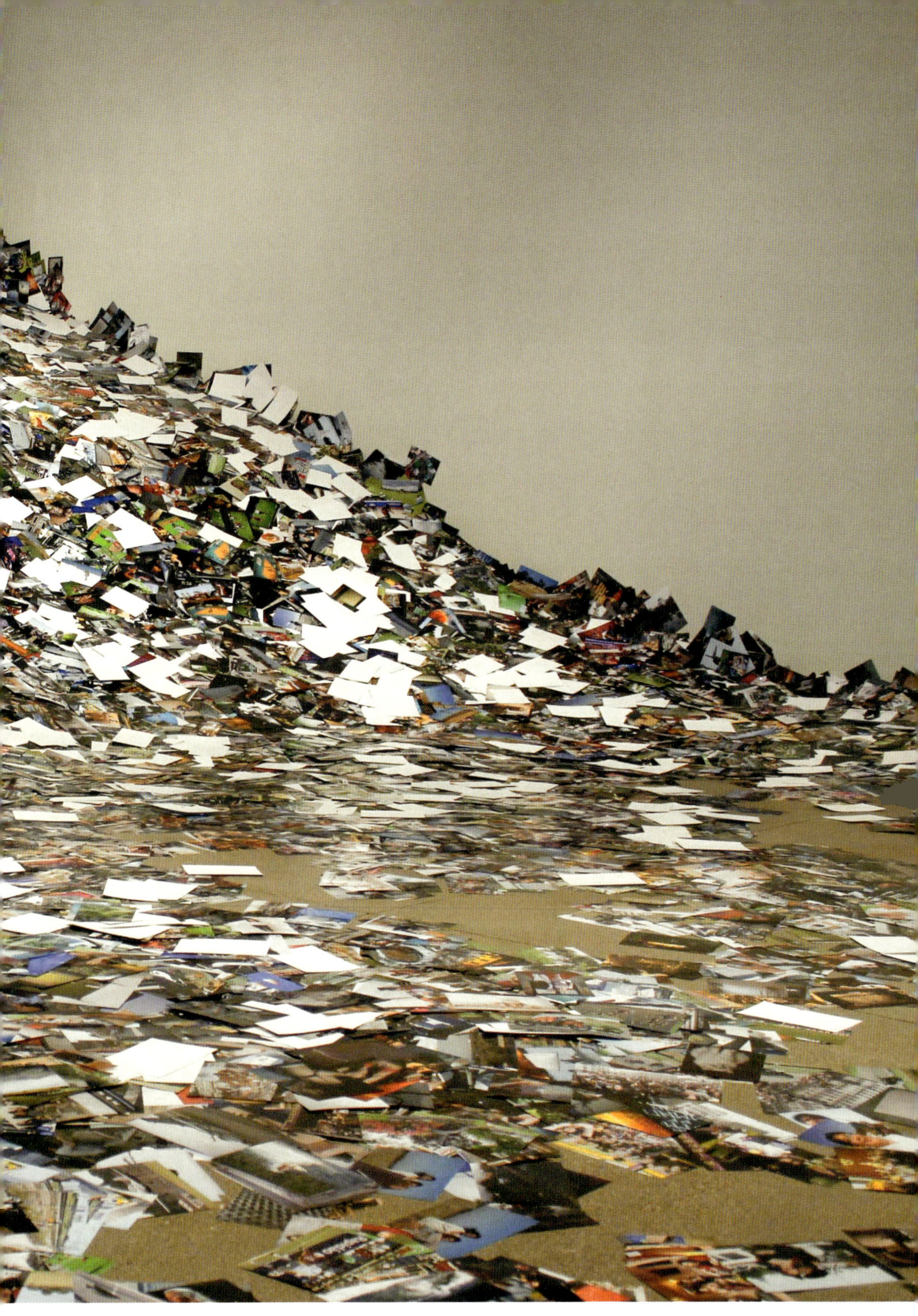

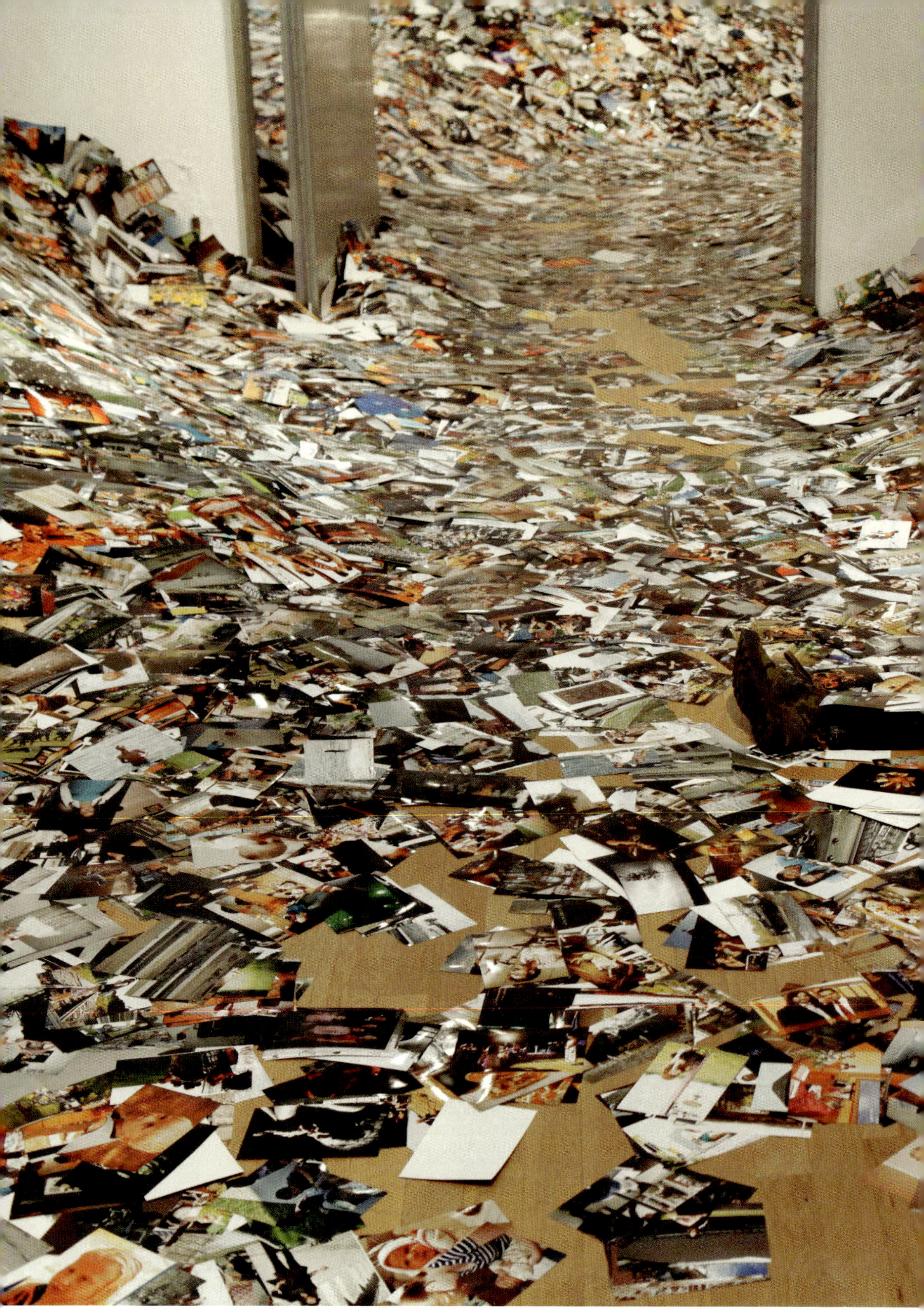

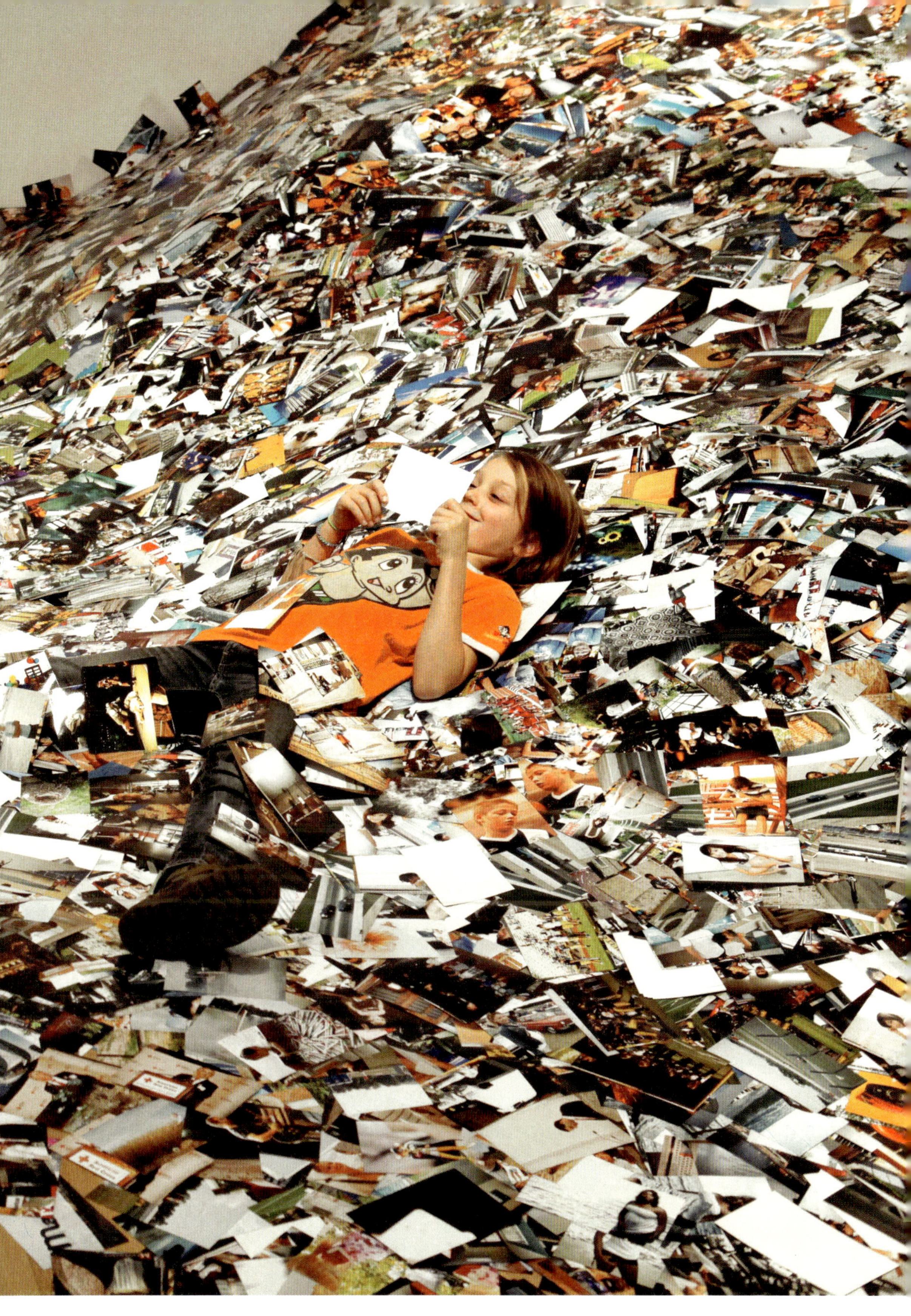

CARTE DE VISITE

Der Begriff Carte de Visite oder Visitkartenporträt bezeichnet nicht nur das Format der Bilder, sondern auch einen ihrer Ursprünge. Denn bevor der Pariser Fotograf André Adolphe-Eugène Disdéri sich diese Anwendung der Fotografie 1854 patentieren ließ, waren zumal in Frankreich Visitenkarten Gegenstand von Moden, die ebenso flüchtig waren wie die der Kleidung. Statt ihres Namens das fotografische Porträt einer Person auf einer solchen Karte zu platzieren, war daher zunächst kaum mehr als eine weitere modische Erscheinung. Doch die kleinen, auf Karton montierten Bilder verselbständigten sich schnell. Frühere Formen fotografischer Porträts, vor allem Daguerreotypien und seltener die oft handkolorierten Porträts auf Albumin- oder Salzpapier, waren meist als Unikate produziert worden. Die Cartes de Visite dagegen wurden in kleinen Auflagen von ein oder zwei Dutzend Abzügen hergestellt und waren vergleichsweise preiswert. Darüber hinaus erlaubte ihr relativ einheitliches Format von etwa 6 x 9 cm, dass sie in dafür eigens produzierten Alben gesammelt werden konnten – sie wurden zu einer sozialen Währung, die zwischen Verwandten und Bekannten ausgetauscht wurde.

Die Cartes-de-Visite-Porträts wurden in der Regel von professionellen Fotograf*innen in Studios oder entsprechend adaptierten Räumen aufgenommen. Sie zeigten die Porträtierten oft in repräsentativen Posen und bester Kleidung und nicht selten mit Accessoires und vor gemalten Hintergründen, die Wohl-

CARTES DE VISITE

The term *carte de visite,* a calling card that included a portrait, describes both the format of such images and their origin. Calling cards were a matter of fashion as ephemeral as clothing trends before the Paris-based photographer André Adolphe-Eugène Disdéri patented this means of using photography in 1854. Initially, putting a photographic portrait of a person in place of their name on such a calling card was a mere whim of fashion. Yet these small card-mounted images swiftly became firmly entrenched. Earlier forms of photographic portraits, chiefly daguerreotypes and rarely also hand-colored salt or albumen-print portraits were generally produced as unique images. In contrast, cartes de visite, produced in small batches of one or two dozen, were comparatively affordable. Moreover, their fairly standardized size of approximately 6 × 9 cm meant they could be collected in specialist albums made for the purpose. Cartes de visite became a form of social currency exchanged by relations and acquaintances.

Generally, professional photographers took portraits for cartes de visite in photo studios or rooms adapted to serve the same purpose. They often portrayed the individuals striking dignified poses in their best clothing, wearing accessories and standing against painted backgrounds that suggest-

stand suggerierten. Zwar waren die Cartes de Visite in den ersten Jahrzehnten vor allem Medien des Bürgertums und des Adels. Dennoch haben für die meisten von ihnen Villen mit ausladenden Gartentreppen, marmorne Säulenstümpfe und Ausblicke in weite Landschaften nicht unbedingt zum Alltag gehört. Die Porträts hatten damit weniger dokumentarischen als vielmehr phantasmagorischen Charakter und zeigten mehr oder weniger idealisierte Selbstentwürfe. Die gemeinsame Arbeit von Porträtierten und Fotograf*innen zielte so einerseits zwar auf die Individualität der Subjekte; weil andererseits die Interessen aller Porträtierten ähnlich waren, gerannen die Posen oft zu Stereotypen, die mit geringen Variationen große Verbreitung fanden.

Ihre Hochzeit hatten die Cartes de Visite etwa zwischen 1860 und 1890. Sie waren damit das erste jener paradoxen fotografischen Massenmedien, bei denen die einzelnen Aufnahmen zwar meist nur in kleinen Auflagen vervielfältigt wurden, die Gesamtzahl jedoch gewaltig war. In jenen Jahren gab es in Städten wie Berlin, Paris und Wien Hunderte von Studios, die pro Jahr Zehntausende von Cartes de Visite produzierten. Bis in die 1920er-Jahre hinein angeboten, mussten sie zunächst mit einer sich immer weiter ausdifferenzierenden Vielfalt von Studioformaten konkurrieren und wurden zusammen mit diesen später von der privaten Fotografie der Amateure und Knipser verdrängt.

ed prosperity. In their first decades, cartes de visite were admittedly a medium most commonly used by the bourgeoisie and the aristocracy. Yet villas with broad garden stairs, marble column pedestals, and views of extensive grounds rarely formed the everyday backdrops of the lives of those pictured. Such portraits were more phantasmorgic in character than documentary and showed a more or less idealized version of the self. On the one hand, the joint efforts of photographer and subject had the goal of capturing the individuality of the person portrayed; yet because everyone having their photograph taken had similar goals, the poses they struck were often standardized with only minor variations.

Cartes de visite had their heyday between 1860 and 1890 and are the first in a series of paradoxically widespread photographic media that were produced in small editions, but on a staggering scale. In those years, there were hundreds of studios in cities such as Berlin, Paris, and Vienna that produced tens of thousands of cartes de visite each year. These photographs, on offer until the 1920s, had to contend increasingly with a differentiated range of possible studio photographs. Ultimately, both were made obsolete when amateurs and hobbyists began taking their own photographs.

Text: Friedrich Tietjen

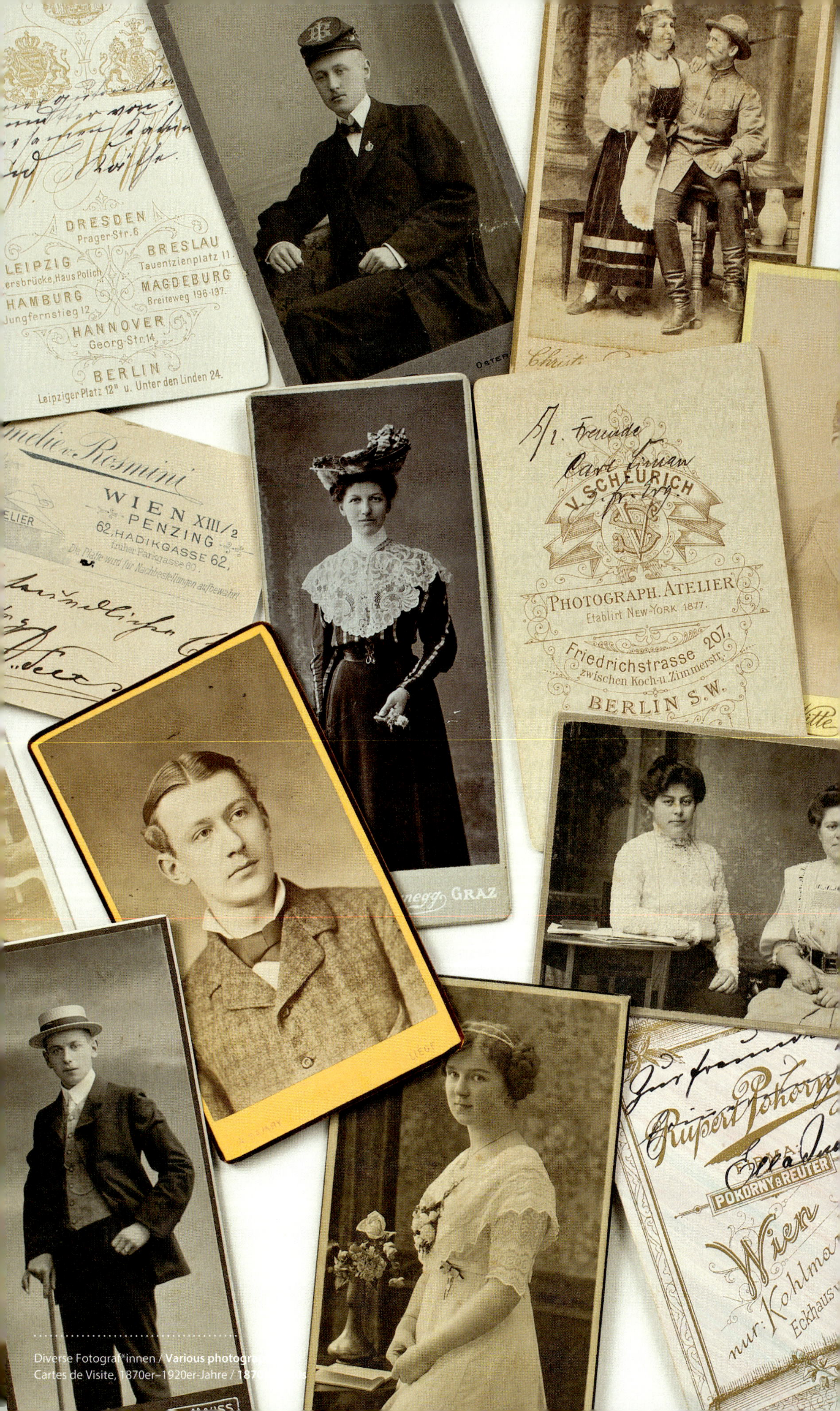

DRESDEN
Prager-Str.6
LEIPZIG
ersbrücke, Haus Polich
BRESLAU
Tauentzienplatz 11.
HAMBURG
Jungfernstieg 12
MAGDEBURG
Breiteweg 196-197.
HANNOVER
Georg-Str.14.
BERLIN
Leipziger Platz 12ᵇ u. Unter den Linden 24.
Atelier v. Resmini
WIEN XIII/2
PENZING
62, HADIKGASSE 62,
früher Parkgasse 60.
Die Platte wird für Nachbestellungen aufbewahrt!
V. SCHEURICH
PHOTOGRAPH. ATELIER
Etablirt New-York 1877.
Friedrichstrasse 207,
zwischen Koch-u. Zimmerstr.
BERLIN S.W.
GRAZ
Rupert Pokorny
POKORNY & REUTER
Wien

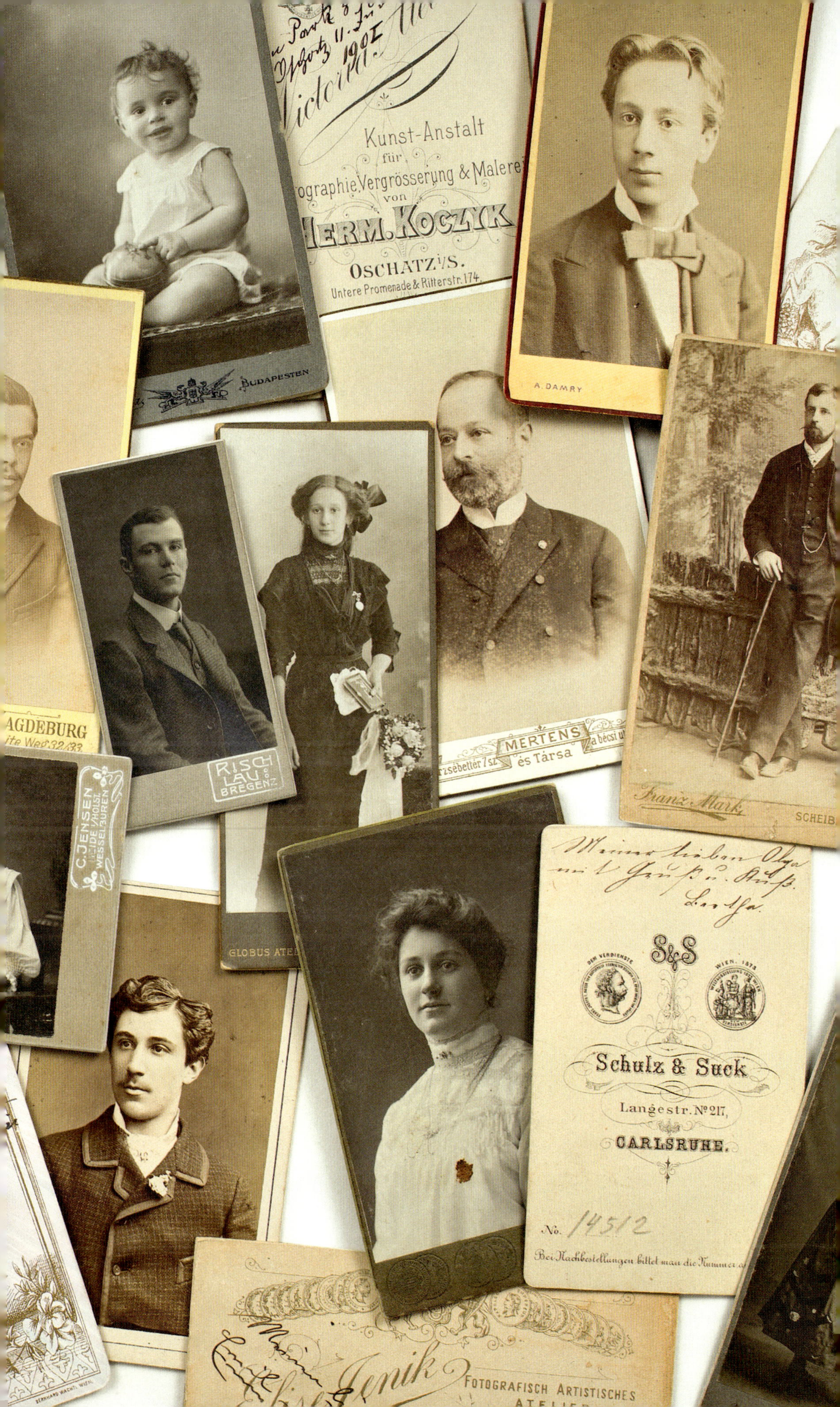

Victoria
Kunst-Anstalt
für
ographie,Vergrösserung & Malerei
von
HERM. KOCZYK
OSCHATZ i/S.
Untere Promenade & Ritterstr. 174.
BUDAPESTEN
A. DAMRY
AGDEBURG
C. JENSEN
WESSELBUREN
RISCH LAU & Co BREGENZ
MERTENS
és Társa
Franz Mark
SCHEIB
GLOBUS ATEL
Schulz & Suck
Langestr. No 217.
CARLSRUHE.
No. 14512
Bei Nachbestellungen bittet man die Nummer a
FOTOGRAFISCH ARTISTISCHES
ATELIER

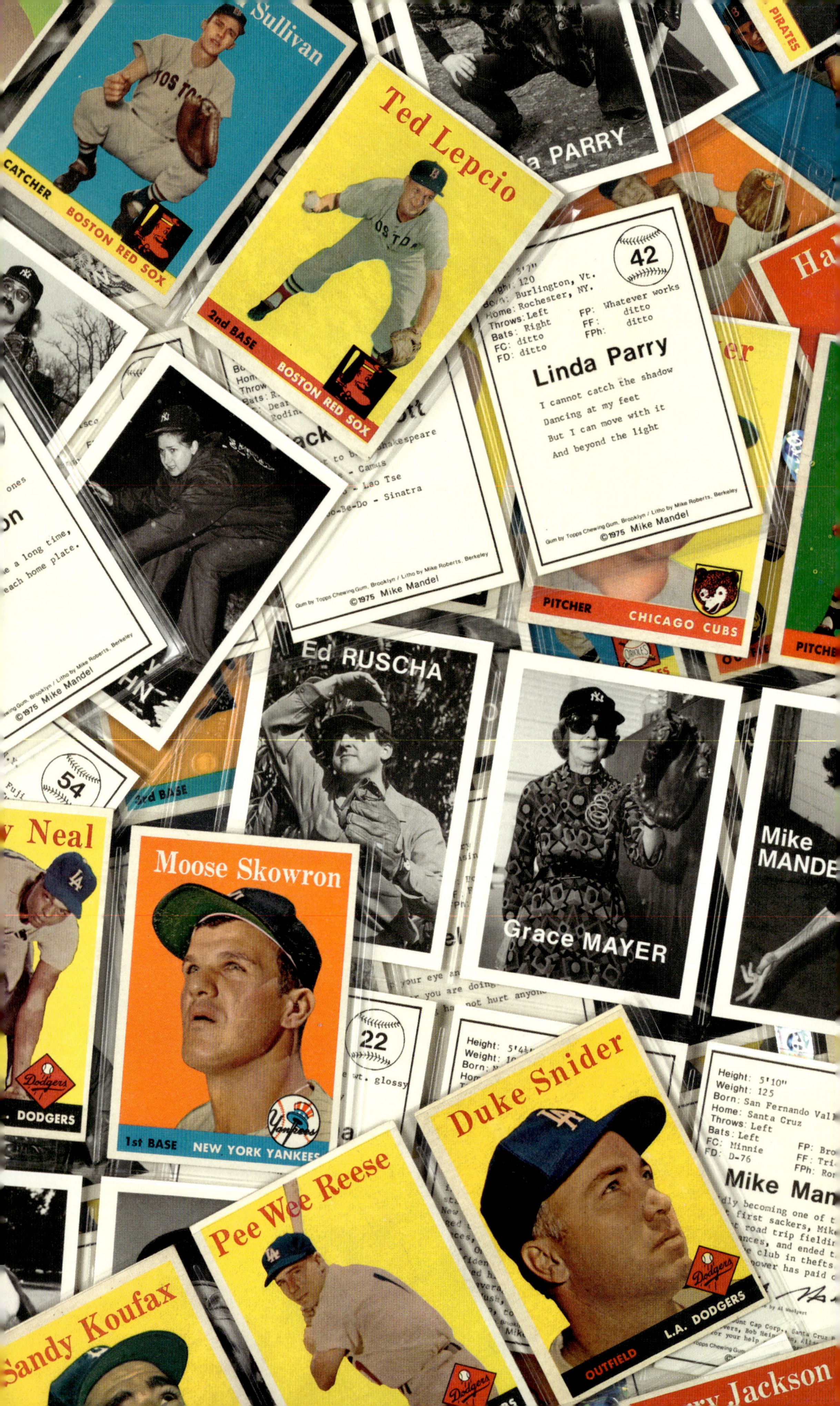
Sullivan
CATCHER
BOSTON RED SOX
Ted Lepcio
2nd BASE
BOSTON RED SOX
PARRY
PIRATES
42
Home: Rochester, NY.
Throws: Left   FP: Whatever works
Bats: Right   FF: ditto
FC: ditto   FPh: ditto
FD: ditto
Linda Parry
I cannot catch the shadow
Dancing at my feet
But I can move with it
And beyond the light
Gum by Topps Chewing Gum, Brooklyn / Litho by Mike Roberts, Berkeley
©1975 Mike Mandel
PITCHER   CHICAGO CUBS
PITCHER
Gum by Topps Chewing Gum, Brooklyn / Litho by Mike Roberts, Berkeley
©1975 Mike Mandel
Ed RUSCHA
Grace MAYER
Mike
MANDEL
54
3rd BASE
Neal
Moose Skowron
Dodgers
DODGERS
1st BASE   NEW YORK YANKEES
22
Height: 5'4"
Weight:
Born:
Height: 5'10"
Weight: 125
Born: San Fernando Val
Home: Santa Cruz
Throws: Left
Bats: Left
FC: Minnie   FP: Bro
FD: D-76   FF: Tri
                FPh: Ron
Duke Snider
Mike Man
OUTFIELD   L.A. DODGERS
Pee Wee Reese
Sandy Koufax
Jackson

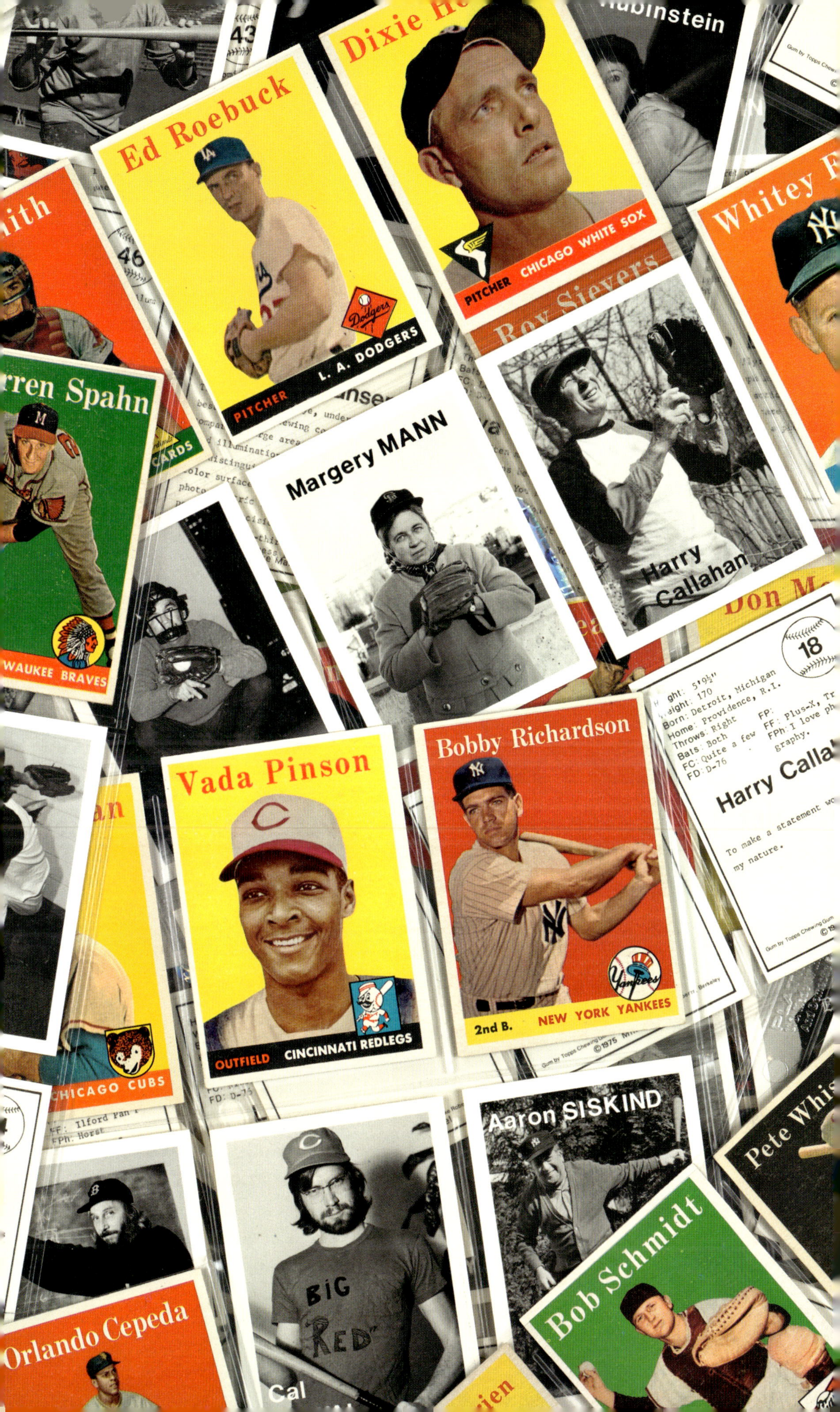

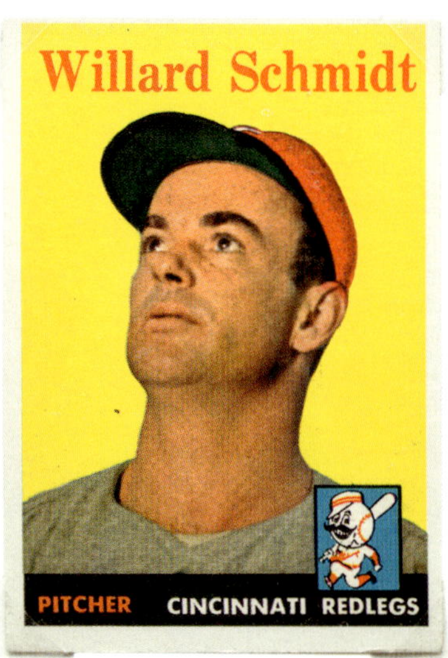

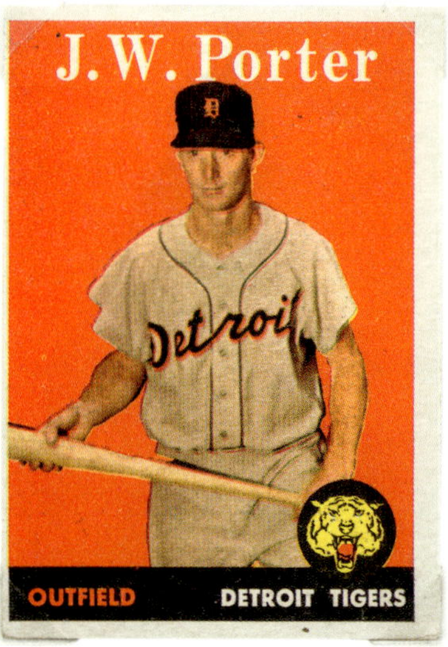

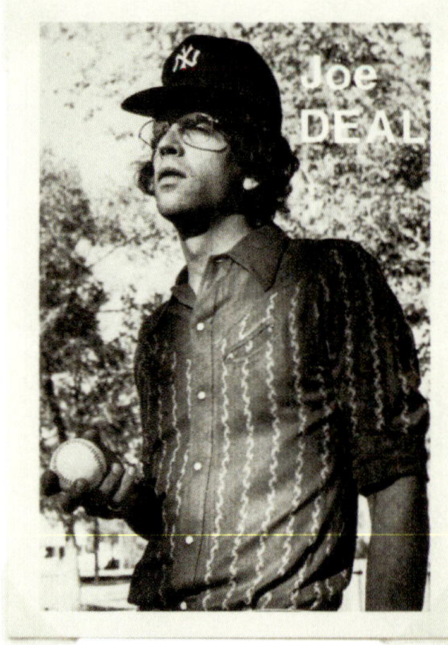

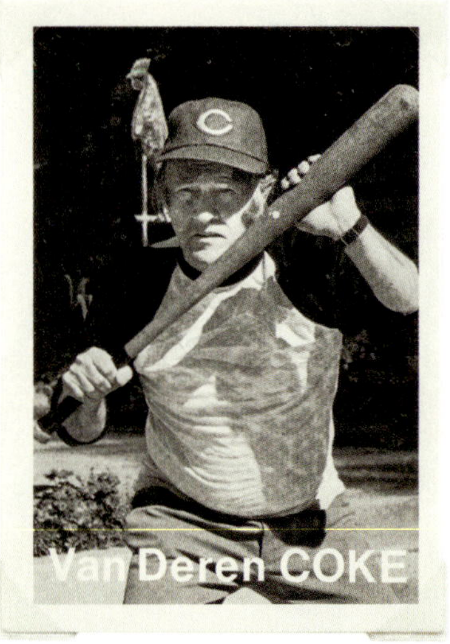

Height:	5'11"	
Weight:	150	
Born:	Topeka, Kansas	
Home:	Rochester, NY	
Throws:	Right	
Bats:	Right	FP: Agfa
FC:	2¼ sq.	FF: Ilford
FD:	Ilford	FPh: Too many

4

Joe Deal

What can I say? For a short period in my life (1954-59), I dreamed that some day I would appear on a baseball card wearing a Yankees cap.

Gum by Topps Chewing Gum, Brooklyn / Litho by Mike Roberts, Berkeley
©1975 Mike Mandel

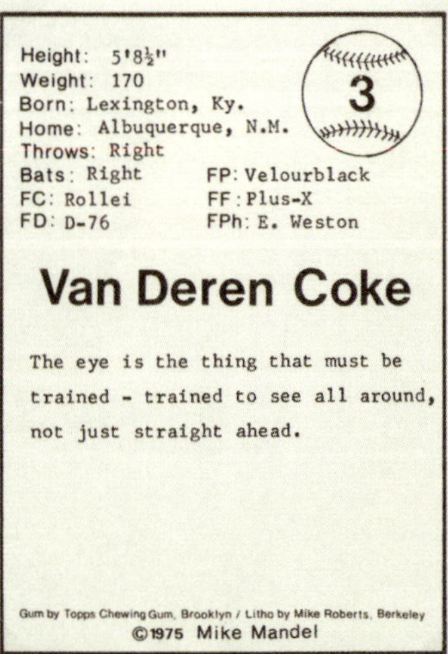

Height:	5'8½"	
Weight:	170	
Born:	Lexington, Ky.	
Home:	Albuquerque, N.M.	
Throws:	Right	
Bats:	Right	FP: Velourblack
FC:	Rollei	FF: Plus-X
FD:	D-76	FPh: E. Weston

3

Van Deren Coke

The eye is the thing that must be trained - trained to see all around, not just straight ahead.

Gum by Topps Chewing Gum, Brooklyn / Litho by Mike Roberts, Berkeley
©1975 Mike Mandel

Mike Mandel
Topps Baseball Cards, 1958 und / **and** *The Baseball-Photographer Trading Cards, 1975*

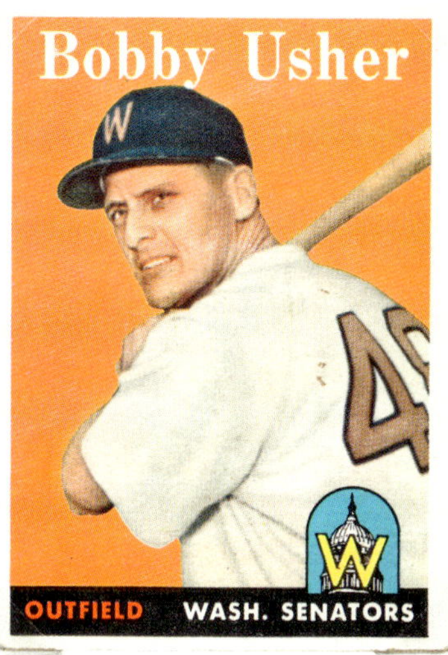

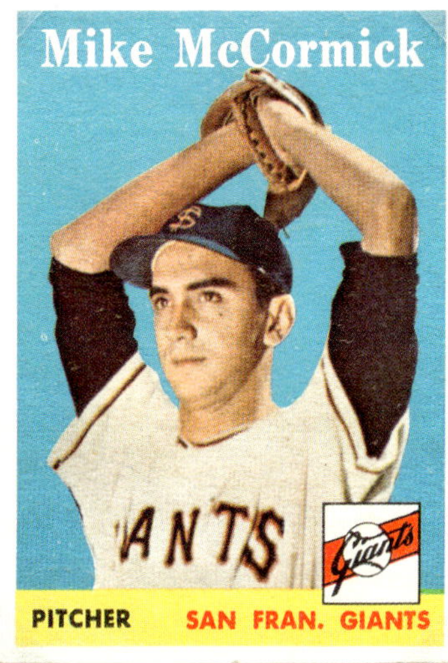

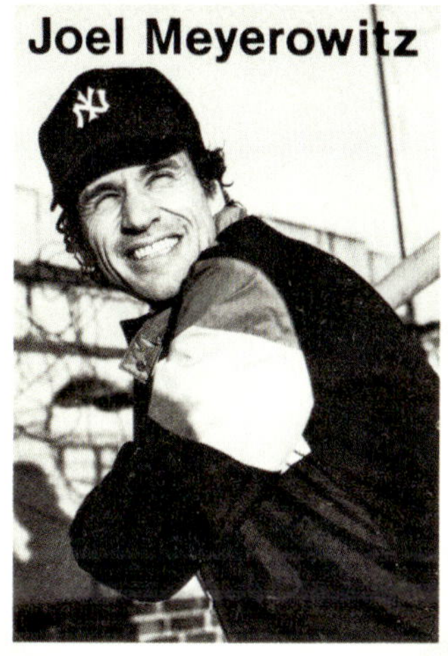

Height: 6'
Weight: 155
Born: The Bronx
Home: New York City
Throws: Right
Bats: Right   FP:
FC: Leica   FF: Kodachrome
FD: FPh: Robert Frank

Joel Meyerowitz

My father was a terrific baseball
player. On summer Saturdays he left
early and played as many as 3 games
on the glass and ash filled lots of
the Bronx. Those were money games,
hard played and sometimes hard fought.
For the tight spots my pop brought a
special bat cut into 3 pieces and
hinged. To the pitcher it appeared
solid even as pop took a warm-up
swing. But at the crucial moment in
mid-windup, my pop would twist his
wrist and down would come his faith-
ful Hillerich and Bradsby and the
composure of any pitcher.

©1975 Mike Mandel

Height: 5'11½"
Weight: 170
Born: Amersfoort, Holland
Home: Champaign, Ill.
Throws: Both
Bats: Both   FP: Agfa
FC: Pentax Spot.   FF: PX 135
FD: FG-7   FPh: Hmm

Bob Flick

Pictures used to be postcards from
a journey the end of which is hoped
for but unknown. That's changed
now.

Gum by Topps Chewing Gum, Brooklyn / Litho by Mike Roberts, Berkeley

©1975 Mike Mandel

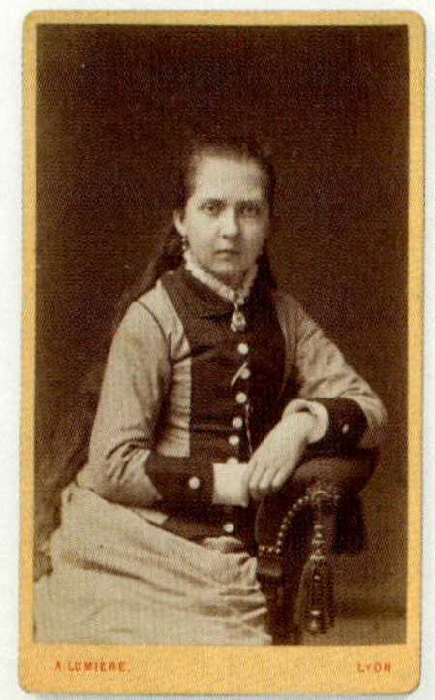
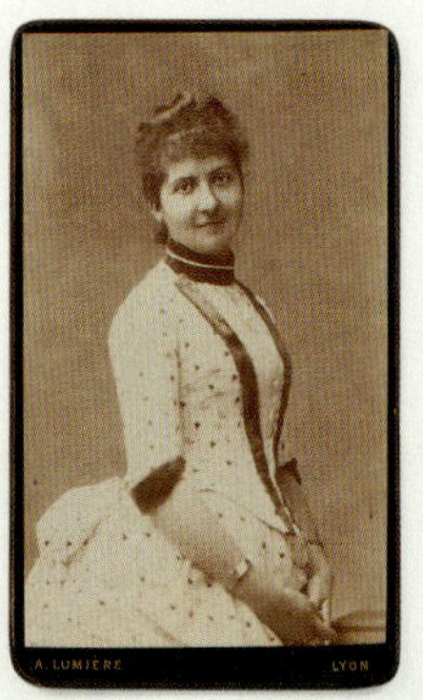
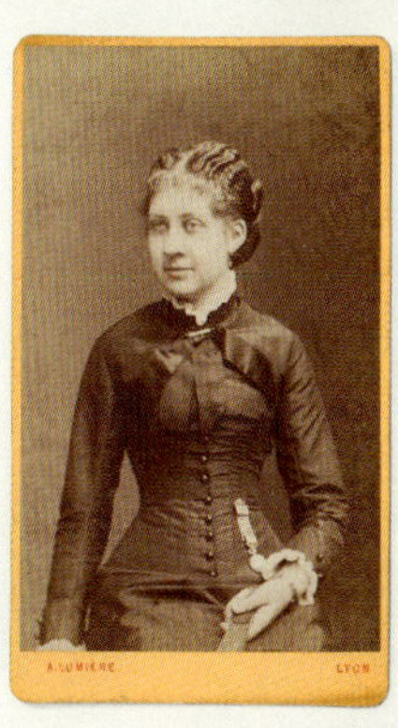
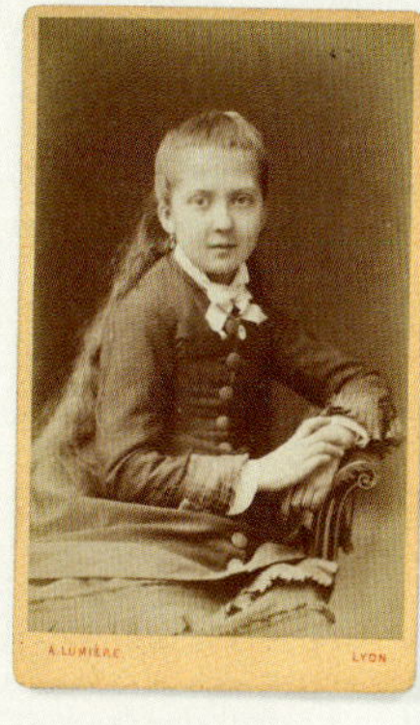
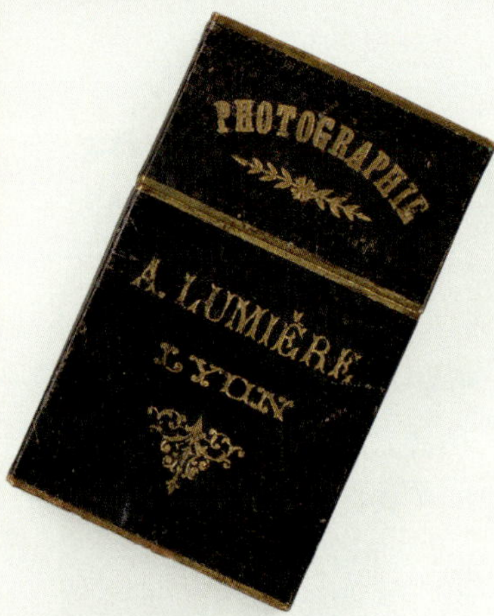
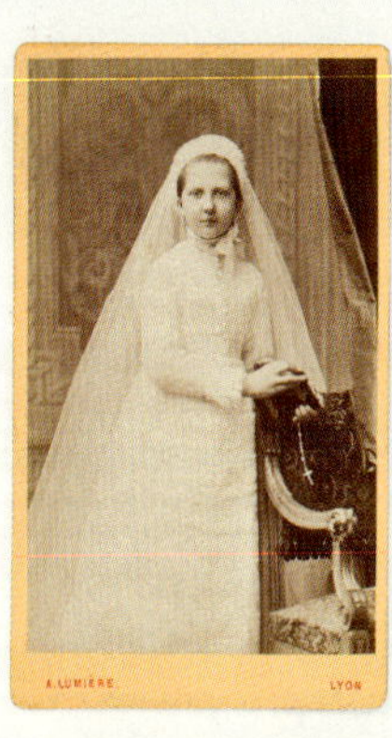
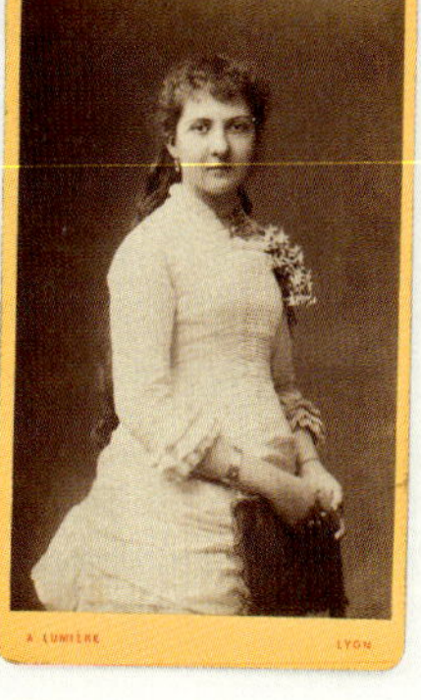
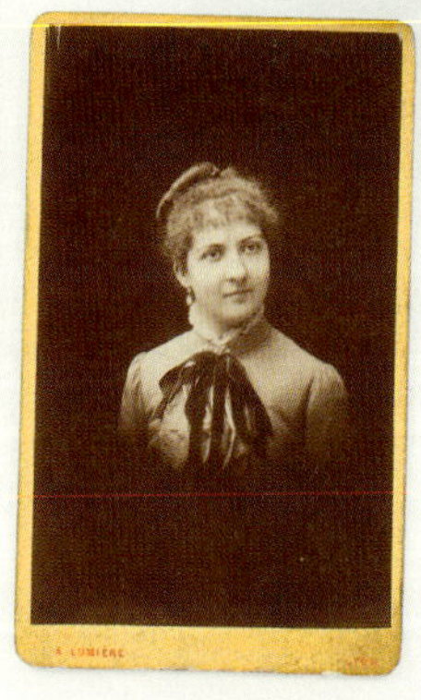

Auguste Lumière
Marguerite & Jeanne Pitrat, Lyon, 1880–1890 , Cartes de Visite

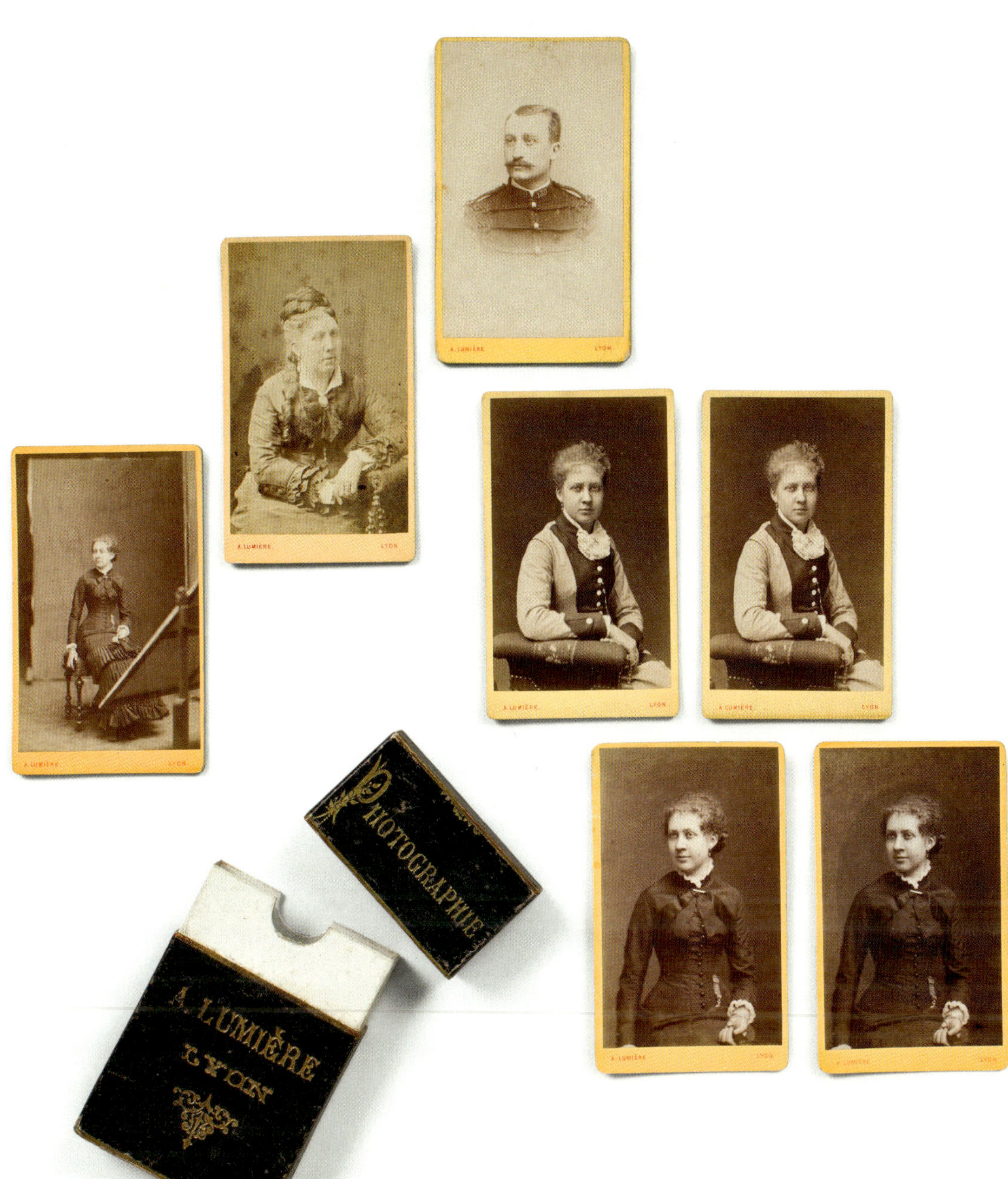

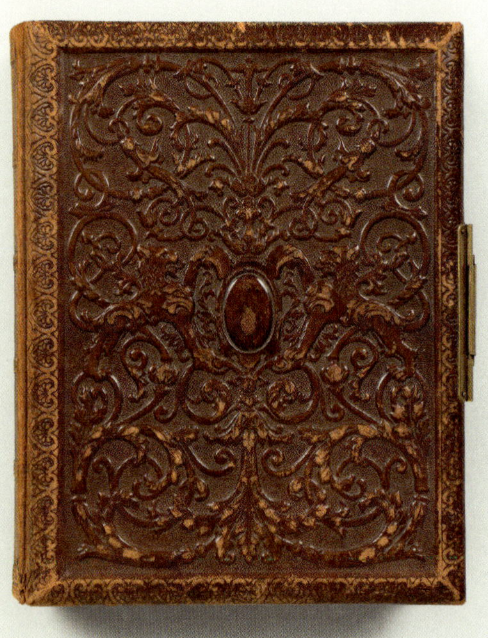

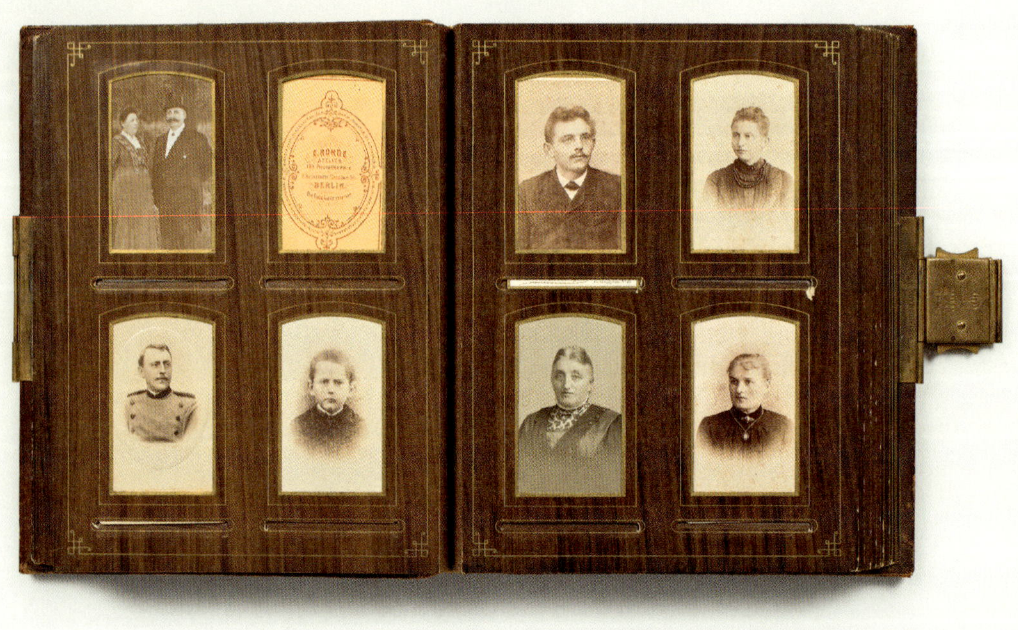

Diverse Fotograf*innen / **Various photographers**
Cartes-de-Visite-Album, 1890er-Jahre / **carte-de-visite album, 1890s**

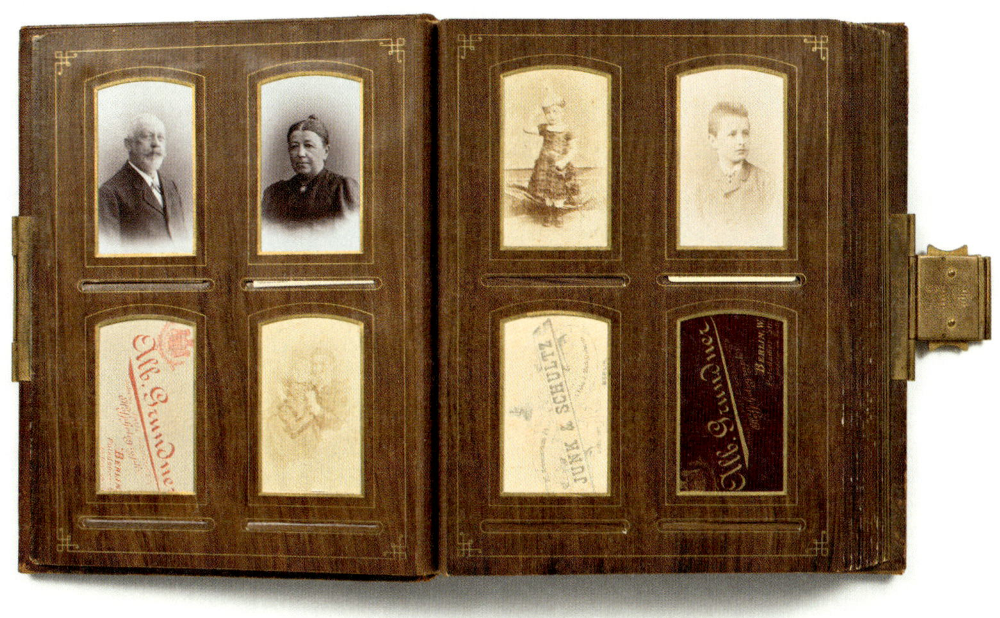

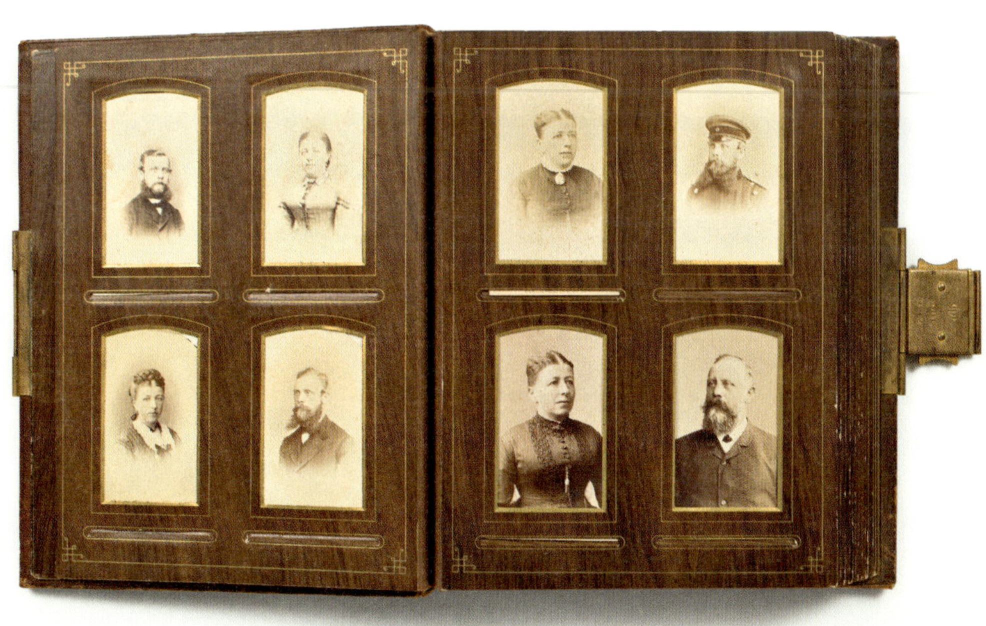

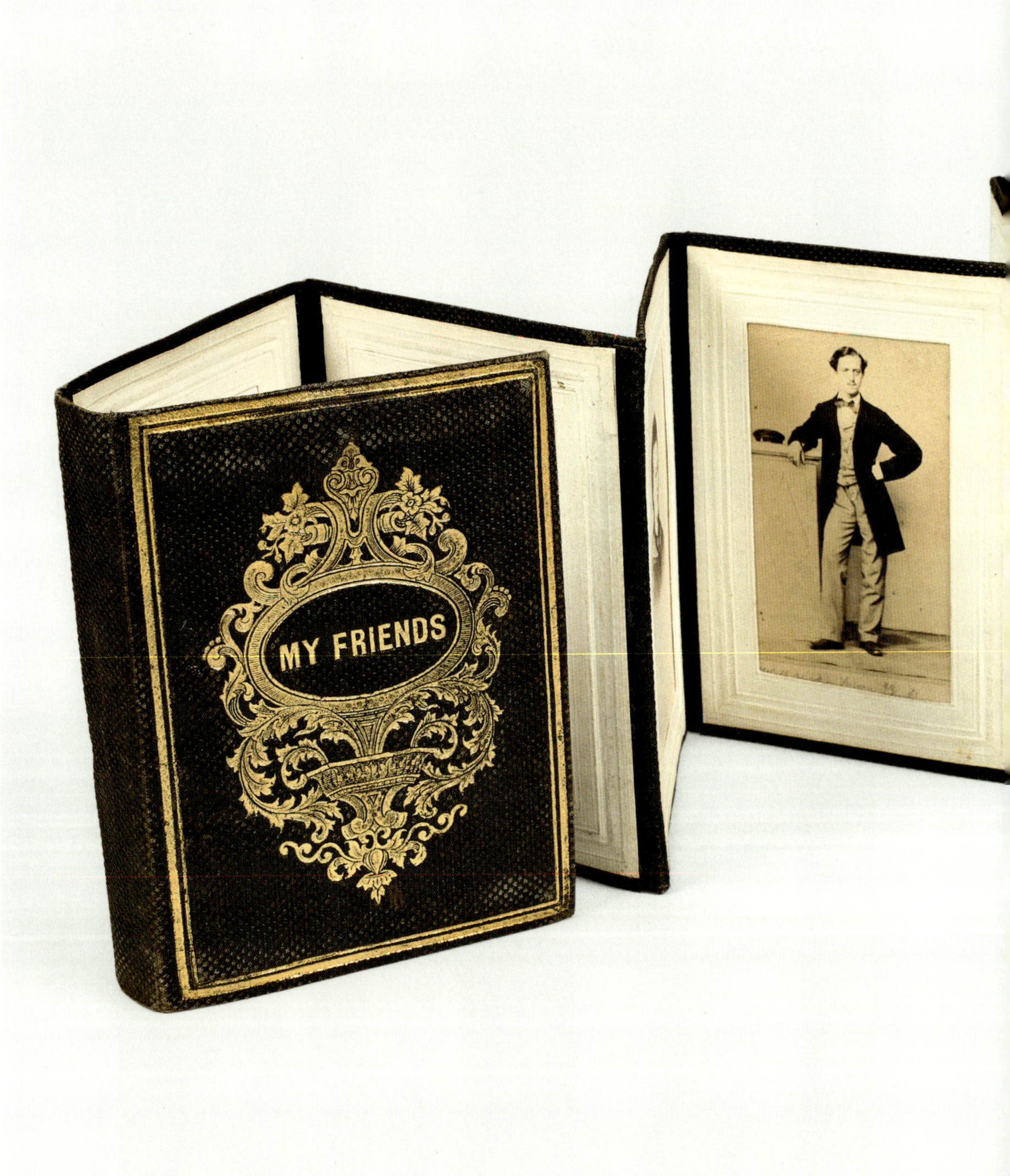

Diverse Fotograf*innen / **Various photographers**
Meine Freunde, Leporello / **My Friends, folding concertina album,** ca. 1870

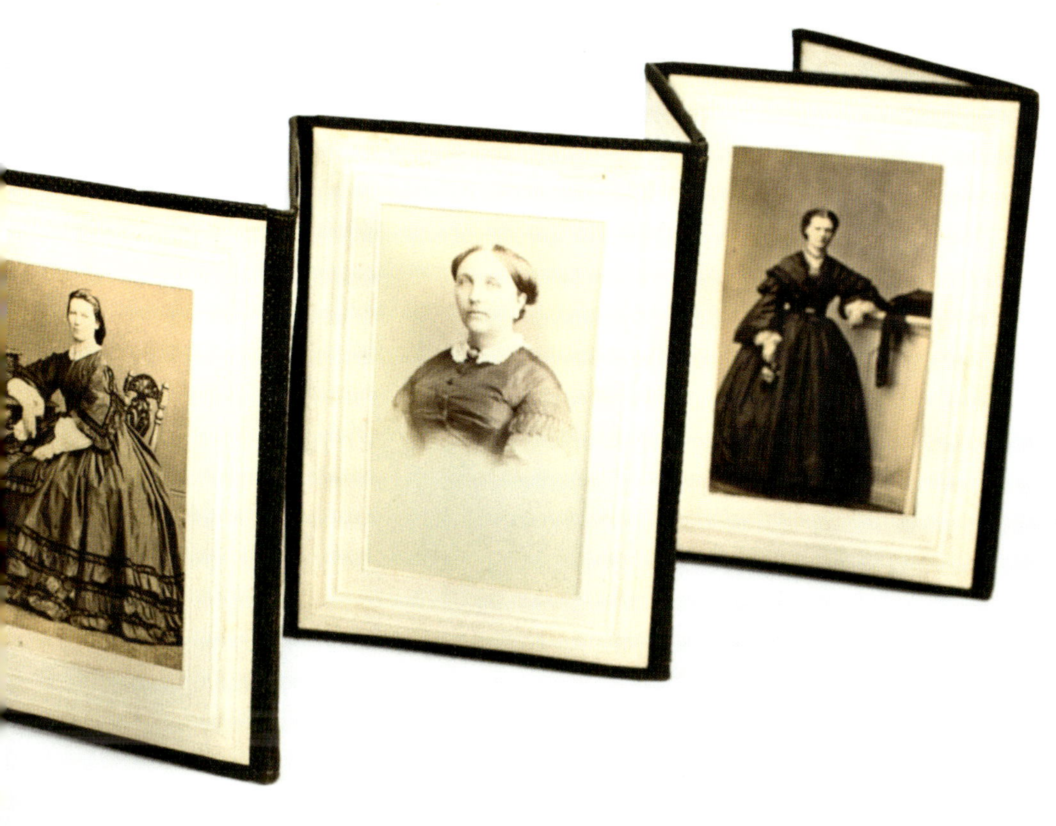

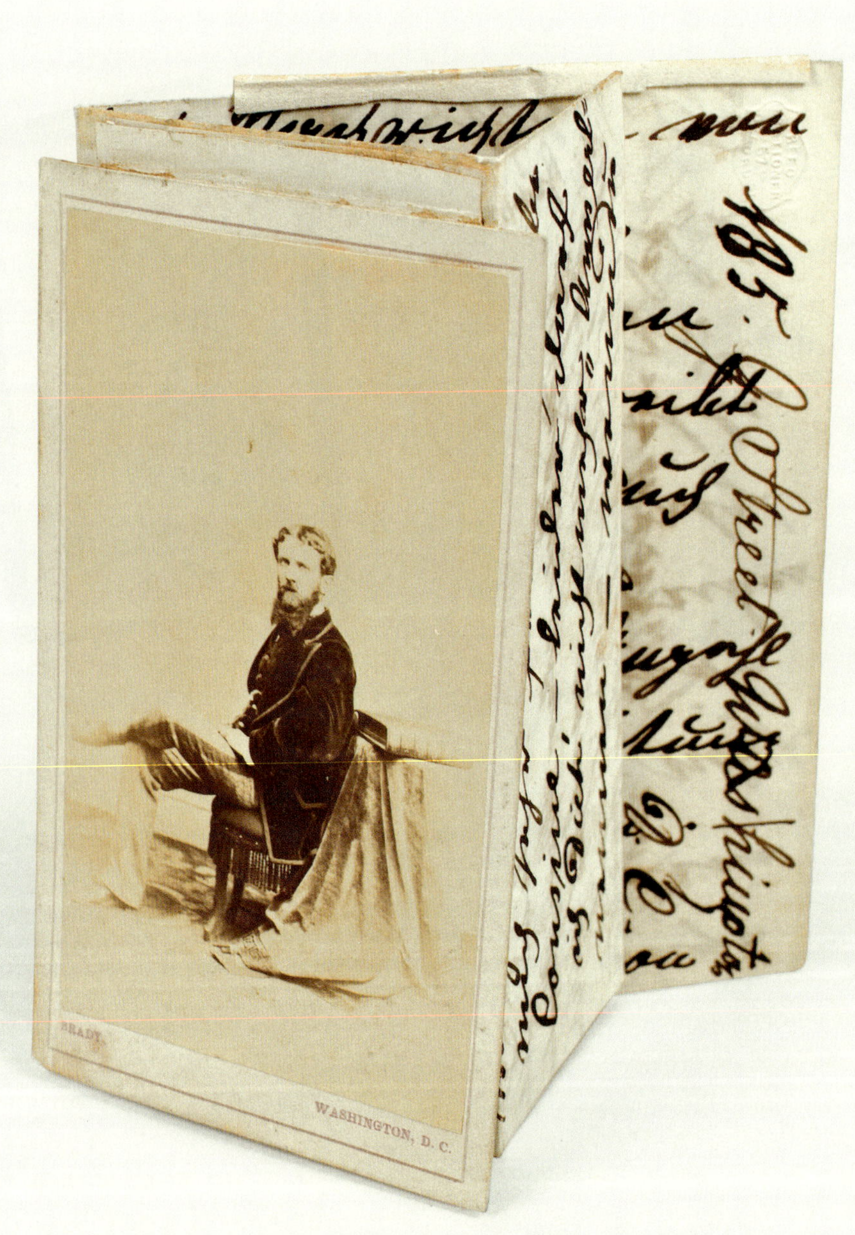

Anonym / **Anonymous**
An Mama, Brief mit montierter / **To Mama, letter with mounted** Carte de Visite 1869
Foto / **Photo** Mathew B. Brady, New York

BRADY.
WASHINGTON, D.C.

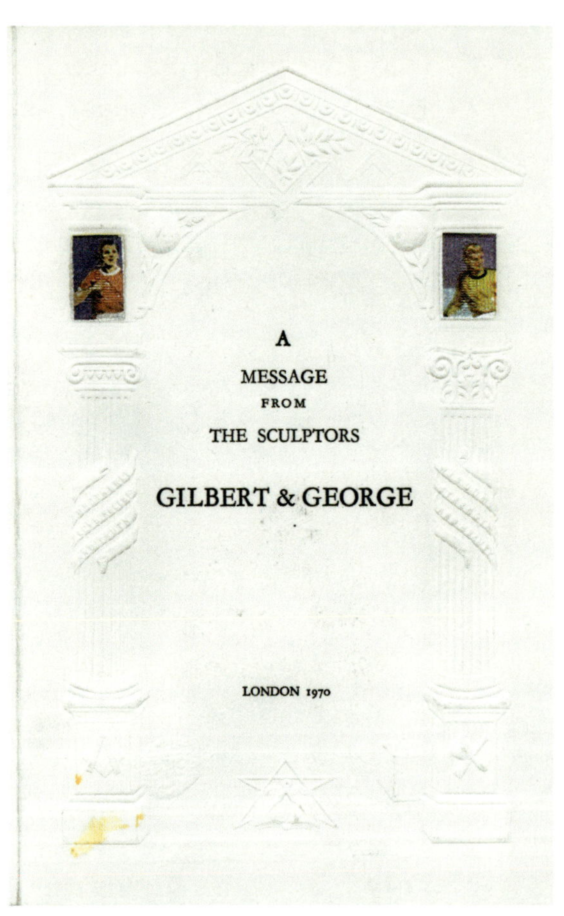

Gilbert & George
A Message from the Sculptors, 1969 (datiert / **dated** 1970)

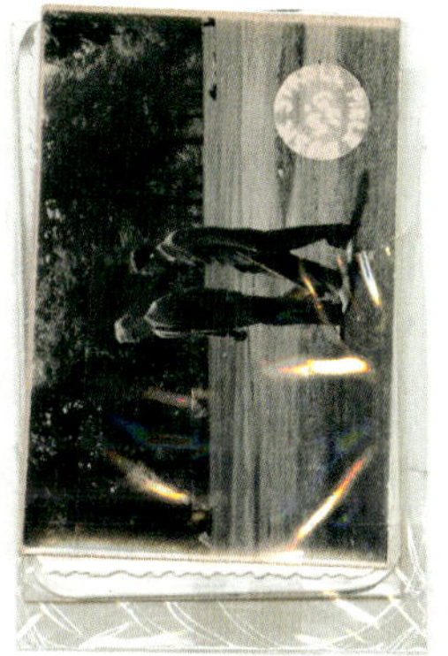

Gilbert and George, the sculptors, are walking along a new road. They left their little studio with all the tools and brushes, taking with them only some music, gentle smiles on their faces and the most serious intentions in the world.

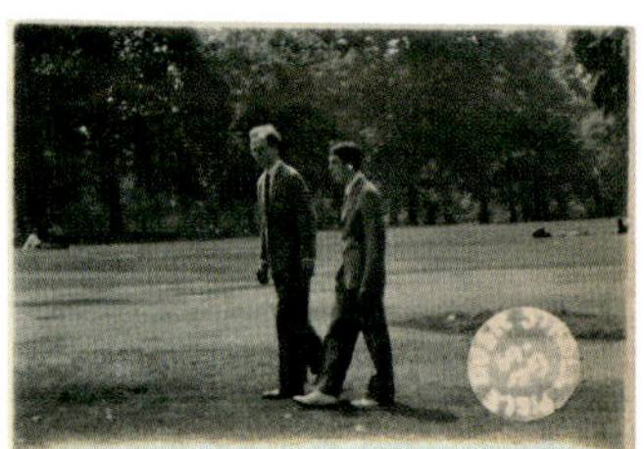

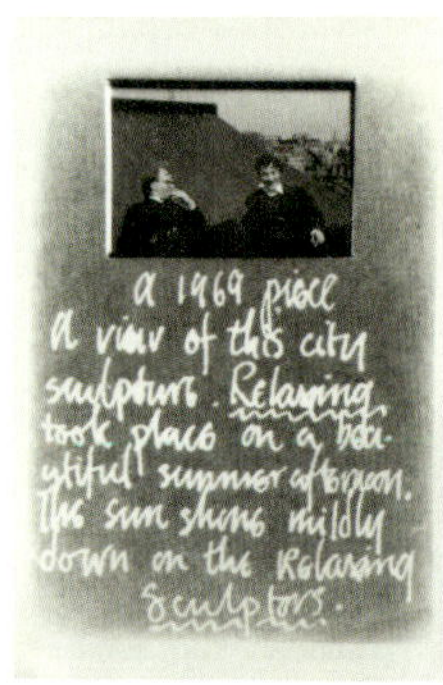

a 1969 piece
a view of this city
sculpture. Relaxing
took place on a beau-
tiful summer afternoon.
The sun shone mildly
down on the Relaxing
Sculptors.

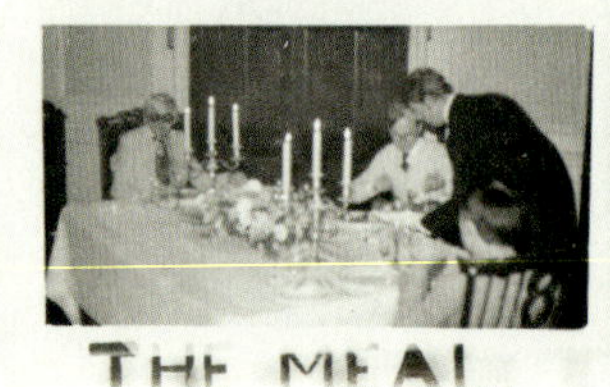

THE MEAL.

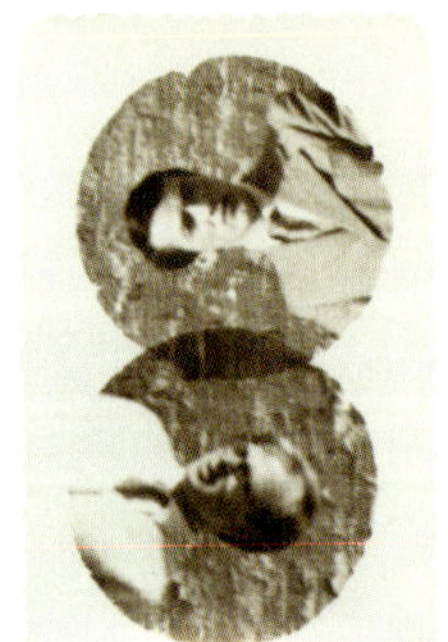

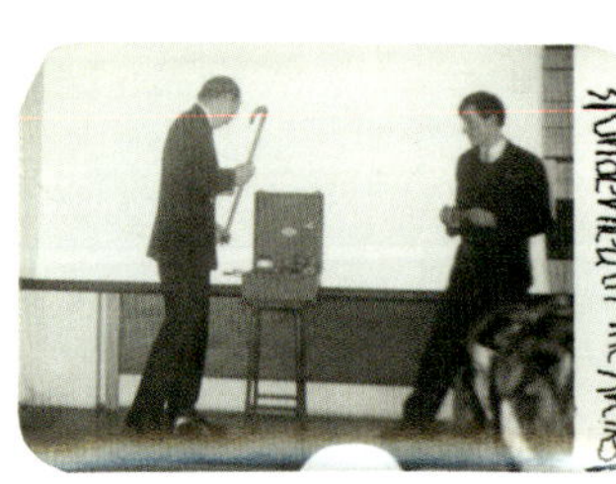

Underneath the Arches

A SCULPTURE SAMPLE
ENTITLED
SCULPTORS' SAMPLES

1.   *G &G's make-up.*

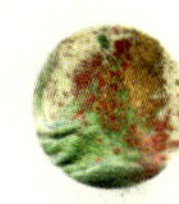

2.   *G &G's tobacco and ash.*

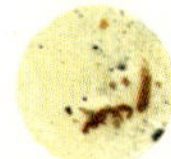

3.   *G &G's hair.*

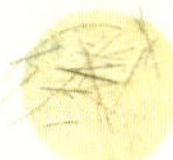

4.   *G &G's coat and shirt.*

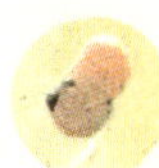

5.   *G &G's breakfast.*

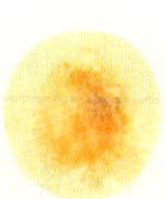

*Gilbert and George **have** a wide range
of **sculptures** for you—singing sculpture,
interview sculpture, dancing sculpture,
meal sculpture, walking sculpture,
nerve sculpture, cafe sculpture, and
philosophy sculpture.*

So do contact us

George and Gilbert

'ART FOR ALL'
12 FOURNIER STREET
LONDON, E.1

Telephone 01 - 247 0161

A.H. & Co.
Briefbögen mit Londoner Stadtansichten / **Stationary with London cityscapes,** 1870

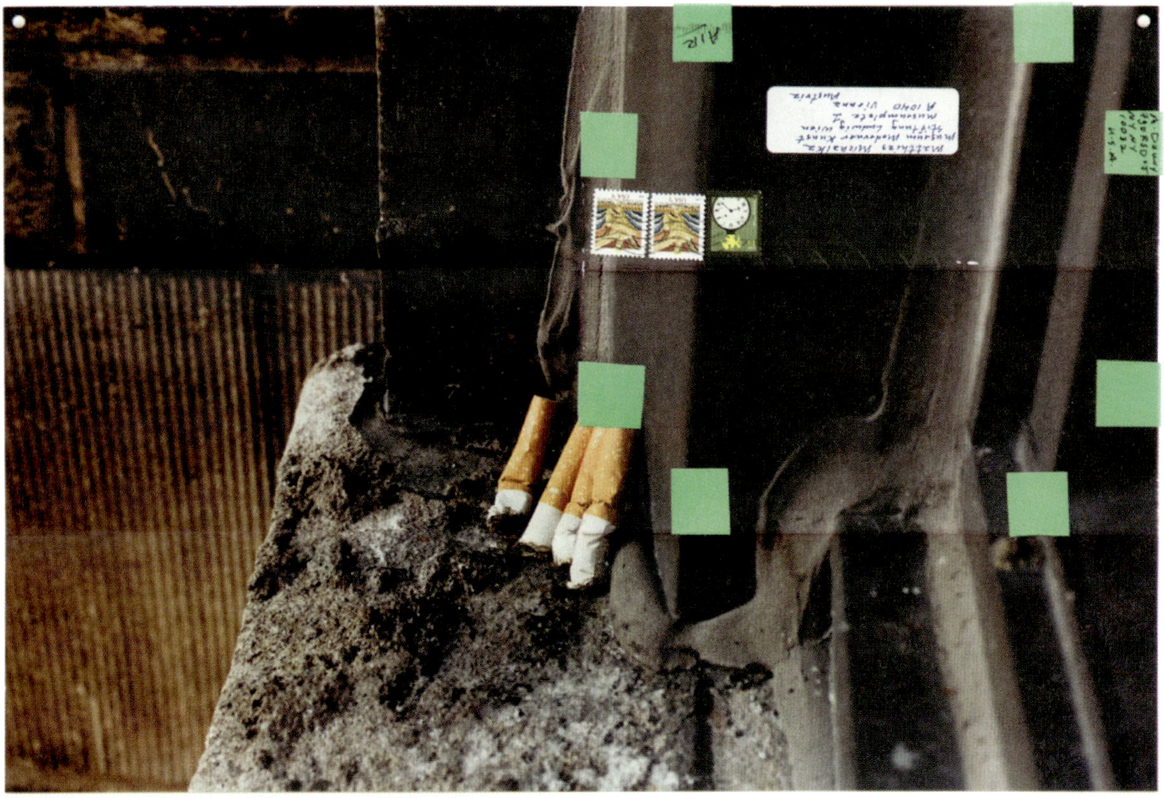

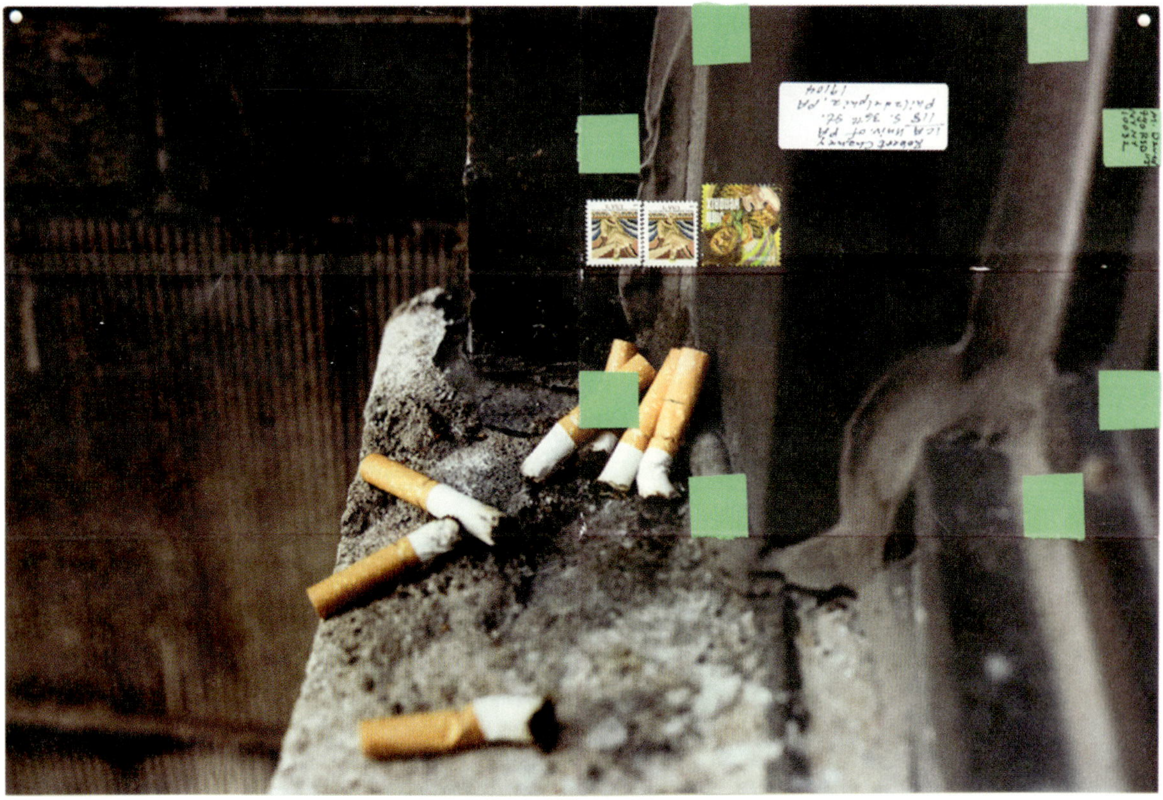

Moyra Davey
Bad Kids, 2014

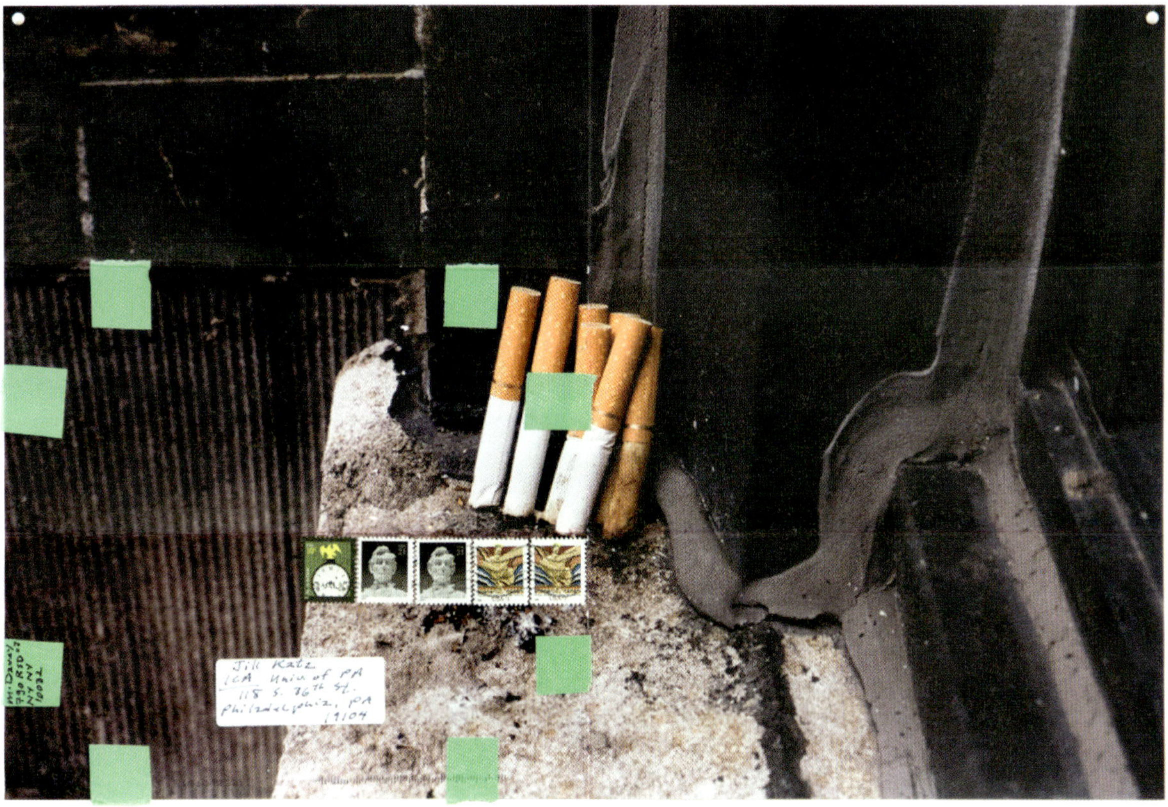

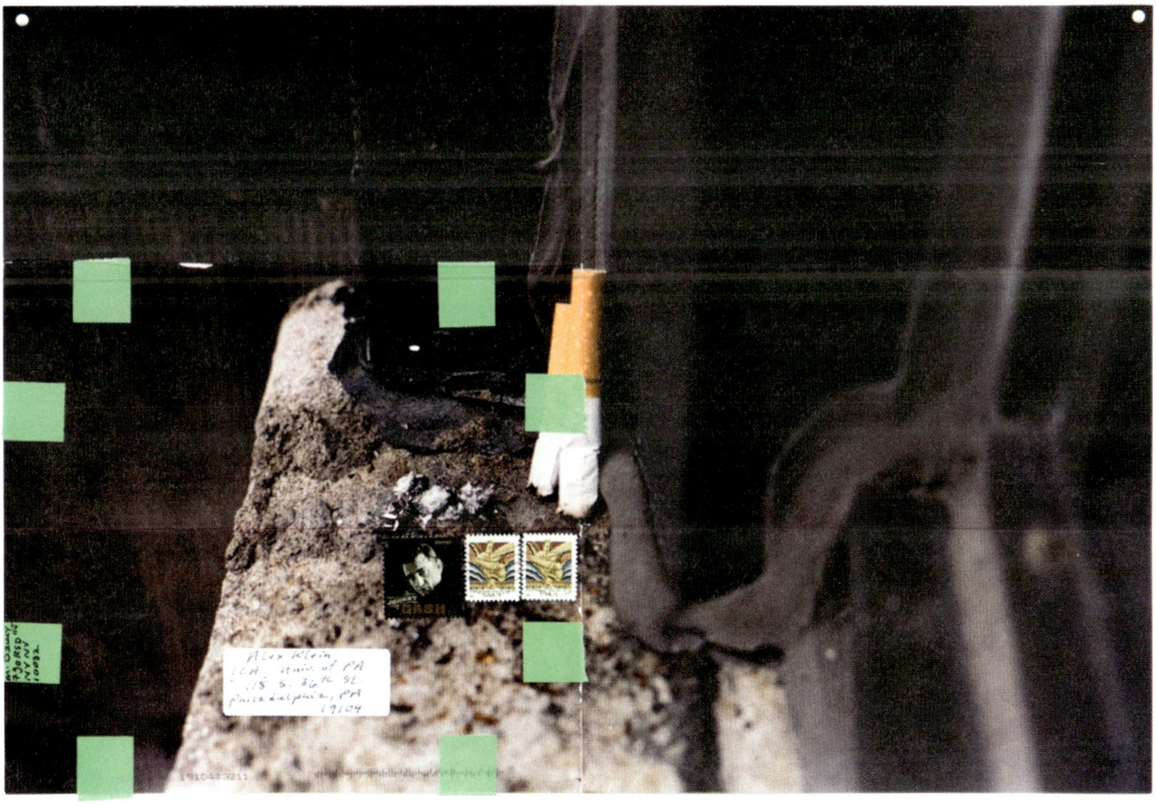

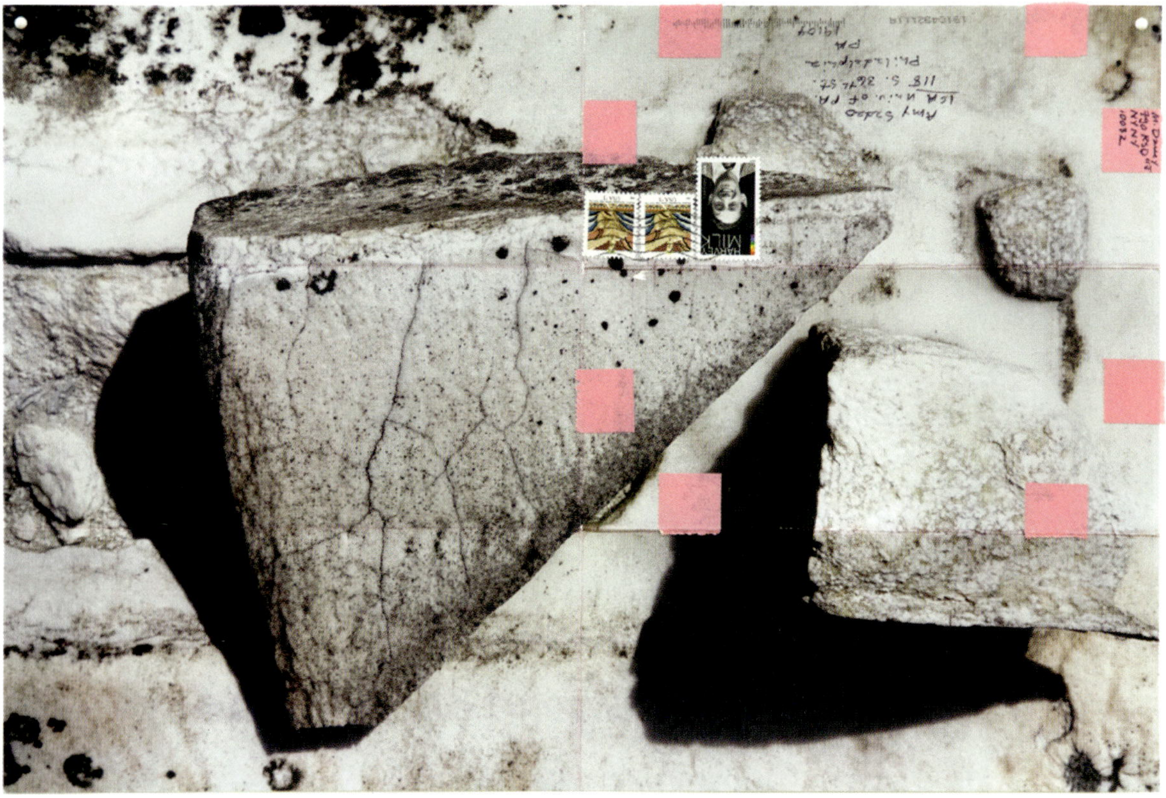

Amy Sadao
ICA Univ. of PA
118 S. 36th St.
Philadelphia,
PA
19104

M. Dowd's
730 RSD
NY NY
10031

HARVEY MILK

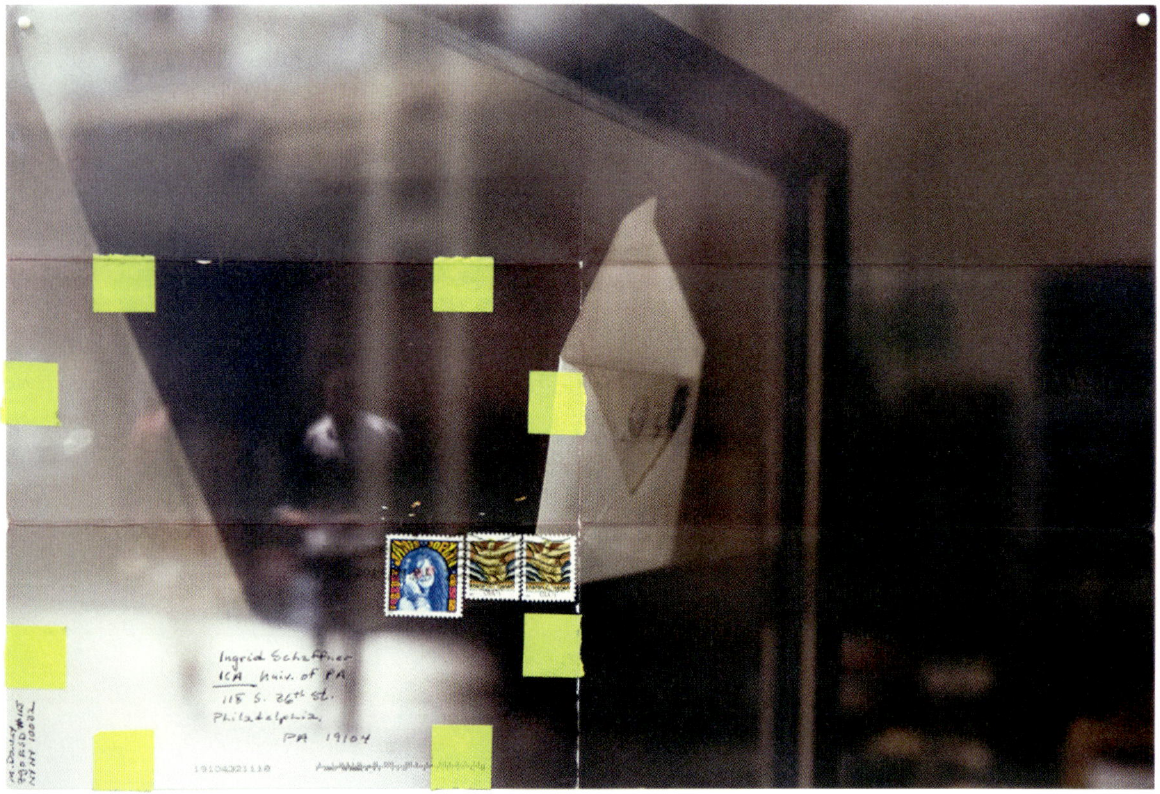

Ingrid Schaffner
ICA Univ. of PA
118 S. 36th St.
Philadelphia,
PA 19104

M. Dowd
730 RSD W103
NY NY 10031

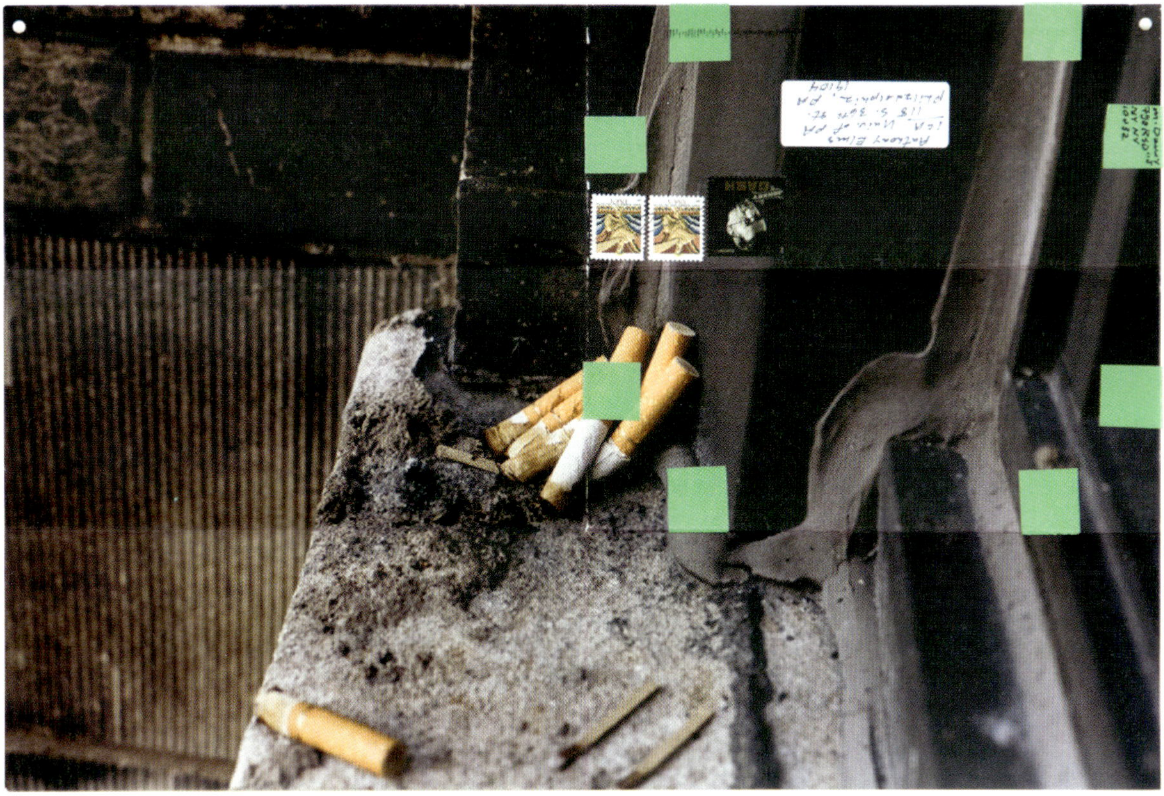

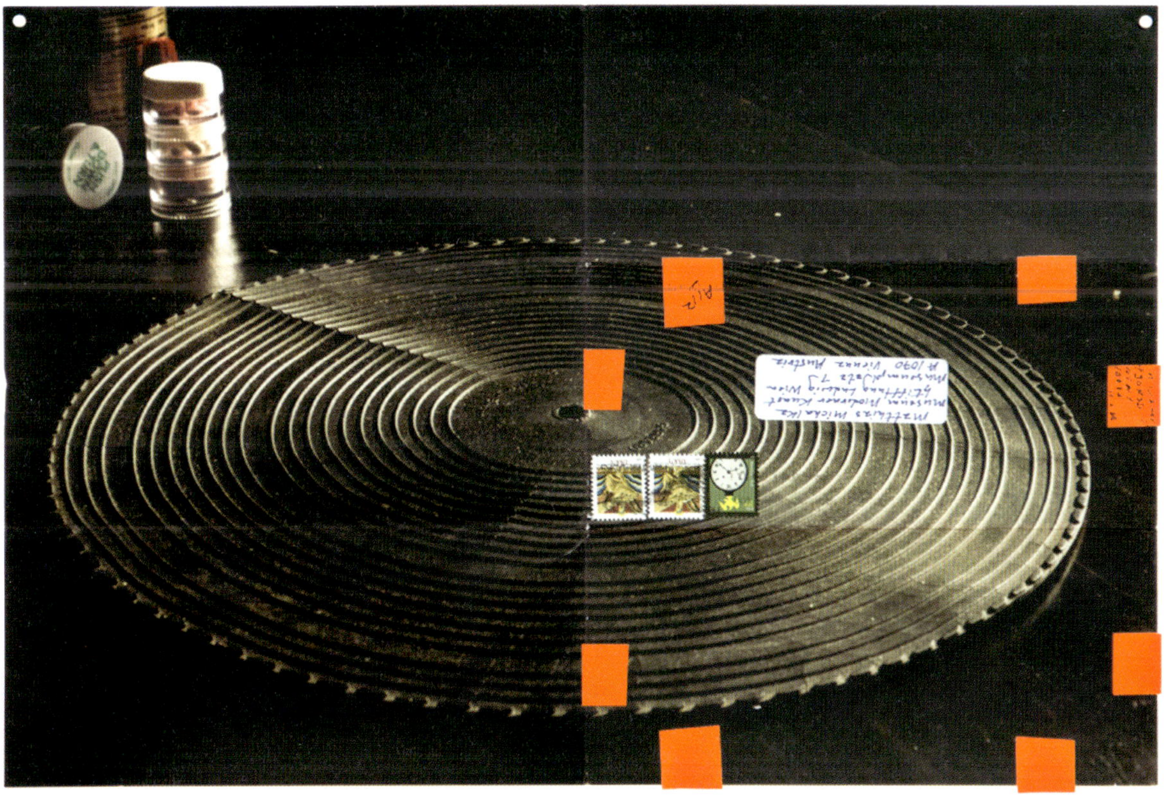

Peter Miller
Envelope, 2020

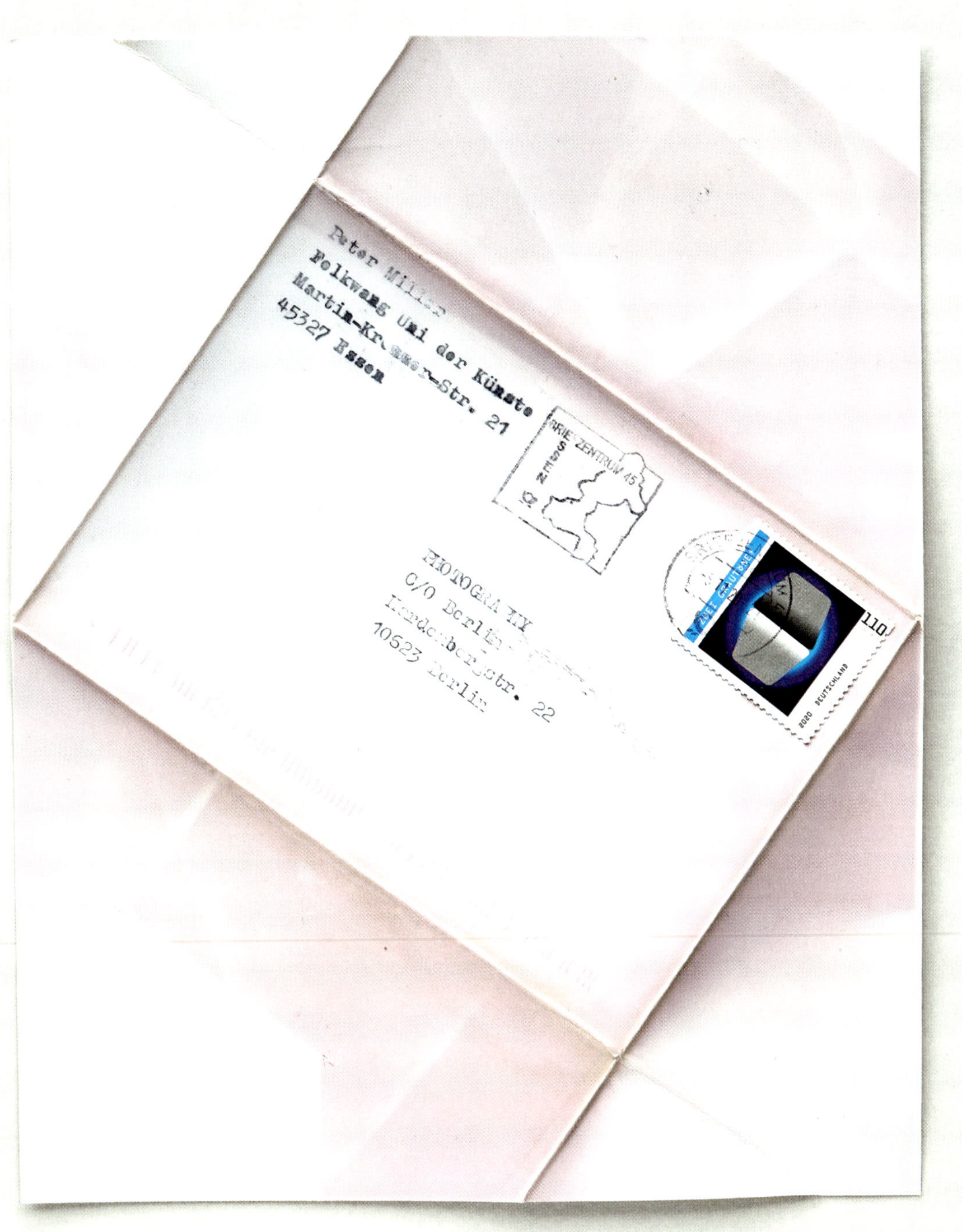

Peter Miller
Folkwang Uni der Künste
Martin-Kremmer-Str. 21
45327 Essen
BRIEFZENTRUM 45
PHOTOGRAPHY
C/O Berlin
...bergstr. 22
10623 Berlin
ZWEI Gedult baxe
DEUTSCHLAND
110
2020

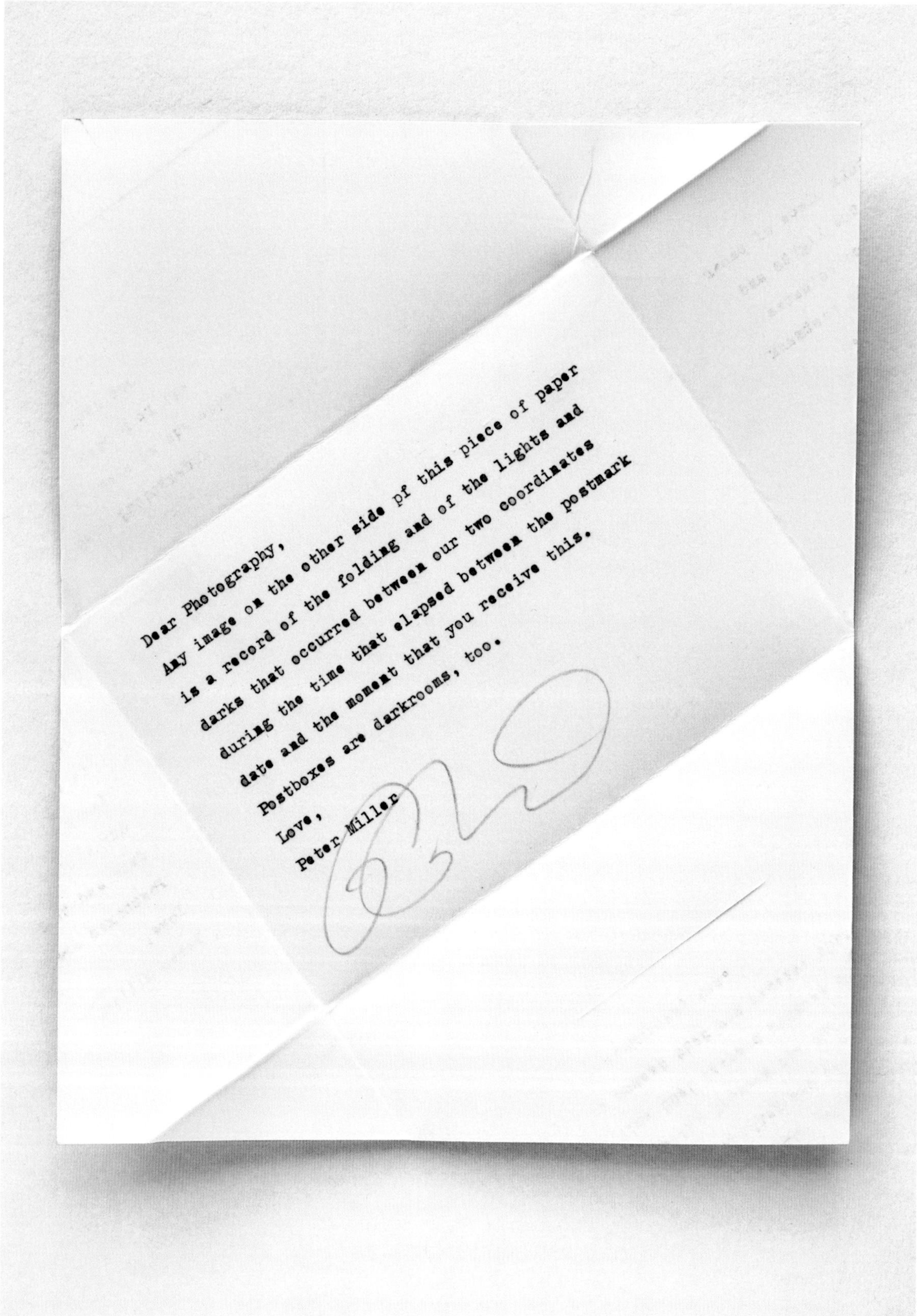

Dear Photography,

Any image on the other side pf this piece of paper
is a record of the folding and of the lights and
darks that occurred between our two coordinates
during the time that elapsed between the postmark
date and the moment that you receive this.

Postboxes are darkrooms, too.

Love,

Peter Miller

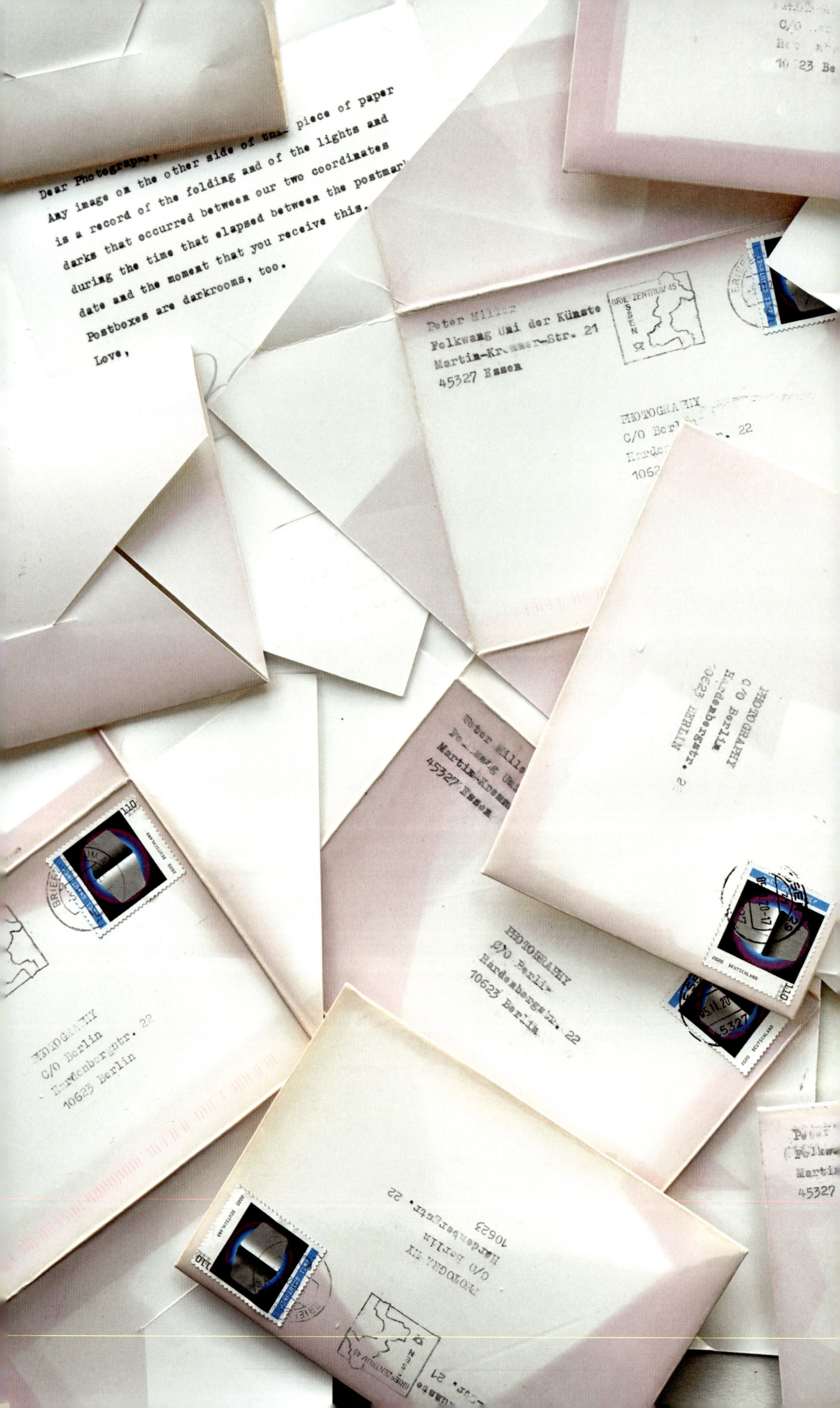

Dear Photographer,
Any image on the other side of this piece of paper
is a record of the folding and of the lights and
darks that occurred between our two coordinates
during the time that elapsed between the postmark
date and the moment that you receive this.
Postboxes are darkrooms, too.
Love,

Peter Miller
Folkwang Uni der Künste
Martin-Kremmer-Str. 21
45327 Essen

PHOTOGRAPHY
C/O Berlin
Hardenbergstr. 22
10623 Berlin

BRIEFZENTRUM 45
ESSEN

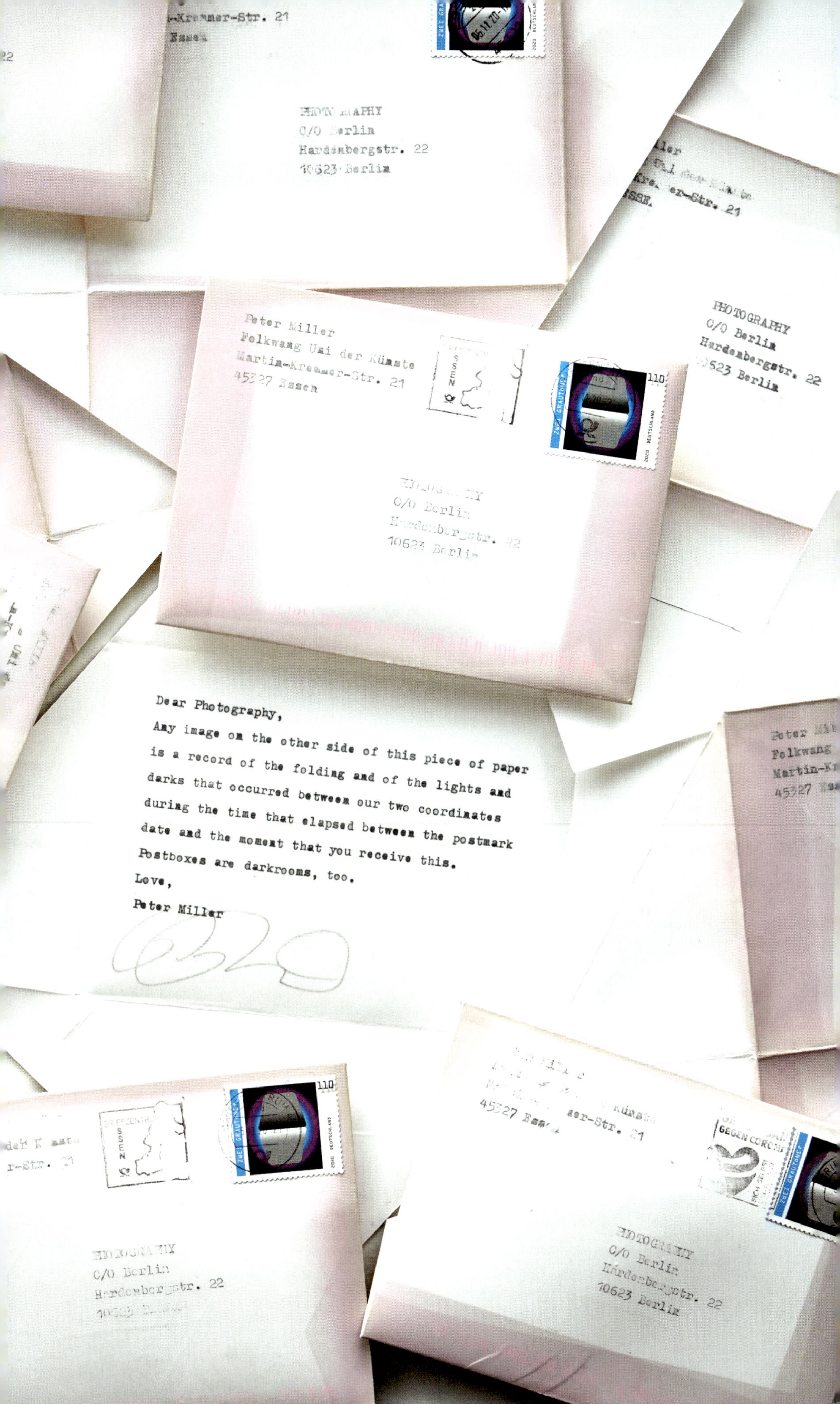
-Kremmer-Str. 21
Essen

PHOTOGRAPHY
C/O Berlin
Hardenbergstr. 22
10623 Berlin

Peter Miller
Folkwang Uni der Künste
Martin-Kremmer-Str. 21
45327 Essen

PHOTOGRAPHY
C/O Berlin
Hardenbergstr. 22
10623 Berlin

Dear Photography,
Any image on the other side of this piece of paper
is a record of the folding and of the lights and
darks that occurred between our two coordinates
during the time that elapsed between the postmark
date and the moment that you receive this.
Postboxes are darkrooms, too.
Love,

Peter Miller

PHOTOGRAPHY
C/O Berlin
Hardenbergstr. 22
10623 Berlin

FOTOBRIEFMARKE

Fotografie und Briefmarke wurden fast zur gleichen Zeit zu öffentlichen Objekten: Die ersten brauchbaren fotografischen Verfahren wurden im Laufe des Jahres 1839 publiziert; ab Mai 1840 wurden Briefe in Großbritannien mit der Penny Black frankiert. Beide Medien verbreiteten sich schnell weltweit, und beide revolutionierten, je auf ihre Weise, wie bürgerliche Gesellschaften sich kommunikativ organisierten: Schon mit den frühen fotografischen Verfahren wurden Porträts so preiswert, dass sie nicht nur den Ober- und Mittelschichten zugänglich waren; mit der Briefmarke und der damit einhergehenden Standardisierung und drastischen Verbilligung des Portos begann überhaupt erst die massenhafte private und geschäftliche Korrespondenz.

Neue Medien sind nie rein. Sie nehmen andere Medien auf, zitieren sich, bringen Hybride hervor. Nicht jede dieser Formen kann sich durchsetzen, nicht jede stirbt deswegen aus. So auch bei der Fotobriefmarke. Zwar wurden Briefmarken mit fotografischen Motiven von den Postbehörden erst in den 1920er-Jahren herausgegeben. Doch erste private Aneignungen des Mediums lassen sich bis in die frühen 1860er-Jahre zurückverfolgen, als in den Fotoateliers die massenhafte Produktion von Porträts auf Papier begann und dabei verschiedene Formate erprobt wurden – bis hinunter zu dem von Briefmarken. Und dann wurden nicht nur die Formate übernommen, sondern auch Zacken-

PHOTO STAMPS

Photography and postal stamps entered common currency at almost the same time: the first usable photographs were published in 1839, and from May 1840, letters in Great Britain were franked with the Penny Black. Both media quickly spread around the world, and both revolutionized, each in its own way, how bourgeois societies organized their communications. Even early photographic processes were affordable enough that portraits were not only accessible to the upper and middle classes. And the stamp, together with the accompanying standardization process and drastic reduction in postage costs, enabled large-scale private and business correspondence for the first time.

New media are never pure: they are hybrids that incorporate and refer to other media. Not every one of these forms will prevail, nor will every one vanish as a result. This is also true for the photo stamp. It was only in the 1920s that postal authorities issued stamps with photographs as subjects. But the first independent appropriations of the medium can be traced back to the early 1860s, when photo studios began producing portraits on paper on a mass scale and testing various formats, including stamps. Not just their formats were adopted, but also their perforated edges, decorative shapes, and indications of value. Instruction books for amateur photographers presented

ränder, Schmuckformen, Wertangaben. Anleitungsbücher für Fotoamateure stellten verschiedene Methoden der Produktion solcher Bilder nebst ausführlichen Rezepten für die Gummierung der Fotopapiere vor, und Großhändler für Fotozubehör boten spezielle Kameras an, mit denen sich schon vorhandene Porträts als Briefmarken vervielfältigen ließen. Die Marken wurden in Alben und auf Postkarten geklebt, sie wurden als Werbe- und Sammelmarken adaptiert, und selbst für Tanzkarten und Briefköpfe wurde ihre Verwendung empfohlen. Große Verbreitung fanden die Fotobriefmarken allerdings nicht – zu groß war wohl die Konkurrenz der Cartes de Visite und anderer Porträtformate, zu klein waren die Bilder, um viel mehr zu sein als ein Scherzartikel oder ein Spielzeug.

Und doch mag genau darin der Reiz bestehen, der dazu führte, dass diese Marken immer wieder aufs Neue produziert wurden. Denn das Spiel endet ja nicht notwendig bei Bild und Zackenrand, sondern zuweilen wird den Marken auch ein Nominalwert gegeben. So wird die Marke zur Maske – war es eigentlich das Privileg gekrönter Häupter und anderer Prominenz, auf Briefmarken porträtiert zu werden, so suggerieren die Fotobriefmarken, dass nun auch der Tante oder dem Bruder solche Ehre zuteil geworden wäre. Zwar ist private Fotografie ohnedies eines der wichtigsten Medien, um die eigene Stellung besser erscheinen zu lassen als sie es tatsächlich ist – doch mit der Fotobriefmarke wird dieses soziale Upgrade gleichsam amtlich.

various means of producing such images, along with detailed recipes for gumming photographic paper. Photography equipment wholesalers offered special cameras that could be used to reproduce existing portraits as stamps. The stamps were stuck into albums and on postcards, they were repurposed as advertising and collector's stamps, and they were even recommended for use with dance cards and as letterheads. Yet photo stamps never became widely used: cartes de visite and other types of portraits offered stiff competition, and photo stamps were too small to be much more than novelty items or toys. And yet, it may be precisely for these reasons that such stamps constantly continued to be revisited. For the fun of stamps does not rest solely on the image and perforated edges; rather stamps sometimes take on a nominal value. In this way, stamps become a mask, and the privilege once reserved for royalty and other prominent figures of being depicted on a stamp may now be conferred on an aunt or brother, or at least this is what a stamp suggests. Regardless of such concerns, personal photographs are one of the most important means of upgrading one's standing, yet a photo stamp is a way of making such a social upgrade feel official.

Text: Friedrich Tietjen

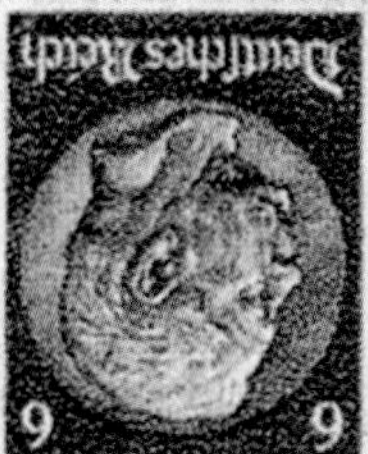
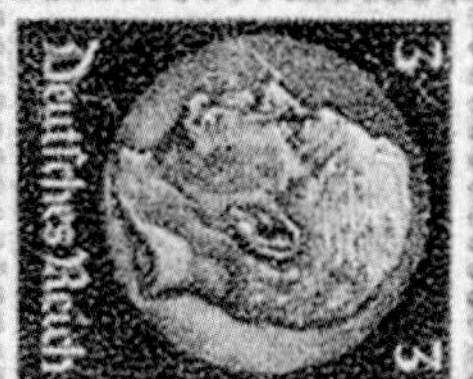
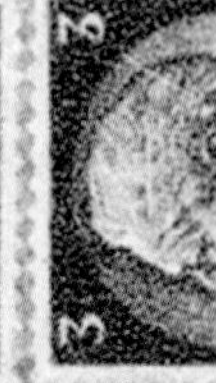
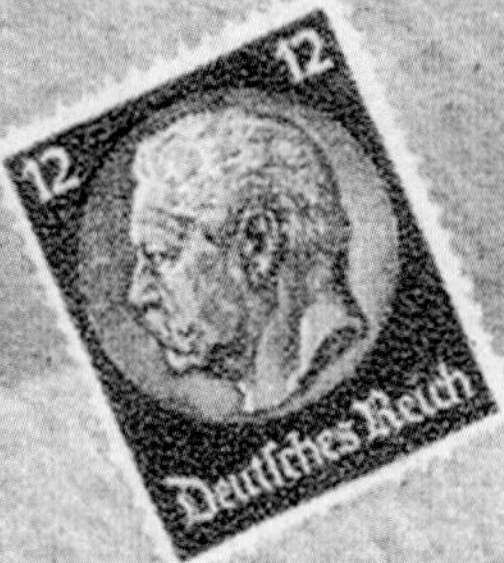
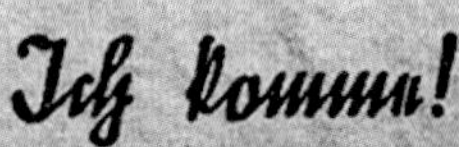
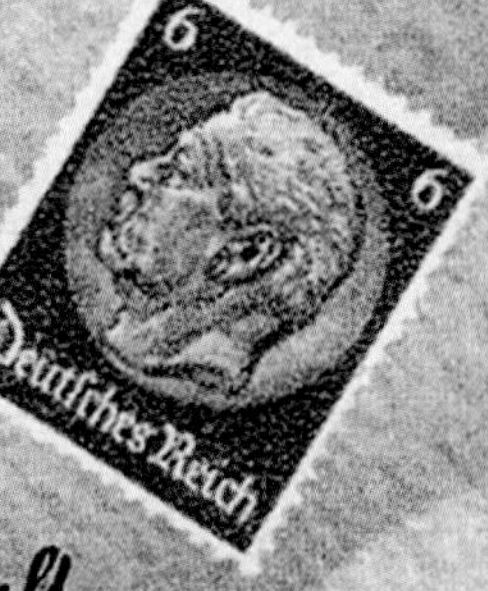
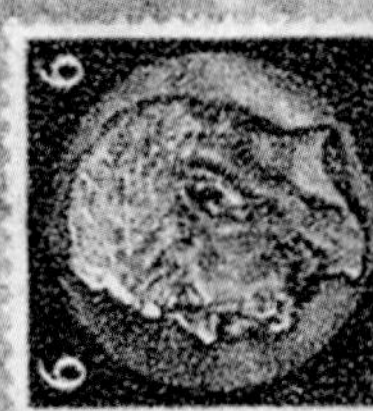
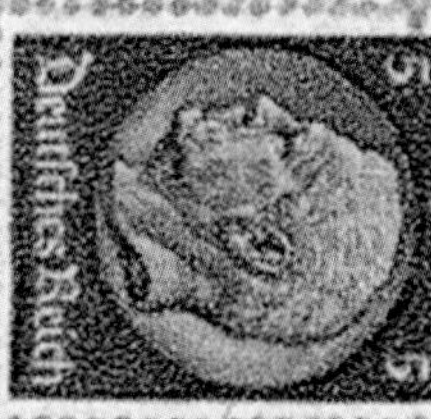
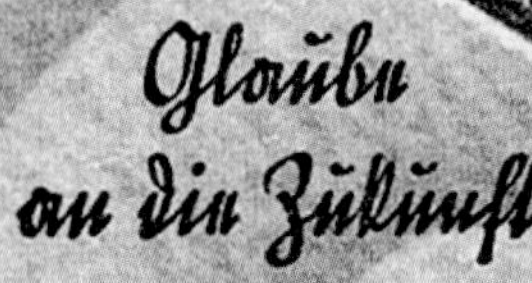
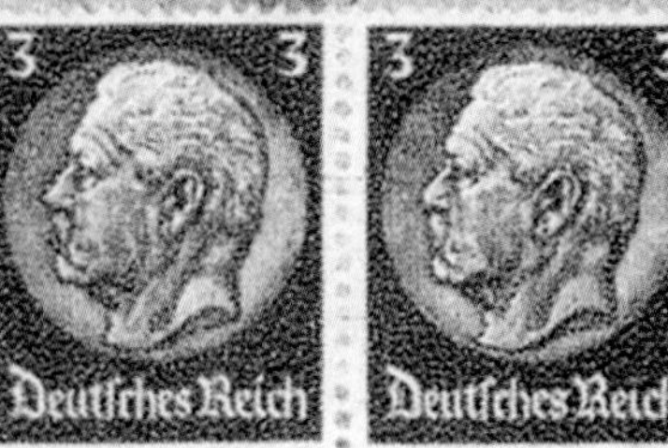
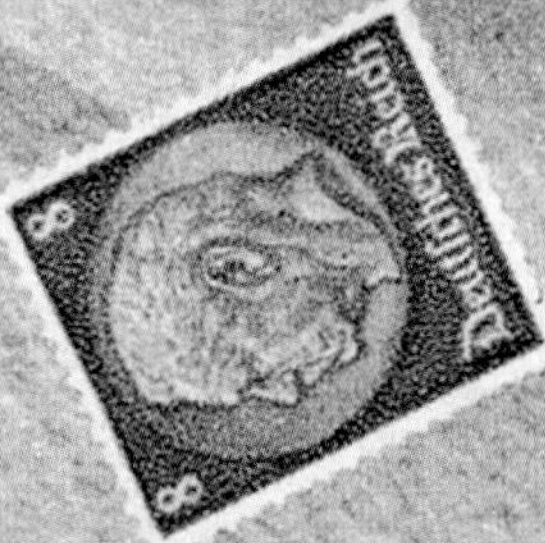
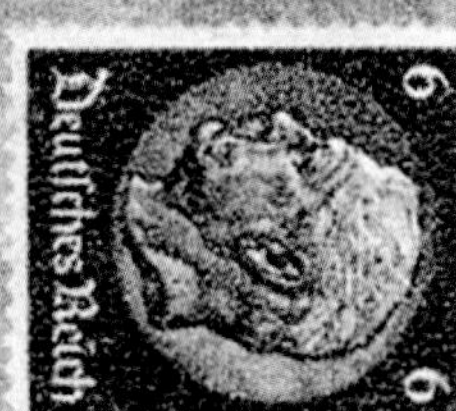

Horns Bild-Postkarten
Briefmarken-Sprache (The Language of Stamps), ca. 1920

Ich bin
Dein,
Du bist
mein

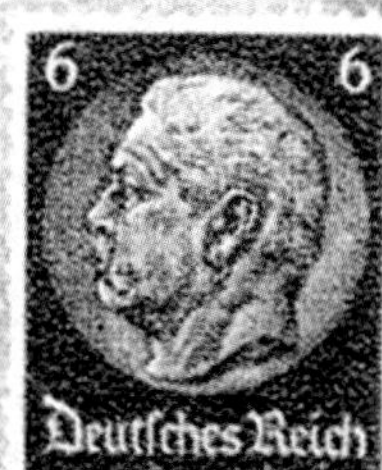

Ich denke stets an Dich

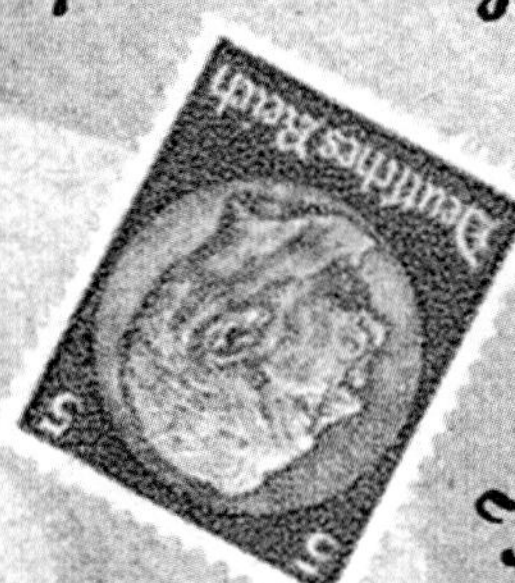

Treib
mich nicht
zur Eifersucht

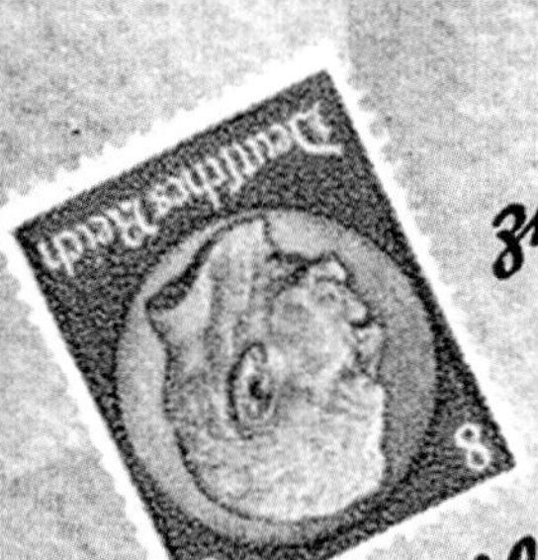

Liebste,
glaub an mich

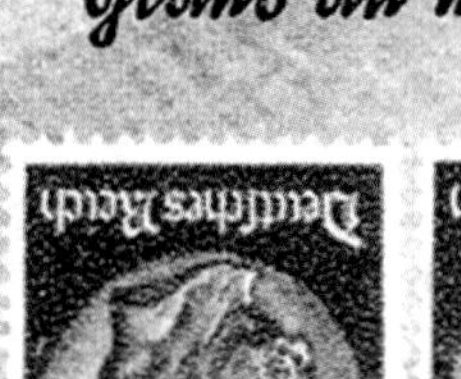

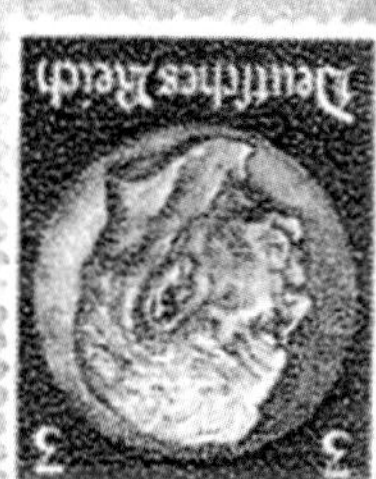

Ich denke nur
an Dich allein

-Sprache

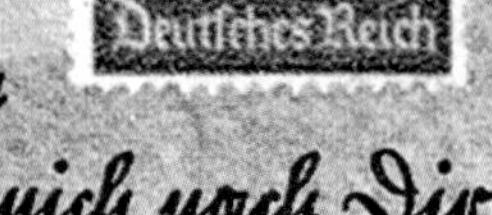

Ich
sehne
mich nach Dir

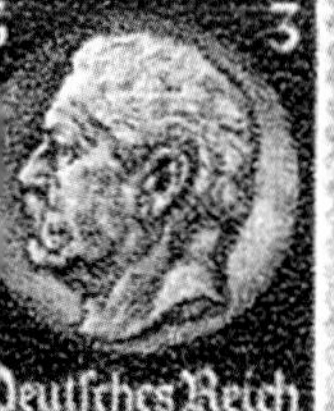

fühle mich
so einsam

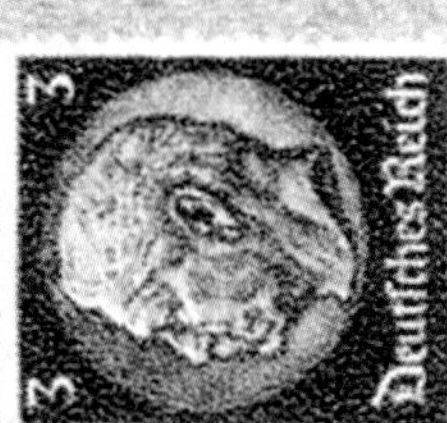

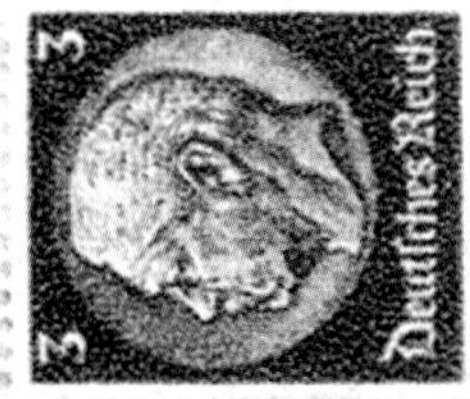

Nur mir allein gehörst Du

Films-Halter für Einzel-Planfilms.

Mit Hilfe dieses Halters können Einzel-Planfilms irgendwelchen Fabrikates in der gewöhnlichen Kassette von Glasplatten verwendet werden. Der Halter besteht aus einer Papp-Rückwand und einem dünnen, steifen Metallrahmen.

per Dutzend: in 6×9 Fr. 2.80   in 9×12 Fr. 3.75   in 13×18 Fr. 6.25

Kassetten- und Camera-Bürste

zum Säubern der Kassetten und des Camera-Innern. Manche Platte geht durch Staubflecken verloren; die Ursache ist meist nicht bei der Platte zu suchen, sondern liegt in dem Umstand, daß sich mit der Zeit Staub in Kassette und Camera-Innern ansammelt, der durch das Herausziehen des Balges aufgewirbelt wird. Preis Fr. 1.—

Filmpack-Kassetten.

Jede Glasplatten-Camera kann durch Anpassung einer Filmpack-Kassette in eine bei Tageslicht zn ladende Films-Camera verwandelt werden. Das Gewicht der in diesen Kassetten zu verwendenden Filmpacks ist ¹/₆ des Gewichtes von Glasplatten. Der Filmpack macht unabhängig vom Dunkelzimmer und ist bequem in beliebigen Mengen nachzutragen.

Zu den in diesem Katalog notierten Cameras suche man die passenden Filmpack-Kassetten an jener Stelle.

Filmpack-Kassetten in Form Fig. 1 (siehe Seite 140) vorhanden in 6×9, 9×12, 10×15, 13×18 cm
" " " " 2 " " 6×9, 9×12, 9×14 cm
" " " " 3 " " 9×12, 10×15, 13×18 cm
" " " " 4 " " 9×12

Preise: Format	6×9	9×12	9×14	10×15	13×18 cm
Fr.	6.60	6.80	9.50	9.50	12.50

Einlage für 9×12 cm Filmpack-Kassetten zur Benützung von Packfilms 8×10¹/₂ cm Fr. —.60
Einfache Filmpack-Kassette 9×12 cm, für Benützung von 8×10¹/₂ cm Packfilms, Form 1, 3 und 5 . . . . Fr. 5.—

Platten-Adapter für Kodaks.

Die Kodaks 3, 3a, 4 und 4a können mit Hilfe dieses Rückdeckels und der Kassetten auch für Platten eingerichtet werden. Die Benutzung der Platten kann neben der des Films geschehen, d. h. es kann nach Belieben abgewechselt werden.

Adapter allein, mit	für Nr. 3	3a	4	4a
Mattscheibe	Fr. 13.—	13.—	13.—	19.—
Doppel-Kassetten p. Stück	5.—	6.—	7.—	8.—

Diese Apparate werden auch mit Einrichtung für Packfilms ausgerüstet. Preise auf Anfrage.

Multiplikator-Kassetten für Briefmarken-Photographien etc.

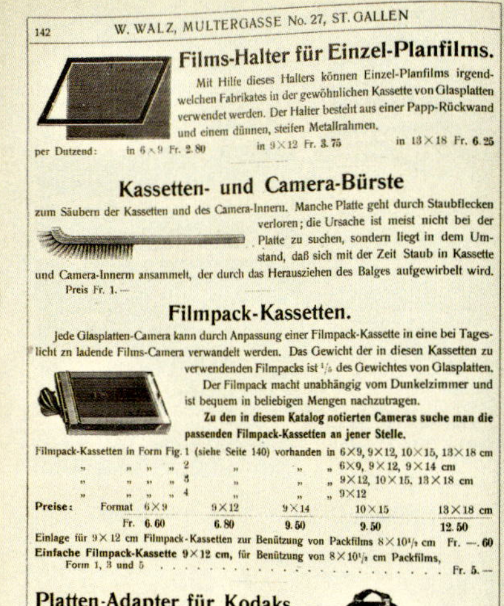

Der Multiplikator besteht aus einem schwarz polierten Rahmen, nicht größer als eine 13×18 cm Kassette, aus einer kleinen Einstellscheibe und einer Kassette 9×12 cm. Mit diesem Multiplikator, der sich an jeder 13×18 cm oder 18×24 cm Camera anpassen läßt, kann man ohne Schwierigkeit auf eine 9×12 cm Platte zwölf Photographien in Briefmarkengröße oder sechs Aufnahmen 40×32 mm in denkbar kürzester Zeit (1 bis 2 Minuten) unter Benutzung des bereits am Apparat befindlichen Objektivs anfertigen. Die Aufnahme kann nach einer als Vorlage dienenden Photographie oder auch direkt nach der Person gemacht werden.

Die Einsendung einer Camera-Kassette ist erforderlich.
Größe I für Cameras bis 13×18 cm komplett . . Fr. 27.—
" II " 18×24 " " . . " 30.—
Anpassungskosten Fr. 4.— bis 7.50

Camera-Ansätze

dienen zur Verlängerung (13 cm) des Camera-Auszuges. Ein Ansatz ist

1. anwendbar für alle 9×12 cm Cameras, die einfachen Auszug haben und die mit Hilfe des Ansatzes Aufnahmen von sehr nahen Gegenständen ermöglichen, oder bei vorhandenem symmetrischem Objektiv die Anwendung der Hinterlinse gestatten, was für Bergaufnahmen von eminentem Vorteil ist;

2. anwendbar für alle 9×12 cm Cameras einfachen oder doppelten Auszuges, um die in Abteilung II (Objektive) aufgeführten Telelinsen Vedo benützen zu können.

Ausführung I dient zur Verlängerung, flach zusammenlegbar Fr. 18.75 Anpassungskosten keine bis ca. Fr. 5.—, je nach Camerasorte.

Ausführung II dient zur Verlängerung des Balges und zur Vergrößerung des Aufnahmeformates auf 13×18 cm, wozu das 9×12 cm Objektiv bei entsprechender Abblendung gut ausreicht. Der Ansatz ist ebenfalls flach zusammenlegbar.

Preis einschließlich Einstellrahmen und Doppel-Kassette Fr. 56.—
Anpassungskosten keine bis Fr. 5.—, je nach Camerasorte. Die Camera ist einzusenden.

Briefmarken-Camera „Stephan"

Praktisch! Elegant! Preiswert!

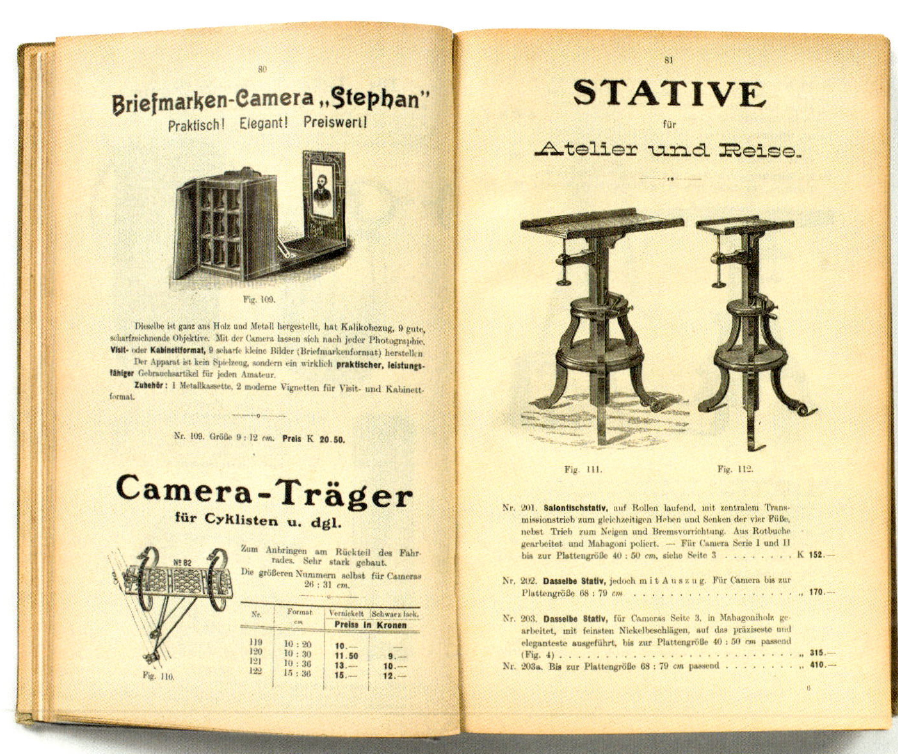

Fig. 109.

Dieselbe ist ganz aus Holz und Metall hergestellt, hat Kalikobezug, 9 gute, scharfzeichnende Objektive. Mit der Camera lassen sich nach jeder Photographie. **Visit-** oder **Kabinettformat,** 9 scharfe kleine Bilder (Briefmarkenformat) herstellen

Der Apparat ist kein Spielzeug, sondern ein wirklich **praktischer, leistungsfähiger** Gebrauchsartikel für jeden Amateur.

Zubehör: 1 Metallkassette, 2 moderne Vignetten für Visit- und Kabinettformat.

Nr. 109. Größe 9 : 12 *cm.* **Preis K 20.50.**

Camera-Träger

für Cyklisten u. dgl.

Zum Anbringen am Rückteil des Fahrrades. Sehr stark gebaut.

Die größeren Nummern selbst für Cameras 26 : 31 *cm.*

Nr.	Format cm	Vernickelt	Schwarz lack.
		Preise in Kronen	
119	10 : 20	10.—	—
120	10 : 30	11.50	9.—
121	10 : 36	13.—	10.—
122	15 : 36	15.—	12.—

Fig. 110.

STATIVE

für

Atelier und Reise.

Fig. 111.   Fig. 112.

Nr. 201. **Salontischstativ,** auf Rollen laufend, mit zentralem Transmissionstrieb zum gleichzeitigen Heben und Senken der vier Füße, nebst Trieb zum Neigen und Bremsvorrichtung. Aus Rotbuche gearbeitet und Mahagoni poliert. — Für Camera Serie I und II bis zur Plattengröße 40 : 50 *cm,* siehe Seite 3 . . . . K **152.—**

Nr. 202. **Dasselbe Stativ,** jedoch m i t A u s z u g. Für Camera bis zur Plattengröße 68 : 79 *cm* . . . . „ **170.—**

Nr. 203. **Dasselbe Stativ,** für Cameras Seite 3, in Mahagoniholz gearbeitet, mit feinsten Nickelbeschlägen, auf das präziseste und eleganteste ausgeführt, bis zur Plattengröße 40 : 50 *cm* passend (Fig. 4) . . . . „ **315.—**

Nr. 203a. Bis zur Plattengröße 68 : 79 *cm* passend . . . . „ **410.—**

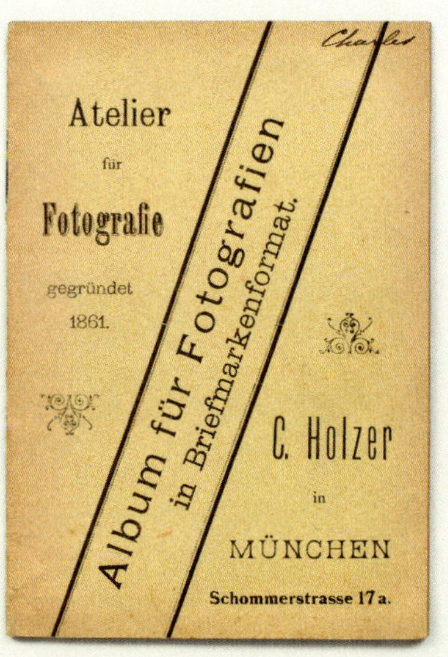

Charles
Atelier
für
Fotografie
gegründet
1861.
Album für Fotografien
in Briefmarkenformat.
C. Holzer
in
MÜNCHEN
Schommerstrasse 17 a.

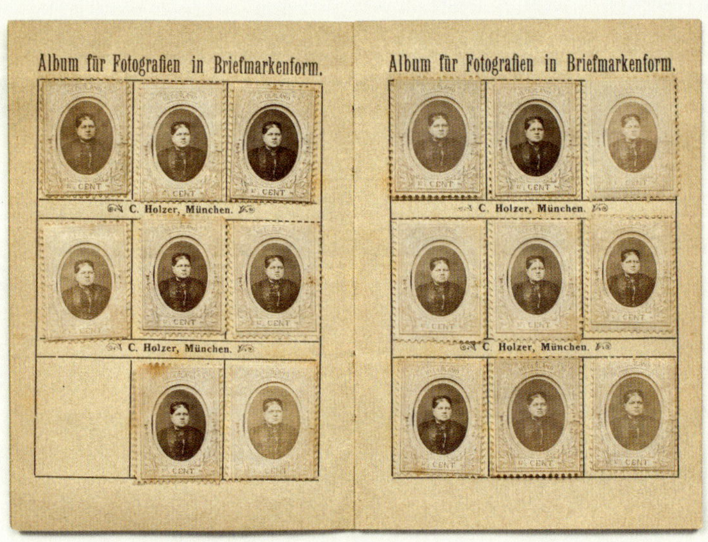

Album für Fotografien in Briefmarkenform.
Album für Fotografien in Briefmarkenform.
C. Holzer, München.
C. Holzer, München.
C. Holzer, München.
C. Holzer, München.

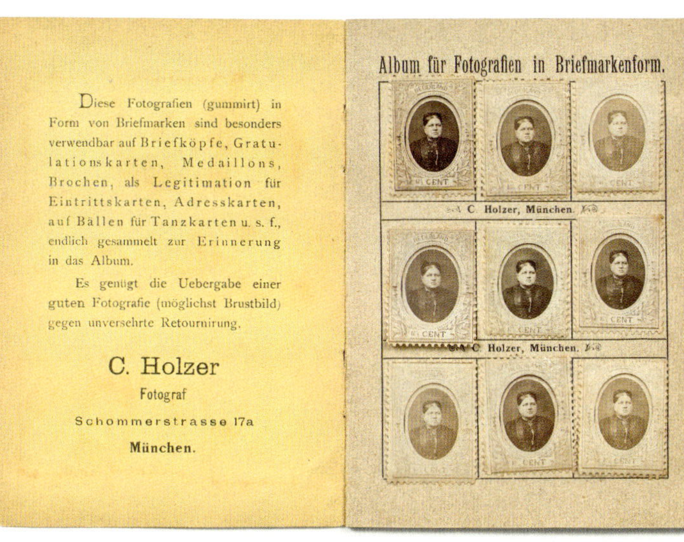

Diese Fotografien (gummirt) in
Form von Briefmarken sind besonders
verwendbar auf Briefköpfe, Gratu-
lationskarten, Medaillons,
Brochen, als Legitimation für
Eintrittskarten, Adresskarten,
auf Bällen für Tanzkarten u. s. f.,
endlich gesammelt zur Erinnerung
in das Album.

Es genügt die Uebergabe einer
guten Fotografie (möglichst Brustbild)
gegen unversehrte Retournirung.

C. Holzer

Fotograf

Schommerstrasse 17a

München

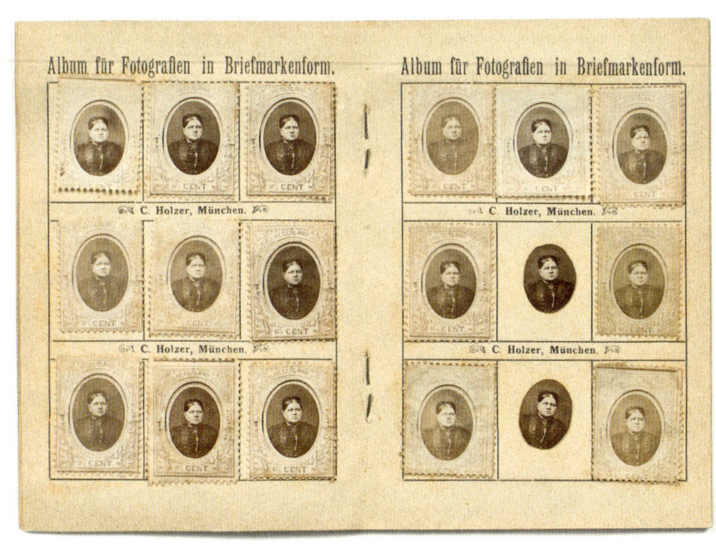

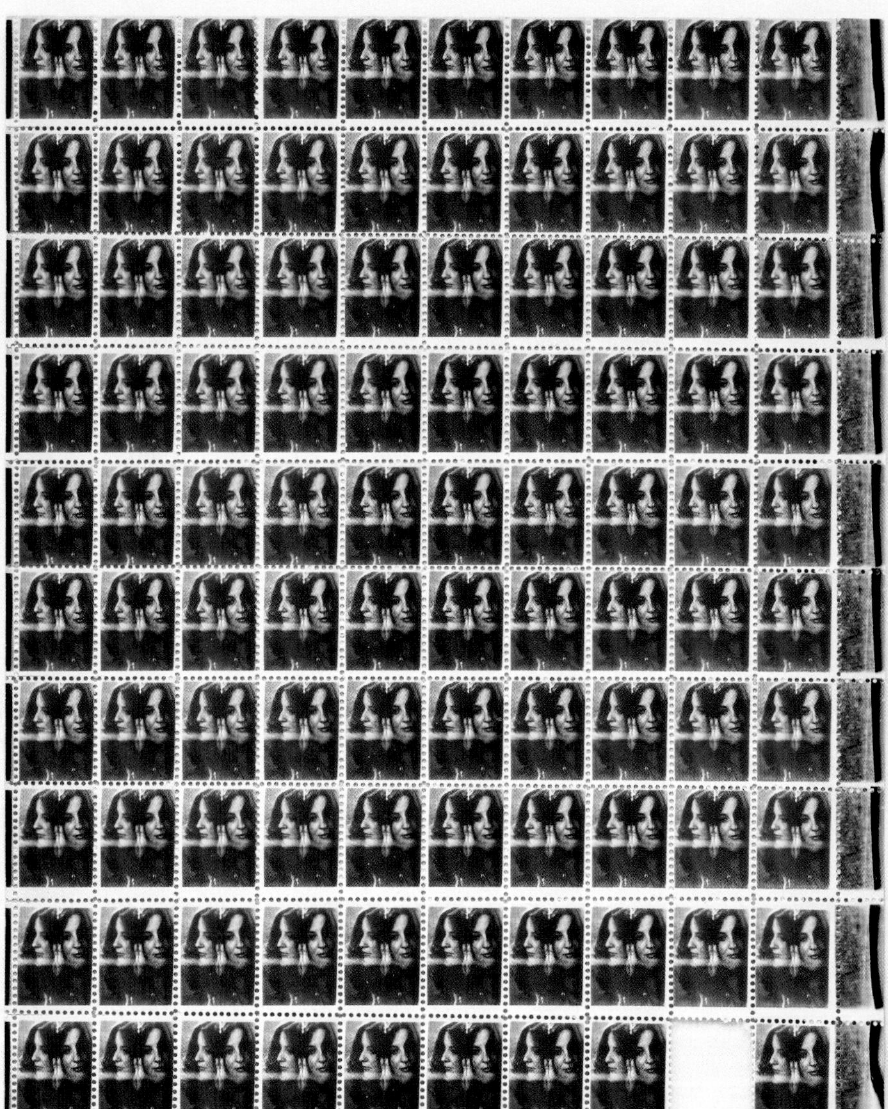

Lynn Hershman Leeson
Identity Face Stamps, 1966–1972

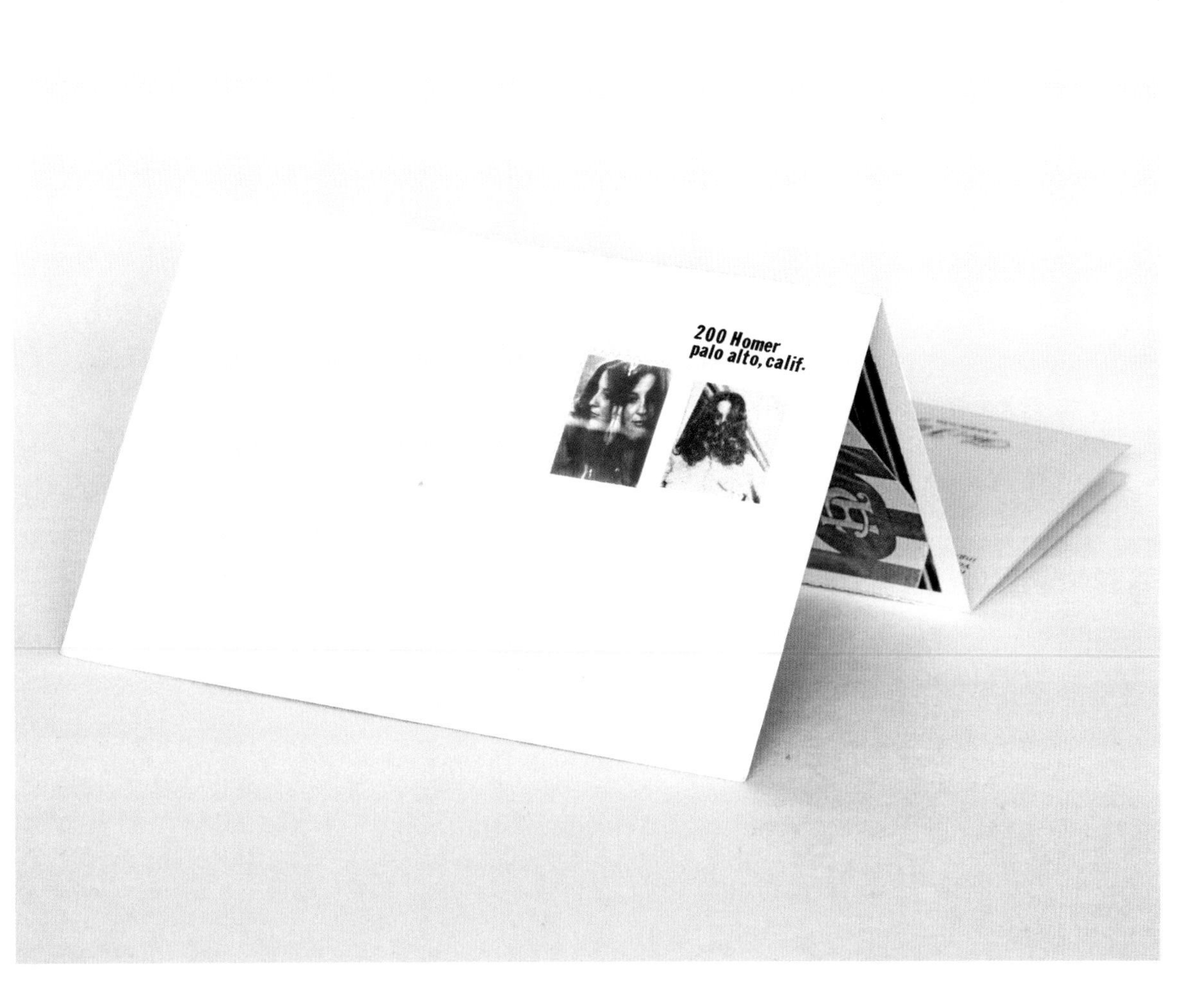

Lynn Hershman Leeson
Museum of Mott Art, 1974, Einladungpostkarte mit montierter Briefmarke / **Postcard invitation with mounted stamp**

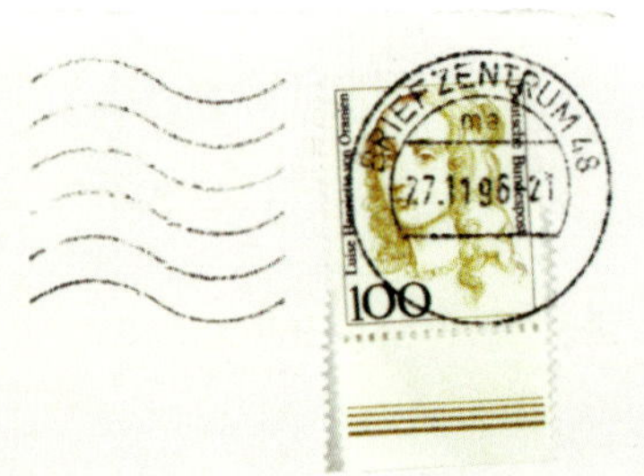

Andreas Slominski
Ohne Titel / Untitled, 1996, Briefkuvert mit von einer Giraffe angefreuchteten Briefmarke /
Envelope with stamp licked by a giraffe

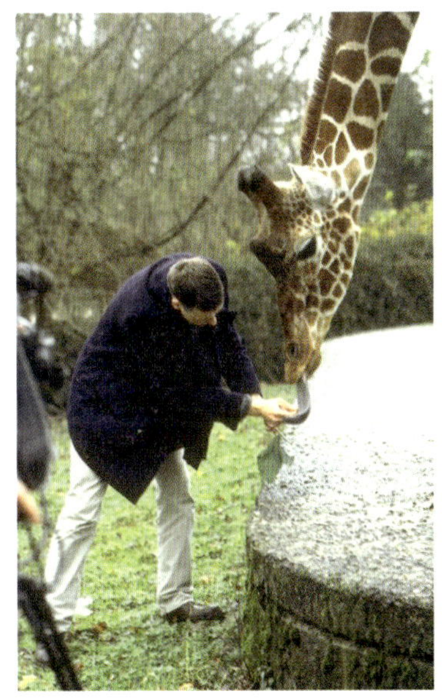

Andreas Slominski
Anfeuchten der Briefmarke / Moistening the Stamp, 1996

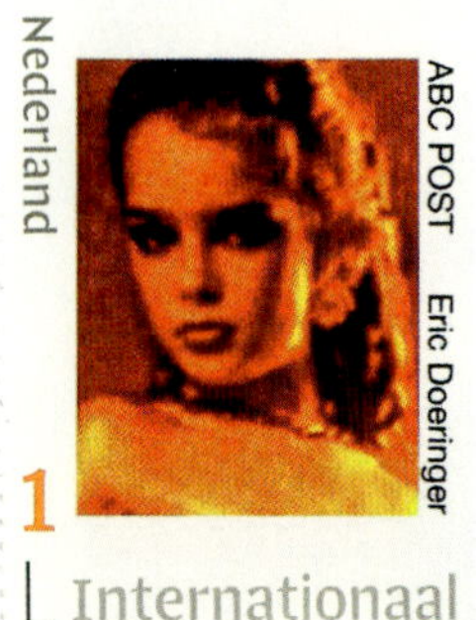

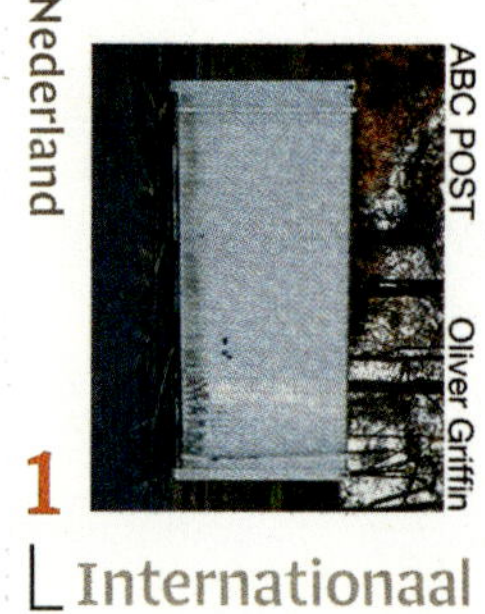

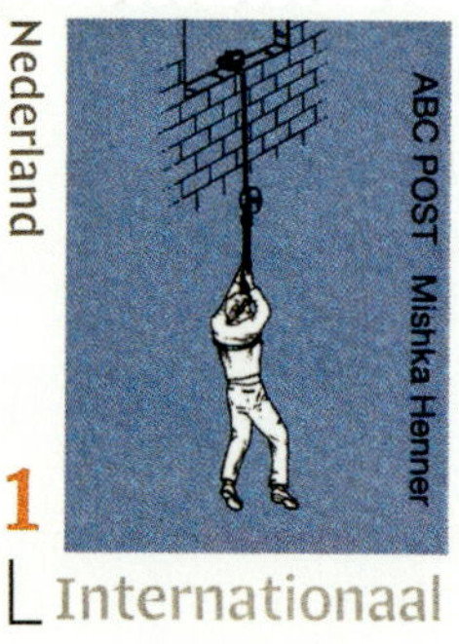

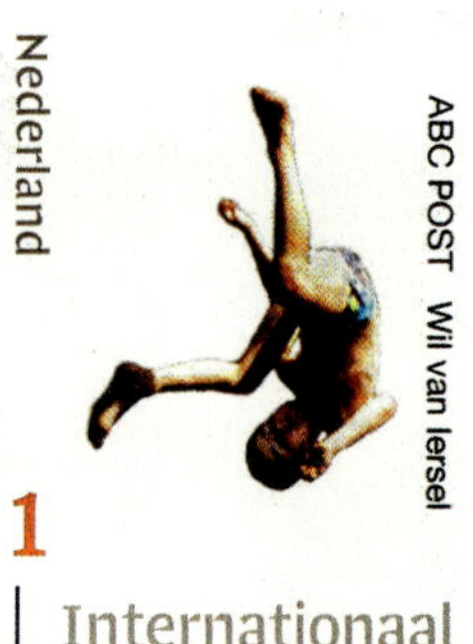

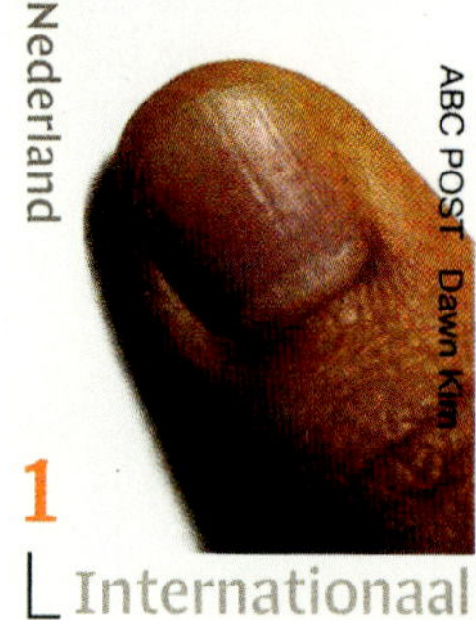

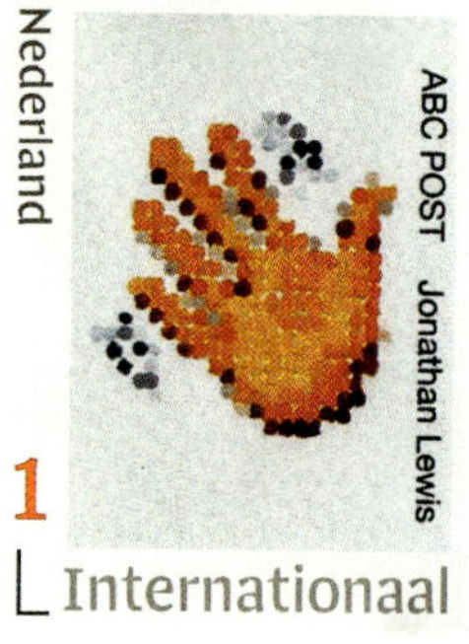

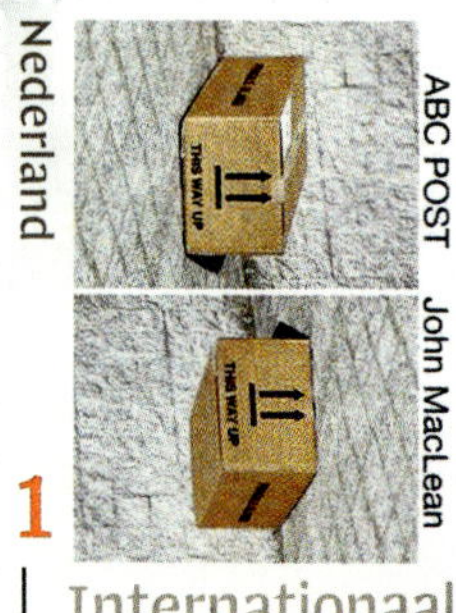

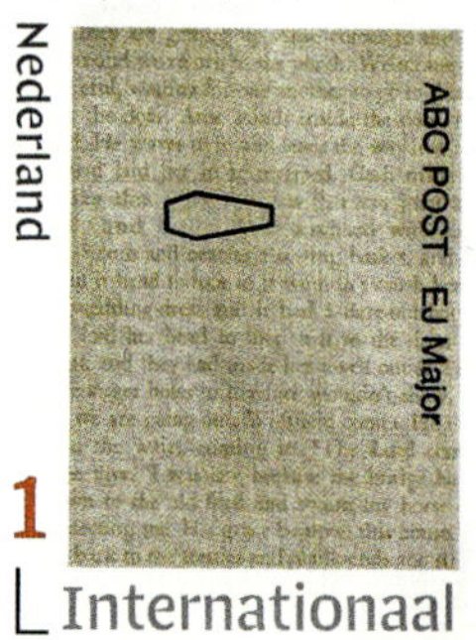

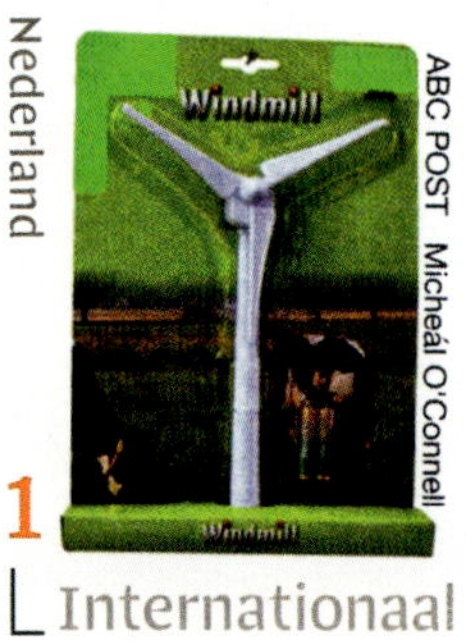

ABC Artists' Books Cooperative
ABC Post, 2020

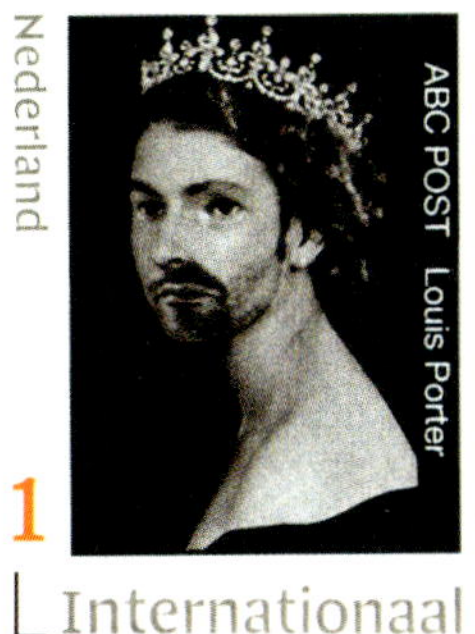

Nederland
ABC POST Louis Porter
1
Internationaal

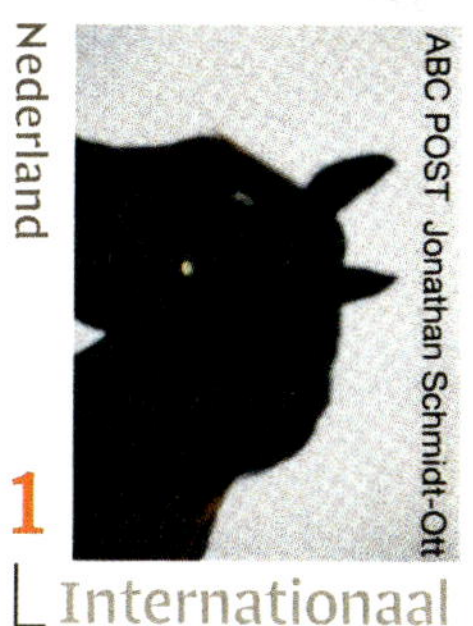

Nederland
ABC POST Jonathan Schmidt-Ott
1
Internationaal

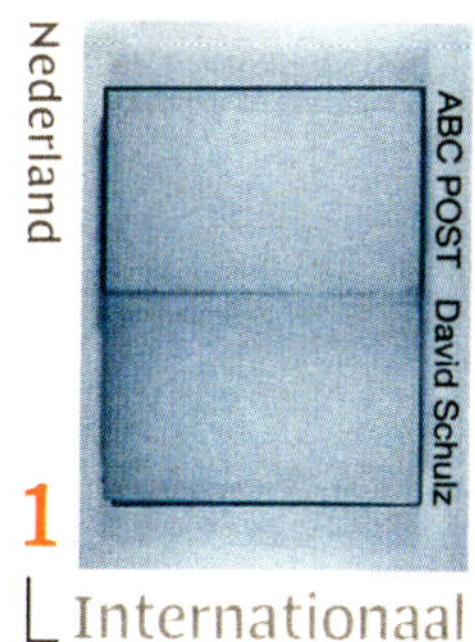

Nederland
ABC POST David Schulz
1
Internationaal

Nederland
ABC POST Travis Shaffer
WASH
BEFORE
READING
1
Internationaal

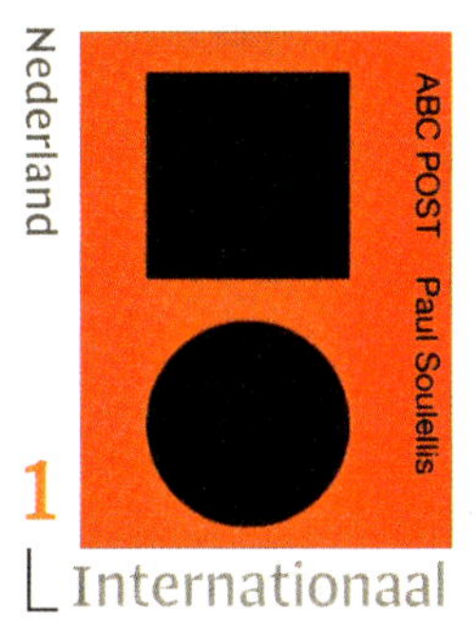

Nederland
ABC POST Paul Soulellis
1
Internationaal

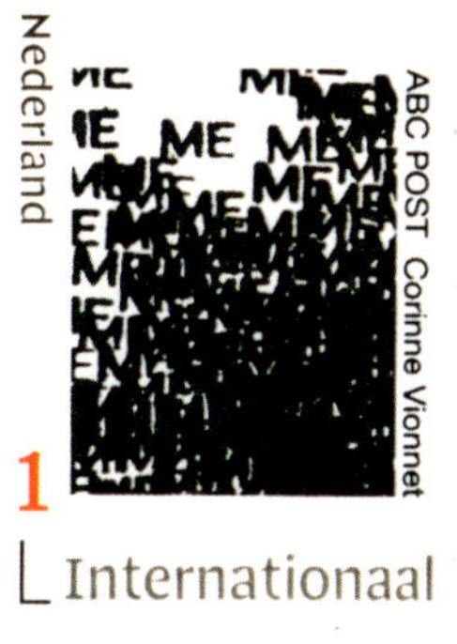

Nederland
ABC POST Corinne Vionnet
1
Internationaal

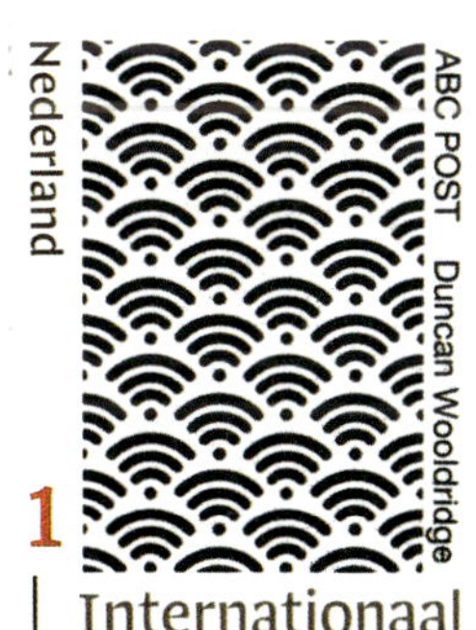

Nederland
ABC POST Duncan Wooldridge
1
Internationaal

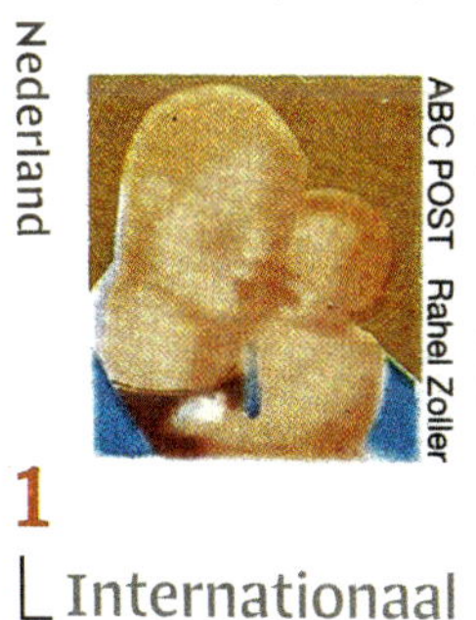

Nederland
ABC POST Rahel Zoller
1
Internationaal

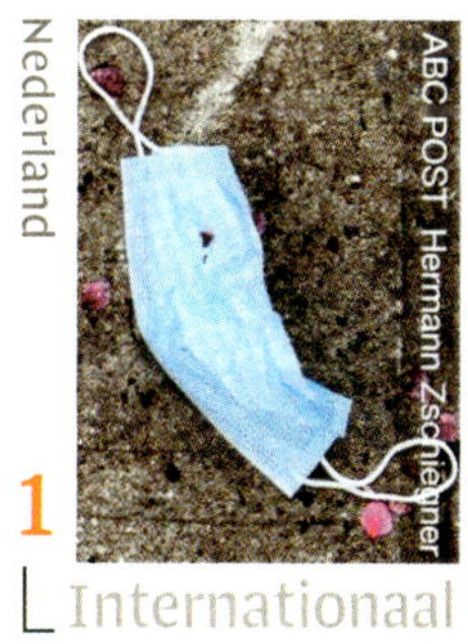

Nederland
ABC POST Hermann Zschiegner
1
Internationaal

ABC POST
https://abcoop.tumblr.com/abcpost

1 Internationaal

The Bucklows

United Kingdom

ABC POST
https://abcoop.tumblr.com/abcpost

1 Internationaal

Jonathan Lewis

USA

ABC POST
https://abcoop.tumblr.com/abcpost

AMSTERDAM
Nederland
ABC POST Jonathan Lewis
1
Internationaal

Mishka Henner

United Kingdom

ABC POST
https://abcoop.tumblr.com/abcpost

AMSTERDAM
Nederland
ABC POST Jonathan Lewis
1
Internationaal

Andreas Schmidt

Germany

Postcon
MAU
049/121-2/013- -13 2003
000004718

POSTKARTE

Obwohl die Postkarte Ende der 1860er-Jahre zunächst auf schriftliche Mitteilungen beschränkt war, sickerten Bilder und Bildlichkeit in Form von Vignetten und kleinen Drucken schon wenig später in das Medium ein. Zur Ansichtskarte wurde sie erst Anfang der 1870er-Jahre; privat hergestellte Karten wurden im Deutschen Reich ab 1872 zugelassen. Wann zuerst fotografische Bilder auf Postkarten erschienen, lässt sich nicht genau bestimmen; erste Beispiele lassen sich in den späten 1880er-Jahren nachweisen. Einen genauen Zeitpunkt festlegen zu wollen ist auch deswegen müßig, weil die Bilder der ab den 1890er-Jahren populären Ansichtskarten zwar meist (chromo-)lithografisch gedruckt, aber oft nach fotografischen Vorlagen angefertigt wurden.

Solche Ansichtskarten wurden schnell populär, und die Motive beschränkten sich keineswegs auf landschaftliche Motive – in Deutschland nutzte das Kaiserhaus das Medium, um sich mal volksnah, mal prunkvoll zu inszenieren, es gab scherzhafte, sentimentale, politische und Werbepostkarten, an Wallfahrtsorten, dem Eiffelturm und Badestränden nahmen ambulante Fotograf*innen Gruppenbilder auf und boten sie später als Karten an, und dass Privatpersonen ihre Studioporträts oder auch eigene Aufnahmen verschickten wurde dadurch befördert, dass auf der Rückseite der entsprechenden Fotopapierformate häufig schon die Adresslinien aufgedruckt wurden.

POSTCARDS

In the late 1860s, postcards were still limited to written messages, yet images and pictoriality permeated the medium shortly thereafter in the form of vignettes and small photo prints. The picture postcard per se only emerged in the early 1870s; privately produced postcards were permitted in the German Reich from 1872. It is impossible to determine when exactly photographs first appeared on postcards; initial examples can be found in the late 1880s. It is also futile to try and determine a specific point in time because images on the postcards popular from the 1890s were printed using chromolithography yet created based on photographs.

Such postcards quickly became widespread, and the subjects depicted were by no means limited to landscapes. In Germany, the imperial family used the medium to depict itself sometimes as close to commoners, and sometimes as grand. There were jokey, sentimental, political, and commercial postcards; postcards sold at places of pilgrimage; traveling photographers at the Eiffel Tower and on beaches took group photographs and later offered them as cards; and the preprinted address lines on the back of the cards encouraged individuals to send their studio portraits and even their own photographs.

Postcards were first used on a large scale to send brief messages quickly during the Franco-Prussian War of 1870–71 and then became perhaps the most important medium of personal communication for several decades. Given the fact that postcards featuring portraits of their senders seldom included

Als Medium knapper und schneller Mitteilungen wurden Postkarten in großer Zahl zuerst während des Deutsch-Französischen Krieges 1870/71 verwendet
und wurden danach für einige Jahrzehnte zum vielleicht wichtigsten Medium
privater Kommunikation. Zumal auf Karten mit den Aufnahmen der Sender steht
häufig nicht mehr als ein freundlicher Gruß oder die Erinnerung an einen gemeinsam verbrachten Tag – wichtig, so scheint es, ist dann nicht der Text oder
das Bild, sondern ihr Zusammenspiel.

Den Porträts aus dem Studio nimmt die beigefügte Notiz zuweilen die steife
Formalität der Pose; private Fotografien können mit Hinweisen auf die Aufnah-
mesituation versehen werden, und solche Hinweise sind auch auf den Ansichtskarten üblich. Mit anderen Worten: Der Text lenkt und verstärkt die Blickrichtung
auf das geschickte Bild: Hier sind wir grade. So sehe ich jetzt aus. Es war schön mit
dir. Herzlichen Glückwunsch! Die Popularität der Postkarte ließ nach dem Ersten
Weltkrieg deutlich nach – vor allem das Telefon löste sie als Mittel für kurze Mitteilungen ab. Dennoch brachte sie weiterhin neue Formen und Anwendungen
hervor – Postkarten werden bei Preisausschreiben eingesetzt, mit Schallrillen als
Klangpostkarten angeboten, Stars versehen ihre Porträts mit Autogrammen für
ihre Fans. Ihr Vorzug blieb dabei, dass sie relativ preisgünstig ist und dennoch
die Empfänger*innen wenigstens potentiell als einzelne adressiert – noch die im
Offset gedruckte Karte einer Wahlkampagne zielt auf Unmittelbarkeit und den
Aufbau einer persönlichen Beziehung. Und vielleicht sorgt eben diese Unmittelbarkeit dafür, dass die Postkarte von der E-Mail nicht verdrängt wird, so dass
auch heute noch in Deutschland jährlich mehr als 200 Millionen Postkarten pro
Jahr verschickt werden.

more than a friendly greeting or a brief recollection of a day spent together,
it seems that the interplay between text and image, rather than either alone,
was of importance.

The note included could ameliorate the stiff formality of studio portraits;
references to the context in which personal photographs were taken could
be included, and such details were indeed common on postcards. In other
words, the text directs and enhances the view of the image sent, declaring:
Here we are now. This is how I look now. I had fun with you. Congratulations!
The popularity of the postcard declined sharply after World War I, mostly
because the telephone replaced it as a means of communicating short messages. Nevertheless, the postcard continued to give rise to new forms and
applications. Postcards were used in competitions for prizes; sound postcards
with phonographic grooves became available; and stars signed portraits for
their fans. Their advantage remained their relative affordability paired with
the ability to address recipients individually: even the offset printed card for
an election campaign aims to establish an immediacy and a personal relationship. And perhaps it is precisely this immediacy that prevents the postcard
from being supplanted by emails, so that even now, Germans send more than
two hundred million postcards each year.

Text: Friedrich Tietjen

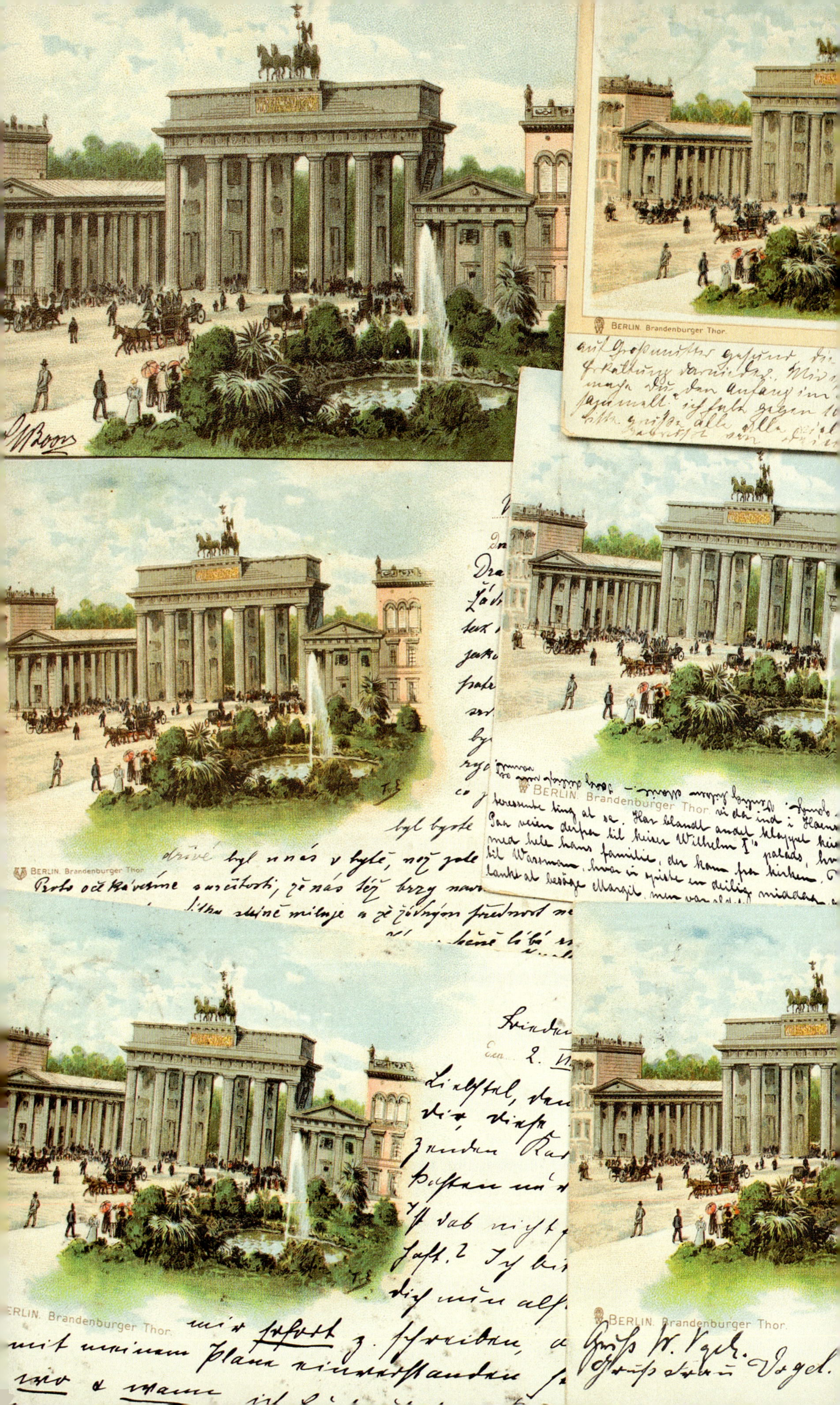

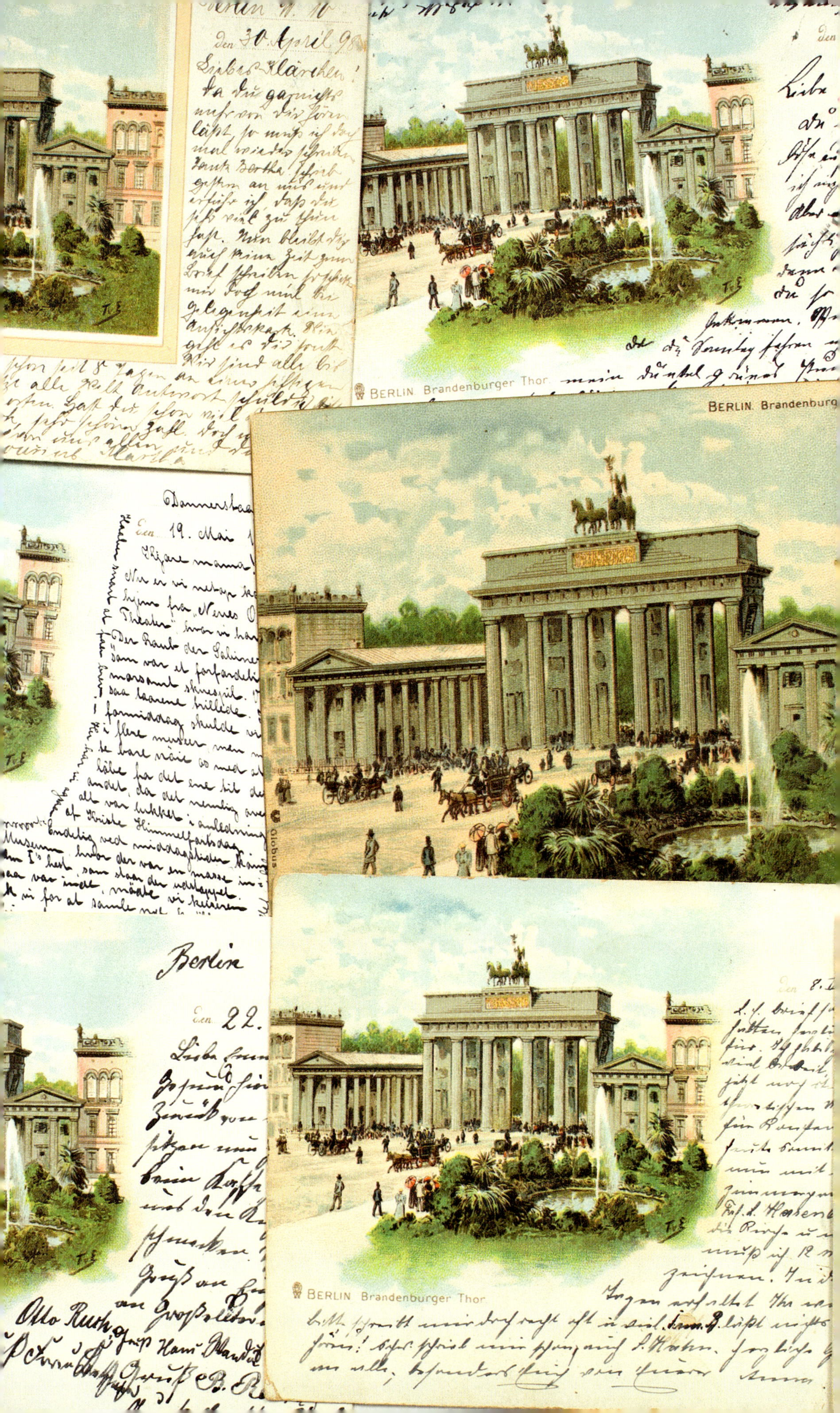
BERLIN Brandenburger Thor.
BERLIN. Brandenburg
Globus
BERLIN Brandenburger Thor.
Berlin
Den 30. April 98

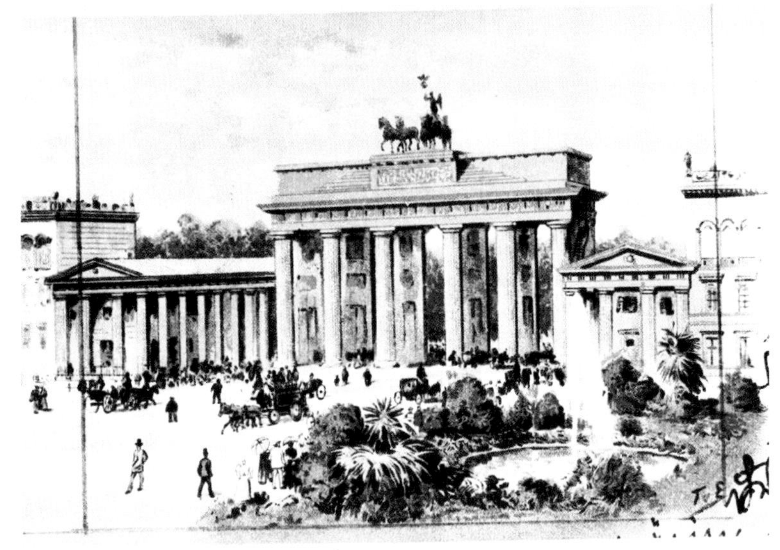

Z 26 432 Berlin, Brandenburger Tor von
NO. (nach altem Foto von 1878)

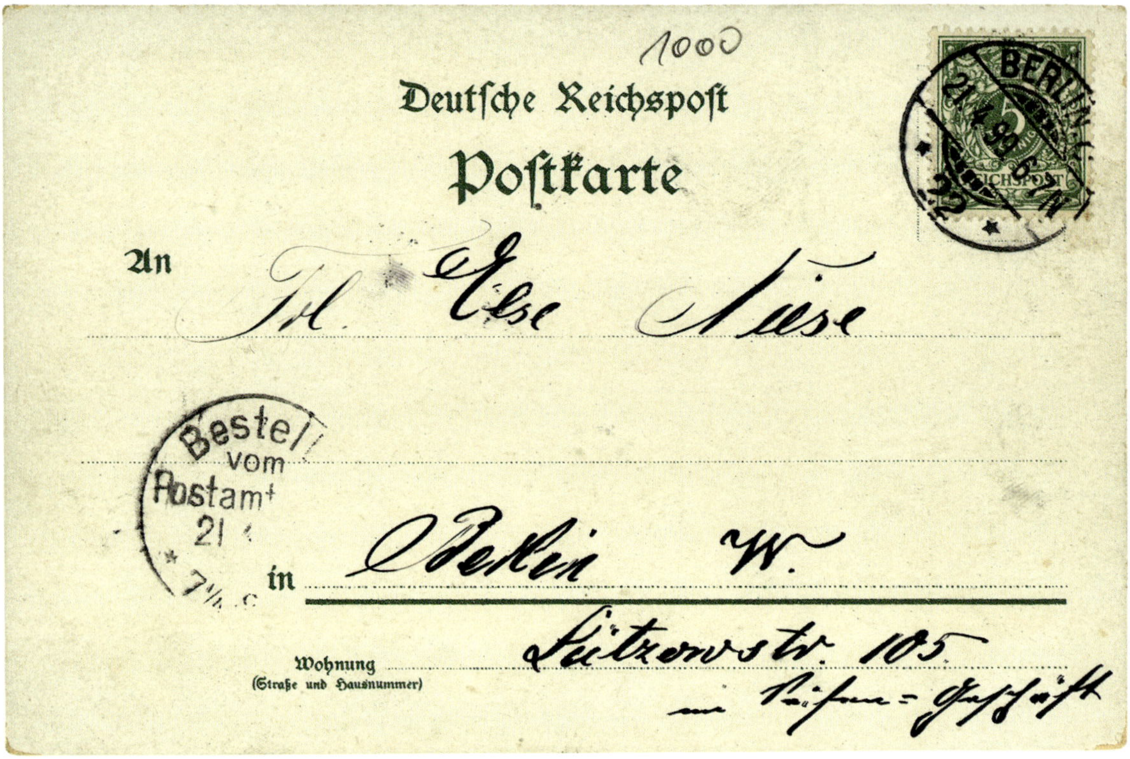

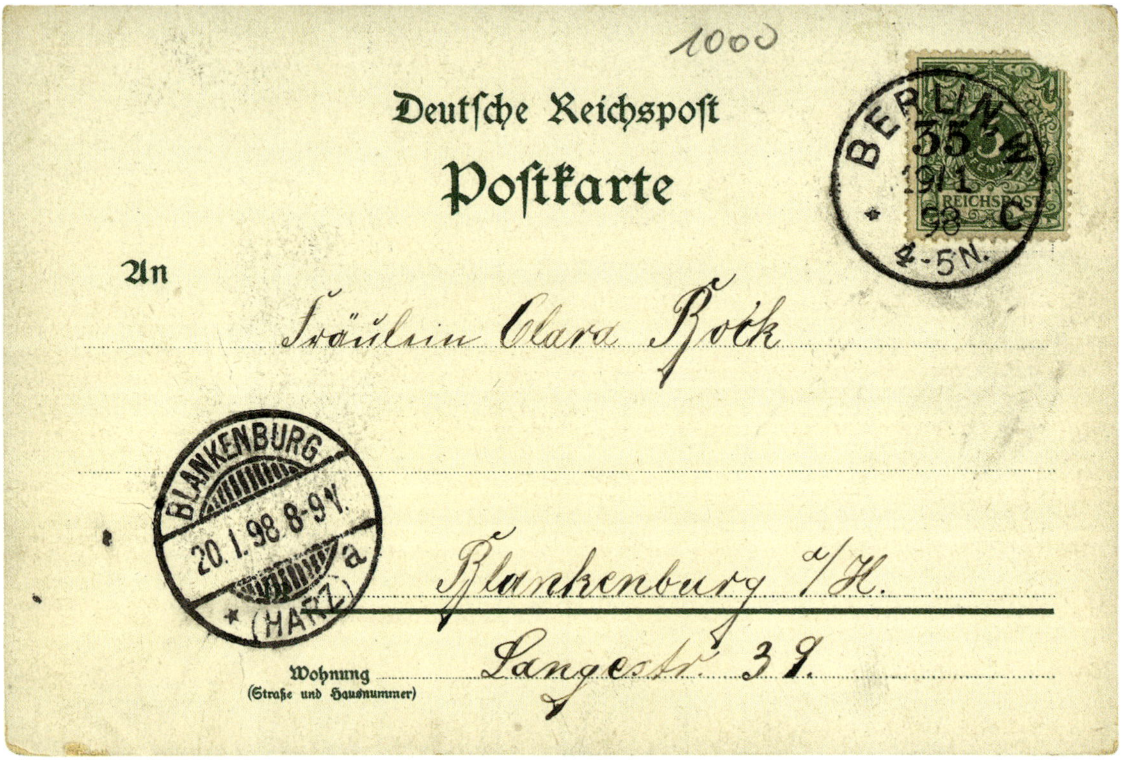

Deutsche Reichspost
Postkarte
An
in
Wohnung
(Straße und Hausnummer)

Deutsche Reichspost
Postkarte
An
Wohnung
(Straße und Hausnummer)

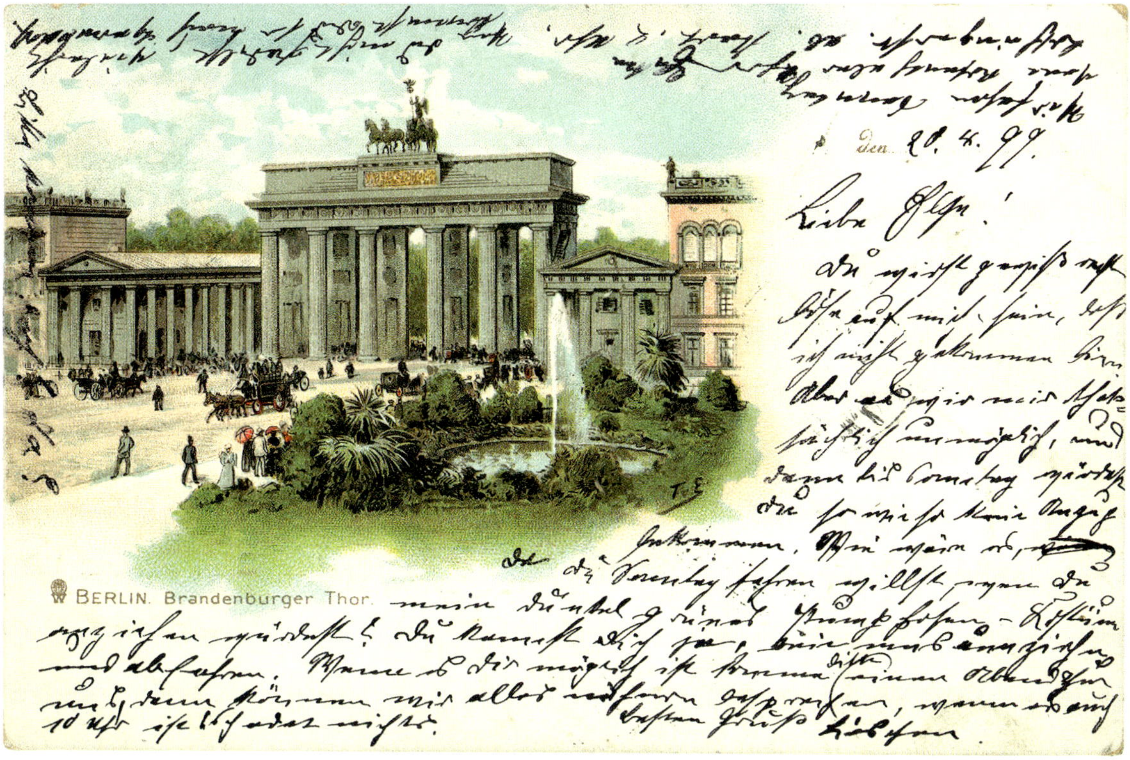

BERLIN. Brandenburger Thor.

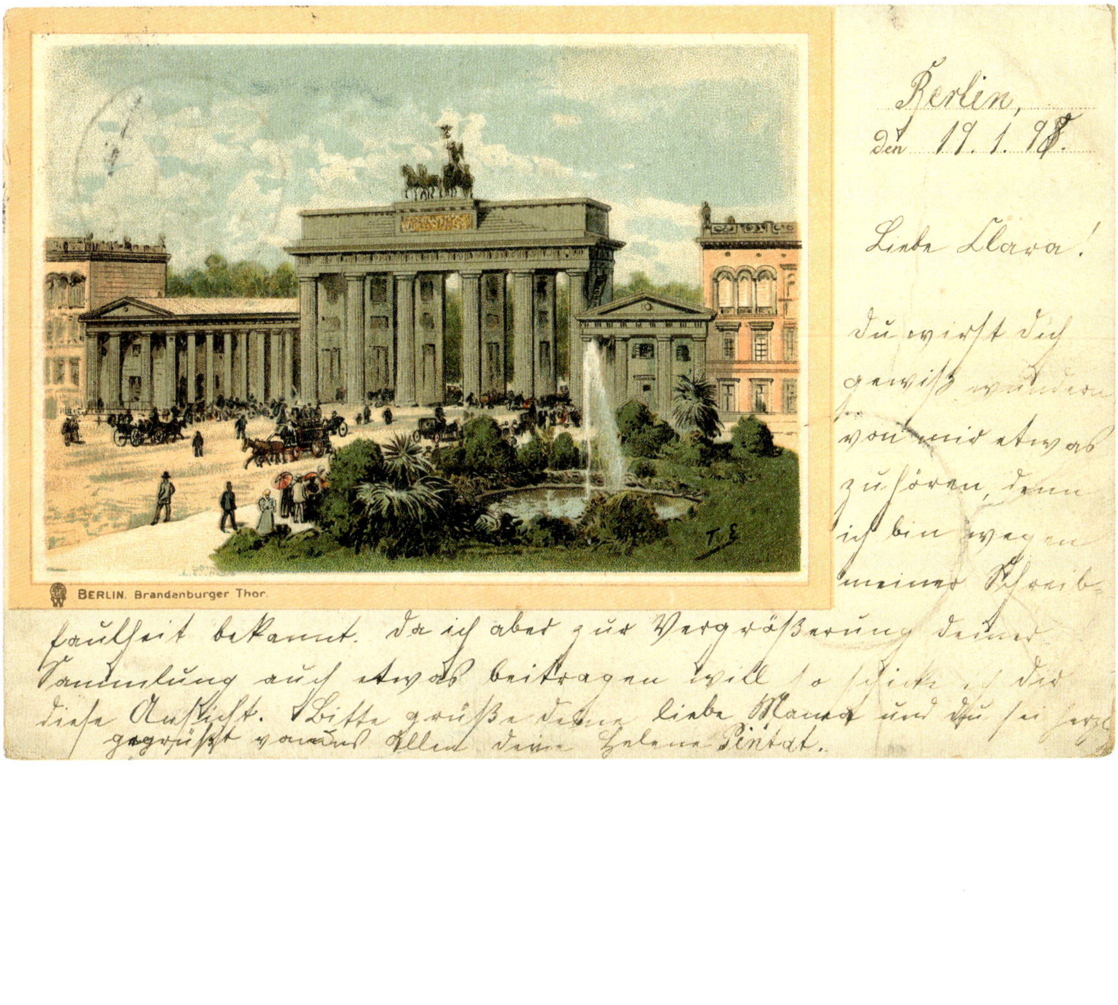

BERLIN. Brandenburger Thor.

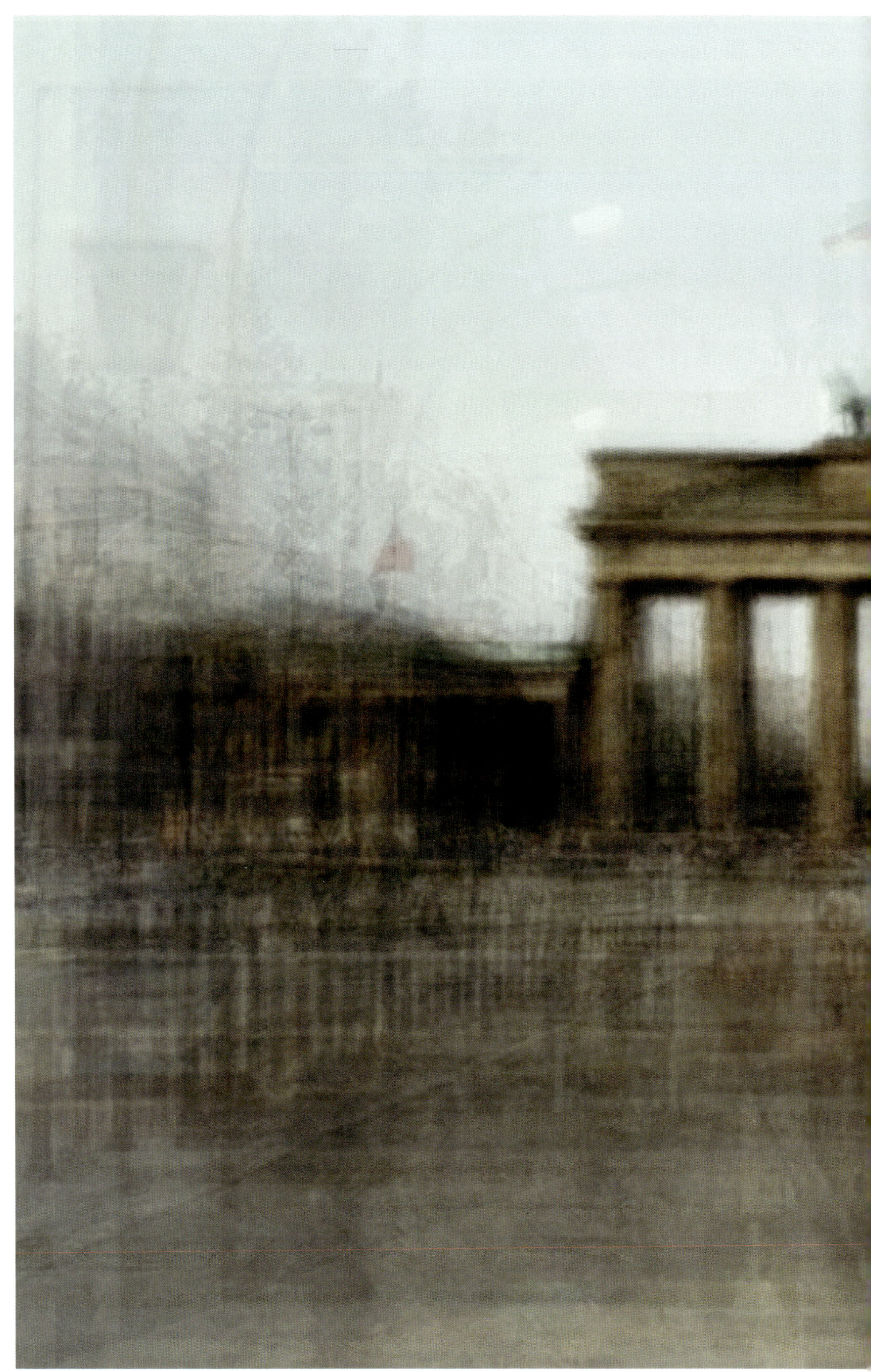

Corinne Vionnet
Berlin, 2006, a.d.S. / **from the series** *Photo Opportunities,* 2005–heute / **present**

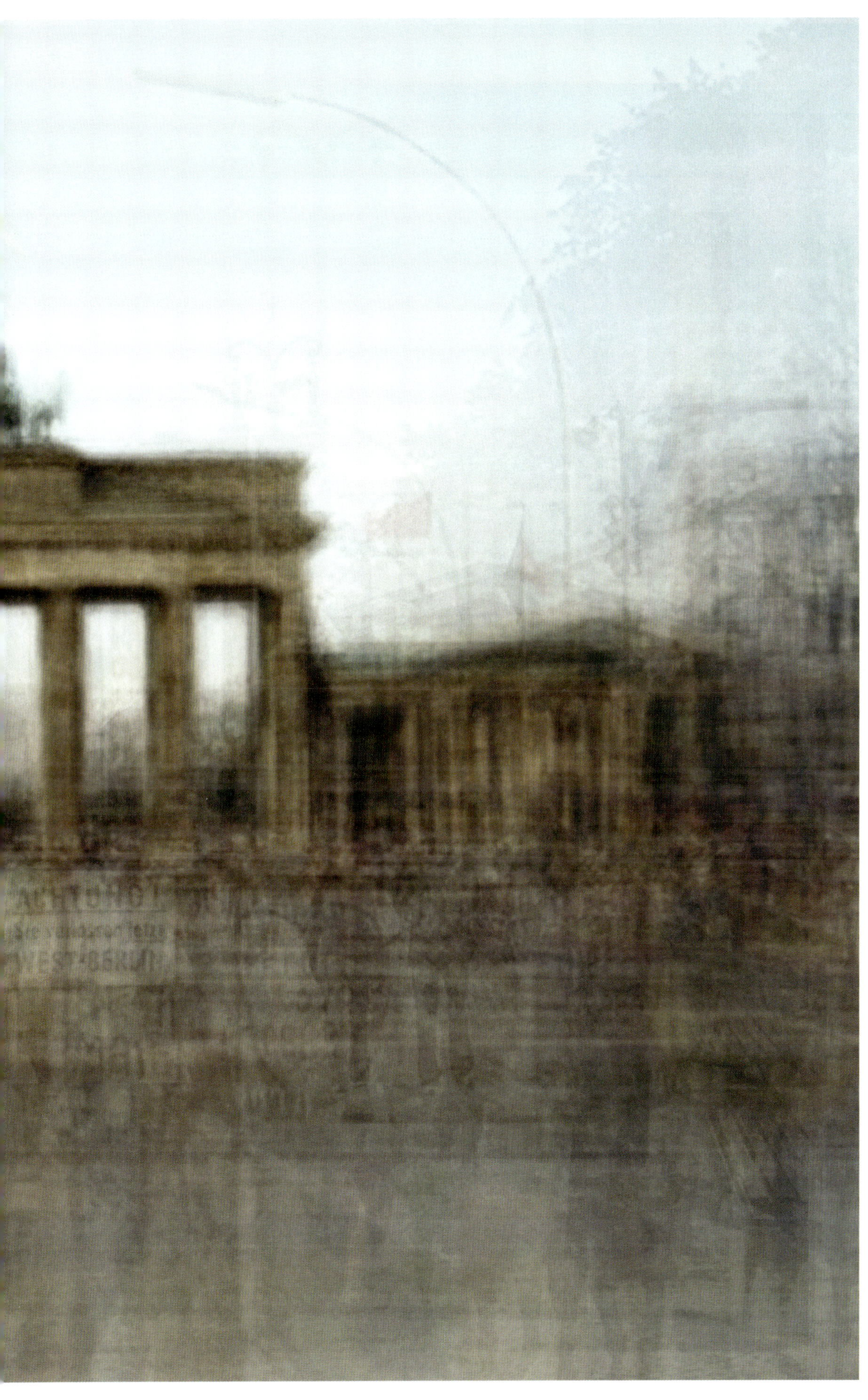

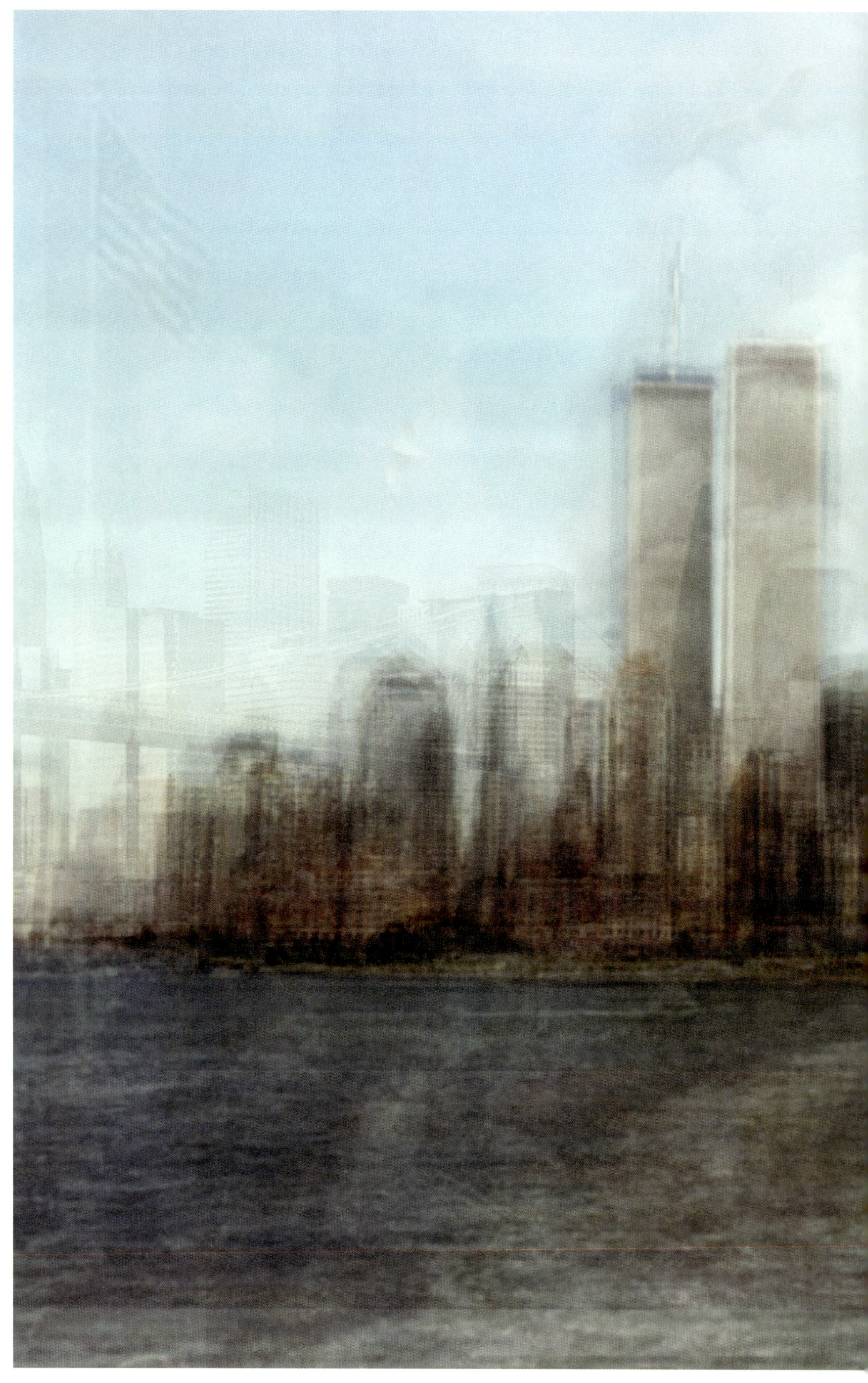

Corinne Vionnet
New York (2), 2007, a.d.S. / **from the series** *Photo Opportunities,* 2005–heute / **present**

Corinne Vionnet
Venezia, 2007, a.d.S. / **from the series** *Photo Opportunities,* 2005–heute / **present**

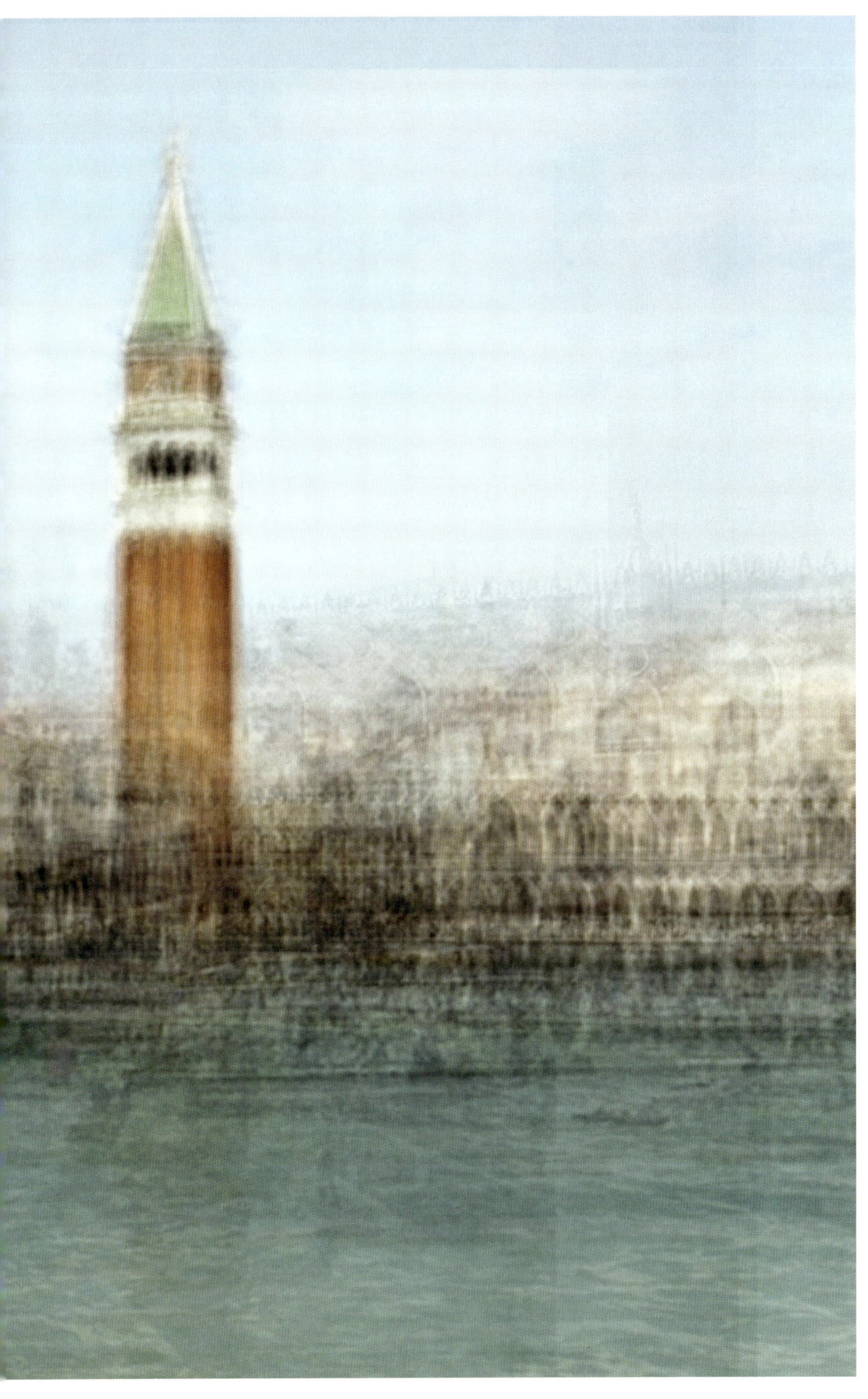

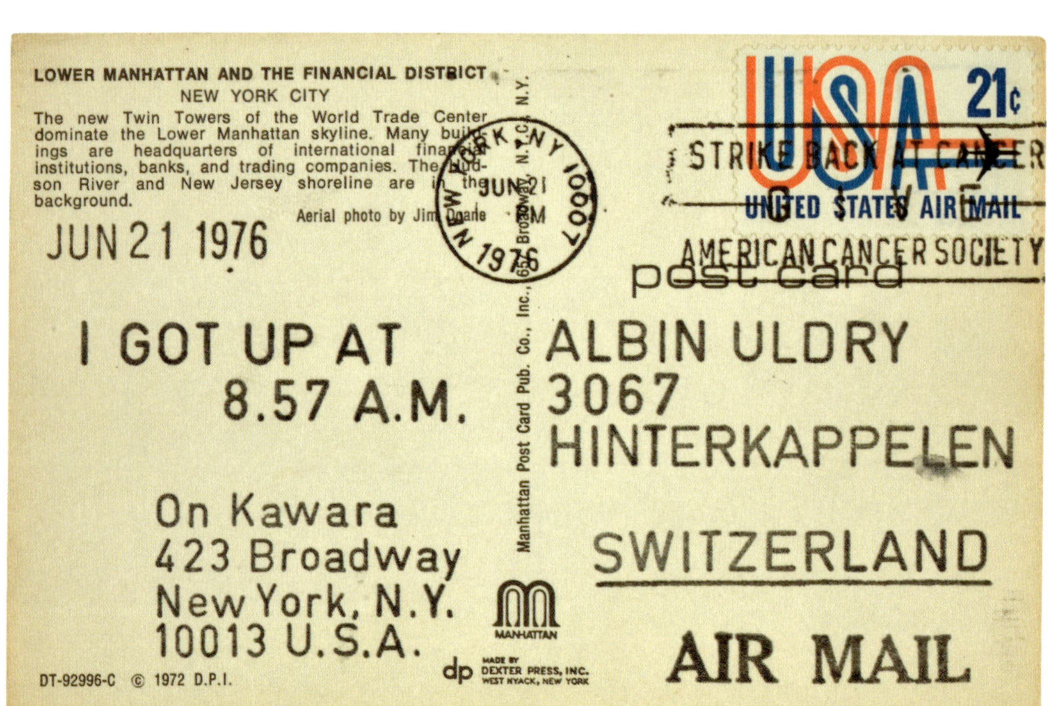

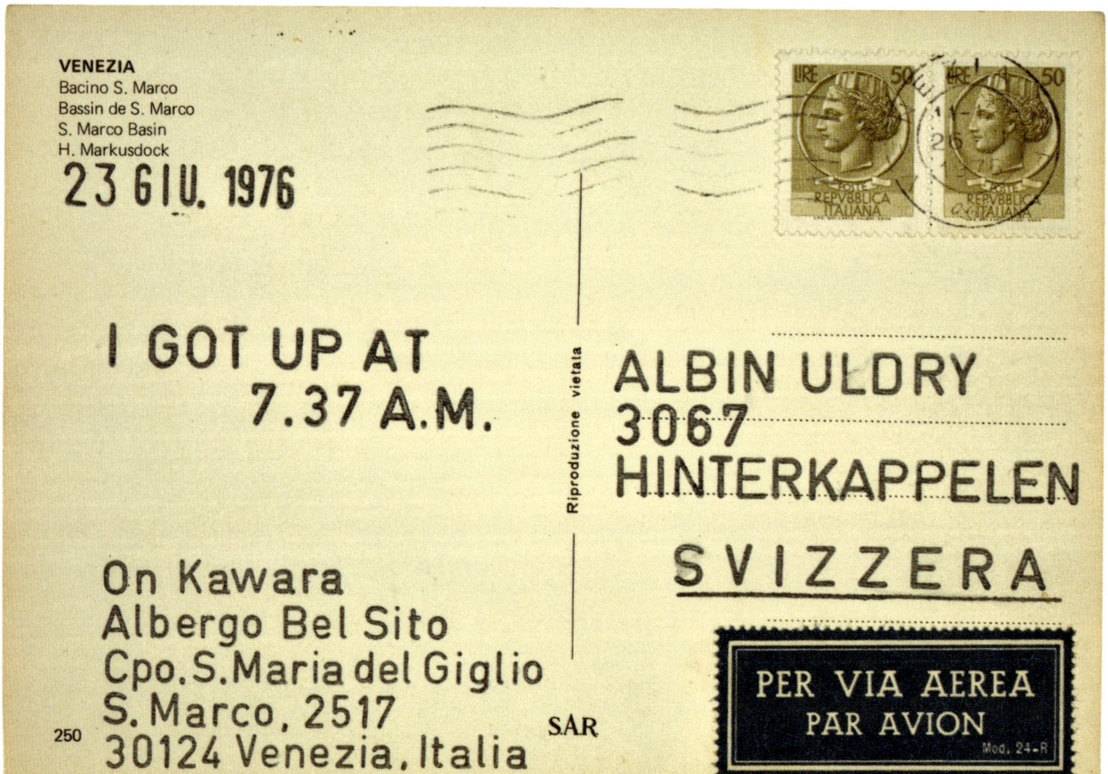

On Kawara
*a.d.S. / **From the series** I GOT UP AT*, 1976

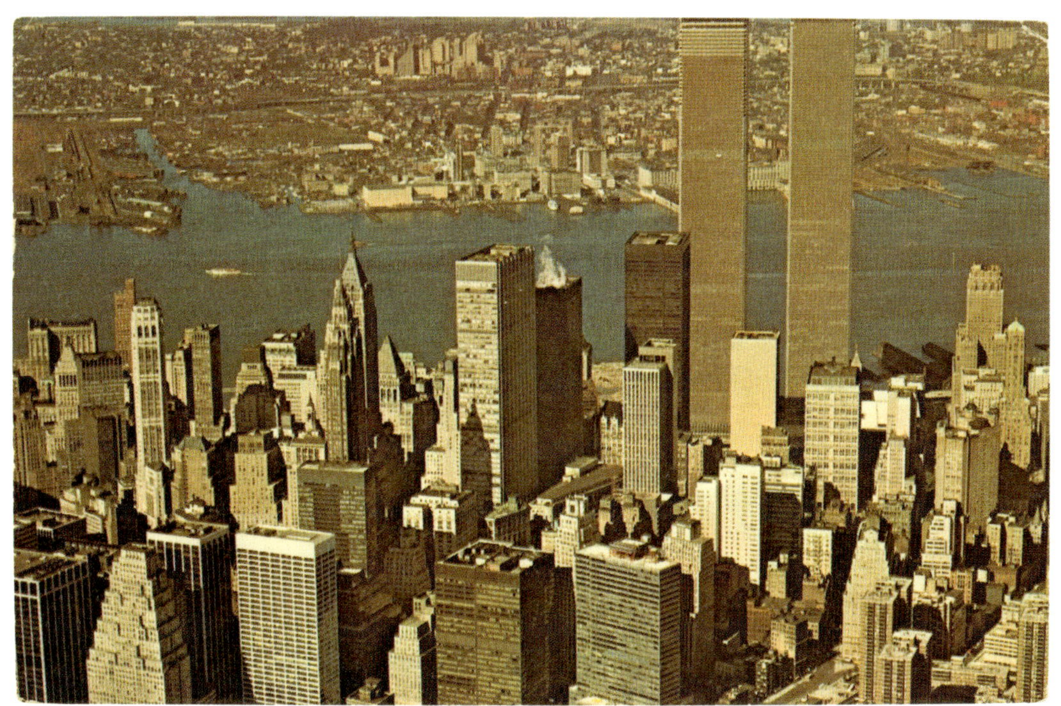

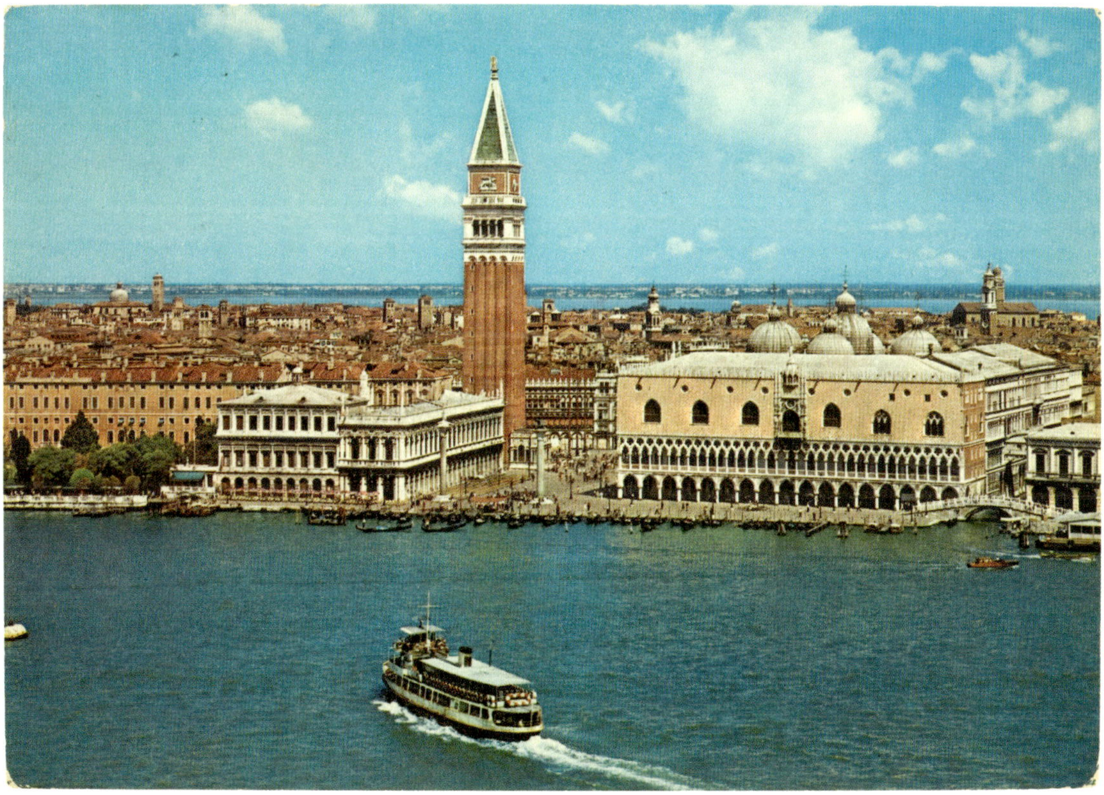

BERLIN
Zentrum mit Kaiser-Wilhelm-Gedächtniskirche
9. Aug. 1976

I GOT UP AT
9.34 A.M.

On Kawara
Damaschkestr.21
1 Berlin 31
Deutschland

ANDRES + CO VERLAG

ANCO

10 DEUTSCHE BUNDESPOST BERLIN
NAHVERKEHRS-TRIEBZUG
30 DEUTSCHE BUNDESPOST BERLIN
RETTUNGS-HUBSCHRAUBER

Deutsche
Industrieausstellung
Berlin
Energie
25
18.-26.9.1976

ALBIN ULDRY
3067
HINTERKAPPELEN

SCHWEIZ

MIT LUFTPOST
PAR AVION

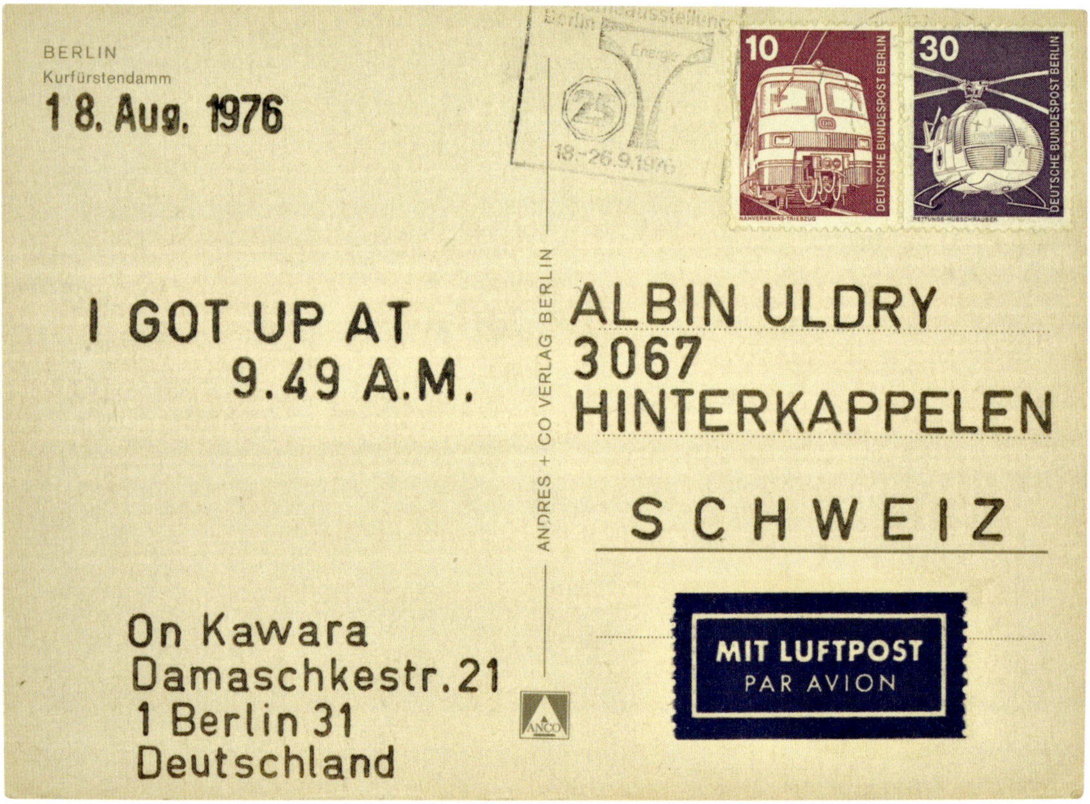

BERLIN
Kurfürstendamm
18. Aug. 1976

I GOT UP AT
9.49 A.M.

On Kawara
Damaschkestr.21
1 Berlin 31
Deutschland

ANDRES + CO VERLAG BERLIN

ANCO

10 DEUTSCHE BUNDESPOST BERLIN
NAHVERKEHRS-TRIEBZUG
30 DEUTSCHE BUNDESPOST BERLIN
RETTUNGS-HUBSCHRAUBER

Berlin
Industrieausstellung
Energie
25
18.-26.9.1976

ALBIN ULDRY
3067
HINTERKAPPELEN

SCHWEIZ

MIT LUFTPOST
PAR AVION

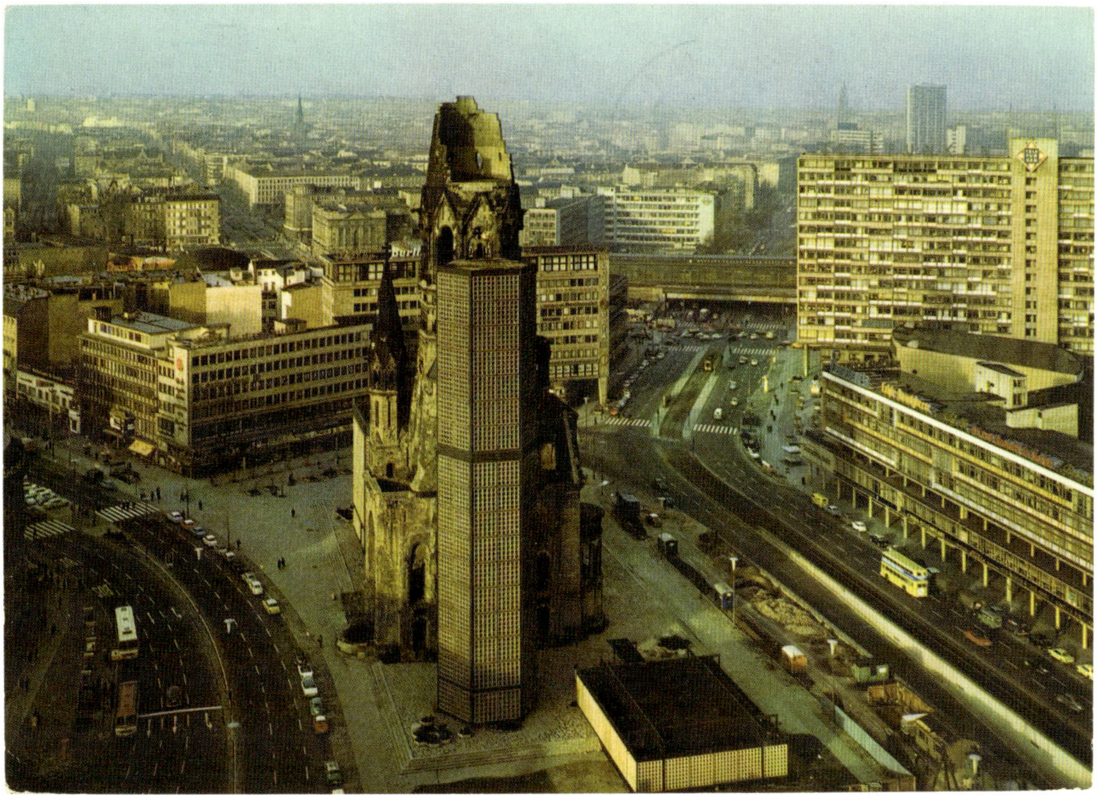

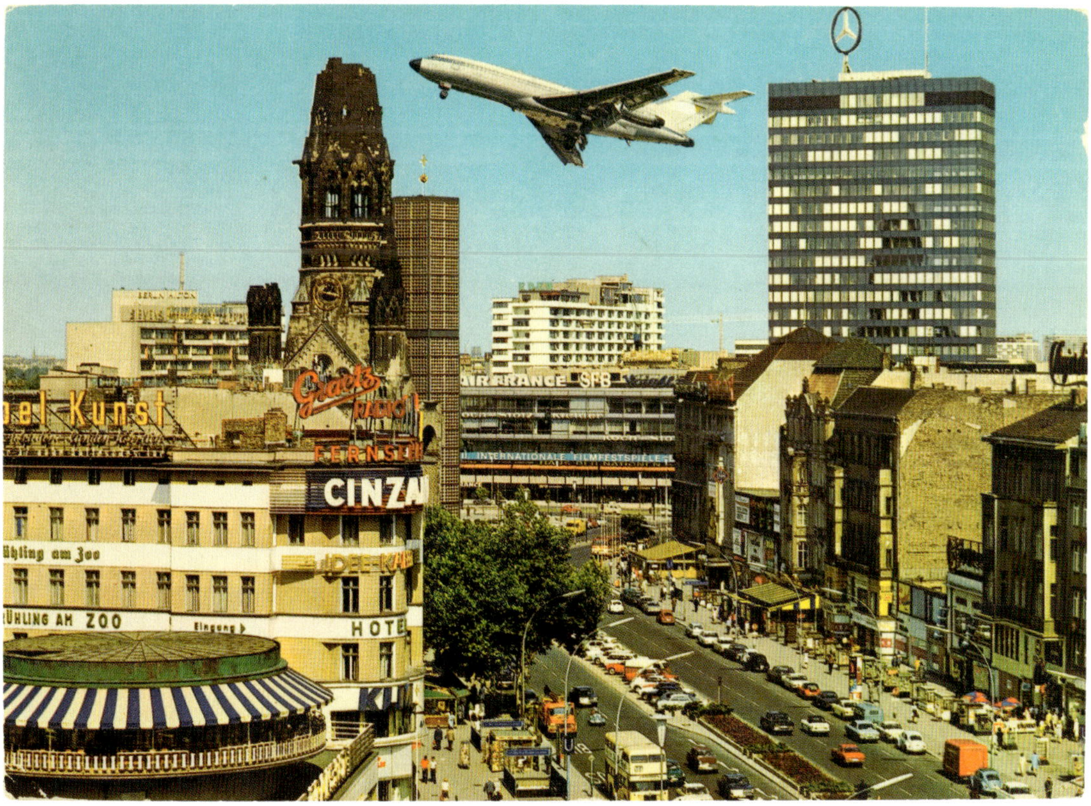

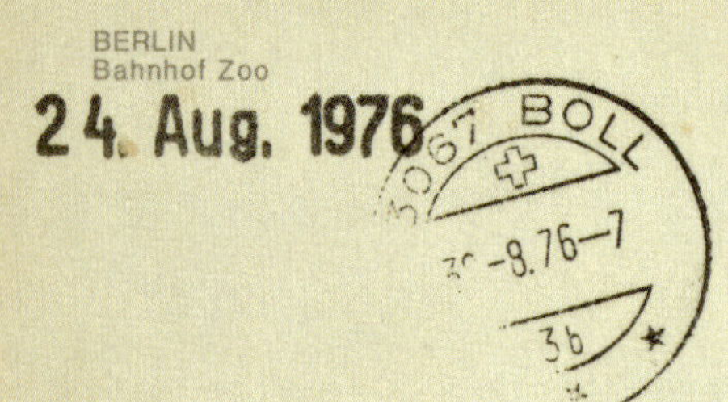

BERLIN
Bahnhof Zoo
24. Aug. 1976

I GOT UP AT
10.25 A.M.

On Kawara
Damaschkestr. 21
1 Berlin 31
Deutschland

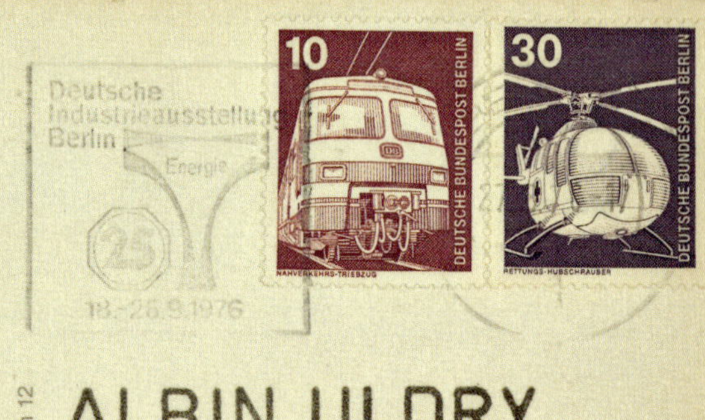

ALBIN ULDRY
3067   3032
HINTERKAPPELEN

SCHWEIZ

MIT LUFTPOST
PAR AVION

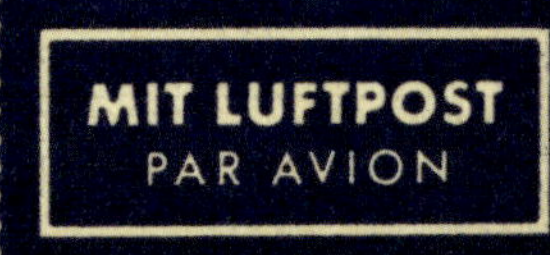
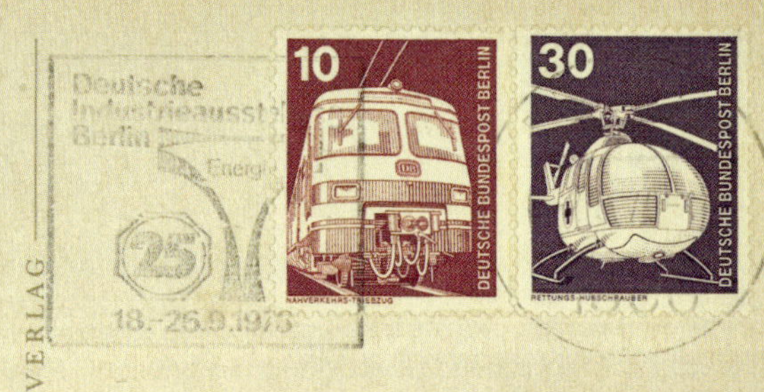

BERLIN
Brandenburger Tor mit Mauer
Brandenburger Tor and Wall
30. Aug. 1976

I GOT UP AT
9.26 A.M.

On Kawara
Damaschkestr. 21
1 Berlin 31
Deutschland

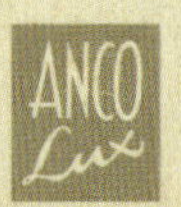

ANCO
Lux

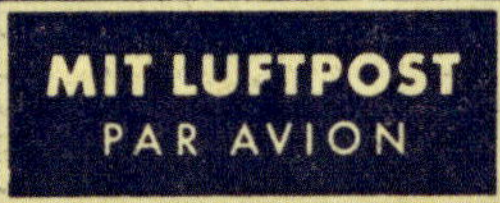

ALBIN ULDRY
3067
HINTERKAPPELEN

SCHWEIZ

MIT LUFTPOST
PAR AVION

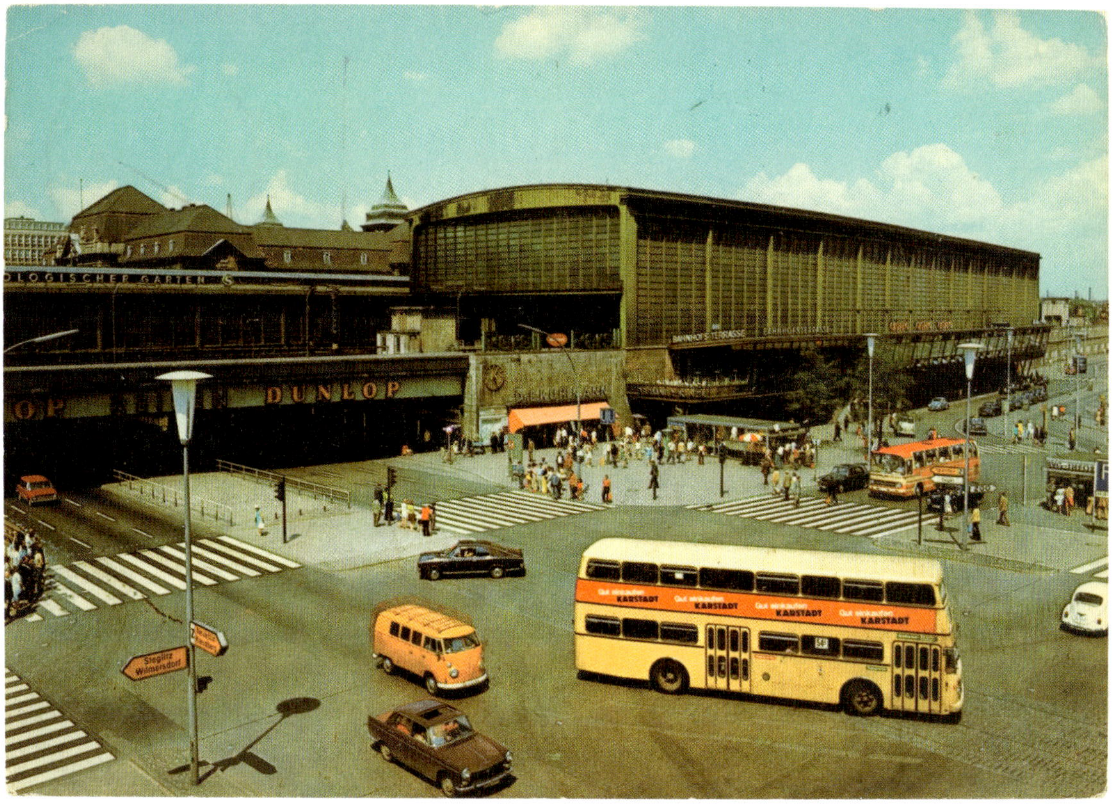

DUNLOP
KARSTADT
Steglitz
Wilmersdorf

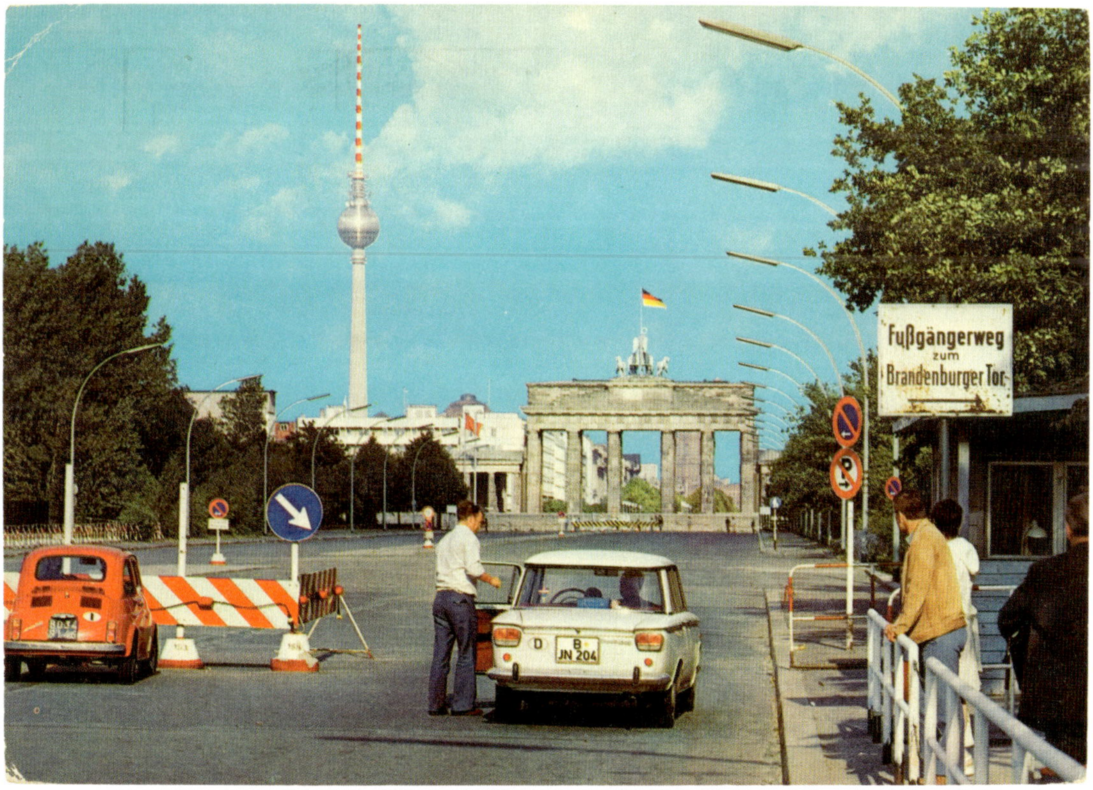

Fußgängerweg
zum
Brandenburger Tor
D B JN 204

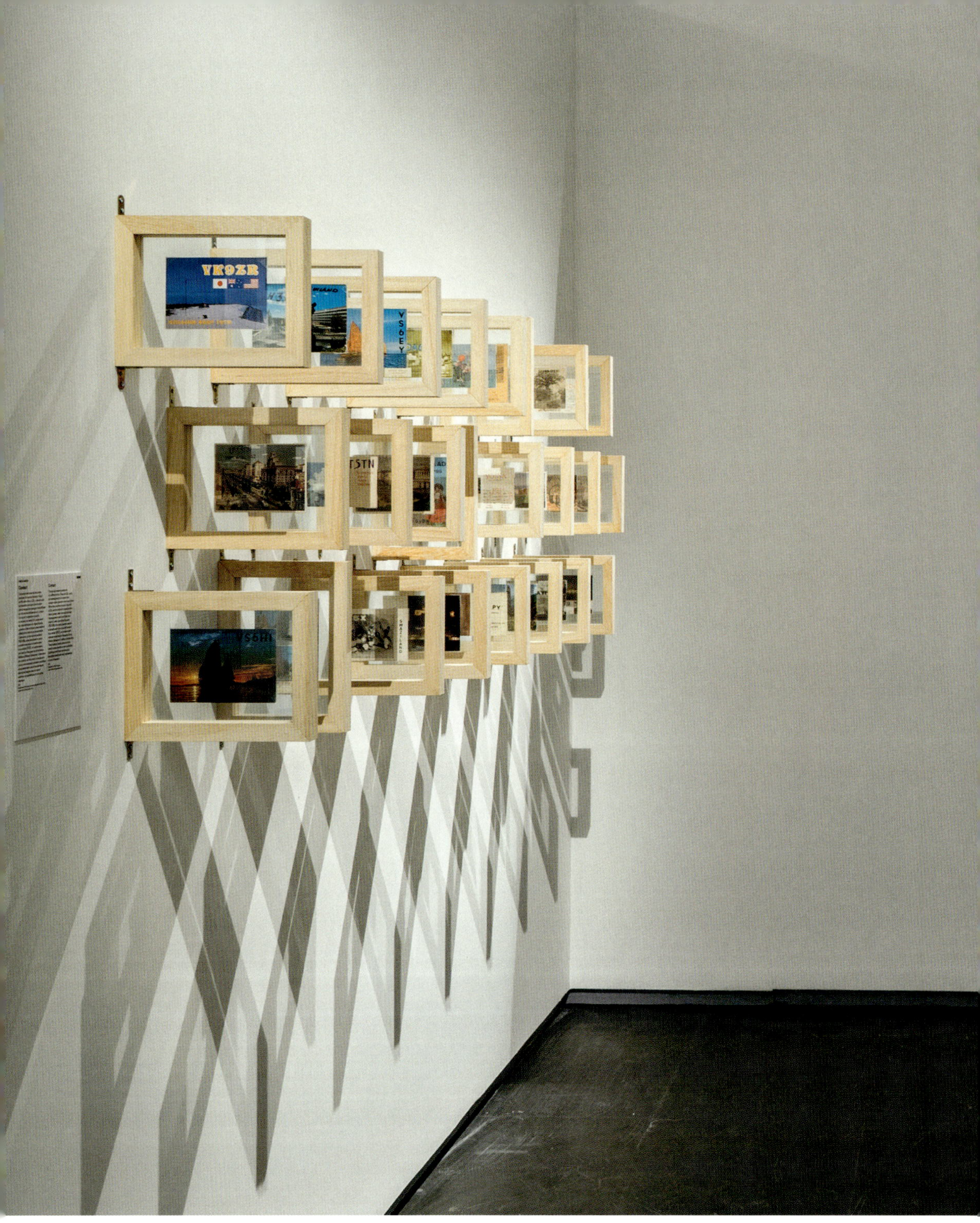

Fredi Casco
Contact, 2014

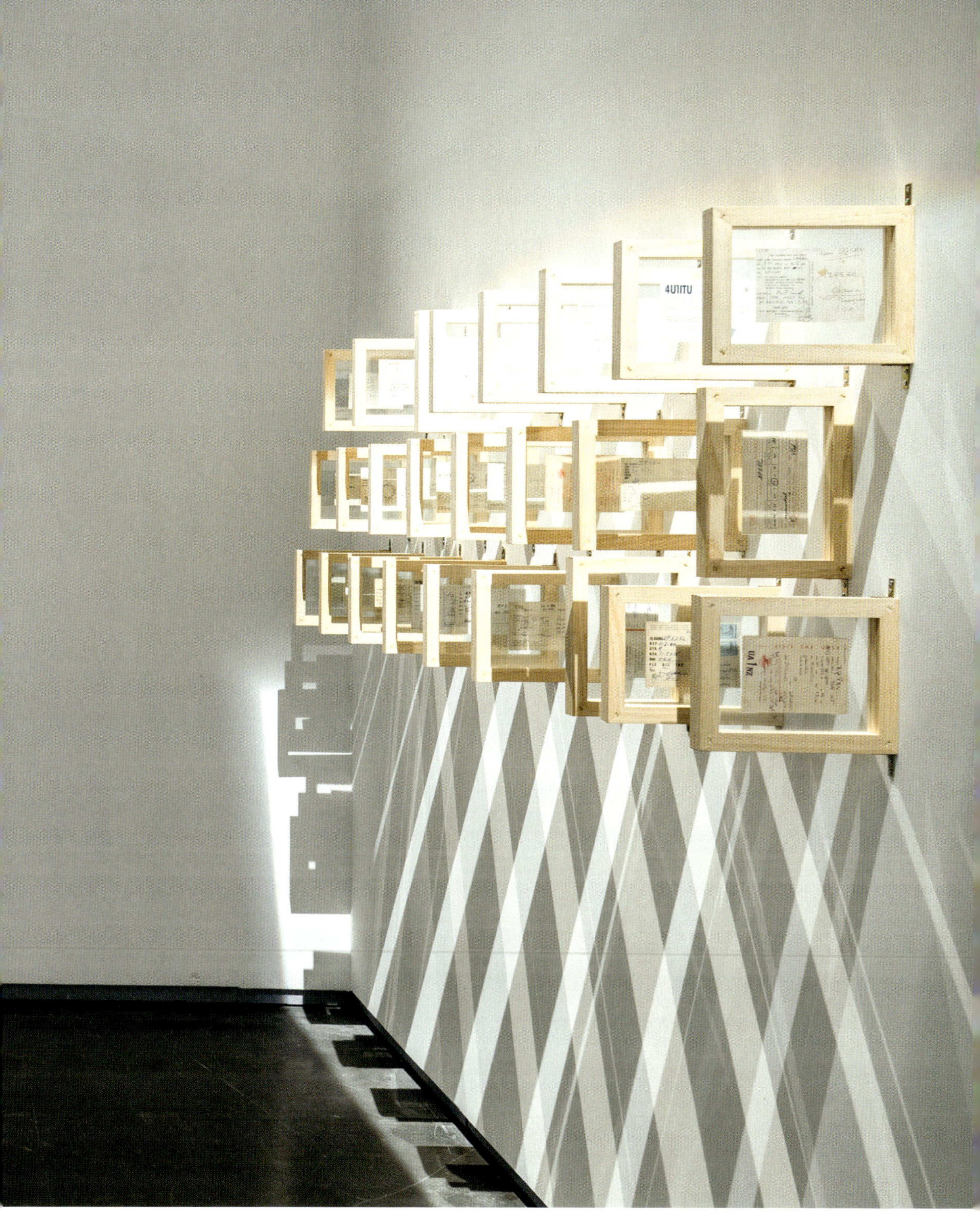

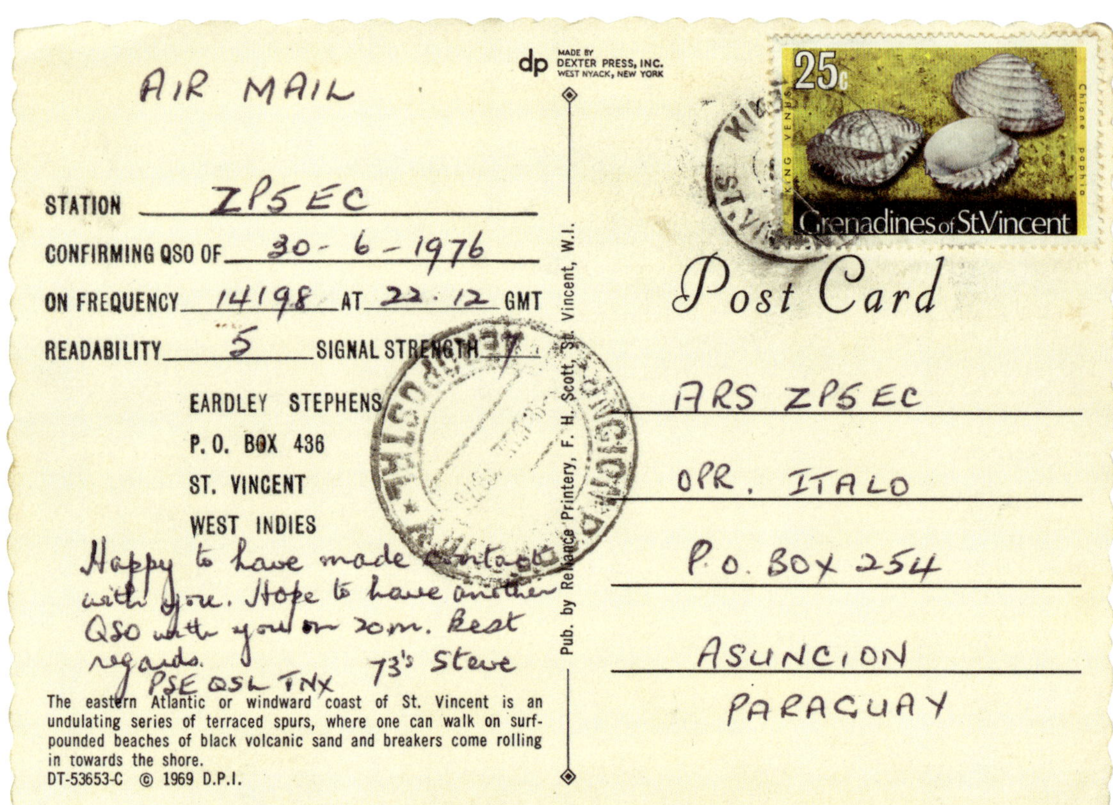

STATION	DATE	AT	MC	ON	YOUR SIGS		
					R	S	T
ZP5EC	13/9/74	1930	14	~~AM~~ 2 x SSB ~~CW~~	5	9	-

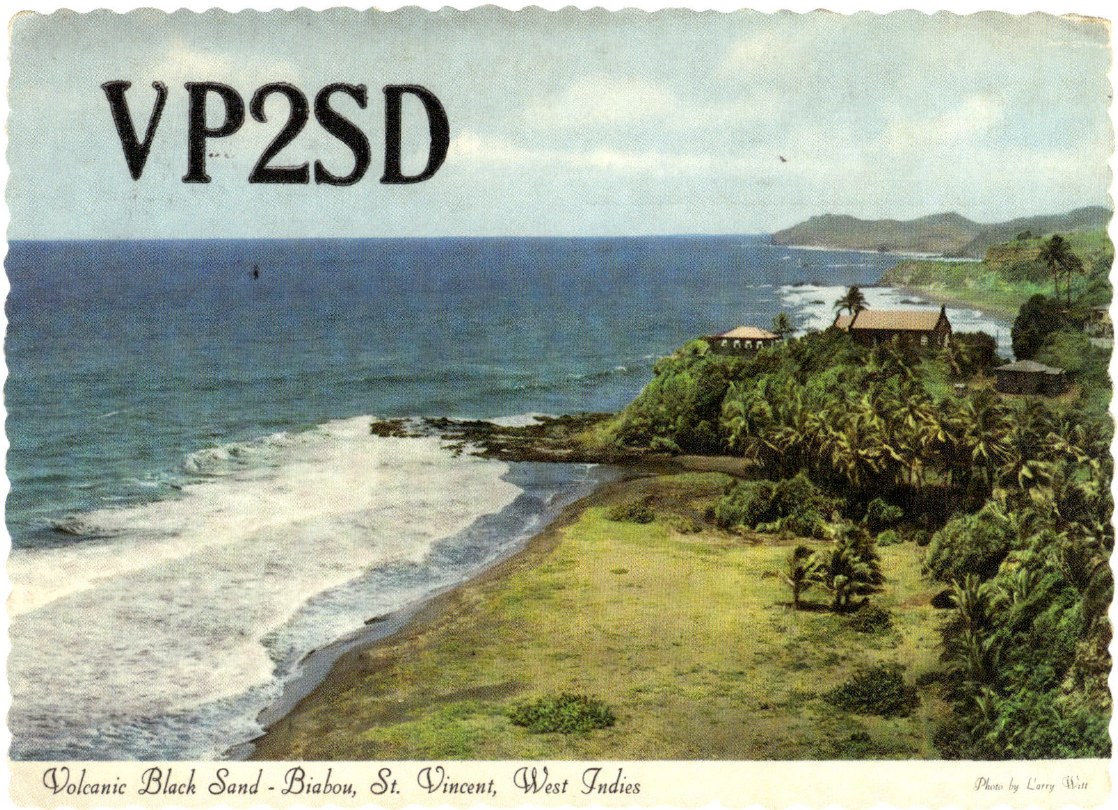

VP2SD

Volcanic Black Sand - Biabou, St. Vincent, West Indies

Photo by Larry Witt

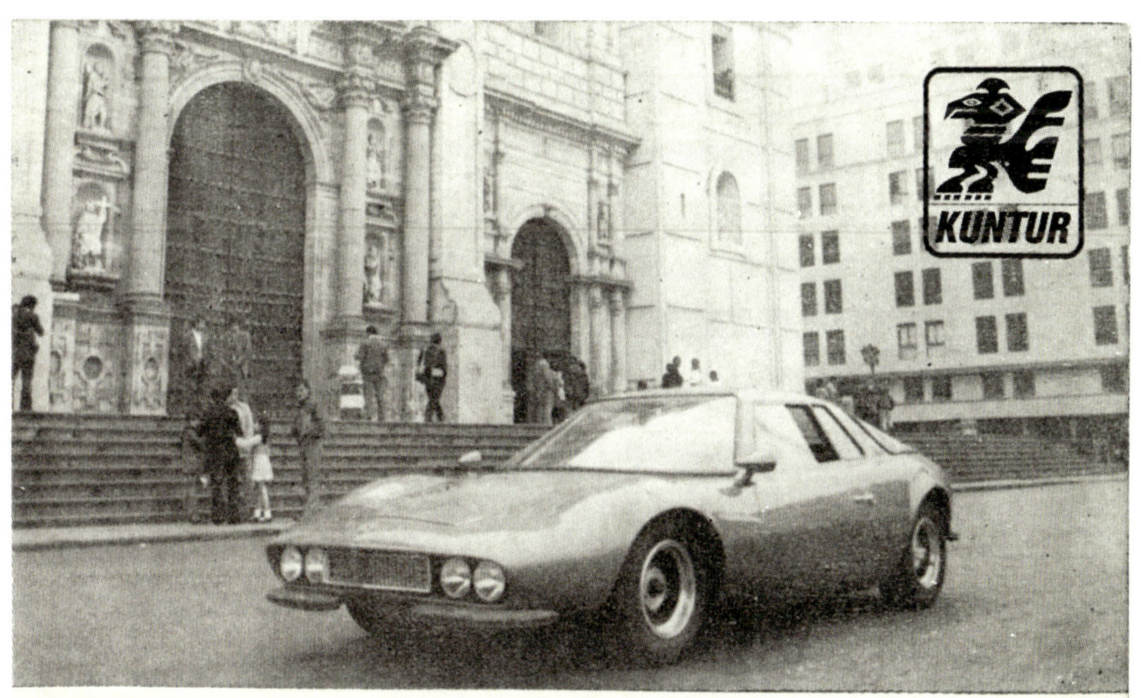

Catedral de Lima. Frente el primer KUNTUR GT, diseñado y construido por OA4MQ.

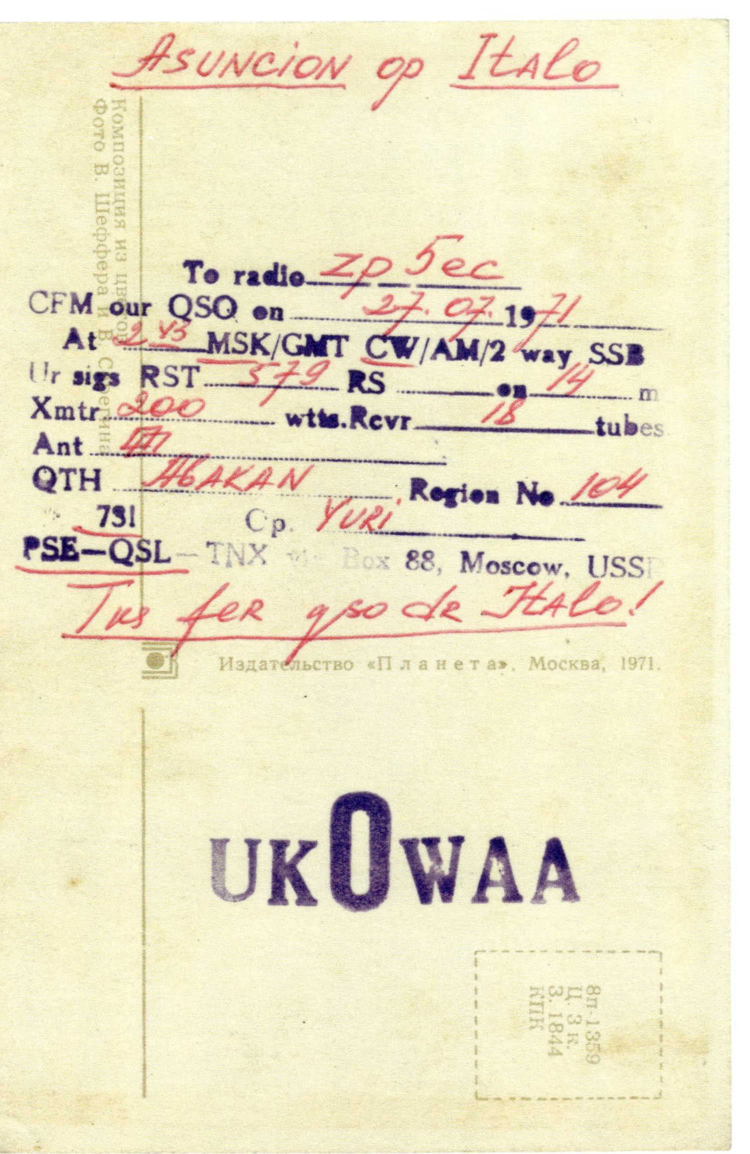

Asuncion op Italo
To radio zp5ec
CFM our QSO on 27. 07. 1971
At 2 v3 MSK/GMT CW/AM/2 way SSB
Ur sigs RST 579 RS on 14 m
Xmtr 200 wtts. Rcvr 18 tubes
Ant 477
QTH Abakan Region No 104
73! Cp. Yuri
PSE–QSL – TNX via Box 88, Moscow, USSR
Tnx fer qso de Italo!
UK0WAA
Композиция из цветов
Фото В. Шеффера и В. Серёгина
Издательство «Планета». Москва, 1971.
8п-1359
Ц. 3 к.
3. 1844
КПК

TO RADIO ZP5EC
QTR 1320
QRG 21
RST 59t
FONE
CW
QSO 10/6/57
TX 600w
ANT 1/2
RX CR100
MNI TNX FER QSO
et QSL. 73
Servicio Q.S.L.
27 ABR 1960
R. C. Paraguayo

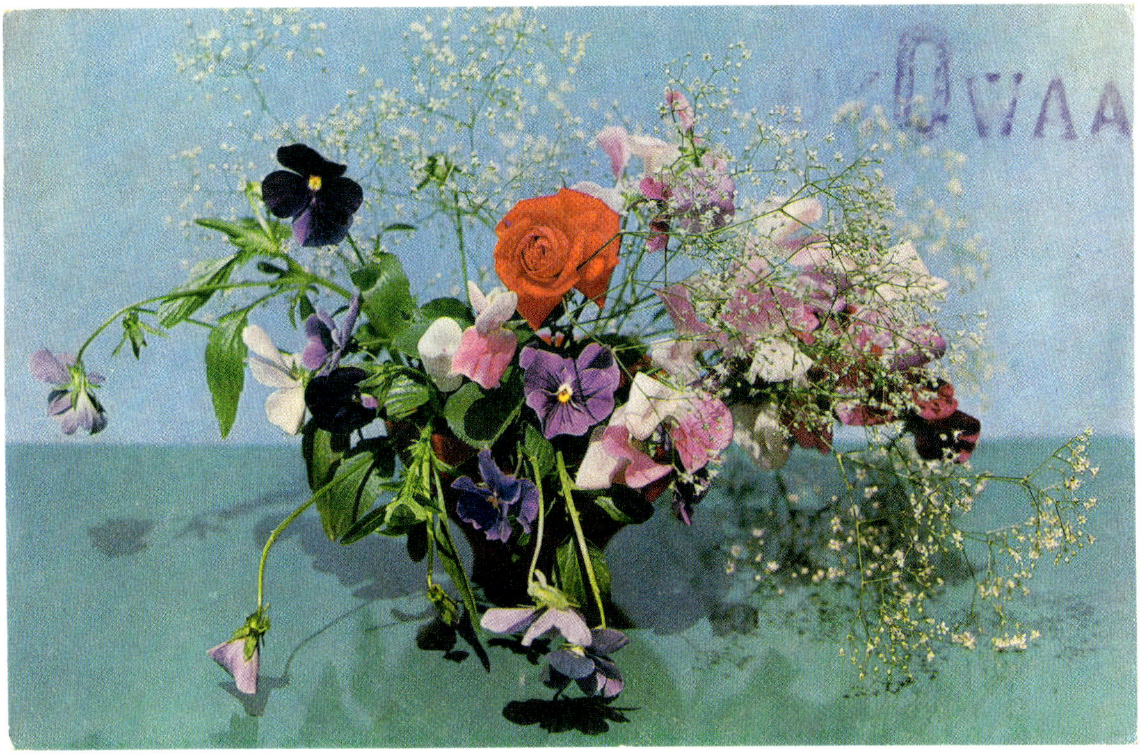

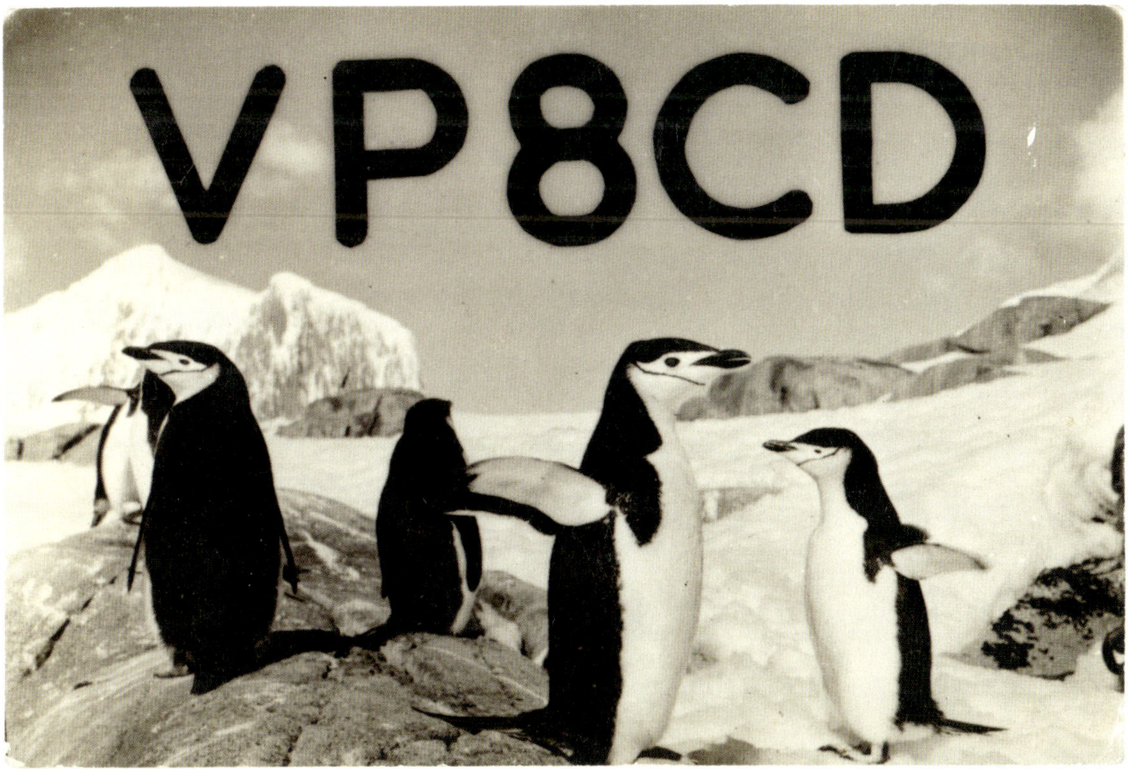

VP8CD

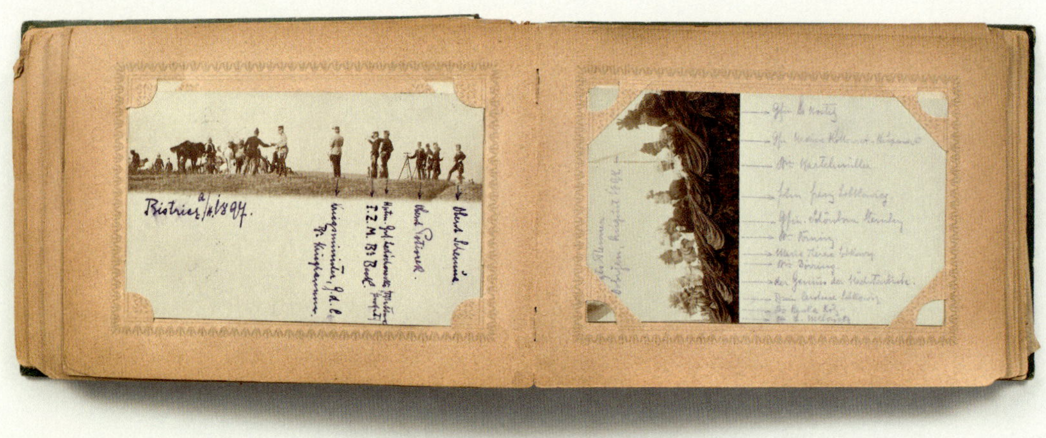

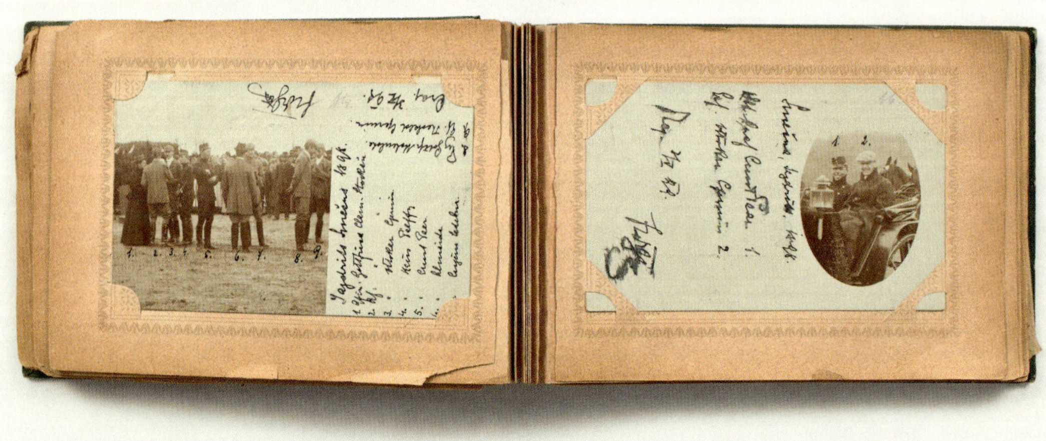

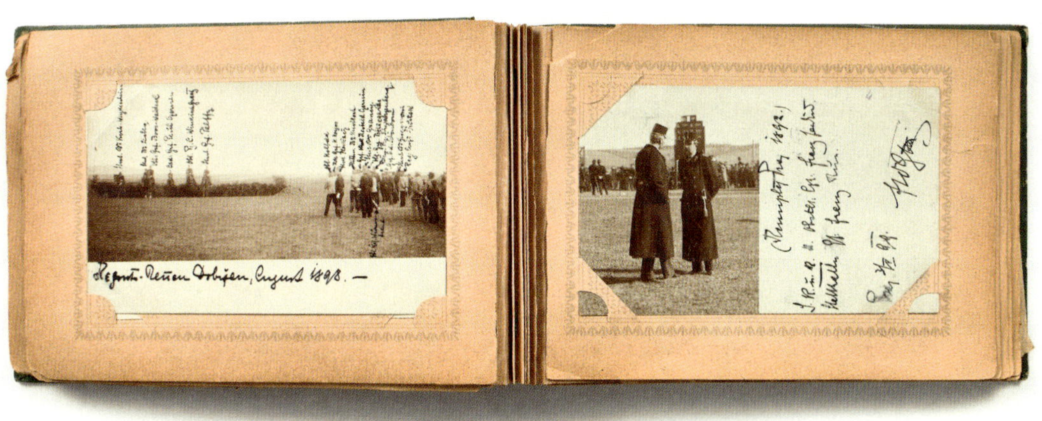

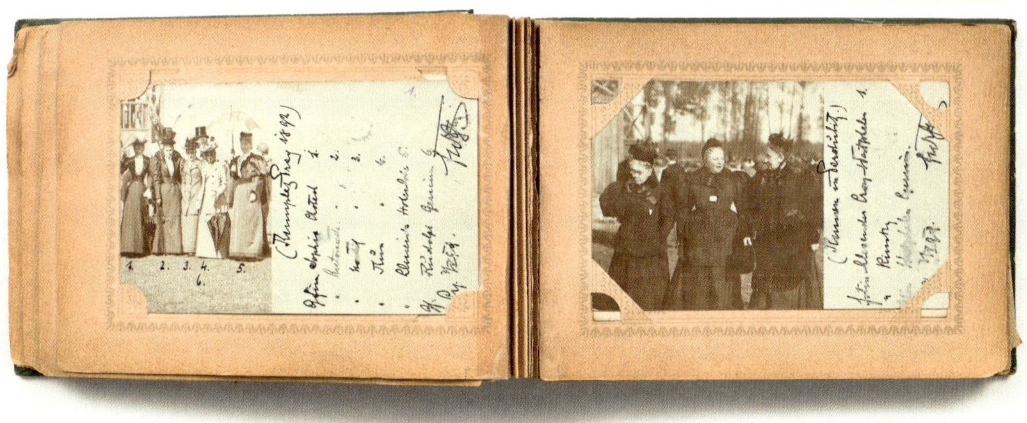

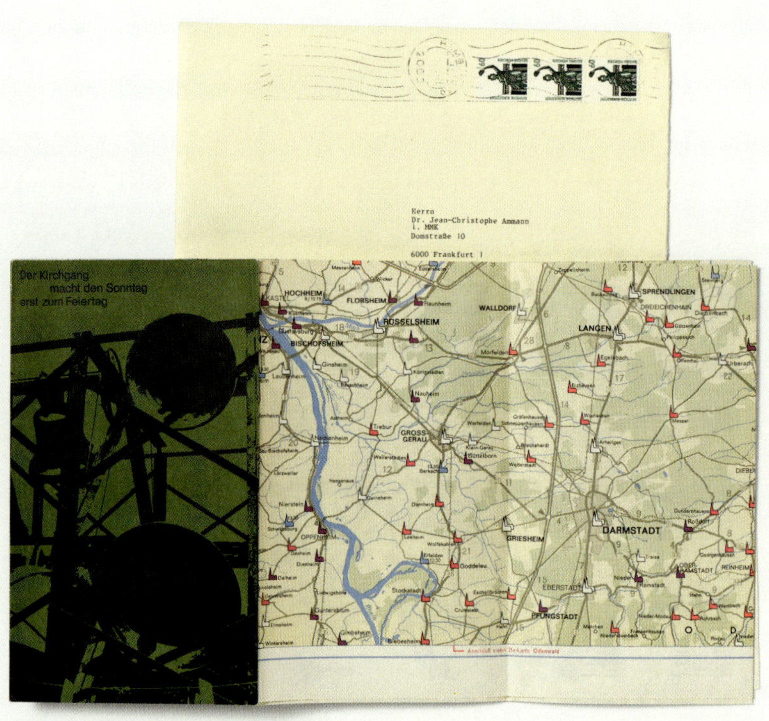

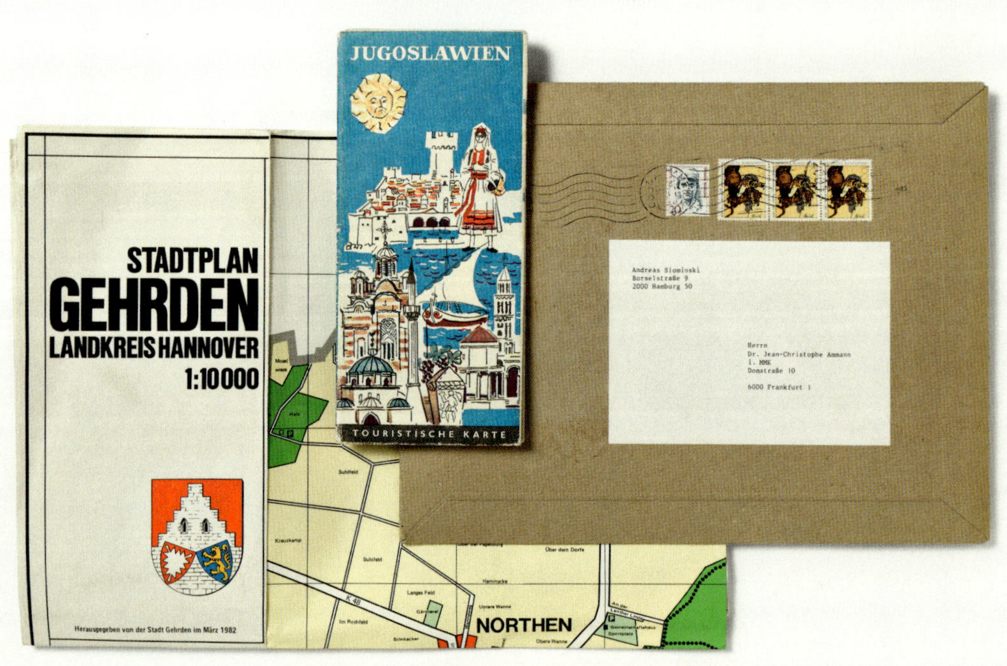

Andreas Slominski
Unkommentierte Sendung von Landkarten und Stadtplänen von Andreas Slominski an Jean-Christophe Ammann /
Mailing of maps and city plans without commentary by Andreas Slominski to Jean-Christophe Ammann, 1992–1997

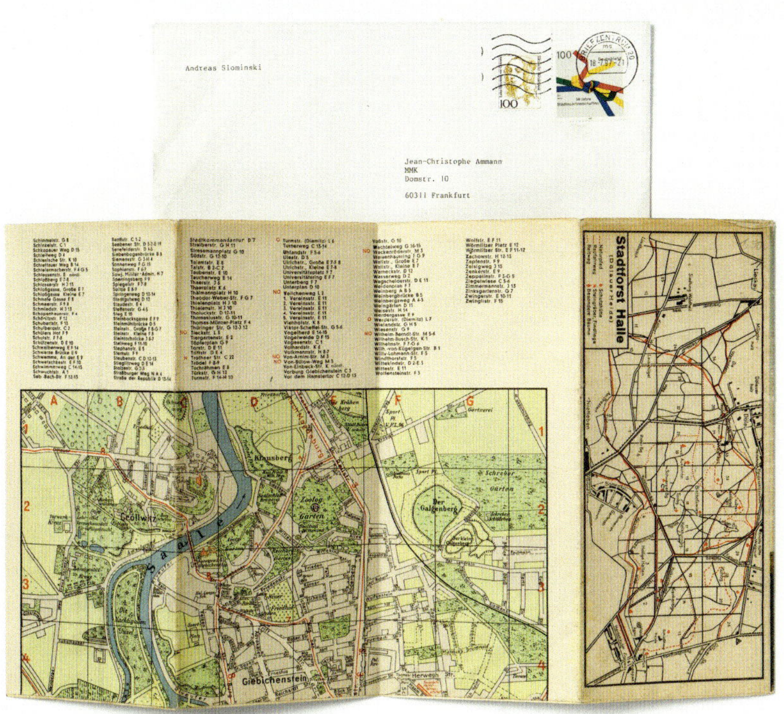

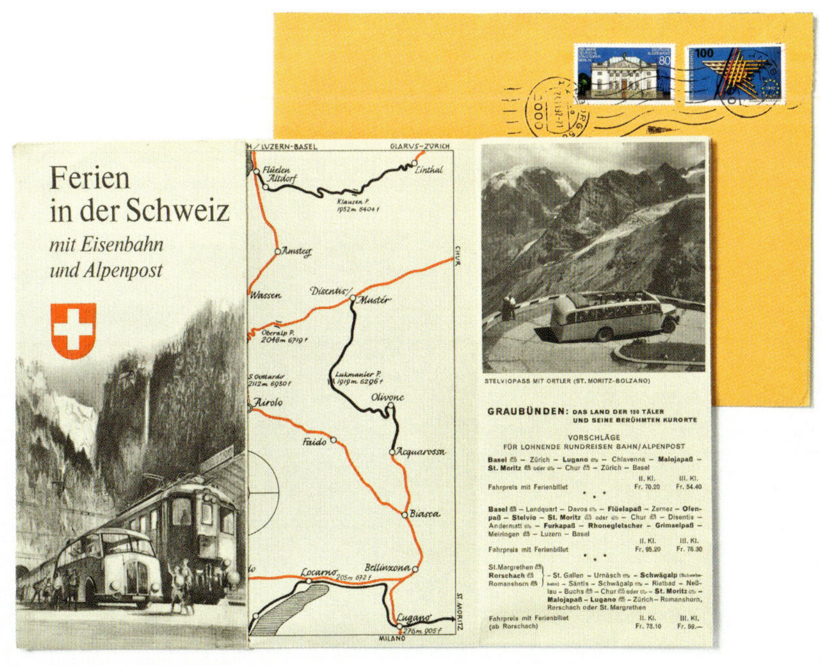

Ferien
in der Schweiz
mit Eisenbahn
und Alpenpost

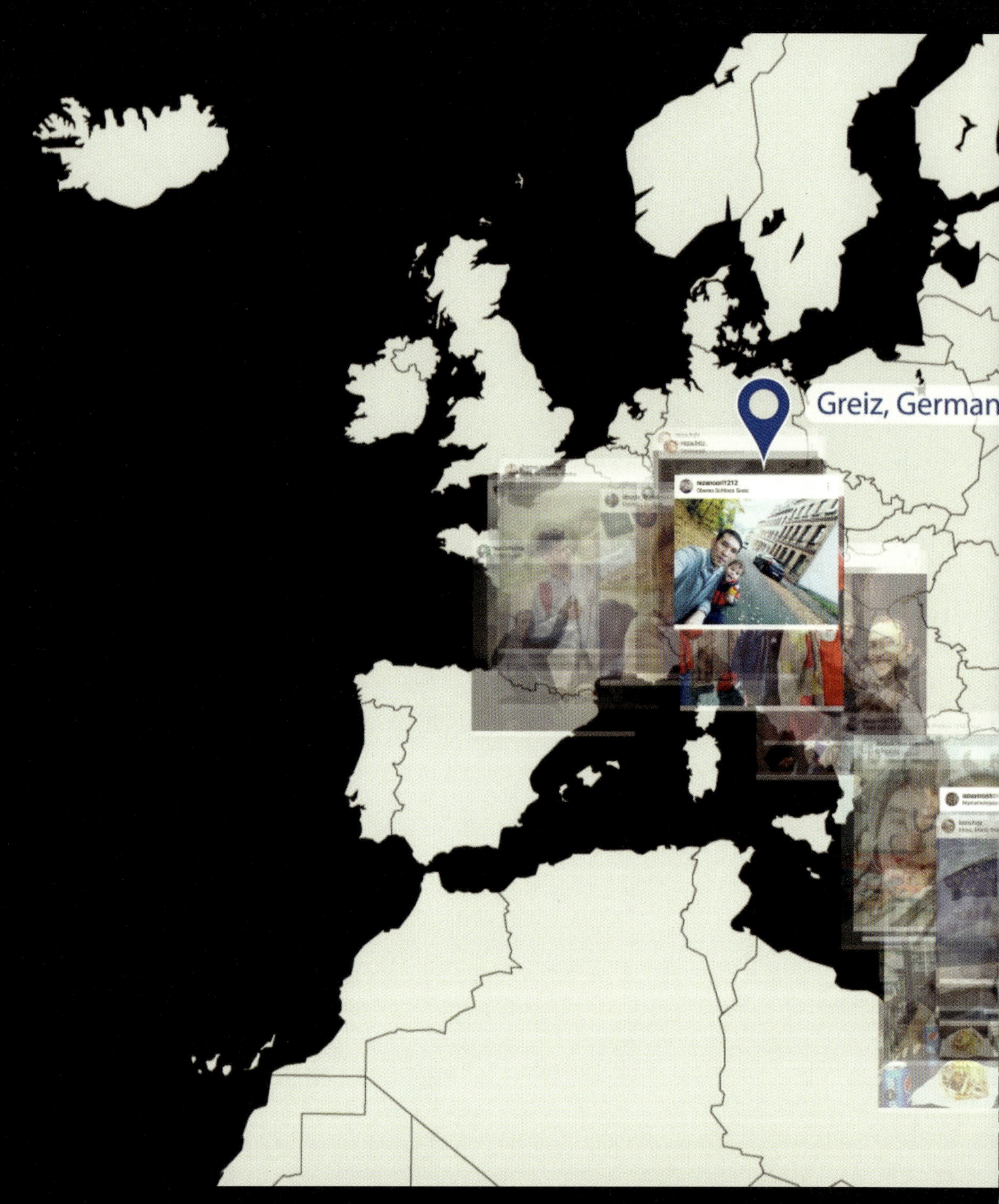

Greiz, German
Oberes Schloss Greiz

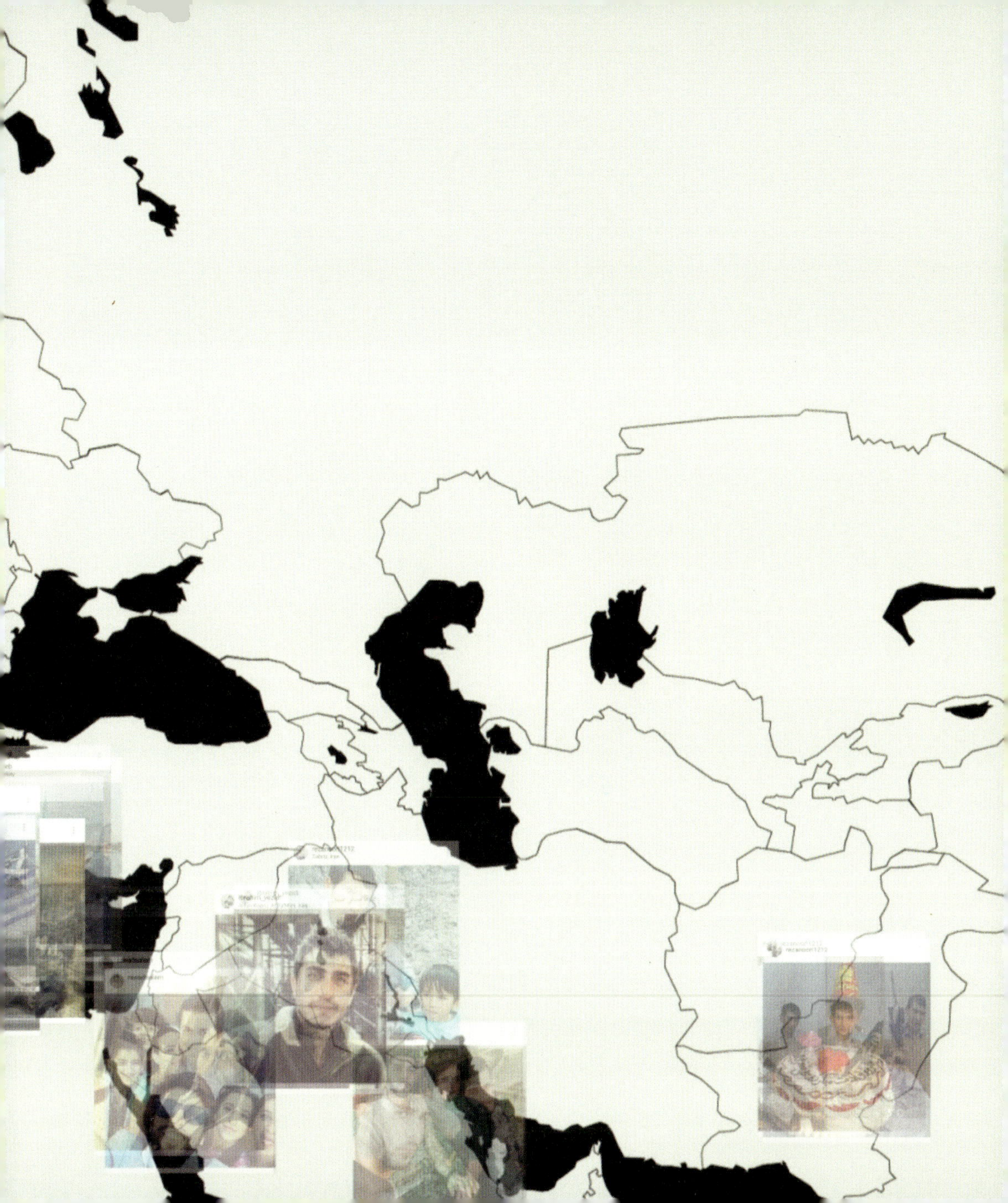

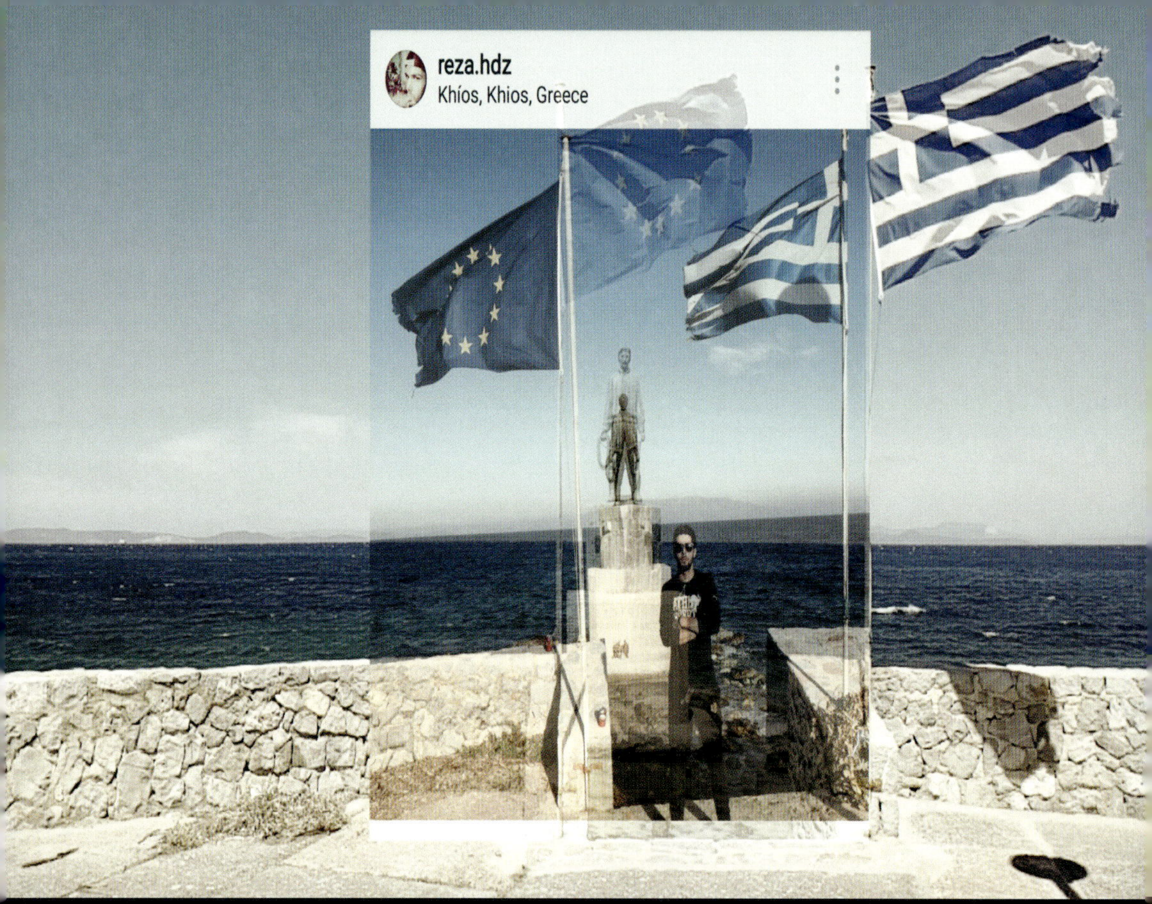

reza.hdz
Khíos, Khios, Greece

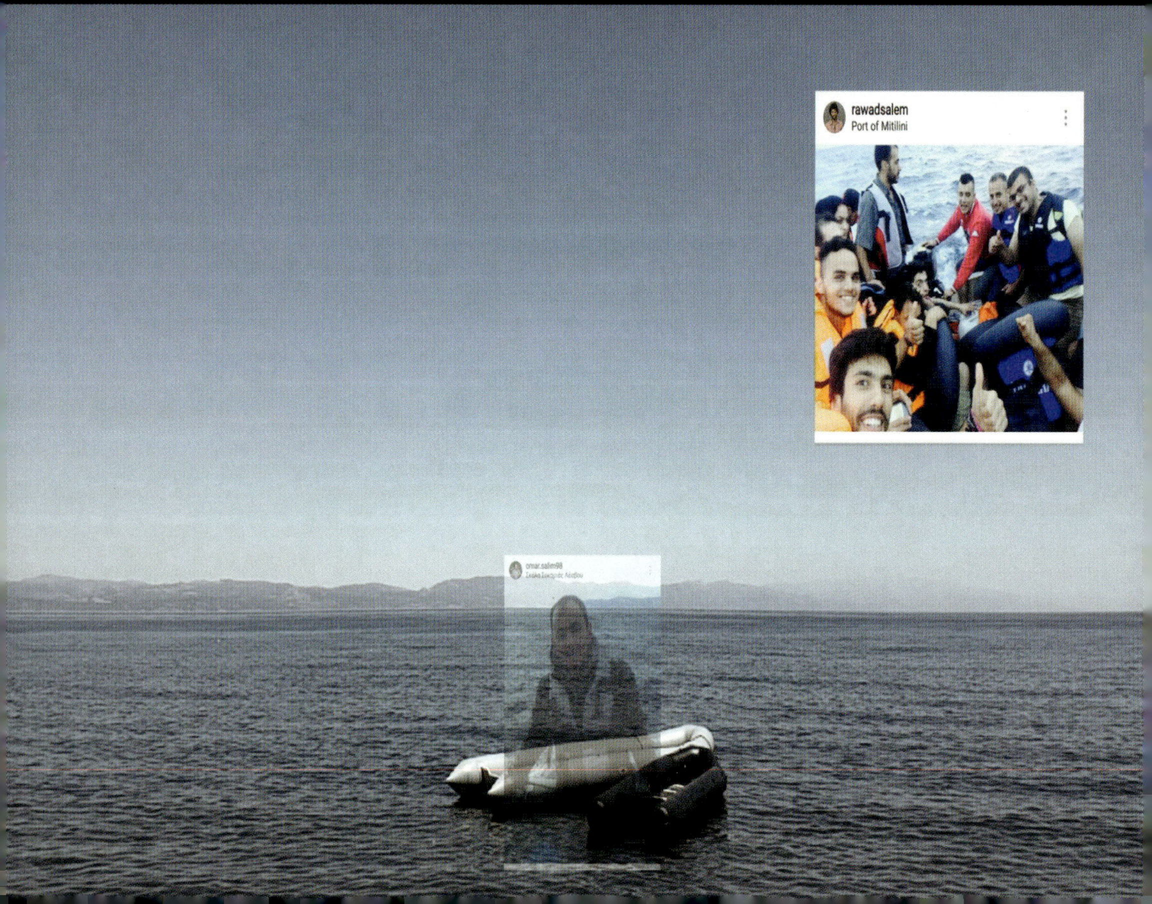

rawadsalem
Port of Mitilini

omar.salem98
Σχολή Σωσίμου Λέσβου

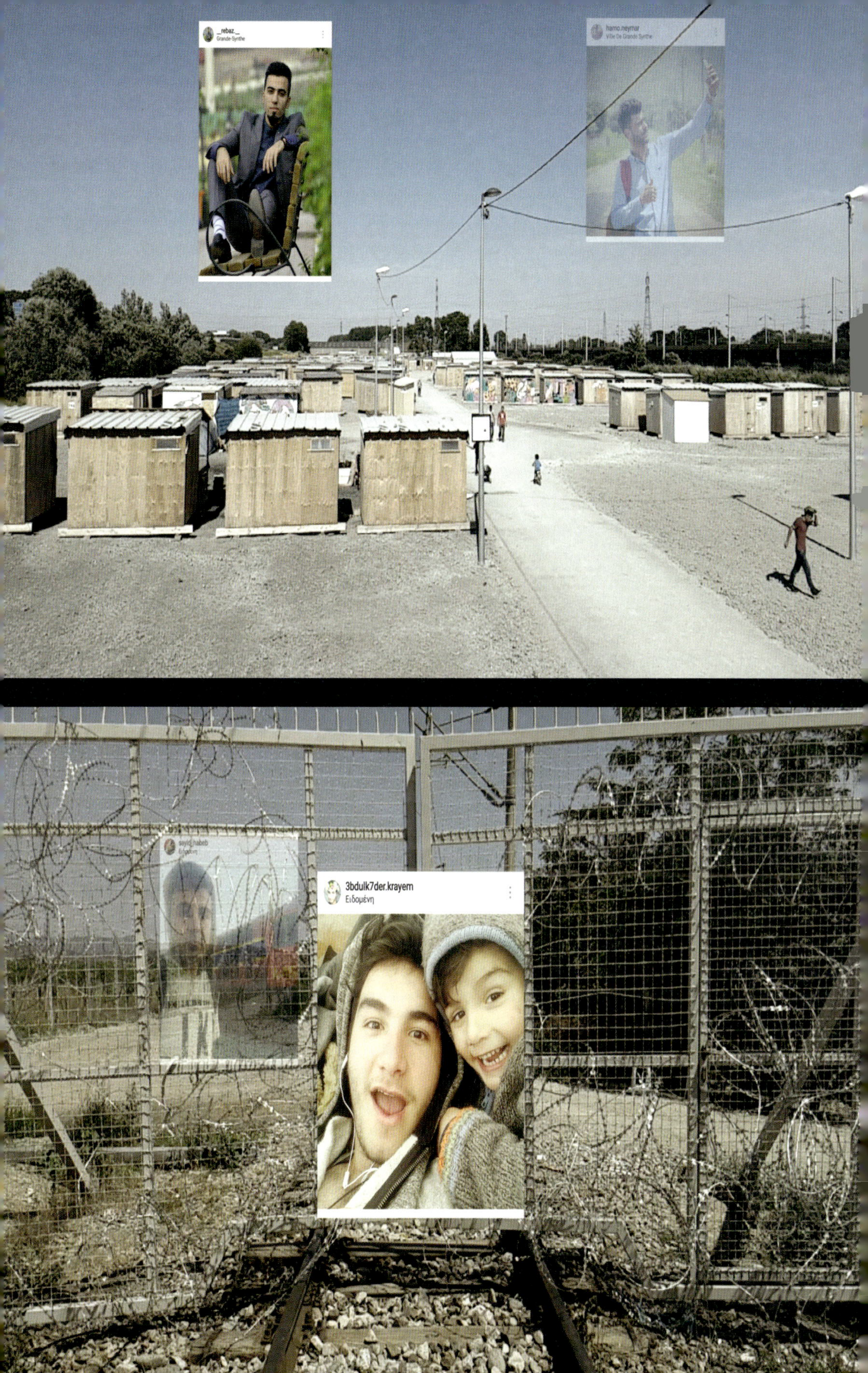

_rebaz__
Grande-Synthe
hamo.neymar
Ville De Grande Synthe
sayid_habib
Ειδομένη
3bdulk7der.krayem
Ειδομένη

BILDTELEGRAFIE

Ende der 1830er-Jahre – und damit ungefähr zeitgleich mit der Veröffentlichung der ersten fotografischen Verfahren – wurden die ersten elektrotelegrafischen Verbindungen geplant und eingerichtet. Um Texte auf diese neue Weise übertragen zu können, wurden sie in der Regel in Buchstaben und Zeichen zerlegt und diese dann codiert – der bekannteste und am weitesten verbreitete dieser Codes wurde von Samuel Morse formuliert, der auch die ersten dazu passenden Telegrafen baute. Durch seine Erfindung wurde nicht nur die Übermittlung von Nachrichten beschleunigt, sondern auch ihre Reichweite vergrößert. Bereits in den 1850er-Jahren existierte an der Ostküste der USA ein dichtes Netz an Kabelverbindungen. Und mit den ersten Ende der 1850er-Jahre verlegten transatlantischen Kabeln konnten zunächst zwar nur wenige Worte pro Minute übermittelt werden, doch das war immer noch deutlich schneller als die schnellsten Schiffsverbindungen, die damals mindestens zehn Tage für die Atlantiküberquerung benötigten. Weil Telegrafie teuer war – vor allem die Verlegung der Kabel verursachte gewaltige Kosten –, wurde sie neben Börsen vor allem von Zeitungen genutzt, die mit Hilfe des neuen Mediums eine aktuelle Berichterstattung gewährleisten konnten, die nicht mehr nur den Ort ihres Erscheinens betraf.

Es sollte allerdings Jahrzehnte dauern bis diese Nachrichten von fotografischen Illustrationen der Ereignisse begleitet werden konnten. Das lag zunächst vor allem daran, dass Fotografien sich nicht im Zeitungsdruck vervielfältigen ließen. Erst mit der Zerlegung in Rasterpunkte verschiedener Größe ab etwa 1890 konnten im Schwarz auf Weiß des Zeitungsdrucks Grauwerte ähnlich denen fotografischer Bilder simuliert werden.

PHOTOTELEGRAPHY

In the late 1830s—around the same time that the first photographs were being taken—the first electro-telegraphic systems were being planned and developed. Texts were reduced to letters and characters and then encoded so that they could be transmitted using this new method. Samuel Morse created the best-known and most commonly used version of such codes, as well as designing the first corresponding telegraph system. His invention not only accelerated the transmission of messages, but also increased their range. In the 1850s, a dense network of cable connections was established on the East Coast of the United States. When the first transatlantic cables were laid in the late 1850s, it was initially only possible to transmit a few words per minute, but that was still significantly faster than the fastest ship connections, which at that time took at least ten days to cross the Atlantic. Because telegraphy was expensive, with the laying of cables being particularly costly, it was mainly used by stock exchanges and above all by newspapers to enable up-to-date reporting on stories relevant beyond their place of publication.

It would, however, take decades before it was possible to include photographs to illustrate the events reported on. Initially, this was mainly due to the fact that the technology used to print newspapers could not repro-

Das Problem war denen der Bildtelegrafie verwandt – auch dort war die Zerlegung in kleine, einfach codierbare Einheiten die Voraussetzung, um Bilder senden zu können. Tatsächlich gab es Versuche, gerasterte Bilder als Vorlagen zu nehmen und die Größe der einzelnen Punkte telegrafisch oder sogar telefonisch nacheinander zu übermitteln; durchgesetzt haben sich schließlich Verfahren, bei denen lichtempfindliche Zellen ein fotografisches Bild in Zeilen abtasten und relative Helligkeiten messen. Die Werte werden sukzessive als Signale übertragen und beim Empfänger in Lichtimpulse umgesetzt, um dort wiederum Zeile für Zeile auf Fotopapier ausbelichtet zu werden.

Erste kommerziell nutzbare Verfahren wurden um 1900 entwickelt, und ab 1907 gab es beispielsweise zwischen Paris, Berlin und London bildtelegrafische Verbindungen, die teils auch für private Bildsendungen benutzt werden konnten. Ihren Durchbruch hatte diese Form der Bildübertragung ab Mitte der 1920er-Jahre, als Agenturen wie Associated Press erst nationale, dann internationale Netzwerke einrichteten, die Redaktionen in vielen Städten und später weltweit mit Meldungen und Bildern versorgten. Ab den 1950er-Jahren wurden Geräte zur drahtlosen Übertragung von Bildern eingesetzt; und in den 1980er-Jahren wurde die Bildtelegrafie von digitalen Verfahren abgelöst, bei denen die Bilder als Dateien versandt werden.

duce photographs. Only when they began to be rasterized around 1890 was it possible to simulate the gray tones of photographs using black-and-white newspaper printing.

The problem was similar to that of image telegraphy, where an image had to be broken down into small, easy-to-encode units to enable transmission. Indeed, attempts were made to use rasterized images as models and transmit the size of individual dots one after the other by telegraph or even by telephone; eventually, processes were established in which light-sensitive cells scan a photograph line by line and measure the relative brightness. The values are successively transmitted as signals and converted into light pulses at the receiving end, which photographic paper is then exposed to line by line.

The first commercially viable processes were developed around 1900, and from 1907 onward there were, for example, phototelegraphy connections between Paris, Berlin, and London, which could sometimes also be used to send personal images. This type of image transmission had its breakthrough in the mid-1920s, when agencies such as Associated Press set up first national, then international networks to supply editorial offices with news and images in many cities and later worldwide. From the 1950s, devices were used to wirelessly transmit images, and in the 1980s, image telegraphy was replaced by digital processes in which images are sent as files.

Text: Friedrich Tietjen

Clare Strand
The Discrete Channel with Noise: Algorithmic Painting, Destination, #11, 2020

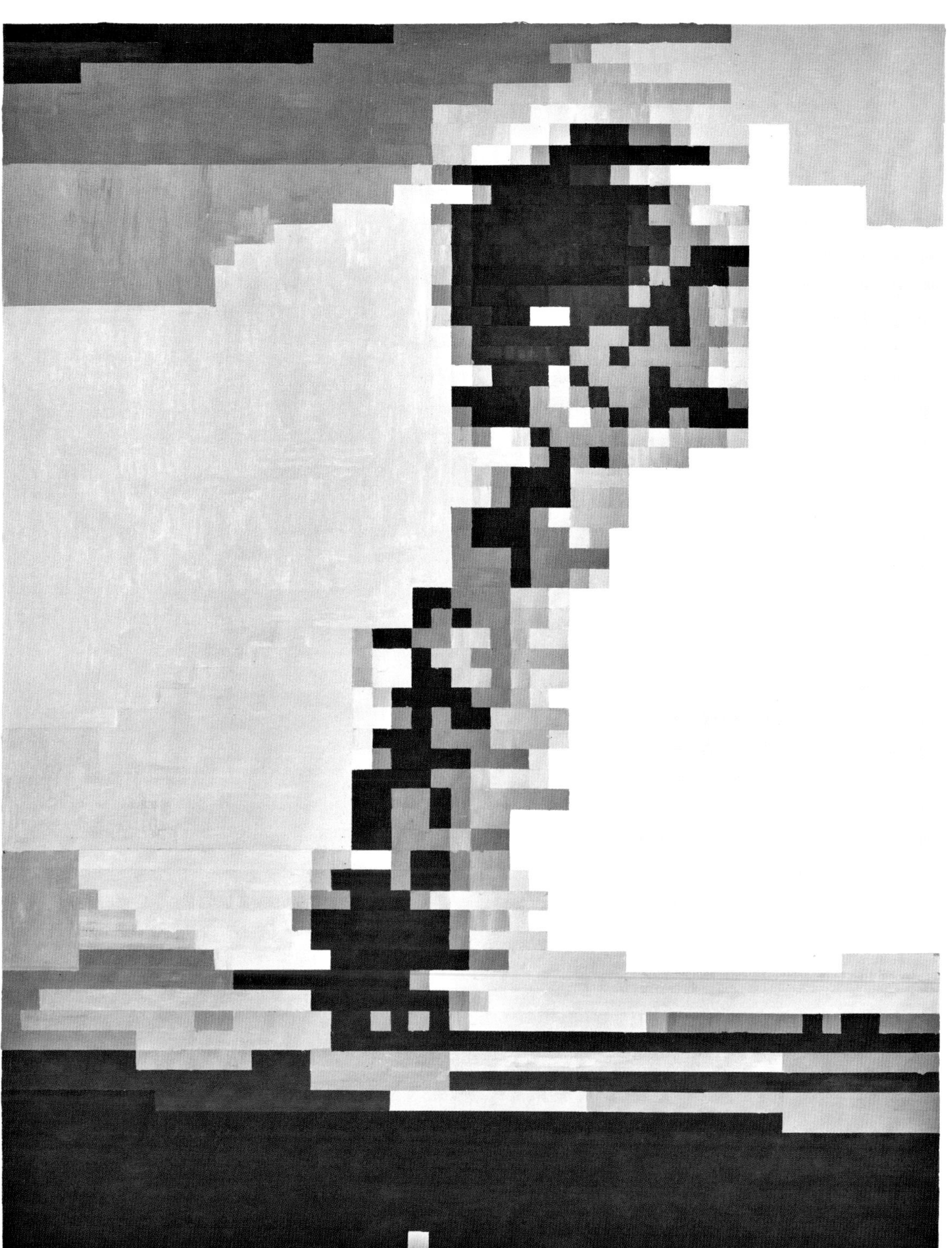

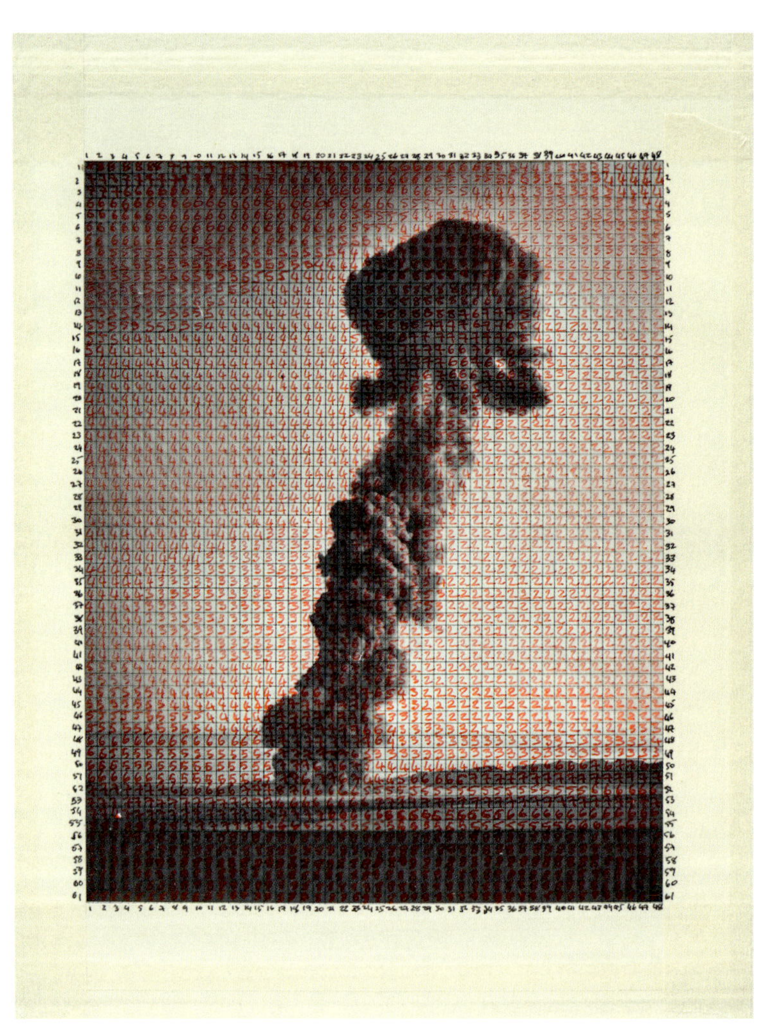

Clare Strand
The Discrete Channel with Noise: Information Source, #11, 2020

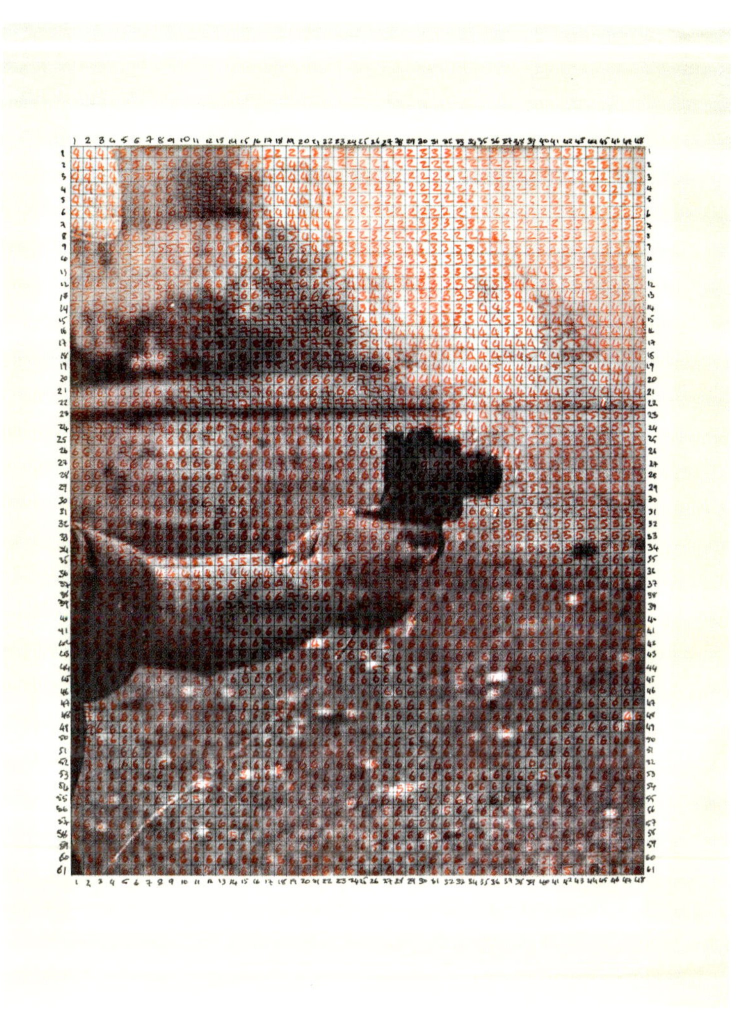

Clare Strand
The Discrete Channel with Noise: Information Source, #12, 2020

Clare Strand
The Discrete Channel with Noise: Algorithmic Painting, Destination, #12, 2020

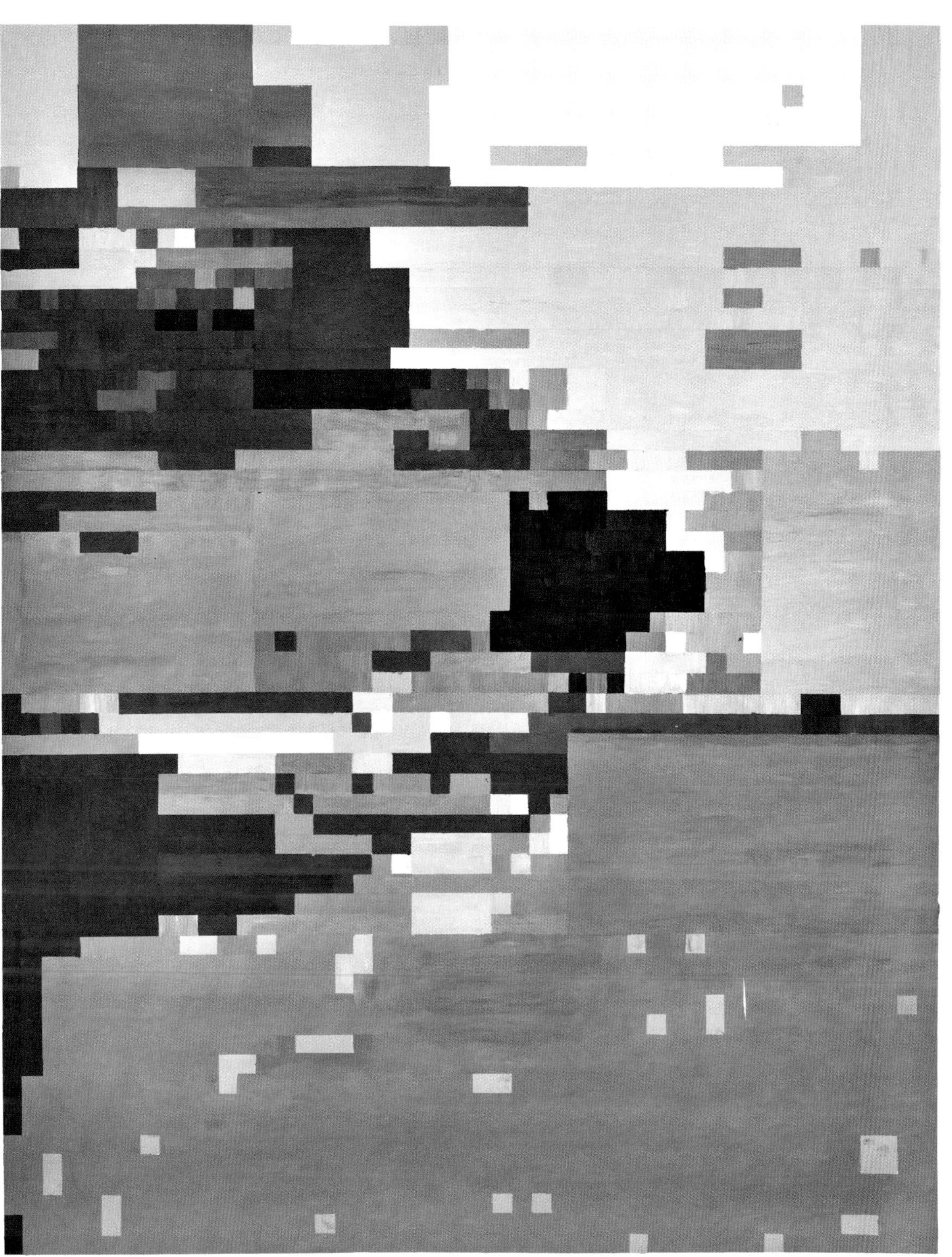

Clare Strand
The Discrete Channel with Noise: Algorithmic Painting, Destination, #13, 2020

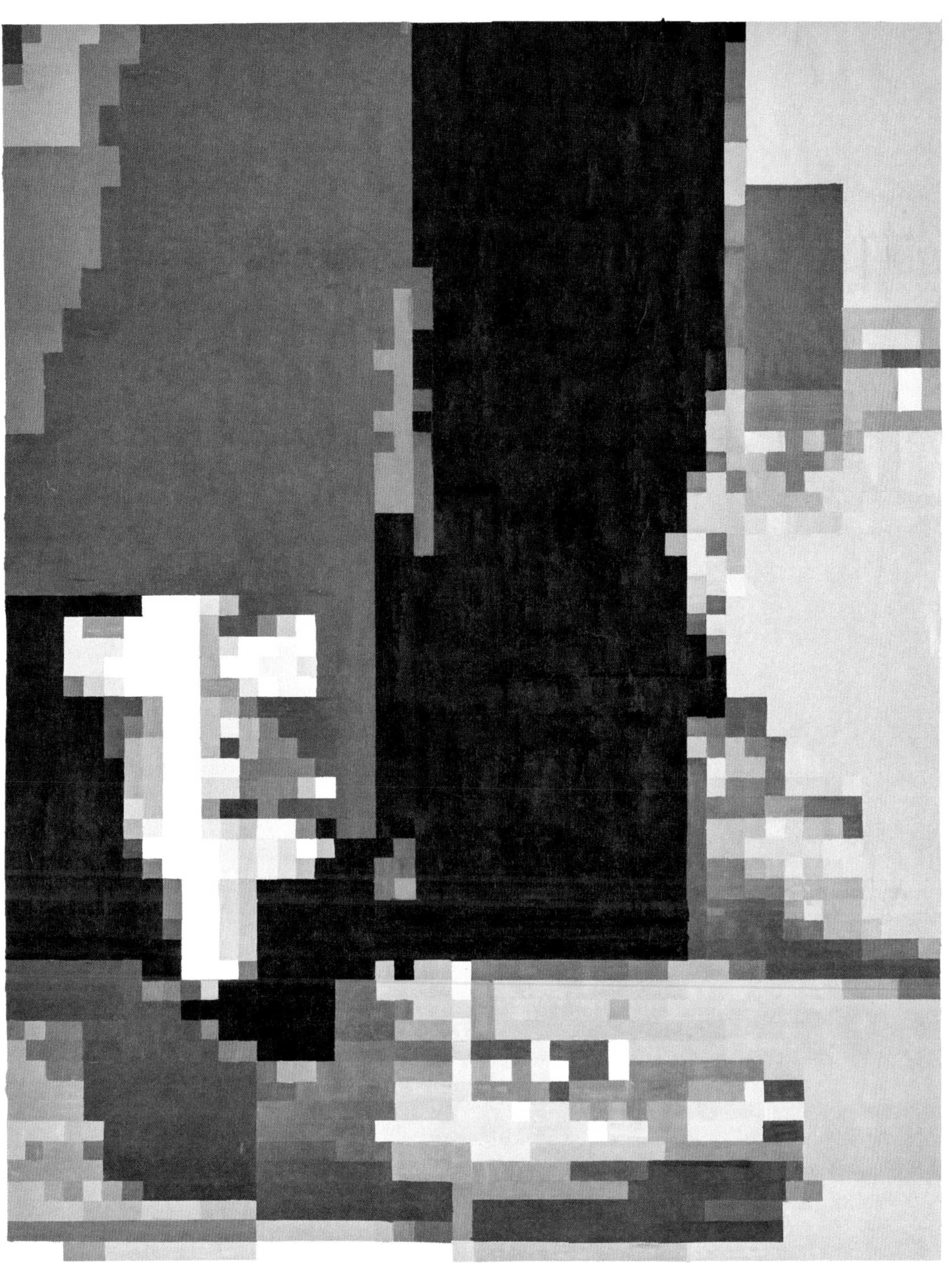

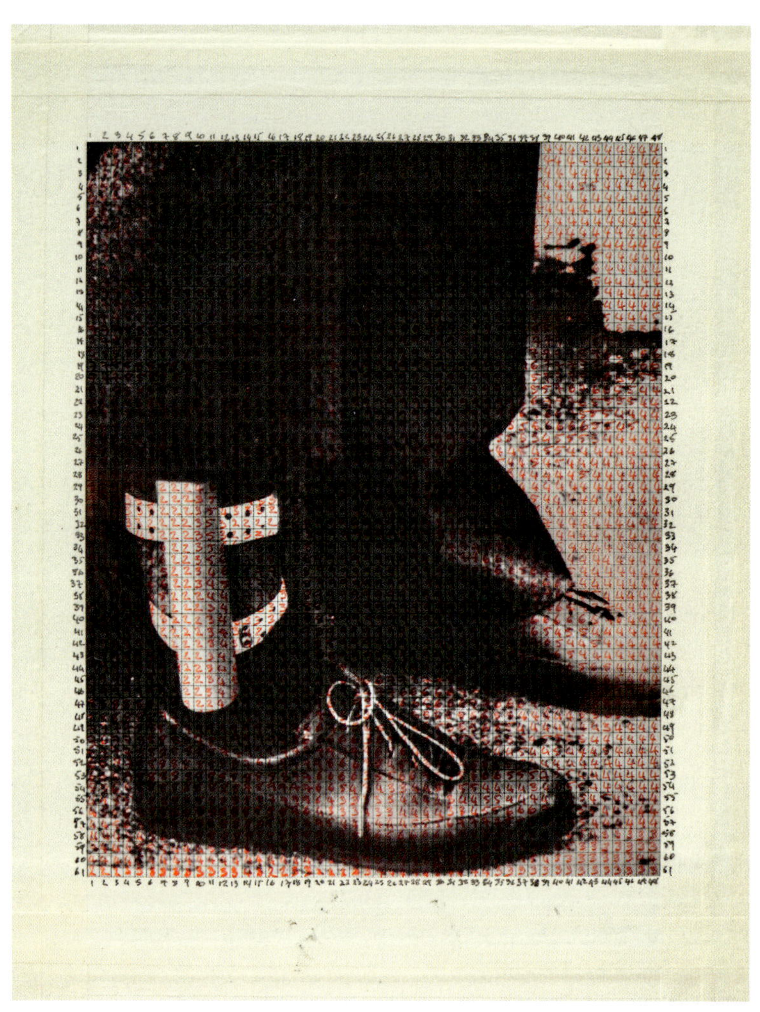

Clare Strand
The Discrete Channel with Noise: Information Source, #13, 2020

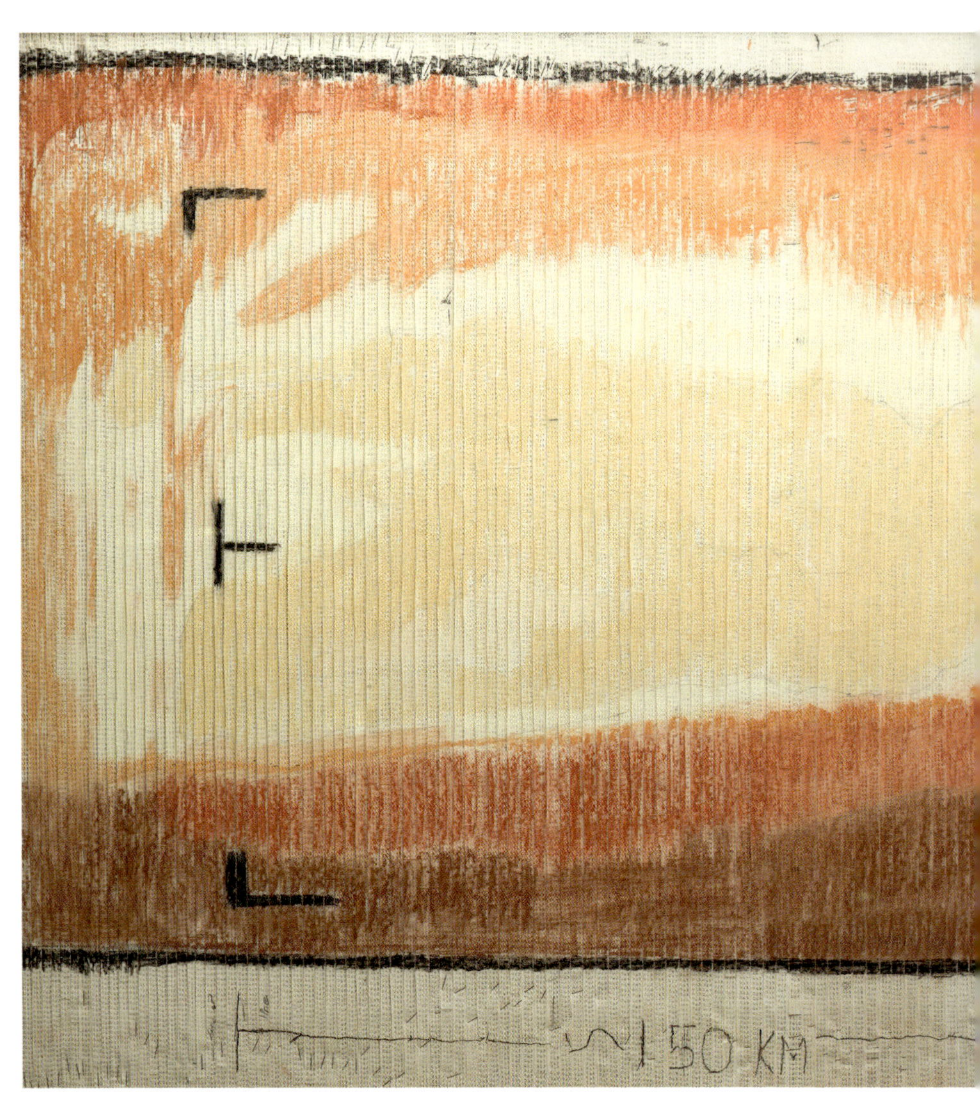

Anonym / **Anonymous** (NASA)
First TV Image of Mars, 15.07.1965 / **July 15, 1965,**
von Hand ausgemalter Ausdruck der übertragenen Daten / **hand-colored diagram of received data**

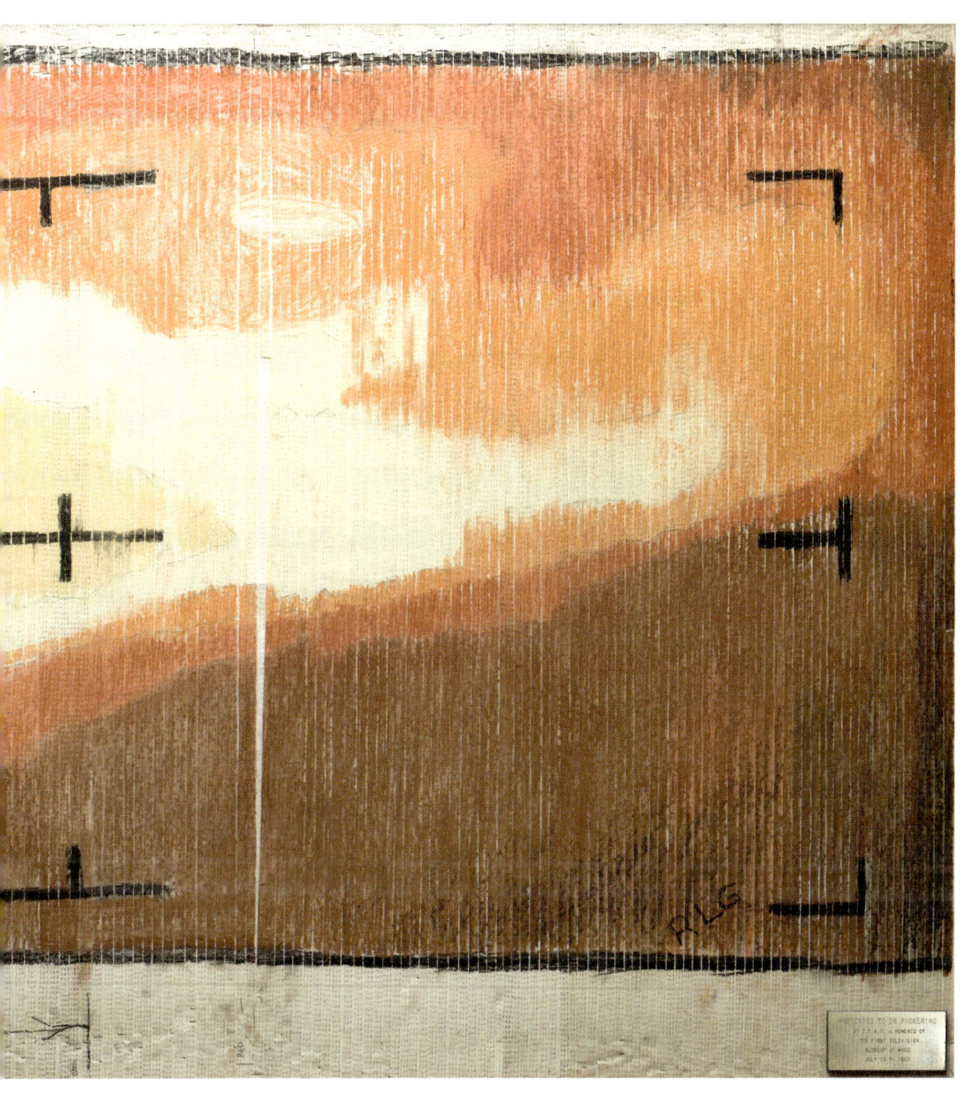
PRESENTED TO DR. PICKERING
BY J.P.L.A.T. A MEMENTO OF
THE FIRST TELEVISION
CLOSEUP OF MARS
JULY 15 TH 1965

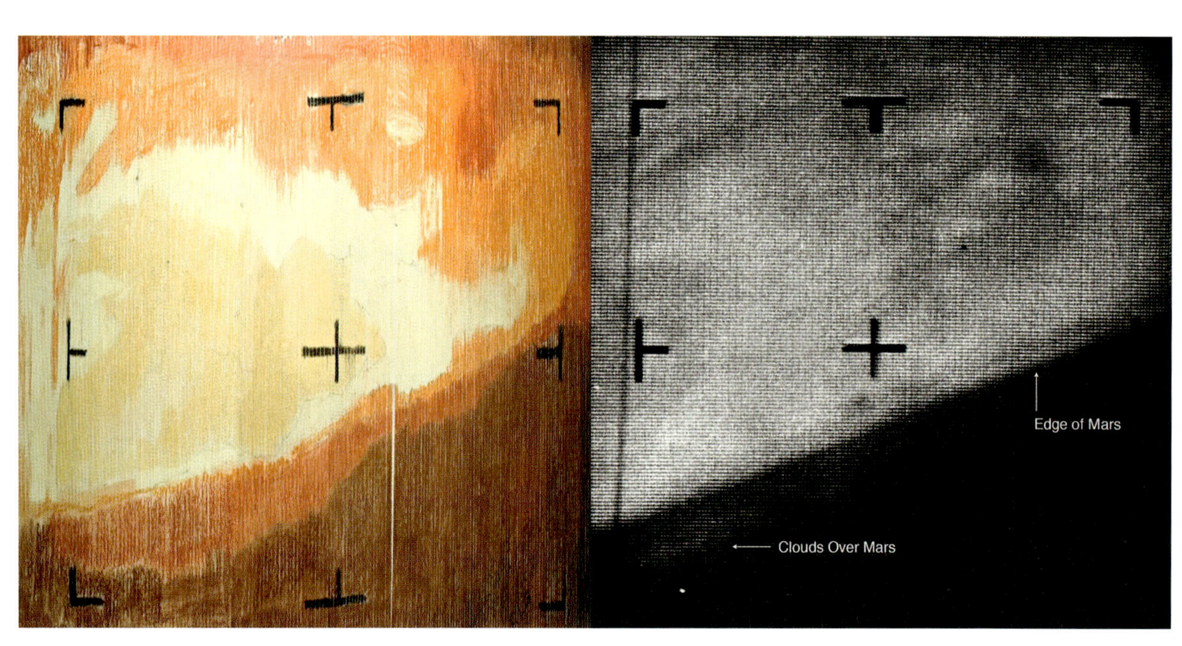

Edge of Mars
Clouds Over Mars

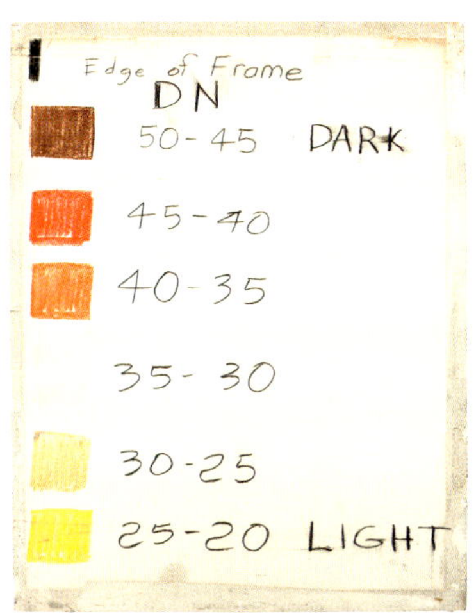

Edge of Frame
DN
50-45   DARK
45-40
40-35
35-30
30-25
25-20   LIGHT

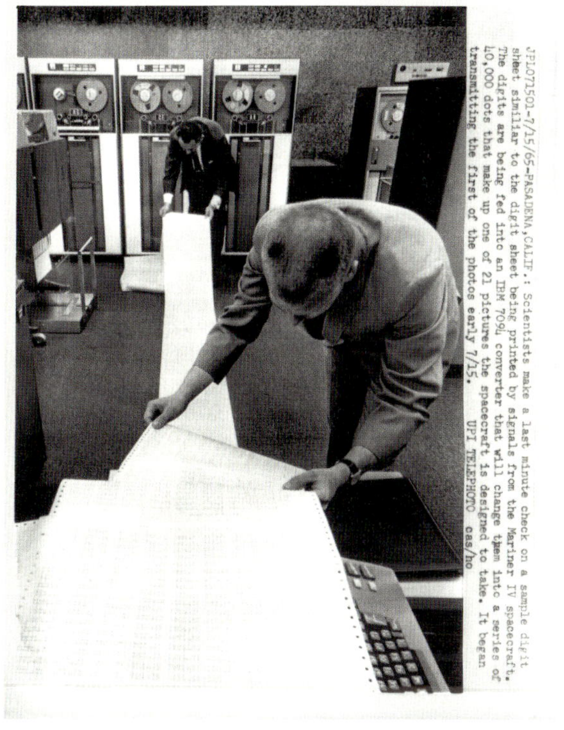

JPL071501-7/15/65-PASADENA,CALIF.: Scientists make a last minute check on a sample digit
sheet similiar to the digit sheet being printed by signals from the Mariner IV spacecraft.
The digits are being fed into an IBM 7094 converter that will change them into a series of
40,000 dots that make up one of 21 pictures the spacecraft is designed to take. It began
transmitting the first of the photos early 7/15.   UPI TELEPHOTO cas/ho

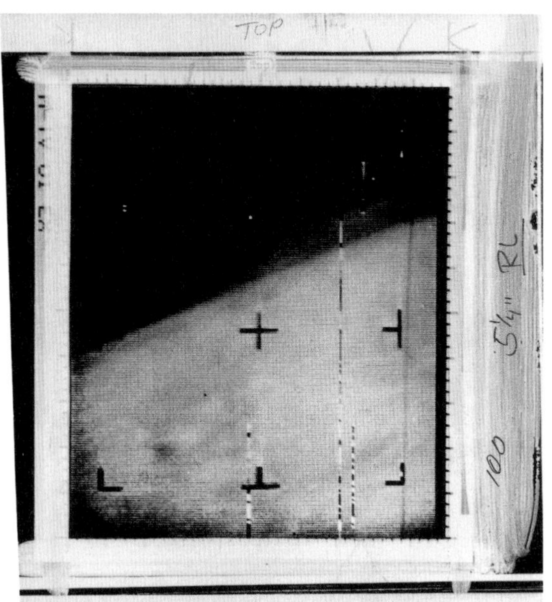
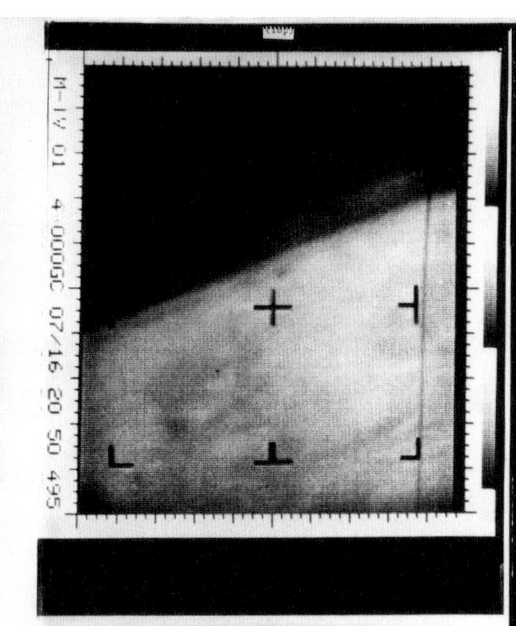

Anonym / **Anonymous** (NASA)
First Mars Photo after "Enhancement," Pasadena, California, 14.07.1965 / **July 14, 1965**

Los Angeles Times

LARGEST CIRCULATION IN THE WEST. 830,118 DAILY; 1,177,588 SUNDAY

VOL. LXXXIV   FIVE PARTS—PART ONE   CC   F   FRIDAY MORNING, JULY 16, 1965   98 PAGES   Copyright © 1965 Los Angeles Times   DAILY 10c

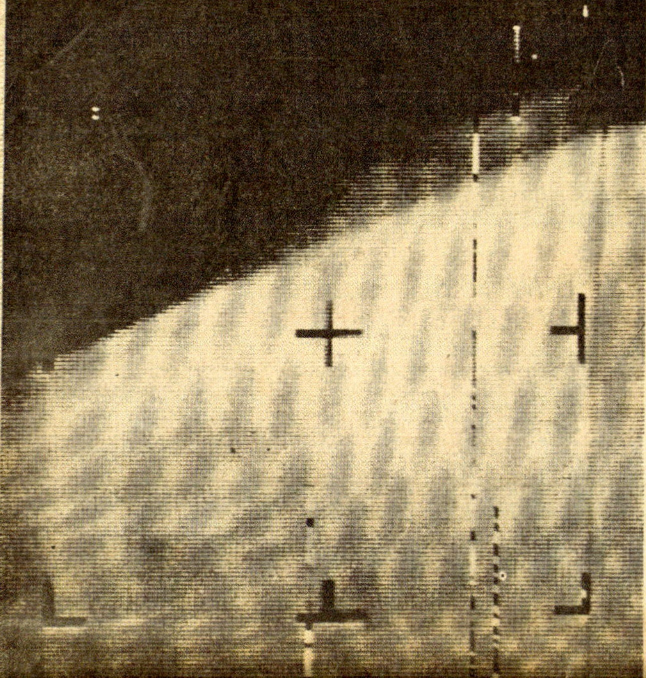

Historic Mars Photos Transmitted to Earth

McNamara Arrives for Viet Survey

War Escalation to Be Weighed; Lodge Accompanies Party

BY ARTHUR J. DOMMEN
Times Staff Writer

SAIGON—Secretary of Defense Robert S. McNamara arrived from Washington early today on a fact-finding trip to Vietnam that started under extremely tight security arrangements at Saigon airport to protect him from Communist Viet Cong terrorism.

McNamara, whose central concern during his visit will be to determine the exact rate of escalation during the two remaining months of the current monsoon season, has been the target of Red plots in the past.

This time, hundreds of U.S. Army and Air Force police reinforced Vietnamese

More news of Vietnam on Pages 2, 10, 11, 12 and 13, Part 1.

security units for the arrival of McNamara and U.S. Am-

First Close-up Picture From Mariner 4 Shows Curved Edge of Planet

BY MARVIN MILES
Times Aerospace Editor

Mariner 4's first close-up picture of Mars was released Thursday night, showing the curved edge of the planet and light and dark areas of the Martian desert Phlegra.

The historic photo, transmitted in the form of numbers across more than 134 million miles of space, was much better than had been anticipated.

In the words of Dr. R. B. Leighton, Caltech's physicist-astronomer and leader of a team of experimenters on the photo project, the first picture marked "a magnificent technical achievement."

Success Presaged

In clarity, the first picture presaged a remarkable success for the Mariner photo mission if the remaining 19 to 20 pictures show expected improvement.

Dr. Leighton said no immediate scientific analysis could be made from the first picture. It will require considerable study and comparison with known information about Mars before this can be done, he added.

The scientist addressed a press conference Thursday night at the Jet Propulsion Laboratory in Pasadena.

the picture itself and brought applause from the audience of newsmen.

The first picture is 10 to 15 times better than the best earth-based pictures taken to date and he expects later photos to be 30 times better, he continued.

As he talked, Mariner's second picture was being transmitted to the Goldstone tracking station near Barstow. It should be available for release today.

Dr. Leighton pointed out that the appearance of the planet's round edge or limb is a fortunate circumstance since there appeared some fogging, apparently due to light in the camera system on the dark area representing space.

Fogging Discerned

Had the picture of the edge not been available, this fogging might not have been recognized and could have materially complicated the problem of photo analysis.

When he was asked what type of terrain appeared in

Los Angeles Times
Historische Mars-Fotos auf die Erde übertragen, 16.07.1965 / **Historic Mars Photos Transmitted to Earth, July 16, 1965**

Thomas Ruff
press++02.20, 2015

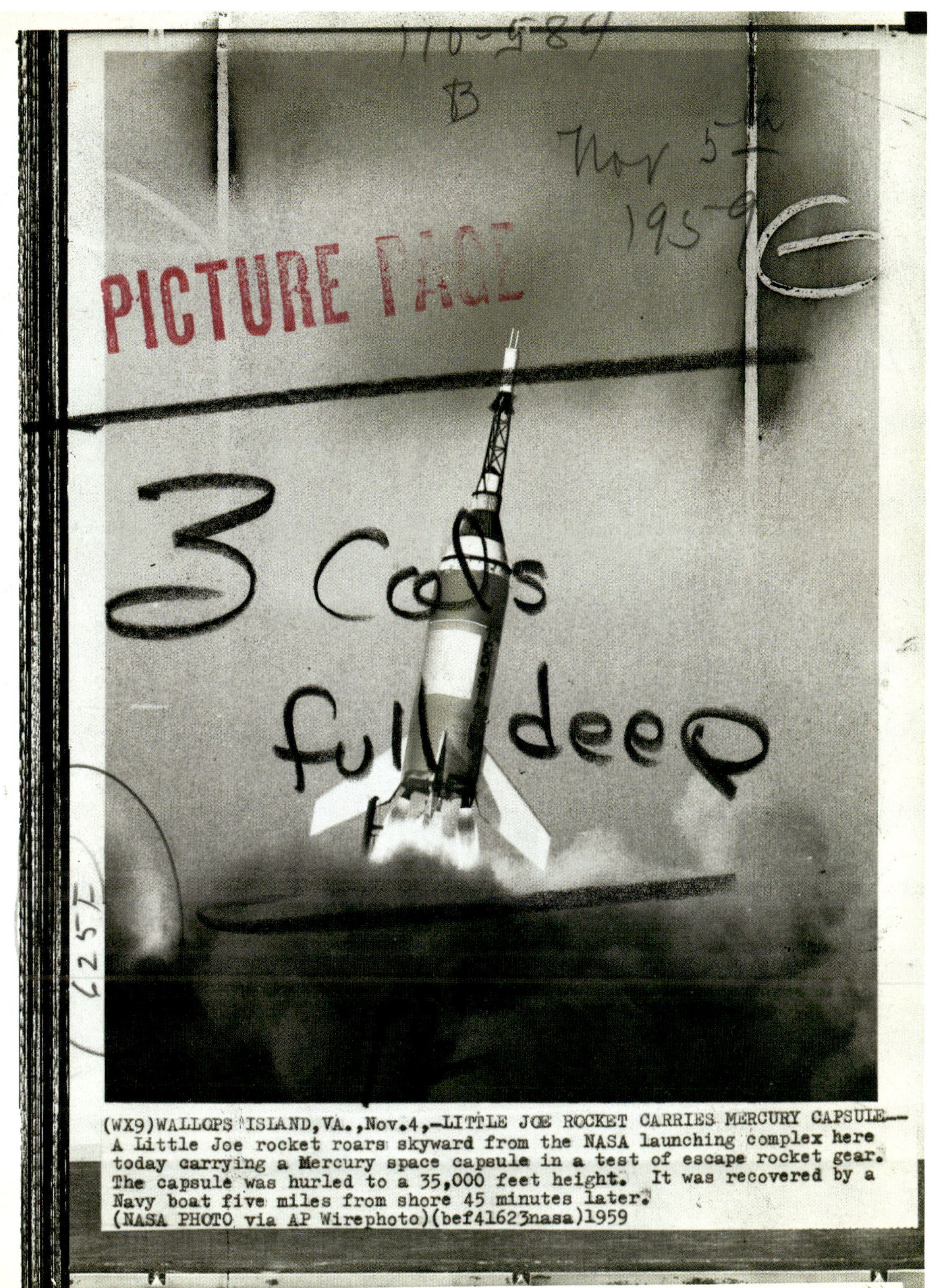

(WX9)WALLOPS ISLAND,VA.,Nov.4,--LITTLE JOE ROCKET CARRIES MERCURY CAPSULE--
A Little Joe rocket roars skyward from the NASA launching complex here
today carrying a Mercury space capsule in a test of escape rocket gear.
The capsule was hurled to a 35,000 feet height. It was recovered by a
Navy boat five miles from shore 45 minutes later.
(NASA PHOTO via AP Wirephoto)(bef41623nasa)1959

Thomas Ruff
press++22.75, 2016

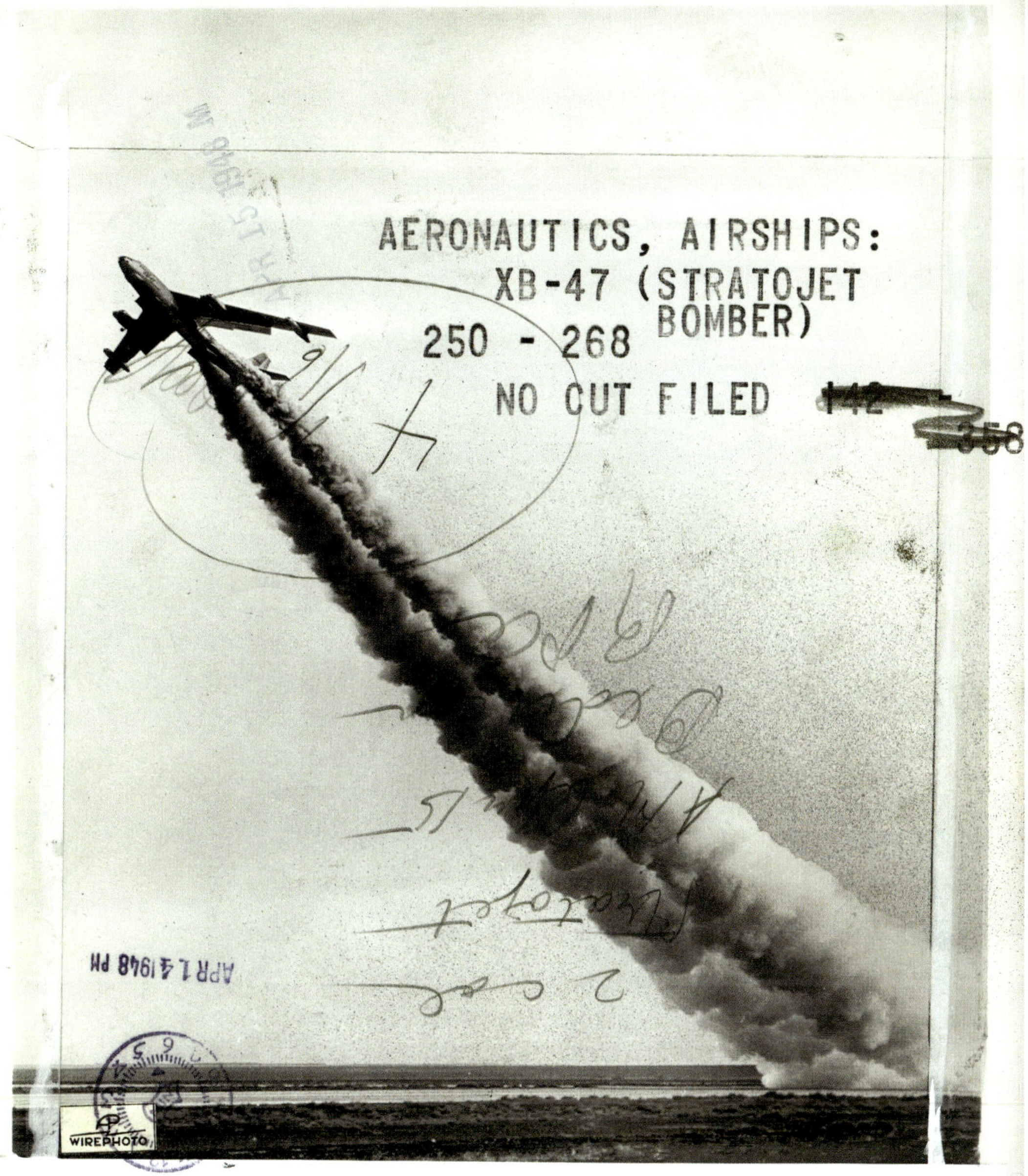

NY10-APRIL 12) STRATOJET IN ROCKET TAKE-OFF--The Boeing XB-47 Stratojet, U.S. Air Force's newest bomber, trails plumes of smoke as it zooms skyward in rocket-assisted take-off at Moses Lake Air Force Base in state of Washington. Eighteen rocket units, mounted nine in each side of the plane's 108-foot fuselage, are used in heavy load take-offs and for emergency power needs. Six turbo-jet engines supply normal power. Plane is first bomber with swept-back wing.(AP Wirephoto)(pjm/pr21045HO)1948
(ADVANCE FOR USE IN AMS OF THURSDAY, APRIL 15)

HANDYFOTO

Im Dezember 1878 erschien in dem Londoner Magazin *Punch* die Abbildung eines sensationellen Gerätes. Mit dem Telephonoskop sollte man miteinander sprechen und sich zugleich sehen können. Natürlich war dieses Gerät eine Fiktion, angeregt durch die öffentlichen Vorführungen der ersten Telefonapparate in den Jahren zuvor. Doch am Telephonoskop wird auch das Potential der Verbindung der beiden Medien Telefon und Kamera deutlich: Werden von Kameras generierte Bilder bei oder unmittelbar nach der Aufnahme gesendet, verschwindet die Nachträglichkeit der Fotografie – was ihre Bilder zeigen, muss nicht Vergangenheit, sondern kann auch Gegenwart sein.

Erste funktionsfähige Geräte, die die Mediensysteme Fotografie und Telefonie miteinander koppelten, lassen sich bis in die 1920er-Jahre zurückverfolgen. Ihren Durchbruch erlebte diese Verbindung jedoch erst in dem Moment, als das Telefon Ende der 1990er-Jahre mobilisiert wurde. Die Ursprungsidee rückte dabei in den Hintergrund: Weil die in den Mobilfunknetzen verfügbaren Übertragungsraten für die Videotelefonie kaum ausreichten, wurden die mit Kameras versehenen Mobiltelefone vor allem für den Versand kleinerer Bilddateien genutzt. Noch heute spielt die Videotelefonie eher eine Nebenrolle; die mit Mobiltelefonen aufgenommenen Bilder haben sich deutlich verändert: 360-Grad-Aufnahmen sind ebenso möglich wie schnelle Serienfotografien und Filme. Auch die für die Geräte verfügbaren Apps zur Bildbearbeitung machen es möglich,

CAMERA-PHONE PHOTOS

In December 1878 the London magazine *Punch* published an illustration of a sensational device. The telephonoscope was said to allow people to talk to and see each other at the same time. Of course, this device was an invention inspired by the recent public demonstrations of the first telephones. But the telephonoscope made clear the potential of connecting the two media of telephone and camera. If images created by cameras are sent while or immediately after being recorded, the retroactive nature of photography vanishes, meaning that images need not only show the past, but can also show the present moment.

The first functioning devices to couple photography and telephony date back to the 1920s. However, this connection only became viable when the telephone became mobile in the late 1990s. The original idea took a back seat: because the transmission speeds available on cell phone networks were insufficient to support video telephony, cell-phones equipped with cameras were used primarily for sending small image files. Still today video telephony continues to play more of a secondary role. Photographs taken with cell phones have significantly changed: 360-degree shots, rapid series of photographs, and films are all possible now. The image-editing apps now available mean it is also possible to make photographs look like watercolors or Polaroids, to animate them, and add comical dog snouts, written messages, or fake film scratches. And because cell phones have increasingly more storage space and are usually within reach all day long, the spectrum of motifs is expanding. The main sub-

Fotografien etwa wie Aquarelle oder Polaroids erscheinen zu lassen, sie zu animieren und mit lustigen Hundenasen, Beschriftungen oder falschen Filmkratzern zu versehen. Und weil diese Telefone immer größere Speicherkapazitäten besitzen und in der Regel den ganzen Tag zur Hand sind, erweitert sich das Spektrum der Motive: Zwar werden auch weiterhin vor allem Kinder, Reisen und Freizeitvergnügen fotografiert. Doch daneben werden Bilder von Menüs in Flugzeugen gemacht, von frisch modellierten Fingernägeln, von Wasserwerfern in den Straßen der Stadt und von Prominenten, die angetrunken in Blumenkübel pinkeln.

Vielleicht am eindrucksvollsten hat sich die Quantität der Bilder verändert. Für das Jahr 2020 wird prognostiziert, dass 1,4 Billionen Fotografien aufgenommen werden, 90 % davon mit den Smartphones, die sich in den Händen von gegenwärtig etwa 3,5 Milliarden Nutzer*innen befinden. Diese Zahlen müssten eigentlich noch größer ausfallen. Denn auch wenn ein großer Teil dieser Bilder nie wieder angesehen wird, so zirkulieren viele andere via Messengerdiensten und Social-Media-Websites, werden geteilt, bearbeitet, reproduziert. Im 19. Jahrhundert hatten die zahllosen fotografischen Verfahren dafür gesorgt, dass die Bindung zwischen Bild und Bildträger immer lockerer und variabler wurde – ein Bild konnte vom Negativ abgezogen, in einem anderen Verfahren vervielfältigt, nochmals abfotografiert und dann gedruckt werden. Mit der digitalen Fotografie, zumal der Mobiltelefone, löst sich diese Bindung fast vollständig auf – die Bilder sind kein chemischer Niederschlag auf objekthaften Bildträgern wie Glasplatten, Filmen oder Papier. Aus gespeicherten Daten übersetzt erscheinen sie auf Bildschirmen, sie haben keinen spezifischen Ort und keine andere Zeit als ihre eigene Gegenwärtigkeit.

jects remain children, travel, and leisure activities. But alongside them, pictures are being of items such as menus on airplanes, freshly done fingernails, water cannons in city streets, and drunk celebrities peeing into flowerpots.

The most impressive change might be the number of images taken. It is estimated that in 2020, 1.4 trillion photographs were taken, 90% of them with smartphones, which are currently used by around 3.5 billion individuals. These figures should be even higher. Even if most of these images vanished into the chaotic darkness of the storage media inside and outside of phones, never to be viewed again, many others will circulate on messenger services and social media sites and will be shared, edited, and reproduced. In the nineteenth century, countless photographic processes loosened the bond between image and image carrier, making the two increasingly interchangeable. An image could be made from a negative, reproduced using another process, photographed again, and then printed. Thanks to digital photography, especially photographs taken with cell phones, this bond has been almost entirely dissolved. The images are no longer a chemical deposit on object-like image supports such as glass plates, film, or paper. Translated from stored data, they fleetingly appear on screens; they no longer even exist in a specific place or time other than their own presence.

Text: Friedrich Tietjen

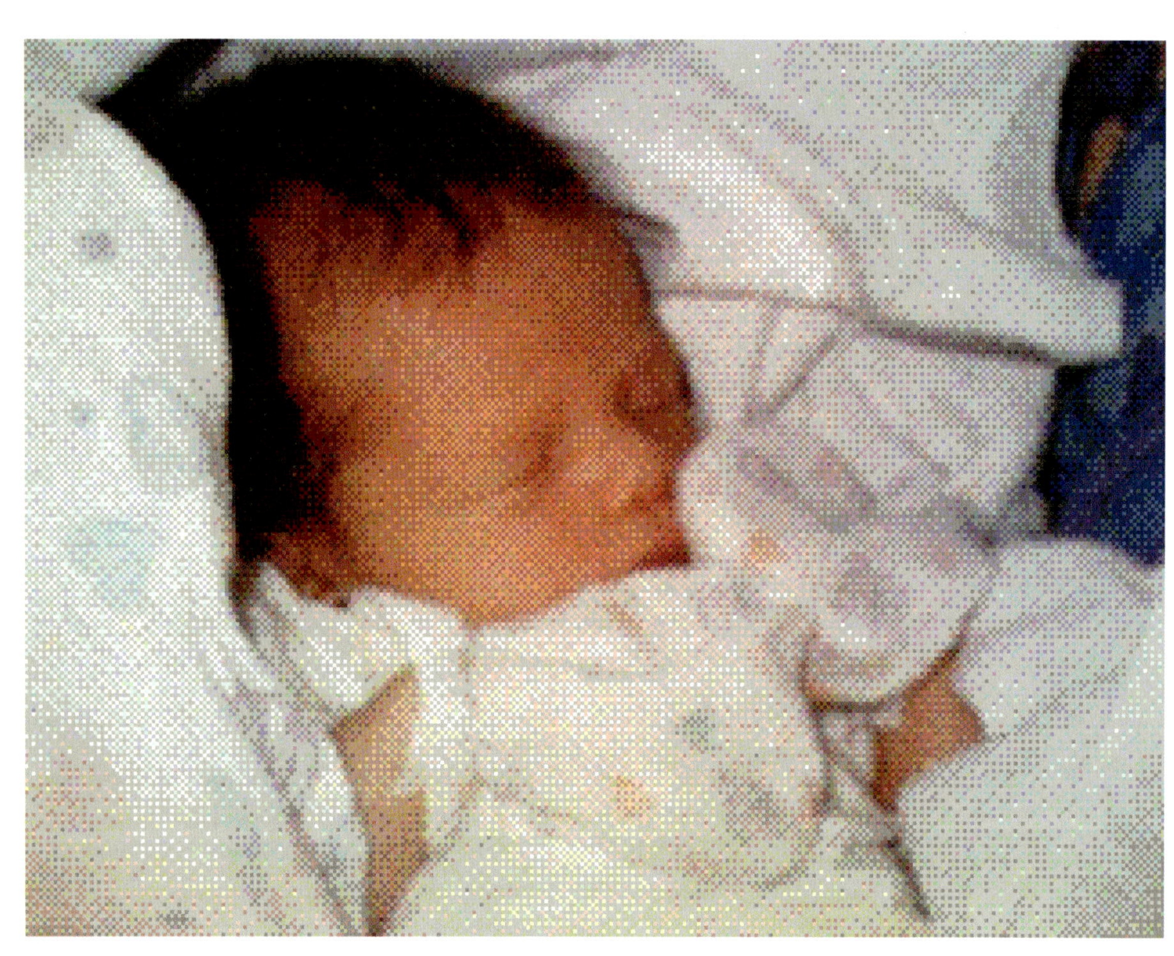

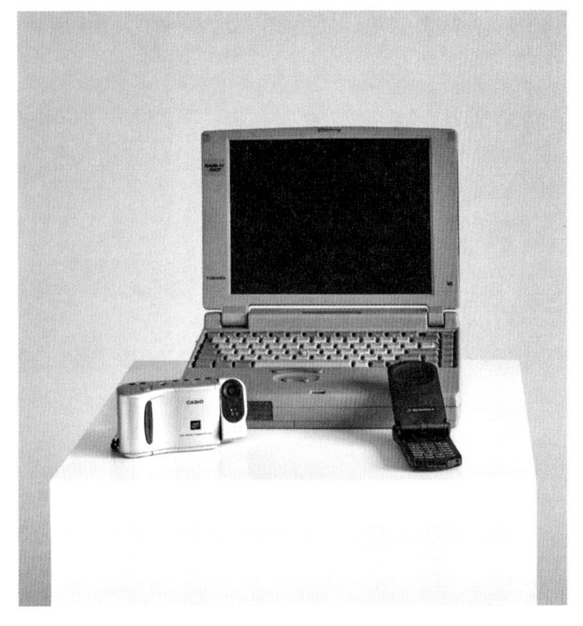

Equipment des ersten Kamera-Handy-Fotos, 11.6.1997 /
Equipment of the first camera-phone photo, June 11, 1997, 2020

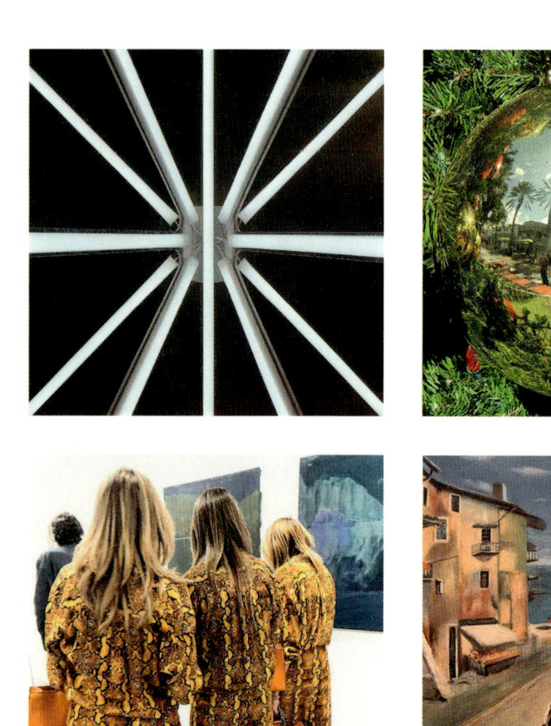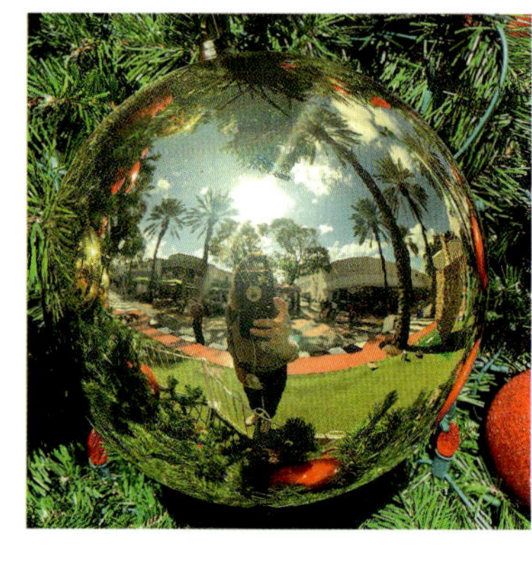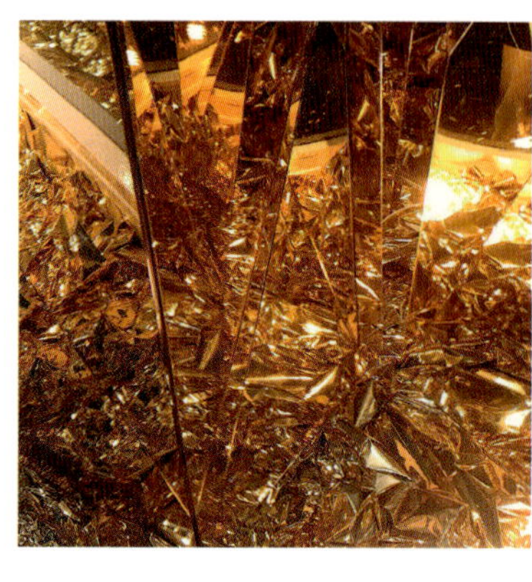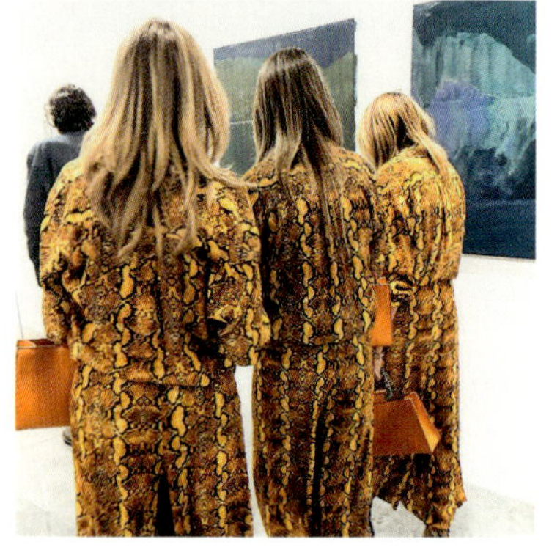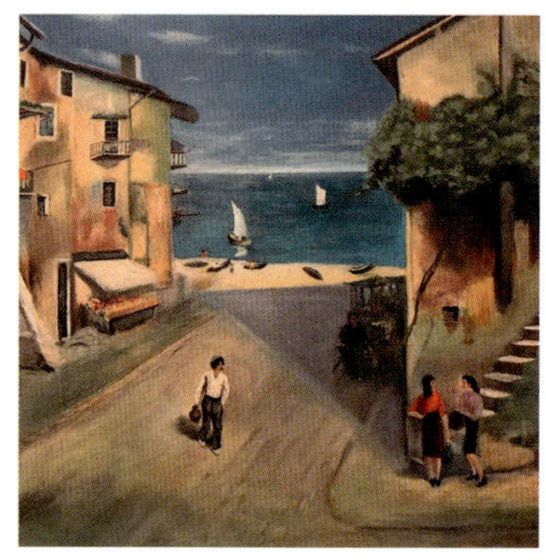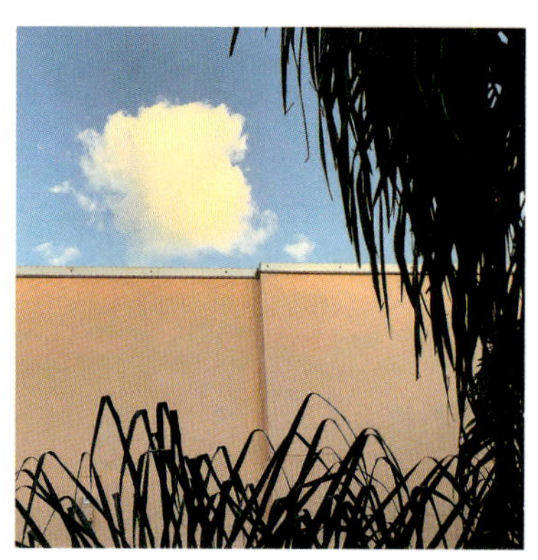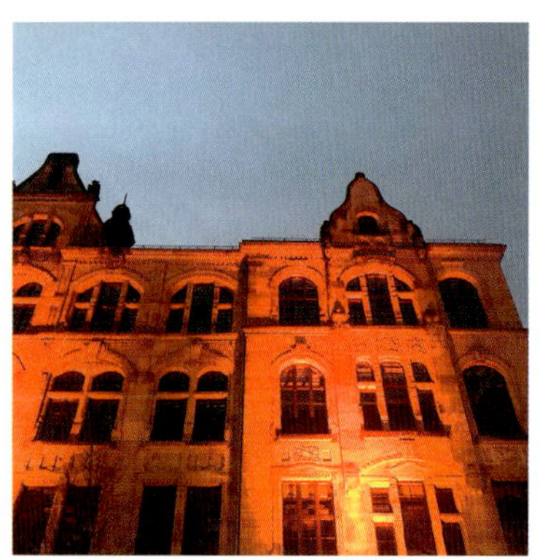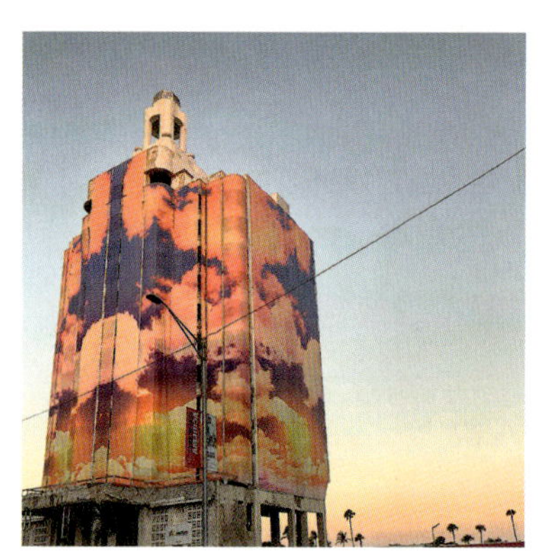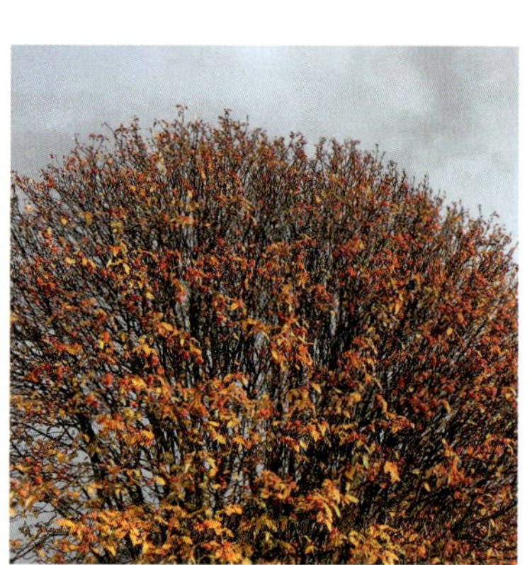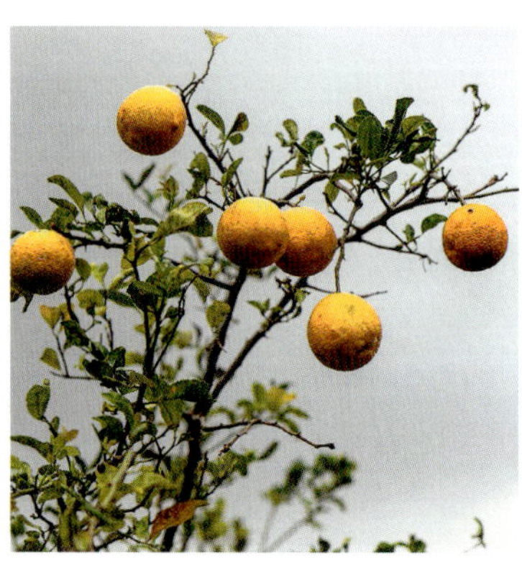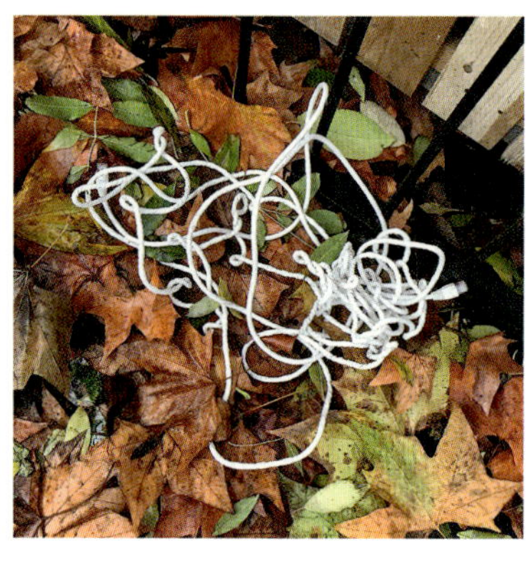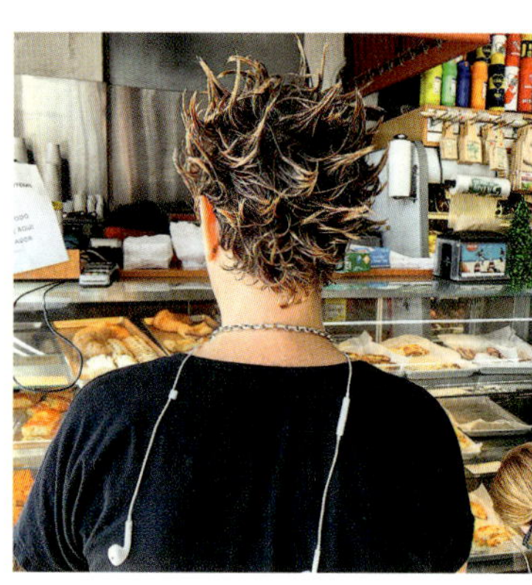

David Campany & Anastasia Samoylova
Untitled, aus Dialog auf / **dialogue on Instagram** 2017–heute / **present**

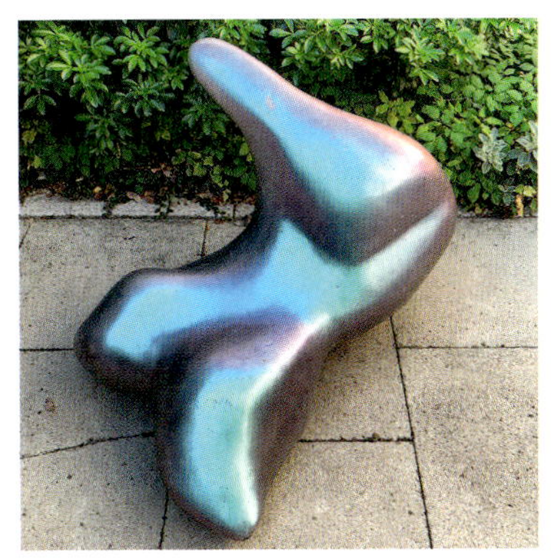
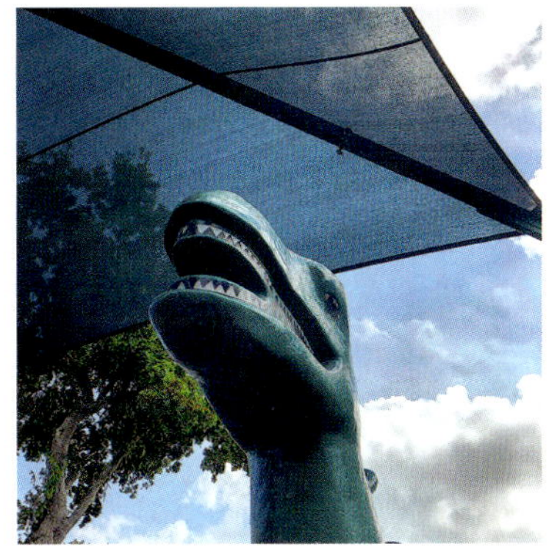
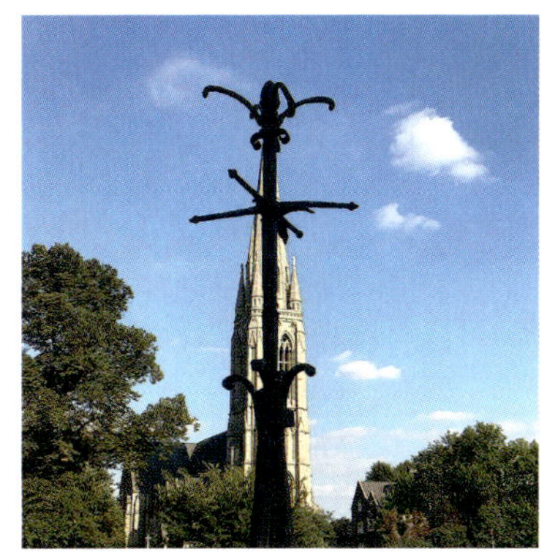
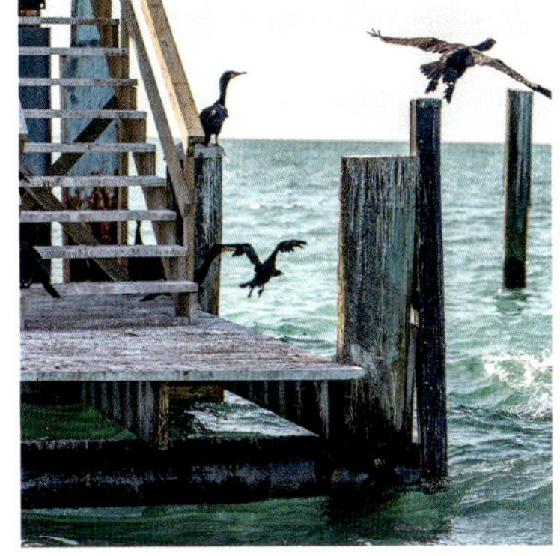
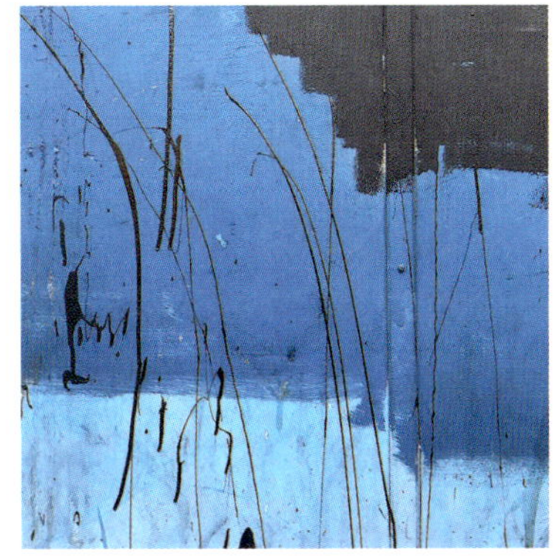
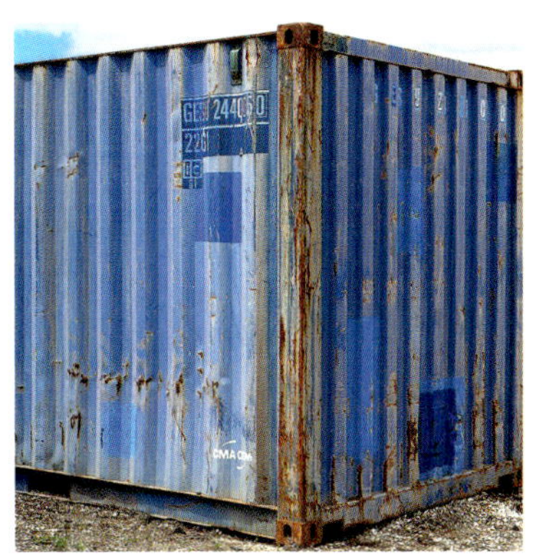
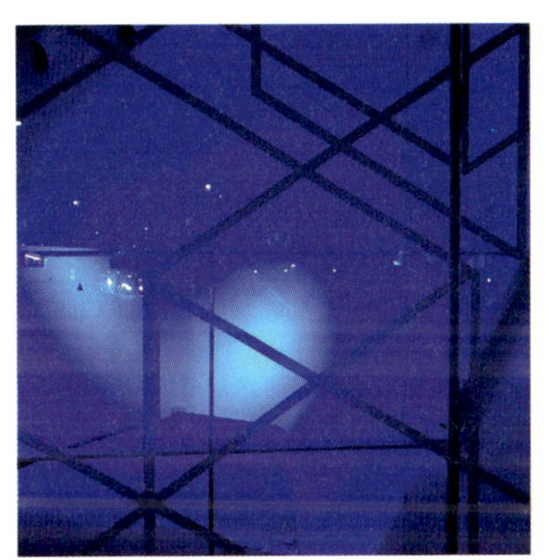
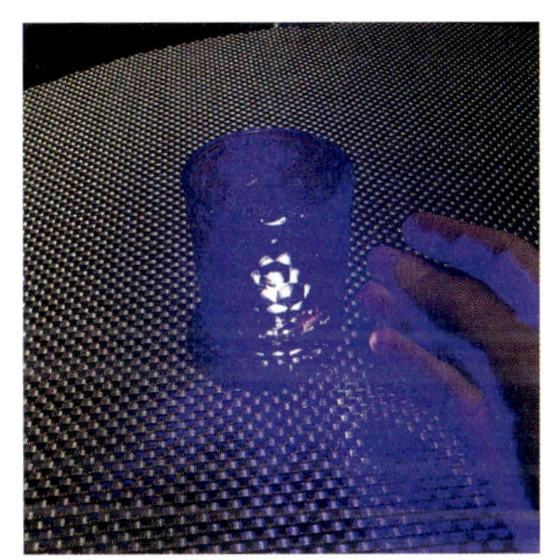
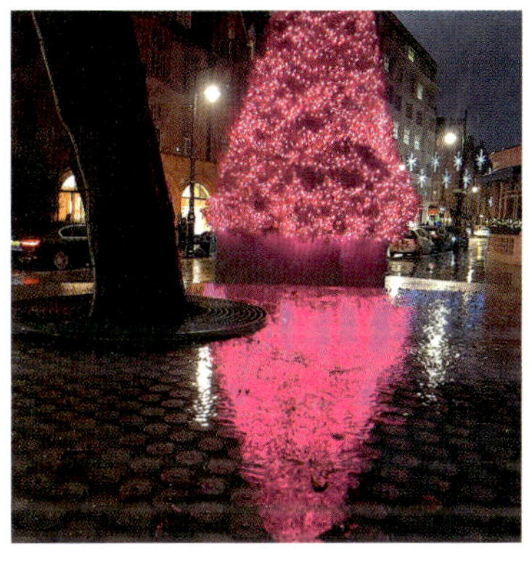
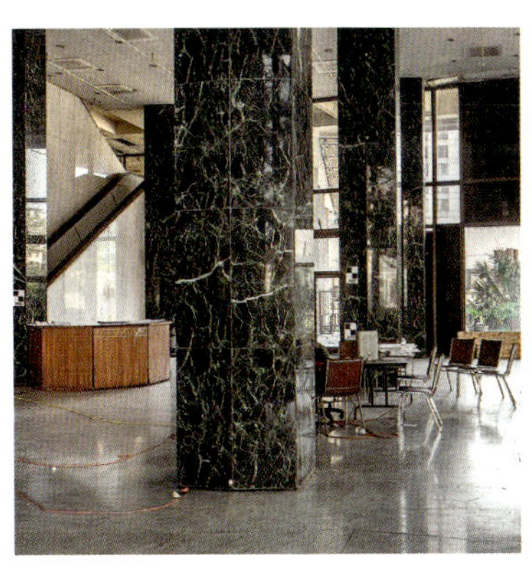
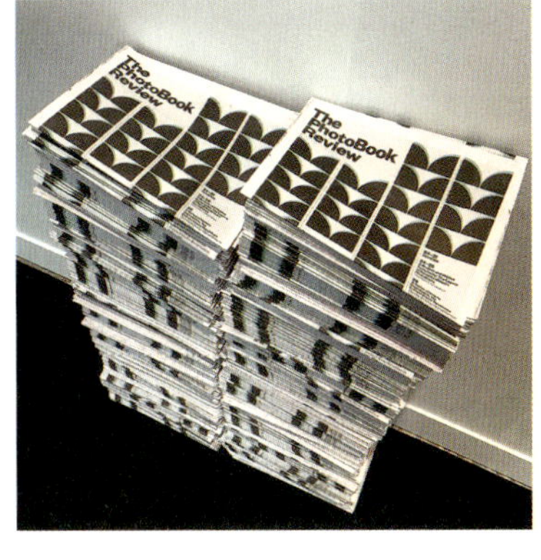
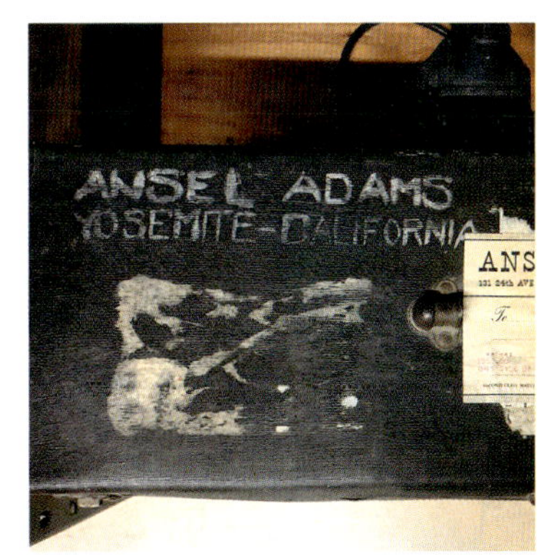

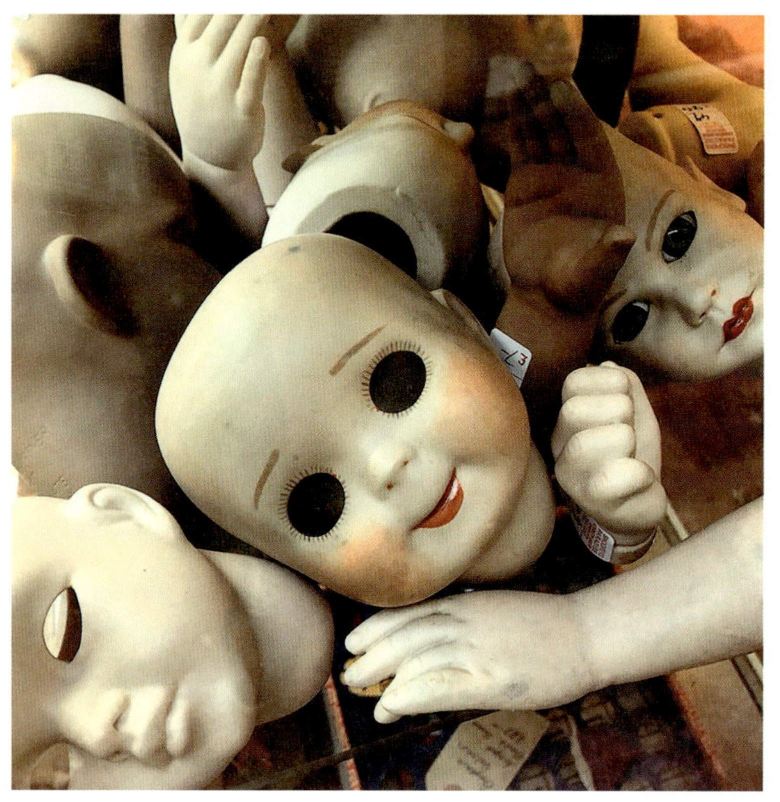
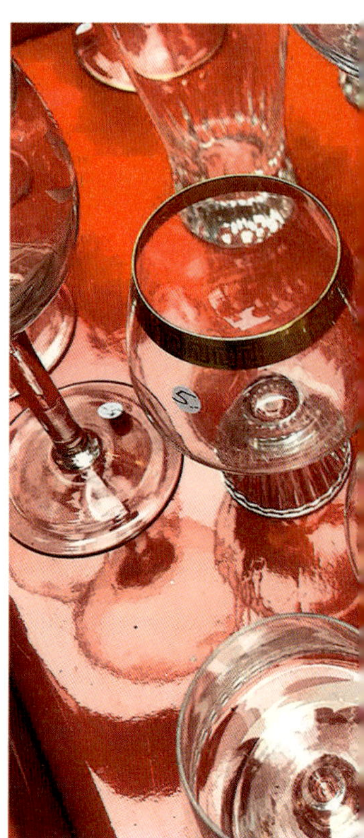

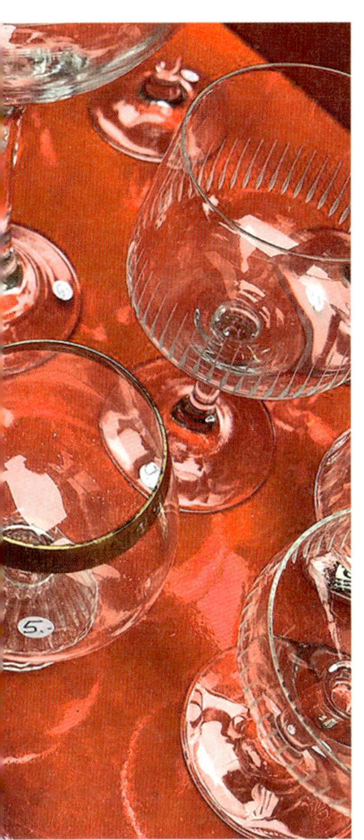
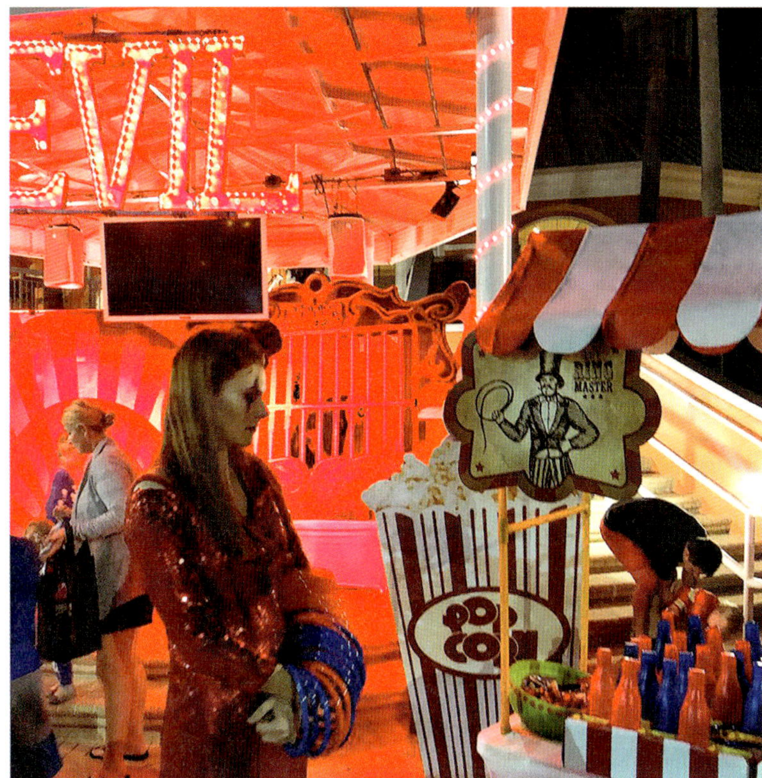

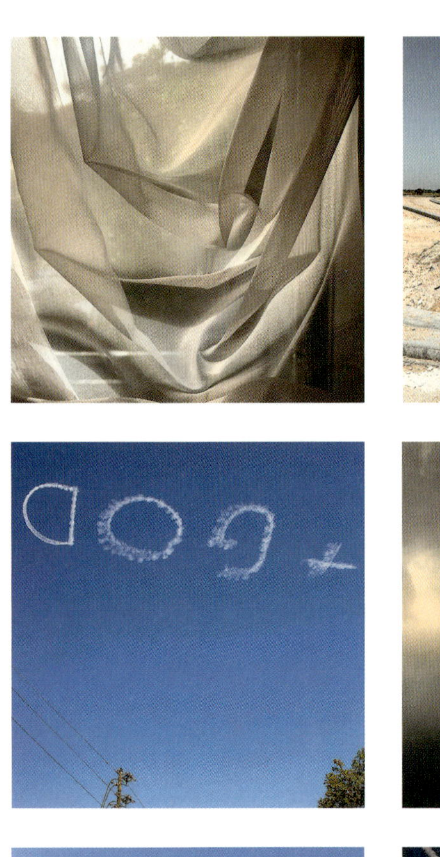
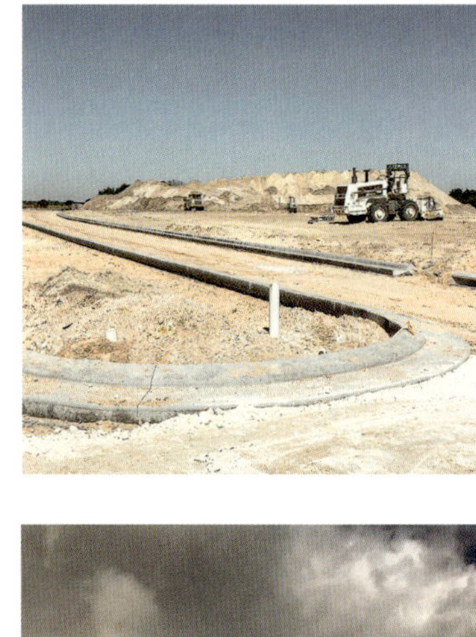
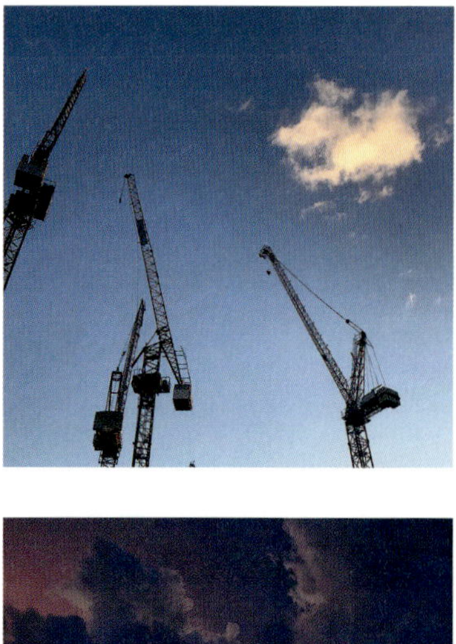
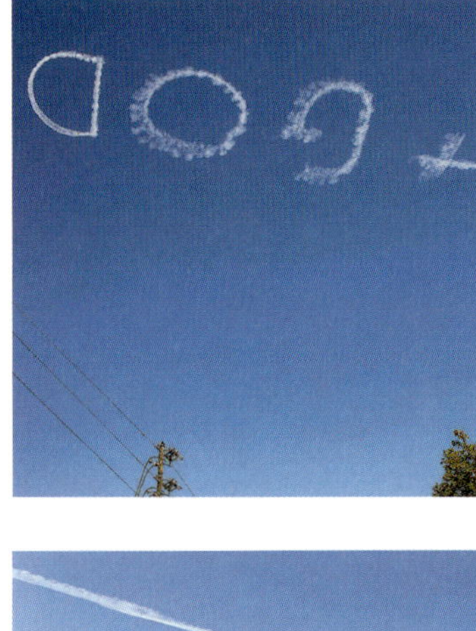
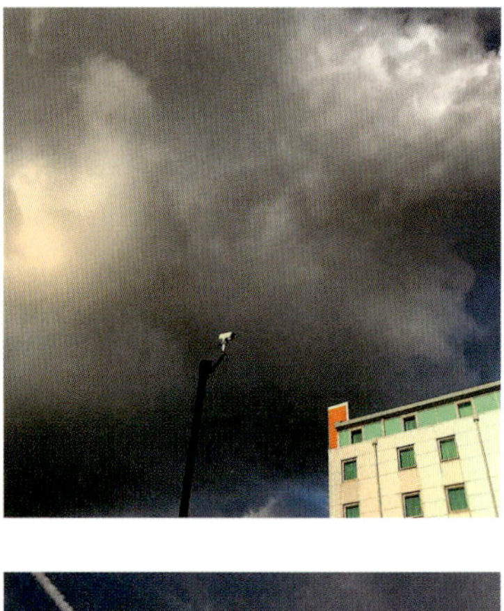
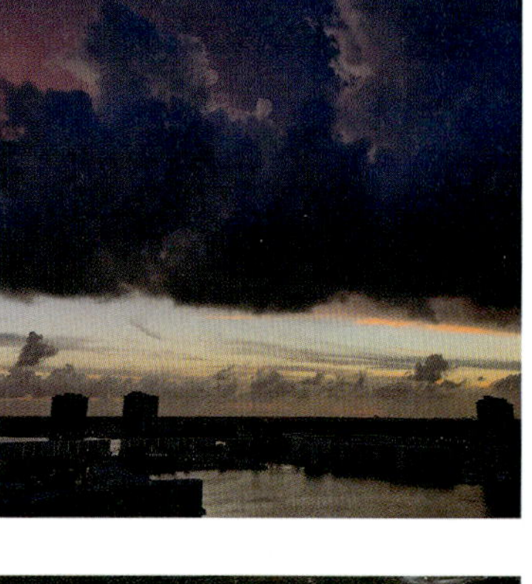
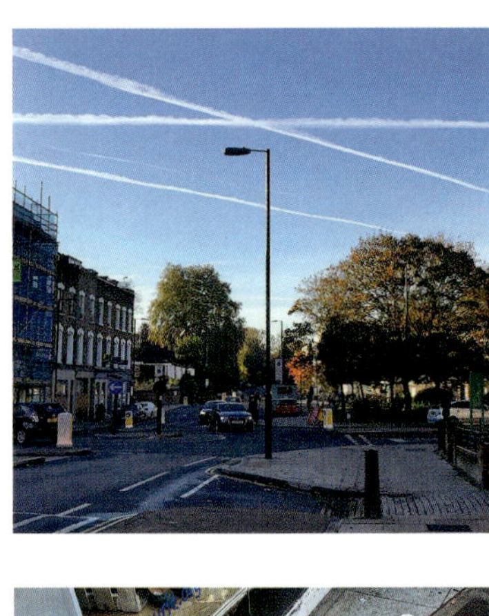
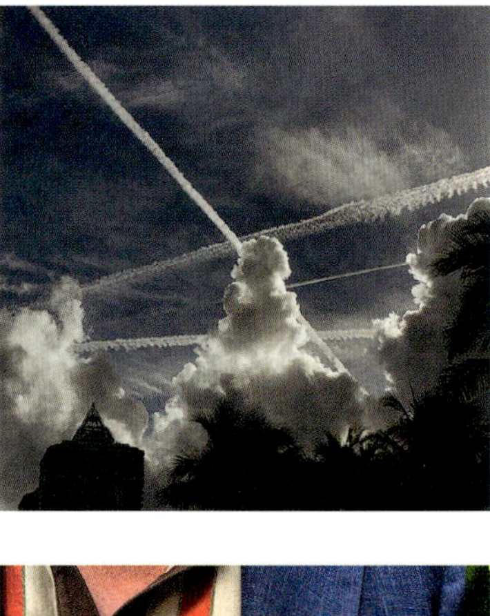
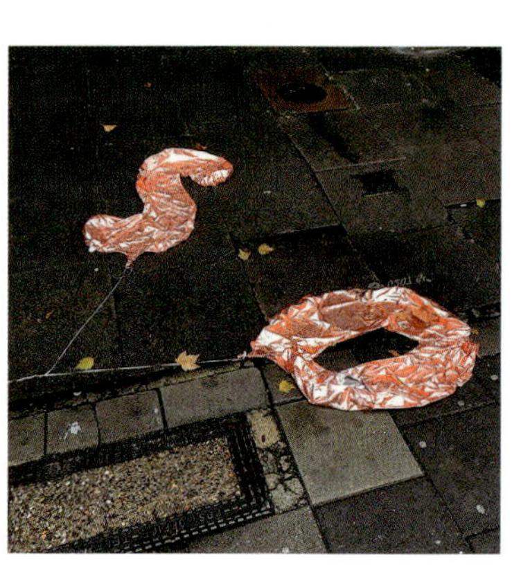
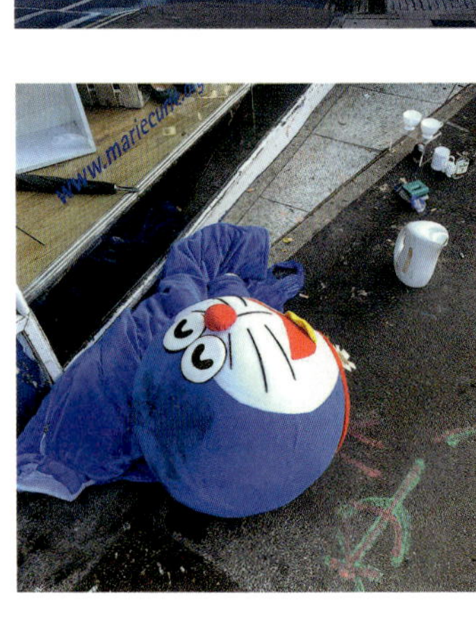
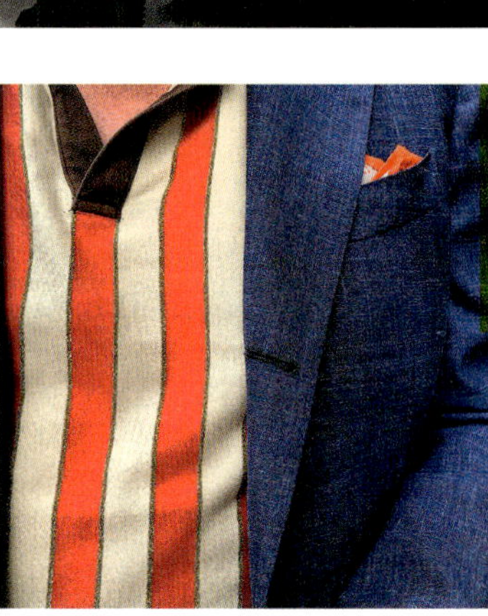
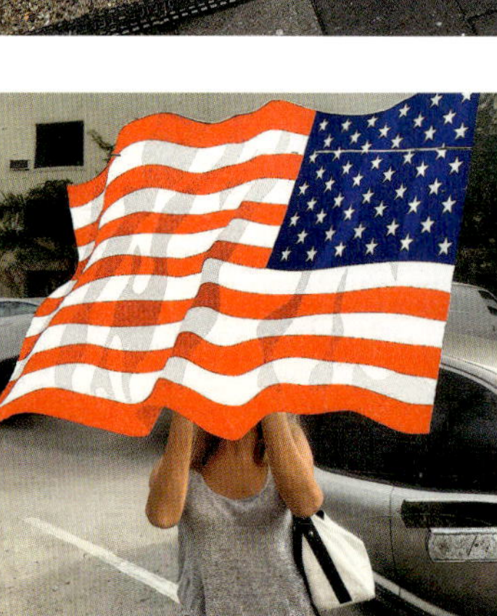

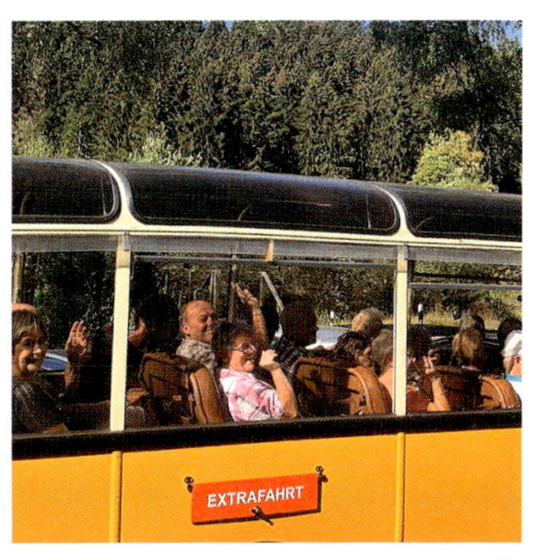
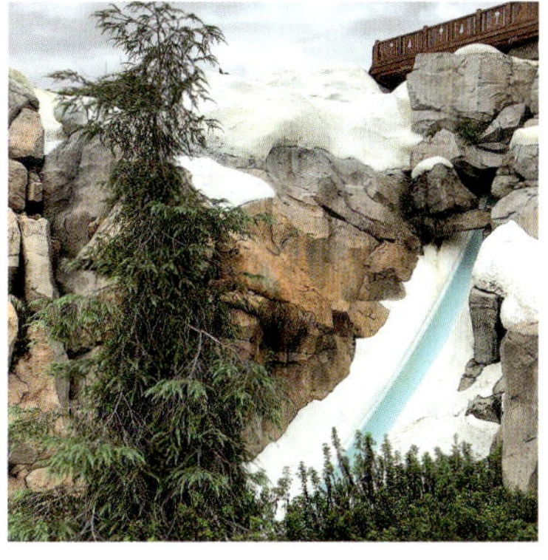
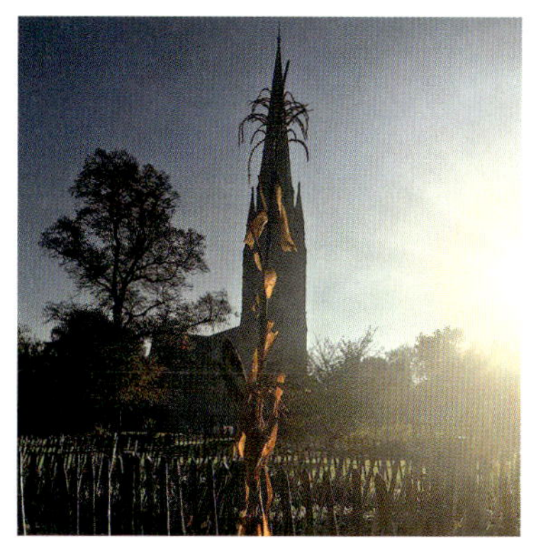
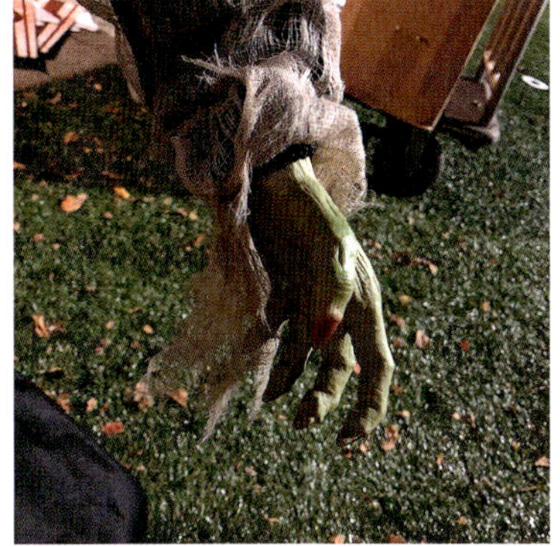
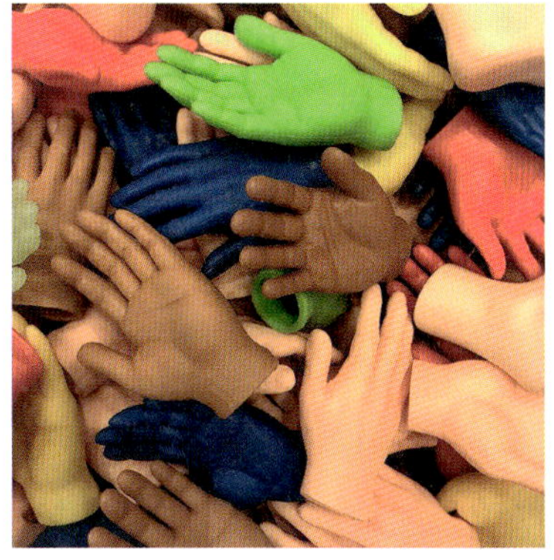
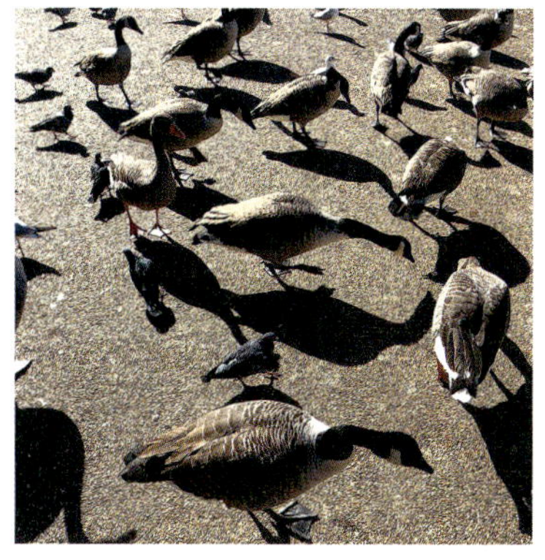
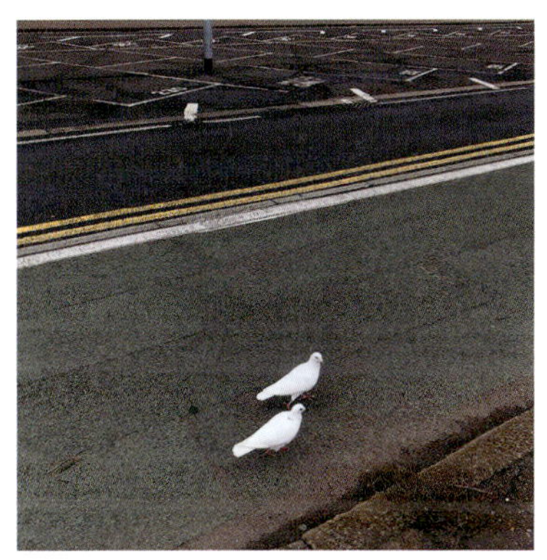
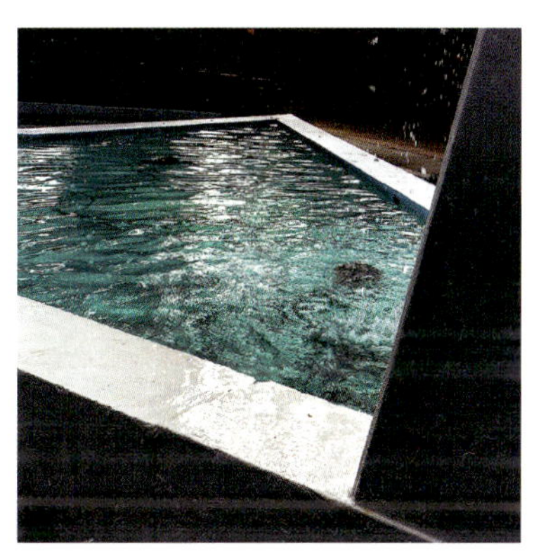
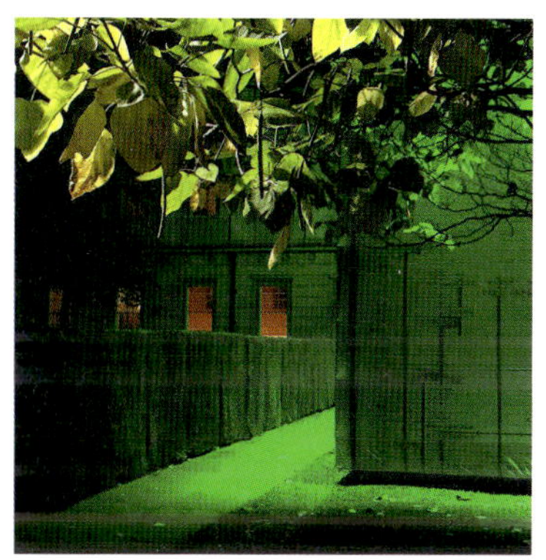
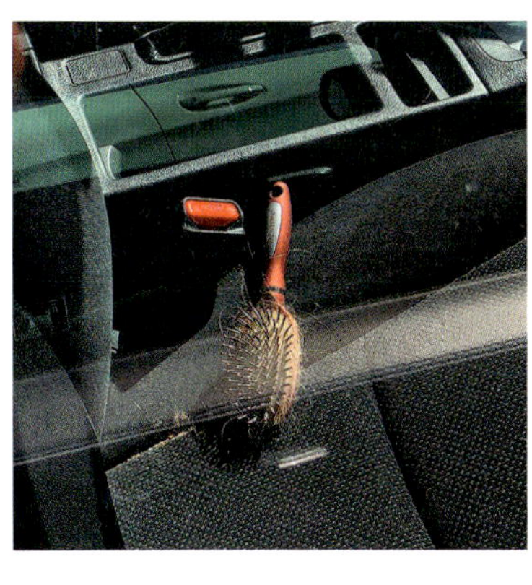
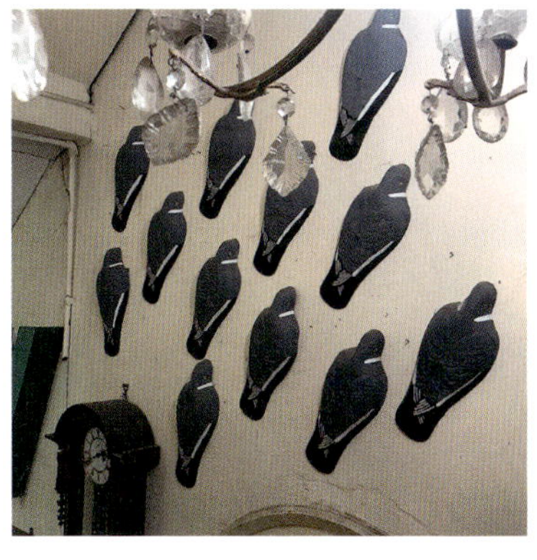
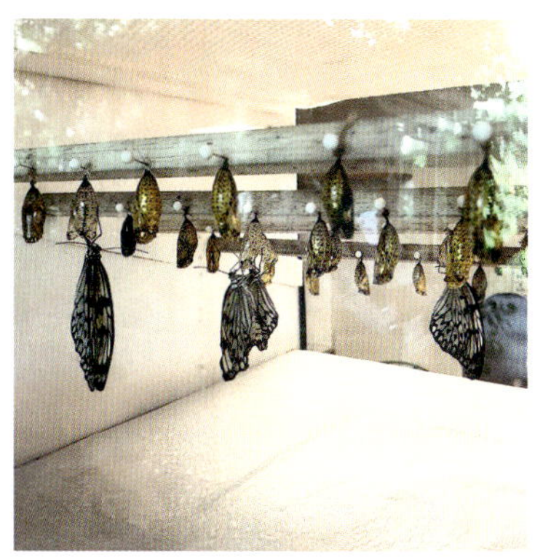

EXTRAFAHRT

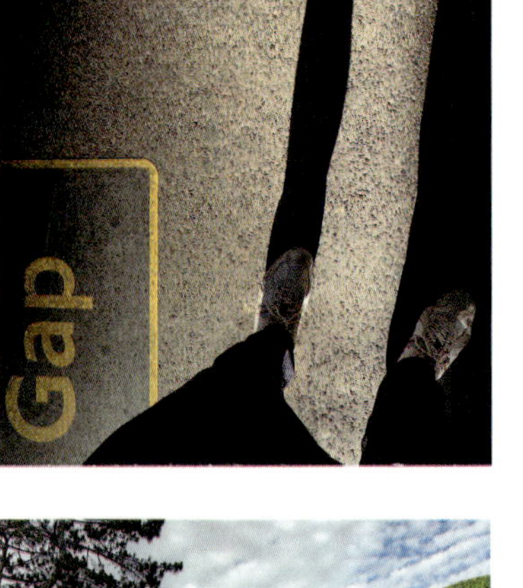
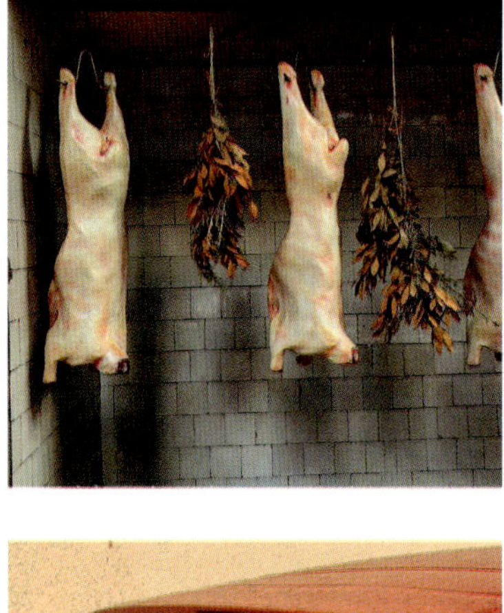
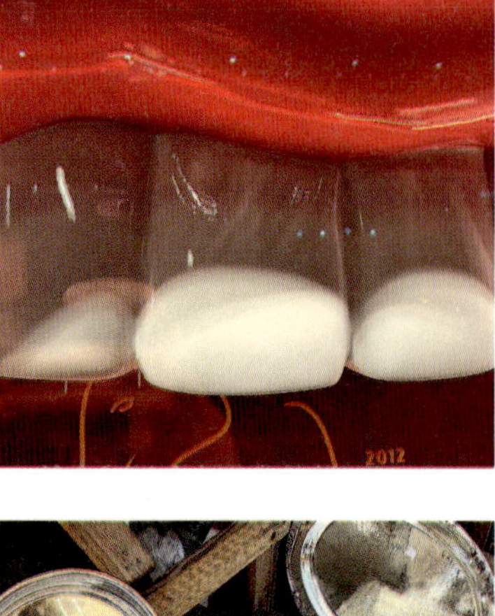
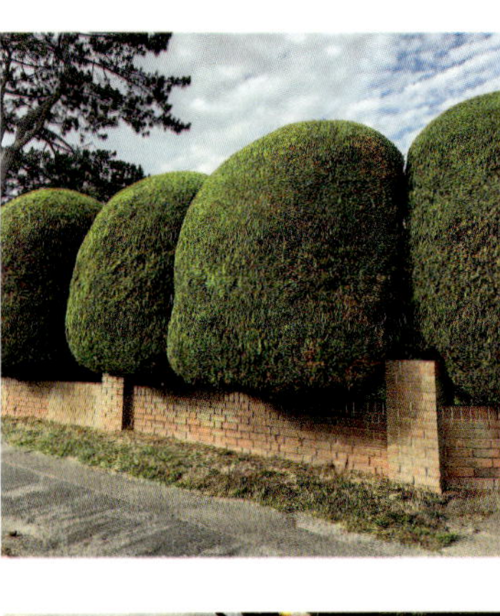
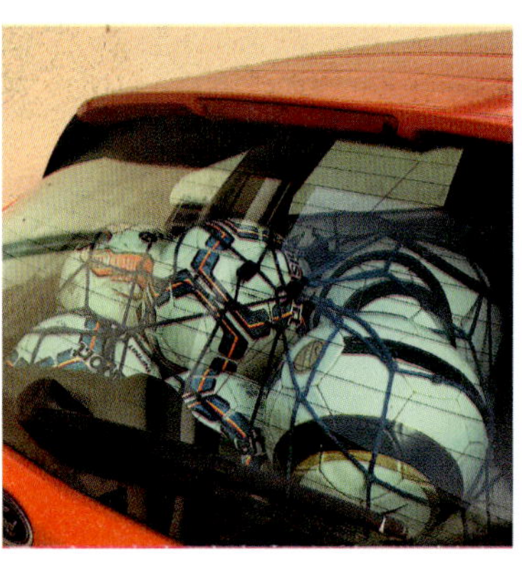
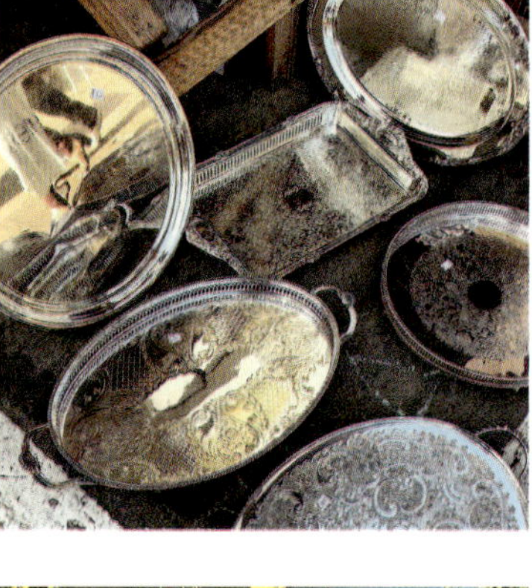
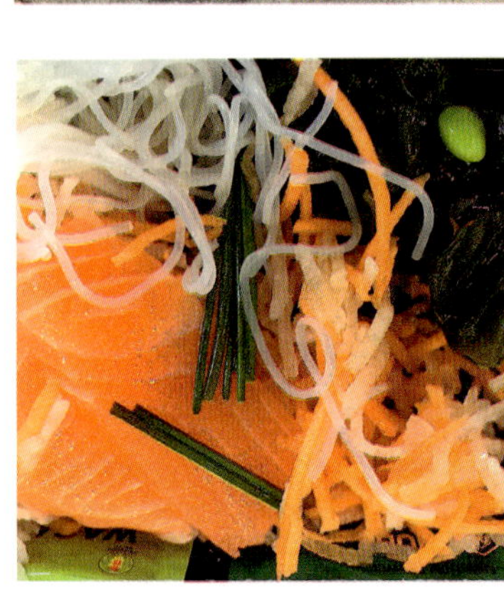
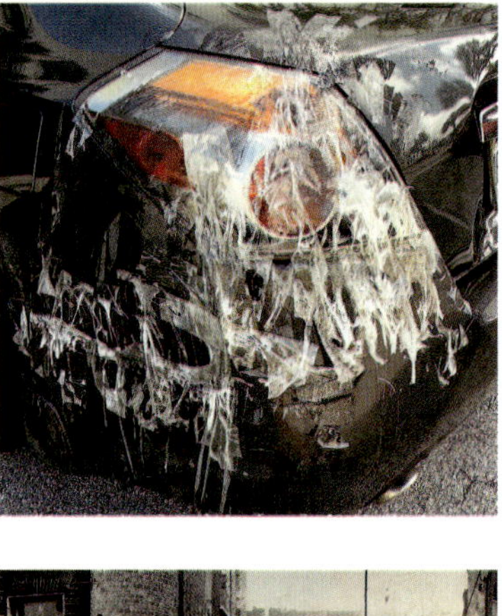
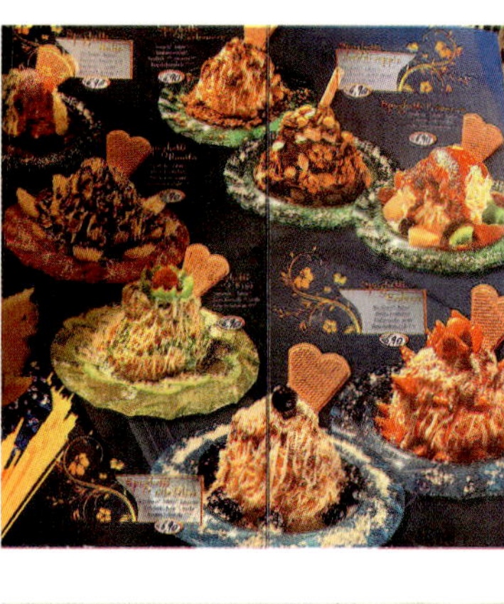
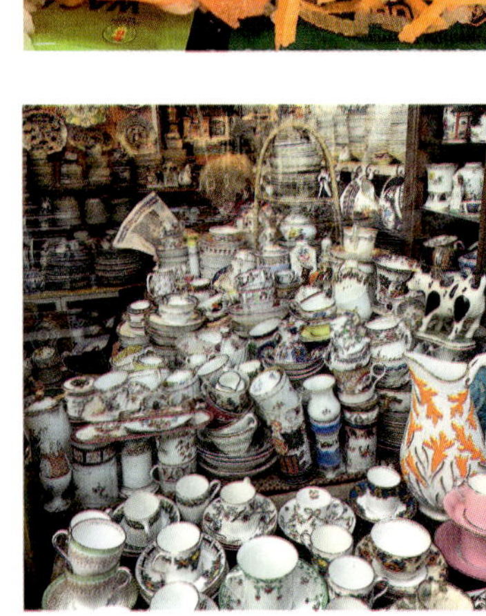
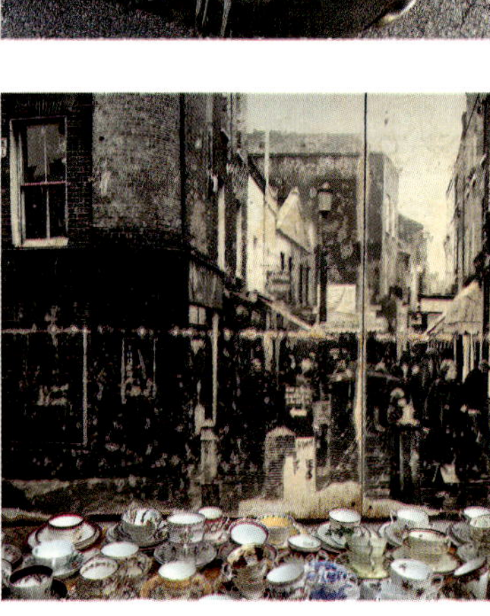
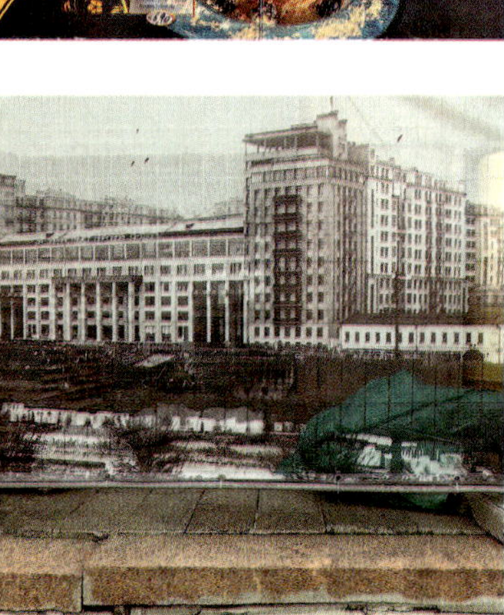

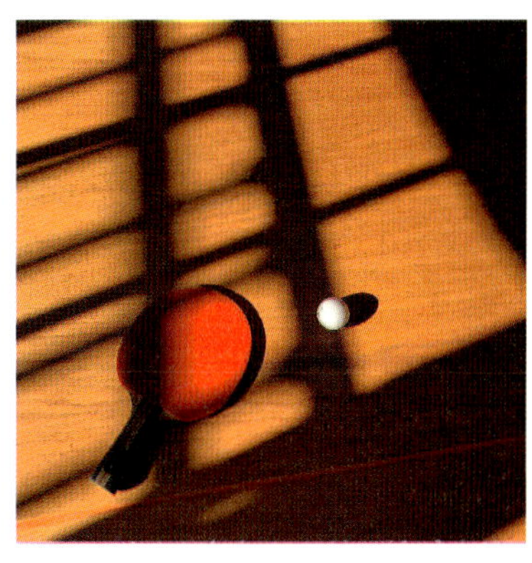
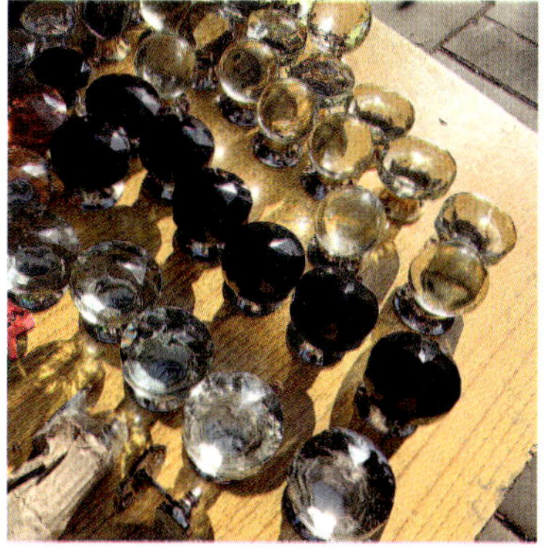
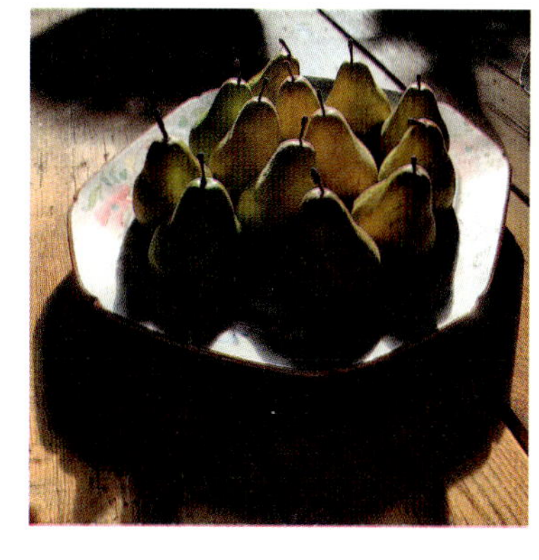
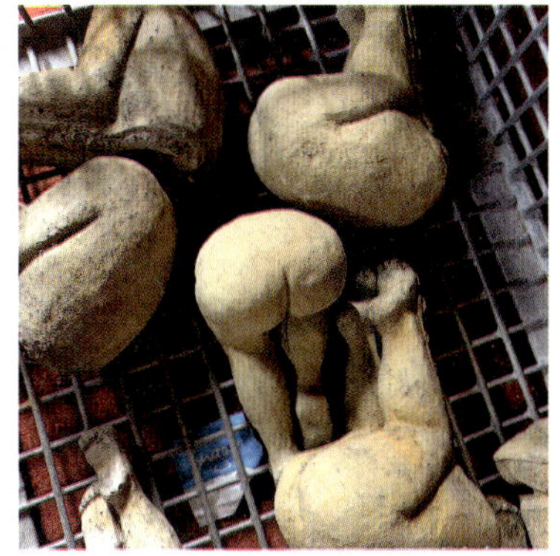
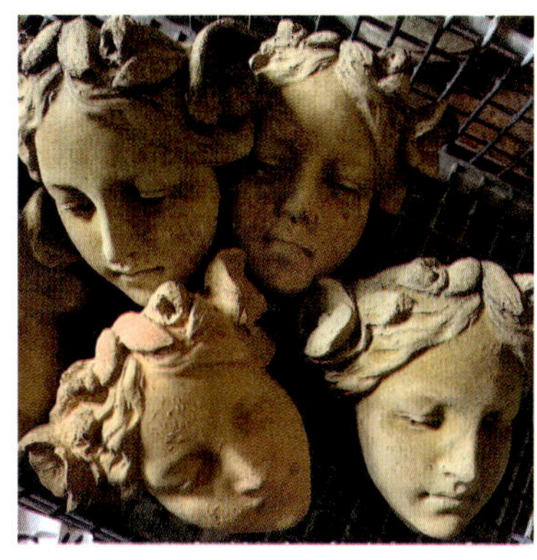
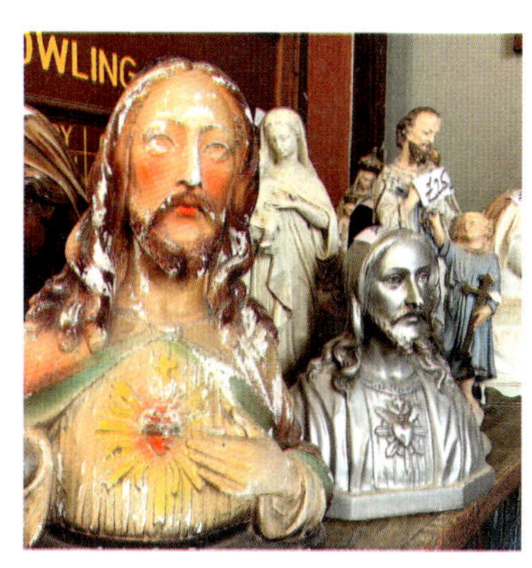
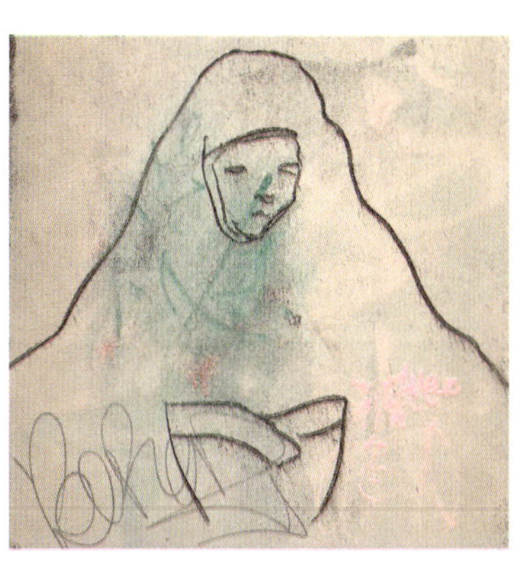
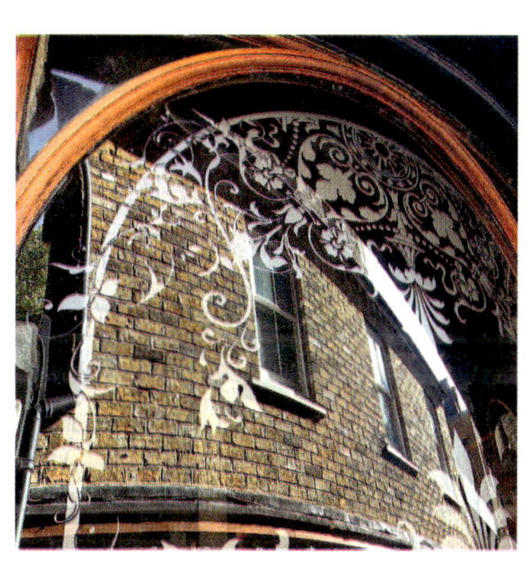
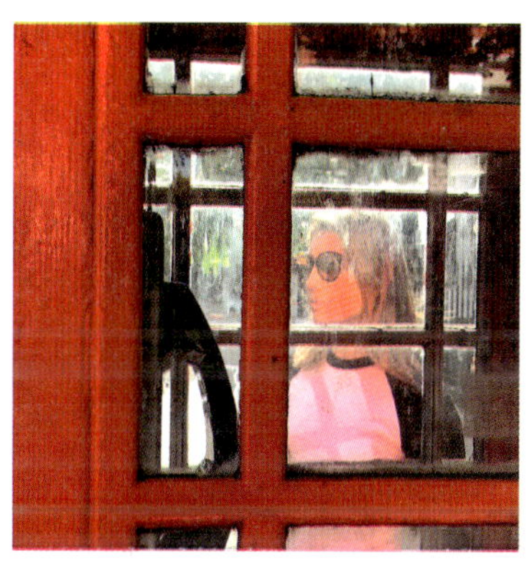
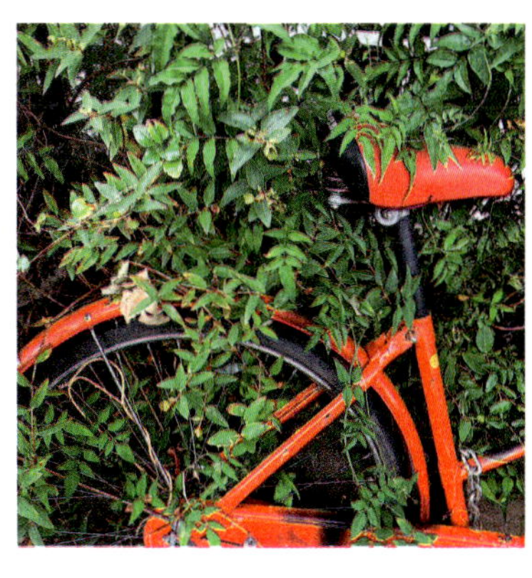
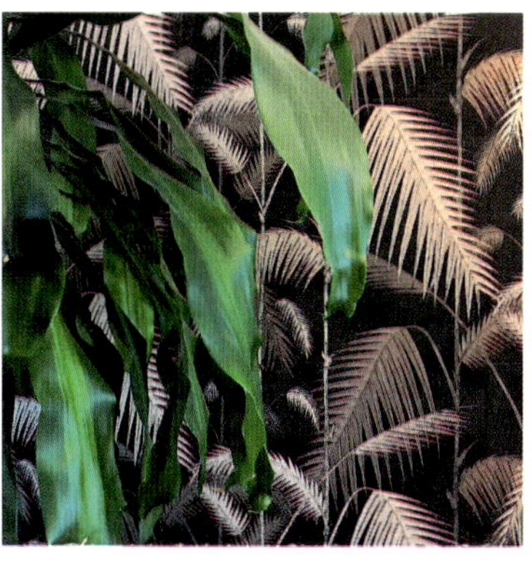
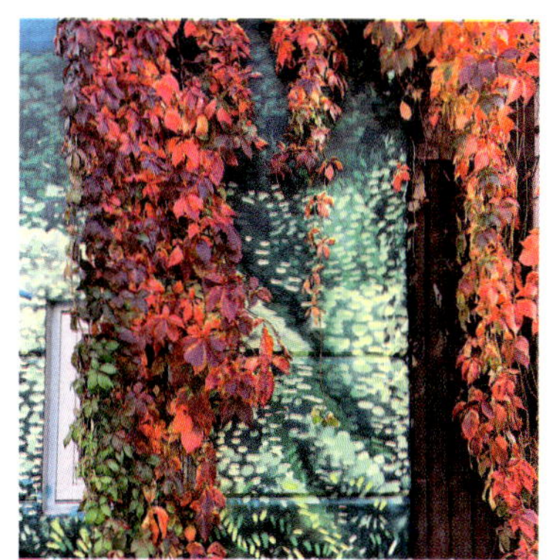

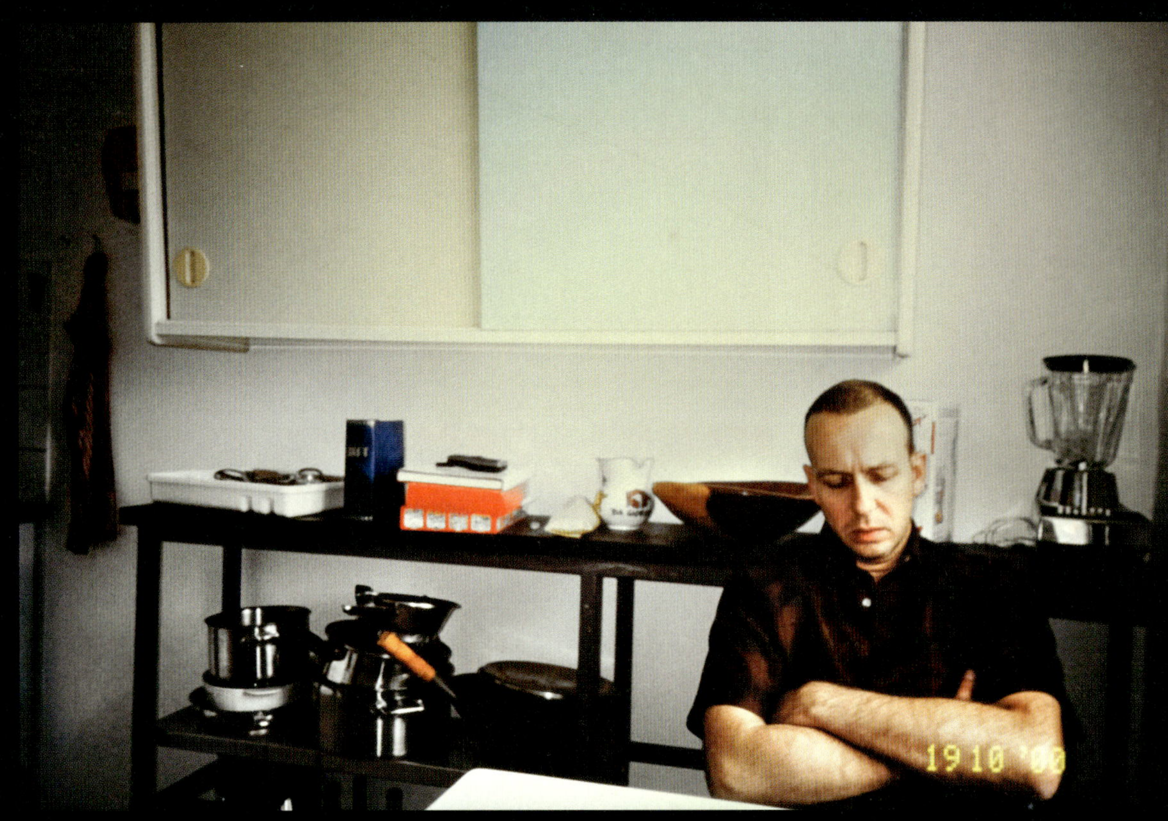

Hallo Jörg, sitze gerade in meiner Küche
und habe dir gleich ein passendes Foto dazu
geschickt. Im Radio lief eine Sendung über
das Wohnen im Alter. Habe Berge von Papier-
arbeit zu erledigen, aber gar keine Lust.
Warte mal wieder auf ganz viel Geld, aber
leider kommt nichts, außer eben den Mahnun-
gen. Grad gar kein guter Moment, wird schon
wieder! Lass es du dir mal in Japan gut
gehen. Freue mich, wenn du wieder da bist.
Alles Liebe, Martin

Martin Fengel & Jörg Koopmann
Post, 2000–2001

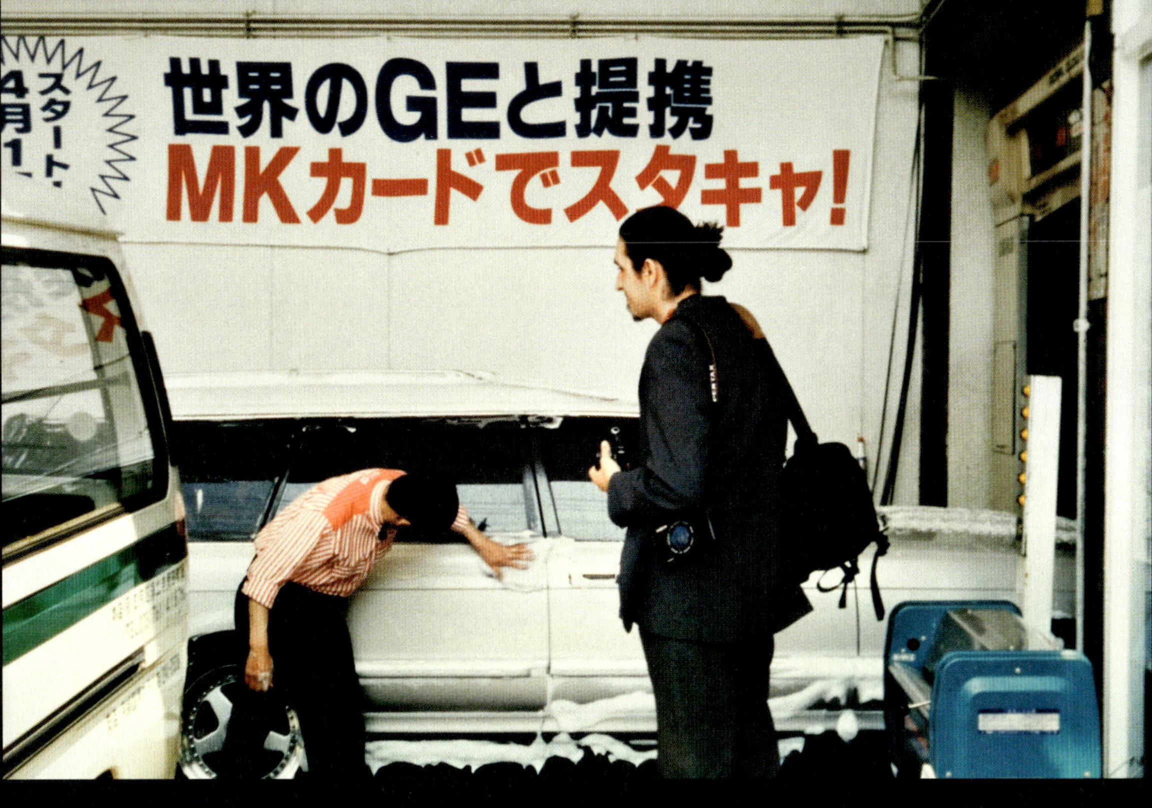

Lieber Martin, eigentlich hätte ich wissen
sollen, dass die Sprachschulkassette *Learn
Japanese in Seven Days* ein Fehlkauf ist.
Takushi heißt Taxi, aber was zu teuer
heißt, weiß ich nicht. Sumimasen, Jörg

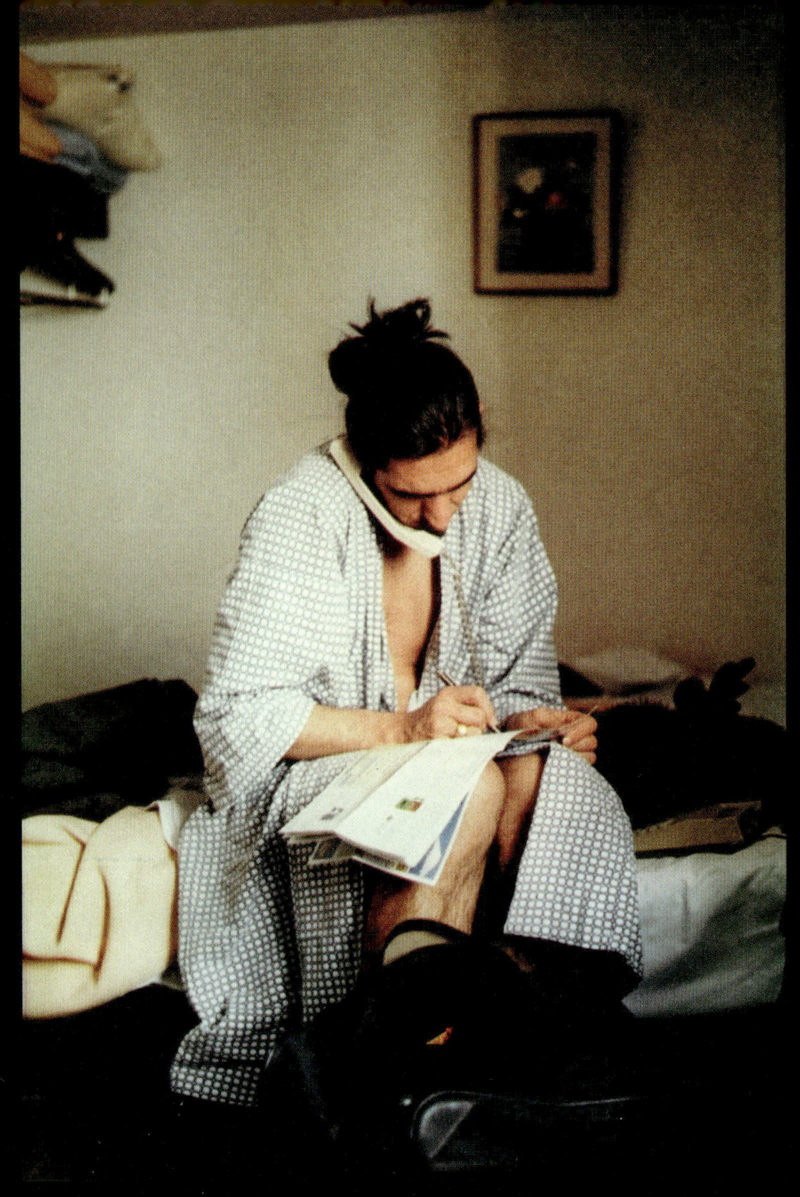

Martin-San, ich habe deine Post noch im
Okura Hotel gekriegt, aber bin nun nach
Shibuya in ein billiges Businesshotel um-
gezogen, das ich selber zahlen muss. Habe
heute bei Parco acht Kilo Fotobücher ge-
kauft. Tolle Arakis zum Beispiel, aber auch
den supertollen Masafumi Sanai entdeckt,

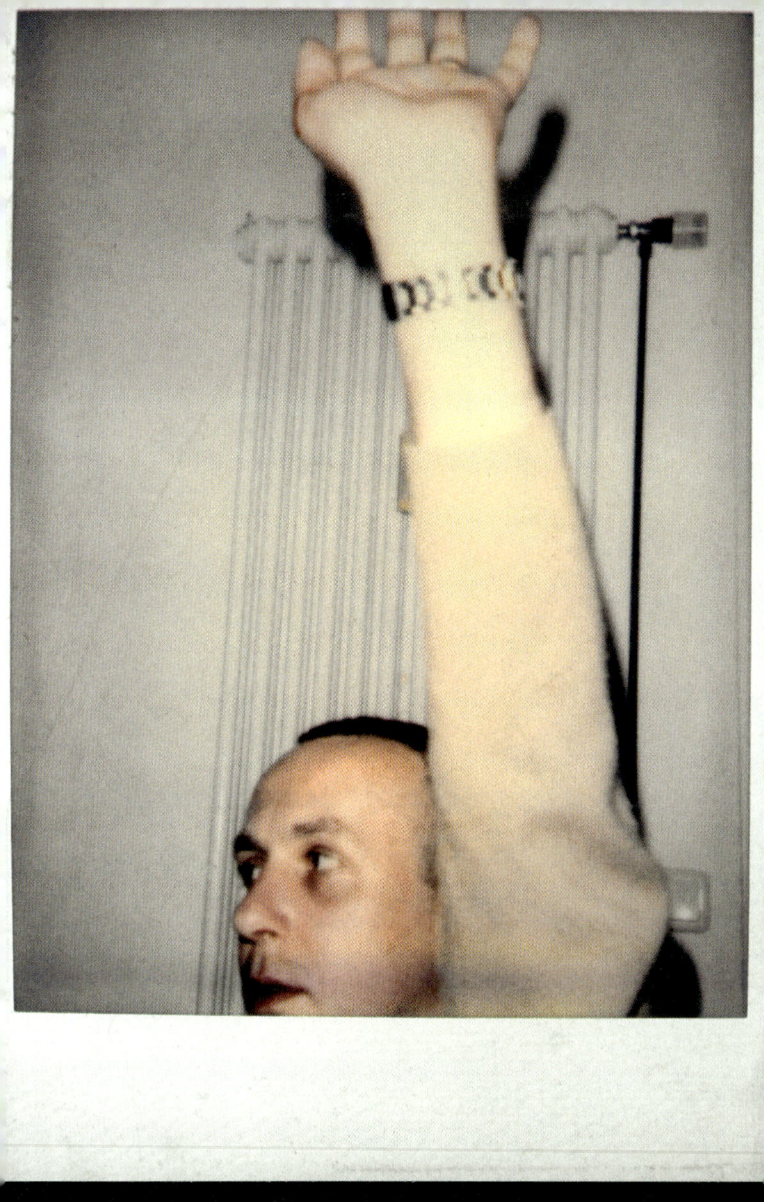

Hallo Jörg, gestern hab ich mich in den
Finger geschnitten. Ich musste den ganzen
Abend mit Arm oben dasitzen. Die schlim-
me Stelle am Finger kannst du auf dem Foto
nicht sehen, es sieht aber wirklich böse
aus. Ich freue mich auf den Urlaub.
Bis bald, Martin

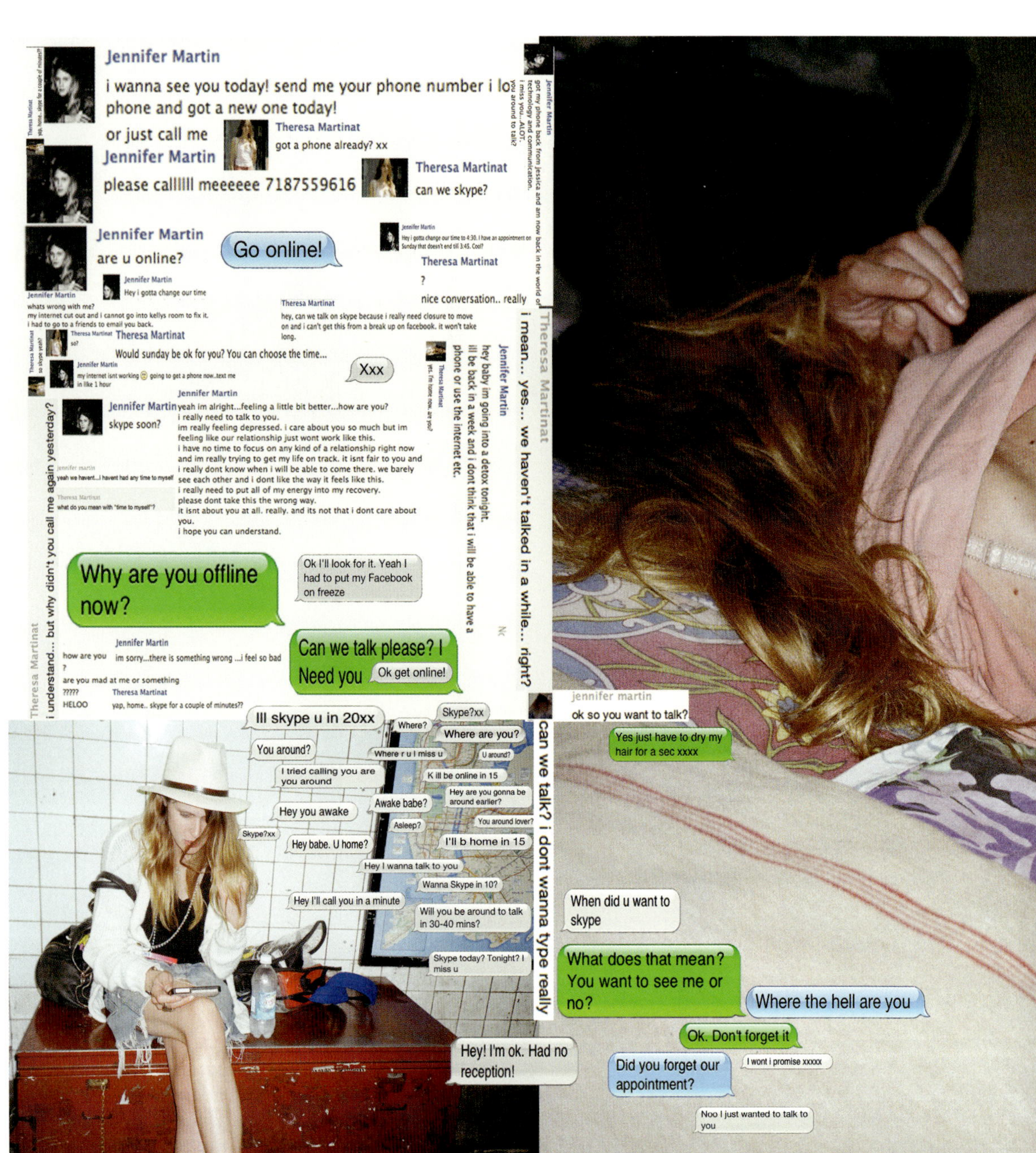

Theresa Martinat
Collage II, I'll Skype You in 20, 2011–2013
a.d.S. / From the series *Like It Never Happened, 2010–2013*

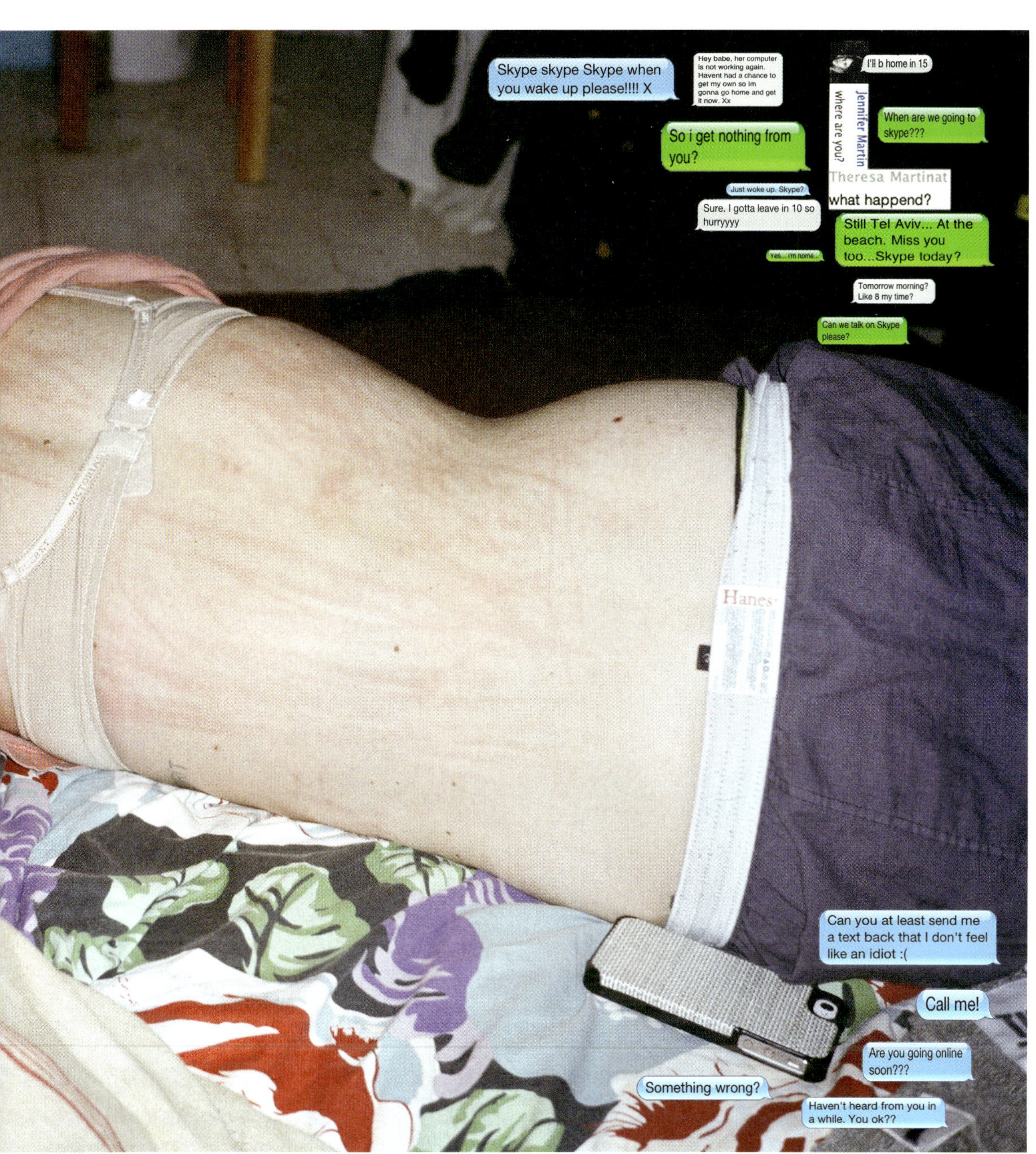

Skype skype Skype when you wake up please!!!! X
Hey babe, her computer is not working again. Havent had a chance to get my own so im gonna go home and get it now. Xx
I'll b home in 15
When are we going to skype???
Jennifer Martin where are you?
So i get nothing from you?
Theresa Martinat
what happend?
Just woke up. Skype?
Sure. I gotta leave in 10 so hurryyyy
Still Tel Aviv... At the beach. Miss you too...Skype today?
Yes.... i'm home...
Tomorrow morning? Like 8 my time?
Can we talk on Skype please?
Hanes
Can you at least send me a text back that I don't feel like an idiot :(
Call me!
Are you going online soon???
Something wrong?
Haven't heard from you in a while. You ok??

Theresa Martinat
Collage I, Jennifer, 2011–2013
a.d.S. / **From the series** *Like It Never Happened,* 2010–2013

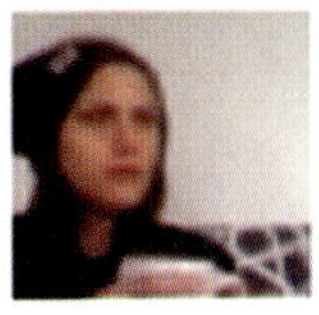

Jennifer Martin December 24, 2010 at 11:37pm Report

Would you be my date for dinner tomorrow?

Sent via Facebook Mobile

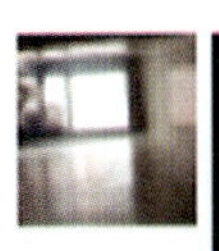

Jennifer Martin she carries around a bag of negativity and just pokes holes in it and leaks it everywhere she goes.

23 minutes ago · Like · 👍 1 person

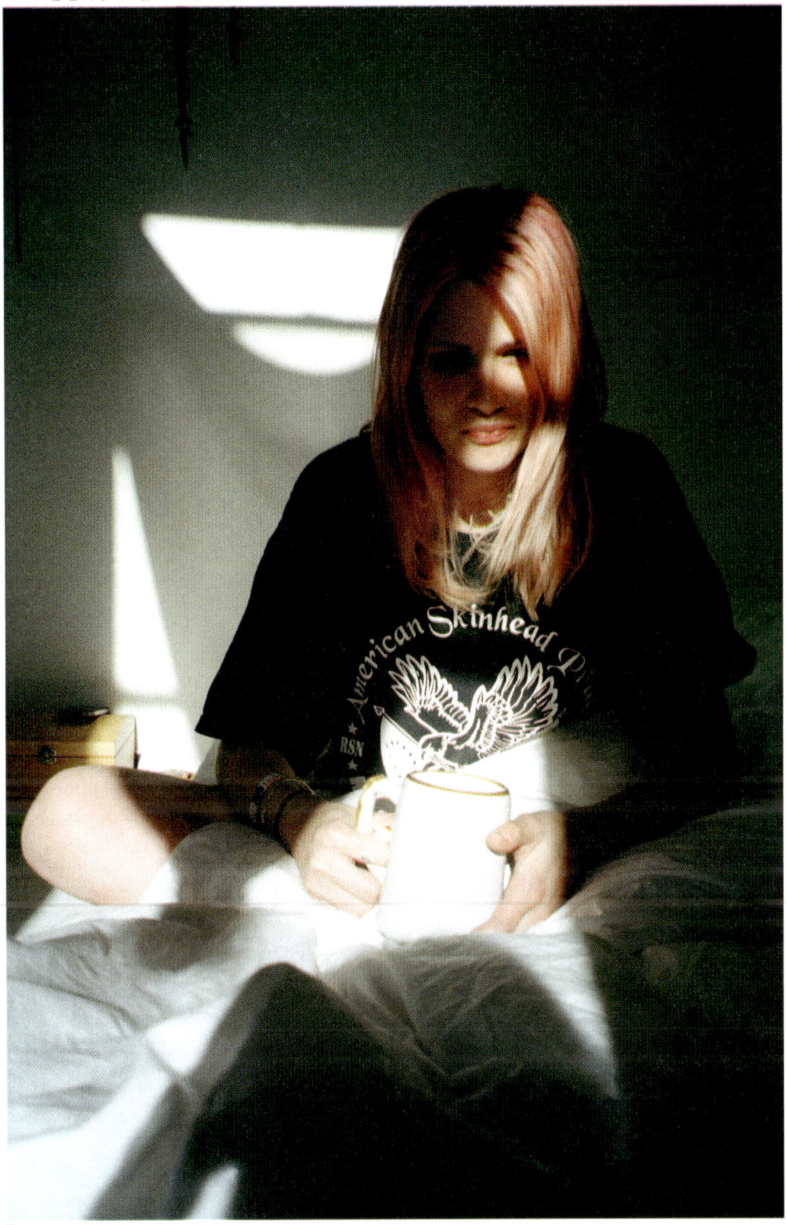

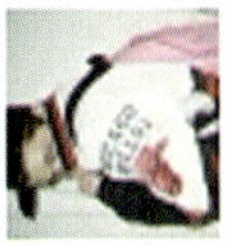

Ricardo Pedaline

January 18, 2011

Theresa she has problems and you Canfield help her yes she is beautiful but there is nothing skin deep and obviously doesn't know how to deal with any type of real life situations ur much better off with someone normal and actually sees what an amazing person u are. Ps if u need anything i am here for you Xo talk soon

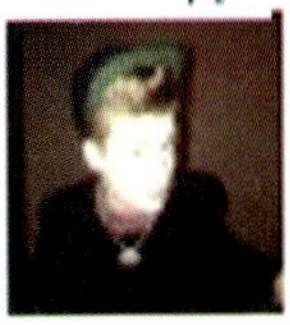

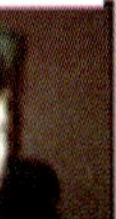

Vala Durvett

you left bags of heroin in my bathroom and my roommate found it. this is disgusting and i hope you realize the situation you have put jennifer and i in. i really have no tolerance for this type of behavior and i cant believe you would do that.

PLATTFORMEN

Wurden in den 1990er-Jahren digitale Bilder in der Regel auf Server hochgeladen und dann per HTML in Websites eingebunden, etablierten sich um 2000 erste Dienste wie Fotki, Photobucket und Flickr, mit denen sich solche Bilder in größeren Mengen speichern lassen. In jüngerer Zeit kamen Google Photos, Instagram, Snapchat und andere Plattformen hinzu, auf denen die Bilder mittlerweile nicht mehr nur gespeichert und gezeigt, sondern auch bearbeitet, geordnet, kommentiert, angeschaut, verknüpft und geteilt werden.

Auf diesen Plattformen bekommt man die Bilder nicht geschickt, sondern zu sehen. Abonnements sorgen dafür, dass man die Aufnahmen der Freund*innen zuverlässig findet; Benachrichtigungen machen darauf aufmerksam, wenn der bewunderte Schauspieler, die verehrte Sängerin Eindrücke aus ihrem Privatleben teilen; Hashtags helfen dabei, Bilder zu bündeln, die aus welchen Gründen auch immer zusammengehören sollen. Man bekommt die Bilder zu sehen, aber man bekommt sie nicht nur gezeigt: Man kann anmerken, wenn man ein Bild mag, man kann es kommentieren, mit einem eigenen Hashtag versehen, man kann sie sich aneignen und mit Filtern und anderen tools bearbeiten und zu etwas werden lassen, das sie vorher nicht waren, zu Memes, GIFs und Montagen, und dann oder wann auch immer kann man sie teilen. Mit Bildplattformen werden Bilder nicht mehr verschickt, sondern verbreitet.

PHOTO SITES

In the 1990s digital photos were uploaded onto servers and integrated into websites with HTML, but around 2000, the first photo sites that allowed larger numbers of images to be saved such as Fotki, Photobucket, and Flickr were set up. More recently, Google Photos, Instagram, Snapchat, and other sites and apps have allowed users to save and display their photos, but also to edit, organize, comment on, view, link to, and share their images.

These sites display rather than send images. Feeds ensure users can find their friends' photographs; alerts notify users when a favorite actor or singer shares an image from their personal lives; hashtags help group images intended to be viewed together for whatever reason. Not only can you see photographs, but also like your favorites, comment, add your own hashtag, or appropriate them and edit them with filters and other tools in order to make them into something they weren't before, such as a meme, GIF, or a montage, to be shared then or later. With image platforms, images are no longer sent but distributed.

Allerdings gilt das nicht für alle Bilder gleichermaßen. Wer bekannt ist oder beliebt, deren Bilder werden gesehen. Die Bilder der anderen werden oft nur ein einziges Mal angeschaut – wenn sie unmittelbar nach der Aufnahme auf dem Display ihrer Smartphones erscheinen. Selbst auf eine der Bildplattformen hochgeladen verschwinden sie im Dickicht der Ordner, im bunten Rauschen der viel zu vielen Bilder, die jeden Blick und jede Wahrnehmung überfordern – außer die der Programme, für die die Milliarden von Bildern zu Big Data geworden sind, mit deren Hilfe sich Software zur Gesichtserkennung trainieren und Modetrends analysieren lassen.

Dass so viele dieser Bilder ungesehen, und das heißt auch: ohne Adressatin bleiben, weist allerdings darauf hin, dass der Blick auf ein Bild und seine Aufnahme sich voneinander gelöst haben. Zu fotografieren ist zu einer Form des Sehens geworden; das Bild scheint dabei oft nur noch ein Nebenprodukt zu sein. Und doch erfüllt es auch ungesehen eine entscheidende Funktion. Wenn Fotografie seit ihren Anfängen eines der oder gar das wichtigste Medium war, sich seines eigenen Lebens zu versichern, dann ist die Aufnahme eines Bildes immer auch ein Akt der Sendung – an uns selbst.

This does not, however, apply equally to all images. The photos of the well-known and well-loved are the ones that are seen. Other people's images are often only seen once, when they pop up on the user's smartphone display after being taken. Even when uploaded to photo sites, they disappear into the thicket of folders; in the colorful torrent of images that overwhelm the eye and the senses, excepting those of the programs that take these billions of images as a source of big data, using them to refine facial recognition technology and analyze fashion trends.

But the fact that so many of these images go unviewed and thus without a recipient also shows that the view of an image and its recording have become detached from one another. Photography has become a way of seeing and the image resulting seems to simply be a by-product. Yet even unviewed, it plays an important role. If photography was one or even the most important means of assuring ourselves of our own existence, then taking a photograph is an act of sending it—to ourselves.

Text: Friedrich Tietjen

Adam Broomberg & Oliver Chanarin
Blame the Algorithm, 2019, *Der Greif,* Ausgabe / **issue 12**
Titelbild / **Front cover** Martha Friedel

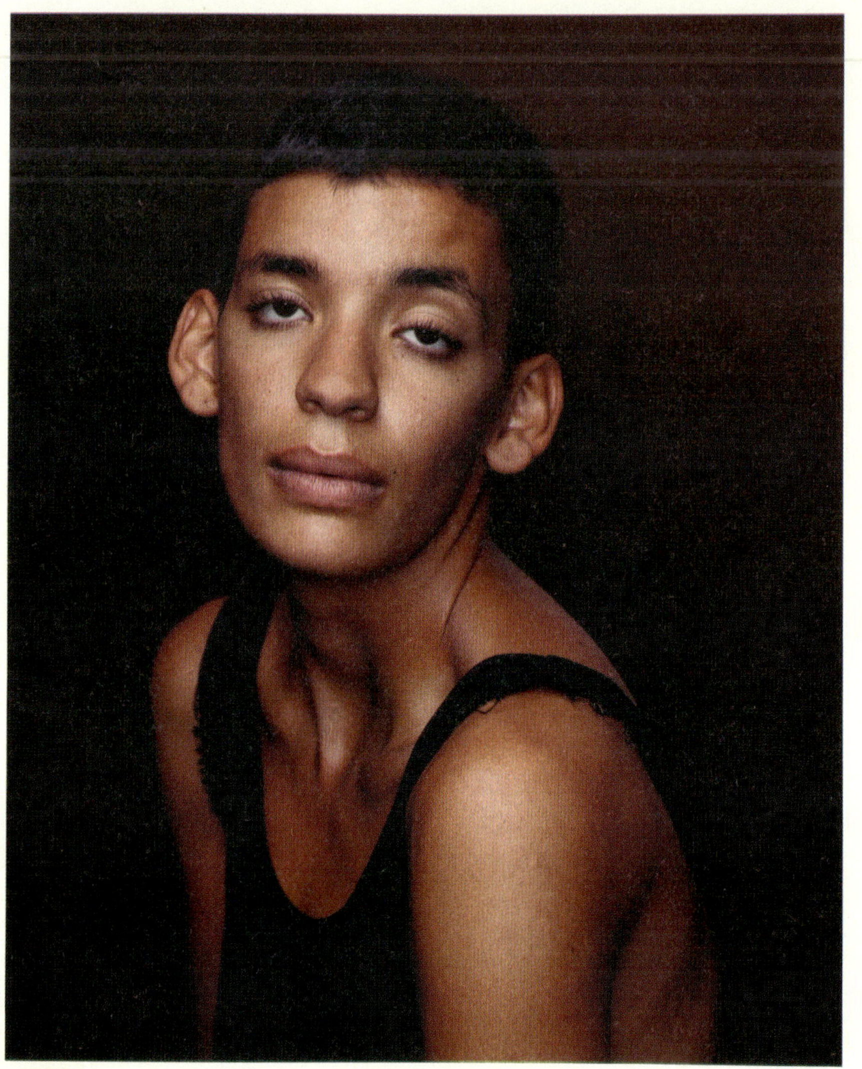
DER GREIF
2019 · ISSUE 12 · ISSN 2191-4524 · GUEST EDITORS: BROOMBERG & CHANARIN

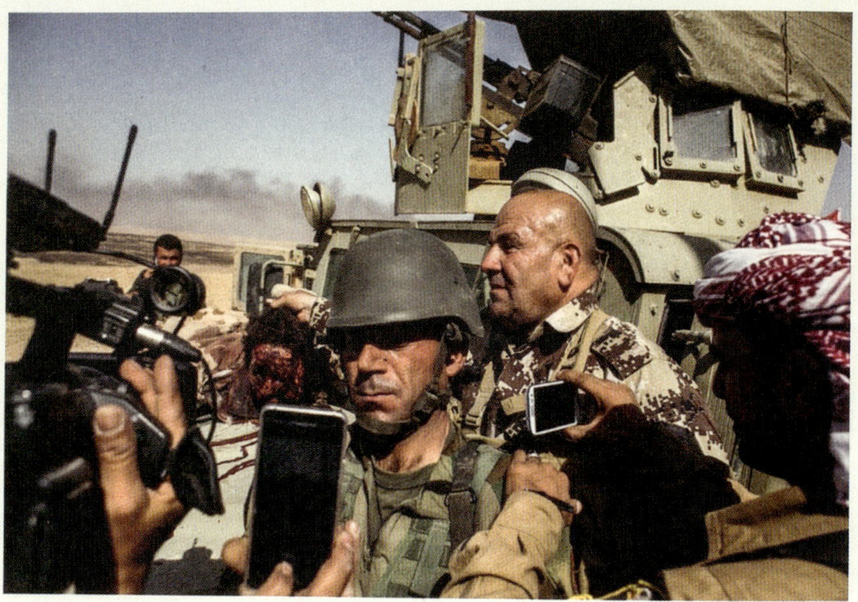

Adam Broomberg & Oliver Chanarin
Blame the Algorithm, 2019, *Der Greif,* Ausgabe / **issue 12**
Fotos / **Photos** Andrea DiCenzo (Bad 7), Paul Breuker (Good 39)

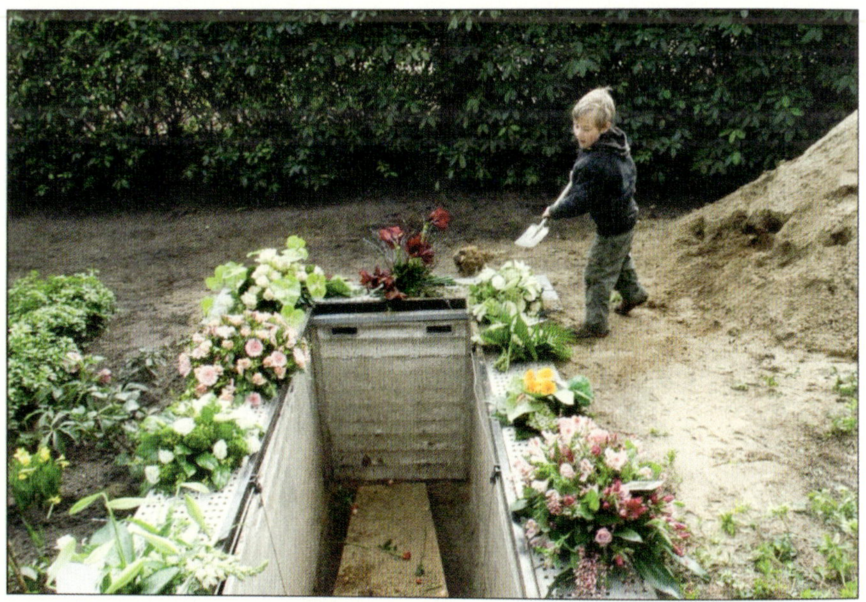

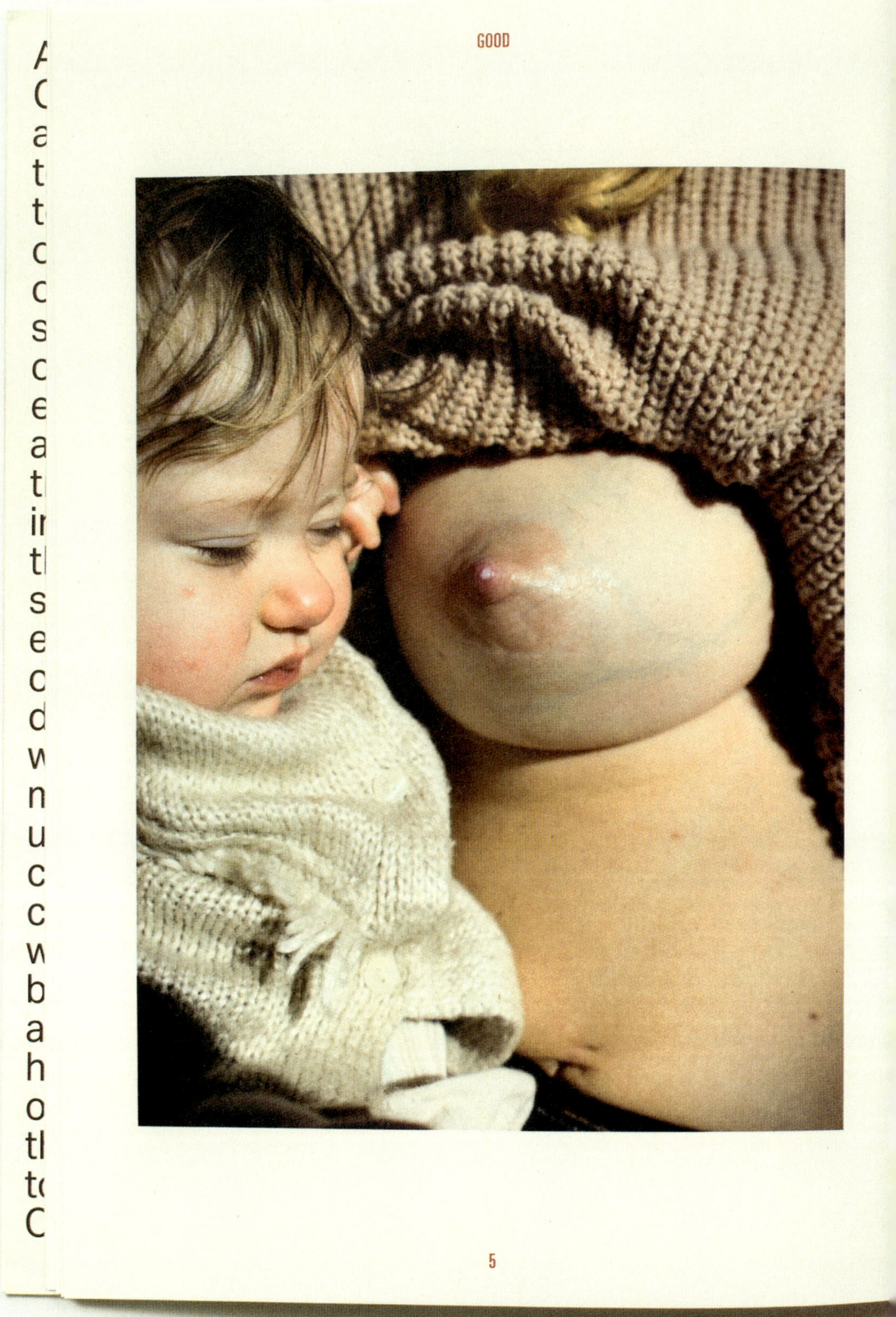

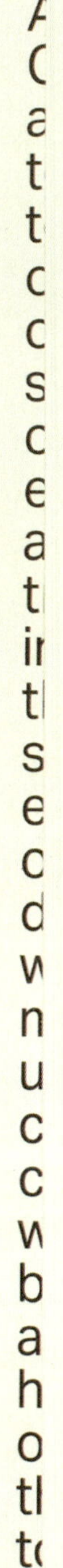

GOOD

....

Adam Broomberg & Oliver Chanarin
Blame the Algorithm, 2019, *Der Greif*, Ausgabe / **issue 12**
Fotos / **Photos** Allison Cherkis (Good 5), Matthew Keenan (Bad 41)

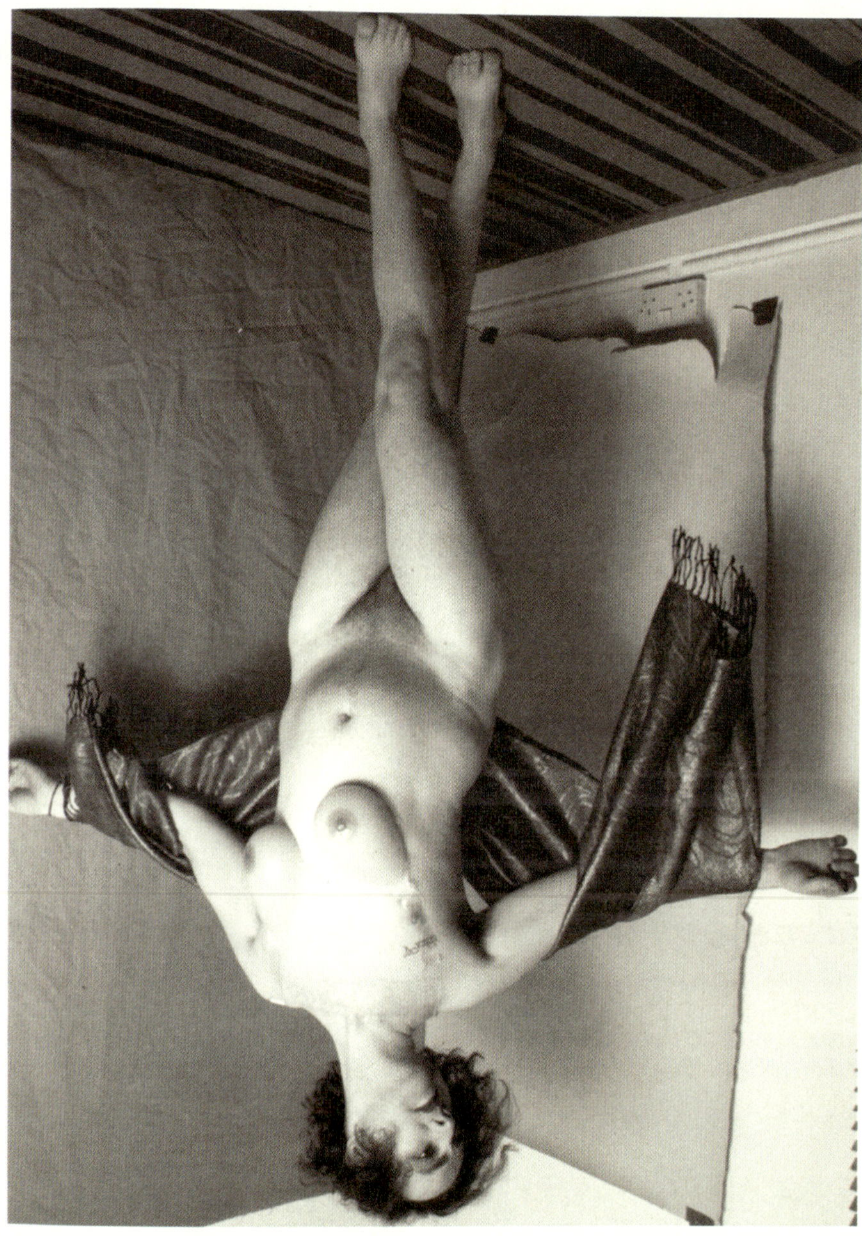

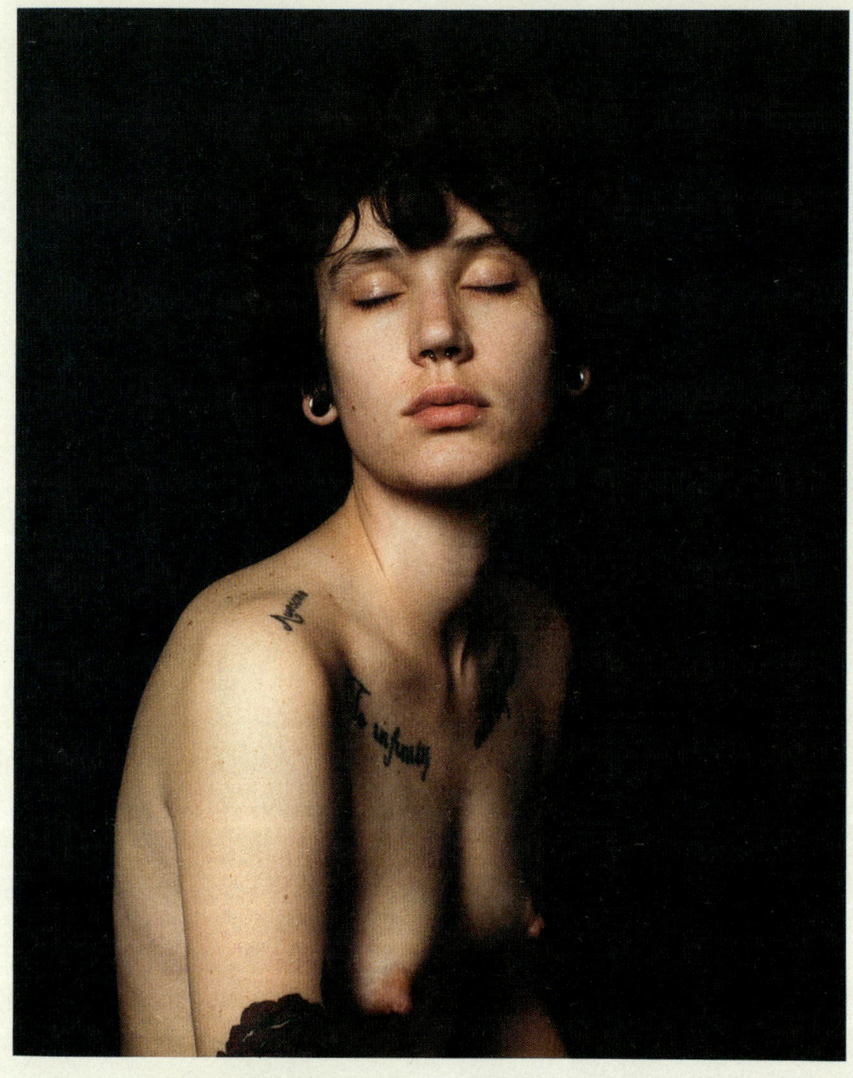

Adam Broomberg & Oliver Chanarin
Blame the Algorithm, 2019, *Der Greif,* Ausgabe / **issue 12**
Foto / **Photo** Rückseite / **Back cover** Milan Gies

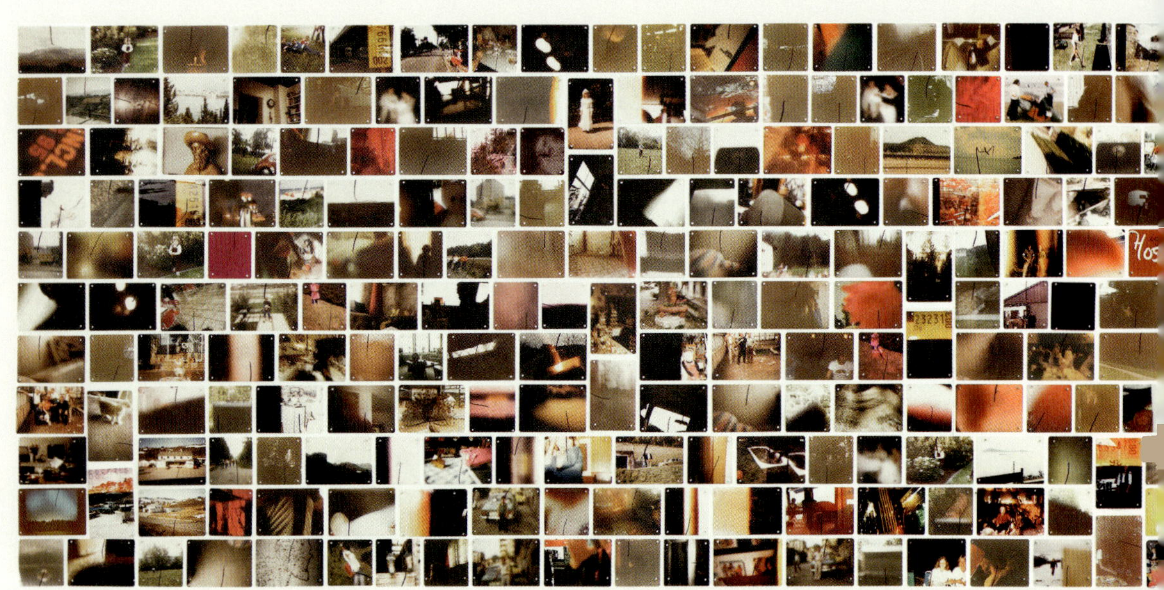

Dieter Hacker
Geprüft und für wertlos befunden, 1980

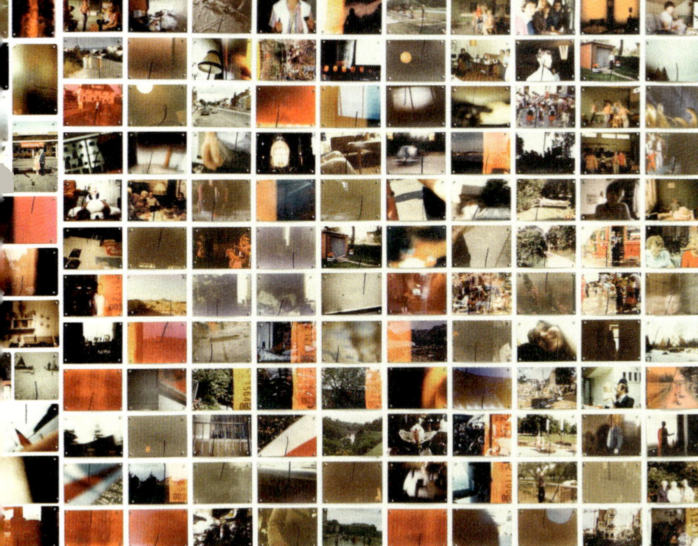
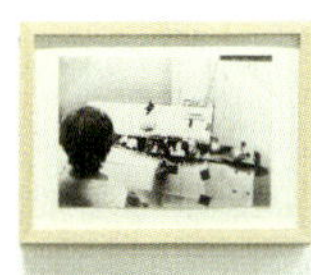

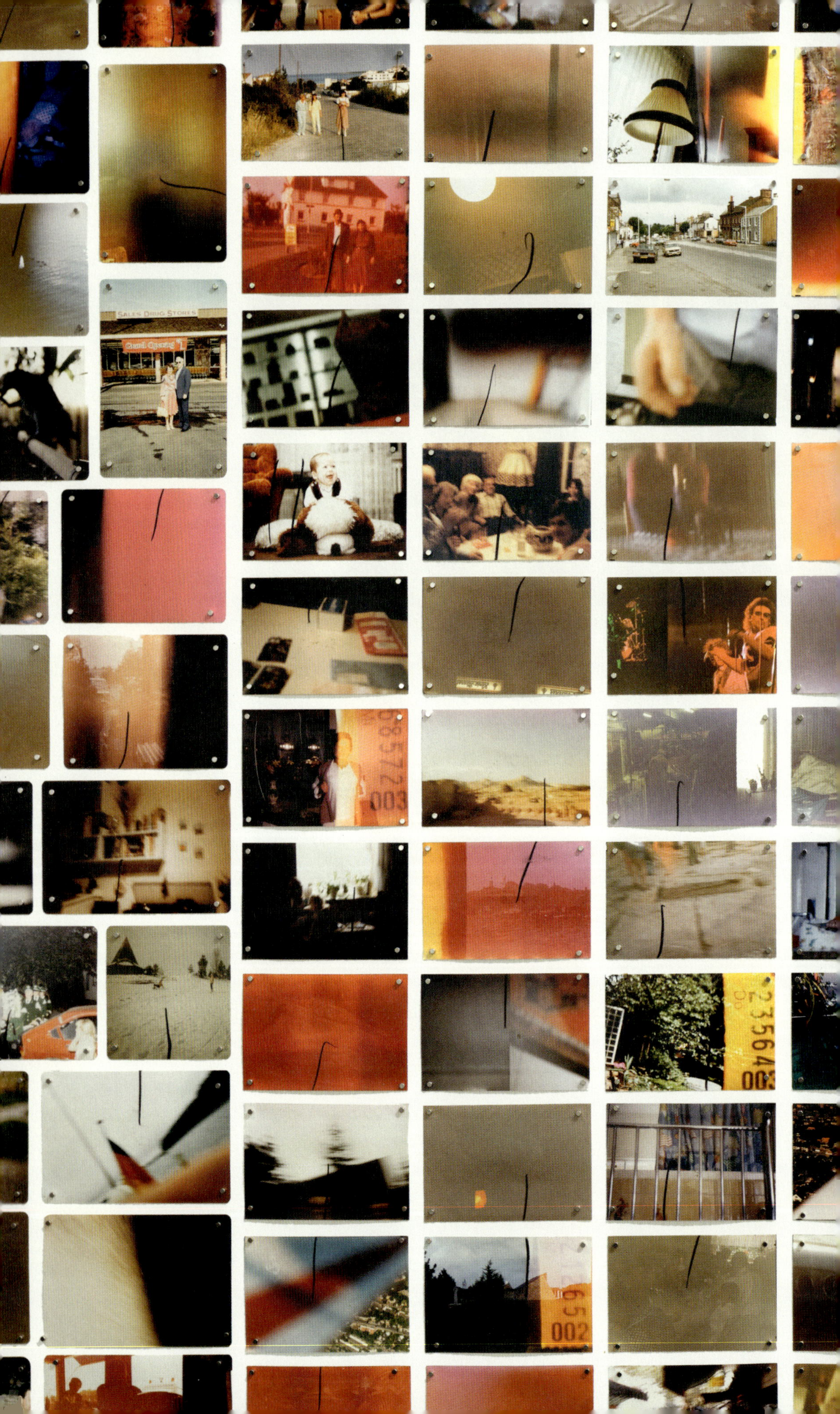

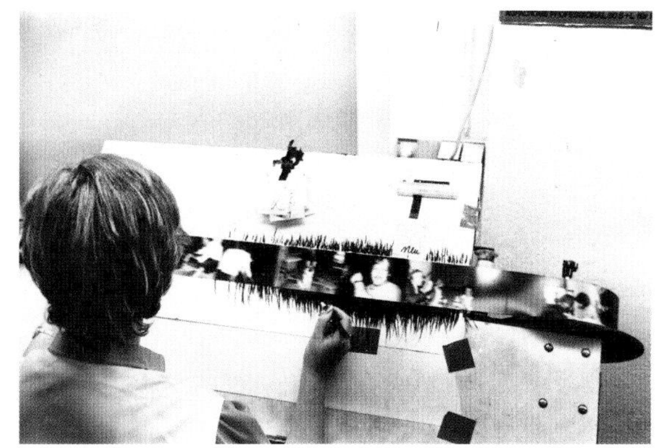

Dieter Hacker
Die Fotokontrolleurin (Detail aus *Geprüft und für wertlos befunden*), 1980

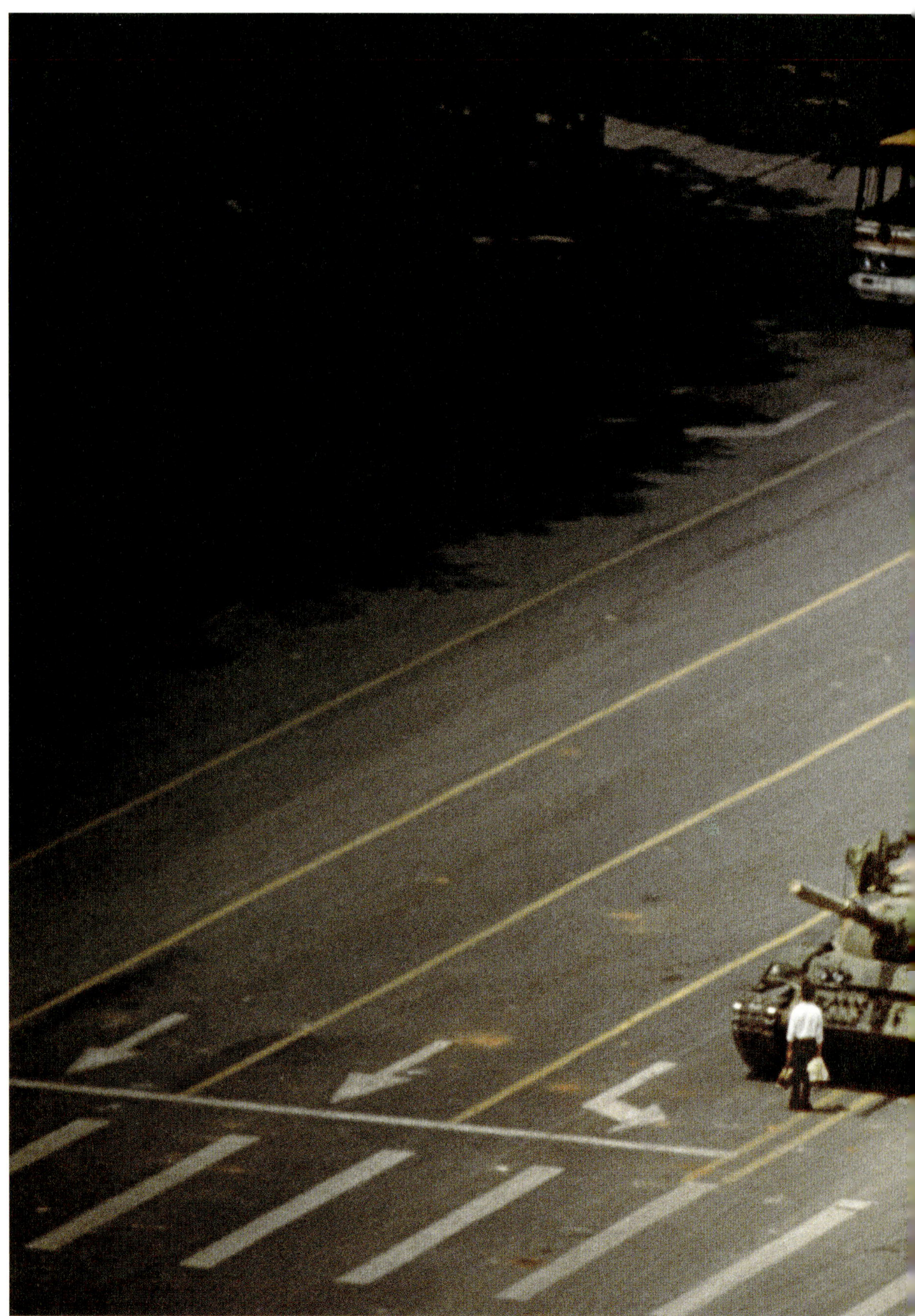

Stuart Franklin
*The Tank Man Stopping the Column of T59 Tanks, Tiananmen Square, 4. Juni 1989 / **June 4,** 1989*

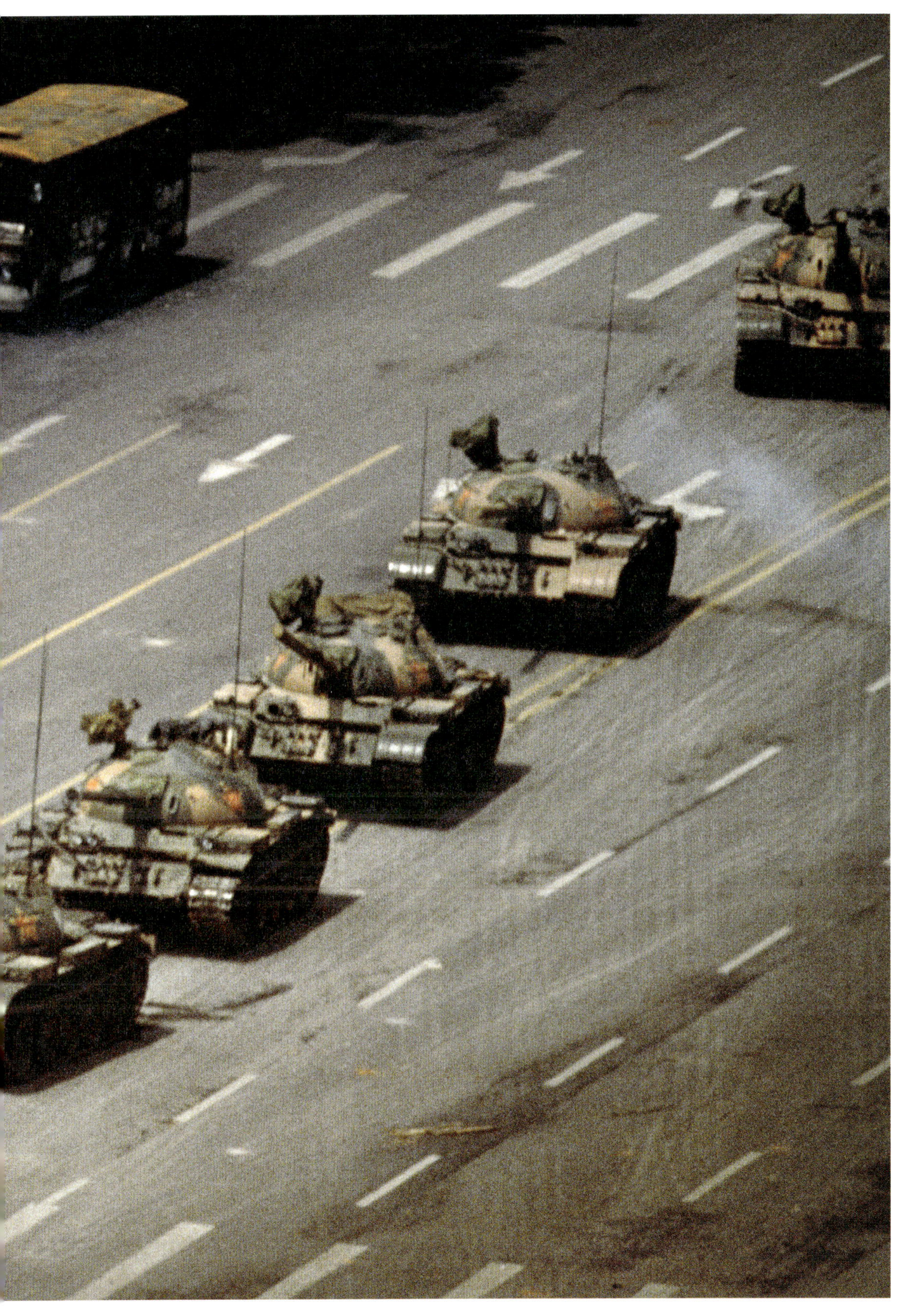

Tank Man und **Unknown Rebel** sind die Bezeichnungen für ei[n]
tionale Bekanntheit erlangte, indem er sich während des Mas
vor einen Konvoi von Panzern stellte und ihr Vorrücken block
Szene zivilen Ungehorsams wurde von zahlreichen Fotografe[n]
der Szene wurden von etlichen Zeitungen und Fernsehsende

Im April 1998 nahm das Time Magazine den *Tank Man* in die

tankman vi[deo]

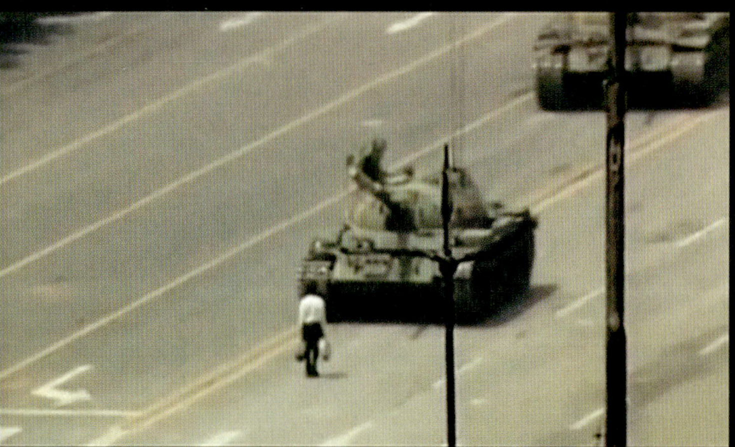

bisher nicht öffentlich identifizierten Mann, der interna-
ers am Platz des himmlischen Friedens (Tian'anmen-Platz)
e, wobei er in jeder Hand eine Einkaufstüte trug. Diese
nd Fernsehteams festgehalten. Verschiedene Aufnahmen
erwendet.

e der 100 einflussreichsten Personen des Jahrhunderts auf.

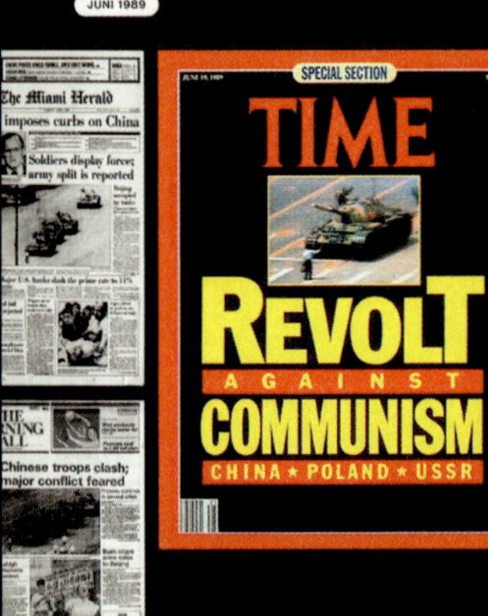

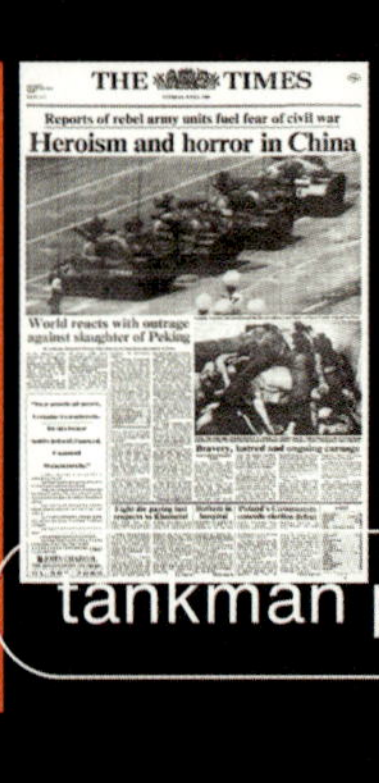

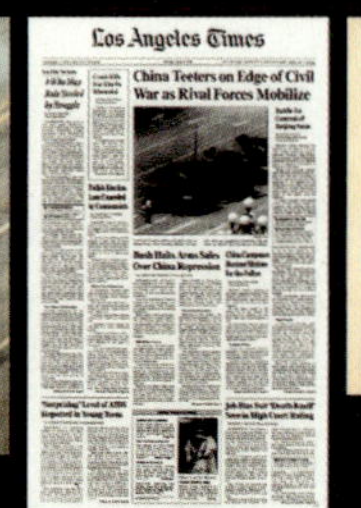

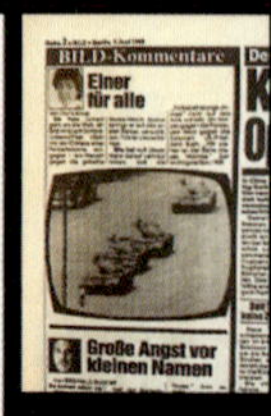

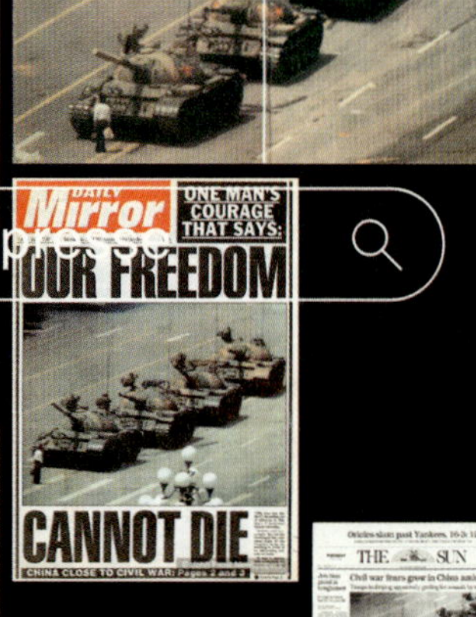

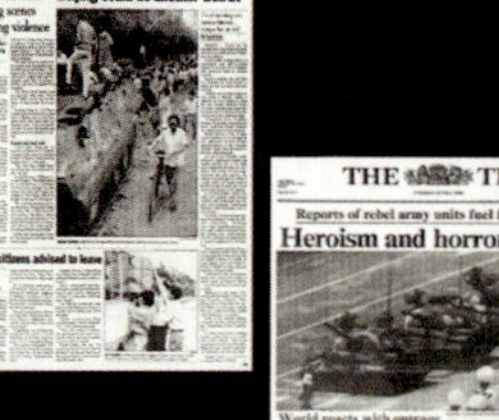

tankman presse

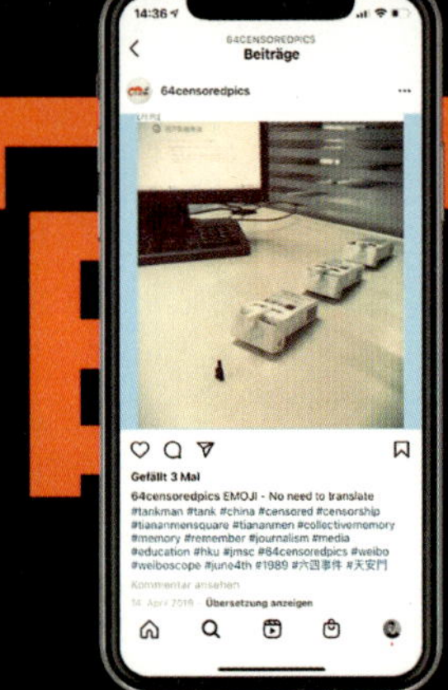

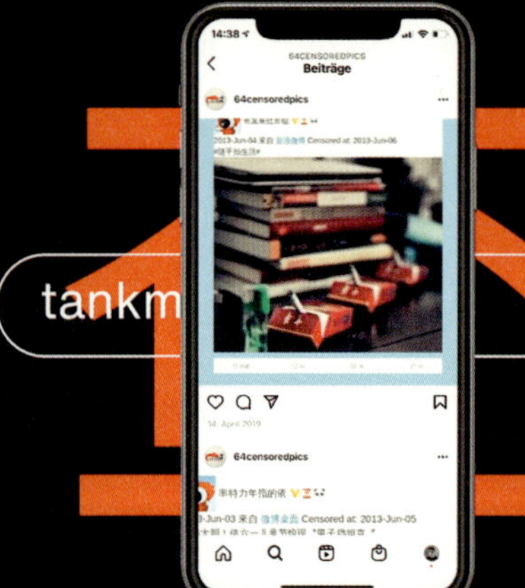

tankm

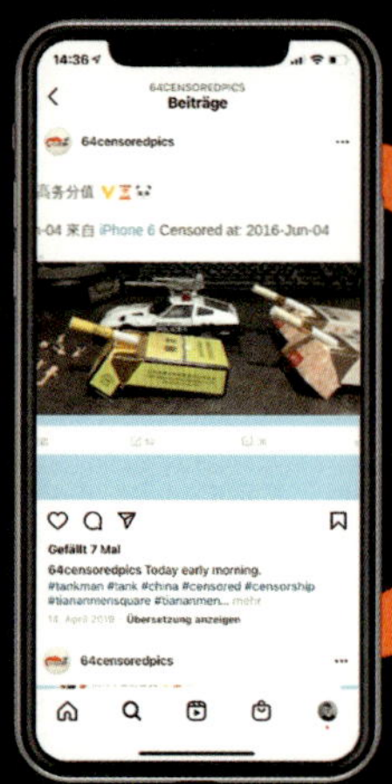

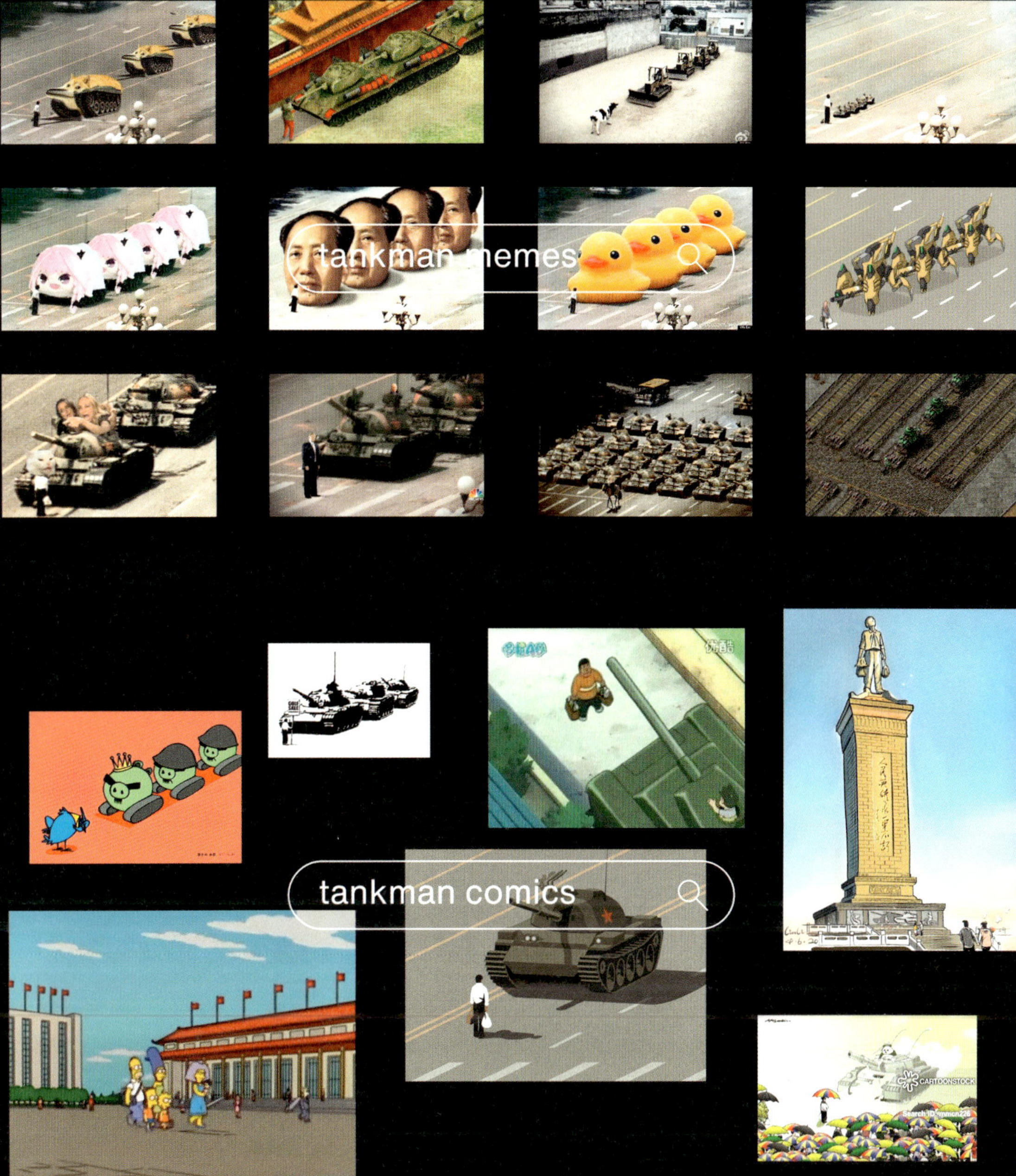
tankman memes
tankman comics
CARTOONSTOCK
Search ID: mmcn226

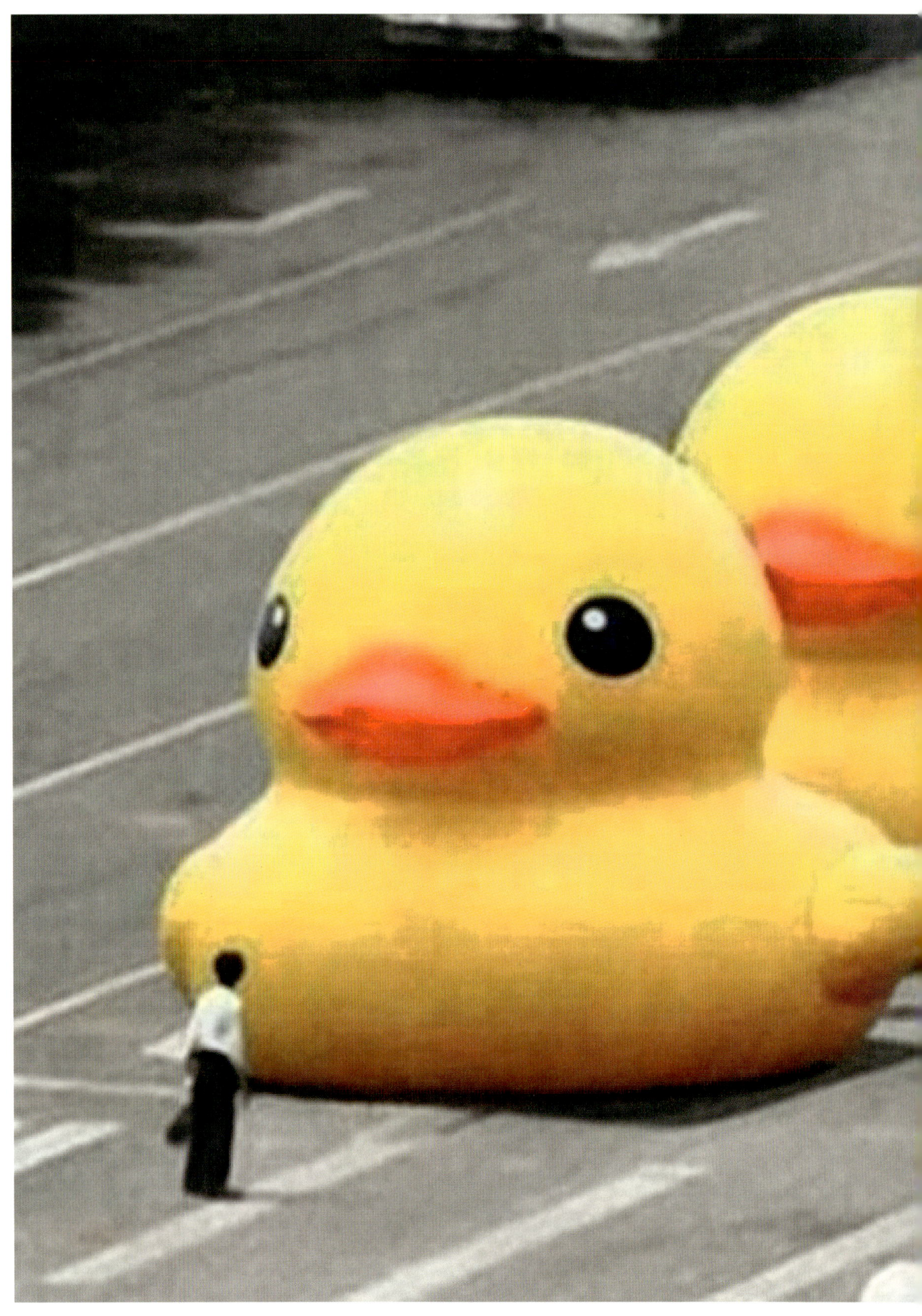

Anonym / **Anonymous**
A Parody of the Iconic 1989 Tiananmen Square Photo of a Chinese Protester Confronting Government Tanks, 2013, Tank-Man-Meme

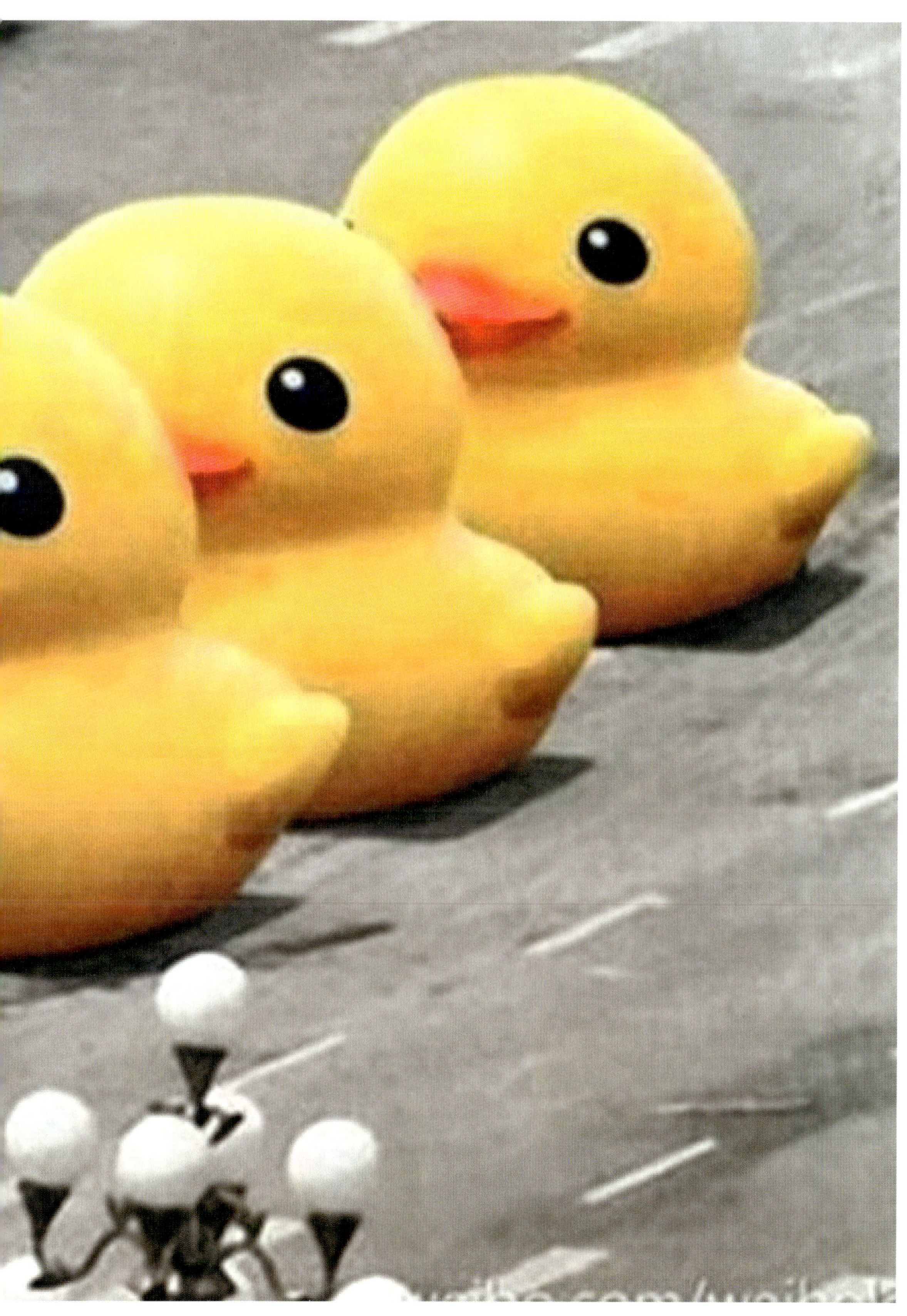

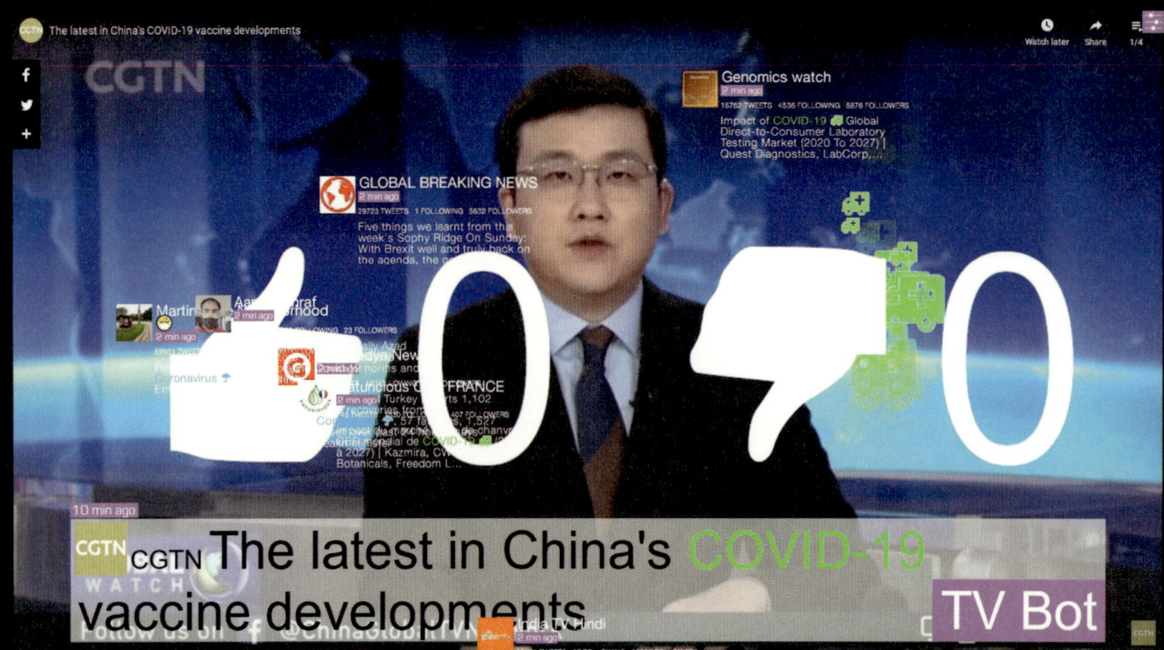

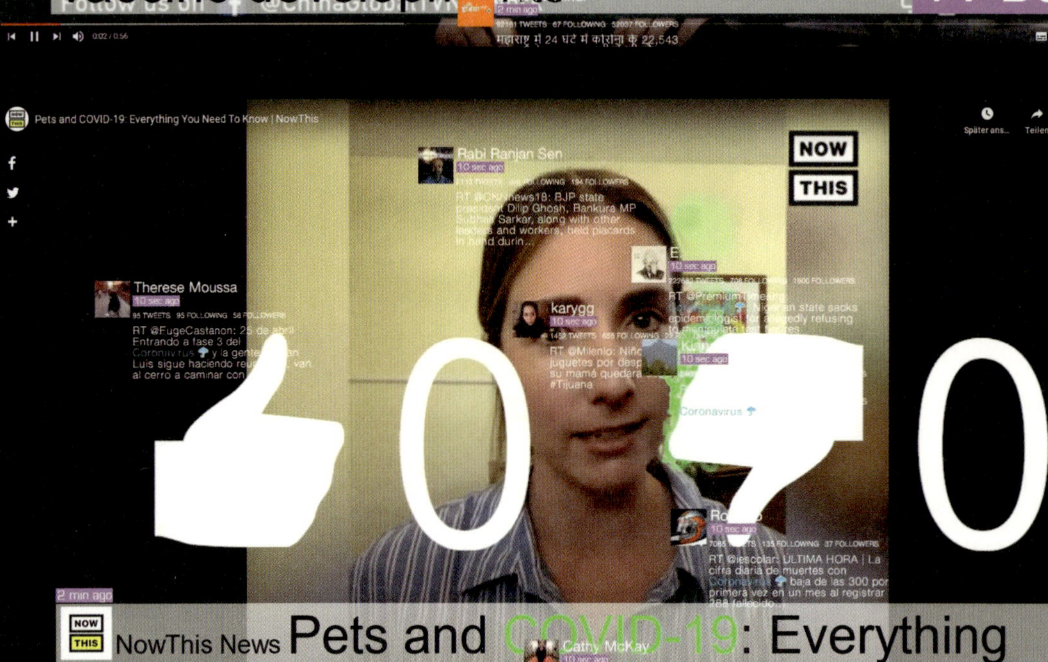

Marc Lee
Corona TV Bot, 2020/2021

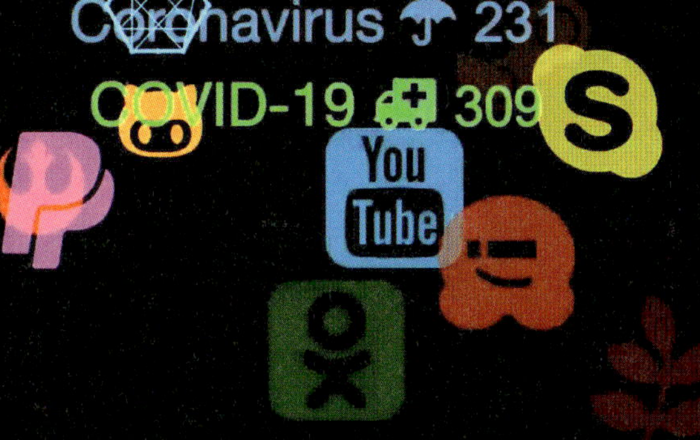

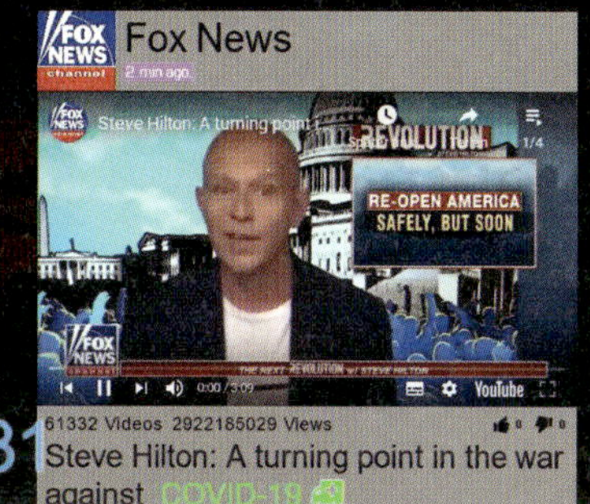

Coronavirus 231
COVID-19 309

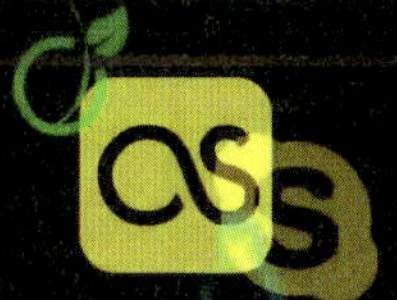

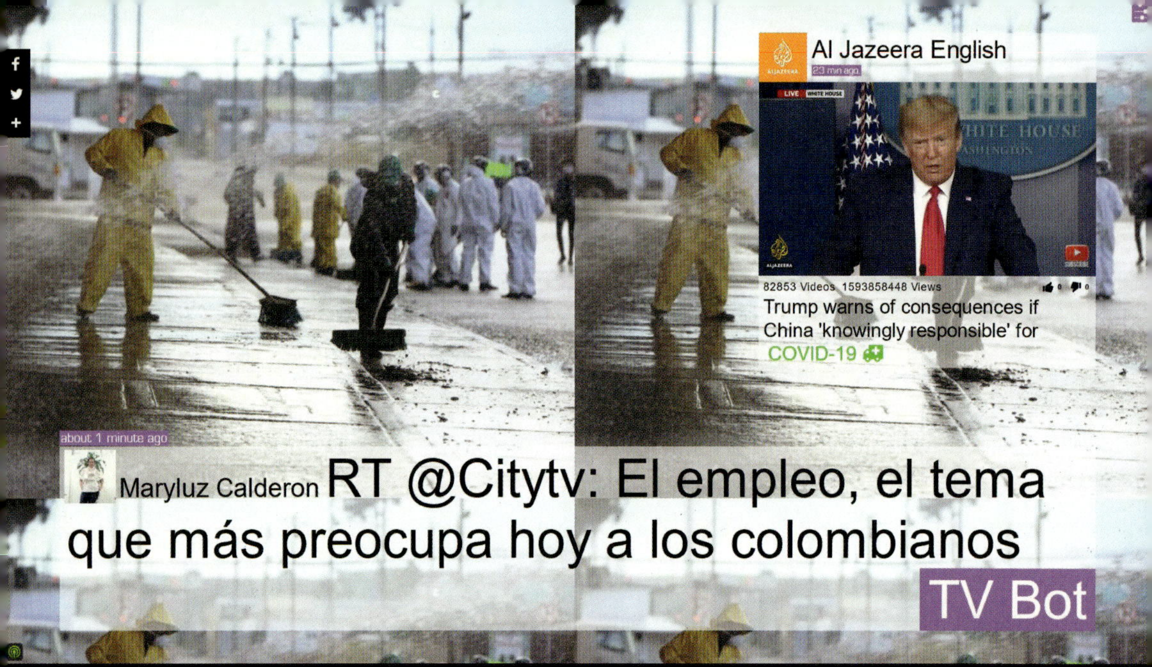

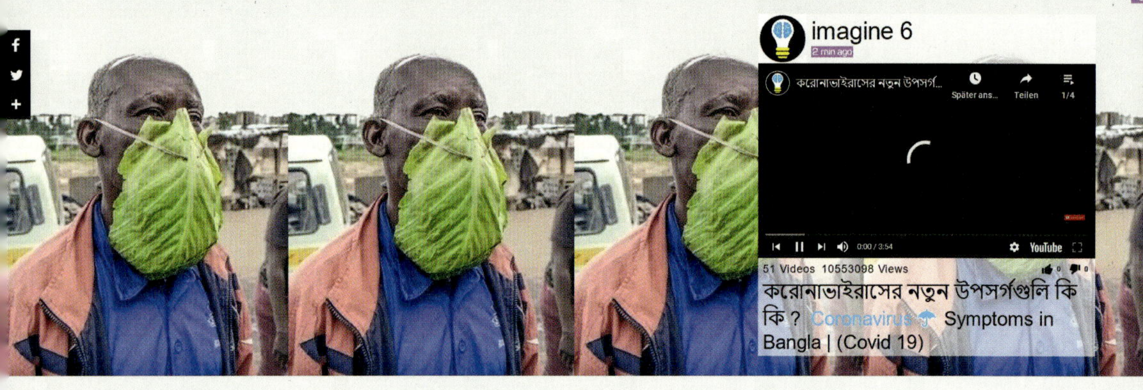
Al Jazeera English
23 min ago
LIVE WHITE HOUSE
WHITE HOUSE
WASHINGTON
82853 Videos 1593858448 Views
Trump warns of consequences if
China 'knowingly responsible' for
COVID-19
about 1 minute ago
Maryluz Calderon RT @Citytv: El empleo, el tema
que más preocupa hoy a los colombianos
TV Bot
imagine 6 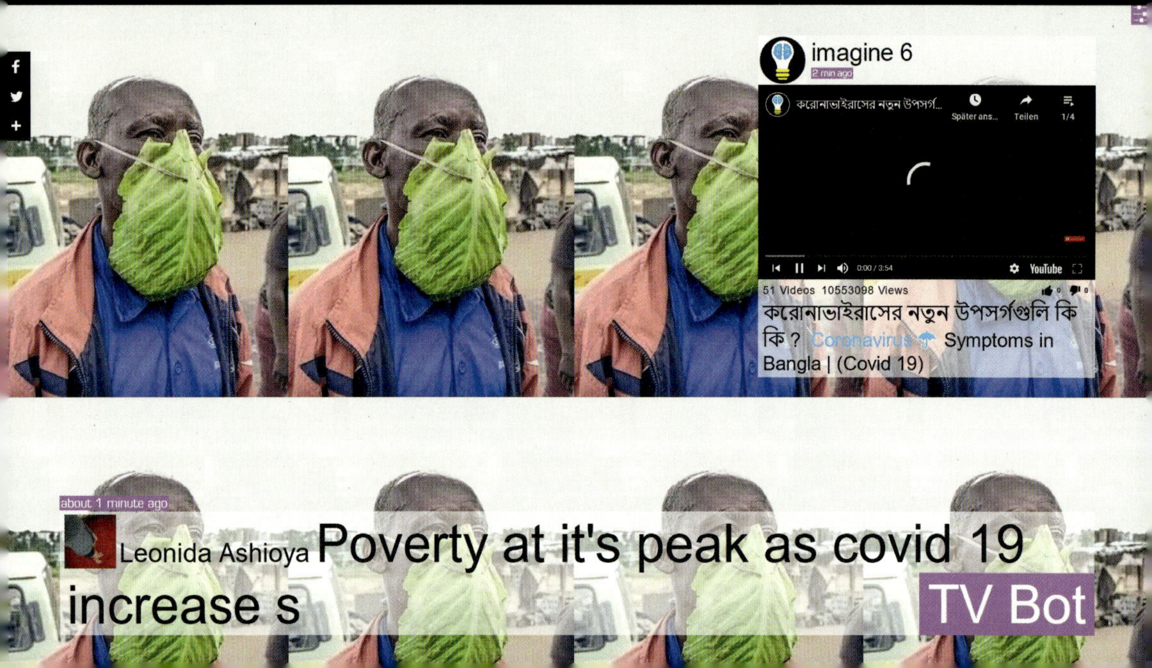
2 min ago
করোনাভাইরাসের নতুন উপসর্গ...
Später ans... Teilen 1/4
0:00 / 3:54
YouTube
51 Videos 10553098 Views
করোনাভাইরাসের নতুন উপসর্গগুলি কি
কি ? Coronavirus Symptoms in
Bangla | (Covid 19)
about 1 minute ago
Leonida Ashioya Poverty at it's peak as covid 19
increase s
TV Bot

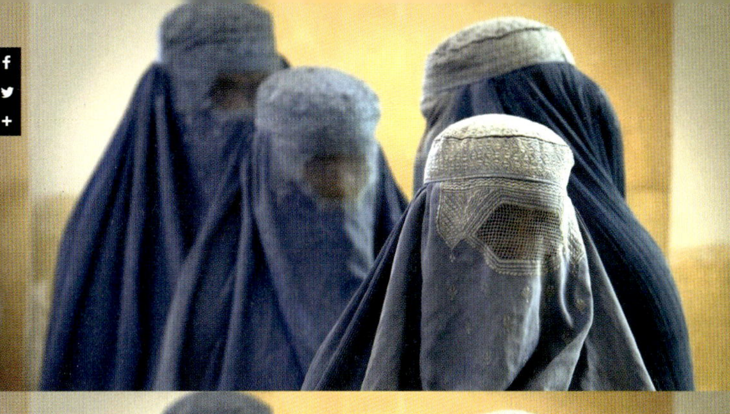
2 min ago
AURORA RT @8balsmusettes8: ¿Covid 19? Ya llegó la máscara facial antiviral de última generación.
TV Bot

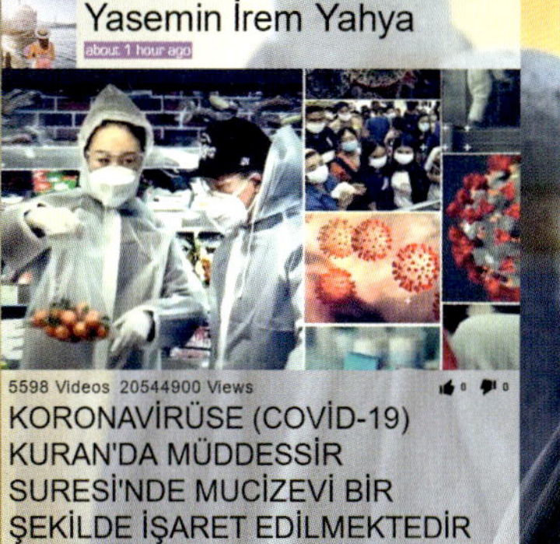
Yasemin İrem Yahya
about 1 hour ago
5598 Videos 20544900 Views
KORONAVİRÜSE (COVİD-19) KURAN'DA MÜDDESSİR SURESİ'NDE MUCİZEVİ BİR ŞEKİLDE İŞARET EDİLMEKTEDİR

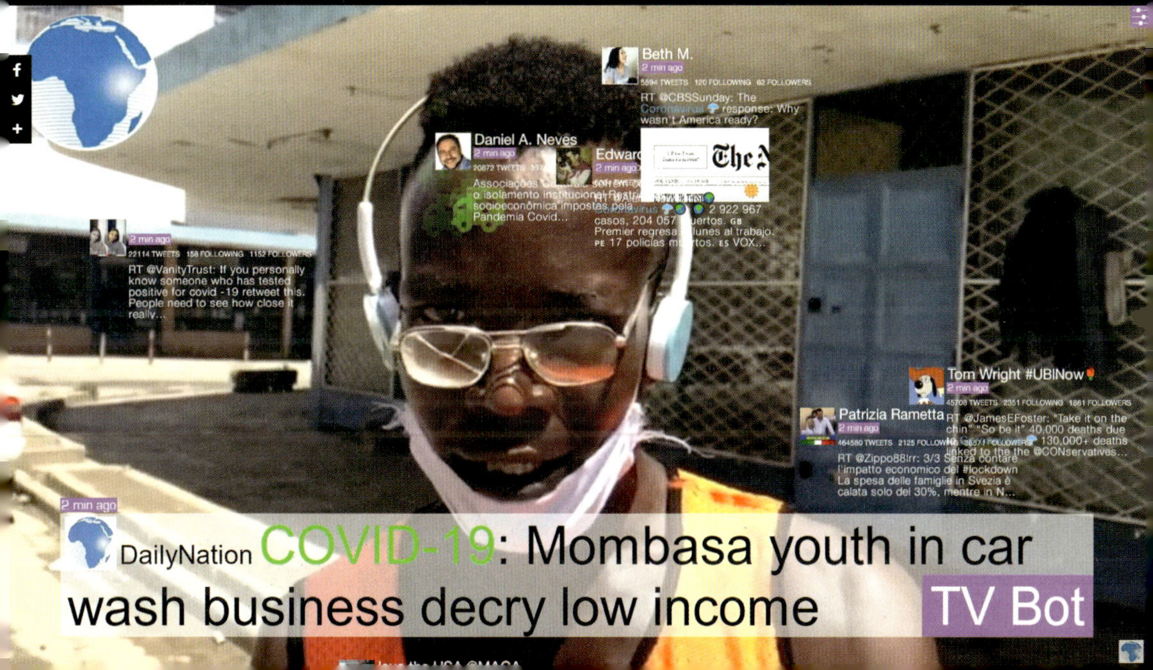

Beth M.
2 min ago
5894 TWEETS 120 FOLLOWING 62 FOLLOWERS
RT @CBSSunday: The Coronavirus response: Why wasn't America ready?

Daniel A. Neves
2 min ago
20872 TWEETS
Associações alertam para o isolamento institucional e a desigualdade socioeconômica impostas pela Pandemia Covid...

Edward
2 min ago
The N

2 min ago
222114 TWEETS 158 FOLLOWING 1152 FOLLOWERS
RT @VanityTrust: If you personally know someone who has tested positive for covid -19 retweet this. People need to see how close it really...

virus 2 922 967 casos, 204 057 muertos. GB Premier regresa el lunes al trabajo. PE 17 policías muertos. ES VOX...

Tom Wright #UBINow
2 min ago
45708 TWEETS 2351 FOLLOWING 1861 FOLLOWERS
RT @JamesEFoster: "Take it on the chin" "So be it" 40,000 deaths due 130,000+ deaths linked to the the @CONservatives...

Patrizia Rametta
2 min ago
464580 TWEETS 2125 FOLLOWING 38571 FOLLOWERS
RT @Zippo88lrr: 3/3 Senza contare l'impatto economico del #lockdown La spesa delle famiglie in Svezia è calata solo del 30%, mentre in N...

2 min ago
DailyNation COVID-19: Mombasa youth in car wash business decry low income
TV Bot

AFGHANISTAN
America / امریکا

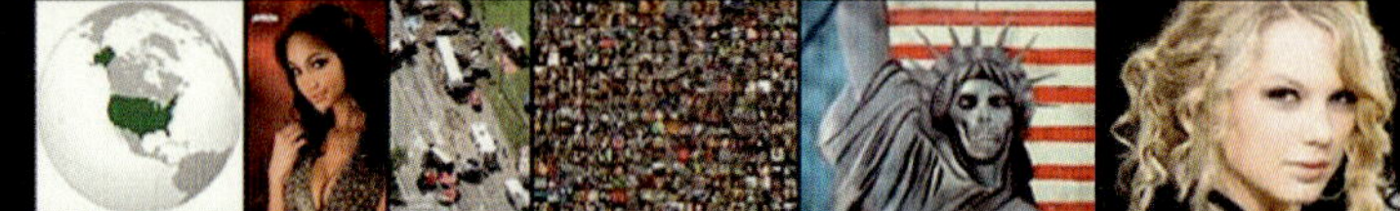

CHINA
America / 美国

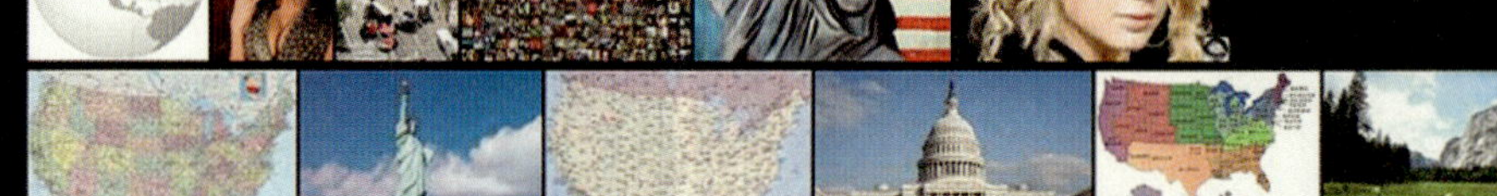

EGYPT
America / امريكا

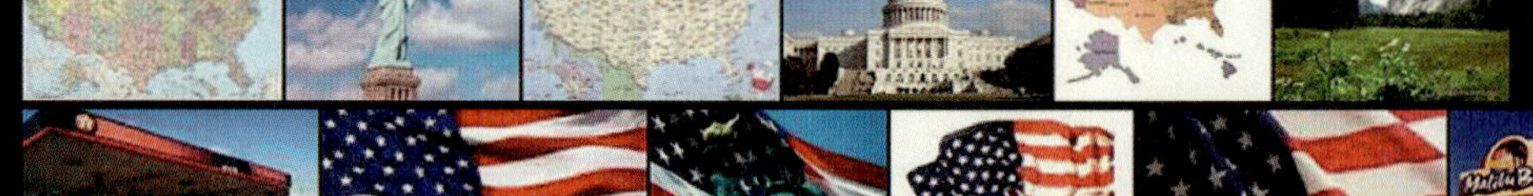

INDIA
America / अमेरिका

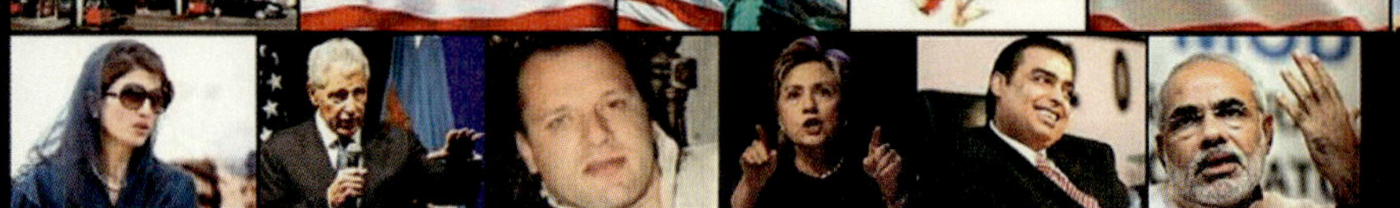

IRAN
America / امریکا

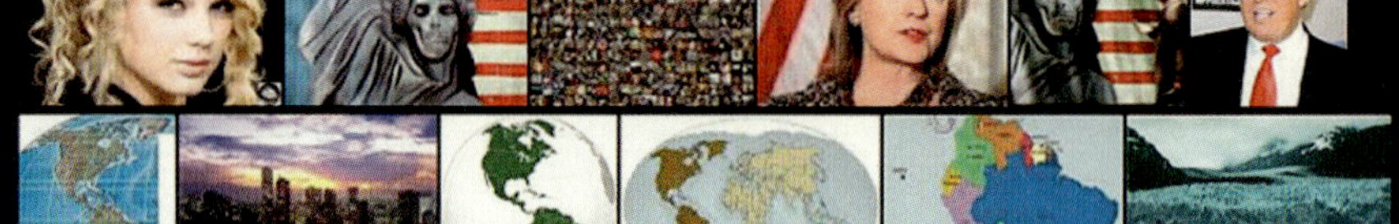

ISRAEL
America / אמריקה

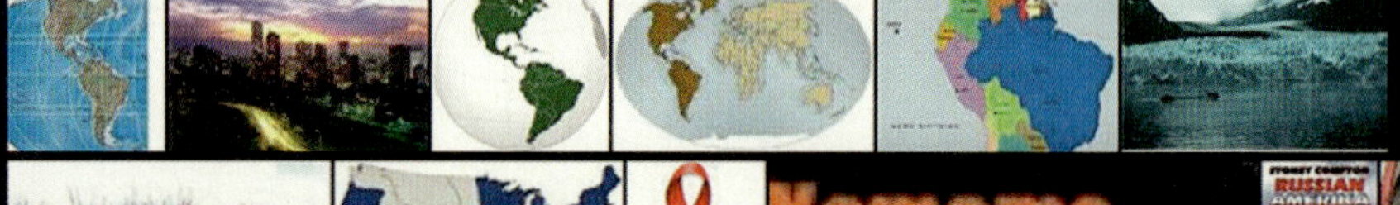

KENYA
America / Amerika

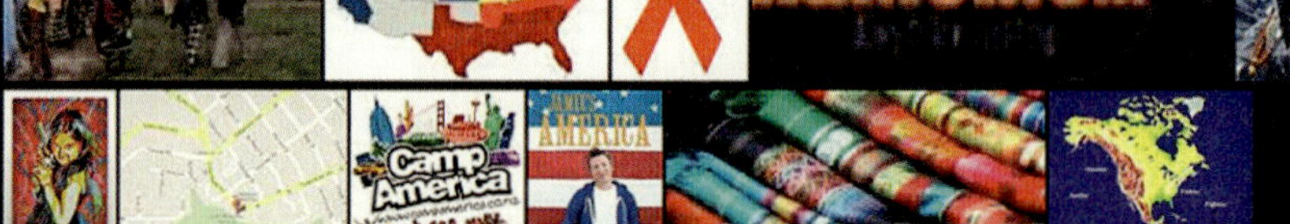

NEW ZEALAND
America / America

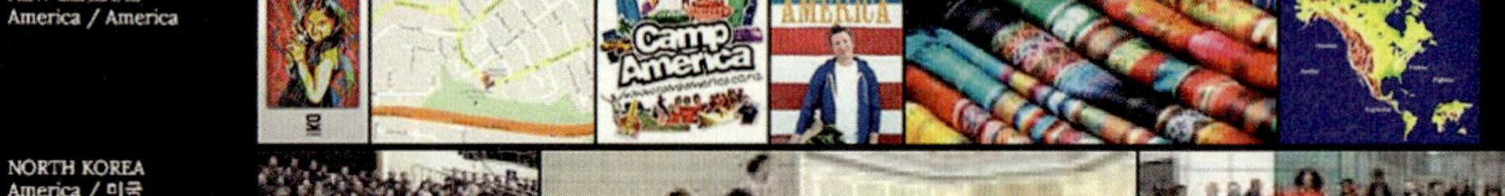

NORTH KOREA
America / 미국

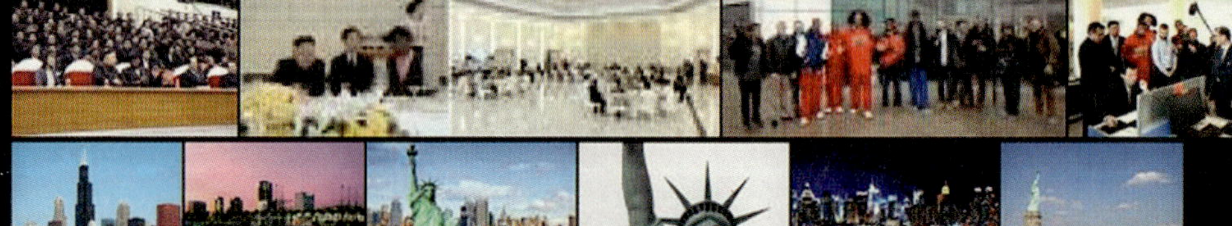

RUSSIA
America / Америка

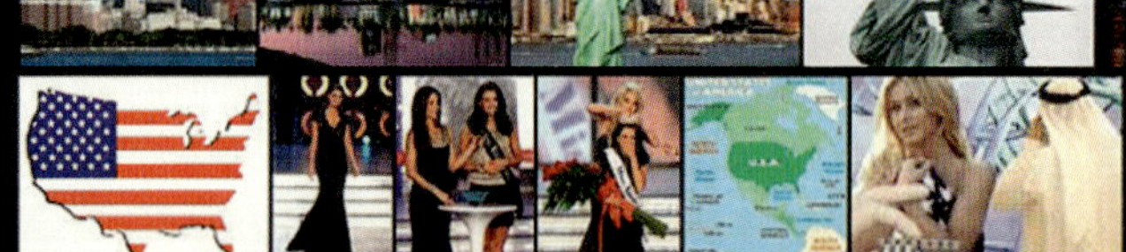

SYRIA
America / امريكا

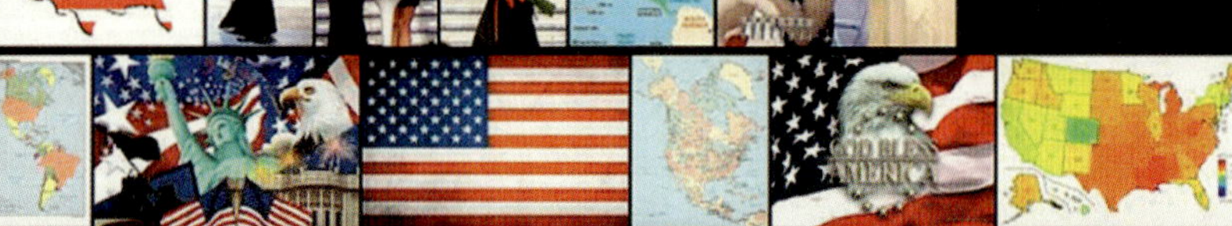

UNITED STATES
America / America

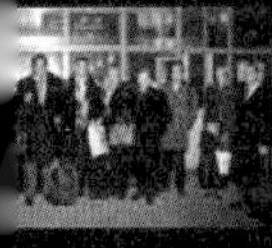

⦿ Sort results alphabetically

⬤ Sort results by GDP

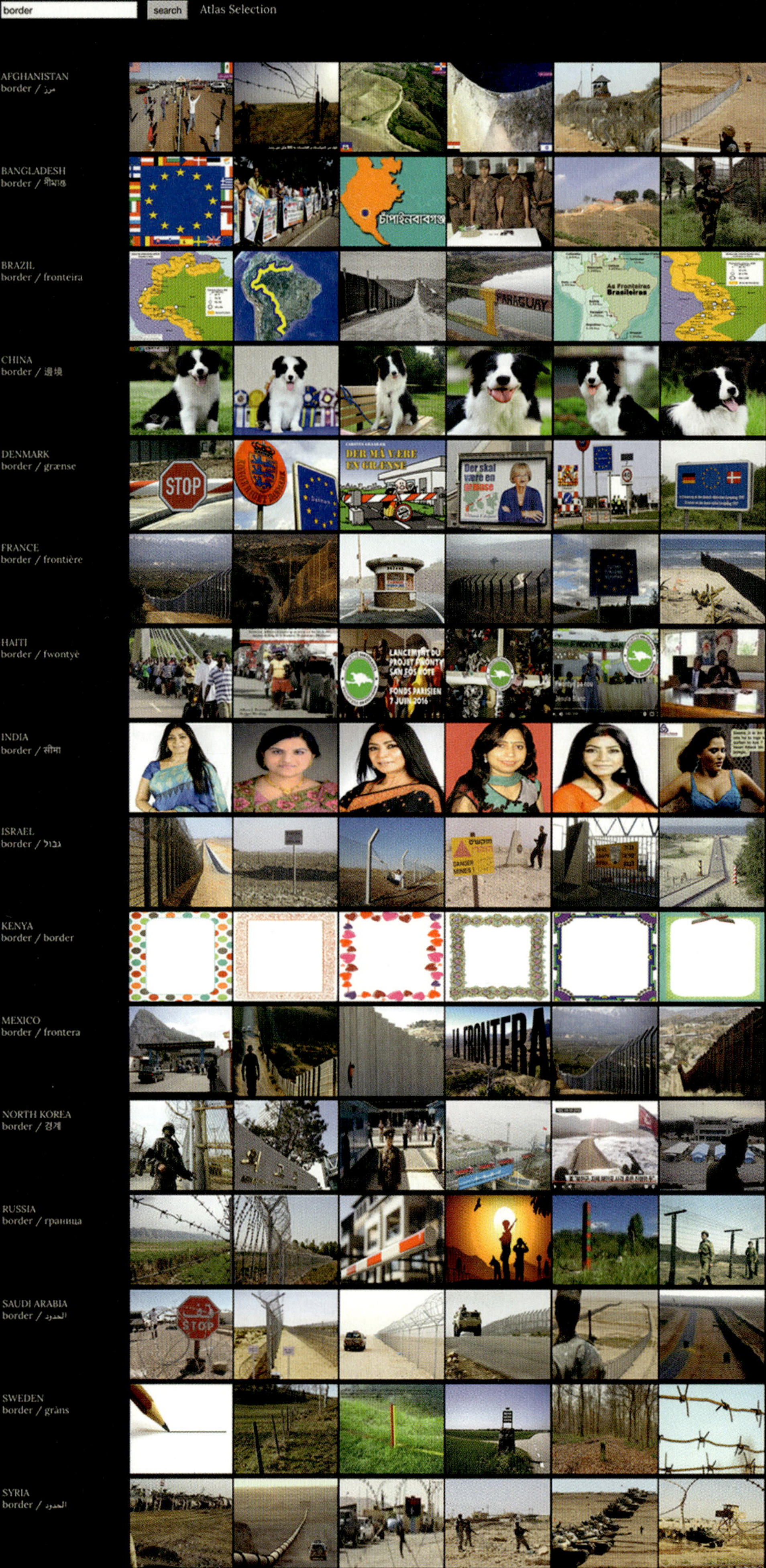

border
search   Atlas Selection
AFGHANISTAN
border / مرز
BANGLADESH
border / সীমান্ত
BRAZIL
border / fronteira
CHINA
border / 邊境
DENMARK
border / grænse
FRANCE
border / frontière
HAITI
border / fwontyè
INDIA
border / सीमा
ISRAEL
border / גבול
KENYA
border / border
MEXICO
border / frontera
NORTH KOREA
border / 경계
RUSSIA
border / граница
SAUDI ARABIA
border / الحدود
SWEDEN
border / gräns
SYRIA
border / الحدود

Taryn Simon & Aaron Swartz
Border, *9/30/16, 12:19 PM (Eastern Standard Time), Image Atlas,* 2012

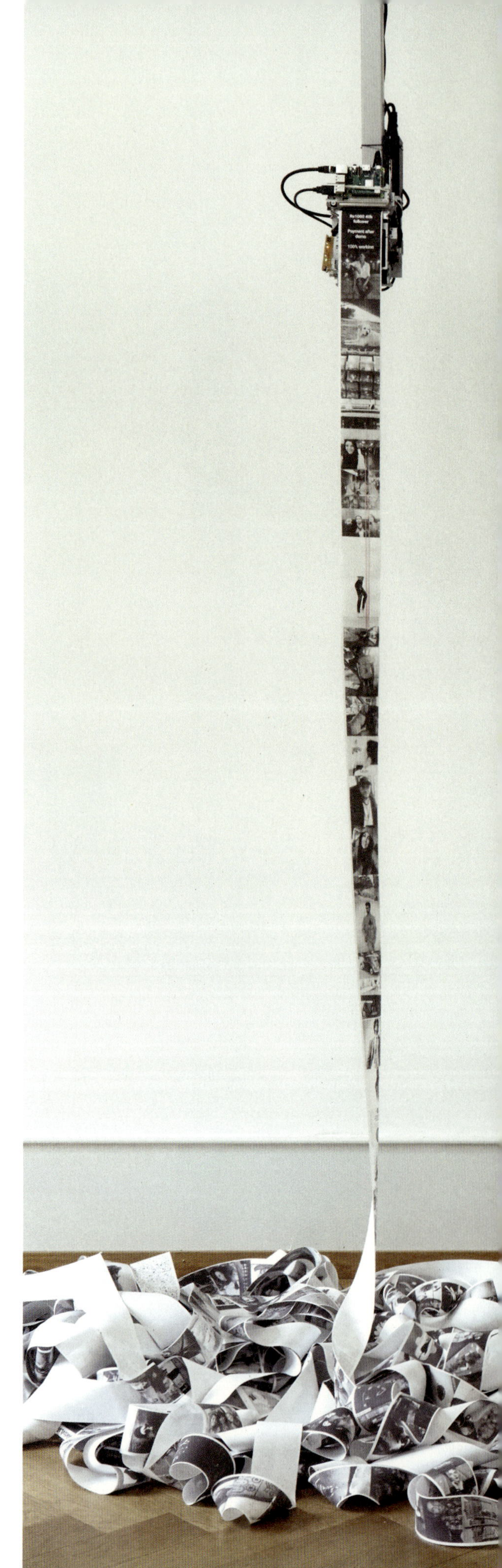

Romain Roucoules
Social Printer, 2018–2021

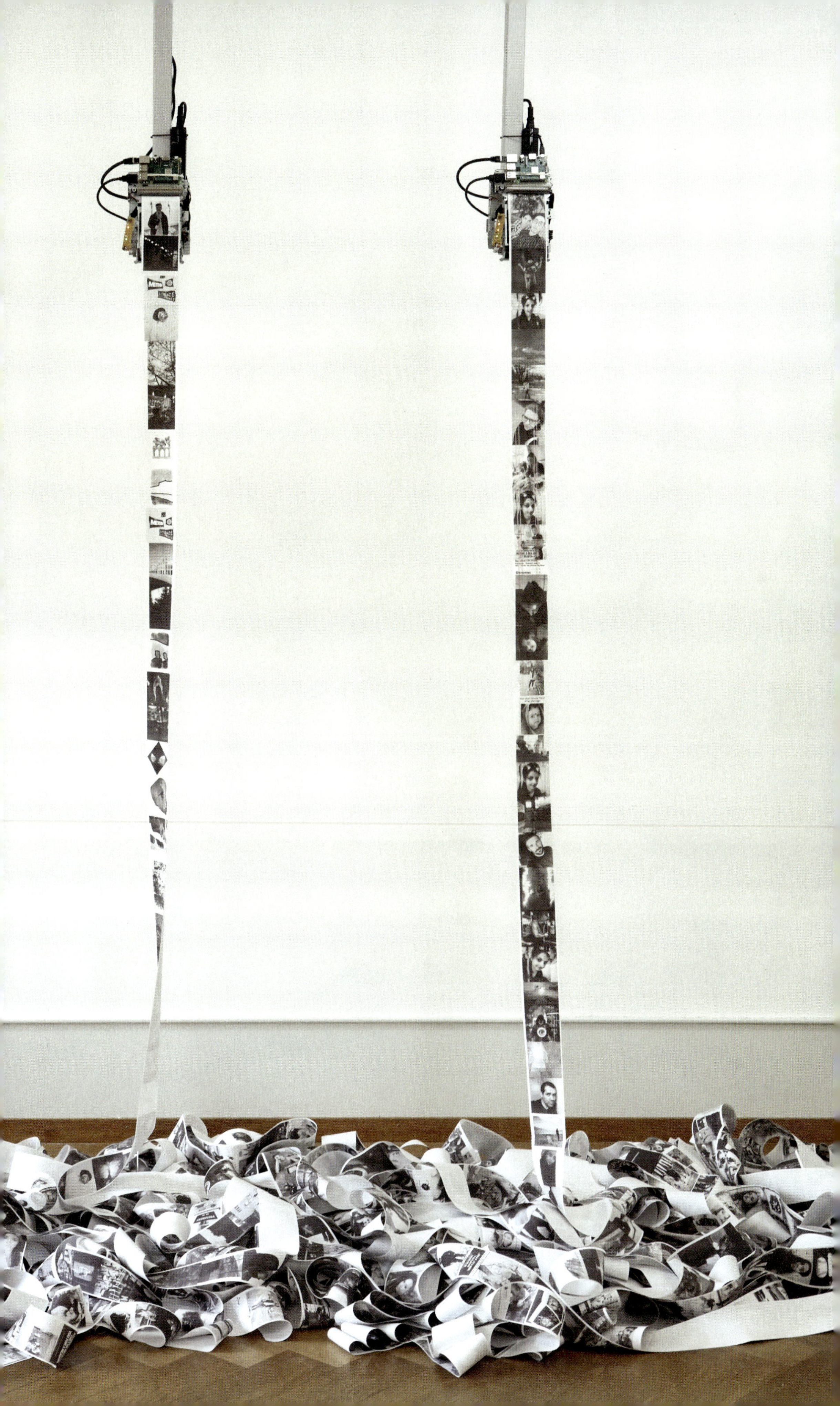

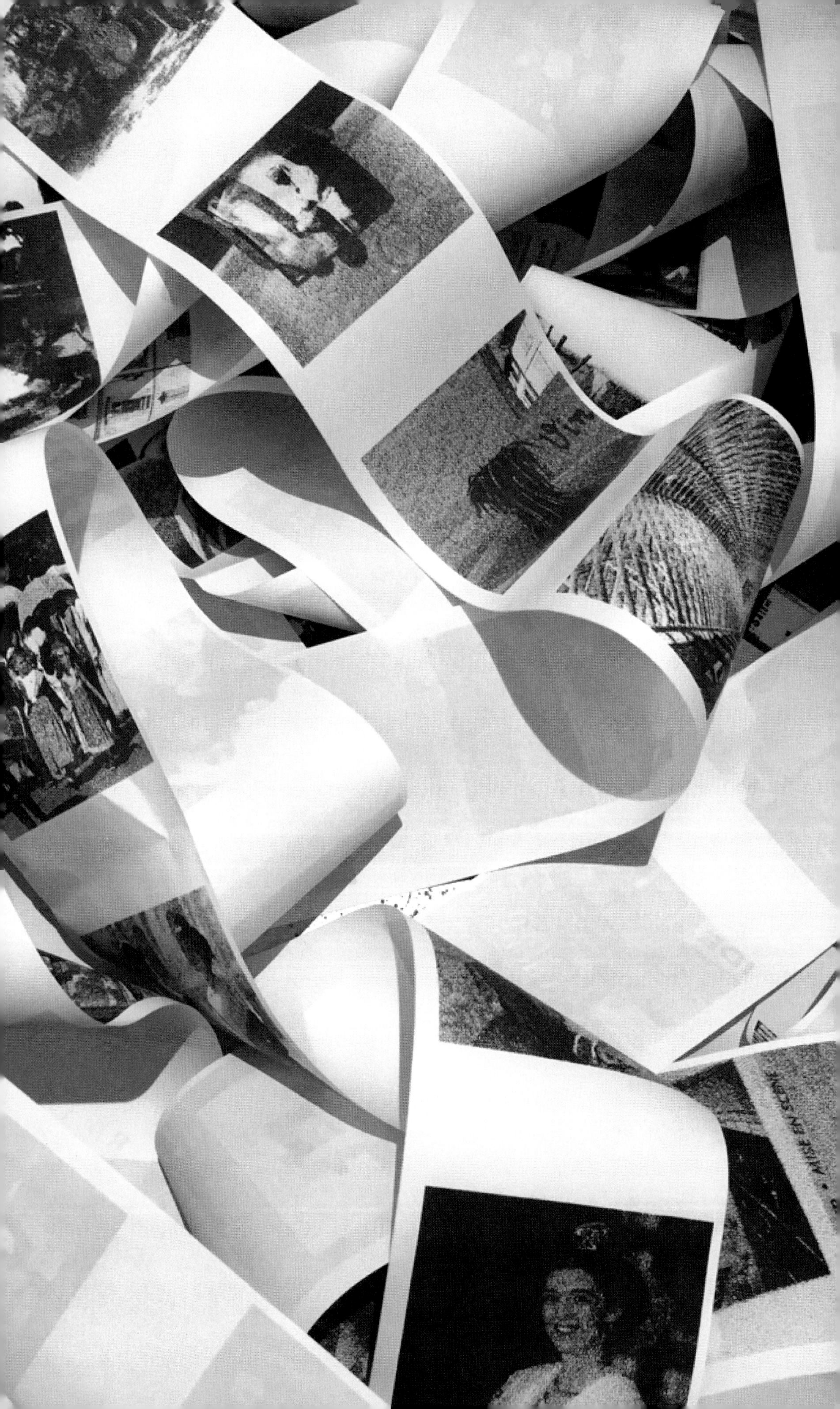

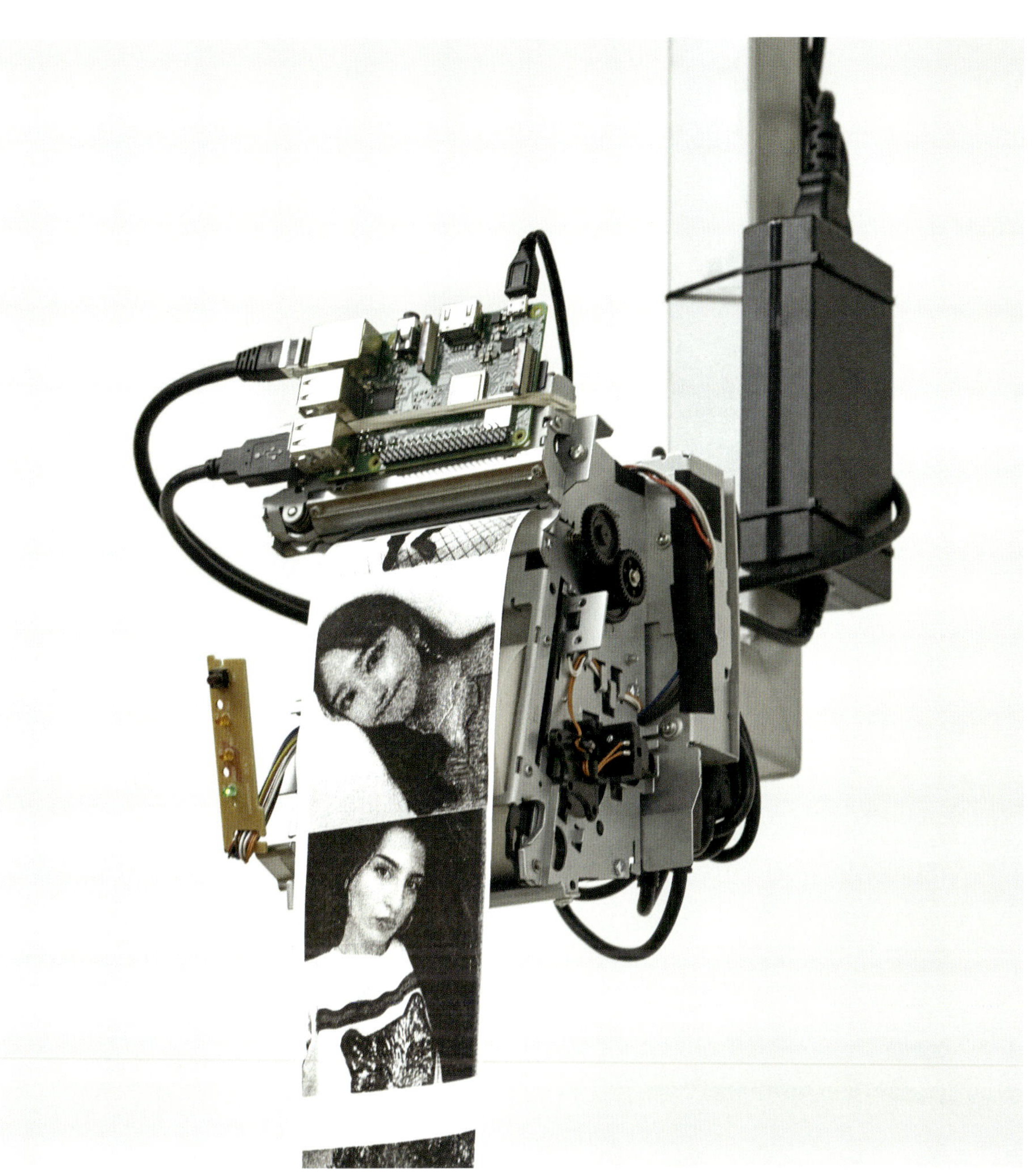

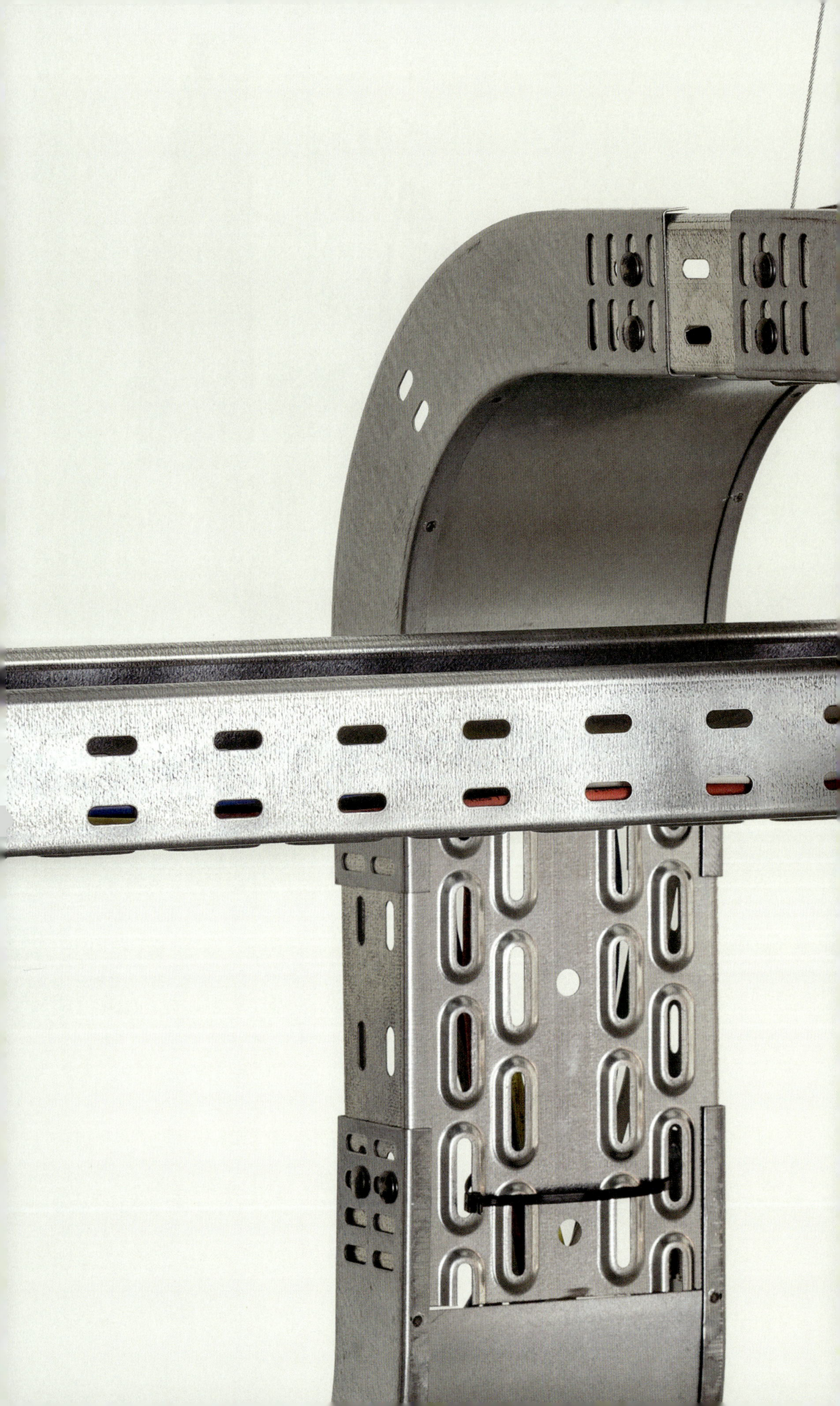

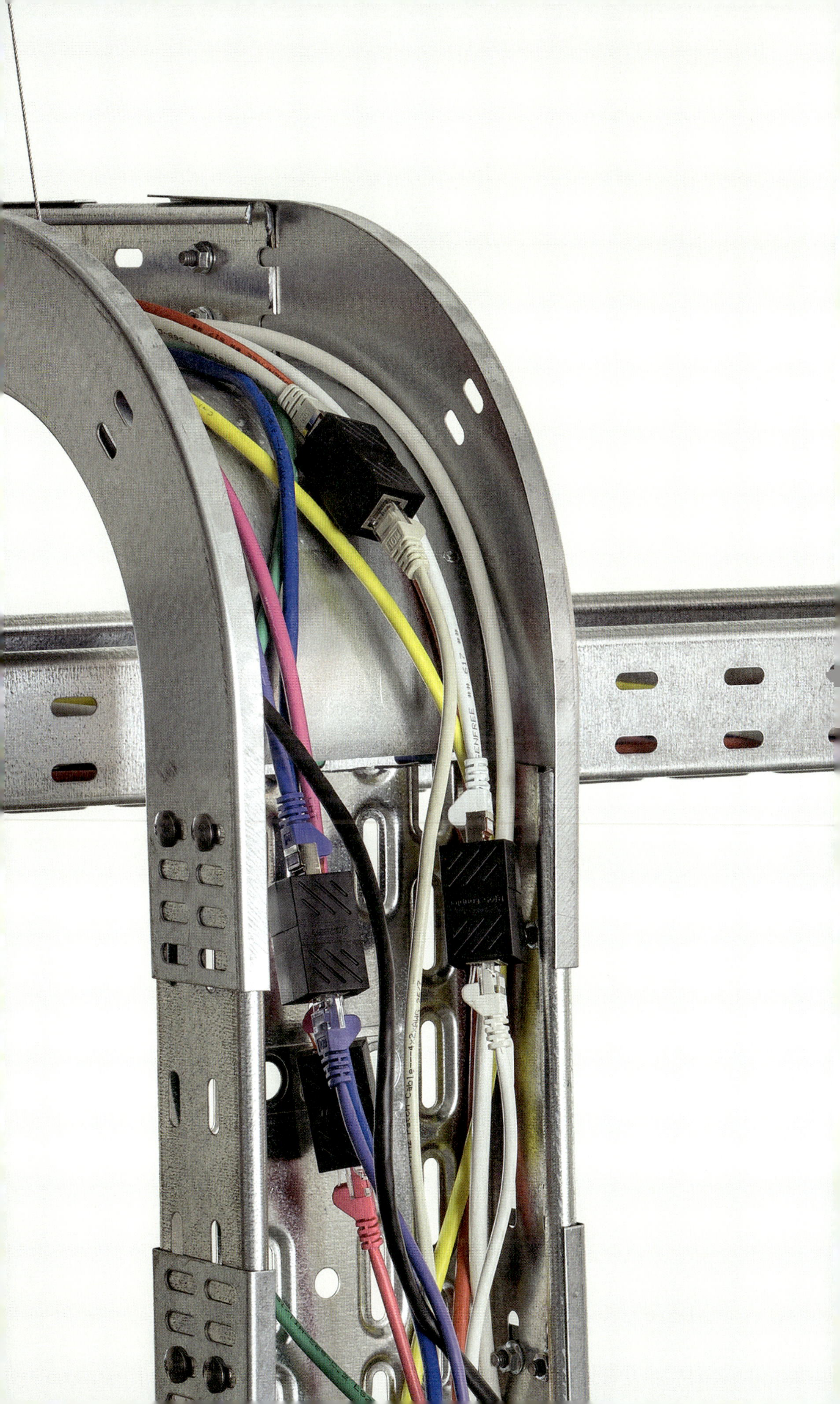

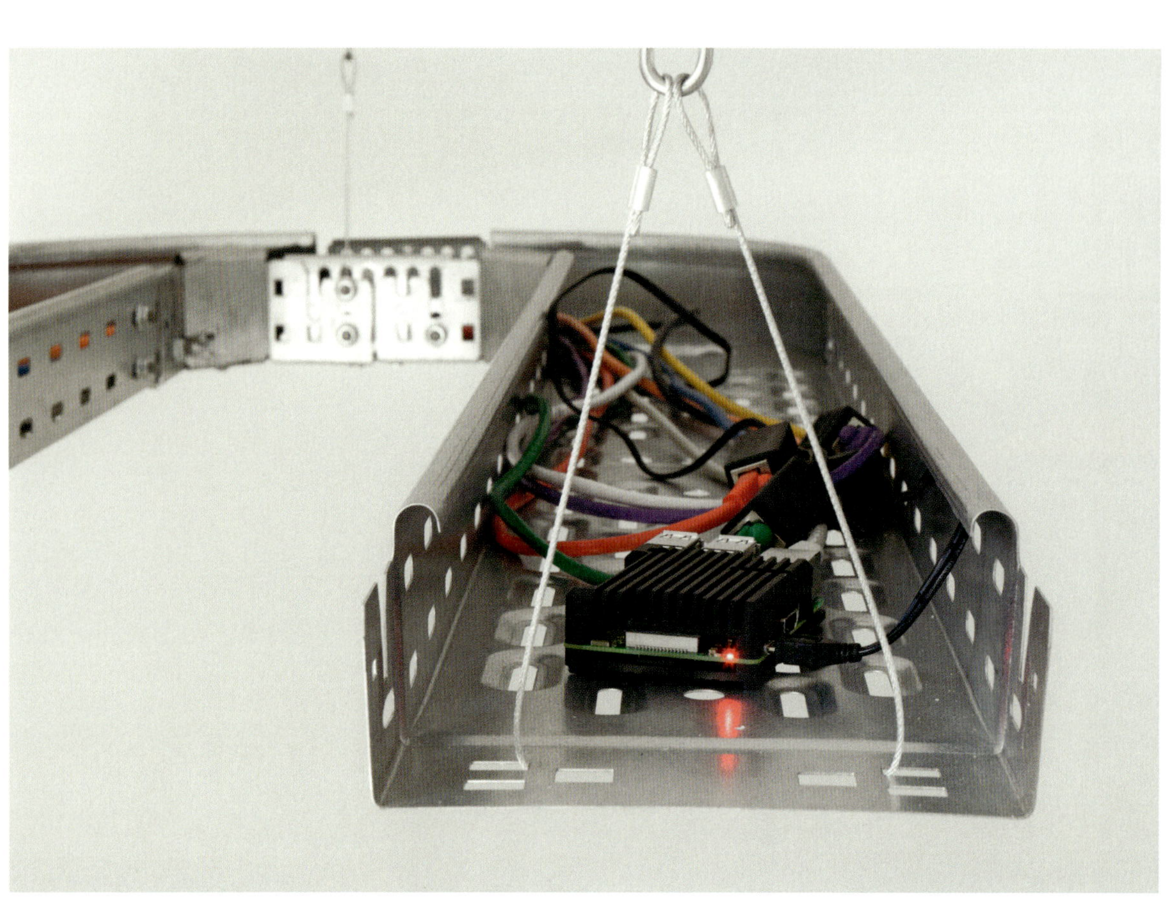

Eva & Franco Mattes
Personal Photographs, September 2009, 2019/2021

receiving	May 10, 2019 at 5:21 PM	--	flushing farm_02.jpg	Oct 6, 20
sending	May 11, 2019 at 9:18 AM	--	foto di blu - 6894.JPG	Sep 21, 2
_BVD7671.JPG	Sep 15, 2009 at 9:09 AM	3.2 MB	foto di blu - 6895.JPG	Sep 21, 2
_BVD7682.JPG	Sep 15, 2009 at 9:09 AM	2.3 MB	foto di blu - 6897.JPG	Sep 21, 2
_BVD7698.JPG	Sep 15, 2009 at 9:09 AM	2.8 MB	foto di blu - 6898.JPG	Sep 21, 2
_BVD7710.JPG	Sep 15, 2009 at 9:09 AM	2.8 MB	GraphicArt1.jpg	Sep 10, 20
_BVD7722.JPG	Sep 15, 2009 at 9:09 AM	3.4 MB	GraphicArt2.jpg	Sep 10, 20
10092009_001.jpg	Oct 6, 2009 at 1:35 PM	498 KB	GraphicArt3.jpg	Sep 10, 20
10092009.jpg	Oct 6, 2009 at 1:35 PM	496 KB	Image002.jpg	Oct 26, 2
12092009_001.jpg	Oct 6, 2009 at 1:35 PM	322 KB	Image003.jpg	Oct 26, 2
12092009.jpg	Oct 6, 2009 at 1:35 PM	351 KB	Image004.jpg	Dec 2, 20
21102009_001.jpg	Mar 5, 2010 at 9:45 AM	116 KB	Image005.jpg	Dec 2, 20
21102009.jpg	Mar 5, 2010 at 9:45 AM	95 KB	IMG_6497.JPG	Sep 21, 2
30112009_001.jpg	Mar 5, 2010 at 9:45 AM	150 KB	IMG_6498.JPG	Sep 21, 2
30112009.jpg	Mar 5, 2010 at 9:45 AM	157 KB	IMG_6499.JPG	Sep 21, 2
20099129754720.JPG.jpeg	Oct 1, 2009 at 4:13 PM	46 KB	IMG_6501.JPG	Sep 21, 2
20099129754721.JPG.jpeg	Oct 1, 2009 at 4:13 PM	46 KB	IMG_6503.JPG	Sep 21, 2
20099129754722.JPG.jpeg	Oct 1, 2009 at 4:13 PM	50 KB	IMG_6505.JPG	Sep 21, 2
20099129754723.JPG.jpeg	Oct 1, 2009 at 4:13 PM	50 KB	IMG_6506.JPG	Sep 21, 2
20099129754724.JPG.jpeg	Oct 1, 2009 at 4:13 PM	56 KB	IMG_6507.JPG	Sep 21, 2
DSCF7204.jpg	Sep 10, 2009 at 10:53 AM	1.5 MB	IMG_6508.JPG	Sep 21, 2
DSCF8923.JPG	Sep 2, 2009 at 4:15 PM	1.9 MB	IMG_6509.JPG	Sep 21, 2
DSCF8935.JPG	Sep 2, 2009 at 5:47 PM	1.8 MB	IMG_6511.JPG	Sep 21, 2
DSCF8971.JPG	Sep 6, 2009 at 11:25 AM	1.9 MB	IMG_6512.JPG	Sep 21, 2
DSCF8972.JPG	Sep 6, 2009 at 11:26 AM	1.9 MB	IMG_6513.JPG	Sep 21, 2
DSCF8975.JPG	Sep 6, 2009 at 11:27 AM	1.9 MB	IMG_6514.JPG	Sep 21, 2
DSCF8980.JPG	Sep 6, 2009 at 11:28 AM	1.8 MB	IMG_6515.JPG	Sep 21, 2
DSCF8981.JPG	Sep 6, 2009 at 12:15 PM	1.8 MB	IMG_6516.JPG	Sep 21, 2
DSCF8984.JPG	Sep 6, 2009 at 12:29 PM	1.9 MB	IMG_6517.JPG	Sep 21, 2
DSCF8987.JPG	Sep 6, 2009 at 6:06 PM	1.8 MB	IMG_6521.JPG	Sep 21, 2
DSCF8988.JPG	Sep 6, 2009 at 6:08 PM	1.9 MB	IMG_6522.JPG	Sep 21, 2
DSCF8990.JPG	Sep 6, 2009 at 7:00 PM	1.8 MB	IMG_6523.JPG	Sep 21, 2
DSCF8992.JPG	Sep 7, 2009 at 4:44 PM	2 MB	IMG_6525.JPG	Sep 21, 2
DSCF8995.JPG	Sep 7, 2009 at 4:53 PM	1.9 MB	IMG_6526.JPG	Sep 21, 2
DSCF8997.JPG	Sep 7, 2009 at 6:12 PM	2 MB	IMG_6527.JPG	Sep 21, 2
DSCF8998.JPG	Sep 7, 2009 at 6:13 PM	2 MB	IMG_6528.JPG	Sep 21, 2
DSCF8999.JPG	Sep 7, 2009 at 11:26 PM	1.9 MB	IMG_6530.JPG	Sep 21, 2
DSCF9001.JPG	Sep 9, 2009 at 8:50 PM	1.9 MB	IMG_6531.JPG	Sep 21, 2
DSCF9003.JPG	Sep 9, 2009 at 8:51 PM	1.9 MB	IMG_6532.JPG	Sep 21, 2
DSCF9004.JPG	Sep 9, 2009 at 10:36 PM	1.9 MB	IMG_6533.JPG	Sep 21, 2
DSCF9005.JPG	Sep 10, 2009 at 4:11 PM	2 MB	IMG_6534.JPG	Sep 21, 2
DSCF9021.JPG	Sep 15, 2009 at 3:02 PM	1.9 MB	IMG_6535.JPG	Sep 21, 2
DSCF9022.JPG	Sep 15, 2009 at 7:21 PM	1.9 MB	IMG_6537.JPG	Sep 21, 2
DSCF9024.JPG	Sep 15, 2009 at 7:21 PM	1.9 MB	IMG_6539.JPG	Sep 21, 2
DSCF9025.JPG	Sep 15, 2009 at 7:22 PM	1.9 MB	IMG_6540.JPG	Sep 21, 2
DSCF9026.JPG	Sep 15, 2009 at 7:22 PM	1.8 MB	IMG_6541.JPG	Sep 21, 2
DSCF9027.JPG	Sep 15, 2009 at 7:27 PM	1.9 MB	IMG_6542.JPG	Sep 21, 2
DSCF9028.JPG	Sep 15, 2009 at 7:28 PM	1.8 MB	IMG_6543.JPG	Sep 21, 2
DSCF9032.JPG	Sep 15, 2009 at 7:30 PM	1.9 MB	IMG_6544.JPG	Sep 21, 2
DSCF9036.JPG	Sep 15, 2009 at 7:33 PM	1.9 MB	IMG_6545.JPG	Sep 21, 2
DSCF9037.JPG	Sep 15, 2009 at 7:34 PM	2 MB	IMG_6546.JPG	Sep 21, 2
DSCF9038.JPG	Sep 15, 2009 at 7:35 PM	1.9 MB	IMG_6547.JPG	Sep 21, 2
DSCF9040.JPG	Sep 15, 2009 at 7:38 PM	2 MB	IMG_6548.JPG	Sep 21, 2
DSCF9042.JPG	Sep 15, 2009 at 7:38 PM	1.9 MB	IMG_6549.JPG_02	Sep 21, 2
DSCF9044.JPG	Sep 15, 2009 at 7:39 PM	1.9 MB	IMG_6550.JPG	Sep 21, 2
DSCF9050.JPG	Sep 15, 2009 at 8:11 PM	1.9 MB	IMG_6551.JPG	Sep 21, 2
DSCF9054.JPG	Sep 16, 2009 at 11:26 PM	1.9 MB	IMG_6552.JPG	Sep 21, 2
DSCF9062.JPG	Sep 16, 2009 at 11:28 PM	1.9 MB	IMG_6553.JPG	Sep 21, 2
DSCF9066.JPG	Sep 16, 2009 at 11:29 PM	1.9 MB	IMG_6554.jpg	Sep 21, 2
DSCF9067.JPG	Sep 16, 2009 at 11:31 PM	1.9 MB	IMG_6555.JPG	Sep 21, 2
DSCF9068.JPG	Sep 17, 2009 at 3:43 PM	1.9 MB	IMG_6556.JPG	Sep 21, 2
DSCF9069.JPG	Sep 17, 2009 at 3:43 PM	1.9 MB	IMG_6557.JPG	Sep 21, 2
DSCF9070.JPG	Sep 18, 2009 at 6:52 PM	1.9 MB	IMG_6559.JPG	Sep 21, 2
DSCF9075.JPG	Sep 20, 2009 at 5:21 PM	2 MB	IMG_6561.JPG	Sep 21, 2
DSCF9076.JPG	Sep 20, 2009 at 5:22 PM	1.9 MB	IMG_6562.JPG	Sep 21, 2
DSCF9078.JPG	Sep 20, 2009 at 5:28 PM	2 MB	IMG_6563.JPG	Sep 21, 2
DSCF9081.JPG	Sep 20, 2009 at 5:32 PM	2 MB	IMG_6564.JPG	Sep 21, 2
DSCF9083.JPG	Sep 20, 2009 at 5:36 PM	2 MB	IMG_6565.JPG	Sep 21, 2
DSCF9084.JPG	Sep 20, 2009 at 5:36 PM	1.9 MB	IMG_6566.JPG	Sep 21, 2
DSCF9085.JPG	Sep 20, 2009 at 5:38 PM	1.9 MB	IMG_6567.JPG	Sep 21, 2
DSCF9089.JPG	Sep 20, 2009 at 8:52 PM	1.9 MB	IMG_6568.JPG	Sep 21, 2

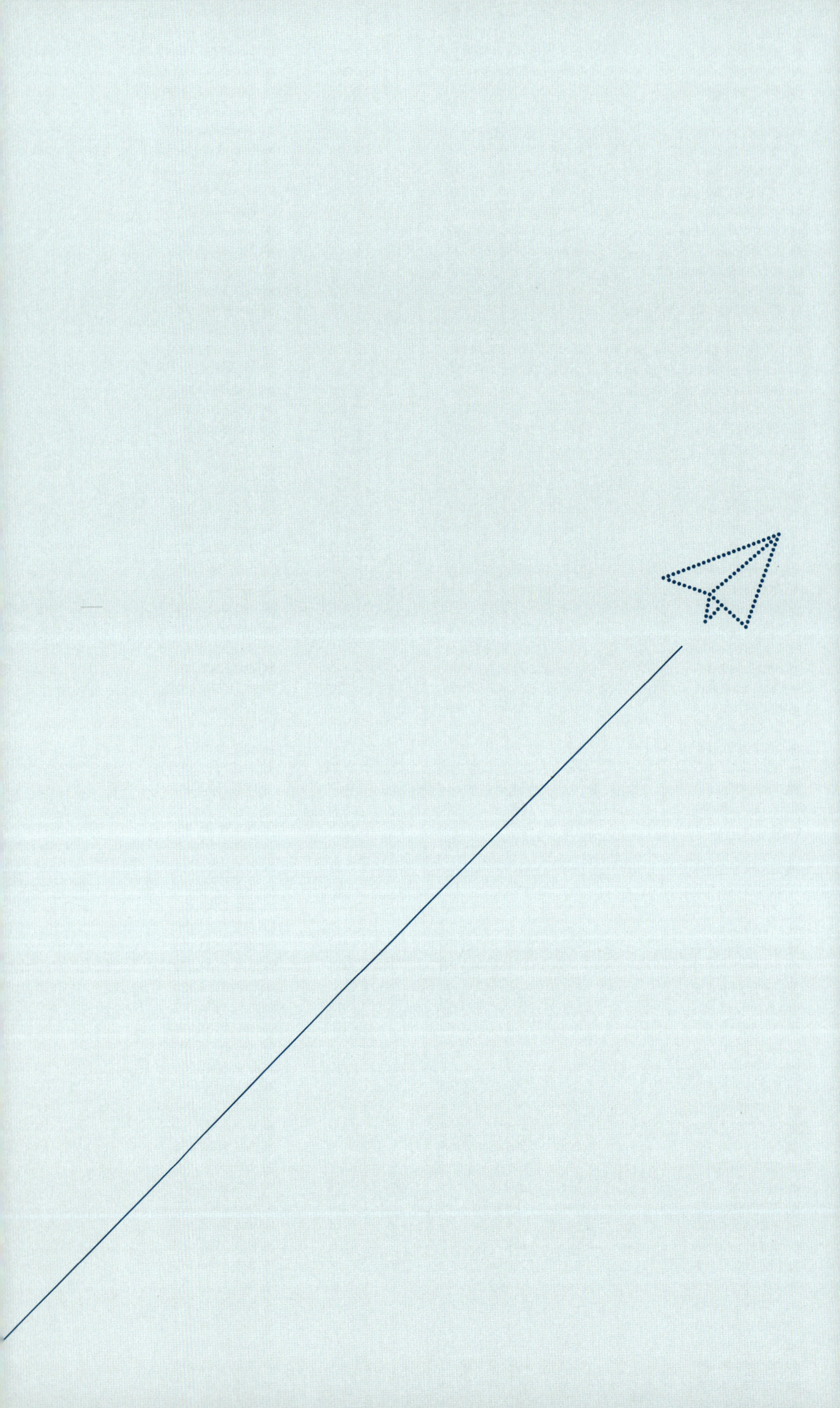

Text: Katja Müller-Helle

TECHNISCHE BILDZENSUR
Infrastrukturen der Löschung

Anfang März 2020, kurz nachdem das Coronavirus als pandemisches Problem Weltöffentlichkeit erlangte, kursierte eine Meldung auf Online-Nachrichten-plattformen und in sozialen Netzwerken, Youtube habe unter den Bedingungen von Covid-19 das Kuratieren und Löschen seiner Inhalte von der Tätigkeit menschlicher Content-Moderatoren verstärkt auf KI-gestützte Systeme verschoben. In den Großraumbüros seien die Abstandsregelungen zur Eindämmung der Pandemie nicht einzuhalten, daher setze man auf die virusfreie Technologie der automatischen Löschung. Nachdem die über 100.000 Mitarbeiter*innen von Google ins Homeoffice geschickt wurden, – inklusive derer, die nach der algorithmischen Erfassung für die Content-Moderation der Inhalte der Sharing-Plattform Youtube verantwortlich sind – müsse allerdings damit gerechnet werden, dass vermehrt Falschzuordnungen und Overblocking stattfinde.[1] Die sonst auf die Kombination aus algorithmischer Erkennung und menschlicher Überprüfung setzende Praxis zur Inhaltsregulierung, „will temporarily start relying more on technology to help with some of the work normally done by reviewers"[2]. Auch andere Plattformen wie Facebook, Twitter und TikTok warnten vorauseilend, „die automatisierten Systeme würden künftig

TECHNICAL PICTURE CENSORS
Infrastructures of Suppression

In early March 2020, shortly after the coronavirus pandemic crisis had gained global attention, a message circulated on online news sites and on social media that YouTube would increasingly be using artificial intelligence instead of humans to review and remove content. The company claimed it was not possible to implement social distancing guidelines introduced to curb the pandemic within their open-plan offices, which is why they were turning to automized removal technology to circumvent risks caused by the virus. Once Google's staff of over one hundred thousand, including those responsible for content moderation of videos flagged by algorithms on YouTube, had been sent home to work, it was inevitable that more videos would incorrectly be flagged and removed.[1] Whereas normally algorithms detect questionable content that is then sent to human reviewers, it was announced that the company "will temporarily start relying more on technology to help with some of the work normally done by reviewers."[2] Other platforms such as Facebook, Twitter, and TikTok, also rushed to warn that "automated systems would independently remove content" and user accounts as soon as algorithms detected issues.[3]

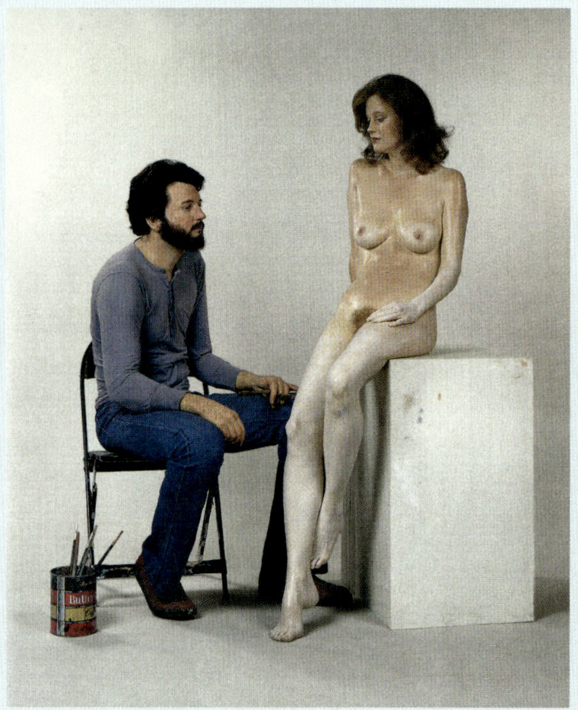

selbstständig Inhalte" und Accounts der User löschen, sobald die Rasterfahndung der Algorithmen greife.[3]

Die durch aktuelle Pandemiebedingungen legitimierte Umstellung auf ein primär KI-gestütztes Löschen anstößiger Inhalte spitzt Effekte einer allgemeinen technologischen Transformation der Öffentlichkeit zu, für die sich in technologischer, juridischer und bildhistorischer Perspektive noch keine klaren Begriffe etabliert haben.[4]

Sind aktuell die globalen Akteure zur Bereitstellung der technischen Infrastrukturen des Bilder- und Nachrichtenteilens verstärkt damit beschäftigt, Fake News zum Coronavirus einzudämmen und auf die offiziellen Seiten der WHO zu verlinken, damit sich Falschinformationen nicht in gefährdende Handlungsweisen übersetzen, waren es zuvor vor allem drei Themenfelder im Internet, die einer Regulierung, Zensur und Moderation bedurften: Darstellungen von Sexualität und Gewalt sowie das Feld der Meinungs- und Kunstfreiheit.

Im Folgenden werde ich zu zeigen versuchen, wie sich im spezifischen Zusammenschluss von Kunst und Nacktheit und deren Mobilisierung durch Bilder in sozialen Netzwerken die Frage nach den Utopien und Grenzen zirkulierender Bilder in der „Digitalmoderne"[5] neu stellt.

TECHNISCHE IDENTIFIZIERUNG

Im November 2018 meldete Hyperallergic, dass der Facebook-Account des an der University of Texas lehrenden Kurators Ruben Cordova gelöscht wurde, welchen er über neun Jahre als fotografisches Archiv genutzt hatte, um seine Bilder mit Annotationen und online-verlinkten Vergleichsbeispielen in seiner vernetzten Community zu teilen und als Ressource für Vorträge an Universitäten

The switch to a primarily AI-guided screening of offensive content, legitimatized by the pandemic, exacerbates the effects of a broader technological transformation of the public domain for which no clear terms have been established, whether from a technological, legal, or art historical point of view.[4] **At the moment, the global players responsible for supplying the technical infrastructure of shared images and news are busy blocking fake news about the coronavirus and substituting links to the official WHO website so that inaccurate information does not lead to dangerous situations. But prior to that, there were three chief topics that required regulation, censorship, and moderation: depictions of sexuality, violence, and the realm of freedom of thought and artistic expression.**

In the following essay, I will attempt to show how the specific intersection of art and nudity as well as the mobilization of the two in images on social media reframe the question of utopias and borders with regard to circulating images in this age of digital modernity.[5]

IDENTIFICATION USING TECHNOLOGY

In November 2018, Hyperallergic reported that Facebook had deleted the account of curator and University of Texas lecturer Ruben Cordova. For the past nine years, he had used his account to archive photographic materials, share his images, link to comparative examples online with his community network, and to draw on as a resource for talks at universities and museums (fig. 1).[6] Facebook's algorithms flagged a photographic reproduction of John de Andrea's 1980 *Self-Portrait with Sculpture* as offensive content and deleted Cordova's account due to an additional number of similar images. This specific work by de Andrea poses a unique challenge for automatic recognition software: with his surface treatment of the statue made from polyvinyl and painted with oils, the artist achieved such a hyperrealistic depiction of a nude female body that the algorithm was unable to distinguish between an artificially created artifact and the human figure. Art historians instantly recognize the grouping of two individuals and painting implements as belonging to the "painter and model" tradition, yet the image slid into the realm of the obscene thanks to the decontextualization of automatized scanning.[7] De Andrea's model so convincingly captures the effect of a naked body—down to the shimmer of the figure's oily skin—that the human eye is bewildered, and an automatic moderator implodes the difference between art work and actual body. The broad spectrum of meaning, the semantic confusion, and the ambiguity of the almost-real were elided to a simple presumption of "naked" thanks to an algorithm-driven identification. "The internal tension in images between the depicted and the depiction that spurn an identifiable accessing of a self-contained object points to the logic of images precisely as not logically connoted, unambiguous attributions but … as a composition of semantically ranging signs."[8] Accordingly, the increased use of AI-guided scanning announced and justified by global social media platforms as a result of coronavirus not only remove questionable

und Museen zu nutzen.[6] Der Facebook-Algorithmus hatte die dort zu findende fotografische Reproduktion von John de Andreas *Self-Portrait with Sculpture* aus dem Jahr 1980 (Abb. 1) als unangemessenen Inhalt erfasst und aufgrund der Vielzahl ähnlicher Beispiele seinen Account gelöscht. Das spezifische Werk Andreas stellte die automatische Erkennung vor eine besondere Aufgabe: Durch die Oberflächenbehandlung der mit dem Material Polyvinyl und in Öl polychromierten Statuen hatte John de Andrea eine solch hyperrealistische Darstellung eines nackten weiblichen Körpers geschaffen, dass der Algorithmus nicht zwischen künstlich hergestelltem Artefakt und menschlichem Körper unterscheiden konnte. Die zweifigurige Gruppe mit Malutensilien, für Kunsthistoriker*innen klar dem traditionsreichen Sujet „Maler und Modell" zugehörig, war in der automatischen Identifizierung und damit De-Kontextualisierung in das Feld des Obszönen abgerutscht.[7] De Andrea hatte den Realitätseffekt des modellierten, nackten Körpers – bis in den Schimmer der öligen Hautoberfläche hinein – so überzeugend gestaltet, dass der menschliche Augensinn irritiert, in der automatischen Erfassung die Unterscheidung zwischen Kunstwerk und realem Körper implodierte. Das semantische Flirren, die Ambiguität des Nahezu-Echten, wurde von der Vielfältigkeit des Bedeutungsspektrums unter der Prämisse ‚nackt' in die Eindeutigkeit einer algorithmischen Identifizierung überführt. „Die innere Spannung von Bildern zwischen Dargestelltem und Darstellung, die einen identifizierenden Zugriff auf ein in sich abgeschlossenes Objekt verwehrt, verweist auf die Logik von Bildern als gerade nicht logisch konnotierte, eindeutige Zuweisungen, sondern [...] semantisch ausgreifende Zeichenkompositionen."[8] Die von den globalen Akteuren der sozialen Plattformen angekündigte Verstärkung der KI-gestützten Abtastung unter Coronabedingungen löschen demnach nicht einfach nur zweifelhafte Bilder aus Newsfeeds. Sie kündigen ein neues Identifizierungsparadigma an, durch das KI-Technologie, Bildzirkulation und Öffentlichkeit in ein neues Verhältnis gebracht werden. Zu diesem müssen sich die klassischen Institutionen der Museen und Bildarchive und ihre Akteur*innen – von Kurator*innen über Kunsthistoriker*innen bis zu Medienhistoriker*innen – verhalten. Dass sich eine Verschiebung von klassischen Institutionen und sozialen Netzwerken als ein Ineinandergreifen von lokalen und netzbasierten Communities in einer neuen Form von Öffentlichkeit herstellt, sei anhand eines weiteren Beispiels dargestellt (Abb. 2). Das Nationalmuseum in Warschau hatte im April 2019 die Arbeit *Consumer Art* der polnischen Künstlerin Natalia LL (Lach-Lachowicz), entstanden in den Jahren 1972 bis 1975, aus den Ausstellungsräumen entfernen lassen. Der damalige Direktor des Museums, Jerzy Miziołek, begründete die Entscheidung mit einem Verweis auf vermeintlich jugendgefährdende Inhalte der Videos und Fotografien, die die Arbeit konstituieren: „he was opposed to showing works that could irritate sensitive young people."[9] Das mehrteilige Werk besteht aus seriellen Fotografien und filmischen Aufnahmen einer blonden Frau im zentral gesetzten Frontalporträt, die eine – mal geschälte, mal ungeschälte – Banane an den Mund heranführt, lustvoll abbeißt oder mit der Zungenspitze berührt. Der rasterartige Aufbau stellt die Wiederholung dieser feministisch zu lesenden Eat-Art in einzelnen, quadratisch gerahmten Fotografien aus, die bis dahin im Kontext einer Kritik an der Pornografisierung des weiblichen Körpers in der Populärkultur der 1970er-Jahre verortet worden war.[10]

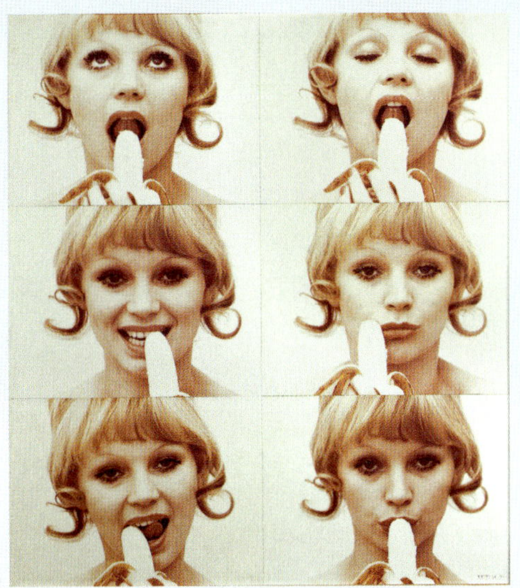

Abb. / **Fig. 2**
Natalia LL
Consumer Art, 1974, Fotografie / **photographs**

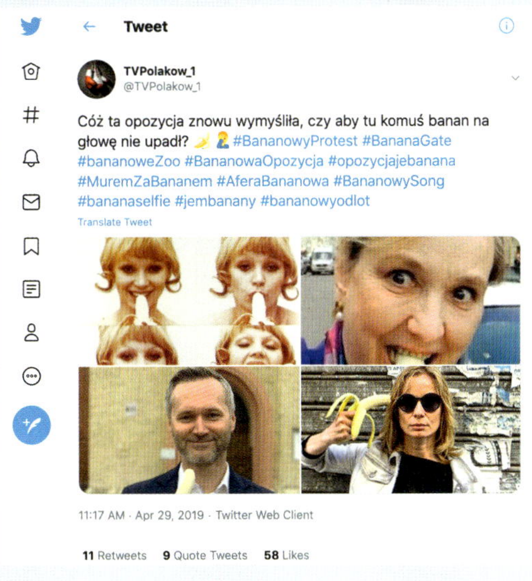

Abb. / **Fig. 3**
TVPolakow_1
Proteste nach der Abhängung von /
Protests following the removal of Natalia LL,
Consumer Art, 1975, 29. April 2019 / **April 29, 2019,**
Twitter Post

images from newsfeeds, it also marks a new paradigm of identification that brings together AI technology, circulating images, and the public in a new way. This is what classical institutions of museums and image archives and those individuals active in them, such as curators, art historians, and media historians, must react to. A further example shows the shift of classical institutions and social media toward an intertwining of local and online communities that form a new type of public (fig. 2). In April 2019, the National Museum in Warsaw removed *Consumer Art*, made between 1972 and 1975 by Polish artist Natalia LL (Lach-Lachowicz), from its galleries. The director at the time, Jerzy Miziołek, justified the decision by suggesting that the contents of the videos and photographs that comprise the work are harmful to juveniles, declaring in a statement that he was "opposed to showing works that could irritate sensitive young people."[9] The multipart work consists of a series of photographs and video footage of a blonde woman front and center with a banana—sometimes peeled, sometimes unpeeled—that she puts to her mouth, lustily bites off, and touches with the tip of her tongue. The individually framed square photographs of this feminist piece of Eat Art are arranged in a gridlike formation, reflecting the repetition in the piece, which had been regarded until that point as a criticism of the pornographization of the female body in 1970s popular culture.[10]

On April 29, 2019, numerous participants gathered at the National Museum in Warsaw for an eat-in to protest the removal of the work from the museum. Alone and in groups, they ate countless bananas and posed for Instagram posts (fig. 3).[11] Within a few hours, the banana-in was being shared across social media with the hashtag #BananaGate and covered by CNN and the *Guardian,* which commented on the banana as a sexualized and subversive icon in critical movements of art history from Warhol to the Guerrilla Girls activists.[12]

Als Protest gegen die Entfernung der Arbeit aus den Museumsräumen kamen am 29. April 2019 vor dem Nationalmuseum in Warschau zahlreiche Teilnehmer*innen zu einem Eat-in zusammen, aßen – allein oder in Gruppen – unzählige Bananen und posierten für den Instagram-Auftritt (Abb. 3).[11] Innerhalb weniger Stunden wurde die Bananenschlacht unter dem Hashtag #BananaGate über die sozialen Netzwerke geteilt und von CNN und dem *Guardian,* der die Banane als sexualisierte Subversionsikonografie in die Kritikbewegungen der Kunstgeschichte von Warhol bis zu den Guerilla-Girls-Aktivistinnen einordnete, kommentiert.[12]

Warum wird *Consumer Art* von Natalia LL gerade jetzt auffällig, während das Werk anscheinend über die Jahrzehnte, in denen es ungestört an der Wand des Nationalmuseums hing, keinen Anstoß erregt hatte? Auf einmal scheinen nicht mehr nur die Jugend, sondern alle Betrachter*innen schutzbedürftig angesichts eines solch wirkmächtigen künstlerischen Motivs wie den lasziv bananenessenden Frauen. Der Akt der Selbstzensur des Museums, vollzogen durch den Direktor des Hauses, kann nicht allein durch die nationalkonservative Regierungspolitik Polens begründet werden, die eine Einhegung der progressiven kulturpolitischen Kräfte vorantreibt, wie es Jonathan Jones im *Guardian* eingeordnet hat.[13] Denn auch in anderen politischen Lagern sind klassische Werke der Kunstgeschichte durch die neuen Netzregulierungen, die von den Plattformbetreibern unter dem Begriff der ‚Netzneutralität' vermarktet werden, einer Neubewertung unterworfen. Nicht das Werk *Consumer Art* hat sich verändert, sondern seine sozio-technische Umgebung.

Entscheidend ist nicht, dass „in den per *cloud computing* vernetzten Speicherinfrastrukturen", in denen schätzungsweise „bis 2022 insgesamt 93 Billionen Digitalbilder liegen"[14], auch Fehlzuschreibungen passieren können.

> Die Virulenz der Umwertung künstlerischer Produktion spitzt sich in der Frage zu, wie und von wem Unterscheidungen getroffen werden – zwischen künstlerischem Artefakt und lebendigem Körper, zwischen Aktbild, Satire oder Pornografie – und wie diese Unterscheidungen über sozio-technische Skripte automatisch und global in das Feld unserer Sichtbarkeit gelangen. Es sind neue Regeln der Opazität, die Entscheidungen über das Zeigen oder Nicht-Zeigen von einer öffentlichen Debatte, wie sie vor Gericht oder in der Presse geführt wird, hin zu privatwirtschaftlich organisierten und nicht mehr staatlich erfassten „Zensurinfrastrukturen"[15] verschieben.

Zieht man ins Kalkül, dass heutige algorithmische Environments Abläufe unterhalb der menschlichen Wahrnehmungsschwelle etablieren, im Blackboxing dazu tendieren, unsichtbar zu wirken und gleichzeitig omnipräsent zu sein[16], sortieren sich die Logiken der Repräsentation von Gemeinschaften (kollektiver Mythen, ikonischer Symbole, gesellschaftlicher Institutionen und ihrer Grenzen) neu. Virulenz erlangt diese Situation insbesondere angesichts einer allumfassenden Sichtbarkeitsmaschine des Internets, in der auf allen Kanälen gesendet zu werden scheint.

PATTERN DISCRIMINATION

Nun könnte man einwenden, dass jedem freigestellt sei, soziale Netzwerke zum Versenden von Bildern nicht zu nutzen oder den Brockhaus und nicht die Such-

What suddenly made *Consumer Art* by Natalia LL so conspicuous when the work had already hung undisturbed for decades on the wall of the National Museum and had raised no objections? All of a sudden, it seems that it is no longer just young people who require protection from such a powerful artistic subject as these lascivious, banana-eating women. The museum's act of self-censorship as performed by the institution's director cannot be solely attributed to Poland's nationalist and conservative government policies and their tendency to contain progressive cultural and political forces, as Jonathan Jones posited in the *Guardian*.[13] New internet regulations sold as instances of "net neutrality" by their enforcers reinterpret classical works of art history regardless of prevalent politics. *Consumer Art* did not change, but rather its socio-technological surroundings.

What was decisive was not the fact that incorrect classifications could be made in the "cloud storage infrastructures," in which estimates suggest "ninety-three billion digital images will be stored by 2022."[14] **The fact that artistic works are being subjected to reevaluation makes the question of how these decisions are made and who makes them all the more urgent—deciding between artistic artifact and living body, between nude depiction, satire, or pornography—and how these distinctions land automatically and globally in our field of vision thanks to socio-technical scripts. There are new rules of opacity, new decisions about whether a public debate will be conducted or not, and if so, whether before a court or in the press, stemming from the "infrastructures of censorship"[15] organized by private companies and not the state.**

If one considers the fact that algorithm-led processes undetectable by humans and operating in black-box environments are now beginning to function in an invisible yet omnipresent way,[16] it is clear that the logics of representing communities (collective myths, iconic symbols, societal institutions and their boundaries) are being reconfigured. This situation becomes especially important when one considers how comprehensively the internet determines what is made visible across the channels through which it disseminates information.

PATTERN DISCRIMINATION

Here, one could counter that everyone can choose not to use social networks to send images and to consult an encyclopedia rather than Google to find information. The decision to give over one's entire art-historical image archive to the economically led guidelines of a US corporation, Facebook Inc., is naive at best given the fact that, since 2012, there has been evidence that images and other content are moderated.[17] The disabling of Ruben Cordova's account has no legal grounds for appeal since a private corporation is at liberty to define its own guidelines. Moreover, strictly speaking, this is not a case of censorship as practiced by such states as China, which removes undesirable political content from its social media site (Weibo). In the case of Facebook, the practice of screening content known as moderation is guided by Facebook's

maschine Google zur Informationsbeschaffung zu konsultieren. Auch erscheint das Vorhaben, sein gesamtes kunsthistorisches Bildarchiv dem unter ökonomischen Richtlinien aktiven US-Großkonzern Facebook Inc. zu überlassen im besten Falle naiv, war ja schon spätestens seit 2012 klar, dass dessen Inhalte und Bilder einer Content-Moderation unterliegen.[17] So stellt die Löschung des Accounts von Ruben Cordova rechtlich erst einmal keinen Fall dar, da ein privatwirtschaftlicher Konzern seine Richtlinien selbst bestimmen kann. Auch handelt es sich, strenggenommen, nicht um einen Akt der Zensur, wie er von Staaten wie dem chinesischen aktuell ausgeübt wird, der unerwünschte politische Inhalte aus seinem Internet (Weibo) entfernt. Die begrifflich als „Moderation" geführte Inhaltsregulierung richtet sich im Fall von Facebook nach dem *Facebook's Operation Manual for Content Moderators*, welches die Bilderströme nach den als problematisch eingestuften Kategorien „Sex and Nudity", „Illegal Drug Use", „Theft Vandalism and Fraud", „Bullying and Harassment", „Hate Content", „Graphic Content", „Self-harm", „Credible Threats" filtert. Dass im Fall der Nudity-Bestimmungen auch Darstellungen von „Mothers breastfeeding without clothes" unterbunden werden, zeigt jedoch, dass hier kein juridisches Problem vorliegt. In die Bestimmungen, die das Regime der Sichtbarkeit im Netz regeln, sind soziale Bewertungen und US-amerikanische Moralvorstellungen implementiert, die durch die Filtersysteme hindurch wirksam werden und querstehen zu sonstigen Kategorisierungen, wie eben in der Unterscheidung von Aktdarstellung und menschlichem Körper. So klingt im englischen Kompositum „pattern discrimination" (dt. Musterunterscheidung) die technische Erkennung bei gleichzeitiger Verkennung vieler sozialer Parameter an, da den scheinbar neutralen Protokollen soziale Voreinstellungen zu Geschlecht, Status, Alter etc. eingeschrieben sind.[18] Das Zeigen oder Verbergen von *Self-Portrait with Sculpture* (1980) hängt an neuen Strukturen der Transparenz und Opazität, die von einer „komplexen soziotechnischen Logistik"[19] abhängen und eine Pornografisierung jedweder Form öffentlicher Nacktheit vorantreiben.

In der algorithmischen Bilderkennung von CVPF-Verfahren (computer vision-based pornography filtering) sind Annahmen über Pornografie, Sexualität und den Körper eingeschrieben, die das Feld von Content-Moderatoren vorstrukturieren:

„[...] that pornographic bodies comport to specific, predictable shapes, textures and sizes."[20] Der „moderation apparatus", wie ihn Tarleton Gillespie nennt, besteht hier aus einer Art technischer Vorzensur, die durch das Verfahren des Hashing operationalisiert wird, und den Abgleich von Bildern mit Hashdatenbanken gewährleistet, die noch vor der moderierenden Nachzensur bzw. Regulierung greifen.[21] Dies kann natürlich auch gute Gründe haben: Kinderpornografie, Copyrightverletzungen oder Jugendschutz, für die es unbedingt juristische Löschungsregelungen geben muss, werden algorithmisch unterbunden. Gleichzeitig können computergestützte Bilderkennungsverfahren nicht zwischen pornografischen Nacktbildern, künstlerischem Akt oder Nacktsatire unterscheiden.

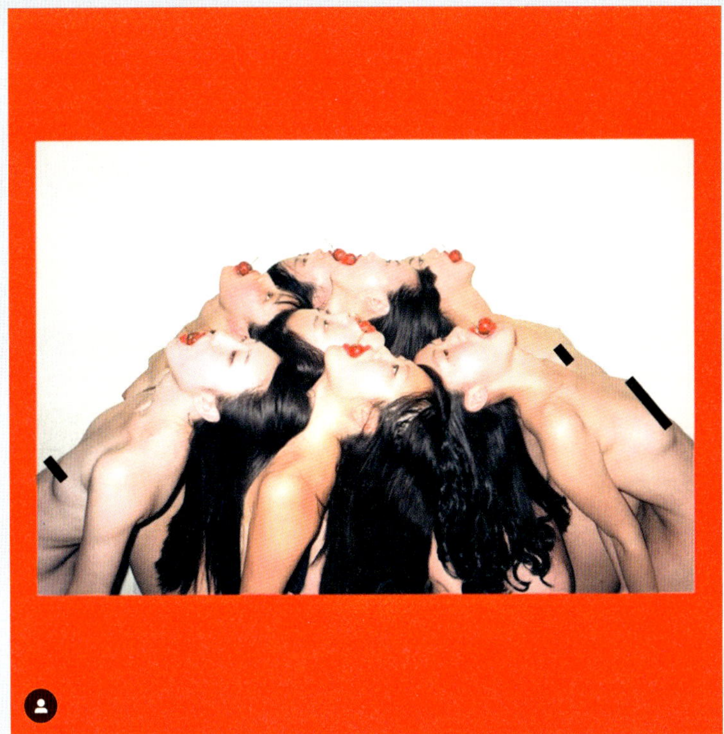

operation manual for content moderators, who filter the flood of images categorized as problematic content, including sex and nudity; illegal drug use; theft, vandalism, and fraud; bullying and harassment; hate content; graphic content; self-harm; and credible threats. The fact that nudity guidelines also prohibit the depiction of "mothers breastfeeding without clothes" shows this is not a juridical problem. The guidelines the company uses to govern online visibility are shaped by societal mores and US attitudes toward morality, imposed by filters, and they clash with other categorizations such as the distinction between artworks depicting nudes and human bodies. The term "pattern discrimination" suggests a technical detection that wrongly gauges numerous social parameters, because social attitudes to sex, status, age, etc. are inscribed in purportedly neutral protocols.[18] Whether *Self-Portrait with Sculpture* (1980) is shown or hidden rests on new structures of transparency and opacity, which in turn are based on "complex socio-technical logistics"[19] that promulgate a pornographization of any form of nudity in public.

Assumptions about pornography, sexuality, and the body are embedded in the algorithmic image recognition processes used in computer vision-based pornography filtering which pre-structure the field of content moderation:

". . . that pornographic bodies comport to specific, predictable shapes, textures and sizes."[20] Here this consists of a type of technical precensorship operationalized through hashing that compares images with hash databases before moderation is exercised as ex post facto censorship or regulation.[21]

TECHNISCHE BILDZENSUR / **TECHNICAL PICTURE CENSORS**

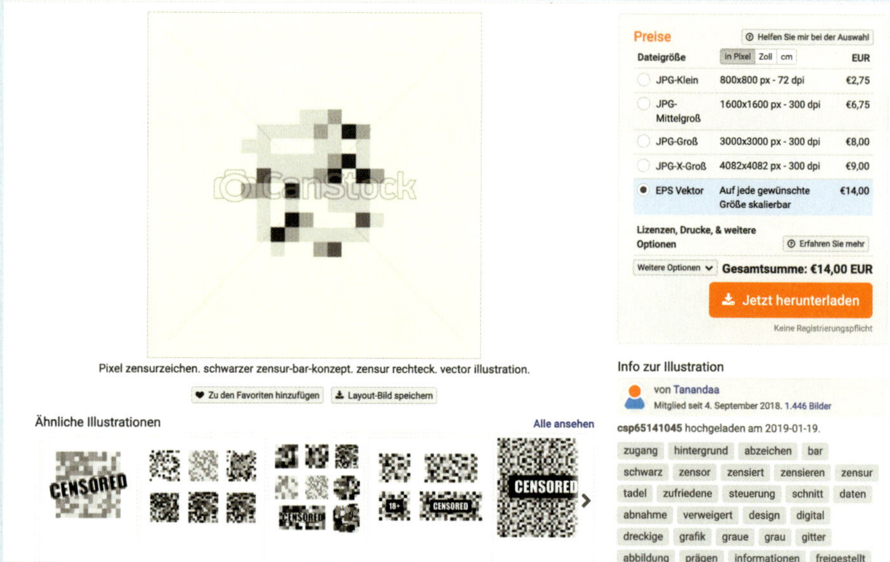

Abb. / **Fig. 5**
canstockphoto.de
Pixel-Zensurzeichen / **Pixel censor sign,**
n.d., Screenshot

Ein Beispiel aus der Ren-Hang-Ausstellung bei C/O Berlin 2019 zeigt, dass nur mit Zensurbalken die „Nipple Policy" der sozialen Netzwerke passiert werden konnte (Abb. 4, 5).

‚FREIE BILDZIRKULATION'

> Die Dominanz der Metapher der Bilderflut, die Beschreibung der Vervielfältigung der Bilder seit dem Aufkommen technischer Reproduktionsmedien und die Vorstellung einer ubiquitär wirksamen Bilderwelt in einem Universum der Bilder des Internets verdecken die opak etablierten Mechanismen technischer Bildzensur bzw. -regulierung.

Dies liegt nicht zuletzt daran, dass das Versenden technischer Bilder seit ihrem Aufkommen Mitte des 19. Jahrhunderts mit wirksamen Utopien einer Senderlogik und einer allumfassenden Konnektivität verbunden wurde, welche sich heute mit der Vorstellung eines demokratischen, freien Netzes amalgamiert. So sprach schon 1873 der Astronom, Spiritist und spätere Science-Fiction-Autor Camille Flammarion in seinem Werk *Lumen* (lat. Licht) angesichts der ersten fotografischen Daguerreotypien, die er in die Hände bekam, von der Lichtgeschwindigkeit der Bildsendung. Der Lichtstrahl sei wie ein Bote, „der uns nicht etwa geschriebene Nachrichten bringt, sondern […] das Bild des Landes, von dem er kommt."[22] Noch Friedrich Kittler beschrieb in *Optische Medien* die Fotografie als Medium der reibungslosen Sendung, indem er ihre Speicherfähigkeit als Überwindungsmaschine von raum-zeitlichen Restriktionen feierte. Die Speicherfähigkeit fotografischer Bilder sei in Differenz zu allen vorhergehenden Medien ein Potential, „um empfangene Bilder über Raum und Zeit hinweg zu übertragen und an einem anderen Punkt in Raum und Zeit wieder senden zu können"[23]. Es kommt jedoch Vilém Flussers „Fotouniversum"[24] zu, die technischen Bilder im

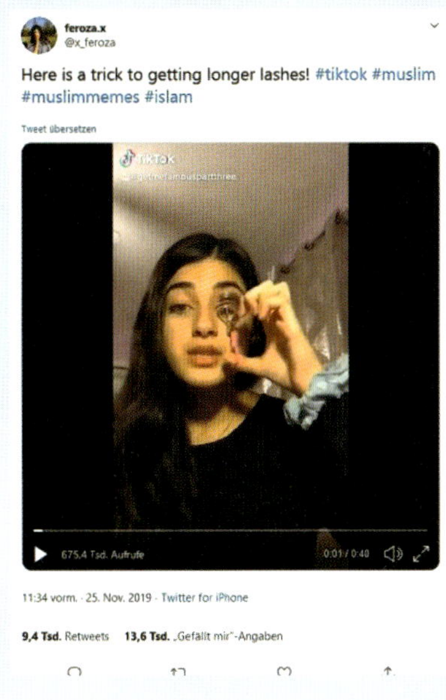

Abb. / **Fig. 6**
Feroza Aziz
Here is a trick to getting longer lashes!
25. November 2019 / **November 25, 2019,**
Twitter Post

Naturally, this can be for good reasons: algorithms are used to suppress child pornography, copyright violations, and for child protection purposes, and legal guidelines necessarily exist for removal of such material. At the same time, computer-aided image recognition cannot distinguish between pornographic nude pictures and nude satire (figs. 4, 5). An example from C/O Berlin's Ren Hang exhibition shows that a censor bar was necessary to avoid being censored by social media's "nipple policy."

"FREE IMAGE CIRCULATION"

The prevalence of the metaphor of a flood of images, which has been used to describe the reproduction of images since the advent of technological reproduction media, and the idea of a ubiquitously effective world of images in the universe of online pictures occlude the opaque established mechanisms of technical image censorship and moderation.

This is due not least to the fact that sending technical images depends on effective utopias of a logic of transmission and all-encompassing connectivity that have become amalgamated with ideas of a democratic and free internet. In 1873, astronomer, spiritualist, and later science-fiction author Camille Flammarion responded to the first photographic daguerreotypes he had held by writing of sending images operating at the speed of light in his book *Lumen* (Latin for "light"). A light beam is a messenger "who brings, not written news, but . . . *the real aspect* of the country from whence he came."[22] As recently as in *Optical Media*, Friedrich Kittler described photography as the frictionless medium of transmission, hailing its ability to preserve as a mechanism for transcending restrictions of space and time. The storage potential of photographic images is different from all preceding media due to its ability

TECHNISCHE BILDZENSUR / **TECHNICAL PICTURE CENSORS**

Kosmos eines nachindustriellen Zeitalters zu verorten, „als einen in sich kreisenden Strudel, in den alle verfügbaren Informationen einfließen, um dort endlos zu zirkulieren."[25]

Diese Mediengeschichte der Bildsendung hat jedoch eine Kehrseite eingeschrieben, welche die Ebene der medientechnischen Ermöglichung, fotografische Bilder in die Distributionswege der Post einzuschleusen, bildtelegrafisch zu nutzen oder in heutigen Netzwerken zirkulieren zu lassen, auf die politische, ethische, juridische (und nicht allein technikhistorische) Frage zuspitzt, welche Informationen überhaupt zirkulieren sollen oder dürfen.

Das Verhältnis von Zirkulation und Regulierung ist aktuell nicht statisch, sondern wird in Formen der Aneignung, in der Meme-Kultur oder mit listigen Tricks immer wieder in Bewegung gebracht.

So überwachen autoritäre Regime wie das chinesische zwar ihr gesamtes Internet, User nutzen jedoch Programme wie TikTok zum Widerstand, indem sie etwa Schmink-Tutorials erstellen, die als Beauty-Video identifiziert werden, um über Unterdrückung und Missstände zu sprechen (Abb. 6). 2019 war der TikTok-Account der damals 17-jährigen Feroza Aziz vorübergehend gelöscht worden, weil sie Chinas Umgang mit muslimischen Uiguren anprangerte, während sie sich die Wimpern richtete.[26] Dass Aziz die Bild- und Tonspur asynchron nutzen muss, um politische Inhalte versteckt zu übermitteln, verstärkt jedoch den Verweis auf die mangelnde Rede- und Kunstfreiheit.

Kurz vor der Jahrtausendwende, im Jahr 1998, hatte Horst Bredekamp in einer Empfehlung an den Deutschen Bundestag auf die Frage hin, wie der neuen Technologie des Internets zu begegnen sei, geantwortet: „Erst wenn sich die Diskussion davon löst, im Internet allein eine globale Befreiung zu sehen, kann sie sich an seinem Beispiel der Frage zuwenden, ob Demokratie im Weltmaßstab ohne globale Kontrollmittel vorstellbar sein kann."[27] Historisch gesehen treten seit dem Buchdruck mit beweglichen Lettern Mechanismen der Zensur und Inhaltsregulierung überall dort auf, wo scheinbar gefährliches Wissen verbreitet wird. Was sich jedoch heute durch automatische Bildlöschungen in ökonomischen Infrastrukturen im Verborgenen vollzieht, sollte wieder einer öffentlichen Debatte zugeführt werden – unter neuen, technologisch geprägten Bedingungen.

1   Youtube-Blog, *Protecting our extended workforce and the community,* 16. März 2020, https://blog.youtube/news-and-events/protecting-our-extended-workforce-and [Zugriff am 5. September 2020]

2   Ebd.

3   Content-Moderation, Die Arbeit lässt sich nicht einfach ins Homeoffice verlagern, in: *Süddeutsche Zeitung,* 27. März 2020, https://www.sueddeutsche.de/digital/coronavirus-facebook-google-content-moderation-1.4859147-2 [Zugriff am 8. August 2020]

4   Zur digitalen Transformation der Öffentlichkeit aus juridischer Perspektive vgl. Jan-Philipp Kruse und Sabine Müller-Mall (Hg.), *Digitale Transformation der Öffentlichkeit,* Weilerswist 2020

5   Zum Begriff der Digitalmoderne und ihrer Regulierungspraktiken im Feld der Kunst siehe Hanno Rauterberg, *Wie frei ist die Kunst? Der neue Kulturkampf und die Krise des Liberalismus,* Berlin 2018, S. 7–48, hier insbes. S. 13–17

"to allow images to be transmitted across space and time and then sent again to another point in space and time."[23] Yet in Vilém Flusser's "photographic universe,"[24] the task is to locate technical images in the cosmos of a post-industrial era, "as a gyrating vortex into which all available information flows and endlessly circulates."[25]

Yet this medial history of image transmission has a flipside due to the way photographic images can be distributed using different media and technologies including the distribution routes of the post, visual telegraphs, and circulation using modern networks, one that raises the political, ethical, juridical (and not only the technical and historical) question of which information should or may be circulated at all.

At the moment, the relationship between circulation and regulation is not static, but rather in constant flux thanks to forms of appropriation, meme culture, and sly tricks.

Authoritarian regimes such as the Chinese government may monitor the entire internet but users can create content for sites such as TikTok as a means of protest, for instance by posting make-up tutorials classified as beauty videos in which they speak about repression and abuse (fig. 6). In 2019, the TikTok account of seventeen-year-old Feroza Aziz was temporarily deleted because she spoke critically about China's treatment of Muslim Uighur population while doing her eyelashes.[26] Yet the fact that Aziz used image and sound asynchronously in order to conceal the political content of her post bolsters the apparent lack of freedom of speech and artistic expression.

Shortly before the new millennium, in 1998, Horst Bredekamp was asked how to deal with new internet technologies. He responded by recommending: "Only when the internet is no longer discussed as a global liberator can we begin considering the question of whether democracy on a global scale is conceivable without a global means of control."[27] From a historical perspective, since the printing press with movable type was invented, mechanisms of censorship and content moderation have emerged whenever the risk of spreading purportedly dangerous information has appeared. Yet what is currently happening covertly within corporate infrastructures should once again be the subject of public debate—under new, technologically defined conditions.

1 "Protecting Our Extended Workforce and the Community," YouTube, last modified March 16, 2020, accessed September 5, 2020, https://blog.youtube/news-and-events /protecting-our-extended-workforce-and.

2 "Protecting Our Extended Workforce and the Community."

3 "Content-Moderation: Die Arbeit lässt sich nicht einfach ins Homeoffice verlagern," *Süddeutsche Zeitung*, March 27, 2020, accessed August 8, 2020, https://www.sueddeutsche.de /digital/coronavirus-facebook-google-content-moderation-1.4859147-2.

4 On the digital transformation of the public sphere from a juridical perspective, see Jan-Philipp Kruse and Sabine Müller-Mall, eds., *Digitale Transformation der Öffentlichkeit* (Weilerswist: Velbrueck Wissenschaft, 2020).

5 On the concept of digital modernity and its regulatory functions in the field of art, see Hanno Rauterberg, *Wie frei ist die Kunst? Der neue Kulturkampf und die Krise des Liberalismus* (Berlin: Suhrkamp Verlag, 2018), 7–48, here especially 13–17.

6   Zachary Small, "Facebook Censors Art Historian for Posting Nude Art, Then Boots Him from Platform", unter: *Hyperallergic,* 27. November 2018, https://hyperallergic.com/472706/facebook-censors-art-historian-for-posting-nude-art-then-boots-him-from-platform/ [Zugriff am 10. August 2020]

7   Vgl. hierzu Katja Müller-Helle, "Noise Bodies. Bildzensur 1967/heute", in: *nach dem film,* Themenschwerpunkt Feminismus und Film, 17, Frühjahr 2019, https://www.nachdemfilm.de/issues/text/noise-bodies-bildzensur-1967heute [Zugriff am 6. September 2020]

8   Gertrud Koch, "Nicht löschbare Bilder", in: *Bildwelten des Wissens. Jahrbuch für Bildkritik*, 16, 2020, im Erscheinen

9   Matthew Robinson, "Protesters stage 'eat-in' as Polish gallery plans to ditch video installation of woman eating banana", *CNN,* 30. April 2019, https://edition.cnn.com/style/article/poland-banana-protest-warsaw-natalia-ll-intl-scli/index.html [Zugriff am 15. August 2020]

10 Vgl. *Consumer Art and Beyond*, Ausst.-Kat. CSW Zamek Ujazdowski, Warschau, 2016; Agnieszka Rayzacher u.a. (Hg.), *Natalia LL Doing Gender*, Warschau 2013; Carmen Lode, *Natalia LL*, Berlin 1991

11 Zur Praxis des Selfie-Protests siehe Kerstin Schankweiler, "Selfie-Proteste. Affektzeugenschaften und Bildökonomien in den Social Media", in: *Working Paper SFB 1171 Affective Societies* 5, 2016, und Wolfgang Ullrich, *Selfies*, Berlin 2019

12 Jonathan Jones, "Bananas in art: a short history of the salacious, disturbing and censored fruit", in: *The Guardian*, 30. April 2019, https://www.theguardian.com/artanddesign/shortcuts/2019/apr/30/bananas-most-political-fruit-history-art-natalia-ll-censored [Zugriff am 6. Mai 2020]

13 Ebd.

14 Simon Rothöler, "Blockieren, Moderieren, Projizieren. Anmerkungen zur technischen Kontrolle digitaler Bildinformation", in: *Bildwelten des Wissens. Jahrbuch für Bildkritik*, 16, 2020, im Erscheinen

15 Elisabeth Niekrenz, "Was sind Uploadfilter?", unter: *Digitale Gesellschaft,* 5. Mai 2020, https://digitalegesellschaft.de/wp-content/uploads/2020/07/DigitaleGesellschaft-Uploadfilter-Interaktiv-V04.pdf, S. 20 [Zugriff am 9. September 2020]

16 Um das Jahr 2000 gewann das Paradigma des Blackboxing an Bedeutung, welches die Relation von technischen Ensembles und menschlicher Wahrnehmung beschrieb. Nach Bruno Latour arbeiten erfolgreiche Technologien – parallel zu ihrem Funktionieren – an ihrer eigenen Unsichtbarkeit: "[Blackboxing is] the way scientific and technical work is made invisible by its own success. When a machine runs efficiently, when a matter of fact is settled, one need to focus only on its inputs and outputs and not on its internal complexity. Thus, paradoxically, the more science and technology succeed, the more opaque and obscure they become." Bruno Latour, *Pandora's Hope. Essays on the Reality of Science Studies,* Cambridge/MA 1999, S. 304

17 Vgl. Simon Rothöhler, "Informationen, die Bilder haben. Zur Moderierbarkeit von visuellem Content", in: *Zeitschrift für Medienwissenschaft*, 2, 2018, S. 85–94, hier S. 85

18 Vgl. Clemens Apprich, Wendy Hui Kyong Chun, Florian Cramer, Hito Steyerl, *Pattern Discrimination*, Lüneburg 2020

19 Rothöhler 2018 (wie Anm. 17), S. 87

20 Robert Gehl, Lucas Moyer-Homer und Sara K. Yeo, "Training Computers to See Internet Pornography: Gender and Sexual Discrimination in Computer Vision Science", in: *Television and New Media*, 6, 2017, S. 529–547, hier S. 530

21 Tarleton Gillespie, *Custodian of the Internet, Platforms, Content Moderation, and the Hidden Decisions that Shape Social Media*, New Haven 2018

22 Camille Flammarion, *Lumen*, Lüneburg 2007 [Erstausgabe 1873], S. 52

23 Friedrich Kittler, *Optische Medien*, Berlin 2002, S. 155

24 Vilém Flusser, *Ins Universum der technischen Bilder*, Göttingen 1990

25 Peter Geimer, *Theorien der Fotografie. Zur Einführung*, Hamburg 2010, S. 159

26 TikTok-Nutzerin prangert Chinas Umgang mit Muslimen an, in: *Frankfurter Allgemeine Zeitung*, 27. November 2019, https://www.faz.net/aktuell/gesellschaft/menschen/tiktok-nutzerin-prangert-chinas-umgang-mit-muslimen-an-16506274.html [Zugriff am 6. September 2020]

27 Horst Bredekamp, "Demokratie und Medien", in: *Bürger und Staat in der Informationsgesellschaft*, hrsg. vom Deutschen Bundestag, Bonn 1998, S. 188–194, hier S. 190

6   Zachary Small, "Facebook Censors Art Historian for Posting Nude Art, Then Boots Him from Platform," *Hyperallergic,* November 27, 2018, accessed August 10, 2020, https://hyperallergic.com/472706/facebook-censors-art-historian-for-posting-nude-art-then-boots-him-from-platform/.

7   On this, see Katja Müller-Helle, "Noise Bodies: Bildzensur 1967/heute, *nach dem film* 17 (Spring 2019), accessed September 6, 2020, https://www.nachdemfilm.de/issues/text/noise-bodies-bildzensur-1967heute.

8   Gertrud Koch, "Nicht löschbare Bilder," *Bildwelten des Wissens. Jahrbuch für Bildkritik* 16 (2020), forthcoming.

9   Matthew Robinson, "Protesters Stage 'Eat-In' as Polish Gallery Plans to Ditch Video Installation of Woman Eating Banana," *CNN,* April 30, 2019, accessed August 15, 2020, https://edition.cnn.com/style/article/poland-banana-protest-warsaw-natalia-ll-intl-scli/index.html.

10 See the exhibition catalog *Consumer Art and Beyond* (Warsaw: CSW Zamek Ujazdowski, 2016); Agnieszka Rayzacher et al., eds., *Natalia LL Doing Gender* (Warsaw: Fundacja Loka Sztuki, 2013); and Carmen Lode, *Natalia LL* (Berlin: ifa, 1991).

11 On the practice of selfie protests, see Kerstin Schankweiler, "Selfie-Proteste: Affektzeugenschaften und Bildökonomien in den Social Media," *Working Paper SFB 1171 Affective Societies* 5 (2016) and Wolfgang Ullrich, *Selfies* (Berlin: Verlag Klaus Wagenbach, 2019).

12 Jonathan Jones, "Bananas in Art: A Short History of the Salacious, Disturbing and Censored Fruit," *The Guardian,* April 30, 2019, accessed May 6, 2020, https://www.theguardian.com/artanddesign/shortcuts/2019/apr/30/bananas-most-political-fruit-history-art-natalia-ll-censored.

13 Jones, "Bananas in Art."

14 Simon Rothöler, "Blockieren, Moderieren, Projizieren: Anmerkungen zur technischen Kontrolle digitaler Bildinformation," *Bildwelten des Wissens: Jahrbuch für Bildkritik* 16 (2020), forthcoming.

15 Elisabeth Niekrenz, "Was sind Uploadfilter?," *Digitale Gesellschaft* 5 (May 2020): 20, accessed September 9, 2020, https://digitalegesellschaft.de/wp-content/uploads/2020/07/DigitaleGesellschaft-Uploadfilter-Interaktiv-V04.pdf.

16 Around 2000, the paradigm of blackboxing, which described the relationship between technical ensembles and human perception, started to gain in significance. According to Bruno Latour, successful technologies work—alongside their regular functioning—by way of their own invisibility: "[Blackboxing is] the way scientific and technical work is made invisible by its own success. When a machine runs efficiently, when a matter of fact is settled, one need to focus only on its inputs and outputs and not on its internal complexity. Thus, paradoxically, the more science and technology succeed, the more opaque and obscure they become." Bruno Latour, *Pandora's Hope: Essays on the Reality of Science Studies* (Cambridge, MA: Harvard University Press, 1999), 304.

17 See Simon Rothöler, "Informationen, die Bilder haben: Zur Moderierbarkeit von visuellem Content," *Zeitschrift für Medienwissenschaft* 2 (2018): 85–94, here 85.

18 See Clemens Apprich, Wendy Hui Kyong Chun, Florian Cramer, and Hito Steyerl, *Pattern Discrimination* (Lüneburg: meson press, 2020).

19 Rothöhler 2018 (see note 17), 87.

20 Robert Gehl, Lucas Moyer-Homer, and Sara K. Yeo, "Training Computers to See Internet Pornography: Gender and Sexual Discrimination in Computer Vision Science," *Television and New Media* 6 (2017): 529–47, here 530.

21 Tarleton Gillespie, *Custodian of the Internet, Platforms, Content Moderation, and the Hidden Decisions That Shape Social Media* (New Haven, CT: Yale University Press, 2018).

22 Camille Flammarion, *Lumen,* trans. AAM and RM (New York: Dodd, Mead, and Company, 1897), quoted in the Project Gutenberg e-book, accessed October 9, 2020, http://www.gutenberg.org/files/43835/43835-h/43835-h.htm, 38.

23 Friedrich Kittler, *Optical Media: Berlin Lectures 1999,* trans. Anthony Emms (Cambridge, UK: Polity, 2010), 118.

24 Vilém Flusser, *Into the Universe of Technical Images* (Minneapolis, MN: University of Minnesota Press, 2011).

25 Peter Geimer, *Theorien der Fotografie. Zur Einführung* (Hamburg: Junius Verlag, 2010), 159.

26 "TikTok-Nutzerin prangert Chinas Umgang mit Muslimen an," *Frankfurter Allgemeine Zeitung,* November 27, 2019, accessed September 6, 2020, https://www.faz.net/aktuell/gesellschaft/menschen/tiktok-nutzerin-prangert-chinas-umgang-mit-muslimen-an-16506274.html.

27 Horst Bredekamp, "Demokratie und Medien," in Deutscher Bundestag, ed., *Bürger und Staat in der Informationsgesellschaft* (Bonn: Deutscher Bundestag, 1998), 188–94, here 190.

Text: Estelle Blaschke

BILDER ORTEN, WELT ORDNEN
Geotagging und die Fotografie

Mitte der 1950er-Jahre wurde die Fotografie ins Weltall geschickt. Zum Zweck der großflächigen und systematischen Spionage einerseits und wissenschaftlichen Forschung andererseits starteten die USA und die Sowjetunion im Wettstreit jeweils eine Reihe von Satelliten-Programmen. Auf Seiten der Vereinigten Staaten sollten die Satelliten, entwickelt unter der Leitung der Abteilung Science & Technology der CIA und der U.S. Air Force, primär die visuelle Überwachung feindlicher Territorien im Kalten Krieg ausbauen und die technologische Dominanz des Landes unter Beweis stellen. Die *imaging systems* Corona und Samos, die unter unterschiedlichen Bezeichnungen und Ausrichtungen bis in die 1980er-Jahre operierten, erlebten, vor allem in den Anfangsjahren, zahlreiche Rückschläge. Diese übertrafen, so die Entwickler, die antizipierten Funktionsstörungen der komplexen physikalischen, chemischen und elektronischen Komponenten um ein Vielfaches: Satelliten stürzten ab, bevor sie den Orbit erreichten. Viele der visuellen Aufzeichnungen waren unscharf oder komplett unbrauchbar. So beschädigten elektrische Ladungen innerhalb der Kamera den fotografischen Film und produzierten „Bilder aus Versehen"[1] (Abb. 1). Manchmal gelangten die Aufnahmen gar nicht erst zur Erde, wenn die Kapsel verlorenging oder auf dem

LOCATING IMAGES, ORGANIZING THE WORLD
Geotagging and Photography

In the mid-1950s photography was sent into space. The United States and the Soviet Union were in competition, building a series of satellite programs for the purpose of large-scale and systematic espionage on the one hand and scientific research on the other. For the US, the satellites, developed under the direction of the CIA's Science & Technology directorate and the US Air Force, were used primarily to expand visual surveillance of enemy territories during the Cold War and to demonstrate the technological dominance of the country. The imaging systems Corona and Samos, which operated under different names and organizations until the 1980s, experienced numerous setbacks, especially in the early years. According to the developers, the malfunctions of the complex physical, chemical, and electronic components were greater than they had anticipated: satellites crashed before they reached orbit. Many of the visual recordings were blurry or completely unusable. Electric charges inside the camera damaged the photographic film and produced "inadvertent images" (fig. 1).[1] Sometimes the images never even made it back to Earth, with the capsule getting lost or bursting. On top

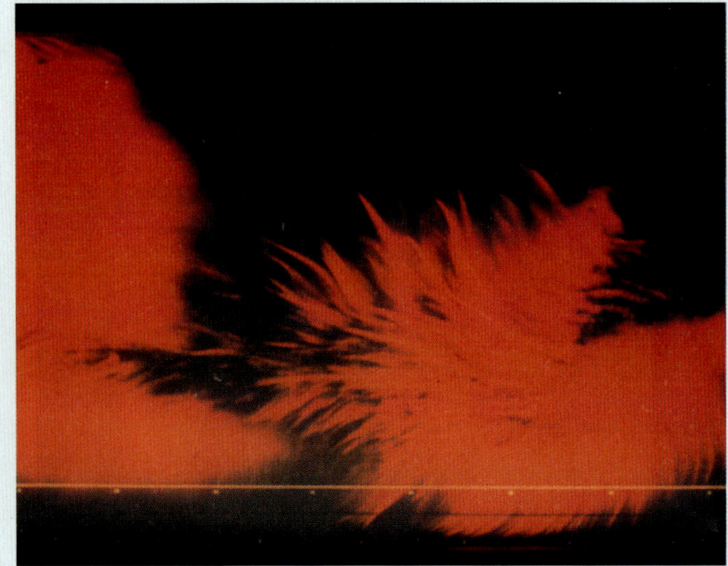

Weg zurück barst. Zudem produzierte das Programm exorbitante Kosten, die über einen längeren Zeitraum politisch nur schwer zu rechtfertigen waren. Doch wie so oft waren es die hoch subventionierten militärischen Anwendungsbereiche, die, im mühsamen trial-and-error-Prinzip, wichtige Entwicklungsschritte in der Technologiegeschichte des Mediums auslösten. Eine Reihe fotografischer Verfahren und Praktiken wurde hier erstmals auf ihre Funktionalität getestet. Eastman Kodak, die mit Lockheed und Columbia Broadcasting System (CBS) zusammenarbeiteten, experimentierten mit dem sogenannten „Bimat-Film", mit dessen Hilfe Bilder in „near real time" übermittelt wurden.[2] Die Fotos sollten, dem Polaroid-Verfahren gleichkommend, an Bord entwickelt werden, von einem hochauflösenden Scanner abgetastet und als elektronisches Signal an die Kontrollstellen zurückgesendet und ausgelesen werden.

Die elektronische, wenn auch noch nicht digitale Form des Bildes war zentral für die Prozessierung und Mobilität der Fotografien.[3]

Die Kameras wurden mit diversen Sensoren (für Temperatur, Licht, Druck etc.) ausgestattet, unter anderem um die Belichtungszeiten bei hoher Geschwindigkeit unmittelbar anzupassen. Es wurde mit Polyester als Alternative zum hochentwickelten Acetat-Film experimentiert, da dieser Bildträger unter den Extrembedingungen spröde wurde. Um einen Flug, ob via Satellit oder Aufklärungsflugzeug, so effizient wie möglich zu gestalten, wurden die Kapazitäten der Filmrollen auf Kilometerlänge ausgeweitet (Abb. 2). Auch kam es in den Kontrollstationen zu Neuerungen: Eastman Kodak testete die Mikrofilm-Suchmaschine Miracode für die Flugauswertung. Auf Mikrofilm reproduzierte Fotografien, Statistiken und Grafiken, also sehr unterschiedliche Bildtypen, wurden mittels der Maschine in Sekundenschnelle abgerufen und auf Großbildschirme

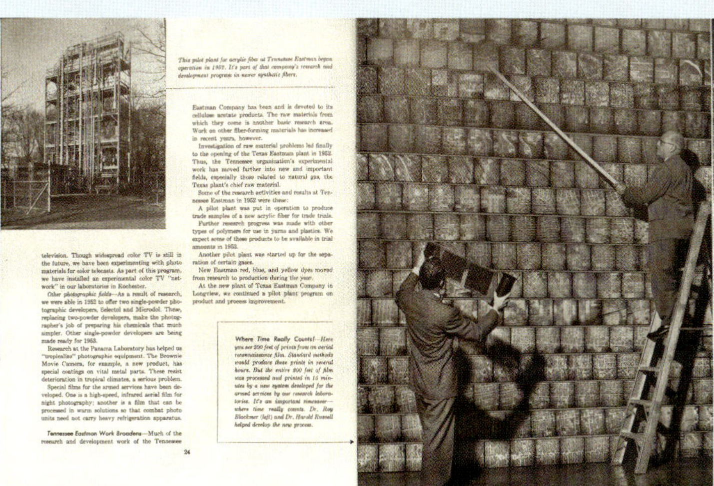

Abb. / **Fig. 2**
Anonym / **Anonymous** (Kodak)
Präsentation des großformatigen Rollfilms und 60-Meter-Prints für die militärische
Luftaufklärung / **Presentation of the large-format roll film and sixty-meter prints
for military air reconnaissance**, 1952, Magazinseite / **magazine spread**

of this, the extortionate costs of the program became difficult to justify po-
litically over a long period of time. But, as is so often the case, photography's
use in heavily subsidized military fields initiated important developmental
steps in the technological history of the medium, using a painstaking trial-
and-error principle. The functionality of a number of photographic processes and practices were tested in this context for the first time. Eastman
Kodak worked with Lockheed and Columbia Broadcasting System (CBS) to
experiment with BIMAT film, which enabled image transmission in "near real
time."[2] Similar to the Polaroid process, the photos were developed on board,
scanned with a high-resolution scanner, and sent back to the control stations to be read as electronic signals.

The electronic, although not yet digital, form of the image was central to the processing and mobility of the photographs.[3]

The cameras were equipped with various sensors (for temperature, light,
pressure, etc.), which, among other things, automatically adjusted exposure times at high velocity. Polyester was trialed as an alternative to the
highly refined acetate film image support, which became brittle under extreme conditions. In order to make a flight as efficient as possible, whether via satellite or reconnaissance aircraft, the capacity of the film reels was
extended to be kilometers long (fig. 2). There were also innovations in the
control stations: Eastman Kodak tested the microfilm search engine Miracode for flight analysis. The machine called up photographs, statistics, and
graphics reproduced on microfilm, all very different types of images, in a
matter of seconds and projected them side by side on large screens. In order
to achieve two- and three-dimensional images at a high resolution (fig. 3),

nebeneinander projiziert. Um die so begehrten hochaufgelösten, zwei- und drei-dimensionalen Bilder zu generieren (Abb. 3), arbeitete die amerikanische Foto-industrie mit gebündelten Kräften an der Weiterentwicklung extrem leistungs-starker Objektive und dualer Kamerasysteme, die vollautomatisch funktionieren mussten. Es wurden Massen an Bildern hergestellt, um präzise und umfassend zu kartografieren.

GPS ALS INFORMATIONELLE ANREICHERUNG

Die Zusammenführung von massenhafter Bildproduktion und geografischer Verortung ist heute einer der wichtigsten Merkmale der Fotografie. Diese Ent-wicklung deutete sich schon in der Ära der Bildsatelliten an und erhielt um 2000 neue Impulse. Im Mai 2000 wurde das Satellitennavigationssystem, bekannt als GPS (Global Positioning System), das ab 1973 vom amerikanischen Verteidi-gungsministerium zur Luft-, Land- und Seefahrtnavigation aufgebaut worden war, unverschlüsselt für die zivile Nutzung freigegeben. Die Aufhebung der selektiven Verfügbarkeit hatte zur Folge, dass die Daten präziser wurden und sich die Anwendungsbereiche erweiterten – am prominesten sind hier die Navi-gationsgeräte für Autos zu nennen.[4] Die Bestimmung von Position und Uhrzeit, die über ein Netz von 24 aktiven Satelliten und stationäre oder mobile Empfän-ger operiert, wurde im selben Jahr erstmals in einem fotografischen Apparat eingesetzt, wenn auch noch in einem sehr begrenzten Maß. Die hochpreisige, digitale Spiegelreflexkamera Nikon D1X, die im Juni 2001 auf den Markt kam, war das erste Modell, das über eine serienmäßig eingebaute GPS-Schnittstelle verfügte. In den Folgejahren multiplizierten sich die entsprechenden Geräte unterschiedlicher Hersteller. Über einen externen oder integrierten GPS-Emp-fänger oder durch das nachträgliche manuelle Geotagging mit spezieller Kar-tensoftware konnten Fotos nun auf Karten referenziert werden.[5] Die Georeferen-zierung ist hier als ein Teil einer umfangreichen, paradigmatischen Veränderung im Wesen der Fotografie zu begreifen.

Mit der digitalen Fotografie bzw. der Speicherung als binärer Code wurden unterschiedliche Typen von Informationen in der hybriden Form des digitalen Files zusammengeführt.

> Fotografien – heute synonym mit dem Bild selbst – setzen sich zusammen aus Bildinformationen sowie administrativen und deskriptiven Metadaten. Sie vereinen Pixel, Geodaten und technische Parameter wie Brennweite und Belichtungs-zeit sowie Bildunterschriften und Urheberrechte. In der Zirkulation werden sie immer häufiger auch durch Kommentare und Hashtags ergänzt.

Dabei unterscheidet man EXIF-Daten, wie sie heute von nahezu allen Digitalka-meras bei der Erstellung eines Bildes abgespeichert werden, von primär manu-ell hinzugefügten IPTC-Daten. Die EXIF-Daten geben Auskunft über die techni-schen Details einer Aufnahme, wie z.B. Kameramodell, Brennweite sowie Datum, Zeit und Ort der Aufnahme. Das Datenformat IPTC wird zur weiteren, qualitati-ven Anreicherung des Informationsgehalts eines Bildes eingesetzt. Je nach Ver-wendung können in diesem Format Informationen z.B. über den Autor, Bildtitel und Bildbeschreibung in Form von Keywords hinzugefügt werden.[6] Mit dieser

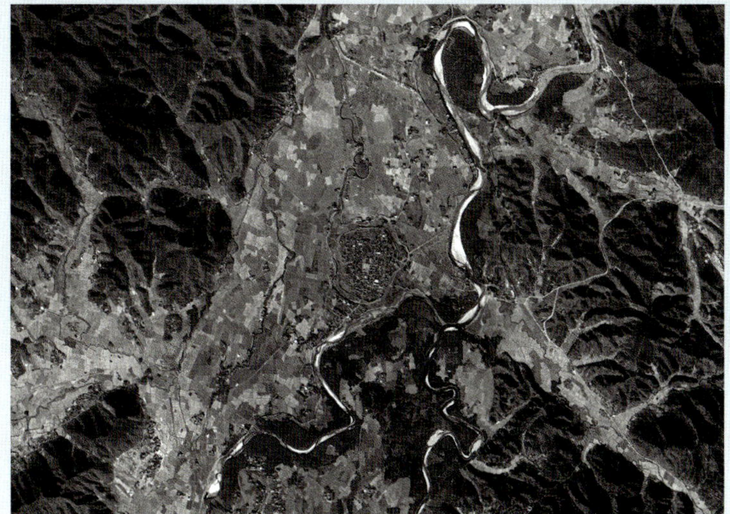

which was highly desired, the American photography industry joined forces to continue developing extremely powerful lenses and dual camera systems that were intended to function fully automatically. In order to map precisely and comprehensively, images were mass-produced.

GPS INFORMATION ENRICHMENT

The confluence of mass-scale image production and geographic location is one of the most important features of photography today. This development, which could already be seen in the era of satellite imagery, gained momentum around 2000. In May 2000 the satellite navigation system known as GPS (Global Positioning System), developed in 1973 by the US Department of Defense for air, land, and sea navigation, was released for civilian use without encryption. By removing selective availability, the data became more precise and the areas of possible use were expanded—the most prominent being as navigation devices for cars.[4] The ability to assign both place and time using a system that operates via a network of twenty-four active satellites and both stationary and mobile receivers was used for the first time in a photographic apparatus that same year, albeit in a very limited capacity. The expensive digital SLR camera Nikon D1X, which entered the market in June 2001, was the first model to have a built-in GPS interface as standard. In the following years, innumerous similar devices from various manufacturers were released. Photos could now be tagged on maps via an external or integrated GPS receiver or through subsequent manual geotagging with specialist mapping software.[5] Georeferencing is to be understood here as part of an extensive, paradigmatic shift in the nature of photography.

With digital photography stored as binary code, different types of information were brought together in the hybrid form of digital files.

Einschreibung von Metadaten und der Anreicherung des Informationsgehaltes eines Bildes entstanden *Bild-Infrastrukturen*, die für die Existenz und die Beständigkeit eines Bildes in digitalen Systemen von entscheidender Bedeutung sind.

Um die Wirkung und Relevanz von Metadaten zu verstehen, ist ein Blick in die Geschichte der analogen Fotografie notwendig. Als Hilfsmittel der Künste und Wissenschaften wurden Fotografien (im Sinne physischer Objekte) seit jeher dazu verwendet, das Abgebildete mit schriftlichen Informationen zu versehen. Bildtitel, Archivnummern, Klassifizierungen, Provenienzen und Bildrechteinhaber*innen wurden auf den Rückseiten der Abzüge oder den Papier- oder Kartonseiten auf denen ein Abzug montiert war, verzeichnet. Die Kamera übersetzte das Abgebildete in ein prozessierbares Format und so wurde es möglich, einen tendenziell homogenen Korpus visueller Aufzeichnungen zu erstellen, der anschließend zu unterschiedlichen Zwecken typologisiert, verglichen und kontextalisiert werden konnte, um Bedeutung zu erzeugen. Die Geschichte der Fotografie war dementsprechend auch stets durch ein Streben nach Ordnung geprägt, um permanent wachsende Bildmengen handhabbar zu machen: von dem Design eines Glasplattenkastens, der Linearität eines Rollfilms, der Struktur des Kontaktbogens bis hin zu den diversen manuellen Ablage- und Suchmethoden wie dem Kartenkatalog oder dem Register. Die wiederkehrende Vorstellung unkontrollierter Bilderfluten, die spätestens seit den 1920er-Jahren zu den Topoi fotografischer Kritik gehörte, war demnach schon immer irreführend. Ordnungssysteme waren und sind die Voraussetzung für die Ansammlung und Zirkulation von Bildern und gleichzeitig als ein Mittel der Disziplinierung zu verstehen.[7]

Die Fotografie war also ein sehr praktisches Medium, um visuellen Repräsentationen schriftliche Informationen hinzuzufügen. Aber auch das Gegenteil war der Fall: Fotografien widerstrebten ihrer Organisation, Systematisierung und eindeutigen Klassifizierung. Das Beschriften der fotografischen Objekte etwa hatte klare praktische und materielle Grenzen. Erschwerend kam noch hinzu, dass Fotografien meist in großen Mengen, Serien und Redundanzen auftraten. Die Beschriftungen reduzierten sich oftmals auf ein Minimum. Fotografien konnten leicht ihrer Lesbarkeit entzogen werden. Sie konnten verstummen und viele Fotos, die in Archiven, Bibliotheken, auf Dachböden, in Schuhkartons oder Alben aufbewahrt wurden, sprechen zu niemandem mehr.

Durch die Zusammenführung von Bilddaten und Metadaten, in Form des digitalen Bildformats, kam es jedoch zu entscheidenden Veränderungen. Die Bilder wurden maschinenlesbar. Der Computer potenzierte die Möglichkeiten, Bilder zu organisieren, in Datenbanken und über Suchmaschinen zu finden und nachzuverfolgen und stellte dementsprechend die Weichen für künftige Ordnungen.

Doch welche Qualität und Funktionen besitzen hierbei die Geodaten? Im Vergleich zu den Keywords, die aufgrund der Bild-Text-Differenz und hermeneutischer Verschachtelungen mehrdeutig sein können – die Grundproblematik der Ekphrasis – sind die Geodaten und die technischen Metadaten eindeutig. Genau *ein* Bild wird *einem* Ort und *einem* Zeitpunkt zugeordnet. Diese Festlegbarkeit ist insofern von Bedeutung als sie den dokumentarischen Cha-

Photographs—synonymous today with the image itself—
are composed of image information as well as administrative and descriptive metadata. They combine pixels,
geodata, and technical parameters such as focal length
and exposure time with captions and copyrights. As
they circulate, they are increasingly supplemented by
comments and hashtags.

A distinction is made here between EXIF data, which is saved by almost all digital cameras today when they create images, and the primarily manually inputted IPTC data. The EXIF data provides information about the technical details of the image, such as camera model and focal length as well as date, time, and place of the image. The IPTC data is used to further qualitatively enrich the information content of an image. Depending on the use, information can be added in the form of keywords, for example, about the author, image title, and image description.[6] With this addition of metadata and the enrichment of the information content of an image, image infrastructures have emerged that are of crucial importance to the existence and durability of an image in digital systems.

To understand the impact and relevance of metadata, it is necessary to take a look at the history of analog photography. As an aid to the arts and sciences, written information has always been used to add to what is depicted in photographs (in the sense of physical objects). Image titles, archive numbers, classifications, provenance, and image rights holders were recorded on the back of the prints or on the paper or card pages on which a print was mounted. The camera translated what was depicted into a processable format, making it possible to create a largely homogeneous corpus of visual recordings that could then be typologized, compared, and contextualized for different purposes to generate meaning. Accordingly, the history of photography has always been shaped by a striving for order; to make a constantly growing numbers of images manageable: from the design of a glass-plate case, the linearity of a roll of film, and the structure of a contact sheet to various manual filing and search methods like card indexes and catalogs. The recurring notion of an uncontrolled flood of images, which has been a topos of photography criticism since at least the 1920s, has therefore always been misleading. Classification systems were and are the prerequisite for the collection and circulation of images and can, at the same time, be understood as a medium of discipline.[7]

Photography was as such a very practical medium for adding written information to visual representations. But the opposite was also true: photographs resisted organization, systematization, and unambiguous classification. The labeling of photographic objects, for example, had clear practical and material limits. A further complicating factor was that photographs mostly appeared in large quantities, series, and duplicates. The captions were often reduced to a minimum. Photographs could easily be made unreadable. They could fall silent; many photos kept in archives, libraries, attics, shoeboxes, or albums no longer engaged in conversation with anyone.

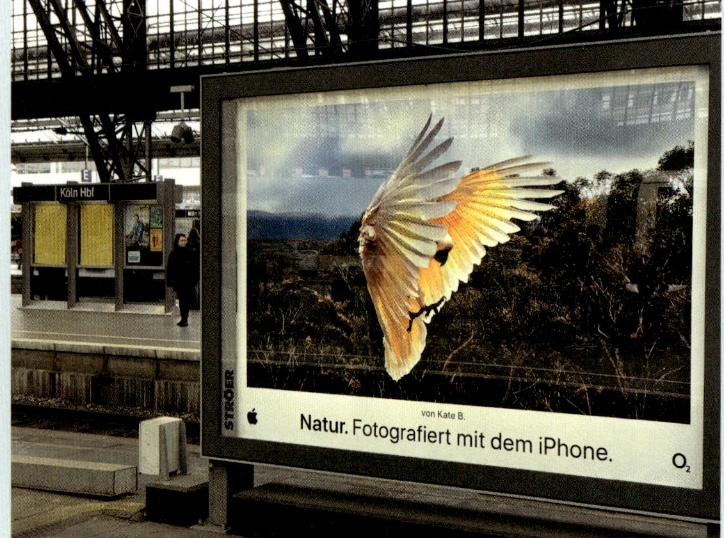

Abb. / **Fig. 4**
Armin Linke
iPhone X Werbeplakat, Hauptbahnhof Köln /
iPhone X Advertisement, Cologne Main Train Station, Mai / **May** 2019, Fotografie / **photograph**

rakter der Bilder hervorhebt und sie auch gerade deshalb für die Wissenschaft, z.B. für die Umweltwissenschaften, zu einem wichtigen Instrument der Beobachtung von Prozessen macht. Die Eindeutigkeit dieser Datentypen stabilisiert und authentifiziert somit digitale Bilder, die gemeinhin als leicht manipulierbar und ephemer gelten.

Aber die Verortung erfüllt noch weitere „urfotografische" Funktionen: das Abbilden und das „Mobilisieren" von Orten[8] und die Bestätigung von Präsenz, das „ich war hier" sowie das systematische Ordnen von Bildern. Abhängig von den jeweiligen Nutzungsintentionen ist die geografische Zuordnung nämlich eine der Basiskategorien, nach denen Fotografien in fotografischen Sammlungen, Fotoarchiven und Bilddatenbanken organisiert sind.[9] Wie Gillian Rose oder Christopher Pinney angemerkt haben, bedeutet dies auch, dass über das „archival grid" (archivarische Raster) bestimmte Lesarten der Bilder konfiguriert werden.[10] Die Geodaten, insbesondere als Teil der administrativen und deskriptiven Metadaten digitaler Bilder, werden somit Schlüssel und Spur zugleich.

MOBILE EMPFÄNGER

Durch das digitale Format sind Fotografien zu Datenbildern geworden. Die Kamera ist zu einem modularen und effizienten Gerät zur Datenerfassung avanciert.

Die Fotokamera ist nicht mehr allein auf das klassische Design des Apparats beschränkt. Als Bildsensorfunktion kann sie in diversen Geräten installiert werden: im Telefon, in der Brille, im Computer, im Auto, in der Drohne, im Satelliten.

However, decisive changes resulted from the confluence of image data and metadata in the form of the digital image format. Images became machine readable. Computers made it possible to organize images, find and track them in databases and search engines, and accordingly set the course for how they would be classified in the future.

But what are the qualities and functions of geodata? Compared to keywords, which can be ambiguous due to the image-text gap and hermeneutic nesting—which is the basic problem of ekphrasis—geodata and technical metadata are unambiguous. One specific image is assigned to a place and point in time. This specificity is important insofar as it emphasizes the documentary character of images and makes them useful in research. In environmental sciences, for example, images have become an important instrument for observing processes. The unambiguity of these data types thus stabilizes and authenticates digital images that are generally considered to be easy to manipulate and ephemeral.

But the location tagging fulfills other ur-photographic functions: the depiction and the "mobilization" of places[8] and the confirmation of presence, the "I was here," as well as the systematic ordering of images. Depending on what the particular intended use is, geographical classification is one of the basic categories by which photographs are organized in photographic collections, photo archives, and image databases.[9] As Gillian Rose and Christopher Pinney have noted, this also means that certain ways of reading images are determined via the archival grid.[10] Geodata, especially as part of the administrative and descriptive metadata of digital images, thus becomes both key and clue.

MOBILE RECEIVERS

The digital format made photographs into data images. The camera advanced to become a modular and highly efficient device to capture data.

The camera is no longer solely limited to the device's classic design. Image sensors can be installed in all manner of devices, including telephones, glasses, computers, cars, drones, and satellites.

Tech companies such as Apple, Samsung, Google, and Huawei were behind the continual push to develop camera performance. When the iPhone 3G was introduced in 2007, it was the first mass-market smartphone capable of taking photos that could be sent instantly. Since then, photographing and filming have become central functions of such devices. Countless advertisements of numerous companies show that the camera, and the quality of the display, are the driving force behind development and therefore the most convincing sales argument for buying a new smartphone (fig. 4). As smartphones comprehensively established themselves as devices for taking photographs and navigating, combining camera and mobile GPS, geodata and geotagging have taken on new relevance. They have become the norm and are used in new ways.

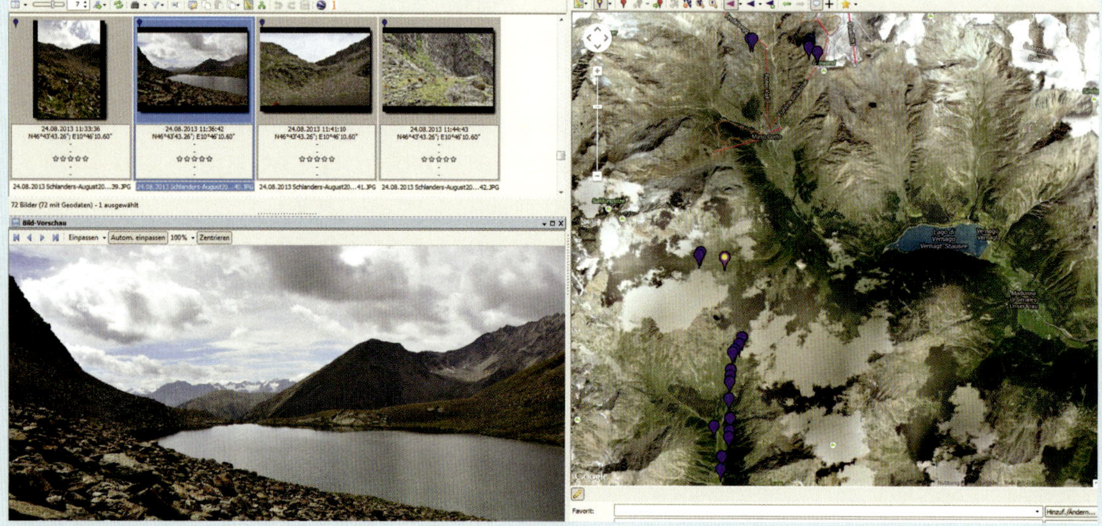

Abb. / **Fig. 5**
Beispiel der Geotagging-Software geosetter /
Example of the geotagging software geosetter,
2020, Screenshot

Dabei waren es insbesondere Tech-Unternehmen wie Apple, Samsung, Google und Huawei, die die Entwicklung der Kamerafunktion kontinuierlich vorangetrieben haben. Seit Einführung des iPhone 3G im Jahr 2007, dem ersten massentauglichen Smartphone, mit dem Bilder gemacht und instantan versendet werden konnten, gehört das Fotografieren und Filmen zu den zentralen Funktionen dieser Geräte. Wie zahlreiche Werbeformate unterschiedlicher Anbieter illustrieren, ist die Kamera – und die Qualität des Displays – der Motor der Entwicklung und folglich das stärkste Verkaufsargument für die Anschaffung neuer Smartphones (Abb. 4). Mit der flächendeckenden Etablierung des Smartphones als Bildmaschine *und* Navigationstool, also der Kombination von Kamera und mobilem GPS-Empfänger, erlangen Geodaten und das Geotagging eine neue Relevanz. Sie wurden zur Norm und fanden neue Anwendungsbereiche.

Dies ist einerseits auf die Betriebssysteme iOS und Android zurückzuführen, die die Georeferenzierung als vorinstallierte Standardeinstellung vorgeben. Wie eine Reihe anderer Dienste muss diese Einstellung gezielt deaktiviert werden. Mit jeder Betätigung des Auslösers entsteht automatisch ein georeferenziertes Bild. Eine weitere entscheidende Rolle spielt das „Bilder teilen" als ein inhärenter Charakter gegenwärtiger Bildproduktion[11] sowie deren Zirkulation auf Social-Media-Plattformen. Dabei lässt sich am Beispiel von Instagram, einer der zentralen Verteilungsplattformen, die Sichtbarkeiten herstellt, organisiert und kontrolliert, der Stellenwert der Georeferenzierung skizzieren. Seit Gründung des Unternehmens im Jahr 2010 war diese als ein zentraler Bestandteil der Plattform konzipiert. Im Markennamen und Logo des Unternehmens schwingt bereits eine Reihe fotohistorischer Assoziationen mit: die Polaroid-Sofortfotografie und das Bildtelegramm, als Verfahren der schnellen Übermittlung, oder der einfachen Bedienung der (1963 eingeführten) Instamatic-Kamera von Kodak, einer vollautomatisierten und kostengünstigen Kleinbildkamera. Instagram

On the one hand, this may be traced back to the iOS and Android operating systems, which specify georeferencing as a preinstalled standard setting. Much as with a host of other defaults, this setting needs to be deliberately deactivated. Every time the camera shutter is released, a georeferenced image is automatically created. The possibility of sharing images has become an inherent part of contemporary image production[11] and plays a further decisive role, as does the circulation of such images on social media. The importance of georeferencing can be seen with regard to Instagram, one of the central social media channels with which forms of visibility are created, organized, and controlled. Ever since the company was founded in 2010, this concept has been a central aspect of the app. The company's name and logo evoke a number of associations from the history of photography: the Polaroid instant camera and the image telegrams as a means of quickly communicating, as well as the easy-to-use Instamatic cameras by Kodak (introduced in 1963), a fully automatic and inexpensive small-format camera. Instagram was meant to be the Twitter for photos. Photos were intended to be shared immediately as ephemeral short messages. The mobile app's look and feel and its functions were reduced to "posting and commenting, liking and following,"[12] and was extremely easy to use. An image could be made, changed using filters, and posted. An image posted on Instagram reinforces one's own presence, the I-was-here of photography. It serves as a tool for communication, exchange, and collective experience (fig. 5). In order to enhance the I-was-here aspect and to be able to organize and visualize the anticipated mass of images, early versions of Instagram were linked to a photo map onto which uploaded images could be mapped (fig. 6).

Thanks to the vigorous support of its users, Instagram amassed a gigantic body of images and data in an extremely short space of time, which made the company interesting for the already established image-based social media

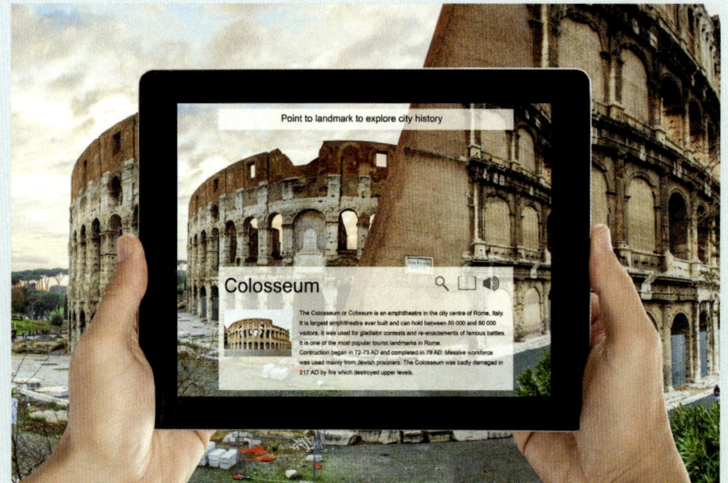

Abb. / **Fig. 7**
Andrey Popov
Modell Colosseum, Augmented Reality
Applikation für die Tourismusbranche /
Application for tourism industry,
ca. 2017, Screenshot

sollte ein Twitter für Bilder sein. Bilder sollten als ephemere Kurznachrichten unmittelbar geteilt werden. Die mobile App war in ihrem Erscheinungsbild und in ihren Funktionen auf das „Posten und Kommentieren, das Liken und Folgen"[12] reduziert und dabei extrem einfach in der Handhabung. Ein Bild wird gemacht, durch das Applizieren von Filtern verändert und veröffentlicht. Ein auf Instagram gepostetes Bild bekräftigt die eigene Präsenz, das *ich-war-hier* der Fotografie. Es dient als Mittel der Kommunikation, des Austauschs und des kollektiven Erlebens (Abb. 5). Um das *ich-war-hier* zu betonen sowie die antizipierten Bildmassen ordnen und visualisieren zu können, waren frühe Versionen von Instagram an eine Photo Map gekoppelt, auf der die hochgeladenen Bilder verortet werden konnten (Abb. 6).

Unter tatkräftiger Mithilfe der User*innen generierte Instagram in kürzester Zeit eine gigantische Bild- und Datenmenge, wodurch das Unternehmen u.a. für den bereits etablierten, bildbasierten Social-Media-Anbieter Facebook interessant wurde. 2012 – zwei Jahre nach der Gründung – kaufte Facebook Inc. Instagram zum Preis von einer Milliarde US-Dollar; zwei Jahre später wurde auch Whatsapp, ein weiterer Umschlagplatz für Bilder, für 19 Milliarden US-Dollar übernommen.

Es ist die umfangreiche Datenerfassung durch die Fotografie, die Bilder zu begehrten digitalen Inhalten machen. Dabei handelt es sich um ein Bildkapital, das massenhaft und zu extrem niedrigen Kosten, da von den User*innen produziert, auf den Servern der Unternehmen gesammelt und gespeichert wird.

Durch das Clustern in annotierten Datenbanken, die u.a. nach geografischen Daten organisiert sind, lassen sich Algorithmen zur Bilderkennung und maschinellem Sehen entwickeln.

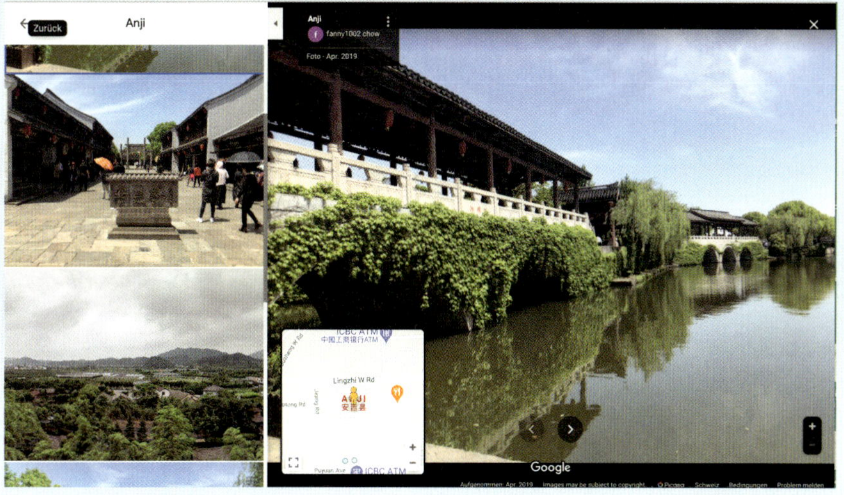

Abb. / **Fig. 8**
fanny1002 chow
Region Anji / **Anji County,** China,
April 2019, Google Maps Screenshot

site Facebook. In 2012, two years after the company was founded, Facebook acquired Instagram for one billion US dollars; two years later, WhatsApp, another platform for exchanging images, was sold for nineteen billion US dollars. **The comprehensive amount of data stored in photographs is what makes images such highly desirable digital content. This image capital is produced en masse and extremely cheaply because it is user generated and collected and saved on company servers.**

Clustering in annotated databases organized according to geographic data (among other factors) allows algorithms for image recognition and machine vision to be developed. These in turn may be used to help produce interactive, intermedial programs based on thousands and hundreds of thousands of shots of tourist sights, such as the Colosseum in Rome (fig. 7). Yet the special potential of location tags is deployed particularly through the linking of different forms of visualization such as photographs, satellite images, and maps; that is, various databases, as is the case with Google Maps in particular (fig. 8).

Digital photography reinforces the characteristics and functions of photography that have always been an integral part of the medium: data collection through the mass development of photographic images as well as the illustration, measurement, construction, and control of the world.

Diese können wiederum in den Dienst interaktiver, intermedialer Formate gestellt werden, basierend auf den Tausenden und Abertausenden betätigten Auslösern vor Sehenswürdigkeiten, wie z.B. dem Kolosseum in Rom (Abb. 7). Doch entfaltet sich das besondere Potential der Verortung gerade durch die Verknüpfung unterschiedlicher Visualisierungsformen: Fotografie, Satellitenaufnahme und Karte, d.h. unterschiedliche Datenbanken, wie dies besonders bei Google Maps der Fall ist (Abb. 8).

Die digitale Fotografie bekräftigt Merkmale und Funktionen der Fotografie, die seit jeher in deren Programm verankert sind: die Datensammlung durch das massenhafte Auftreten von fotografischen Bildern sowie die Bebilderung, Vermessung, Konstruktion und Kontrolle der Welt.

1   Peter Geimer, *Bilder aus Versehen. Eine Geschichte fotografischer Erscheinungen*, Hamburg 2010

2   R. Cargill Hall, *SAMOS to the Moon: The Clandestine Transfer of Reconnaissance Technology Between Federal Agencies*, Washington D.C. 2001, URL: https://www.nro.gov/Portals/65/documents/history/csnr/programs/docs/prog-hist-01.pdf

3   Die hohe Störanfälligkeit und das enorme Gewicht der Konstruktion bewirkten jedoch schnell ein Umdenken. Bei anschließenden Flügen wurden die Filme in Kapseln geborgen und analog entwickelt. Zu Vorgeschichte der Analog-Digital-Umwandlung vgl. Jens Schröter, „Das Ende der Welt. Analoge vs. Digitale Bilder – mehr oder weniger ‚Realität'?", in: Jens Schröter, Alexander Böhnke (Hg.), *Analog/Digital – Opposition oder Kontinuum? Zur Theorie und Geschichte einer Unterscheidung*, Bielefeld 2004, S. 335–354, hier S. 340f.

4   James F. Zumberge und Gerd Gendt, "The Demise of Selective Availability and Implications for the International GPS Service", in: *Physics and Chemistry of the Earth,* 6–8, 2001, S. 637–644

5   GPS ist natürlich nicht immer störungsfrei bzw. akkurat, wenn etwa das Signal durch einen bedeckten Himmel oder Baum beeinträchtigt wird.

6   Vgl. hierzu u.a. Winfried Gerling, Susanne Holschbach, Petra Löffler: *Bilder verteilen. Fotografische Praktiken in der digitalen Kultur*, Bielefeld 2018, S. 106–119

7   Vgl. Estelle Blaschke, Davide Nerini, "Vers l'image augmentée", in: *Transbordeur. Photographie. Histoire. Société No. 3: Photographie et technologies d'information*, Paris/Genf 2019, S. 7–13 und Estelle Blaschke, *Banking on Images. The Bettmann Archive and Corbis*, Leipzig 2016. Dem wäre noch hinzuzufügen, dass für kommerzielle Bildagenturen wie auch für Unternehmen die Bilddaten kommerzialisieren, das ökonomische Potential einer Sammlung in der Ordnung liegt.

8   Die Vorstellung der Mobilisierung von Orten und Bauwerken durch das fotografische Abbild ist gerade in den frühen Plädoyers für die Fotografie wie etwa bei Jules Janin, François Arago und Auguste Belloc sehr präsent.

9   Unterschiedlichen Nutzungsintentionen sind erkennbar, wenn man z.B. kunsthistorische Phototheken, die die Fotografie als Medium verwenden, um Architektur, Malerei, Skulptur etc. handhabbar zu machen und die nach Epochen, Ort, Künstler*innen, Material etc. organisiert sind, mit künstlerischer Fotografie vergleicht, die primär nach Autor*innen organisiert sind.

10 Vgl. hierzu Gillian Rose, "Practising Photography: An Archive, a Study, some Photographs and a Researcher", *Journal of Historical Geography*, 4, 2000, S. 555–571. Christopher Pinney, "The Parallel Histories of Anthropology and Photography", in: Elizabeth Edwards, *Anthropology and Photography 1860–1920*, New Haven/London 1992, S. 74–95

11 Vgl. hierzu: André Gunthert, *L'image partagée. La photographie numérique*, Paris 2015; Gerling/Holschbach/Löffler 2018 (wie Anm. 6); Simon Rothöler, *Das verteilte Bild. Stream – Archiv – Ambiente*, München 2018

12 Gerling/Holschbach/Löffler 2018 (wie Anm. 6), S. 49

1   Peter Geimer, *Inadvertent Images: A History of Photographic Apparitions* (Chicago, IL: Chicago University Press, 2018).

2   R. Cargill Hall, *SAMOS to the Moon: The Clandestine Transfer of Reconnaissance Technology between Federal Agencies* (Washington, DC: National Reconnaissance Office, 2001), https://www.nro.gov/Portals/65/documents/history/csnr/programs/docs/prog-hist-01.pdf.

3   The high likelihood of failure and the huge weight of the apparatus soon necessitated a change of plan, however. In subsequent flights, the films were secured in capsules and developed by analog methods. For background information on the change from analog to digital, see Jens Schröter, "Das Ende der Welt: Analoge vs. Digitale Bilder—mehr oder weniger 'Realität?,'" in Jens Schröter and Alexander Böhnke, eds., *Analog/Digital—Opposition oder Kontinuum? Zur Theorie und Geschichte einer Unterscheidung* (Bielefeld: transcript Verlag, 2004), 335–54, here 340–41.

4   James F. Zumberge and Gerd Gendt, "The Demise of Selective Availability and Implications for the International GPS Service," *Physics and Chemistry of the Earth* 6–8 (2001): 637–44.

5   Of course, GPS technology is neither completely without flaws nor completely accurate, for example, if there is interference from clouds or trees affecting the signal.

6   On this subject see, for example, Winfried Gerling, Susanne Holschbach, and Petra Löffler, *Bilder verteilen: Fotografische Praktiken in der digitalen Kultur* (Bielefeld: transcript Verlag, 2018), 106–19.

7   See Estelle Blaschke and Davide Nerini, "Vers l'image augmentee," in *Transbordeur: Photographie, histoire et société*, no. 3: *Photographie et technologies d'information* (Paris and Geneva: Macula Éditions, 2019), 7–13, and Estelle Blaschke, *Banking on Images: The Bettmann Archive and Corbis* (Leipzig: Spector Books, 2016). The economic potential of a collection for commercial image agencies and companies that commodify image data should also be noted.

8   The notion of mobilizing places and buildings through the photographic image already had a strong presence in the work of photography's early proponents, such as that of Jules Janin, François Arago, and Auguste Belloc.

9   One can tell the different intentions for which photography is employed by looking at, for example, art-historical photo libraries in contrast to fine-art photography. The former use photography as a medium to make architecture, painting, and sculpture more accessible, and are organized by era, place, artist, material etc., whereas the latter are primarily organized by photographer.

10 On this subject, see Gillian Rose, "Practising Photography: An Archive, a Study, Some Photographs and a Researcher," *Journal of Historical Geography* 4 (2000): 555–71; Christopher Pinney, "The Parallel Histories of Anthropology and Photography," in Elizabeth Edwards, *Anthropology and Photography 1860–1920* (New Haven, CT, and London: Yale University Press, 1992), 74–95.

11 On this subject, see André Gunthert, *L'image partagée. La photographie numérique* (Paris: Textuel, 2015); Gerling, Holschbach, and Löffler 2018 (see note 6); Simon Rothöler, *Das verteilte Bild: Stream—Archiv—Ambiente* (Munich: Wilhelm Fink Verlag, 2018).

12 Gerling, Holschbach, and Löffler 2018 (see note 6), 49.

Text: Kerstin Schankweiler

DIE *MEMEIFICATION* DES TANK MAN

Am 25. Januar 2011 entstand vom Balkon einer Wohnung in Kairo ein verwackeltes, unscharfes Handyvideo, dass eine spektakuläre Szene der sich formierenden Straßenproteste festhält. Darin stellt sich ein einzelner unbewaffneter Mann einem Wasserwerfer der Sicherheitskräfte entgegen (Abb. 1). Das Video verbreitete sich viral, als es noch am selben Tag unter dem Titel „Egyptian Tank Man" hochgeladen wurde. Der Vorfall ereignete sich am Beginn der Ägyptischen Revolution 2011, dem ersten von 18 Tagen bis zum Rücktritt des damaligen Staatschefs Husni Mubarak. Die Hashtags #Jan25 und #egypt gingen in der Folge in den Sozialen Medien um die Welt.[1] Das Datum wurde namensgebend, denn in Ägypten nannte man die Proteste die „Revolution des 25. Januar" – in der westlichen Welt eher bekannt unter dem Namen „Arabischer Frühling", womit eine ganze Reihe von Aufständen in Nordafrika und dem Nahen Osten, beginnend mit der Revolution in Tunesien 2010, gemeint ist.

THE *MEMEIFICATION* OF TANK MAN

A shaky, out-of-focus video taken on a smartphone from an apartment balcony in Cairo on January 25, 2011, shows a spectacular scene of protest forming on the street. A single unarmed man faces a water canon mounted onto a military riot-control vehicle (fig. 1). The video went viral the same day it was posted under the title "Egyptian Tank Man." This incident took place at the start of the 2011 Egyptian revolution, on the first of eighteen days leading up to the resignation of then president Hosni Mubarak. As a result, the hashtags #Jan25 and #egypt crisscrossed the world on social media.[1] The protests came to be known as the January 25 Revolution, or more widely in the Western world as the Arab Spring, a term used to refer to a wide array of protests in northern Africa and the Middle East, beginning with the Tunisian revolution in 2010.

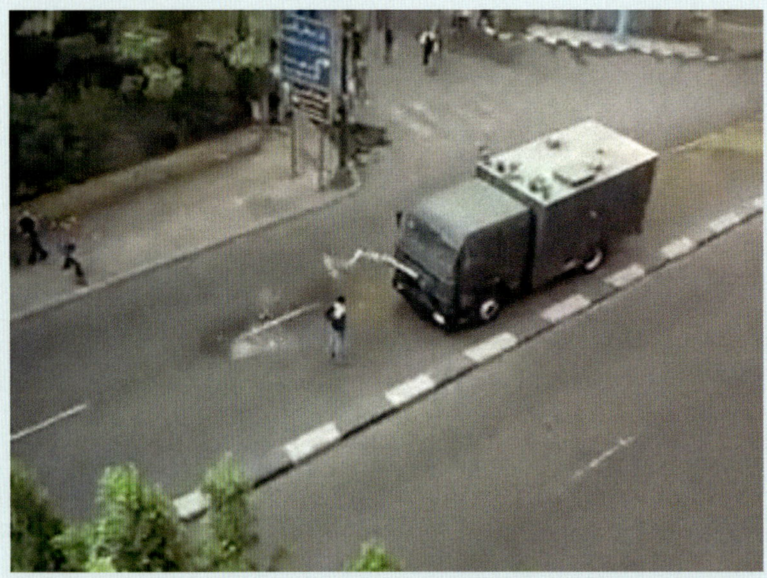

Abb. / **Fig. 1**
MFMAegy
Egyptian Tank Man,
25. November 2001 / **November 25, 2001**
YouTube Standbild / **video still**

Fotografien und Videos, die im Kontext von politischem Protest in den Sozialen Medien zirkulieren, habe ich als „Bildproteste" diskutiert.[2]

Sowohl Bilder als auch Protestbewegungen haben in den Sozialen Medien Konjunktur.

Allein auf Facebook werden jede Sekunde circa 4.000 Fotos gepostet, das sind ca. 350 Millionen Fotos am Tag.[3] Auf YouTube werden pro Minute 500 Stunden Videomaterial hochgeladen.[4] Wolfgang Ullrich hat konstatiert, dass Bilder durch die heutigen Gebrauchsweisen, die vor allem kommunikativ sind (nicht mehr so sehr im Modus der Erinnerung), sprachähnlicher werden, eine fast schon mündliche Qualität erlangen.[5]

Vor diesem Hintergrund verwundert es nicht, dass Fotografien und Videos auch in politischen Konflikten eine zentrale Rolle spielen. Die Aufstände in Ägypten 2011 wurden (nicht ohne Kritik) als „Facebook-Revolution" dargestellt und der syrische Konflikt als der „erste YouTube-Krieg"[6] bezeichnet. Dies deutet darauf hin, dass den Sozialen Medien heute eine tragende Rolle in politischen Konflikten zugeschrieben wird.

Natürlich wurden Bilder auch vor dem Zeitalter der Sozialen Medien in Revolutionen und Protesten strategisch eingesetzt. Doch heute kann praktisch jeder zu jeder Zeit mit der Handykamera Ereignisse dokumentieren und seine Bilder und Botschaften in Umlauf bringen.

Die Omnipräsenz von Bildern, ihre neuen technischen Bedingungen und Gebrauchsweisen, ästhetischen Qualitäten und transnationalen Ökonomien sowie ihr Einsatz in politischen Konflikten und sozialen Bewegungen – all das fordert dazu heraus, über das Versprechen und die Potentiale digitaler Bildkultu-

Previously, I have discussed photographs and videos of political protests circulated via social media as "image protests."[2]

Both images and protest movements are in much demand on social media.

Every second, around four thousand images are posted on Facebook, equivalent to about 350 million photos each day.[3] Five hundred hours of video material are uploaded onto YouTube every minute.[4] Wolfgang Ullrich has stated that the current way images are used is less as a means of remembering than as a communicative tool similar to speech, with an almost oral quality.[5]

Viewed against this background it is unsurprising to consider that photographs and videos also play a central role in political conflicts. The protests in Egypt in 2011 were (not without criticism) depicted as a Facebook revolution, and the Syrian conflict was termed the "first YouTube war."[6] This indicates that social media are ascribed a substantial role in political conflicts.

Naturally, images were strategically deployed in revolutions and protests before the era of social media. Yet today, basically anyone can document events with their smartphones at any time and circulate the resulting images and messages.

The omnipresence of images, their latest technological requirements and applications, their aesthetic qualities and transnational economies, and their use in political conflicts and social movements all call for a consideration of both the promises and potential of digital visual cultures as well as their boundaries, limitations, and attendant asymmetries of power, which I will illuminate using image protests as an example.

First of all, the circulation of images in an era of algorithmizing requires that content is tagged in order to be found in the first place. The naming of image files and video titles are equally important in this context.

Automatic text recognition continues to work much better than does image recognition. Staying with our example of the Egyptian Tank Man from Cairo: the video was circulated so widely around the world because it was titled in both English and Arabic, and uploaded numerous times under different titles.[7]

A large number of videos posted to YouTube, for instance, have very few clicks or indeed are never viewed. They are described as the "gigantic underbelly of the internet" or "the lonesome net."[8] Many of these videos still have the names automatically assigned by the devices they were filmed on, which do little to convey their content (such as "MOV 4861," "IMG 0071 May 2018," or "DSC 0008"). A low number of clicks means the contents are classed as less relevant and thus do not appear on site feeds. Therefore we can assume that we are able to apprehend only a tiny fraction of the protest online, even if largely ignored images and videos are just as public and theoretically capable of being accessed.

ren ebenso nachzudenken wie über die Grenzen, Einschränkungen und Macht-
asymmetrien, die ich am Beispiel von Bildprotesten beleuchten werde.

Zunächst einmal ist es für die Zirkulation in Zeiten von Algorithmisierung zentral, dass Inhalte so mit Tags verschlagwortet werden, dass sie überhaupt gefunden werden.

Auch die Benennung von Bilddateien und die Betitelung von Videos ist in diesem Zusammenhang wichtig. Automatische Texterkennung funktioniert immer
noch wesentlich besser als Bilderkennung. Bleiben wir bei unserem Beispiel des
„Egyptian Tank Man" aus Kairo. Das Video konnte unter anderem deshalb breit
und international zirkulieren, weil es neben Arabisch zusätzlich auf Englisch benannt und außerdem mehrfach mit verschiedenen Titeln hochgeladen wurde.[7]

Eine große Zahl an Videos, die tagtäglich etwa auf YouTube hochgeladen
werden, haben sehr niedrige Klickzahlen oder wurden gar nie aufgerufen. Sie
werden als „gigantischer Unterbauch des Internets" oder „das einsame Netz"
bezeichnet.[8] Viele dieser Videos tragen Namen, die von den Aufnahmegeräten
automatisch vergeben wurden und wenig aussagekräftig sind (wie „MOV 4861",
„IMG 0071 May 2018" oder „DSC 0008"). Niedrige Klickzahlen wiederum führen
dazu, dass die Inhalte als wenig relevant eingestuft werden und in den Feeds
der Plattformen nicht auftauchen. Wir können deshalb davon ausgehen, dass
wir nur einen kleinen Bruchteil des Widerstands im Netz wahrnehmen können,
auch wenn kaum rezipierte Bilder und Videos ebenso öffentlich und zumindest
theoretisch zugänglich sind.

Doch die Gründe für die Viralität des Videos „Egyptian Tank Man" sind wesentlich komplexer. Ein weiterer Grund liegt in dem Bildnetzwerk, zu dem das
Video gehört. Bereits der Titel bezieht sich nämlich auf einen berühmten historischen Vorläufer des mutigen Ägypters, auf den uns eine weitere Benennung
des Videos, „Tiananmen-like Courage in Cairo", explizit hinweist. Die Betitelun-
gen erinnern an die ikonischen Pressefotografien des „Tank Man" vom Tian'anmen-Platz in Beijing 1989, der sich einer Panzerkolonne entgegengestellt hatte
(Abb. 2). Der chinesische und der ägyptische „Tank Man" sind nicht die einzigen
Beispiele. Die David-gegen-Goliath-Bildformel, in der sich eine einzelne helden-
hafte Person einer Übermacht entgegenstellt, ist äußerst stabil. Sie kann als Warburg'sche Pathosformel bezeichnet werden und gehört regelrecht zum Bilder-
repertoire von Protestkulturen.[9]

Die Echokammer der Bilder führt im Internet meiner These nach zu einer
Verschiebung, vom „discrete icon" zum „generic icon". Der Medien- und Kommu-
nikationswissenschaftler David Perlmutter bezeichnet mit „discrete icon" eine
einzigartige Ikone, und mit „generic icon" einen ikonischen Bildtypus, der zwar
auf das gleiche Motiv rekurriert, bei dem aber Akteur*innen, Orte oder Situationen wechseln können.[10] Es handelt sich also um eine affizierende Bildformel,
die einen hohen Wiedererkennungswert besitzt, und es geht um die Relationen,
die Bilder untereinander ausbilden. Zunächst einmal möchte ich festhalten, dass
Medienzeugenschaft immer eine Transformation beschreibt, die die Grundlage
für die Entwicklung zur generischen Formel ist: Etwas Individuelles, Ephemeres,
Situatives, das sich auf ein bestimmtes Ereignis des Bezeugens bezieht, wird zu

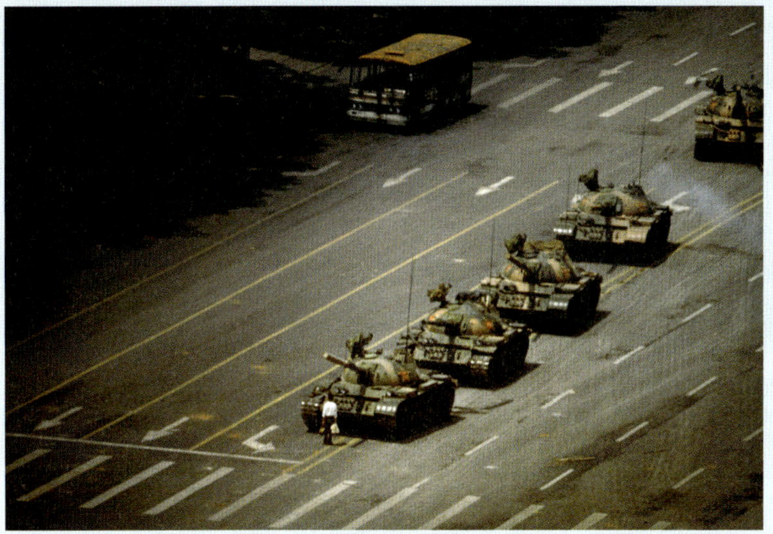

Abb. / **Fig. 2**
Stuart Franklin
"The Tank Man" Stopping the Column of T59 Tanks, Tiananmen Square,
4. Juni 1989 / **June 4, 1989,** C-Print

Yet the reasons behind the virality of the Egyptian Tank Man video are significantly more complex. A further reason is the image network this video belongs to. The title itself references the brave Egyptian's well-known historical antecedent, explicitly referenced in a second video name, "Tiananmen-like Courage in Cairo." The title evokes the iconic press photographs of Tank Man at Tian'anmen Square in Beijing in 1989 when he stood and faced down a colonnade of tanks (fig. 2). The Chinese and Egyptian "Tank Men" aren't the only examples. The David and Goliath construct in which lone heroic figures stand up to a superpower is firmly established. It can be described as a pathos formula à la Aby Warburg and is a firm fixture in the visual repertoire of protest cultures.[9]

According to my thesis, the echo chamber of online images leads to a shift from the "discrete icon" to the "generic icon." The media and communications scholar David Perlmutter uses the term "discrete icons" to refer to singular icons, whereas "generic icons" are iconic image types in which the individuals, places, and situations depicted change, even as the same setup is repeated.[10] So a potent formula with high recognition value is in operation, one that forms a set of interrelated images. First of all, I would like to note that such media witnessing always describes a transformation that is the basis for being developed into a generic formula: something individual, ephemeral, situation-specific, and related to a particular event of witnessing becomes a generic testimony that is lasting and enables circulation and repetition. Experiencing the described moment in Cairo was doubtless an exceptional event in space and time that one would struggle to match. Yet when it becomes a medial event of witnessing, it is no longer singular, but repeatable in other times and spaces. With regard to 9/11, Paul Frosh and Amit Pinchevski have made reference to what they termed "repeatable singularity."[11] Icons, like

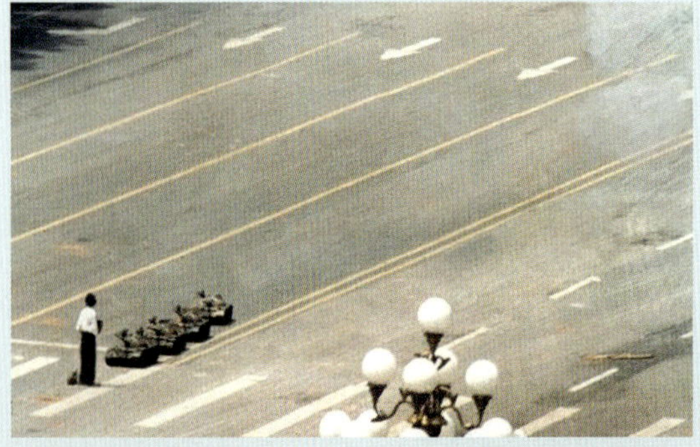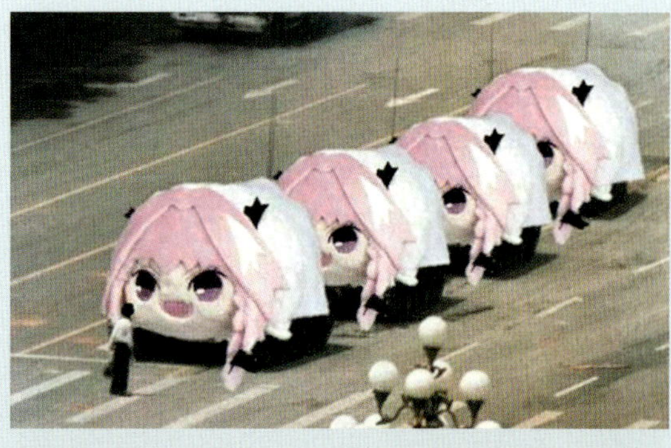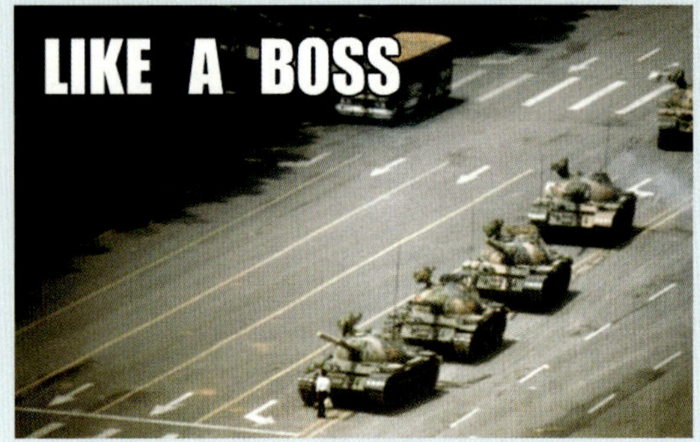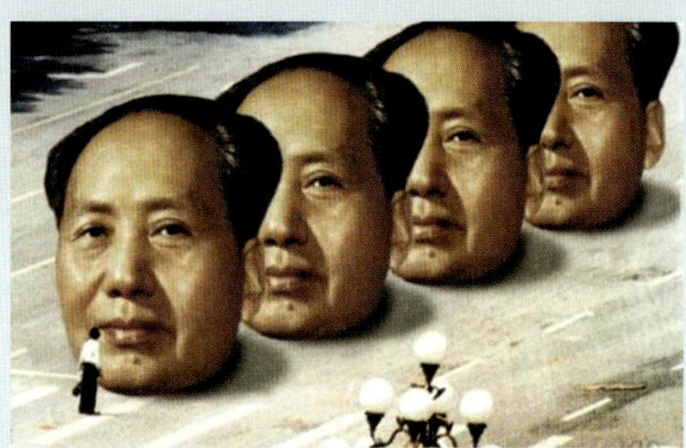

einem generischen Zeugnis, das dauerhaft ist und Zirkulation und Wiederholung ermöglicht. Die Szene in Kairo zu erleben, war zweifellos ein außergewöhnliches Ereignis in Zeit und Raum, das man nur schwerlich vergleichen kann. Aber wenn sie zu einem medialen Ereignis des Bezeugens wird, ist sie nicht mehr einzigartig, sondern in anderen Zeiten und Räumen wiederholbar. Paul Frosh und Amit Pinchevski haben das bezogen auf 9/11 die „wiederholbare Singularität"[11] genannt. Ikonen sind, ebenso wie Zeugnisse, wiederholbar geworden. Fast ist es so, als würden diese Bilder immer wieder aufgeführt und verkörpert, als würden sie regelrecht zum Reenactment animieren. Dieser Effekt hat sich im Zeitalter der Sozialen Medien potenziert.

Bilder scheinen also die Produktion weiterer, ähnlicher Bilder anzuregen.

Dies eröffnet nicht nur einen Raum für unzählige Wiederholungen, sondern auch für Aneignungen und Weiterentwicklungen, wie sie so typisch für unsere aktuelle Social-Media-Kultur geworden sind, nämlich im Internetphänomen der Memes.

Als Meme bezeichnet man eine Bildidee, die sich in den Sozialen Medien verbreitet und auf Nachahmungen in Form von Parodien oder Remixen basiert (Abb. 3)[12].

Die digitalen Bildkulturen unterliegen einer regelrechten *Memeification*. Angelehnt an den Begriff der *Datafication* (alles wird zu Datenmaterial) meine ich mit diesem Begriff, dass Bilder zu Bildnetzwerken werden.[13] Die *Memeification* der Bildkulturen ist mit dem generisch-ikonischen Charakter direkt verbunden, denn Memes beziehen sich besonders auf ikonische Bilder, weil ihr Witz nur durch wiedererkennbare Bezüge funktionieren kann. Der Kunst- und Fotohistoriker André Gunthert hat gerade diese Praxis und „Ästhetik der Appropriation"[14] als grundlegend für die „Kultur des Sharing"[15] und die Zirkulation von Bildern beschrieben.

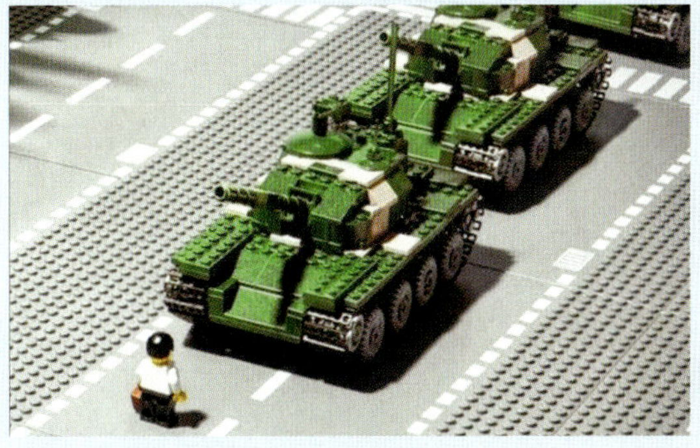

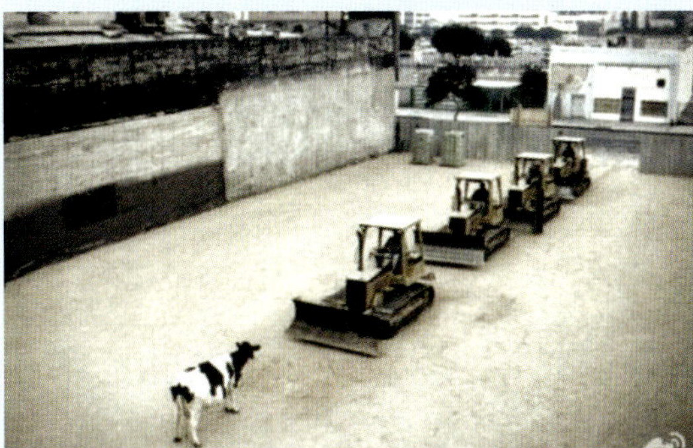

testimonies, have become repeatable. It is almost as if these images can constantly be experienced afresh and embodied, as if they are veritably animated into functioning as reenactments. This effect has been intensified in an era dominated by social media.

Thus images spark the production of further, similar images.

This opens up space not only for countless repetitions but also for appropriations and further developments as has become characteristic of current social media culture, to wit: the internet phenomenon of the meme.

A meme is an image or other content spread on social media that is based on imitations in the form of parodies or remixes (fig. 3).[12]

Digital visual culture has become subject to a downright memeification. I intend this term, much like "datafication" (where everything becomes potential data), to indicate how images are made into image networks.[13] The memeification of visual culture is directly tied to memes' generically iconic character, for memes reference iconic images in particular, because their humor only works through recognizable references. Art and photography historian André Gunthert described the "aesthetics of appropriation"[14] as fundamental to a "culture of sharing"[15] and the circulation of images.

Thus this memeification demands circulation on the one hand, while simultaneously limiting the pool of images and encouraging normification and canonization.

Well-known images become better known, while this poses a hindrance to many other

DIE *MEMEIFICATION* DES TANK MAN / THE *MEMEIFICATION* OF TANK MAN

Die *Memeification* befördert also einerseits die Zirkulation, andererseits wird der Bilderpool dadurch jedoch limitiert und Normierung und Kanonisierung vorangetrieben.

Bekannte Bilder scheinen immer bekannter zu werden, während dies für viele andere Bilder, die sich nicht so leicht an die Bildnetzwerke anschließen lassen, eine Einschränkung bedeutet.

Trotzdem erlauben die neuen Bildnetzwerke einer viel größeren Zahl an Bildern, sozusagen im Windschatten bekannter Bilder, sichtbar zu werden. Dabei geht das Einzelbild im Schwarm der Memes geradezu unter. Die *Memeification* bedeutet also zugleich Einschränkung wie Erweiterung des Bilderpools.

Die Bilder des Tank Man, die wie kein anderes an die Studierendenproteste und die Demokratiebewegung in China 1989 sowie deren gewaltsame Niederschlagung durch den Staat erinnern, dürfen in China nicht gezeigt werden. Interessant in diesem Zusammenhang ist ein Meme, in dem die Panzer durch gelbe Gummienten ersetzt wurden (Abb. 4). Mit diesem Meme gelang es im Jahr 2013, am 24. Jahrestag des Massakers am Tian'anmen-Platz, auf Sina Weibo, dem chinesischen Twitter, die Zensur in China temporär zu umgehen und so im Netz das Gedenken wachzuhalten. Die gelben Gummienten beziehen sich dabei auf eine bekannte und beliebte Kunstinstallation des niederländischen Künstlers Florentijn Hofman, die *Rubber Duck*, die neben vielen anderen Städten auch im Victoria Harbour von Hongkong ihren Auftritt hatte. Drei Wochen vor dem Jahrestag der Proteste auf dem Tian'anmen-Platz jedoch verlor das Objekt die Luft, woraufhin das Hashtag #bigyellowduck zum meistgesuchten Keyword aufstieg. Dies machte sich das Tank-Man-Meme zunutze, um die Zensur zu umgehen. Diese Durchmischungen von Kunst, Populärkultur und Bildpolitiken sind ein zentrales Merkmal der Bildproteste in den Sozialen Medien.

Es zeigt sich, dass die Frage nach den Möglichkeiten und Grenzen zirkulierender Bilder nicht leicht zu beantworten ist, weil die digitalen Bildkulturen in ihrer Fluidität[16] zwar immer neuen Einhegungen unterliegen (der Logik der Algorithmen, Bildzensur, Normierungen etc.), diese aber auch kreativ umgangen werden.

Auch die eingangs erwähnten Videos, die sehr niedrige Klickzahlen haben oder sogar niemals aufgerufen wurden, werden längst auf eigenen Seiten zusammengestellt, die diese nicht gesehenen Bilder als Raritäten mit hohem Authentizitätsversprechen anpreisen und damit ihre vermeintliche Unzulänglichkeit und mangelnde Viralität wenden.[17]

Abschließend möchte ich eine künstlerische Arbeit vorstellen, die das Video des ägyptischen Tank Man als *found footage* aufgreift. Die Arbeit steht exemplarisch dafür, dass Bilder aus den Sozialen Medien, ebenso wie die damit verbundenen Sehgewohnheiten, Praktiken, Politiken und Trajektorien, heute für die Gegenwartskunst eine wachsende Bedeutung besitzen.

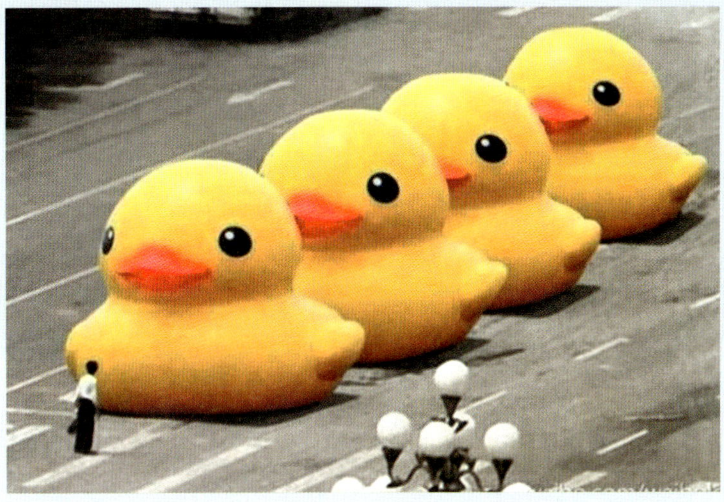

Abb. / **Fig. 4**
Anonym / **Anonymous**
A Parody of the Iconic 1989 Tiannmen Square Photo of a
Chinese Protester Confronting Government Tanks, 2013,
Tank-Man-Meme

images that cannot so easily be fit into such image networks.

Nevertheless new image networks enable a far larger number of images to become more visible in the slipstream, as it were, of well-known images. Yet in this, the single image becomes lost in the swarm of memes. The memeification thus indicates both the limitation and expansion of the pool of images.

Images of Tank Man, which are unparalleled in summoning up the student protests and democracy movement in China in 1989 as well as their brutal suppression by the Chinese state, are not permitted to be shown in China. A meme in which the tank is replaced by a yellow rubber duck is an interesting meme viewed in this context (fig. 4). This meme succeeded in temporarily evading censors in China on Sina Weibo (the Chinese Twitter) in 2013, on the twenty-fourth anniversary of the massacre at Tian'anmen Square, and thus in commemorating the anniversary online. The yellow rubber duck references a well-known and beloved art installation by Dutch artist Florentijn Hofman, whose *Rubber Duck* was shown at Victoria Harbour in Hong Kong as well as in many other cities. Three weeks before the anniversary of the Tian'anmen Square protests, however, the sculpture deflated, boosting the hashtag #bigyellowduck to a frequently searched-for keyword. The Tank Man meme took advantage of this to sidestep the censors. This mix of art, pop culture, and image policies is a central trait of visual protests on social media.

It is clear it is not easy to say what possibilities and limitations are faced by circulating images because digital visual culture and its fluidity[16] constantly faces new boundaries (the logic of algorithms, image censorship, normification, etc.)—which, however, can be creatively sidestepped.

Es handelt sich im eine Drei-Kanal-Videoarbeit der libanesisch-ägyptischen Künstlerin Lara Baladi, die während der Aufstände in Kairo lebte und selbst bei den Protesten aktiv war (Abb. 5). Bereits der Titel *Alone, Together,… In Media Res* (2012) liest sich wie ein Kommentar auf die digitale Gegenwart, in der die User vereinzelt an ihren Bildschirmen sitzen, und eben doch zusammen sind. Die lateinische Phrase „in medias res" (was so viel heißt wie „mitten in die Dinge hinein", oder „gleich zur Sache kommen") wandelt sie in „in media res" ab und weist damit auf die Bedeutung der Medien für aktuelle Protestkulturen hin. Videos der Proteste in Ägypten collagiert Baladi mit anderen YouTube-Fundstücken wie Ausschnitten von Zeichentrick- und Spielfilmen, Musikvideos, Clips von politischen oder philosophischen Reden und historischen Revolten. Die Aufstände in Ägypten werden so mit anderen sozialen Bewegungen, ihrem Motivkanon und ihren Bildpolitiken in Verbindung gebracht. In dem Video taucht auch der „Egyptian Tank Man" auf (Abb. 6), hier kombiniert mit der Rede von Malcom X „Democracy is Hypocrisy" auf der rechten Seite und weiteren Videos von Straßendemonstrationen auf der linken Seite. Jeder Screen wird aus einem separaten Pool von Videos gespeist, wobei ein Programm die Abfolge variiert, so dass immer neue Kombinationen entstehen. Lara Baladi thematisiert in dieser Arbeit YouTube als eine Kontaktzone von Bildern, die sich über Zeit und Raum hinweg gegenseitig zu affizieren scheinen und verwobene, nicht-lineare Genealogien ausbilden. Die Künstlerin erklärt: „Gerade als das YouTube-Video ‚Tiananmen-Cairo Courage in Cairo' viral wurde, postete ein Freund auf Facebook eine Rede, die Jean-Paul Sartre 40 Jahre zuvor vor einem Publikum streikender französischer Arbeiter gehalten hatte. Als die politischen Spannungen zunahmen, erschienen auf YouTube und anderen Websites immer mehr Bilder und Videos von einem überfüllten Tahrir-Platz. Sie waren ein Echo auf Bildmaterial von anderen Aufständen im Nahen Osten und in Nordafrika, aber auch die Eindrücke und Stimmen einer Vielzahl früherer sozialer Bewegungen. Es war, als ob Sartre mit uns in Tahrir protestierte."[18]

In Baladis Arbeit wird das Social Web als Echokammer von Bildern offenbart, sie beleuchtet die Dynamik und die Relationen zwischen Bildern im Netz, sei es Fiktion oder Dokumentation, in einer historischen Perspektive.

In Werken der Gegenwartskunst, wie denen von Lara Baladi, zeigt sich nicht nur die neue Ästhetik der Bildnetzwerke. Sie leisten auch eine wichtige Medienreflexion und die nachhaltige Archivierung der digitalen Bilder über den Hype des Internets hinaus.

Sie beleuchten die politischen Potentiale der Bildpraktiken in den Sozialen Medien und eröffnen zugleich neue Zirkulations- und Resonanzräume für diese Bilder, wenn der „Egyptian Tank Man" uns etwa in einer Ausstellung begegnet. Die künstlerische Praxis kann in diesem Sinne die Fortführung der Bildproteste mit anderen Mitteln bedeuten.

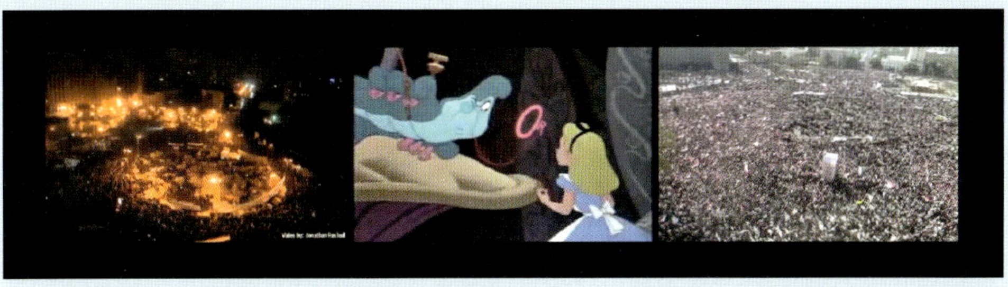

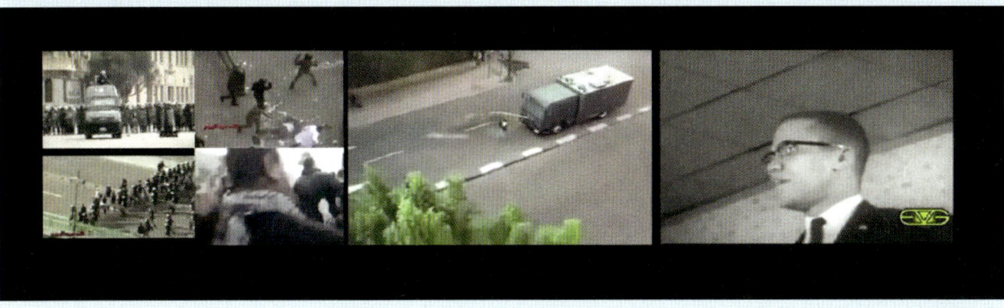

Abb. / **Figs. 5–6**
Lara Baladi
Alone, Together,… In Media Res, 2012, 3-Kanal-Videoinstallationen /
three-channel video installations, 42 Min., Standbilder / **video stills**

Even the videos mentioned at the start with only a few or perhaps even no clicks at all have long been gathered on dedicated pages that present these unseen images as rarities hailed as highly authentic, thus flipping their supposed inaccessibility and lack of virality.[17] To close, I would like to mention an artwork that makes use of the video of the Egyptian Tank Man as found footage. The work is an example of how images from social media carry growing significance in contemporary art, as do the habits of seeing, practices, policies, and trajectories that social media has formed.

The three-channel video piece is by Lebanese-Egyptian artist Lara Baladi, who was living in Cairo at the time of the protests and herself took an active role (fig. 5). The title itself, *Alone, Together,. . . In Media Res* (2012), sounds like a commentary on the digital present where users sit before their monitors, alone yet virtually together. By transforming the Latin phrase *in medias res* (which roughly means "in the middle of things," or "without preamble") into *in media res,* she calls attention to the significance of the media in current protest cultures. Baladi collaged videos of protests in Egypt with other YouTube found footage such as snippets from animated and feature films, music videos, clips from political and philosophic speeches, and historical revolts, thus conflating the uprisings in Egypt with other social movements and their fixed images and uses of pictures. The video also includes footage of the Egyptian Tank Man (fig. 6), combined in the artwork with Malcom X's speech "Democracy is Hypocrisy" on the right and additional videos of street demonstrations on the left. Each screen draws its images from a separate pool of videos, and a program varies the order so that new combinations constantly emerge. In this work, Baladi thematizes YouTube as a contact zone of images that seem to be affecting one another across space and time, weaving together non-linear genealogies. The artist explains: "Just as the YouTube video *Tiananmen-Cairo*

1 Zizi Papacharissi, *Affective Publics: Sentiment, Technology, and Politics,* New York 2015

2 Kerstin Schankweiler, *Bildproteste,* Berlin 2019. In diesem Buch wurden Teile des vorliegenden Beitrags bereits publiziert.

3 https://www.omnicoreagency.com/facebook-statistics/ [Zugriff am 18. September 2020]

4 https://www.statista.com/statistics/259477/hours-of-video-uploaded-to-youtube-every-minute/ [Zugriff am 18. September 2020]. Diese Zahl gibt den Stand von Mai 2019 an.

5 Wolfgang Ullrich, *Selfies,* Berlin 2019, S. 55f.

6 Zit. in O. Al-Ghazzi, "'Citizen Journalism' in the Syrian Uprising: Problematizing Western Narratives in a Local Context", in: *Communication Theory*, 24, 2014, S. 435–454, hier S. 441

7 "Egyptian Tank Man", "Tiananmen-like courage in Cairo: Egypt's 25 Jan protests", "From Tiananmen square to Cairo"

8 Kathrin Klette, „Das ‚einsame Netz' ist der radikalste Teil des Internets", in: *Neue Zürcher Zeitung,* 21. August 2020, https://www.nzz.ch/gesellschaft/das-einsame-netz-wo-das-internet-am-radikalsten-ist-nzz-ld.1567168 [Zugriff am 18. September 2020]

9 Schankweiler 2019 (wie Anm. 2), S. 25–30

10 David Perlmutter, "Hypericons. Famous News Images in the Internet-Digital-Satellite Age", in: Paul Messaris, Lee Humphreys (Hg.), *Digital Media. Transformations in Human Communication,* New York u.a. 2006, S. 51–64, hier S. 54

11 Im Original: "the repeatable singularity of 9/11". Paul Frosh, Amit Pinchevski, "Introduction. Why Media Witnessing? Why Now?", in: Dies. (Hg.): *Media Witnessing: Testimony in the Age of Mass Communication,* Basingstoke u.a. 2009, S. 1–19, hier S. 9

12 Limor Shifman, *Meme. Kunst, Kultur und Politik im digitalen Zeitalter*, Berlin 2014, S. 10; siehe auch Dirk von Gehlen, *Meme,* Berlin 2020

13 Schankweiler 2019 (wie Anm. 2), S. 50–64. Vgl. auch Marina Bulatovic, "The imitation game: The memefication of political discourse", in: *European View*, 18, Issue 2, 2019, S. 250–253. Der Begriff wird zunehmend in öffentlichen Debatten und der Presse verwendet.

14 André Gunthert, *Das geteilte Bild. Essays zur digitalen Fotografie,* Konstanz 2019, S. 105

15 Ebd., S. 109

16 Ebd., S. 13–21

17 http://astronaut.io/, https://petittube.com, https://underviewed.com [Zugriff am 18. September 2020]

18 Im Original: "Just as the YouTube video 'Tiananmen-Cairo Courage in Cairo' went viral, a friend posted on Facebook a speech Jean Paul Sartre had delivered to an audience of striking French autoworkers 40 years earlier. As the political tension grew, more and more images and videos of a packed Tahrir Square appeared on YouTube and other websites. They echoed footage from other uprisings across the Middle East and North Africa, as well as the sights and sounds of a vast array of past social movements. It was as though Sartre was protesting with us in Tahrir." Lara Baladi, "Alone, Together", in: *Guernica. A Magazine of Art & Politics,* 25. Januar 2013, https://www.guernicamag.com/daily/lara-baladi-alone-together/ [Zugriff am 18. September 2020]

Courage in Cairo went viral, a friend posted on Facebook a speech Jean-Paul Sartre had delivered to an audience of striking French autoworkers forty years earlier. As the political tension grew, more and more images and videos of a packed Tahrir Square appeared on YouTube and other websites. They echoed footage from other uprisings across the Middle East and North Africa, as well as the sights and sounds of a vast array of past social movements. It was as though Sartre was protesting with us in Tahrir."[18]

In Baladi's work, social media is revealed as an echo chamber of images. She illuminates the dynamics and relationships between online images, whether fictions or documentations, from a historic perspective.

Contemporary artworks such as Baladi's do not merely reveal the new aesthetics of image networks. Far from mere internet hype, they also reflect crucially on the use of media and the sustainable archiving of digital images. They at once illuminate the political potential of visual practices on social media and open up new spaces for these images to circulate and resonate, for instance when we encounter "Egyptian Tank Man" in an exhibition. In this sense, such art practices can constitute the continuation of protest using other means.

1   Zizi Papacharissi, *Affective Publics: Sentiment, Technology, and Politics* (New York: Oxford University Press, 2015).

2   Kerstin Schankweiler, *Bildproteste* (Berlin: Klaus Wagenbach Verlag, 2019). Parts of the present chapter appeared in that book.

3   "Facebook by the Numbers: Stats, Demographics & Fun Facts," Omnicore Agency, accessed September 18, 2020, https://www.omnicoreagency.com/facebook-statistics/.

4   "Hours of video Uploaded to YouTube Every Minute as of May 2019," Statista, accessed September 18, 2020, https://www.statista.com/statistics/259477/hours-of-video-uploaded -to-youtube-every-minute/. This figure is accurate as of May 2019.

5   Wolfgang Ullrich, *Selfies* (Berlin: Verlag Klaus Wagenbach, 2019), 55–56.

6   Quoted in O. Al-Ghazzi, "'Citizen Journalism' in the Syrian Uprising: Problematizing Western Narratives in a Local Context," *Communication Theory* 24 (2014): 435–54, here 441.

7   "Egyptian Tank Man," "Tiananmen-like courage in Cairo: Egypt's 25 Jan protests," "From Tiananmen square to Cairo."

8   Kathrin Klette, "Das 'einsame Netz' ist der radikalste Teil des Internets," *Neue Zürcher Zeitung,* August 21, 2020, accessed September 18, 2020, https://www.nzz.ch/gesellschaft /das-einsame-netz-wo-das-internet-am-radikalsten-ist-nzz-ld.1567168.

9   Schankweiler 2019 (see note 2), 25–30.

10 David Perlmutter, "Hypericons: Famous News Images in the Internet-Digital-Satellite Age," in Paul Messaris and Lee Humphreys, eds., *Digital Media: Transformations in Human Communication* (New York et al.: Peter Lang Publishing, 2006), 51–64, here 54.

11 The reference is to "the repeatable singularity of 9/11." Paul Frosh and Amit Pinchevski, "Introduction: Why Media Witnessing? Why Now?," in Frosh and Pinchevski, eds., *Media Witnessing: Testimony in the Age of Mass Communication* (Basingstoke et al.: Palgrave Macmillan, 2009), 1–19, here 9.

12 Limor Shifman, *Meme: Kunst, Kultur und Politik im digitalen Zeitalter* (Berlin: Suhrkamp Verlag, 2014), 10; see also Dirk von Gehlen, *Meme* (Berlin: Verlag Klaus Wagenbach, 2020).

13 Schankweiler 2019 (see note 2), 50–64. See also Marina Bulatovic, "The Imitation Game: The Memefication of Political Discourse," *European View* 18, no. 2 (2019): 250–53. The term has recently also been used more frequently in public discourse.

14 André Gunthert, *Das geteilte Bild: Essays zur digitalen Fotografie* (Konstanz: Konstanz University Press, 2019), 105.

15 Gunthert, *Das geteilte Bild*, 109.

16 Gunthert, *Das geteilte Bild*, 13–21.

17 See http://astronaut.io/; "Harangue," PetitTube, https://petittube.com; Underviewed, https://underviewed.com, all accessed September 18, 2020.

18 Lara Baladi, "Alone, Together," *Guernica: A Magazine of Art & Politics,* January 25, 2013, accessed September 18, 2020, https://www.guernicamag.com/daily/lara-baladi-alone -together/.

Text: Matthias Bruhn

POST PICTURES
Visuelle Reichweite

Das Wort *Post* hat einen Doppelsinn, der auf zwei unabhängige lateinische Wurzeln zurückgeht: Die Post als Versanddienst kommt vom Posten und von der Position (lat. *ponere, positum* für stellen, gestellt), sie bezieht sich also begriffsgeschichtlich auf einen Weg anhand seiner Rast- und Zielpunkte; Varianten wie das *Poster* an der Wand gehen auf dieselbe Wurzel zurück. Im Unterschied dazu meint das Präfix oder Adverb *post* ein Dahinter oder Danach, in Entsprechung zum ebenfalls lateinischen *ante* oder griechischen *anti*.

Etymologisch gelesen, könnten *Post Pictures* also zweierlei sein, nämlich Bilder, die auf die Post gegeben werden, und Bilder sekundärer Art, die etwas nachbilden oder in denen etwas nachwirkt. Es könnten z. B. jene Netzhauteffekte sein, die um 1800 als „Nachbilder" die optische Forschung beschäftigt haben, weil sie die Frage aufwarfen, ob sie Abbildungen oder Einbildungen zeigen. Denkbar wären aber auch Bildformen und -konzepte, die sich durch eine historische Nachträglichkeit auszeichnen, wie sie im Begriff des *Postfotografischen* zum Ausdruck kommt.

POST PICTURES
Visual Reach

The word *post* has two meanings that can be traced back to two separate Latin roots: *post* meaning a delivery service is derived from posts and positions (from the Latin verb *ponere*, meaning "to place," and *positum*, "placed"), so in terms of its conceptual history, the term refers to a path based on its rest and end points; variants of this such as a wall *poster* can be traced back to the same root. By contrast, the prefix or adverb *post* indicates "behind" or "beyond," also corresponding to the Latin *ante* or the Greek *anti*.

Seen at from an etymological point of view, *post pictures* could therefore be two things: on the one hand, they could be images sent by post as well as secondary images reproducing or echoing something. They could, for example, be the retinal effect of afterimages, which were studied by optical researchers around 1800, raising as they did the question of whether they were images viewed or mere illusions. But on the other hand, they could also be pictorial forms and concepts marked by their retrospective historical character, as expressed by the concept of *post-photography*.

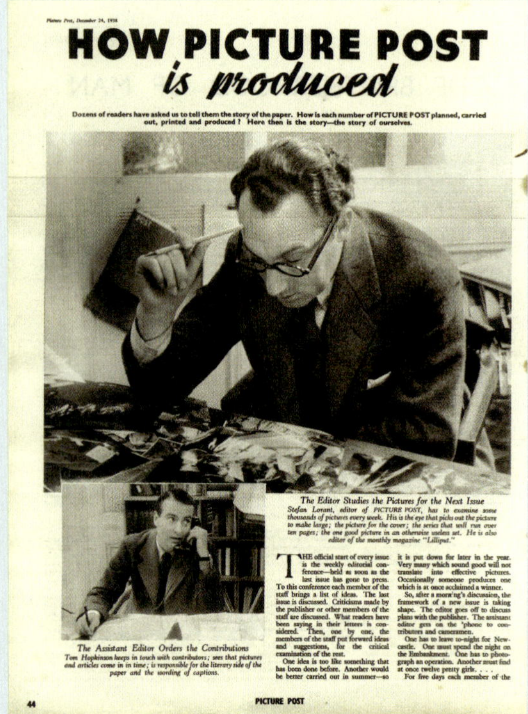

Abb. / **Fig. 1**
Anonym / **Anonymous**
Picture Post
Wie Picture Post produziert wird /
How Picture Post Is Produced,
Bildredakteur Stefan Lorant bei der Arbeit /
Picture Editor Stefan Lorant at Work, 1938,
Magazinseite / **magazine page**

Es gibt durchaus eine Beziehung zwischen beiden Sinndimensionen, und zwar nicht nur, weil auch Postsendungen verspätet eintreffen können.

Denn Bilder erfüllen von alters her eine kommunikative und nachrichtliche Funktion, sei es als nonverbale Zeichensprache oder konkrete Tauschform.

Ihre Trägermedien haben eigene Wege des visuellen Austauschs hervorgebracht, die von Flugblättern und Steckbriefen bis zu den diversen Kanälen elektronischer Übertragung reichen. Im modernen Pressewesen fanden Bild und Nachricht immer wieder zusammen, etwa in der Fotoreportage oder im Telefax, und so wie sich die Presse als Kurier, Herold und Merkur verstand, hat auch das Bild eine eigene Form der Berichterstattung begründet.

Besonders einflussreich war die britische *Picture Post*, initiiert von dem aus Ungarn stammenden Fotografen Stefan Lorant (Abb. 1), der wie viele seiner Landsleute in Berlin tätig war, ehe er in Folge der nationalsozialistischen Machtergreifung in die Emigration gezwungen wurde – zunächst nach Ungarn, dann nach England. Nach mehreren Anläufen gelang Lorant dort 1938 mit der Herausgabe der Zeitschrift *Picture Post* ein Erfolg, der für die Entwicklung des Fotojournalismus wegweisend bleiben sollte. Indem sie anderen Emigrierten ein Auskommen bot, war die *Post* sowohl Sendung als auch Haltung, *Flagpost* und Mission. Noch zum Ende des Zweiten Weltkrieges betrug ihre Wochenauflage fast zwei Millionen Exemplare (Abb. 2), und als das Blatt 1957 mit dem Siegeszug des Fernsehens eingestellt wurde, waren es immer noch deutlich über eine halbe Million, was die Auflage vieler heutiger Magazine übertrifft.

Die *Picture Post* steht aber nicht nur für eine innovative Form der Reportage, sondern auch für die Entwicklung eines globalen Systems der Bildbeschaffung

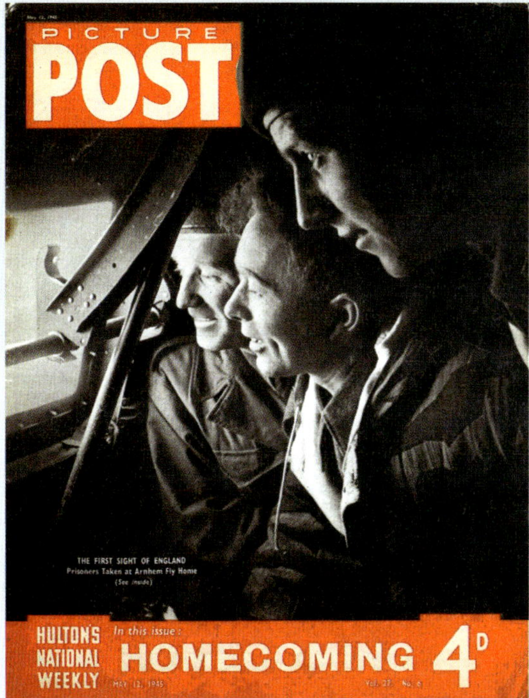

Abb. / **Fig. 2**
Anonym / **Anonymous**
Picture Post
Der erste Blick auf England – in der Schlacht von Arnheim
gefangengenommene britische Soldaten fliegen nach Hause /
The First Sight of England—Prisoners Taken at Arnhem Fly Home,
1945, Magazintitel / **magazine cover**

There is certainly a relationship between these two aspects of meaning, and not only because messages sent by post have a habit of turning up late.

Pictures have always played a role in communicating and informing, whether as a nonverbal pictorial language or a concrete form of exchange.

Media containing pictures has created its own methods of visual exchange, ranging from flyers and "wanted" posters to the various channels of electronic transmission. Image and message have fused again and again in the modern press, for example, in photojournalism and faxes. And, just as the press sees itself as a courier, herald, and messenger, so too has the image established its own form of reportage.

Britain's *Picture Post*, established by Hungarian-born photographer Stefan Lorant (fig. 1), was particularly influential. Like many of his compatriots, Lorant worked in Berlin before being forced to emigrate after the National Socialists seized power—initially to Hungary, then on to England. After several attempts, Lorant achieved success in 1938 with the founding of the *Picture Post* magazine, which was a pioneer in the development of photojournalism. By providing a livelihood for other emigrants, the *Post* was both a message and an attitude, both a flag post and a mission. By the end of World War II, the magazine's weekly circulation had almost reached two million (fig. 2), and when the periodical was discontinued in 1957 as a result of TV's dominance, it was still at well over half a million, exceeding the circulation of many magazines today.

The *Picture Post* not only represents an innovative form of reporting, but also the development of a global system of image making and distribution that

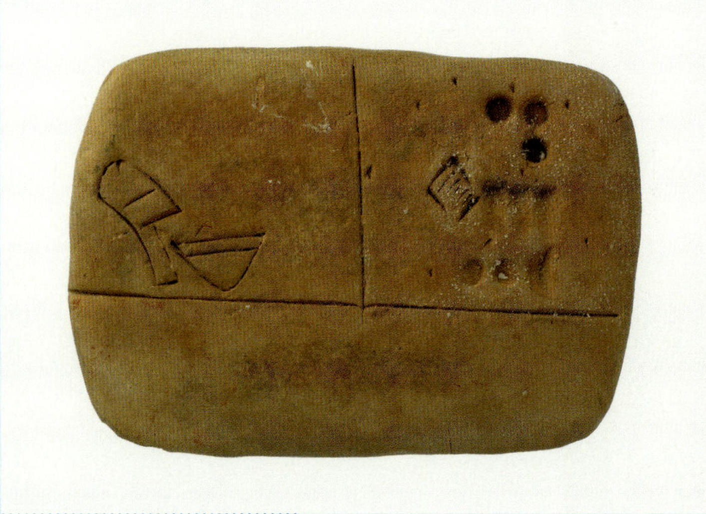

und -verteilung, das im Stile antiker Imperien auf die Zentren aufstrebender Industrienationen ausgerichtet war. Das illustrierte Pressewesen war ein durchweg technisiertes, auf Masse und Geschwindigkeit angelegtes Geschäft, das mit anderen Kommunikationsmitteln verschaltet und auf die laufende, individuelle Einlieferung von Bildmaterial angewiesen war. In dieser Hinsicht nahm es eine Problemlage sozialer Medien vorweg, in denen mächtige Informations- und Bildtechnologien auf das Bedürfnis nach ungehinderter Kommunikation treffen. Es weist aber auch historisch weit zurück:

Schon die Bildformen der Frühgeschichte waren an Prozesse des Austauschs, des Handels und der Warenzirkulation gebunden.

Bild, Schrift und Zahl dienten etwa in den Stadtkulturen des Zweistromlandes als grafische Inhalts- und Echtheitsangabe oder als Vertrag. Tontafeln wurden mit schriftbildlichen Darstellungen versehen, die wie Formulare mithilfe von Linien und Kartuschen zu Sinneinheiten zusammengefasst wurden (Abb. 3). Ihre Qualität lag in der Regelhaftigkeit und Einfachheit, die dazu beitrug, dass sich bestimmte Zeichen und Praktiken – etwa die Bildnisproduktion oder die Praxis der Signatur – über Jahrtausende und auch über Medien hinweg nur wenig geändert haben.

Bilder fungieren seither als eine Art Währung. Aufschlussreich ist in diesem Zusammenhang, dass das Deutsche bei der Begriffsbildung den Aspekt der *Gewährleistung* betont, während die englische *Currency* die Geläufigkeit hervorhebt. Genau genommen beschreibt nur beides zusammen die Wechselwirkung, den Wechselkurs alltäglicher grafischer Praktiken. Denn der Handel erfordert nicht nur Informationen, sondern auch Kurrentschriften und Kurrentbilder, also Formen der Straße, des Verkehrs, der marktmäßigen und politischen Effizienz.

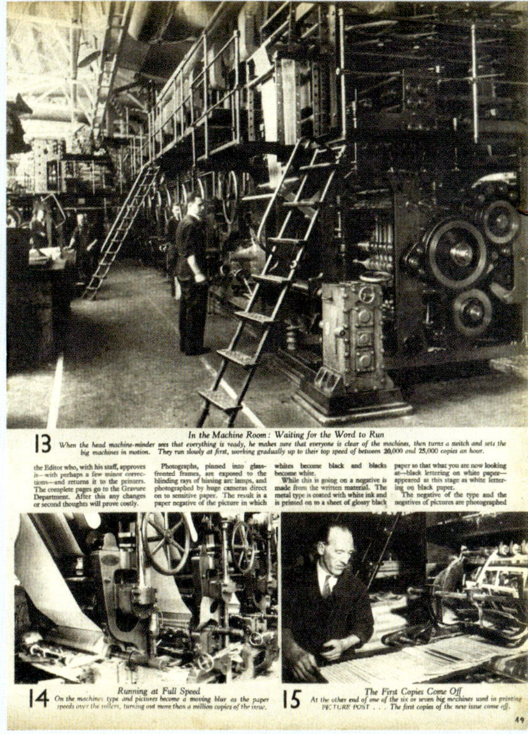

Abb. / **Fig. 4**
Anonym / **Anonymous**
Picture Post
Im Maschinenraum, Fortsetzung der Dokumentation /
In the Machine Room: Waiting for the Word to Run,
1938, Magazinseite / **magazine page**

was oriented, in the style of ancient empires, toward the centers of emerging industrial nations. The illustrated press was an industrialized business in every respect, designed for mass production and speed. It was interconnected with other means of communication and reliant on the constant, individually tailored delivery of image material. In this way, it anticipated the problematic aspects of social media, where powerful information and image technologies collide with a thirst for unimpeded communication.

At the same time, it speaks to a long history: **Even in early history, pictorial depictions played a role in the exchange, trade, and circulation of goods.**

In the urban cultures of Mesopotamia, for example, images, writing, and numbers served as graphic depictions of contents or authenticity, or as a contract. Clay tablets contained pictograms formed using lines and cartridges into units of meaning, much like paperwork (fig. 3). Their benefit lay in their uniformity and simplicity, which is part of the reason that certain symbols and practices—such as the production of portraits or the use of the signature—have hardly changed over millennia and across media.

Since then, images have acted as a kind of currency. In this context, it is illuminating that the German term *Währung* emphasizes the way money acts as a *guarantee*, while the English word *currency* emphasizes fluidity. Strictly speaking, it is only taken in tandem that the two words describe the interaction, the exchange that occurs in everyday graphic practices. After all, trade not only requires information, but also contemporary writing and images, that is, forms of the street and exchange, and of market-based and political efficiency. It is the reproduction of signets and coins with their stereotyped, resilient engraved and stamped patterns that guarantees that recurring patterns are recognized across borders and languages. Even in

Insbesondere im Siegel- und Münzwesen mit seinen stereotypen, stabilen Gravur- und Stempelformen gewährleistet die Vervielfältigung, dass wiederkehrende Muster grenz- und sprachübergreifend anerkannt werden. Schon in der Antike musste sich das Gesicht eines Fürsten dazu dem Schema der Bildgestaltung unterwerfen, um münzhoheitlich anerkannt zu sein; eine Wechselwirkung von Vor- und Nachbild, Druck und Gegendruck, die sich bis in die Bildkommunikation unserer Tage fortgesetzt hat.

Es lag daher nahe, wenn Politik und Wirtschaft um 1900 in Berlin, London und New York selbstbewusste Parallelen zu den antiken Hochkulturen herzustellen versuchten, wie in D. W. Griffith' Monumentalfilm *Intolerance* von 1916, der eine Brücke von Babylon bis in die USA schlägt. Auch die Freilegung und Ausstellung archäologischer Stätten bot Gelegenheiten, um zurück in die Zukunft zu reisen, denn die historischen Praktiken wiesen Ähnlichkeiten zur Turbokommunikation und zum industriellen Imperialismus auf. Der Selbstvergleich spielte nicht nur auf babylonische Sprachverwirrung oder den Turmbau der rasant wachsenden Städte an, sondern auch auf die elektrisierende Vorstellung, mit kulturtechnischen Leistungen wie dem Rad, der Töpferscheibe und dem Rollsiegel gleichziehen zu können. Neben Setzmaschine und Rohrpost waren es erstaunlich oft Zahn- und Au토räder, Reifen und Kugellager, der ‚Rundfunk' und die rotierende Filmspule, welche die Fantasie beflügelten (vgl. Abb. 4). Stimme und Sound konnten auf Walzen und Scheiben aufgezeichnet und reproduziert werden. Zumindest in der Selbstwahrnehmung der Zeit wurde damit das Rad tatsächlich neu erfunden.

DIE WELT AUF KNOPFDRUCK

Zu jener Zeit entstand in den westlichen Kapitalen auch der moderne Bildjournalismus. Nachdem es möglich geworden war, Fotografien mit handlichen Kameras auf Knopfdruck zu erstellen und sie durch Rasterung für den Hochdruck aufzubereiten, konnten Fotos kurz nach 1900 auch im Rotationsverfahren auf billiges Zeitungspapier gepresst und so an ein Millionenpublikum gebracht werden (Abb. 5). Das städtische Großpublikum bekam nun nicht nur Stahlstiche oder wöchentliche Fotobeilagen zu sehen, sondern tagesaktuelle Knüller, womöglich Schnappschüsse, die vom Boulevard kamen und für den Boulevard gedacht waren.

Mit Vereinfachung der Fototechnik wuchs auch der Vorrat an Bildern.

Gegen Ende des 19. Jahrhunderts war der Markt für Studiofotografie bereits gesättigt, nun kam die Bildreportage hinzu. Fotobetriebe wie George Grantham Bain in New York oder das Berliner Büro Zander & Labisch übertrugen in dieser Situation die Logik und Logistik der Telegrafendienste auf die Fotografie, um Redaktionen mit Nachschub zu versorgen und den Bildertausch zu organisieren. Einige dieser Agenturdienste hatten ihrerseits Bedeutung für die Bildkommunikation, wie die US-amerikanische UPI, die 1971 mit dem Unifax II einen markttauglichen Thermodrucker für Faxkopien etablierte.

Da die Negative meist im Archiv verblieben und nur Abzüge zirkulierten, veränderte sich der Charakter der Ware, der von den Illustrationsbetrieben ge-

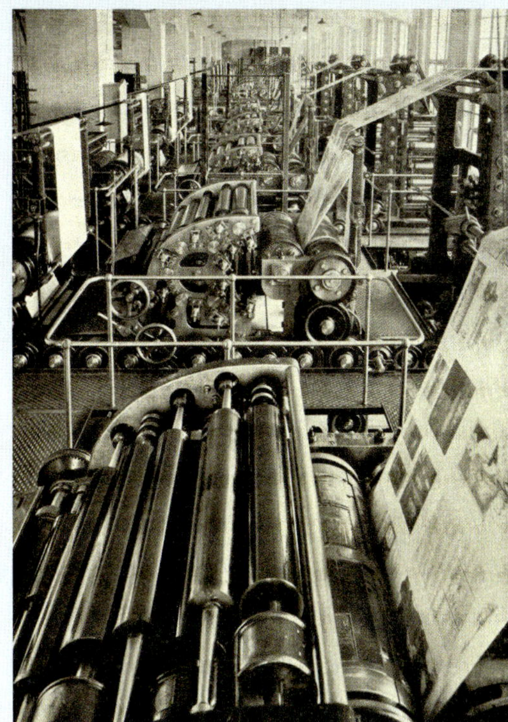

antiquity, the face of a prince had to fit into the schemata of the image design in order for sovereign coins to be recognized; the interaction between model and illustration, pressure and resistance, which still remains part of image communication today.

It was natural for politics and business in Berlin, London, and New York around 1900 to try to create self-conscious parallels to the advanced civilizations, as in D. W. Griffith's monumental 1916 film *Intolerance*, which draws a connection between Babylon and the United States. The excavation and exhibition of archaeological sites and findings also offered opportunities to travel back to the future, as historical practices showed similarities to turbo-communication and industrial imperialism. The self-comparison not only played with the Babylonian confusion of tongues and the building of towers in rapidly growing cities, but also with the electrifying idea of being able to create equally astounding cultural and technical achievements such as the wheel, the potter's wheel, and the cylinder seal. In addition to the typesetting machine and pneumatic tubes, it was surprisingly often gears and car wheels, tires and ball bearings, the radio and the rotating film reel that stoked the imagination (fig. 4). Voice and sound could be recorded and replayed on rollers and discs. In that way, at least in the self-experience of the time, the wheel was actually reinvented.

THE WORLD AT YOUR FINGERTIPS

At this time, modern photojournalism also emerged in Western capital cities. Shortly after 1900, once it became possible to take photographs with handy cameras at the push of a button and to prepare them for printing by a process of rasterization, they could be printed on cheap newsprint by using rollers and brought to an audience of millions (fig. 5). Thus the urban public

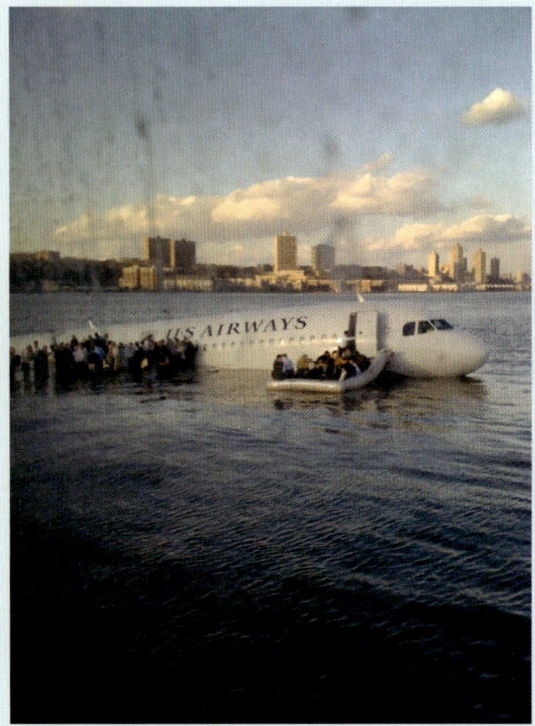

Abb. / **Fig. 6**
Janis Krums
Notlandung des US-Airways-Fluges 1549 im Hudson River /
Emergency landing of US Airways Flight 1549 in the Hudson River,
New York, 15. Januar 2009 / **January 15, 2009,**
Smartphone-Aufnahme / **smartphone picture**

handelt wurde. Fotografie verwandelte sich in eine Lizenz, in eine zeitlich und räumlich begrenzte Genehmigung, ein bestimmtes Motiv für einen bestimmten Zweck oder Zeitraum verwenden zu können. Dies setzte wiederum die Festschreibung, Verwaltung und Nachverfolgung von Urheberrechten voraus. Ebenso wichtig wie die Bildmotive wurden Adresslisten und Kundenstämme. Durch vorausschauende Verschlagwortung konnten ältere oder allgemeingültige Bildmotive wiederverwertet werden.

> Das fotografische Negativ wurde zum Ausgangspunkt einer neuerlichen visuellen Besitzanzeige zwischen geistigem Eigentum und der Goldwährung originaler Aufnahmen.

Aus der Beschleunigung der Prozesse selbst erwuchs dem System allerdings auch eine permanente innere Konkurrenz. Nach Kodaks fertig bestückter Kamera von 1888 markierte vor allem die Einführung der Leica 1924 eine weitere Stufe der technischen Vereinfachung, die man als eine Geschichte von „Knopfdruckmedien" oder „One-button media" bezeichnen könnte, bei der ein Fingerzeig genügt, um ein Ergebnis zu erzielen. Ihre Schnelligkeit und Einfachheit war für Agenturen ein Argument, Arbeitskräfte als namenlose „Operatoren" einzustellen und zu entgelten, weshalb die in diesem Feld tätigen (wie z. B. Stefan Lorant oder Gisèle Freund) umso mehr auf die ästhetische und politische Eigenständigkeit ihrer Arbeit pochen mussten. Die Gründung des Fotograf*innen-Verbundes *Magnum Photos* war Folge dieses Anspruchs.

Für die frühen Bilderdienste zählte außerdem weniger die Qualität oder Autorschaft ihres Materials als ihre Aktualität und Rarität. Die Kundschaft ver-

not only got to see steel engravings and weekly photo supplements, but also daily scoops including candid shots that were both taken on the streets and intended for them.

With the simplification of photo technology, the cache of images also grew.

Toward the end of the nineteenth century, when the market for studio photography was already saturated, photojournalism emerged. Photography agencies such as George Grantham Bain in New York and the Berlin office Zander & Labisch transferred the logic and logistics of telegraph services to photography, supplying editors with a stock of images and organizing the exchange of images. Some of these news services also played important roles in image communication, such as United Press International (UPI), which established a mass-marketable thermal printer for fax printouts in 1971 with the Unifax II.

Since the negatives mostly remained in archives and only prints circulated, the character of the product being exchanged by illustration firms changed. Photography became a licensed good with limited permission to use a given image for a certain purpose and period. This, in turn, required the establishment, management, and tracking of copyright permissions. Address lists and client bases became just as important as images. Through forward-looking keywording, older or timeless images could be reused.

The photo negative became the starting point for a new visual display of ownership existing between intellectual property and the golden standard of the original photograph.

Yet a constant internal competition arose from the acceleration of the very processes. After the release of Kodak's preassembled camera in 1888, the introduction of the Leica in 1924 marked a further level of technical simplification, which could be described as the story of push-button or one-button technology, where raising a finger is enough to achieve a result. Such cameras' speed and simplicity made the case for agencies to hire and pay workers to be nameless "operators." As a result, those working in the field (Stefan Lorant and Gisèle Freund, for instance) had to fight all the harder for the aesthetic and political sovereignty of their work. The founding of the Magnum Photos association of photographers grew out of this demand.

The quality and authorship of photographic material was less important for early photography services than the images' topicality and rarity. This is what customers demanded and the conflict persisted. No photography agency was present when Latvian entrepreneur Janis Krums saw a US Airways plane floating in the Hudson River from a ferry in New York in January 2009, and shared his picture on Twitter, so editors immediately resorted to using his photo (fig. 6). Agencies lament such circumventions of their sourcing and quality assurances, but the citizen journalism of social media has actually

langte es so, und der Konflikt blieb bestehen. Als der lettische Unternehmer Janis Krums im Januar 2009 in New York von einer Fähre aus eine Maschine der US Airways im Hudson River treiben sah und seine Aufnahme via Twitter verteilte, war keine Fotoagentur zur Stelle, weshalb Redaktionen umgehend auf sein Foto zurückgriffen (Abb. 6). Agenturen bedauern solche Umgehungen ihrer Quellen- und Qualitätssicherung, doch hat der *Citizen Journalism* der sozialen Medien eigentlich nur da angeknüpft, wo das Agenturwesen einst begann. Bereits damals wurde beklagt, dass die neue fotografische Produktivität geradewegs in die gesellschaftliche Verdummung führen müsse.

DIGITALE ERINNERUNG

Das *Selfie* verleitet den Kulturpessimisten zu einer vergleichbaren Melancholie. Aus welchem Narzissmus, so fragt er sich, rührt der Impuls, sich im Badezimmer mit Fischmund zu fotografieren? Welchen Gewinn verspricht es, den Internet-Leviathan mit Selbst-Duplikaten zu füttern, einem imaginären Über-Ich beizutreten und sein Leben als Avatar, *digital twin* oder intermediales Schema zu führen? Finden Jahrtausende der technischen Evolution, verbunden mit der Stromleistung von Atomkraftwerken, ihre Erfüllung darin, in der U-Bahn *Candy Crush* spielen zu können?

Bemerkenswert bleibt, dass ausgerechnet das Selfie eine so große Produktivität freigesetzt hat, dass sie eine Stilepoche am Übergang vom *Global Village* Marshall McLuhans zum *Global Bedroom* der Videokonferenzen prägen könnte. Im Unterschied zum Zeitalter des Live-TV und zu McLuhans futuristischer Begeisterung für die visuelle Instant-Zukunft ist das Selfie im Badezimmer ein „Post"-Bild im mehrfachen Sinne: Es ist postmodern im Gestus, es wird in der Öffentlichkeit des *www* zeitversetzt wahrgenommen, es ist Nach- und Abbild mit formalen Codes. Es fließt in einen fast autopoetischen Kommunikationsstrom ein und verbindet sich mit diesem. Aufnahmen werden im doppelten Sinne ‚geschöpft', als eine liquide Formgebung.

> Mit dem digitalen Knopfdruck kehren Bilder außerdem zur Alltagspraxis von Bild, Schrift und Zahl zurück, der Klick ist eine neue Keilschrift. Eine Telefonnummer wird abfotografiert, um sie nicht aufschreiben zu müssen. Sonnenuntergänge und Denkmäler müssen nicht unbedingt qualitätvoll sein, um zu imponieren oder touristische Planerfüllung zu vermelden. Mit jeder Aufnahme werden neue Erwartungen erzeugt.

Weil günstige Technik und Speicherkarten es ermöglichen, wird dabei mehr aufbewahrt, als jemals angeschaut werden kann. Da es nicht das Ziel ist, Archive anzulegen, nimmt die visuelle Entropie zu, aber erst beim nächsten Medienwechsel oder technischen Defekt wird dieser offene Strom zum Problem.

Mit zunehmender Erfahrung und zeitlichem Abstand setzt andererseits bei den Teilnehmenden ein Prozess ein, der noch einmal an die Sortiervorgänge der Bilderdienste um 1900 erinnert. Denn mit wachsenden Beständen geht die Möglichkeit des Selbstabgleichs mit Kopien der eigenen Person, der eigenen Umwelt und ihrer Wahrnehmung einher. Es entwickelt sich womöglich das Bedürfnis nach Kontrolle dieses *Image*, das seine eigene Lebensdauer hat. Aus dem Selfiestar kann die Schauspielerin oder der Ich-Agent werden, der aus Klickzah-

merely picked up where the agency system once began. At that time, people already complained that the productivity of new photography would lead straight to social dumbing down.

DIGITAL MEMORY

The selfie induces a comparable melancholy in cultural pessimists. What narcissism, they wonder, gives rise to the impulse to take a photo of yourself in the bathroom posing with a duck face? Who gains from feeding the Internet Leviathan with duplicates of oneself, assuming an imaginary super-ego and leading one's life as an avatar, digital twin, or intermedial scheme? Do millennia of technical evolution, combined with the power output of nuclear power plants, reach their acme in the ability to play Candy Crush on the subway?

What remains noteworthy is that the selfie, of all photographic forms, has unleashed such a rampant productivity that it could define the era, interleaved as it is between Marshall McLuhan's global village and today's videoconferenced global bedroom. In contrast to the era of live television and McLuhan's futuristic enthusiasm for the visual instant-future, the selfie taken in the bathroom is a post: an image in a number of ways. This postmodern gesture is apprehended after a time lag in the online agora, a model and illustration that follows formal strictures, that flows and melds into an almost autopoietic stream of communication. Photographs are "made" in two senses, just as liquid is given a form.

At the press of a digital button, images return to the everyday use of image, letter, and numeral; a click is our cuneiform. We photograph telephone numbers so we don't have to bother writing them down. Sunsets and monuments need not possess special qualities to impress or convey that our travel plans have been fulfilled. Every photograph awakens a new set of expectations.

More photographs are saved than can ever be reviewed thanks to cheap equipment and memory cards. With the goal no longer being to establish an archive, a visual sense of entropy mounts, but only when we switch media or experience technological difficulties does this coursing stream present itself as a problem. On the other hand, those participating find themselves embarking on a process not dissimilar to the sorting processes used by photo services circa 1900 as they gained experience and temporal distance. For with increasing stores of photographs, the possibility increases to compare one's self with copies of the same, one's environment with the way that environment has been perceived. A desire might well develop to control this image, which has its own lifespan. The selfie star can morph into an actor or become their own agent, earning cash with every click. Like photographic avant-gardes, Fluxus artists, and net artists, selfies and GIFs reflect exchange processes. People pose before a camera as if in front of a shopwindow, trying out a scowl, and as we well know from photo booths, when you've got four takes, you can use one as a commentary. In any case, most users must realize by now that their data is not truly sent, but rather publicized or shared. Copies of the digital delivery are usually retained much as ancient seal stamps or negatives in photo archives.

len Geld generiert. Nicht nur fotografische Avantgarden, Fluxus und Netzkunst begleiten und thematisieren also die mediale Entwicklung, auch Selfie- und Giphy-Stile sind Spiegelbilder des Aushandlungsprozesses. Menschen posieren vor der Kamera wie vor einem Schaufenster und grimassieren auf Probe, und wie schon im Fotoautomaten gilt: Wer vier Aufnahmen frei hat, darf eine als Kommentar nutzen. Mehr oder weniger dürfte außerdem den meisten *Usern* bewusst sein, dass ihre Daten nicht wirklich verschickt, sondern strenggenommen publiziert oder geteilt werden. Kopien der digitalen Lieferung werden in der Regel einbehalten wie der antike Siegelstempel oder das Negativ im Fotoarchiv.

Dieses unscheinbare technische Detail soll nicht nur andeuten, dass viele digitale Prozesse keine moderne Erfindung sind, sondern umgekehrt auch unterstreichen, dass es sehr wohl medienhistorische Sprünge gibt, die nicht ohne Folgen für die Wahrnehmung bleiben, darunter die Verfügbarmachung des Bildlichen durch fotografische und digitale Reproduktion. Ein Maler wie der Franzose Nicolas Poussin, der Mitte des 17. Jahrhunderts eine Gemäldeserie zum Thema *Die Sieben Sakramente* ein zweites Mal anfertigen sollte, musste sich im vorfotografischen Zeitalter noch mit anderen Mitteln behelfen.

Da Poussin in Rom lebte, trieb seinen französischen Auftraggeber die Sorge und Ungeduld um, dass der kränkelnde Maler sein Werk in der pestilenten Stadt nicht zu Ende bringen werde. Aufgerollt in einer Trommel ging daher eine Leinwand nach der anderen mit dem Kurier via Ostia und Marseille nach Paris, während die Farbe trocknete. Eine entscheidende Folge war, dass der Maler seine zweite Version nie komplett gesehen hat. Poussin konnte ihre Gesamtwirkung nicht abschätzen, sondern musste mit jeder Tafel neu ansetzen. Informationen wie der Farbaufbau wurden nicht in Skizzen festgehalten, sondern blieben in den Pigmenten und auf der Palette gespeichert. Erst vor diesem Hintergrund wird auch deutlich, welche praktische Bedeutung eine auf Jahre angelegte, konzeptionelle Arbeit für einen Maler des 17. Jahrhunderts haben konnte.

SOZIALE INDEXIKALITÄT, ODER: NACH DEM BILD IST VOR DEM BILD

Der Knopfdruck verstärkt dagegen die filternde Bedeutung von groben Klassifikatoren wie Format, Genre und Stil. Je mehr Aufnahmen es gibt, desto deutlicher werden sie zu Sichtbarkeitsregeln einer Zeit. Sie sind *Content* nach vorgespurten Kriterien und zeigen Motive, die sich schnell als *Gesichter, Körper, Dinge* und *Sites* mit entsprechender Binnenvariation erfassen lassen. Mathematisch gesehen eine Normalverteilung, betrieblich gesehen nicht mehr als ein Sortierungsproblem. Sie sind Container für Metadaten, Beziehungs- und Bewegungsmuster, sie sind Gegenstand und Ergebnis von Analyseverfahren und Algorithmen. Vor dem Hintergrund der Debatten um Macht und Missbrauch globaler Netzwerke scheint immer gleichgültiger, was Bilddateien eigentlich enthalten, ganz zu schweigen von gestalterischen und künstlerischen Ansprüchen, sie stehen eher für das Bedürfnis, die Hoheit über das Bild und seine Produktion und Zirkulation, die Münzhoheit im Digitalen, zurückzuerlangen.

Der Begriff des *Content* deutet aber auf ein Problem hin, das auch die bildwissenschaftliche Diskussion der letzten Jahrzehnte durchzogen hat. In dieser Diskussion war „das Bild" ebenfalls ein Containerbegriff für teilweise völlig ver-

This seemingly minor technical detail should not only suggest that many digital processes are far from modern inventions, but rather in turn serve to underscore that there are definite advances in media history that are not without consequence for human perception, such as the way photographic and digital reproductions make the pictorial available. A painter in the mid-seventeenth century such as Frenchman Nicolas Poussin, who was tasked with duplicating his *Seven Sacraments* painting series, had to turn to other means in an era predating photography.

His French clients were anxious and impatient as to whether Poussin, living as an ailing painter, would be able to complete his work in the plague-ridden city of Rome. Thus one canvas after the next traveled by courier via Ostia and Marseilles to Paris, rolled up in a barrel as the paint dried. A significant consequence was that the painter never saw his second version as a complete set. Poussin was unable to evaluate its effect taken in toto, but rather had to begin anew with every new panel. Information such as the use of color was not recorded in sketches, and instead remained "saved" in his paints and on his palette. Only viewed against this background can one grasp what practical significance a years-long conceptual undertaking could have on a seventeenth-century painter.

SOCIAL INDEXICALITY, OR POST-PHOTO IS PRE-PHOTO

In contrast, the press of a button heightens the significance of broad means of classification such as size, genre, and style as filters. The more photographs there are, the more clearly they determine the rules by which visibility is achieved in an era. They are content made according to predetermined criteria and show subjects that can be easily apprehended as faces, bodies, things, and sites with appropriate internal variations. Viewed mathematically, this is a normal distribution, and seen from a business point of view, it is nothing more than a problem of sorting. They are containers for metadata, relationships, and movements; they are the object and result of analytic processes and algorithms. Against the backdrop of debates over power and the misuse of global networks, what the image data actually contains seems less and less relevant, never mind the images' artistic and design demands; instead, they are more significant as representations of the need to reassert control over the image, its production, and its circulation as the digital equivalent of the coin's sovereignty.

Yet the term *content* touches on a problem that has made itself felt over the past decades in the field of visual studies. In this discussion, too, "the image" was a container term for sometimes entirely different levels, points of view, and interests. Instead of differentiating between medium and process, painting and photograph, or monitor and image signal, an über-term was sought that would encompass many of these possible nuances. The resulting visual theory was one that sidestepped technological and economic dimensions and avoided such categories as dissemination, address, effect, and reception, even though the "iconic"—a central term in this discussion—must come into play with regard to serial printed images and images on coins.

In an argument based on media technology, visual studies have all the more vehemently countered that essential processes in image production take

schiedene Ebenen, Blickwinkel und Interessen. Anstelle zwischen Medium und Verfahren, Gemälde und Fotografie oder Bildschirm und Bildsignal zu differenzieren, wurde ein Superbegriff gesucht, der viele dieser möglichen Unterscheidungen ausschlug. Das Ergebnis war eher eine Bildertheologie, die mit technisch-ökonomischen Dimensionen wenig zu tun und Kategorien wie Verbreitung und Adressierung, Wirkung und Rezeption vermieden hat, obwohl das „Ikonische" – ein Schlüsselbegriff dieser Diskussion – am ehesten in seriellen Münz- und Druckbildern zutage treten müsste.

Eine medientechnisch argumentierende Bildwissenschaft hat umso vehementer dagegengehalten, dass wesentliche Prozesse der Bildproduktion auf der unsichtbaren elektronischen Ebene der Datenverarbeitung und der Infrastrukturen verlaufen, während Visualität nur an einigen Schnittstellen aufleuchte. Aus dieser Perspektive war die Konjunktur des Bildbegriffs in den 1990er-Jahren eher eine Abwehrreaktion als eine Antwort auf die sogenannten neuen Medien.

> Die Wahrheit liegt vermutlich in der breiten Grauzone dazwischen: Technische Mittel haben zweifellos entscheidenden Anteil am Erfolg bestimmter Bildmuster, sie sind die materielle Bedingung dafür, aber sie sind vor allem Verstärker einer *Visuality*, die nach gesellschaftlichen Regeln abgefüllt und dargereicht wird. Aus schön wurde fotogen, aus fotogen wurde *instagrammable*.

Diese Regeln haben sich über lange Zeiträume entwickelt, genau wie die Bereitschaft zur kosmetischen Ausrichtung des eigenen Lebens auf ein vorgegebenes Image hin. Sie strukturieren die Ressorts der illustrierten Presse und weite Teile des katalogisierten Alltags, sie führen zur medialen Selbstähnlichkeit und Selbstzensur.

Die kollektiven Aufnahme- und Auswahlmechanismen dahinter könnten als ‚soziale Indexikalität' bezeichnet werden, als Spur eines Daseins im Licht der Gesellschaft. Sie ist in ihren historischen Grundzügen schon in Gisèle Freunds Dissertation von 1935 beschrieben, in der die junge Fotografin den Bogen vom Schattenriss und Scherenschnitt zur fotografischen *Carte de visite* geschlagen hat, um die Dialektik von technischer und ästhetischer Entwicklung, industrieller und individueller Produktion soziologisch nachzuzeichnen.

In den anschließenden Jahrzehnten florierte die populäre Fotografie, dabei wurden vermeintlich unscharfe Aufnahmen im Fotolabor von den Entwicklermaschinen vollautomatisch aussortiert, später folgten Photoshop und digitale Lächelautomatik (also der Mechanismus, bei dem die Kamera automatisch auslöst, sobald eine Person lächelt). In Mustererkennung und KI-Training werden Aufnahmen nach Helligkeitsverteilungen und Bewegungsmustern durchsucht, also nach Kategorien, die der formalen Ästhetik und der frühen Gestaltforschung entnommen sein könnten. Grafikprozessoren und neuronale Netze wiederholen teilweise eine Frühphase der Kunstwissenschaft – mit dem Effekt, dass dann noch eine Reihe anderer „Trainingsprogramme" zu durchlaufen wäre, von der

place on the invisible electronic level of data processing and infrastructures, while visuality only makes itself apparent through certain interfaces. Viewed from this perspective, the boom in the concept of the image in the 1990s was more a defensive reaction than a response to "new media."

Most likely, the truth lies in the vast gray area between the two. Technical means have doubtless played a decisive role in the success of certain patterns of image. They are their material precondition. But most of all, they amplify a visuality that is packaged and presented according to societal rules. Beautiful became photogenic, and photogenic became *Instagrammable*.

These rules have developed over long periods of time, as has cosmetic adjustment of one's own life toward a given image. They determine the departments of glossy magazines and newspapers, and broad swathes of catalogued everyday life, leading to medial self-similarity and self-censorship.

The collective reception and selection mechanisms behind this could be described as "social indexicality," as a trace of existence seen under society's light. Gisèle Freund described its elementary historic characteristics back in her 1935 dissertation, when the young photographer managed to connect silhouettes and photographed *cartes de visite* in order to adumbrate the dialectic of technical and aesthetic development, industrial and individual production, from a sociological point of view.

Popular photography flourished in subsequent decades, with shots deemed out-of-focus in the photo lab discarded by the developing machines in a fully automated process. Photoshop followed, and digital smile detection (that is, the mechanism that triggers a camera to take a picture when a person smiles). Photographs are scanned for brightness distributions and movement patterns, in other words, for categories that could be taken from formal aesthetics and early design research as a part of pattern recognition and AI training. Graphic processors and neural networks partially replicate an early phase of art studies with the effect that a number of other "training programs" would then have to be run, from iconology and cultural studies to the Frankfurt School and reception aesthetics. Although knowledge of digital processes is fundamental to understanding why photographed objects look different depending on the make and model of camera and sensor, the data they generate also has a pictorial-historical basis and requires specific vocabularies. This is evident not least in human-led content moderation of social media and in the training of machines that reproduce social prejudices or tastes in visual matter.

With an eye to the beginnings of photography and photojournalism, it is hardly surprising that in an age of unbridled capitalism across social media, people "prosume" images of all kinds,

Ikonologie und Kulturwissenschaft bis zu Frankfurter Schule und Rezeptionsästhetik. Die Kenntnis der digitalen Verfahren ist zwar grundlegend, um zu verstehen, warum fotografierte Gegenstände je nach Kamera- und Sensorfabrikat unterschiedlich aussehen; aber auch die mit ihnen erzeugten Daten haben bildhistorische Grundlagen und erfordern spezifische Vokabulare. Dies zeigt sich nicht zuletzt in der von Menschen ausgeführten *Content-Moderation* sozialer Medien oder beim Training von Maschinen, das mit dem Bildmaterial auch gesellschaftliche Vorurteile oder Geschmäcker reproduziert.

Mit Blick auf die Anfänge der Fotografie oder der Fotoreportage ist es wenig überraschend, dass die Menschen im Zeitalter des ungebremsten Plattform-Kapitalismus Bilder aller Art „prosumieren",

die wiederum von Marodeuren aller Art als Ressource ausgebeutet werden. Interessant dürfte es aber werden, wenn im Gegenzug *jpeg*-Artefakte und andere *Glitches* maschinellen Ursprungs imitiert werden, um sich mithilfe von Schminke und Botox in künstlich erzeugte Gesichter zu verwandeln. Das ist dann definitiv nicht nur ein Fall für die Soziologie oder Psychologie, sondern auch für eine kunstwissenschaftliche Bildtheorie.

which are in turn exploited as a resource by marauders of all persuasions. However, things might become interesting if people begin to imitate jpeg artifacts and other machine-made glitches, making artificially created faces using make-up and Botox. This, then, would most certainly be a case not only for sociologists and psychologists, but also for an art-historical theory of images.

WERKLISTE / **LIST OF WORKS**

ERIK KESSELS
* 1966 in Roermond (NL), lebt / **lives** in Amsterdam (NL)
Erik Kessels setzt sich in seinen Arbeiten mit Fragen um Materialitäten von kollektivem Amateur-Bildmaterial – ob aus privaten Fotoalben des 20. Jahrhunderts, Flohmarktfunden oder anderen kollektiven Bildquellen – auseinander. In *24HRS in Photos* macht er die an einem Tag von Usern auf der Internetplattform flickr hochgeladene Zahl (ca. 350.000 Bilder) an visuellem Bildmaterial transparent und überführt dieses als Installation physisch in einen dreidimensionalen (Ausstellungs-) Raum.

Erik Kessels considers issues of materiality in his work using amateur image material found in personal photo albums of the twentieth century, discoveries made at flea markets, and other sources of collective images. In *24HRS in Photos* he makes tangible how much visual imagery is uploaded every day on the internet platform flickr (around 350,000 images) by physically presenting the images in a three-dimensional installation.

> *24HRS in Photos*, 2004/2013/2021
> Installation aus ca. 350.000 Fotografien /
> **Installation with ca. 350,000 photographs**
> Installationsansicht / **Installation view**
> Erik Kessels, Pier24 San Francisco
> © Erik Kessels
> Seiten / **Pages** 4–5, 76–77

> *24HRS in Photos*, 2004/2011/2021
> Installation aus ca. 350.000 Fotografien /
> **Installation with ca. 350,000 photographs**
> Installationsansicht / **Installation view**
> Erik Kessels, Foam Amsterdam
> © Erik Kessels
> Seiten / **Pages** 78–79

> Diverse Fotograf*innen / **Various photographers**
> Ohne Titel 1870er–1920er-Jahre / **Untitled 1870s–1920s**
> Abzüge in diversen fotografischen Verfahren /
> **Prints in various photographic processes,**
> Cartes de Visite, Sammlung / **Collection** Friedrich Tietjen,
> Wien / **Vienna** & Leipzig
> Seiten / **Pages** 82–83

MIKE MANDEL
* 1950 in Los Angeles (USA), lebt / **lives** in Watertown (USA)
Mit Werbe-, Nachrichten- und Archivbildern hinterfragt Mike Mandel die Bedeutung der Fotografie in der Populärkultur. Die Arbeit stammt aus einer Zeit, in der Fotografie vermittelt über die Konzeptkunst in den Kunstmarkt einzog. Sie kombiniert ein Set handelsüblicher Sammelkarten bekannter Baseballspieler mit vom Künstler angefertigten Bildern, die bekannte Fotograf*innen im Sportoutfit inszenieren. Wie beim Tauschmedium sind charakterisierende Eigenschaften wie Größe, Gewicht und Lieblingskamera vermerkt.

Using images culled from advertisements, news, and archives, Mike Mandel challenges the meaning of photography in pop culture. This piece is from a period in which photography entered the art market by way of Conceptual Art. The artist combined a set of ordinary baseball cards showing famous players with his own pictures of famous photographers in sport clothing. Similar to the trading cards, his cards also list characteristics including height, weight, and favorite camera.

> *Topps Baseball Cards,* 1958 und / **and** *The Baseball-Photographer Trading Cards,* 1975
> 3 Sets, je 135 Tauschkarten / **3 sets, each with 135 trading cards**
> 1 Set originale Tauschkarten von 1958 / **1 set of original trading cards from 1958**
> Sammlung / **Collection** Fotomuseum Winterthur
> © Mike Mandel
> Seiten / **Pages** 84–87

Auguste Lumière
Marguerite & Jeanne Pitrat, Lyon, 1880–1890
14 Cartes de Visite in 2 Schachteln / **boxes**
Sammlung / **Collection** Bernd Stiegler, Konstanz
Seiten / **Pages** 88–89

Diverse Fotograf*innen / **Various photographers**
Ohne Titel 1890er-Jahre / **Untitled 1890s**
Album von / **by** Eduard Kade, Berlin, Cartes de Visite
Sammlung / **Collection** Friedrich Tietjen, Wien / **Vienna** & Leipzig
Seiten / **Pages** 90–91

Diverse Fotograf*innen / **Various photographers**
Meine Freunde / **My Friends,** ca. 1870
Leporello / **Folding concertina album,** Cartes de Visite
Sammlung / **Collection** Friedrich Tietjen, Wien / **Vienna** & Leipzig
Seiten / **Pages** 92–93

Anonym / **Anonymous**
An Mama / **To Mama,** 1869
Brief mit montierter / **Letter with mounted** Carte de Visite
Foto / **Photo** Mathew B. Brady, New York
Sammlung / **Collection** Friedrich Tietjen, Wien / **Vienna** & Leipzig
Seiten / **Pages** 94–95

GILBERT & GEORGE
Gilbert * 1943 in San Martin de Tor (IT), lebt / **lives** in London (GB)
George * 1942 in Plymouth (GB), lebt / **lives** in London (GB)

A Message from the Sculptors, 1969 (datiert / **dated 1970**)
Lebendige Skulptur / **Living sculpture**
6 Silbergelatineausbelichtungen, 3 Briefbögen und Umschlag /
6 gelatin silver prints, 3 letterheads, and envelope
Museum MMK für Moderne Kunst, Frankfurt am Main
© Gilbert & George, **Courtesy** Archiv Jean-Christophe Ammann
Seiten / **Pages** 96–99

A.H. & Co.
Londoner Stadtansichten / **London cityscapes,** 1870
5 Briefbögen, je mit 2 montierten Fotografien /
5 letterheads, each with 2 mounted photographs
Sammlung / **Collection** Bernd Stiegler, Konstanz
Seiten / **Pages** 100–101

MOYRA DAVEY
* 1958 in Toronto (CAN), lebt / **lives** in New York City (USA)
In ihren Fotografien, Videos und Texten kreist Moyra Davey stets um die Objekte, Zufälle und Störungen des täglichen Lebens. Für ihre *Mailer*-Serie nahm sie Fotografien auf, faltete sie, verklebte
sie mit Tape, versah sie mit Briefmarken und Adressen, und versendete sie über die Post. Wie überdimensionierte Postkarten kommunizieren diese Fotobriefe nicht über Schrift, sondern über das
Bild. Während die Absenderin stets dieselbe blieb, änderten sich Sujets und Empfänger*innen im
Fortgang der Serie.

**Moyra Davey's photographs, videos, and texts revolve around the objects, coincidences, and
disturbances of everyday life. For her *Mailer* series she folded photographs, sealed them with
tape, added addresses and stamps, and sent them by mail. Like oversized postcards, these photo letters communicate through images instead of through writing. While the sender always
remained the same, the subjects and addressees changed over the course of the series.**

Bad Kids, 2014
8 C-Prints, Klebeband, Briefmarken, Tinte /
8 C-prints, tape, postage stamps, ink
Courtesy of the artist and Galerie Buchholz,
Berlin, Köln / **Cologne,** New York
Seiten / **Pages** 102–105

PETER MILLER
* 1978 in Burlington (USA), lebt / **lives** in Essen (DE) und / **and** Paris (FR)
Peter Miller erforscht Geschichte, Magie und Konstitution der analogen Medien. Seine für C/O Berlin entwickelte Arbeit ist ein romantischer Brief an die Fotografie, den er im Dunkeln auf Fotopapier getippt, zu einem Briefumschlag gefaltet und in die Post gegeben hat. Auf dem Weg zum Ausstellungsort belichtete sich das Papier, wobei sich die Spuren der Reise als abstraktes Bild präsentieren. Auch der öffentliche Briefkasten und die Transportkisten der Postunternehmen können Dunkelkammern sein.

Peter Miller investigates history, magic, and the constitution of analog media. For C/O Berlin he wrote a love letter to photography, which he typed in the dark on photo paper, folded into an envelope, and then mailed. In transit to the exhibition venue, the paper was exposed, resulting in an abstract image that shows the traces of traveling, proving that even public mailboxes and post-office crates can serve as darkrooms.

Envelope, 2020
Installation aus Lumen Prints / **Installation of lumen prints**
Courtesy of the artist and Galerie Crone, Berlin & Wien / **Vienna**
© Peter Miller, VG Bild-Kunst, Bonn 2020
Seiten / **Pages** 107–108, 110–111

Horns Bild-Postkarten
Briefmarken-Sprache / **The Language of Stamps,** ca. 1920
Postkarte / **Postcard**
Sammlung / **Collection** Bernd Stiegler, Konstanz
Seiten / **Pages** 114–115

W. Walz, Optische Werkstätten
Photographische Apparate und Zubehör,
No. III, St. Gallen 1913, S. / **pp.** 142f.,
Katalog mit gebundener Preisliste, Doppelseite /
Catalogue with bound price list, double-page spread
Sammlung / **Collection** Friedrich Tietjen, Wien / **Vienna** & Leipzig
Seite / **Page** 116

Leopold Loebenstein
Fabrik und Lager sämtlicher photographischer Artikel,
Wien / **Vienna** VIII/2, 1905, S. / **pp.** 80f.
Katalog mit gebundener Preisliste, Doppelseite /
Catalogue with bound price list, double-page spread
Sammlung / **Collection** Friedrich Tietjen, Wien / **Vienna** & Leipzig
Seite / **Page** 117

Atelier C. Holzer, München / **Munich**
Album für Fotografien in Briefmarkenformat /
Album for photographs in stamp format, ca. 1900
Broschüre mit montierten Fotobriefmarken /
Brochure with mounted photo stamps
Sammlung / **Collection** Friedrich Tietjen, Wien / **Vienna** & Leipzig
Seiten / **Pages** 118–119

LYNN HERSHMAN LEESON
* 1941 in Cleveland (USA), lebt / **lives** in San Francisco (USA)
Als wichtige Protagonistin der Medienkunst hat die US-amerikanische Multimediakünstlerin Lynn
Hershman Leeson ihr Werk in die Zeit Before Computers (B. C.) und After Digital (A.D.) unterteilt.
Die Arbeit *Face Stamps* stammt aus der ersten Schaffensperiode. Sie zeigt ein doppeltes Selbst-
porträt auf Fotobriefmarken, die die Künstlerin auf Einladungskarten klebte. Diese warben für ihre
ortsspezifische Installationen in New Yorker Hotelzimmern und wurden an Künstler*innen und Kol-
leg*innen gesandt.
/
**As an important protagonist of Media Art, the American multimedia artist Lynn Hershman Lee-
son has divided her work into the periods B.C. (Before Computer) and A.D. (After Digital). Her
Face Stamps are from the first period. Featuring a double self-portrait, she affixed these photo
stamps to the invitations that she sent to artists and friends for her site-specific installations in
New York hotel rooms.**

> *Identity Face Stamps,* 1966–72
> Briefmarken / **Postage stamps,** Edition 1/8
> **Courtesy of the artist &** Bridget Donahue, New York
> Seite / **Page** 120

> *Museum of Mott Art,* 1974
> Einladungspostkarte mit montierter Briefmarke /
> **Postcard invitation with mounted stamp**
> **Courtesy of the artist &** Bridget Donahue, New York
> Seite / **Page** 121

ANDREAS SLOMINSKI
* 1959 in Meppen (DE), lebt / **lives** in Werder an der Havel (DE)
Im Juni 1996 ließ der Konzeptkünstler Andreas Slominski eine gewöhnliche Briefmarke von einer
Giraffe im Münsteraner Zoo befeuchten. Mit der Marke frankierte er anschließend einen Brief. Der
Briefumschlag blieb leer – bis auf Absender und Adressat. Die Aktion war für die Skulpturenprojekte
Münster, für die die Arbeit entstanden war, schon vor deren Eröffnung nicht mehr sichtbar. Lediglich
die Erzählungen, die Dokumentation und der Briefversand zeugen von der Performance und
verschmolzen zur eigentlichen Botschaft.

**In June 1996 Conceptual artist Andreas Slominski had a giraffe lick an ordinary postage stamp
in the Münster zoo. He then affixed the stamp on a letter. The envelope, which was empty, only
bore the addresses of the sender and the recipient. Although the action was part of the Sculpture Projects Münster, this work could not be viewed, even before the opening. Only the story,
the documentation, and the sending of the letter tell of the performance, and the three elements merge into the actual message.**

> *Ohne Titel /* **Untitled,** 1996
> Briefkuvert, frankiert und gestempelt /
> **Envelope, franked and stamped**
> Museum MMK für Moderne Kunst, Frankfurt am Main
> © Andreas Slominski, Foto / **Photo** Axel Schneider
> Seite / **Page** 122

> *Anfeuchten der Briefmarke /* **Moistening the Stamp, 1996**
> Aktion im / **Performance at** Allwetterzoo Münster
> © Andreas Slominski
> Seite / **Page** 123

ABC ARTISTS' BOOKS COOPERATIVE
Gegründet / **Founded** 2009 in Berlin (DE)
ABC ist ein internationales Künstler*innenkollektiv, das sich mit alternativen und kollaborativen
Formen der Distribution beschäftigt. Im Mai 2020, auf dem ersten Höhepunkt der Corona-Pande-
mie in Europa, entwickelten ABC ein Mail-Art-Projekt, um während der erzwungenen Distanz in
Kontakt zu bleiben. Die Mitglieder des Kollektivs entwarfen Motive für Briefmarken und produzier-
ten diese über die niederländische Post. Diese wurden dann auf Blankopostkarten geklebt und um
den Globus versendet.

ABC is a collective of international artists that engages in alternative and collaborative forms of distribution. In May 2020, during the first peak of the Corona pandemic in Europe, ABC developed a mail art project so that they could stay in contact during the period of enforced distancing. The members of the collective designed postage stamps and produced them in collaboration with the Dutch postal service. These were then affixed to blank postcards and sent all over the world.

ABC Post, 2020
Briefmarken / **Stamps**
Gestaltung / **Design** Eric Doeringer (USA), Oliver Griffin (UK/DE), Mishka Henner (UK), Wil van Iersel (NL), Dawn Kim (USA), Jonathan Lewis (USA), John MacLean (UK), EJ Major (UK), Micheál O'Connell (UK), Louis Porter (UK), Jonathan Schmidt-Ott (DE), David Schulz (DE), Travis Shaffer (USA), Paul Soulellis (USA), Corinne Vionnet (CH), Duncan Wooldrige (UK), Rahel Zoller (UK), Hermann Zschiegner (USA)
Courtesy ABC Artists' Books Cooperative
Seiten / **Pages** 124–125

ABC Post, 2020
Versendete Postkarten / **Dispatched postcards**
Gestaltung / **Design** Jonathan Lewis (USA)
Courtesy ABC Artists' Books Cooperative
Seiten / **Pages** 126–127

THEMISTOKLES VON ECKENBRECHER
* 1842 in Athen / **Athens** (GR), † 1921 in Goslar (DE)

Schon im 19. Jahrhundert war das Brandenburger Tor ein beliebtes Postkartenmotiv. Die Vorlage lieferte eine Fotografie aus dem Jahre 1878, die Themistokles von Eckenbrecher überarbeitete. Über die Poststempel auf der Rückseite wird deutlich, dass im Medium Postkarte Bild und Ort miteinander verbunden sind. Alle diese Bilder wurden in Laufnähe des Berliner Wahrzeichens auf die Post gegeben. Nicht erst heute, sondern bereits damals gab das Motiv darüber Aufschluss, wo sich die Versender*in der Postkarte gerade befand.

The Brandenburg Gate in Berlin was a favorite postcard subject even in the nineteenth century. The original image was a photograph from 1878 that was reworked by Themistokles von Eckenbrecher. The postmark on the back makes it clear that the medium of the postcard merges images and places. All of these images were mailed within walking distance of the Berlin landmark. This demonstrates that it is not a modern development for images to serve as an indication of the sender's location.

Globus Verlag, Berlin
Brandenburger Thor / **The Brandenburg Gate,** 1898–1904
12 Postkarten / **postcards** (recto / verso)
Seiten / **Pages** 130–131, 134–135

Das Brandenburger Thor / **The Brandenburg Gate,** ca. 1890
Druckgrafik nach einer Fotografie von 1878 /
Print based on a photograph from 1878
© Bildarchiv Foto Marburg
Seite / **Page** 133

CORINNE VIONNET
*** 1969 in Monthey (CH), lebt / lives in Vevey (CH)**

Corinne Vionnet zählt zu den Pionier*innen in der Auseinandersetzung mit webbasierten Bildern. Für ihre Serie hat sie auf Photo-Sharing-Webseiten eine Schlagwortsuche nach berühmten Monumenten durchgeführt und Tausende der gefundenen touristischen Schnappschüsse gespeichert und übereinandergeblendet. Die appropriative Arbeit setzt sich mit der Homogenisierung individueller Erfahrung auseinander. Unser Aufsuchen ikonischer Orte bringt die immer gleichen Bilder und ähnlichen Perspektiven hervor.

Corinne Vionnet is one of the pioneers in the investigation of web-based images. For this series she did keyword searches for monuments on photo-sharing websites and found thousands of tourist snapshots, which she archived and layered. The appropriative method investigates the homogenizing of individual experience. Our individual visits to iconic places always produce the same images and result in similar perspectives.

Berlin, 2006
a.d.S. / **From the series Photo Opportunities,** 2005–heute / **present**
Tapete und 10.000 Postkarten / **Wallpaper and 10,000 postcards,** 2021
© Corinne Vionnet, 2021
Courtesy Parrotta Contemporary Art, Köln / **Cologne**
Seiten / **Pages** 136–137

New York (2), 2007
a.d.S. / **From the series** *Photo Opportunities,* 2005–heute / **present**
Archivpigmentdruck / **Archival pigment print,** 2020
© **Corinne Vionnet, 2021**
Courtesy Parrotta Contemporary Art, Köln / **Cologne**
Seiten / **Pages** 138–139

Venezia, 2007
a.d.S. / **From the series** *Photo Opportunities,* 2005–heute / **present**
Archivpigmentdruck / **Archival pigment print,** 2020
© Corinne Vionnet, 2021
Courtesy Parrotta Contemporary Art, Köln / **Cologne**
Seiten / **Pages** 140–141

ON KAWARA
* 1933 in Kariya (JP), † 2014 in New York City (USA)
Mit *I Got Up* entstand in mehr als 12 Jahren ein gigantisches Werk, für das On Kawara mehr als 8.000 Postkarten weltweit verschickte – zwei an jedem Tag. Jeweils mit genauer Entstehungszeit, Adresse von Absender und Empfänger versehen, umspannten die Postkarten ein Netzwerk der Kunstwelt. Die Botschaften zeigen die globale Wanderung des Künstlers und die zeitlich unregelmäßige Stempelung der Postkarten: Allein 1973 wurden Postkarten aus 28 Städten verschickt, woran sich immer sein Standort ermitteln lässt. Interessanterweise beschreibt die Sammlung an Postkarten des MMK Frankfurt seine Reisen von New York City über die 37. Biennale in Venedig bis zu seinem Aufenthalt in Berlin als DAAD-Stipendiat.

Over a period of more than twelve years, On Kawara sent more than eight thousand postcards all over the world—two each day—in the context of his huge series *I Got Up.* Always listing the exact time of creation and the addresses of the sender and the recipient, these postcards spanned a network of the artworld. The messages express the artist's global movement and postmarks at irregular intervals: in 1973 alone, the postcards were sent from twenty-eight cities, thus always giving evidence of his location. The collection of postcards held by the Museum für Moderne Kunst in Frankfurt documents his trips from New York City to the 37th Venice Biennale and finally his sojourn in Berlin as a DAAD grant recipient.

I Got Up, 19.06.1976–09.09.1976 / **June 19–September 9, 1976**
42 Farbpostkarten / **42 color postcards**
Museum MMK für Moderne Kunst, Frankfurt am Main
© One Million Years Foundation, Foto / **Photo** Axel Schneider
Seiten / **Pages** 142–147

FREDI CASCO
* 1967 in Asunción (PY), lebt / **lives in Asunción (PY)**
Contact besteht aus gefundenen QSL-Karten, die im Kommunikationswesen dazu dienten, ein empfangenes Funksignal zu bestätigen und seine Charakteristika mitzuteilen. Zwischen 1953 und 1986 wurden diese Karten von überall auf der Welt zu einem Amateurfunker mit dem Kürzel ZP5EC gesendet, der unter dem damals herrschenden Diktator Alfredo Stroessner in Paraguay lebte. In einer Zeit, in der Kommunikation kontrolliert wurde, repräsentiert der Austausch mit der Welt außerhalb eine Form der Freiheit.

Contact consists of found QSL cards that were sent to confirm a received radio signal and to describe its characteristics. Between 1953 and 1986 these cards were sent from all over the world to an amateur radio operator using the code ZP5EC, who lived in Paraguay under the then ruling dictator Alfredo Stroessner. In a period in which communication was carefully controlled, such an exchange with the outside world represented a form of freedom.

Contact, 2014
49 QSL-Karten / **49 QSL cards**
Installationsansicht / **Installation view,** Cartes Postales,
Rencontres d'Arles, 2019
© Fredi Casco, 2021, **Courtesy** mor charpentier, Paris
Foto / **Photo** Aurore Valade
Seiten / **Pages** 148–153

Ruda Bruner-Dvořák, Prag / **Prague**
Album für Frau Gräfin / **Album for Countess** Elisabeth Thun, 1890er-Jahre / **1890s**
Album, Beschriftete Postkarten / **Inscribed postcards**
Sammlung / **Collection** Friedrich Tietjen, Wien / **Vienna** & Leipzig
Seiten / **Pages** 154–155

ANDREAS SLOMINSKI

* 1959 in Meppen (DE), lebt / **lives** in Werder an der Havel (DE)
Über einen längeren Zeitraum verschickte Andreas Slominski an den damaligen Direktor des Museum für Moderne Kunst in Frankfurt am Main Landkarten und Stadtpläne – unkommentiert. Einfach in einen Umschlag gesteckt, kamen diese visuellen Botschaften als Ortsangaben bei Jean-Christophe Ammann an und verweisen als Kommentare lediglich darauf, wo sich Slominski gerade aufgehalten haben mag. Visuelle Botschaft, Ort und Zeit verschmelzen zu einem puren Ortungssignal.

Over an extended period, Andreas Slominski sent maps and city plans without any commentary to the then director of the Museum für Moderne Kunst in Frankfurt am Main. Merely inserted into the envelope, these visual messages were received by Jean-Christophe Ammann, thus informing him about Slominski's whereabouts. Visual message, place, and time merge to create a pure indication of location.

Unkommentierte Sendung von Landkarten und Stadtplänen von Andreas Slominski an Jean-Christophe Ammann / **Mailing of maps and city plans without commentary by Andreas Slominski to Jean-Christophe Ammann,** 1992–1997
Landkarten, Stadtpläne und Umschläge / **Maps, city maps, and envelopes**
Museum MMK für Moderne Kunst, Frankfurt am Main
© Andreas Slominski, Foto / **Photo** Axel Schneider
Seiten / **Pages** 156–157

TOMAS VAN HOUTRYVE

* 1975 in San Francisco (USA), lebt / **lives** in Paris (FR)
Als Folge der Flüchtlingswelle nach Mitteleuropa im Jahr 2015 reflektierte van Houtryve 2016/17 eine Reihe von Instagram-Posts Geflüchteter, die mit einem bestimmten Ort verknüpft waren und folgte deren digitaler Spur durch Europa: Er reiste genau an jene Orte, auf denen die Geflüchteten sich selbst auf der Flucht fotografiert hatten. Im Nachhinein kombinierte er die Bilder zu einer Landkarte der Exilbewegung, die von den Instagram-Fotos überlagert wurde.

In response to the 2015 wave of refugees in central Europe, Tomas van Houtryve reflected a series of Instagram posts by refugees that were linked to a specific location and followed their digital traces through Europe. He traveled to the exact places where the refugees had photographed themselves during their exodus. He later combined the pictures to create a map of their movement, which was layered using Instagram photos.

Traces of Exile, 2016/17
Ein-Kanal-Video-Installation /
Single-channel video installation,
Standbilder / **video stills**
© Tomas van Houtryve / VII
Seiten / **Pages** 158–161

CLARE STRAND

* 1973 in Croydon (UK), lebt / **lives** in Brighton (UK)

Während eines temporären Studioaufenthalts bei C/O Berlin, fungierte die konzeptuell arbeitende Künstlerin Clare Strand als menschliche Bildübertragungsmaschine. Ihr Ehemann übermittelte ihr nach einem festgelegten Farbcode von 1 für Weiß bis 10 für Schwarz Fotografien aus ihrem Archiv per Telefon. Wie beim Malen nach Zahlen füllte sie mit Pinsel und Farbe Quadrat für Quadrat. Es entstanden großformatige, gemalte Reproduktionen der Fotografien, deren Motive die Künstlerin bis zum Ende des Prozesses nicht kannte.

During a temporary studio residency at C/O Berlin Clare Strand, who works in a conceptional mode, made herself into a human image-transferring "machine." Her husband conveyed photographs from her archive to her by telephone, using a predetermined grid and color-code system of 1 for white and 10 for black. Similar to painting by numbers, she filled in each square using a paintbrush and paint to create large-format, painted reproductions of photographs whose subjects the artist did not know during the entire process.

The Discrete Channel with Noise: Algorithmic Painting, Destination, #11–13, 2020
Gemälde, Acrylfarbe auf Papier / **Painting, acrylic paint on paper**
© Clare Strand, 2021, **Courtesy** Parrotta Contemporary Art, Köln / **Cologne**
Seiten / **Pages** 165, 169, 171

The Discrete Channel with Noise: Information Source, #11–13, 2020
Archivarische Inkjet-Prints, überlagert mit gerastertem Acetatblatt und handgeschriebener roter Tinte / **Archival inkjet prints overlaid with gridded acetate sheet and handwriting in red ink**
© Clare Strand, 2021, **Courtesy** Parrotta Contemporary Art, Köln / **Cologne**
Seiten / **Pages** 166–167, 172

NASA

Gegründet / **Founded 1958** in Washington, D.C. (USA)

Das Mariner-Programm der NASA erkundete zwischen 1962 und 1973 erdähnliche Planeten des Sonnensystems. Am 15. Juli 1965 flog Mariner 4 als erste irdische Raumsonde in knapp 10.000 Kilometern am Mars vorbei. Die 22 Ansichten sind die ersten eines fremden Planeten, die aus dem Weltall aufgenommen wurden. Da die Übertragung der Bilder mehrere Stunden dauerte, behalfen sich die Ingenieure damit, die Datenmenge aus Einsen und Nullen auszudrucken und sie nach einem vorher festgelegten Farbencode anzumalen.

NASA's Mariner program explored earthlike planets of the solar system between 1962 and 1973. On July 15, 1965, Mariner 4 was the first spacecraft to fly by Mars at a distance of only ten thousand kilometers. The twenty-two views are the first close-ups to be taken of another planet from space. Since it took several hours to transmit the images, engineers printed out the data, consisting of ones and zeros, and painted them out according to a predetermined color code.

First TV Image of Mars, 15.07.1965 / **July 15, 1965**
Farbige Kreide auf Papierstreifen, gerahmt /
Colored chalk on paper strips, framed
Installationsansicht / **Installation view**
© NASA/JPL-Caltech/Dan Goods
Seiten / **Pages** 174–175

First TV Image of Mars, 16.07.1965 / **July 16, 1965**
Seitenvergleich von gemaltem Bild und Bildtelegrafie /
Side-by-side comparison of drawn image and wirephoto
© NASA/JPL-Caltech
Seite / **Page** 176

First TV Image of Mars, Color Key, 1965
Kreide und Bleistift auf Karton /
Chalk and pencil on cardboard
© NASA/JPL-Caltech/Spencer Lowell
Seite / **Page** 177

Anonym / **Anonymous** (NASA)
Scientists make a last-minute check,
Pasadena, **California,** 15.07.1965 / **July 15, 1965**
Telephoto
© NASA/JPL-Caltech
Seite / **Page** 177

Anonym / **Anonymous** (NASA)
First Mars Photo after "Enhancement,"
Pasadena, **California,** 14.07.1965 / **July 14, 1965**
Bildtelegrafie / **Wirephoto**
© NASA/JPL-Caltech
Seite / **Page** 178

Anonym / **Anonymous** (NASA)
First Mars Photo after "Enhancement,"
Pasadena, **California,** 14.07.1965 / **July 14, 1965**
Retuschierte Bildtelegrafie / **Retouched wirephoto**
© NASA/JPL-Caltech
Seite / **Page** 178

Los Angeles Times
Historische Fotos vom Mars auf die Erde übertragen, 16.07.1965 /
Historic Mars Photos Transmitted to Earth, July 16, 1965
Tageszeitung, Titel / **Newspaper front page**
Seite / **Page** 179

THOMAS RUFF

* 1958 in Zell am Harmersbach (DE), lebt / **lives** in Düsseldorf (DE)

Für *press++* eignete sich der Fotograf Thomas Ruff gefundenes Pressematerial aus dem 20. Jahrhundert an. Ab den 1920er-Jahren war es im Pressewesen üblich, die retouchierten, rückseitig gestempelten und mit erklärendem Text versehenen Fotografien über Radiokabel um die Welt zu senden. Ruff blendete die Vorder- und Rückseite dieser historischen Tele- bzw. Wirefotografien digital übereinander und befragt so den Aussagewert der unbeschriebenen fotografischen Oberfläche.

For his *press++* series, the German photographer Thomas Ruff appropriated twentieth-century press material. Starting in the 1920s, it was customary to send retouched photographs, with rubber stampings and a description on the back, around the world by radio transmission. Ruff digitally combined the fronts and backs of these historical telephotos and wirephotos in layered images, thus questioning the meaningfulness of the photographic surface without inscriptions.

press++02.20, 2015
C-Print
Courtesy Sprüth Magers
© Thomas Ruff, VG Bild-Kunst, Bonn 2020
Seite / **Page** 181

press++22.75, 2016
C-Print
Courtesy Sprüth Magers
© Thomas Ruff, VG Bild-Kunst, Bonn 2020
Seite / **Page** 183

PHILIPPE KAHN

* 1952 in Paris (FR), lebt nahe / **lives near** Santa Cruz (USA)

Philippe Kahn gilt als Erfinder des Handy-Fotos. 1997 bastelte er aus einem Computer, einer Kamera und einem Mobiltelefon die erste Apparatur, mit der ein Bild direkt nach der Aufnahme an mehrere Tausend Empfänger gesandt werden kann. Mit diesem legendären Foto seiner neugeborenen Tochter Sophie, für das er die klassische Fotokamera mit einem mobilen Telefon verband, nahm Kahn die heutige Social-Media-Praktik vorweg, die Bildaufnahme und Bildverteilung in einem Gerät – dem Smartphone – vereint.

Philippe Kahn is considered the inventor of the camera-phone photograph. In 1997 he built the first apparatus, using a computer, camera, and a cellphone, with which he was able to send an image to thousands of people directly after it was taken. With the legendary photograph of his newborn daughter, Sophie, for which he connected the classic camera to a mobile telephone, Kahn anticipated today's social media practice by combining the taking and sending of pictures in one device: the smartphone.

> Fotografie nach der Geburt von Sophie Lee-Kahn 11.06.1997 /
> **Sophie Lee-Kahn birth picture, June 11, 1997**
> Digitale Fotografie auf Bildschirm /
> **Digital photograph on screen**
> **Courtesy the** Lee-Kahn Foundation
> Seite / **Page** 186
>
> Erstes Kamera-Handy Foto 11.06.1997 (Apparate) /
> **First camera-phone photo, June 11, 1997 (apparatus)**
> Installationsansicht / **Installation view,** 2020
> **Courtesy the** Lee-Kahn Foundation
> Seite / **Page** 187

DAVID CAMPANY & ANASTASIA SAMOYLOVA

David Campany * 1967 in London (UK), lebt / **lives** New York City (USA)
Anastasia Samoylova * 1984 in Moskau / **Moscow** (RU), lebt / **lives** in Miami (USA)
In den vergangenen drei Jahren haben David Campany und Anastasia Samoylova über Instagram einen experimentellen Bildaustausch durchgeführt (www.instagram.com/dialogue_aandd/). Sie fotografieren und veröffentlichen Fotos, auf die sie in einem nicht endenden visuellen Gespräch reagieren. Manche der Antworten sind formal – Farbe, Muster – manche thematisch-assoziativ. Ihr Projekt ist spezifisch für die globalisierte Welt des Smartphones und der sozialen Medien ausgerichtet und umfasst derzeit etwas mehr als 4.500 Bilder.

Over the past three years, David Campany and Anastasia Samoylova have conducted an experimental exchange of images on Instagram (www.instagram.com/dialogue_aandd/). They photograph and publish photographs that they react to in an endless visual conversation. Many of the responses are formal—color, patterns—while others are thematic or associative. The project is specifically designed for the globalized world of smartphones and social media, currently consisting of over 4,500 images.

> *Untitled,* aus / **from** *Dialogue,* 2017–heute / **present**
> Standbilder / **Video stills,** 2020
> **Courtesy of the artists**
> Mit Dank an die / **With thanks to** Galerie Andreas Schmidt, Berlin
> Seiten / **Pages** 188–195

MARTIN FENGEL & JÖRG KOOPMANN

Martin Fengel * 1964 in München / **Munich** (DE), lebt / **lives** in München / **Munich** (DE)
Jörg Koopmann * 1968 in München / **Munich** (DE), lebt / **lives** in München / **Munich** (DE)
Die Arbeit *Post* (2000/01) beschreibt einen fiktiven, visuellen Dialog zwischen den beiden Künstlern Martin Fengel und Jörg Koopmann, die sich über einen längeren Zeitraum Botschaften zu schicken schienen. In der Dia-Installation wird dem/r Betrachter*in suggeriert, dass beide nicht gemeinsam, sondern getrennt verreist sind. Tatsächlich sind die Porträts und Bilder auf gemeinsamen Reisen vom jeweils anderen gemacht worden und im Text, der an einen Postkartentext erinnert, kommentiert worden.

The work *Post* describes a fictive visual dialogue between Martin Fengel and Jörg Koopmann in which the two artists seem to send each other messages over an extended period. Although the slideshow suggests to viewers that the two were traveling on separate journeys, the portraits and pictures were in fact taken on trips taken together. The images showing one artist were always taken by the other artist, who also wrote the text commentaries that are reminiscent of a postcard text.

Post, 2000–2001
Dia Installation mit Ton / **Slide installation with sound,** 80 Dias / **slides**
Courtesy of the artists
Seiten / **Pages** 196–199

THERESA MARTINAT
* 1989 in Ludwigsburg (DE), lebt / **lives** in Berlin (DE)
In zwei Künstlerbüchern von Theresa Martinat verweben sich Bilder und Exzerpte aus Emails sowie Nachrichtenfetzen aus Social-Media-Kanälen zu Collagen. Teile von diesen wurden als eigenständige Arbeiten aus den Büchern herausgelöst. Mit diesen Einblicken in ein persönliches Foto- und Internettagebuch macht sie Begegnungen und Freundschaften transparent. Dieser Blick in eine intime Innenwelt macht uns Betrachter- und Leser*innen zu Privatdetektiv*innen und Voyeur*innen – ungewollt, aber nicht unbedingt gegen unseren Willen.

Two artist books by Theresa Martinat consist of images and excerpts from emails and bits of messages from social media channels that are combined in collages. Parts of these were removed from the books to create independent works. These glimpses into her personal photo and internet diary make her encounters and friendships transparent. This look into an intimate interior world transforms the viewer/reader into private detectives and voyeurs—involuntarily, but not necessarily against our will.

Collage II, I'll Skype You in 20, 2011–2013
a.d.S. / **From the series** *Like It Never Happened,* 2010–2013
35mm, **Screenshots**
Investitionsbank Berlin
© Theresa Martinat, 2021
Seiten / **Pages** 200–201

Collage I, Jennifer, 2011–2013
a.d.S. / **From the series** *Like It Never Happened,* 2010–2013
35mm, **Screenshots**
© Theresa Martinat, 2021, **Courtesy of the artist**
Seite / **Page** 203

ADAM BROOMBERG & OLIVER CHANARIN
Adam Broomberg * 1970 Johannesburg (ZA), lebt / **lives** in London (UK) und / **and** Berlin (DE)
Oliver Chanarin * 1971 London (UK), lebt / **lives** in London (UK) und / **and** Berlin (DE)
Als Gastredakteure des Magazins *DER GREIF* sammelten die Künstler Bilder, die zu privat, zu ruhig, zu gewalttätig, zu politisch, zu subversiv oder zu explizit sind, um sie online zu veröffentlichen. Sie erhielten eine Lawine von Einsendungen. Konfrontiert mit der gewaltigen Aufgabe, das Material zu selektieren, wandten sie sich in einem zweiten Schritt an einen ehemaligen Facebook-Moderator. Schließlich beschlossen sie, sowohl die „guten" als auch die „bösen" Bilder einzubeziehen.

As guest editors of the magazine *DER GREIF* the artists collected images that are too private, too quiet, too violent, too political, too subversive, or too explicit to be published online. In response to the callout, they received an avalanche of submissions. Confronted with the daunting job of selecting material, they turned in a second step to a former Facebook moderator. They ultimately decided to include both the "good" and the "bad" images.

Blame the Algorithm, 2019
Der Greif, Ausgabe / **Issue 12**
Gast-Editoren / **Guest editors:** Broomberg & Chanarin
Magazin, Doppelseite / **Magazine, double-page spread**
Titelbild / **Cover:** © Martha Friedel, **Courtesy** Der Greif
Seite / **Page** 207

Blame the Algorithm, 2019
Der Greif, Ausgabe / **Issue 12**
Gast-Editoren / **Guest editors:** Broomberg & Chanarin
Magazin, Doppelseite / **Magazine, double-page spread**
Foto / **Photo** Bad 7: © Andrea DiCenzo, **Courtesy** Der Greif
Good 39: © Paul Breuker, **Courtesy** Der Greif
Seiten / **Pages** 208–209

Blame the Algorithm, 2019
Der Greif, Ausgabe / **Issue** 12
Gast-Editoren / **Guest editors:** Broomberg & Chanarin
Magazin, Doppelseite / **Magazine, double-page spread**
Foto / **Photo** Bad 41: © Matthew Keenan, **Courtesy** Der Greif
Good 5: © Allison Cherkis, **Courtesy** Der Greif
Seiten / **Pages** 210–211

Blame the Algorithm, 2019
Der Greif, Ausgabe / **Issue** 12
Gast-Editoren / **Guest editors:** Broomberg & Chanarin
Magazin, Doppelseite / **Magazine, double-page spread**
Foto Rückseite / **Back Cover:** © Milan Gies, **Courtesy** Der Greif
Seite / **Page** 212

DIETER HACKER

* 1942 in Augsburg (DE), lebt / **lives** in Berlin (DE)
Die Arbeiten stellen Amateurfotografien in den Fokus. *Geprüft und für wertlos befunden* ist eine Fotosammlung der anderen Art: In einem Großlabor wurden „Fotokontrolleur*innen" beschäftigt, die eingesandte Filmrollen sichteten und dabei unscharfe, angeschnittene und anderswie als fehlerhaft empfundene Bilder aussortierten. Dieses Verfahren weist auf die heutige Form der Content-Moderation voraus, bei der menschliche und algorithmische Aktanten eingesetzt werden, um unsere Internetbeiträge zu ordnen.

The works focus on amateur photographs. *Geprüft und für wertlos befunden* (Tested and Deemed Worthless) is a different sort of photo collection: "photo inspectors" were hired to review the rolls of film that had been sent to a large lab and to sort out the ones that were out of focus, badly framed, and images that were considered faulty in other ways. This process reflects the current form of content moderation in which human agents and algorithms are used to organize our contributions to the internet.

*Geprüft und für wertlos befunden / **Tested and Deemed Worthless,*** 1980
Installation aus Silbergelatineausbelichtungen und C-Prints /
Installation of gelatin silver prints and C-prints
Installationsansichten / **Installation views,**
ZKM | Zentrum für Kunst und Medien Karlsruhe, 2018
ZKM | Zentrum für Kunst und Medien Karlsruhe
© Dieter Hacker, 2021, Foto / **Photo** Jonas Zilius
Seiten / **Pages** 214–216

Die Fotokontrolleurin (Detail aus *Geprüft und für wertlos befunden*) /
***The Photo Inspector* (Detail from *Tested and Deemed Worthless*),** 1980
Silbergelatineausbelichtung / **Gelatin silver print**
ZKM | Zentrum für Kunst und Medien Karlsruhe
© Dieter Hacker, 2021, Foto / **Photo** Tobias Wootton
Seite / **Page** 217

JONAS MEYER & CHRISTIN MÜLLER

Jonas Meyer * 1982 in Saarbrücken (DE) lebt / **lives** in Berlin (DE)
Christin Müller * 1983 in Leipzig (DE) lebt / **lives** in Leipzig (DE)
1989 erlangte ein unidentifizierter Mann als „Tank Man" internationale Berühmtheit. Er stellte sich einem Panzerkonvoi bei den Protesten am Tian'anmen-Platz in Peking entgegen. Die Szene ging zum 24. Jahrestag des Massakers viral. Unter dem Hashtag *#BigYellowDuck* luden Unbekannte ein Meme ins Netz, bei dem die Panzer durch überdimensionierte Quietscheenten ersetzt worden waren. Für kurze Zeit wurde so die chinesische Zensur umgangen, die jegliche Referenz auf die Ereignisse im Jahr 1989 unterbindet. Nach einer Recherche von Christin Müller hat der Mediendesigner Jonas Meyer das historische Phänomen und sein Nachleben in den sozialen Netzwerken für C/O Berlin in ein Video übersetzt.

In 1989 an unidentified man rose to international fame as "tank man" for standing up to a convoy of tanks at Tian'anmen Square in Beijing. On the twenty-fourth anniversary of the massacre the scene went viral. Under the hashtag *#BigYellowDuck,* an unidentified person uploaded a

meme in which the tanks were replaced by oversized rubber ducks, thus briefly eluding the Chinese censors who had forbidden all references to the 1989 events. After research by Christin Müller, media designer Jonas Meyer translated the historical phenomenon and its afterlife in social networks into a video for C/O Berlin.

Stuart Franklin
"The Tank Man" Stopping the Column of T59 Tanks,
Tiananmen Square, 4. Juni 1989 / **June 4, 1989**
C-Print © Stuart Franklin / Magnum Photos / Agentur Focus
Seiten / **Pages** 218–219, 279

Tank Man, 2021
Video mit Sound / **with Sound**
© Jonas Meyer
Seiten / **Pages** 220–223

Anonym / **Anonymous**
*A Parody of the Iconic 1989 Tiananmen Square Photo of
a Chinese Protester Confronting Government Tanks,* 2013
Tank-Man-Meme
https://www.kqed.org/lowdown/13161/on-tiananmen-square
-anniversary-using-creative-memes-to-circumvent-censorship
[Zugriff am 15.10.2020 / **Accessed on October 15, 2020**]
Seiten / **Pages** 224–235, 283

MARC LEE
* 1969 in Knutwil (CH), lebt / **lives** in Zürich (CH)
Für C/O Berlin hat der multimedial arbeitende Künstler Marc Lee, der sich mit dem Informationsaustausch beschäftigt, einen sogenannten Bot, d.h. eine Software programmiert, die aktuellste Twitter-, Instagram und Youtube-Meldungen rund um den Globus nach den Schlagworten „Corona" und „Covid-19" durchsucht. Die Tweets, Posts und Videoschnipsel werden vom Algorithmus nach Aktualität geordnet und zu einer wilden Live-TV-Sendung verwoben, die die Meldungen zur Pandemie in Echtzeit über den Bildschirm flimmern lässt.

The multimedia Swiss artist Marc Lee, who is fascinated by the exchange of information, created a bot for C/O Berlin, that is, a program that searches the current Twitter, Instagram, and YouTube posts around the world for the keywords "Corona" and "COVID-19." The tweets, posts, and video clips are then organized according to topicality by algorithms and interwoven into a wild, live TV show that presents the news on the pandemic in real time.

Corona TV Bot, 2020/2021
Screenshots von Live-TV Sendung, 20.04.2020 /
Screenshots from live TV broadcast, April 20, 2020
3-teilige Video-Installation mit Sound /
Three-part video installation with sound, 2021
Courtesy of the artist
Seiten / **Pages** 226–229

TARYN SIMON & AARON SWARTZ
Taryn Simon * 1975 in New York City (USA), lebt / **lives** in New York City (USA)
Aaron Swartz * 1986 in Chicago (USA), † 2013 in New York City (USA)
Der von Taryn Simon in Zusammenarbeit mit dem Programmierer Aaron Swartz entwickelte *Image Atlas* untersucht kulturelle Ähnlichkeiten und Unterschiede, indem er die besten Bilergebnisse für bestimmte Suchbegriffe in lokalen Suchmaschinen auf der ganzen Welt verschlagwortet. *Image Atlas* hinterfragt die vermeintliche Unschuld und Neutralität der Algorithmen, die von Suchmaschinen verwendet werden, und stellt die Möglichkeit einer universellen Bildsprache in Frage.

Created by Taryn Simon in collaboration with the programmer Aaron Swartz, *Image Atlas* examines cultural similarities and differences by indexing top image results for given search terms across local search engines throughout the world. *Image Atlas* challenges the purported innocence and neutrality of the algorithms that are used by search engines and questions the possibility of a universal visual language.

America, 06/21/2013, 8:18 PM (Eastern Standard Time) Image Atlas, 2012
Mixed Media
imageatlas.org
© **Taryn Simon in collaboration with Aaron Swartz, Courtesy Gagosian**
Seiten / **Pages** 230–231

Border, 9/30/16, 12:19 PM (Eastern Standard Time) Image Atlas, 2012
Mixed Media
imageatlas.org
© **Taryn Simon in collaboration with Aaron Swartz, Courtesy Gagosian**
Seiten / **Pages** 232–233

ROMAIN ROUCOULES
* 1991 in Vincennes (FR), lebt / **lives** in Paris (FR)
Der französische Künstler Romain Roucoules befragt die alltägliche Verwendung neuer Technologi-
en. *Social Printer* ist eine ortsspezifische Installation, die handelsübliche Quittungsdrucker mit einer
Software verbindet, die alle Bilder, die auf Instagram mit dem Hashtag *#coberlin* verbunden sind,
auf Thermopapier ausdruckt. Die stetig wachsende Papierskulptur materialisiert den digitalen Bil-
derfluss in Echtzeit und regt zugleich zum Aufnehmen neuer Bilder an, die ins Netz hochgeladen
und getagged werden, um zu zirkulieren.

The French artist Romain Roucoules surveys the everyday use of new technologies. *Social Printer*
is a site-specific installation that links ordinary receipt printers with a program that prints out all
Instagram images with the hashtag #coberlin on thermal paper. The constantly growing paper
sculpture makes the digital flow of images tangible in real time and also stimulates taking new
images that are uploaded to the internet and tagged for circulation.

Social Printer, 2018–2021
Installation aus Thermodruckern und Thermopapier /
Installation of thermal printers and thermal paper
Installationsansichten / **Installation views,**
Photoforum Pasquart, Bienne, 2019
© Romain Roucoules
Seiten / **Pages** 234–237

EVA & FRANCO MATTES
* 1976 in Italien / Italy, leben / **living** in New York City (USA)
Das multimediale Werk kreist um ethische und politische Fragen des Internets und um die Subversion sozialer Medien. *Personal Photographs* nimmt den Gedanken des Netzwerks wörtlich: Die Arbeit
besteht aus Trassen mit bunten Kabeln darin, die sich durch die Ausstellungsräume winden und
den Informationsfluss unserer digitalen Infrastrukturen repräsentieren. Unsichtbar für die Betrachter*in zirkulieren darin alle Bilder, die das Künstlerduo während eines einzelnen Monats aufgenommen und gespeichert hat.

The multimedia work circles around ethnic and political questions of the internet and around the
subversion of social media. *Personal Photographs* takes a literal look at the concept of network:
the work consists of cable trays with colorful cables that wind their way through the exhibition
rooms and represent the information flow in our digital infrastructures. Invisible to the viewers,
all images taken by the artist duo during a period of one month circulate in these cables.

Personal Photographs, October 2006, 2019/2021
Installation aus Kabelrinnen, Ethernet-Kabeln, digitalen Bildern, Raspberry Pi single-board
Computern, Mikro-SD-Karten, USB-Flash-Laufwerken, kundenspezifischer Software /
Installation of Cable tray, ethernet cables, digital images, Raspberry Pi single-board
computers, micro SD cards, USB flash drives, custom software
Installationsansichten / **Installation views, Careof,** Milan, 2019
© Eva & Franco Mattes, **Courtesy of the artists**
Foto / **Photo** Delfino Sisto Legnani & Melania Dalle Grave für / **for** DSL Studio
Seiten / **Pages** 238–241, 328

Personal Photographs, September 2009, 2019/2021
Installation aus Kabelrinnen, Ethernet-Kabeln, digitalen Bildern, Raspberry Pi single-board
Computern, Mikro-SD-Karten, USB-Flash-Laufwerken, kundenspezifischer Software /
**Installation of Cable tray, ethernet cables, digital images, Raspberry Pi single-board
computers, micro SD cards, USB flash drives, custom software**
Installationsansicht / **Installation view,** Team Gallery, Los Angeles, 2019
© Eva & Franco Mattes, **Courtesy of the artists,** Foto / **Photo** Jeff McLane
Seite / **Page** 240

Personal Photographs, September 2009, 2019
Screenshot der Bilddaten / **Screenshot of the content**
© Eva & Franco Mattes, **Courtesy of the artists**
Seite / **Page** 241

Personal Photographs, September 2009, 2019/2021
Installation aus Kabelrinnen, Ethernet-Kabeln, digitalen Bildern, Raspberry Pi single-board
Computern, Mikro-SD-Karten, USB-Flash-Laufwerken, kundenspezifischer Software /
**Installation of Cable tray, ethernet cables, digital images, Raspberry Pi single-board
computers, micro SD cards, USB flash drives, custom software**
Installationsansicht / **Installation view,** Team Gallery, Los Angeles, 2019
© Eva & Franco Mattes, **Courtesy of the artists,** Foto / **Photo** Jeff McLane
Seite / **Page** 240

Personal Photographs, September 2009, 2019
Screenshot der Bilddaten / **Screenshot of the content**
© Eva & Franco Mattes, **Courtesy of the artists**
Seite / **Page** 241

AUTOR*INNEN / **AUTHORS**

ESTELLE BLASCHKE ist Fotohistorikerin und vertritt die Professur Medien, Kommunikation, Gesellschaft am Seminar für Medienwissenschaft der Universität Basel. Forschungsschwerpunkte sind: Fotografie als Informationstechnologie, Fotografie und Ökonomie, Theorie und Geschichte von fotografischen Archiven. Sie lebt in Basel.

Estelle Blaschke is a photo historian and professor of media, communication, and society at the seminar for media studies at the Universität Basel. Her research interests are photography as information technology, photography and economics, and the theory and history of photographic archives. She lives in Basel.

MATTHIAS BRUHN ist Professor für Kunstwissenschaft & Medientheorie mit dem Schwerpunkt *Technische Imagination* an der Staatlichen Hochschule für Gestaltung in Karlsruhe. Er leitet u.a. das Teilprojekt *Adaptive Bilder* im DFG-Schwerpunktprogramm *Das digitale Bild* und ist Mitherausgeber der 2003 gegründeten Schriftenreihe *Bildwelten des Wissens.* Ein Beitrag zum Tagungsthema ist 2020 im Katalog der Ausstellung *Le supermarché des images* (Jeu de Paume Paris) erschienen. Er lebt in Berlin und Karlsruhe.

MATTHIAS BRUHN is a professor of art and media theory at the Staatliche Hochschule für Gestaltung in Karlsruhe with a focus on the technical imagination. He directs the Adaptive Bilder subproject within the Deutsche Forschungsgemeinschaft focus program *Das digitale Bild* and coedits the publication series *Bildwelten des Wissens,* begun in 2003. He published an article on the topic of this symposium in the 2020 catalog for the exhibition *Le supermarché des images* (Jeu de Paume, Paris). Bruhn lives in Berlin and Karlsruhe.

FELIX HOFFMANN ist Kunsthistoriker und Kulturwissenschaftler und seit 2005 Hauptkurator der C/O Berlin Foundation. Er hat zahlreiche Ausstellungen kuratiert zuletzt *Das letzte Bild . Fotografie und Tod* (2019). Er lebt in Berlin.

FELIX HOFFMANN is an art historian and art theorist, and has been head curator of the C/O Berlin Foundation since 2005. He has curated numerous exhibitions, including most recently *The last Image . Photography and Death* (2019). He lives in Berlin.

CHRISTIAN KASSUNG ist Professor für *Kulturtechniken und Wissensgeschichte* an der Humboldt-Universität zu Berlin. Seine Forschungsschwerpunkte sind die Wissensgeschichte der Physik, Kulturtechniken der Industrialisierung, Geschichte und Praxis technischer Medien sowie nicht hegemoniale Wissensproduktion. Im Herbst erscheint sein neues Buch *Fleisch. Die Geschichte einer Industrialisierung*. Er lebt in Berlin.

CHRISTIAN KASSUNG is a professor of cultural technologies and the history of knowledge at the Humboldt Universität zu Berlin. His research focuses on the history of knowledge in physics, cultural technologies of industrialization, the history and practice of technical media, and nonhegemonic knowledge production. His new book, *Fleisch: Die Geschichte einer Industrialisierung* will be published in fall 2020. He lives in Berlin.

KATJA MÜLLER-HELLE ist Leiterin der Forschungsstelle *Das Technische Bild* an der Humboldt Universität zu Berlin. Ihre Forschungsschwerpunkte sind die Geschichte und Theorie der Fotografie, technische Bilder und die Historiografie bildlicher Evidenzerzeugung. 2014-2015 und 2018 war sie Fellow am Getty Research Institute in Los Angeles. Sie ist Mit-Herausgeberin der *Bildwelten des Wissens. Jahrbuch für Bildkritik.* Zuletzt erschienen: Peter Geimer/Katja Müller-Helle (Hg.): *Das Sichtbare und das Sagbare. Evidenz zwischen Text und Bild in Roland Barthes' Mythen des Alltags*, Göttingen: Wallstein Verlag 2020.

KATJA MÜLLER-HELLE the head of the research center *Das Technische Bild* at the Humboldt Universität zu Berlin. Her research covers the history and theory of photography, technical images, and historiographies of pictorial evidence. In 2014–15 and 2018 Katja Müller-Helle was a fellow at the Getty Research Institute in Los Angeles. She is coeditor of *Bildwelten des Wissens: Jahrbuch für Bildkritik.* Her most recent publication is Peter Geimer/Katja Müller-Helle (ed.): *Das Sichtbare und das Sagbare: Evidenz zwischen Text und Bild in Roland Barthes' Mythen des Alltags* Göttingen: Wallstein Verlag 2020.

SIMON ROTHÖHLER arbeitet als Juniorprofessor für Medientechnik und Medienphilosophie an der Ruhr-Universität Bochum. Seine Forschungsschwerpunkte sind Digitale Medien und Bildtheorie, Medienhistoriografie, Film- und Serienästhetik sowie die Theorie und Geschichte des Dokumentarischen. Zuletzt erschienen: *Theorien der Serie zur Einführung* (Hamburg, Junius Verlag 2020).

SIMON ROTHÖHLER is a junior professor for media technology and media philosophy at Ruhr-Universität Bochum. His research interests include digital media and image theory, media historiography, the aesthetics of film and TV series, and the theory and history of the documentary. His most recent publication is *Theorien der Serie zur Einführung* (Hamburg: Junius Verlag, 2020).

KERSTIN SCHANKWEILER ist Professorin für Bildwissenschaft im globalen Kontext an der Technischen Universität Dresden. Sie forscht zu digitalen Bildkulturen, Affektökonomien, Gegenwartskunst aus Afrika sowie zu transkulturellen und postkolonialen Fragestellungen. Zuletzt erschien ihr Buch *Bildproteste. Widerstand im Netz* (Berlin 2019) sowie der Band *Image Testimonies. Witnessing in Times of Social Media* (hg. mit Tobias Wendl und Verena Straub, London/New York 2019).

KERSTIN SCHANKWEILER is a professor of the science of images in a global context at the Technische Universität Dresden. Her research specialisms include digital image cultures, economies of affect, contemporary African art, and transcultural and postcolonial issues. Her book *Bildproteste: Widerstand im Netz* (Berlin, 2019) was recently published, along with the volume *Image Testimonies: Witnessing in Times of Social Media* (co-edited with Tobias Wendl and Verena Straub, London/New York, 2019).

KATHRIN SCHÖNEGG ist Fotografiehistorikerin und Kuratorin der C/O Berlin Foundation, wo sie u.a. das Förderprogramm *C/O Berlin Talent Award* leitet. Zuletzt erschien ihre Monografie *Fotografiegeschichte der Abstraktion*, Verlagsbuchhandlung Walther König 2019. Sie lebt in Berlin.

KATHRIN SCHÖNEGG is a photography historian and curator at C/O Berlin Foundation, where she directs the *C/O Berlin Talent Award* development program, among other responsibilities. Her monograph *Fotografiegeschichte der Abstraktion* was recently published (Cologne: Verlagsbuchhandlung Walther König, 2019). She lives in Berlin.

FRIEDRICH TIETJEN lebt und arbeitet in Leipzig, Berlin und Wien. Er co-organisiert die jährlich in St. Petersburg stattfindende Tagung „After Post-Photography" und forscht und publiziert zu privaten fotografischen Medien in Ostdeutschland, serieller Kunst und Hitlers Bart – dazu erscheint *Hitler abstempeln. Drei defacements* in den Bildwelten des Wissens (Band 16).

FRIEDRICH TIETJEN co-organizes the conference After Post-Photography, which takes place annually in St. Petersburg. He researches and publishes work on personal photographic media in East Germany, serial artworks, and Hitler's moustache. On the latter he has published *Hitler abstempeln: Drei defacements* in *Bildwelten des Wissens* (volume 16). Tietjen lives and works in Leipzig, Berlin, and Vienna.

WOLFGANG ULLRICH lebt als freier Autor und Kulturwissenschaftler in Leipzig, er forscht und publiziert zur Geschichte und Kritik des Kunstbegriffs, zu bildsoziologischen Fragen sowie zu Konsumtheorie. Seit 2019 ist er Mitherausgeber der Reihe *Digitale Bildkulturen* im Verlag Klaus Wagenbach und publizierte darin den Band *Selfies. Die Rückkehr des öffentlichen Lebens* (2019).

WOLFGANG ULLRICH is a freelance author and cultural researcher. He researches and writes on the history of and criticism on the concept of art, questions of visual sociology, and consumer theory. Since 2019, he has coedited the series *Digitale Bildkulturen* for Verlag Klaus Wagenbach, and written the volume, *Selfies: Die Rückkehr des öffentlichen Lebens* (2019) for the series. Ullrich lives in Leipzig.

BILDNACHWEIS ESSAYS / **ESSAY IMAGE CREDITS**

WOLFGANG ULLRICH
Abb. / **Fig.** 1: https://commons.wi+D2:D9kimedia.org/wiki/File:Gamshurst-St_Nikolaus
-Kreuzweg-06-Veronika_reicht_Jesus_das_Schweisstuch-gje.jpg
(Zugriff am 15.10.2020 / **accessed on October 15, 2020), Photo Gerd Eichmann** © CC BY-SA
Abb. / **Fig.** 2: https://de.wikipedia.org/wiki/Datei:Hans_Memling_026.jpg
(Zugriff am 15.10.2020 / **accessed on October 15, 2020**)
Abb. / **Fig.** 3: https://apkpure.com/selfie-camera-auto/com.kkachur.autoselfie
(Zugriff am 15.10.2020 / **accessed on October 15, 2020**)
Abb. / **Fig.** 4: https://www.instagram.com/p/CALeYxJp0e4/
(Zugriff am 15.10.2020 / **accessed on October 15, 2020**)
Abb. / **Fig.** 5: https://www.laboiteverte.fr/photobomb-lancienne-en-1840/?l=at1
(Zugriff am 15.10.2020 / **accessed on October 15, 2020**)
Abb. / **Fig.** 6: https://www.instagram.com/p/5YO0OsvmBx/
(Zugriff am 15.10.2020 / **accessed on October 15, 2020**)

FRIEDRICH TIETJEN
Für alle Objekte / **For all images: Courtesy** Sammlung /
Collection Friedrich Tietjen, Wien / **Vienna** & Leipzig

CHRISTIAN KASSUNG
Abb. / **Fig.** 1: Alexander Bain, Patentschrift / **Patent Specification,** 1843,
Blatt / **Sheet** 6, Figs. 1 und / **and** 2
Abb. / **Fig.** 2: *L'Illustration,* Magazin / **magazine,** 64 (3326),
24.11.1906 / **November 24,** 1906, Titelbild / **cover image**
Abb. / **Fig.** 3: *Die Woche,* Magazin / **magazine,** 11 (4)
23.01.1909 / **January 23, 1909,** S. / **p.** 142
Abb. / **Fig.** 4: *Le Matin,* Tageszeitung / **daily newspaper,** 80 (9105),
31.01.1909 / **January 31, 1909,** S. / **p.** 1
Abb. / **Fig.** 5: *The Daily Mirror,* Tageszeitung / **daily newspaper,**
17.03.1908 / **March 17, 1908,** S. / **p.** 4
Abb. / **Fig.** 6: *The Daily Mirror,* Tageszeitung / daily newspaper,
18.03.1908 / **March 18, 1908,** S. / **p.** 3
Abb. / **Fig.** 7: Philippe Bata, „Patrice A. Carré, Presse, Photographie et Télécommunications
de 1850 à 1940", in: *Revue française des t*élécommunications, 56, 1985, S. / **p.** 54

KATJA MÜLLER-HELLE
Abb. / **Fig.** 1: Luke Syson, Sheena Wagstaff, Emerson Bowyer und /
and Brinda Kumar, *Like Life, Sculpture, Color, and the Body*, New York 2018, S. / **p.** 143
Abb. / **Fig.** 2: Courtesy Natalia LL Archive / ZW Foundation, Toruń
Abb. / **Fig.** 3: https://twitter.com/TVPolakow_1/status/1122791957414068225
(Zugriff am 15.10.2020 / **accessed on October 15, 2020**)
Abb. / **Fig.** 4: https://www.instagram.com/p/B8jnsJtnU05/?igshid=1htdj9fogmd2c
(Zugriff am 15.10.2020 / **accessed on October 15, 2020**)
Abb. / **Fig.** 5: https://www.canstockphoto.de/rectangle-bar-zeichen-zensor-65141045.html
(Zugriff am 15.10.2020 / **accessed on October 15, 2020**)
Abb. / **Fig.** 6: https://www.faz.net/aktuell/gesellschaft/menschen/tiktok-nutzerin-prangert
-chinas-umgang-mit-muslimen-an-16506274.html
(Zugriff am 15.10.2020 / **accessed on October 15, 2020**)

ESTELLE BLASCHKE
Abb. / **Fig.** 1: https://www.nro.gov/FOIA/Major-NRO-Programs-and-Projects/CAL-Photographs/
(Zugriff am 15.10.2020 / **accessed on October 15, 2020**) © NRO
Abb. / **Fig.** 2: Eastman Kodak Company, *Annual Report 1952,* Rochester 1953, S. / **p.** 25
Abb. / **Fig.** 3: https://commons.wikimedia.org/wiki/File:City_of_Anji_in_1969_by_CORONA
_satellite.jpg#globalusage
(Zugriff am 15.10.2020 / **accessed on October 15, 2020**) © CIA/NRO/USGS
Abb. / **Fig.** 4: © Armin Linke
Abb. / **Fig.** 5: http://gps-camera.eu/wissen/Was-ist-Geotagging-Welche-Moeglichkeiten-gibt-es
(Zugriff am 15.10.2020 / **accessed on October 15, 2020**)
Abb. / **Fig.** 6: https://www.theverge.com/2016/9/6/12817340/instagram-photo-map-removals
(Zugriff am 15.10.2020 / **accessed on October 15, 2020**)

Abb. / **Fig.** 7: https://arpost.co/2019/07/24/3-applications-of-augmented
-reality-in-the-travel-industry/
(Zugriff am 15.10.2020 / **accessed on October 15, 2020**)
Abb. / **Fig.** 8: https://www.google.de/maps/
(Zugriff am 15.10.2020 / **accessed on October 15, 2020**)

KERSTIN SCHANKWEILER
Abb. / **Fig.** 1: https://www.youtube.com/watch?v=kWr6MypZ-JU
(Zugriff am 15.10.2020 / accessed on October 15, 2020)
Abb. / **Fig.** 2: © Stuart Franklin / Magnum Photos / Agentur Focus
Abb. / **Fig.** 3A: https://www.memecenter.com/fun/19250/unusual-tank-man
(Zugriff am 15.10.2020 / **accessed on October 15, 2020**)
Abb. / **Fig.** 3B: http://www.quickmeme.com/meme/358noc
(Zugriff am 15.10.2020 / **accessed on October 15, 2020**)
Abb. / **Fig.** 3C: https://knowyourmeme.com/photos/1356359-haunted
-doll-that-drinks-all-your-pepsi-and-calls-you-a-bitch
(Zugriff am 15.10.2020 / **accessed on October 15, 2020**)
Abb. / **Fig.** 3D: https://meduza.io/feature/2014/12/17/shutka-po-pekinski
(Zugriff am 15.10.2020 / **accessed on October 15, 2020**)
Abb. / **Fig.** 3E: https://www.buzzfeednews.com/article/kevintang/how-the
-chinese-internet-remembers-tiananmen-on-its-24th-ann
(Zugriff am 15.10.2020 / **accessed on October 15, 2020**)
Abb. / **Fig.** 3F: https://twitter.com/lexiphanic/status/341882864977186816
(Zugriff am 15.10.2020 / **accessed on October 15, 2020**)
Abb. / **Fig.** 4: https://www.kqed.org/lowdown/13161/on-tiananmen
-square-anniversary-using-creative-memes-to-circumvent-censorship
(Zugriff am 15.10.2020 / **accessed on October 15, 2020**)
Abb. / **Fig.** 5, 6: © Lara Baladi

MATTHIAS BRUHN
Abb. / **Fig.** 1: *Picture Post,* 24.12.1938 / December 24, 1938, Innenseite / magazine page
Abb. / **Fig.** 2: https://blogs.nottingham.ac.uk/manuscripts/2020/05/08/victory-in-europe-day
/picture-post-page-001/ (Zugriff am / accessed on 15.10.2020) Courtesy Manuscripts and
Special Collections, The University of Nottingham
Abb. / **Fig.** 3: © bpk Berlin / Vorderasiatisches Museum, SMB / Olaf M.Teßmer
Abb. / **Fig.** 4: *Picture Post,* 24.12.1938 / Decmeber 24, 1938, S. / **p.** 49
Abb. / **Fig.** 5: Ullstein Verlag (Hg.), *50 Jahre Ullstein, 1877–1927,* Berlin 1927, S. / **p.** 299
Abb. / **Fig.** 6: © Janis Krums mit freundlicher Genehmigung / **with kind permission**

DANK / **ACKNOWLEDGMENTS**

Die Kurator*innen danken /
The curators would like to thank
Peggy Sue Amison
Friedrich Balke
Hartmut Böhme
Clement Chéroux
Ludger Derenthal
Veit Didczuneit
Bogomir Ecker
Eva Ehninger
Daniel Goods
Daniel Herleth
Paul Mellenthin
Jonas Meyer
Roland Meyer
Christin Müller
Boaz Levin
Ulrich Pohlmann
Margarete Pratschke
Bernd Stiegler
Friedrich Tietjen

Besonderer Dank / **Special thanks to**
Gerhard Steidl

LEIHGEBER*INNEN / **LENDERS**

Galerie Buchholz, Berlin, Köln / Cologne, New York
Galerie Crone, Berlin, Wien / Vienna
Bridget Donahue, New York
Fotomuseum Winterthur
Gagosian, New York
Der Greif, München / Munich
Investitionsbank Berlin
Lee-Kahn Foundation, Scotts Valley
Museum für Moderne Kunst / MMK, Frankfurt am Main
mor charpentier, Paris
Parrotta Contemporary Art, Köln / Cologne
Sprüth Magers, Berlin, London, Los Angees
Bernd Stiegler, Konstanz
Friedrich Tietjen, Wien / Vienna, Leipzig
ZKM | Zentrum für Kunst und Medien Karlsruhe

C/O BERLIN FOUNDATION

Vorstand / **Executive Board**
Stephan Erfurt (CEO), Dr. Andreas Behr

Kurator*innen / **Curators**
Felix Hoffmann, Hauptkurator / **Chief Curator**
Dr. Kathrin Schönegg

Registrar*innen & kuratorische Assistenz /
Registrars & curatorial assistants
Carolin Bollig, Martin Granderath

Kaufmännische Leitung / **Managing director**
Karin Hänsler

Rechnungswesen / **Finances**
Kirsten Mintert, Leitung / **Head**
Katrin Zech

Education
Sibylle Kufus, Leitung / **Head**
Frauke Menzinger

Kommunikation / **Communications**
Magnus Pölcher, Leitung / **Head**
Anna Falck-Ytter, **Digital Media**
Cecilia Ritter, Tourismusmarketing /
Tourism marketing

Development
Louisa Seelis

Technical resources / **Installation**
Björn Rohde, Leitung / **Head**
Teunis van Panhuis

Bookshop
Raluca Blidar, Leitung / **Head**
Friedrich Franke, Peter Odinzow, Ulrike Olms

Besucherbetreuung, Empfang /
Visitor support, reception
Sandra Sydow, Leitung / **Head**
Yanina Raspa
Julian Hemelberg, Emma Hutton, Catharina Krüger,
Pol Merchan, Jacintha Nolte, Gwen Schlüter,
Jérôme Sklorz, Matthias Walendy, Sven Wolfgang

Projektassistenz / **Back office**
Ksenia Disterhof

Design
Marc Naroska, Leitung / **Head**
Nadja Metzinger

C/O Berlin Friends
Sibylle Kufus

PUBLIKATION / **PUBLICATION**

Diese Publikation erscheint anlässlich der Ausstellung/
This publication accompanies the exhibition

Send Me an Image . From Postcards to Social Media
März bis September / **March to September** 2021

C/O Berlin Foundation
Hardenbergstraße 22–24
10623 Berlin
www.co-berlin.org

Kurator*innen / **Curators**
Felix Hoffmann
Dr. Kathrin Schönegg

Herausgeber*innen / **Editors**
Felix Hoffmann & Dr. Kathrin Schönegg für/
for C/O Berlin Foundation

Gestaltung / **Design**
Naroska, Berlin

Kuratorische Assistenz / **Curatorial assistants**
Carolin Bollig, Martin Granderath

Lektorat / **Copyediting**
H von G – Katrin & Hans Georg Hiller von Gaertringen
(deutsch / **German**)
Tas Skorupa (englisch / **English**)

Übersetzung / **Translations**
Sylee Gore

Scans & Triton-Trennungen /
Scans & tritone separations
Steidl image department, Göttingen

Bildbearbeitung / **Image processing**
Steidl image department

Herstellung / **Production**
Bernard Fischer, Gerhard Steidl

Gesamtherstellung / **Production and printing**
Steidl, Göttingen

Titel / **Cover image**
Anonym / **Anonymous**
*A Parody of the Iconic 1989 Tiananmen Square Photo
of a Chinese Protester Confronting Government Tanks,*
2013, Tank-Man-Meme

Erste Auflage 2021 / **First edition 2021**

© 2021 für die abgebildeten Werke wie vermerkt
in der Werkliste / **for the reproduced works as
mentioned in the list of works**

© 2021 für die Texte bei den Autor*innen /
for the texts: the author**s**
© 2021 für diese Ausgabe / **for this edition:**
Steidl Verlag, Göttingen/ **Steidl Publishers**

Alle Rechte vorbehalten. Kein Teil dieses Buches darf
in irgendeiner Form (Druck, Fotokopie oder einem
anderen Verfahren) ohne schriftliche Genehmigung
des Verlages reproduziert oder unter Verwendung
elektronischer Systeme verarbeitet werden. /
**All rights reserved. No part of this publication may
be reproduced or transmitted in any form or by
any means, electronic or mechanical, including
photocopy, recording, or any other storage and
retrieval system, without prior permission in
writing from the publisher.**

STEIDL
Düstere Str. 4, 37073 Göttingen, Germany
Phone +49 551 49 60 60
mail@steidl.de
steidl.de

ISBN 978-3-95829-962-7

Printed in Germany by Steidl

Gefördert durch / **Supported by**

ART FOUNDATION
MENTOR LUCERNE

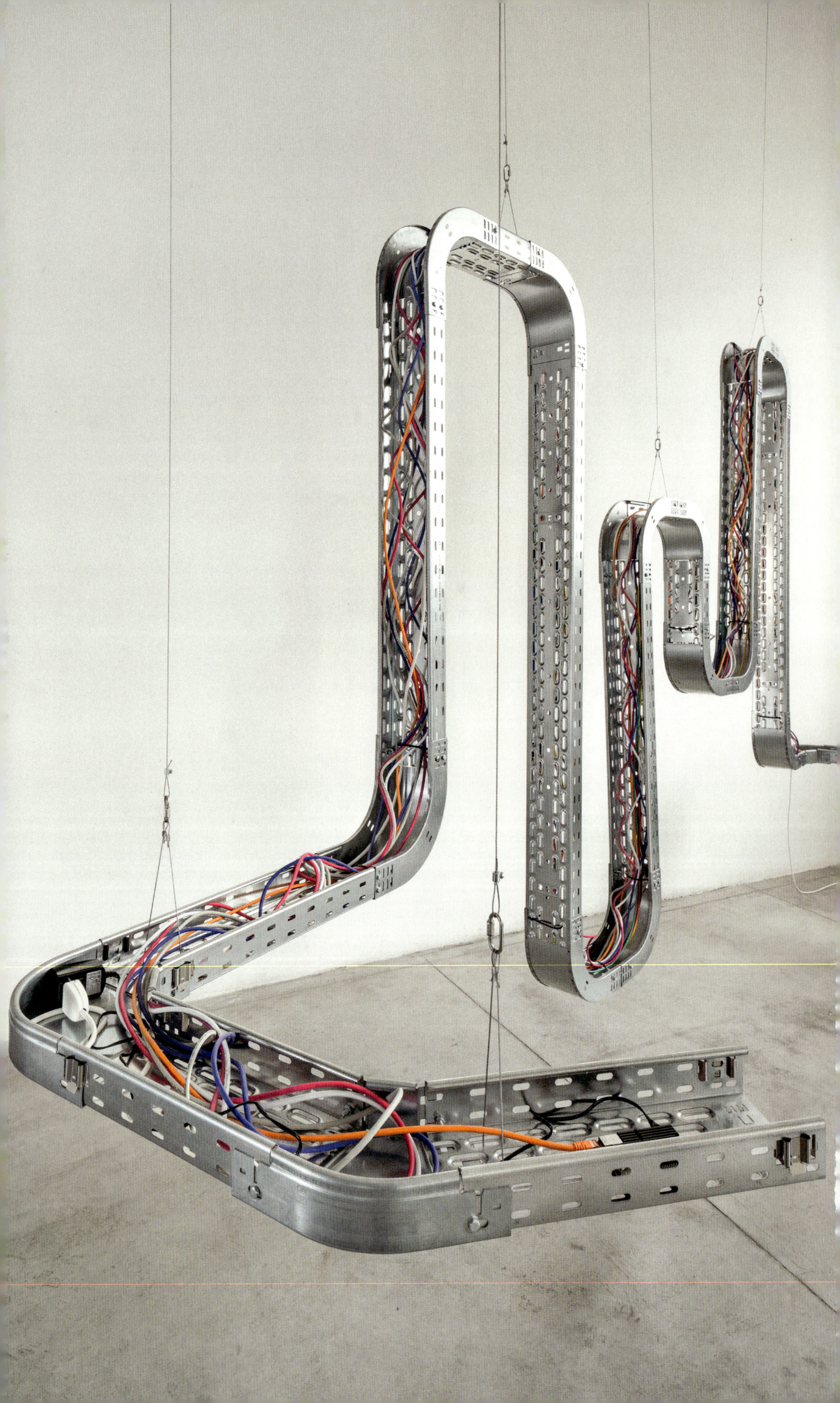